GREEK AND ROMAN CLASSICS

UNICIO J. VIOLI
ASSOCIATE PROFESSOR OF ENGLISH
FAIRLEIGH DICKINSON UNIVERSITY

MONARCH
PRESS

TABLE OF CONTENTS

GREEK EPIC

INTRODUCTION

HOMER'S *ILIAD* AND *ODYSSEY*

PREFACE: In order to appreciate the *Iliad* and the *Odyssey* more fully, it is necessary to know as much as possible of the background of the work. We must try, to the best of our ability, to put ourselves in the place of Homer's audience. This introduction will give a summary of the material needed for a proper understanding of the *Iliad*. Consult the Bibliography for a list of books presenting this background material in greater detail.

GREECE AND THE TROJAN WAR: There are two epics that Homer is said to have written: the *Iliad* and the *Odyssey*. The story of the *Iliad* unfolds toward the end of the Trojan War—a war between the Greeks and the Trojans. The *Odyssey* is the story of the return of one of the Greek generals who had fought in the Trojan War. All readers of the *Odyssey* are expected to know the story of the *Iliad* and the Trojan War.

THE TROJAN WAR, ALL FABLE? Is there any truth to the tale of this war? Or is it merely a story that gained great popularity in Greece, even though it has no historical basis?

The Greeks after Homer believed in his geography, even to the point of assigning actual locations to places that are a part of Homer's fabled land. But for many years during the modern era, people thought that there had never been a Trojan War. Some people thought that there had never even been a city named Troy.

THE BIRTH OF ARCHEOLOGY: There was one person, however, who did believe in Troy. Heinrich Schliemann, a German industrialist, had read Homer as a boy and had gained a great enthusiasm for the *Iliad* and the *Odyssey* — an enthusiasm that stayed with him for the rest of his life. In 1870 he started digging at the town of Hissarlik in Turkey, where he believed Troy was buried.

His discovery, which confirmed his belief, surprised everyone and forced scholars to admit the existence of this fabled city. He also uncovered Pylos, Nestor's city, and Mycenae, the city ruled by Agamemnon, the leader of the Greek forces in the Trojan War.

Archeologists can now tell us where many of Homer's cities were. And from the excavations of these cities they have found many of the objects described by Homer—mixing bowls, armor, bows, etc. Their research also clarifies the details of the Homeric house, which is difficult to reconstruct on the basis of Homer alone.

But their research also raised problems, for this new archeological evidence shows that Homer was describing no particular period of history. Thus, a warrior in the *Iliad* might ride into battle on a chariot of the ninth century B.C.; he might fight in a battle formation of the eighth century, holding a spear of the twelfth. This disregard of historical accuracy has been used as evidence by some scholars to demonstrate that more than one person composed each of the epics. This problem will be considered in the section dealing with the "Homeric Question."

THE FIRST GREEKS: Thus, from these contemporary sources, as well as from the *Iliad* and the *Odyssey,* a fairly complete picture of life during the Mycenaean period can be obtained.

The Greeks of this time were the descendants of the original Greek colonists, who had entered the Greek mainland from the north about 2000 B.C. and had merged with the original inhabitants of this land. They brought with them horses, and wheel-made pottery, the idea of fortified towns, and, of course, the Greek language.

THE MYCENAEANS: By the middle of the sixteenth century B.C. the most powerful Greek city was Mycenae (my SEE nee). Through foreign trade, mostly with Egypt, Mycenae was able to gain great wealth and power.

1. Its citizens conquered Crete, the strongest outpost of the pre-Greek people of the Aegean Sea.

2. For 400 years (1550-1150 B.C.) Mycenae ruled the Aegean, founding many colonies as its trade expanded.

3. Many of these colonies became famous on their own in later classical times as, for example, Miletus and Rhodes.

The period of Mycenaean power ended about 1150 B.C. with the invasion of the Dorians. The Dorians, the last race of Greeks to overrun the mainland, brought about the downfall of Mycenaean civilization, starting what is known as the "Dark Ages" of Greece (1150-900 B.C.).

ECONOMY DURING MYCENAEAN TIMES: During the period of the Trojan War, Greece was broken up into many small kingdoms, living under a social and economic system similar to that of the Middle Ages in Europe.

1. The main economic unit was the *oikos,* the equivalent to the manor of the later feudal system.

2. Surrounding the *oikos* was enough farm and pasture land to support the *oikos*-owner, his family, his servants, and his slaves. The servants had various functions to perform, such as herding the pigs, goats, and cattle kept by all *oikoi* (the plural of *oikos*). They also had duties to perform in the house.

3. Since the main source of slaves was through warfare, most of the slaves in any household were women, for it was the practice among victorious Greeks to kill all the men they conquered. The female slaves helped the mistress of the house in weaving, washing and nursing. Many also served as concubines for the master of the house.

THE CLASSES:

1. The householders and their families formed an aristocracy based on the farm. Each *oikos* was a nearly self-sufficient unit, independent of every other household, although the *oikos*-owner did owe allegiance to the king of his land.

2. Servants and slaves, few of whom had specialized skills, were attached to an *oikos.*

3. The ministrels, carpenters, metal-workers, doctors, and prophets formed a class by themselves. They were not attached to any one house, but went wherever their services were called for.

4. All other people, whatever their position, were part of the masses.

WARFARE: It was only during a war that the household-owners acted together. The wars in which they engaged were probably not fought for the acquisition of land, but rather to obtain metals: gold, silver, copper, iron. (Some scholars think that the historical Trojan War was actually a raid to obtain iron.) The Greeks themselves saw no difference between a war and a private raid. Odysseus and his men, for example in Book IX of the *Odyssey,* saw nothing wrong with interrupting their journey home to sack the city of Ismaros, taking all the booty and women they could carry.

ASSEMBLIES: During peacetime the only official place for the nobles to meet was the Assembly, which was called by the king.

1. These Assemblies were called whenever the king had an important decision to make concerning the nobles (that is, all the *oikos*-owners) in his land.

2. Although he had the power to make decisions without consulting them, he rarely did so.

3. At an Assembly the nobles would discuss the problem before them, judging it on the basis of local traditions. It is no wonder that Homer considered the Assembly a vital part of any civilized society.

For example, when in the *Odyssey* he describes the barbaric Cyclopes (Book IX), Homer is quick to point out that they have no Assemblies, and live without traditions.

On the other hand, the Phaeacians (*Odyssey,* Books VI, VII, VIII), whom Homer considers to be overly civilized, are constantly having Assemblies. On the battlefield, far from home, Agamemnon in the *Iliad* carries on this custom by continuing to hold Assemblies to discuss matters of importance to the Greek warriors.

GUEST AND HOSTS: In a world in which contact among nobles living in the same country was limited to these infrequent Assemblies, meetings among nobles living in different lands were even more irregular. There was no king and no law to regulate such "international" affairs. Instead, people had to depend on their faith in each other. From this dependence, an elaborate tradition developed concerning the relationship between travellers and their hosts.

1. For example, hosts were expected to protect their guests from harm.

2. Of course, the guest had responsibilities to his host. The traditional cause of the Trojan War is a breach of faith on the part of a guest. Paris (also called Alexander), who was a guest in the house of Menelaus, King of Sparta, seduced Menelaus' wife Helen and ran away with her to his native city of Troy. Menelaus and his brother (Agamemnon) led an army of Greeks to Troy in order to destroy the city for harboring such a villain as Paris, who had broken a sacred guest-host tradition.

3. The importance in the Greek mind of the guest-host relationship can be seen in the fact that Zeus, the mightiest of the gods, was considered to be the guardian of these relations.

GREECE AFTER THE TROJAN WAR:　From the preceding section it is easy to see that scholars have a great deal to say about the social and historical background of both the *Iliad* and the *Odyssey*.

But if we ask about Greece during the 400 years following the Trojan War, we are on less sure ground.

1. The Trojan War was fought about a century before the influx of Dorian Greeks to the mainland.

2. These Dorians spread out over western Greece, bringing about the end of the system of government described heretofore.

3. The Dorian invasion also meant that Greece was now without an alphabet, for the knowledge of writing was lost with the destruction of the major towns by the Dorians.

4. For a period of about 400 years (1150-750 B.C.) until writing was reintroduced, there was no body of written literature in Greece. But this is not to say that there was no literature being composed, for poems were composed to be recited orally.

COMMUNITY SPIRIT IN MAINLAND GREECE:　The type of poem that was composed depended on the society in which it was produced. The Dorians were a communal people. That is, they lived and worked together with very little conflict among individuals. It was this community spirit which produced the Spartans, the foremost of the Dorians in the fifth and fourth centuries B.C. The poetry that developed from such a society—choral songs—aptly reflected the communal feelings of its inhabitants. These poems were not only sung by groups of people, but frequently exalted the very group spirit that gave rise to choral songs.

INDIVIDUALITY IN IONIA:　In the eastern part of the Greek-speaking world and on the coast of Asia Minor, as well as on the islands of the Aegean, were the Ionian Greeks. Many of these Ionians were living in towns founded by the Mycenaeans during the period of expansion and trade. Here trade was still carried on with Egypt and other lands, although not to the extent that it was in the period of Mycenaean supremacy. Instead of the community spirit that evolved in the West, a sense of individuality was maintained throughout *Ionia* (as the Aegean islands and the coast of Asia Minor were called). Quite naturally, the poetry of Ionia reflected this individuality.

1. Instead of poems sung by many people, as among the Dorians, the poems in Ionia were recited by one person, and, what is more important, instead of poems about the community spirit, these were poems that exalted the spirit of the individual.

2. The two long poems we have from this period, the *Iliad* and the *Odyssey*, praise individual accomplishments.

THE ORAL TRADITION AND THE EPIC: One of the first questions to arise concerning the *Iliad* and the *Odyssey* is how, since there was no writing, anyone could memorize a poem the length of these two epics (about 350 pages in most books).

1. It has been found to be generally true that in societies where there is no writing, people's memories are better than those of people living in literate societies. Even today there are poets living in Yugoslavia capable of reciting, from memory, poems longer than the *Iliad*.

2. But a good memory is not the complete answer; for the minstrel, the bard who recited the poem, was expected to compose his own story, even though it might be based on traditional tales, such as those centering around the Trojan War.

3. A precise understanding of how a bard was able to compose and recite his poems was not to be had until recently. Before we can learn the answer to this question, however, we must first learn precisely what a Greek epic is.

EPIC METER: An *epic* is a long poem, each line of which is in the same meter. The meter of the *Iliad* and the *Odyssey* (and because of their great influence, most subsequent epics) is *dactylic hexameter*, that is, each verse contains a rhythmic pattern of six dactyls (/ ∪ ∪ = a dactyl). Of course there were variations on the basic rhythm.

ORAL TRADITION AND THE FORMULA: These useful words, phrases, and lines were passed down from poet to poet until, by Homer's time (800-750 B.C.) it was possible to compose a long epic of great complexity and originality that was made up largely of formulas (as these standard words, phrases, and lines are called). It is thought that some of these formulas date back to the Trojan War itself. They were kept alive by generations of poets even though the meanings of some of the words were lost, perhaps even to Homer.

For example, Hermes is frequently called "argeiphontes." Some people translate the word as "the slayer of Argos," others as "brightly appearing." Over a period of centuries more and more phrases were originated and retained in the collective memory of the minstrels, thus increasing the store of formulas.

By Homer's time, every common word appeared in a number of formulas: The Greek word for ship, for example, appears in several phrases: *balanced ship* (2 feet), *dark-prowed ship* (3 1/4 feet), and *curved ship* (2½ feet). These three formulas fit at the end of the line. Thus, as the singer recites the first part of the line, he plans ahead to have 2, 2½, or 3 1/4 feet left at the end of the line so that he may fit in one of the "ship" formulas. Those who maintain that these "epithets" have no meaning are led astray by the way that they phrase the problem. It is true, that given a set number of feet at the end of the line and a name to go with this number, there is usually only one adjective appropriate to the name to fill out the line. Therefore, they conclude, these adjectives are chosen for solely metrical convenience. The conclusion would be true if their hypothesis were true—but it is not. The poet is not "given" a set number of feet to fill up with a name and an adjective.

He controls the first half of the line as much as the last half. He decides whether there will be 2, 2 1/2, 3 1/4, or any other number of feet left; and therefore he can decide in advance exactly which epithet he will use.

THE EPIC CYCLE: The *Iliad* and the *Odyssey* are only two epics that revolve around the Trojan War. We know of other epics, now lost, that fill out the story from the judgement of Paris to the tale of Telegonus, a sequel to the *Odyssey*. Our main source for these epics is Proclus, a grammarian of the second century A.D., who summarized their plots in his *Chrestomathy*:

1. *Cypria*: this epic by Stasinus or Hegesias opens on Olympus where Zeus and Themis, the goddess of custom, are planning the forthcoming Trojan War. Hera, Athena, and Aphrodite dispute among themselves which of them is the most beautiful; they choose Alexander (Paris) to be the judge; but he chooses Aphro-

dite solely because she promises that he can marry Helen if he judges in her favor. Paris visits Menelaus, the husband of Helen, a man foolish enough to leave the beautiful Helen behind with his guest while he sails to Crete on a trip. Paris and Helen waste no time in "getting together"; then they set sail for Troy, after filling the boats with treasures from Menelaus' storeroom. When Menelaus learns what has occurred, he returns home and plans a punitive expedition against Troy with his brother Agamemnon, and Nestor, the oldest reigning king in Greece. They travel through Greece gathering a fighting force. (Odysseus pretends to be insane to avoid the draft, but he is found out by Palamedes, who accompanies Menelaus.) When they are assembled in Aulis, the incident of the sparrows and the snake, described in Book II of the *Iliad*, takes place.

They start out for Troy, but a storm disperses the ships, and they are forced once more to gather in Aulis. (Achilles' ship is driven to Scyros, where he marries Deidameia; he then rejoins the fleet in Aulis.) Before their second departure, Agamemnon angers Artemis, the goddess of the hunt, with his boast of his hunting prowess. She keeps the fleet in Aulis by means of strong winds until Calchas, the prophet, suggests that Agamemnon appease her wrath with the sacrifice of his daughter Iphigenia; this ritual is then performed.

The Greeks set sail again and this time reach their destination, although they lose some time when they decide to leave behind Philoctetes, who is bitten by a snake and has developed a smelly, festering wound, on Lemnos. Some of the battle scenes are described in which Achilles plays the major role. Zeus plots to have Achilles withdraw from the fighting.

2. Homer's *Iliad* continues the story where the *Cypria* ends.

3. The *Aethiopis* by Arctinus of Miletus continues the action of the *Iliad* where Homer left off. Achilles is killed by Paris with the aid of Apollo, and Aias and Odysseus argue over which of them should have the armor of Achilles.

4. The *Little Iliad* by Lesches of Mitylene continues the tale. Achilles' arms are awarded to Odysseus. Aias commits suicide. Diomedes brings Philoctetes, who is already healed, to Troy, after which he slays Paris. Epeius builds the wooden horse. Odysseus then disguises himself as a beggar so that he may enter Troy undetected

and plot with Helen the taking of Troy (cf. Book IV of the *Odyssey*). This epic ends with the Trojans taking the wooden horse into Troy.

5. *Sack of Troy* by Arctinus of Miletus. The trick of the wooden horse succeeds: Troy is taken and the long war is over. Priam is slain by Neoptolemus, Achilles' son.

6. *Returns* by Agias of Troezen. In this epic are related the home-comings of all the major Greek generals except Odysseus, whose return is thoroughly detailed in Homer's *Odyssey*. Nestor and Diomedes arrive home safely; Menelaus reaches Sparta only after losing five ships. Agamemnon arrives safely in his native land, but is slain by his wife and her lover.

7. Homer's *Odyssey*. After many travails and travels, Odysseus reaches Ithaca, his native land, where he slays the entire pack of suitors besieging his wife.

8. *Telegony* by Eugammon of Cyrene. This is a haphazardly planned continuation of the *Odyssey* wherein Odysseus indulges in many adventures and even marries again, although his wife Penelope is still living. Telegonus, his son by Circe (see Book X of the *Odyssey*), comes to Ithaca to find Odysseus and unwittingly kills him.

HOMERIC QUESTION: Not too long ago, the prevailing opinion among Homeric scholars was that there was no such person as Homer. His epics were nothing but a patchwork of poems built around a central theme. These "analysts" also argued about the subsequent stratification of the poems of Homer—some maintaining that they grew gradually, others that they incorporate scattered material.

J. A. Scott, Sheppard, and Drerup (see Bibliography) were the first to see the *Iliad* and *Odyssey* as unified epics. They stressed Homer's originality, even to the point of denying the existence of Troy.

Most modern criticism dates from 1928, when the first work of Milman Parry was published. Now that scholars could be fairly certain that they were dealing with the work of one poet, they could proceed to give the analysis Homer's epics deserve. Some few scholars however, still cling to the analytic theory.

THE *ILIAD*

BOOK I: THE PLAGUE AND THE WRATH

INVOCATION AND THEME: "An angry man—there is my story: the bitter rancour of Achilles, prince of the house of Peleus, which brought a thousand troubles upon the Achaean host."

> **COMMENT:** *Menis* (wrath or anger) is a principal theme of this epic, and hence it is stated outright at the very beginning. The *Odyssey* starts with the word for *man,* and Virgil's epic, the *Aeneid,* begins with "arms and the man"— both epics, then, center their stories around man. Also, like the *Odyssey,* Homer's other epic masterpiece, the *Iliad* commences with an invocation to the muse of lyric poetry. The invocation is really a prayer that his memory and ability to compose an epic will not fail him. The Muses or the *Pierides* (after their birthplace, Pieria, a spring on the side of Mount Olympus) are goddesses who inspire artists and poets to create. They are the daughters of Zeus and Mnemosyne (goddess of memory). The sense is that the arts are the product of divine inspiration and memory.

THE QUARREL OVER BRISEIS: The story of the *Iliad* begins with *Chryses* (KRY seez), a priest of Apollo, pleading for the return of his daughter Chryseis (kry SEE iss), who had been captured in a previous raid on the city of Chryse, and in a later division of the spoils, had been awarded to Agamemnon (ag uh MEM non), the leader of the Greek forces. Agamemnon is not pleased with Chryses' request: "The woman I will not release! She shall live to old age in our house, far away in our house, far away in Argos, working the loom and lying in my bed. Begone now! don't provoke me, or it will be the worse for you."

> **COMMENT:** These were barbaric times. On the raids, men were slain and women taken as booty to serve as mistresses and servants. Note Agamemnon's open declaration that she will live to old age in his house "far away in Argos, working the loom and lying in my bed." Beds and looms are important to Homer as we shall see.

The furious priest returns home and prays to his god, Apollo, to unleash his arrows upon the Greek forces.

COMMENT: Apollo, the sun god, armed with bow and arrow could shoot with deadly aim. Here he is called "Smintheus" (the mouse-god). This is a symbolic way of saying mice bring the deadly plague with them. Homer uses the vivid imagery of an arrow massacre to picture the spread of a deadly plague among the ranks of the Greek army. To these primitive people all illnesses sprang from the actions of hostile spirits and gods.

The plague rages for nine days, killing both animals and men. Achilles (uh KILL eez) calls an Assembly of warriors and bids Calchas (KAL kuss), the prophet, to reveal the cause of the plague. Calchas: "Mark what I say, and swear me an oath that you will defend me with all your might in word and deed. For I think I shall provoke a man who rules all our people, one whom all the people obey."

COMMENT: A wise prophet, he makes Achilles swear a solemn oath of protection before revealing that the cause of the plague is Apollo's wrath at Agamemnon's treatment of Chryses. We will see charming and delightful displays of this kind of—shall we say—"prudence" throughout Homer's works.

When the news is brought that Calchas has revealed that Agamemnon is the cause of the deadly massacre by arrow, the mighty chief of the Achaeans (uh KEE uhnz), Homer's term for the Greeks, becomes livid with fury: "Why I like her better than my own wife Clytemnestra; she is just as good in face or figure, brains or fingers."

COMMENT: Note that sex alone is not the slave girl's only virtues: he also notes her face, figure, brains, and *fingers*. She is valuable for he skill with the loom (a most important Homeric virtue) and her intelligence.

Achilles, the mightiest of the Greeks, reminds Agamemnon that all the prizes have already been distributed, that the chief should wait for the next raiding expedition. Achilles accuses his king of greediness, of always grabbing the best prize for himself. Nevertheless, the chief asks for Achilles' mistress Briseis (bry SEE iss) in exchange for his giving up of Chryseis. This in turn enrages Achilles, the wrathful one, who is just about to pull out his sword to slay his chief when Athena (uh THEE nuh) appears, visible only to Achilles, bids him to control his wrath, and holds him back by pulling on his long red hair. She tells him that the time will come when three times the value of what he is giving up will be offered him in return for this insult. The petulant Achilles swears a mighty oath that he will fight no longer, throws down his sceptre (the sign of the privileged speaker) and sits down.

THE YIELDING OF BRISEIS: *Nestor,* the aged king of Pylos, chides the two warriors, and advises Agamemnon not to take Briseis, and Achilles not to stay angry; but he is ineffective. The Assembly breaks up, and two heralds are sent to fetch Briseis from Achilles' tent. Achilles yields up his beloved Briseis (his favorite captive female slave) and weeping, calls upon his mother, Thetis (THEE tiss), to aid him: "O my mother! I was born to die young, it is true, but honour I was to have from Zeus (ZOOS), Olympian Thunderer on high! And now he has insulted me! He has taken my prize and keeps it, he has robbed me himself"

> **COMMENT:** If we get the impression that two spoiled brats greedily quarrel over prizes and booty like schoolboys over a lost marble, we are very likely right. One cannot over-emphasize that the Greek army are primitive warriors on a raiding expedition looking for booty in metals and women. The hot-headed Agamemnon, who, to save his lost face, seizes upon the booty of Achilles, and the mightiest of warriors, Achilles, who weeps like a babe wailing for his mother, may seem ridiculous to us. But the portraits are human and truthful and above all—psychologically true!

Thetis, his goddess mother, appears, and agrees to help her son in his plea. She will go to Zeus and plead for his aid in helping Achilles to wreak revenge upon his fellow Greeks. Zeus is to favor the Trojans in battle so much that the Greeks will come to Achilles begging for his help in battle. Thus, her son's honor (an all-important ideal in those days) will have been avenged. Odysseus (oh DISS seeoos) returns Chryseis to her father and the plague is ended. Achilles remains for the next fifteen days sulking within his tent.

ZEUS, HERA, AND HEPHAISTUS: Twelve days pass before Thetis visits Mount Olympus, the home of the immortal gods; and kneeling before Zeus (she clasps his knees with her left hand and touches his beard with her right hand, the traditional position of the suppliant) and obtains her request. After Thetis' departure, Hera, Zeus' wife, quarrels with her husband, suspecting that he has consented to help the Trojans, her enemies (see Introduction). Zeus petulantly replies: "My dear Hera, do not expect to know everything I say. You must not expect as much as that, although you are my wife. Whatever is proper for you to hear, you shall be the first to hear before any in heaven or earth; but when I choose to consider things by myself, do not be inquisitive and ask questions about everything." Queen Hera, opening her fine eyes, answers: "O you dreadful creature, what a thing to say! I inquisitive? I ask you questions? I never did such a thing in my life!" The stern husband tells her to shut up and sit down or else he will beat her up. This silences her, but the master-craftsman of Olympus (and their son), Hephaistus takes his mother's side and advises her to give in. He tells her her loves her but cannot help her "for the Olympian is hard to tackle"; he relates another unfortunate time he had crossed his father's wrath. Then the craftsman, ugly and lame, serves wine to all, and the sight of this misshapen creature raises "laughter unquenchable among the blessed gods." And so after feasting they go to bed, and Zeus sleeps with Queen Hera by his side.

> **COMMENT:** The quarrel between husband and wife, the sympathy shown by the monstrous son, the laughter of the gods—all this reveals a comic spirit among the immortal gods that is downright human.

THE *ILIAD*

BOOK II: THE DREAM AND CATALOGUE

THE DREAM AND TEST: Zeus in his plan to favor the Trojans sends a deceptive dream to Agamemnon, the content of which is that if he attacks now he will win over Troy. Agamemnon holds a council with his generals and broaches his plan. But before battling, there will be a test of the soldiers' courage and will to fight. He will offer them a chance to go home right away. Then an Assembly is held of the soldiers and generals. This is followed by the first simile of the *Iliad*.

COMMENT: A simile is a comparison in the form "like . . . so. . . ." Here the Achaean soldiers are compared to bees swarming and buzzing. Homer frequently makes use of similes to relieve and illuminate the morbidly sombre battle scenes. Thus, there are four times as many similies in the *Iliad* as in the *Odyssey*, where there is a greater variety of scenes. Thus, there are four times as many similes in the battle scenes as innon-battle scenes. The subject matter of these similes usually represents the domestic life of Homer's time rather than of the time of the Trojan War. They frequently come at the start or close of an important episode. Although they "take us away from the action" of the *Iliad* in the sense that we leave the battle, they relate back to the action in a metaphorical sense, and should always be closely examined. By means of his similes, Homer interweaves scenes of peace into the martial atmosphere of the poem, showing that thoughts of war must always involve thoughts of peace.

Agamemnon addresses the Assembly and reminds them that ten years of fighting have not brought them victory, even though they outnumber the Trojans ten to one. He tests his men by suggesting that they leave Troy and go home to their families.

"Then as a strong west wind stirs a deep cornfield (corn = wheat) rustling the ears and bending them low, so all that gathering was stirred; with loud clamour they rushed towards their ships . . ." Athena stirs Odysseus to action. He persuades the leaders to return to battle, and the lower classes of soldiers he beats into submission to his orders to return to battle. But one commoner is blustering and railing. It is *Thersites* (Thehr SIGHT eez), the man with the ready tongue, "always ready to talk, with no manners and no sense, anything to annoy the princes, anything to raise a laugh: and he was the ugliest man ever seen before Ilion (another name for Troy). He was bandy-legged and lame of one foot, a hump-back, with his two shoulders crushed together into his chest; on the top he had a sugar-loaf head with a few tufts of fluff. Achilles hated him heartily and so did Odysseus, for he was always badgering them." But this time he laces into Agamemnon for his "greediness" and his insult to Achilles. The crowd has no sympathy for Thersites; nor does Odysseus, who curses and beats him: ". . . May I no longer be called the father of Telemachus, if I don't strip the clothes from your body, strip off the cloak and shirt that cover your nakedness, and send you off to the ships roaring with pain after a good sound drubbing!" He beats Thersites with a great sceptre borrowed from the king. The rest howl with laughter: "Now he has stopped this damned word-slinger from his speechifying. I don't think he will pluck up courage to rail at kings again with his foul tongue."

> **COMMENT:** Thersites, with his sensible analysis of the fighting and his reasonable suggestion, is out of place in a tribal society where honor and glory in battle form the very base of their value system. We must remember that kings and nobles ruled with absolute power, and that commoners were looked upon as almost sub-human and simian, even though the labor and fighting of the commoners was vital to the interests of the aristocrats. Note the comic attitude of Homer toward that other laborer-commoner so skilled with his hands— the god Hephaestus. We are being historically anachronistic should we display sympathy toward commoners like Thersites or Hephaestus.

Both Odysseus and Nestor tell the men that the gods are with them in battle, as indicated by symbolic signs, such as that of the serpent (sent by Zeus) who leaped into a tree, ate up eight sparrow-chicks and their mother, and then turned to stone before their very eyes.

> **COMMENT:** Birds, serpents, and other creatures in nature formed part of a vast symbolic system by which the intent of the gods was determined. The serpent episode here is interpreted to mean (by Calchas the prophet, their official sign-reader) that the war will last nine years (i.e., the eight chicks plus the mother sparrow), but Troy will be taken in the tenth. One of the functions of the prophet was to interpret

"signs" for the benefit of the people so they could follow the will of the gods.

A sacrifice is performed and the sacrificial feast eaten, and then the troops are marshalled. Athena (invisible) runs through the ranks filling the men's hearts with courage, "And as goat-keepers easily sort out of the solid flocks of goats, when they are mixed together at pasture, so their leaders arrayed the men in this place and in that place, ready for battle."

COMMENT: Homer is fond of using everyday scenes from domestic and farm life for his similes. This is what makes them so delightful. They are taken from man's everyday experience, the simple, homely joys of labor in and around the home. You will never find a false note in Homer. He unerringly hits home to the heart of things.

CATALOGUE OF SHIPS: A list of the leaders and their ships is given—of both the Greeks and Trojans.

COMMENT: Many of the places mentioned did not exist in Homer's day. Many seem to be taken from centuries-old oral traditions originating in the thirteenth century B.C.

THE *ILIAD*

BOOK III: OATHS; THE BATTLE OF ALEXANDER AND MENELAUS

THE CHALLENGE: Paris (Alexander) leaps in front of the Trojan ranks with a challenge to the Achaeans, a challenge accepted by Menelaus (men uh LAY us), the husband of Helen, whom Paris had taken from Menelaus' very house, thereby causing the Trojan War. Paris regrets his challenge and slinks suddenly for cover. Hector, his brother, scolds him for his cowardice, which is admitted by Paris: "That is true enough, Hector, that is true enough. Your heart is always as hard as steel. Like a shipwright's axe, when he slices off a spar from a tree with all the strength of a man! A hard heart indeed! Don't taunt me with Aphrodite's adorable gifts. You can't throw away a god's gifts, offered unasked, which none could win by wishing." Nevertheless, Paris agrees to a duel.

THE WATCH FROM THE WALL: The watch from the wall (*Telchoskopia*) is enacted by seven Trojan elders, "old men, long past their fighting days, but excellent speakers," and Priam, the elderly king of the Trojans. They sit on the watchtower, chirruping in their thin old voices "like so many crickets on a tree"; when they see Helen (running to watch the duel between her husband and her lover, with herself as the prize), they whisper to one another in plain terms: "No wonder Achaeans and Trojans have been fighting for such a woman! I do declare she is like some divine creature come down from heaven." Priam calls upon her to name some of the more outstanding figures below them on the field of battle. She identifies Agamemnon, every inch a king even though a head shorter than many others; she points out Odysseus, a head shorter than the king "but broader in shoulders and chest . . . patrolling the ranks of men like a tame wether." There is no trick or invention which he does not know, and "he is never at a loss" for words or schemes. When speaking (says one elder) "he would stand with his eyes fixt on the ground, [he] didn't move the staff backwards or forwards, but held it stiff, like a dull fellow; you would call him surly and stupid both. But as soon as he let out his great voice from his chest, and a shower of words [fell] thick and soft like snowflakes in winter time, no other man alive could come near Odysseus. But then we did not think him so very much to look at."

COMMENT: This is deservedly a famous scene. Helen's beauty, the cause of nine years of a deadly and frustrating war, is described indirectly by its impression on withered old men staring from a wall tower. Instead of describing her beauty directly, Homer *indicates* it indirectly by its effect on others—a far more powerful method of description.

Aias (Ajax) is pointed out next, a real tower of strength; and Idomeneus (eye doh MEEN oohs), the great Cretan captain.

THE DUEL: Paris is the first to throw a spear, which is stopped by Menelaus' shield. Then Menelaus pierces Paris' shield with his spear and rushes in, brandishing his sword, which breaks Paris' helmet; he starts to strangle Paris with Paris' own chin strap, but it breaks. At this point Aphrodite, alarmed, conveys her beloved Paris to his own bedroom, to which place the scornful Helen is brought also. In spite of her taunts, Paris is unrepentant: "You need not scold me, my dear. This time Menelaus has won because Athena helped him. Next time it will be my turn; for I have my gods too. Let us love and be happy! I was never so much in love before, not even when I carried you off in my ship from Lacedaemon (LASS uh DAY moan), and we shared our first love in that island." She enters into bed with him.

COMMENT: An odd fellow, Paris—defeated in a duel, an arrant boaster, knave, and coward, a violator of hospitality (a primary crime in those days), he is yet the darling of the goddess of love herself, Aphrodite. Handsome and filled with sex-appeal, how could the most virtuous of wives resist him?

THE *ILIAD*

BOOK IV: THE BREAKING OF THE OATHS

THE BROKEN TRUCE: The observers of the battle are the gods on Olympus. Zeus tries to anger Hera by saying that Aphrodite, by saving Paris, has outwitted Athena and Hera (who favor the Greeks). Zeus is grieved at the extent of Hera's hatred for the Trojan host. Troy is a favorite city of his: "I have always loved best sacred Ilios (Troy, hence the *Iliad*) and King Priam, and the people of that fine old soldier king! My altar where never lacked public feast, or the savour of burnt-offering and drink-offering which is our solemn right."

> **COMMENT:** The gods were very careful to make sure that humans paid them due sacrifice in burnt meat and wine offerings. Failure by a mortal to appease the gods' wrath, or entreat their favor by skimping or eliminating the food sacrifice and its accompanying prayer, could result in great harm or even death to that mortal by the particular god who was neglected. Note that the *smell* of the sacrifice was supposedly inhaled by the god through the smoke of the fire as it ascended upward. It was that *savour* that pleased their appetites.

Zeus pleases his wife-sister Hera by sending Athena down to break the truce. She induces Pandarus, an archer (archers were considered cowardly warriors because they fought away from the front lines), to shoot an arrow. Menelaus is hit by Pandarus' arrow, thus breaking the solemn, cease-fighting truce. The wound is not serious, thanks to Athena's aid.

THE BATTLE RECOMMENCES: Both sides begin fighting, and Agamemnon spurs his troops with words of encouragement or abuse or even bribing promises:

> "Stick to it, men, to it with all your might! . . . Those who began it, those who broke their solemn oath, shall be a dainty meal for the cultures! (To be consumed by vultures or dogs was the ultimate humiliation.) And we will take their city and carry off their wives and children in shiploads!"

> **COMMENT:** These men are bloodthirsty indeed! All men taken prisoner were killed, but the women and children were used as mistresses and slaves. We must see this savagery, not

in the light of our own Judeo-Christian ethics, but in terms of pre-Christian tribal values.

Agamemnon has special words of encouragement for Idomeneus, the king of Crete: "Idomeneus, you are the man for me! First at a feast, and first in the field!" Next he encourages Aias, son of Telamon, and Aias, the son of Oileus (the Aiantes). Then he speaks to the reminiscing Nestor, who is still spry in spirit. Then to Odysseus and Menestheus, who are both holding back—but not from fear. Stinging words of cowardice evoke an angry retort from Odysseus, which is what King Agamemnon wants. "What a thing to say, Prince!" retorts Odysseus; "bite it back, and let it stay behind your teeth." Agamemnon apologizes. Next, Agamemnon reminds Diomedes of his father's prowess in battle. Diomedes, not having Odysseus' way with words, has no answer. Yet he chides his friend for talking rudely to their leader.

COMMENT: Here we see how Homer can characterize a person with a very few words. From this brief episode Diomedes (dy oh MEE deez) emerges as a modest warrior, respectful of his superiors. Odysseus, on the other hand, is always ready with a speech. (Men are killed and armor is regularly stripped as booty (armor was a symbol of a hero's identity, and the stripping signified complete victory over the enemy).

"Then the Danaan battalions moved on to battle line after line, as the long billows roll to the shore line after line when the west wind drives: the swell gathers head far out on the sea, then bursts on the land in thunder, rearing and curving its crest about the headlands and spitting out the salt spray. So the army moved, each mass with its own leaders; their words of command were heard, and the rest marched in silence."

Simoeisius is slain by Aias, son of Telamon, and "there he lay like a poplar tree which has grown up in the hollow of a great marsh, a smooth stem with branches growing at the top; some cartwright has cut it down with his axe to bend into the felloe of a fine car, and there it lies drying on the river-bank. So lay Simoeisius, when Asias struck him down." (Such exquisite similes are the stuff of the greatest poetry.) The Trojans retreat.

THE *ILIAD*

BOOK V: THE ARISTEIA OF DIOMEDES

THE INSPIRED VALOR (ARISTEIA) OF DIOMEDES: Diomedes kills Phegeus (FEE joos) and takes his horses and chariot; the Trojans are dismayed by his death. Meriones, a nephew and companion of Idomeneus, kills Phereclus, "an artist who knew how to make all sorts of lovely and precious things with his own hands. . . . Meriones chased him and caught and struck him in the right groin; the point ran through the bladder under the bone. He fell groaning upon his knees, and death covered him up." Then Meges slays Pedaios, a bastard son of Antenor. Meges struck him on the sinew behind the head, and the blade cut his tongue at the root and went through the teeth. He fell in the dust, biting hard on the cold metal.

> **COMMENT:**   The vivid details, the specific routes of spears and swords—all add to the stark realism. Without apparent emotion Homer gives us the gore and blood of battle; perhaps there is even a kind of exultation in heroic duel, for this is epic battle and elemental savagery at its starkest. Homer is not for the weak-minded.

Diomedes continues his slaughter of the Trojans. In a duel with Aeneas (ee NEE uhs) Diomedes "lifted a large stone, such as two men could not lift as men are now, but he handled it easily himself. This he crashed down upon the hip of Aeneas, where the thigh turns in the socket, what they call the cup; the jagged stone smashed the cup and burst both the sinews, and tore away the skin. The hero fell forward on his knees and leaned with one hand upon the ground: then black night covered his eyes." Diomedes then pursues the goddess Aphrodite (aff roh DYE tee) and manages to cut her in the hand with his spear. Ichor, which flows from the veins of the immortal gods, runs from her wound. With a scream she hastens to Olympus (the mountaintop home of the gods) where she is consoled by her mother; and of course such wounds are easily healed.

THE *ILIAD*

BOOK VI: HECTOR AND ANDROMACHE

HELENUS' ADVICE: The battle rages on. Telamonian Aias slays Acamas; Diomedes kills Axylus; Teucer, a half-brother of Telamonian Aias, slays Aretaon. Menelaus captures Adrestus, whose chariot has broken down, and who then tries to bribe Menelaus; but Agamemnon reminds him of how he was treated when Paris visited his house and urges the kill. Adrestus is pushed away and speared by Agamemnon. Nestor then calls out in a loud voice:

> "Friends and Danaans! you are the servants of Arês, and no one must linger and throw himself on spoils. Our business is not to go back to the camp laden, but to kill. Then you can strip the bodies lying dead, and get all that booty afterwards at your leisure."

COMMENT: The blood-curling cries to kill and seize booty may seem horribly cruel in our eyes, but we must remember that Homer's warriors lived by a different code. Might and courage in the face of the enemy and a merciless homicide upon the enemy were valued. Booty seized after the call was an honorable reward for battlefield valor. Tribal values are centered around courage, honor, reputation, and glory won against the enemy.

Helenus (HELL uh nuss), Hector's brother, asks Hector and Aeneas to stop the Trojan retreat by raising the troops' will to fight. Then Hector must tell his mother Hecuba (HEK you buh) to offer a finely woven robe to Athena as well as a sacrifice of twelve heifers a year—all in order to keep Diomedes away from Troy. Hector does as advised.

DIOMEDES AND GLAUCUS: Diomedes meets Glaucus (GLAW kuss), a Trojan, and holds his spear back at the sight of this god-like youth. Glaucus replies that his lineage is of little matter when he is asked for his name. Says Glaucus: 'The generation of men is like leaves; wind may sweep leaves to the ground, but others grow when spring comes. Thus it is with men." Glaucus tells about his forebears, especially the thrilling story of Bellerophon (bell AIR oh fun), who earned the enmity of Proetus, the king. Proetus dared not kill him—instead he gave him a folded tablet with secret marks that would cause his death when he handed the tablet to the Lycian king, as Proetus had directed Bellerophon to do.

COMMENT: This is one of the two passages in Homer's works that refers to writing. The description of the tablet agrees with actual tablets found in Knossos and Pylos which were written on in the Linear B alphabet.

Bellerophon, as one of his deadly tasks, is told to slay the Chimaera (ky MEE rah), a fire-breathing monster with a snake's tail, a lion's head, and a goat's body. He also succeeds against the fierce Solymi and the Amazons. The upshot is that the king offers him his daughter's hand and half his kingdom, both of which are accepted by Bellerophon. Diomedes refuses to fight Glaucus because his grandfather was once host to Bellerophon for three weeks, after which they had exchanged gifts of friendship. Diomedes suggests that they not fight, either now or in the future, and that, to seal their friendship, they exchange armor.

COMMENT: Diomedes makes the greatest act of faith in Glaucus that a Homeric hero can offer, for exchanging armor is equivalent to exchanging identities. Homer, however, cannot resist speaking in his own character by saying that Glaucus was a fool to exchange his golden armor for Diomedes' bronze one; a hundred oxen's worth for none—a very commercial note. One reason for Homer's greatness is his very practical eye and his frank directness of vision.

HECTOR AND ANDROMACHE: Hector meets his mother Hecuba (or Hecabe) who, like a good mother, offers him wine, but Hector refuses the wine and her motherly advice about his welfare. He relays Helenus' message to her—that she offer Athena the robe and the twelve yearly heifers in order to keep Diomedes from Ilium (Troy). Hecuba does as requested, but Athena rejects the offerings (a bad sign).

Next Hector visits Paris, who has not left his bedroom since Aphrodite put him there. Paris accepts his brother's rebukes and arms for battle. Helen blames herself for all their woes. Then Hector finds his wife Andromache (an DRAHM uh kee) with his son Astyanax (ass TY uh nax), otherwise known as Scamandrius. (Notice that as Hector has gone through the city, the people he meets are progressively more related to him.) She pleads with her husband not to return to war, and reminds him that Achilles had slain her father, mother, and brothers. Hector is now her father, mother, brother, as well as husband; and she does not want to lose him to the mighty Achilles. Hector, of course, rejects her pleas, but he is concerned as to her fate:

"To think that you should live in a foreign land, and ply the loom at the orders of another woman; that you should carry water from strange fountains . . . May I be dead and buried deep in the earth before I hear your cries and see you dragged away!"

Then Hector holds out his arms for his boy, but the boy weeps and shrinks from his father, "for he was afraid of the gleaming metal and the horsehair crest, when he saw that dreadful thing nodding from the top of the helmet." The parents laugh aloud; Hector removes his gleaming helmet, kisses and dandles his son, praying to Zeus that his son will be a mighty warrior: "May he kill his enemy and bring home the blood-stained spoils, and give joy to his mother's heart!" Then Hector leaves Troy to return to battle, followed by Paris.

THE *ILIAD*

BOOK VII: THE BATTLE BETWEEN HECTOR AND AIAS

HECTOR AND AIAS DUEL: Athena, witness to a Trojan advance, hastens from Olympus to help the Greeks, but is intercepted by Apollo. He suggests that they stop the fighting for this day. Apollo suggests that a duel should be fought between two great warriors while the armies rest. Helenus, through his ability as a seer, suggests this very plan to Hector, who consents. Hector then challenges any Achaean to a duel. Menelaus consents but is dissuaded by Agamemnon. Old Nestor tries to shame them by mentioning his own former bravery in combat. If he were young now as he was formerly, he says, he would not hesitate to accept Hector's challenge. Immediately, nine Achaeans volunteer. Lots are marked and then (this and the episode of Bellerophon in Book VI contain the only Homeric references to writing) put in a helmet, which is shaken until a lot flies out. Telamonian Aias wins the lot to fight the redoubtable Hector, the mightiest of the Trojans. The duel is on: spears, rocks, and swords, but the two are evenly matched. Finally, darkness ends the fight with neither the victor. As customary, gifts are exchanged between combatants, Aias offering his silver-studdend sword in return for a finely embroidered belt. Both sides then retire.

PARIS' OFFER: An argument develops over Helen: whether to return her to her husband Menelaus or to let Paris still enjoy her. Paris will not give her up, but he does offer to return all the possessions seized from the Spartans (Menelaus' countrymen and Menelaus himself) as well as stock from his own wealth. Priam, the king of the Trojans, bids the herald Idaeus to inform Agamemnon of the offer. Diomedes recommends that the Danaans (i.e., the Greeks) reject the offer since they will win anyway. They do accept the offer of a temporary truce however (Agamemnon did not let it be known that he was about to make the same offer of a truce). There is a truce; corpses are gathered and washed and piled on funeral pyres for burning. The Greeks also build a wall behind a trench, for protection against the enemy, and to save their ships from destruction. A shipment of wine arrives, which is paid for in bronze, iron, and cattle. Then all go to sleep.

THE *ILIAD*

BOOK VIII: THE SHORT BATTLE

ZEUS' ORDERS: Zeus tells the gods to refrain from helping either side so that he can fulfill his promise to Thetis—that he would make the Trojans victorious. He promises exile in dark Tartarus (the penal sector of the underworld) to any disobeying god. Zeus leaves Olympus in his flying chariot. He goes to Mount Ida, which overlooks the battlefield.

THE ACHAEANS IN RETREAT: The fight resumes with neither side in ascendancy, until Zeus holds out his divine balance scales, the fate of the Trojans on one pan, and the fate of the Achaeans on the other. The Achaean pan sinks down, giving the Trojans the decision.

> **COMMENT:** Zeus' scale portends victory for the Trojans, at at least in *this* battle. The balances are used again in Book XXIV in deciding the duel between Achilles and Hector.

Zeus' thunder from the heavens puts the frightened Greeks on the run. Nestor cannot retreat, for his horse has been speared by Paris. He had "shot it on the top of the skull where the first hairs grow on a horse's head, a fatal spot. The arrow pierced the brain; the horse leapt high in agony writhing about the barb, and threw horses and all into confusion (there were two pole-horses to a car or chariot)." Diomedes rescues Nestor, but the heroes of Achaea are all on the run. The confident Hector and his exulting troops rankle Hera, but both she and Poseidon dare not break Zeus' command. Just as the ships are about to be set on fire by the Trojans, the Achaeans rally and drive them back. Teucer, hiding behind his brother's shield (Telamonian Aias), shoots off his arrows.

> **COMMENT:** Archers are degraded fighters who shoot from behind the battleline. It is a special practice of the Lycians, who are led by Pandarus, the Carians, and the Paeonians, all allies of Troy. Meriones and Teucer are the only Achaean archers mentioned. The Achaeans made small use of the bow.

Teucer fells eight Trojans and is finally hit by a rock thrown by Hector. Athena and Hera decide to help the Achaeans in spite of Zeus' orders, but Zeus' messenger Iris warns them and they quickly desist. Zeus returns to Olympus, gloats over the downcast

Athena and Hera and provokes them further by stating the Trojans will advance even farther the next day.

HECTOR VICTORIOUS: The sun sets, ending the hostilities for the day. Hector addresses his assembled men, telling them to keep fires burning throughout the night so that the Achaeans may not escape in their ships. Now that the Trojans command an area outside the town walls where they can spend the night, they let the old men of Ilium keep guard, thereby preventing a surprise attack on Troy in their absence. At dawn they will attack and, Hector says confidently, destroy the Achaeans. The Trojans stay up during the night tending the fires and thinking of victory.

THE *ILIAD*

BOOK IX: THE EMBASSY TO ACHILLES

AGAMEMNON'S COMPENSATION: In a speech (like that in Book II) "with tears running down his cheeks, as a clear spring trickles over a rock," Agamemnon suggests that the Danaans leave Troy. His men sit uneasily, wondering whether he is tricking them again. Diomedes denounces Agamemnon for suggesting flight, and Nestor, "that grand old man whose counsel was always thought the best, spoke with honesty and good courage, setting out his thoughts neat and clear, like a weaver weaving a pattern upon his loom."

> **COMMENT:** The old wise counsellor, whose advice is almost always taken, is famous for his somewhat comic garrulity and pomposity. The type was made famous also by Shakespeare in his own Nestor as well as his Polonious and Justice Shallow. Note the admiration expressed by Homer in the neat clearness of his thoughts, splendidly capped by the simple, homely, weaving image. No image in Homer is false or artificial; they are all taken from life and experience. Only Dante and Shakespeare had the gift, but Homer towers over them both in that special art.

Nestor in a long-winded speech suggests that sentries be placed along the wall; he adds that an apology be offered Achilles so that he will forget his anger and rejoin the army of the Achaeans. Agamemnon admits his error and offers Achilles tripods, gold, copper cauldrons, race horses, and seven captive women, including Briseis, of whom Agamemnon swore an oath:

> "And I will swear a solemn oath that she has never lain in my bed, and I have never touched her in the way of a man with a woman. In addition, Achilles will be given his choice of the booty when Troy is captured, and one of Agamemnon's daughters for his wife—and her dowry will be seven cities!"

> **COMMENT:** The usual practice in Greece was for the husband to give gifts to his new father-in-law, although there are other examples to the contrary in both the *Iliad* and the *Odyssey*.

THE EMBASSY: Phoenix (FEE nix), Achilles' beloved teacher, Telamonian Aias, and Odysseus are chosen to plead with Achilles, in accordance with Nestor's plan for an embassy. They set out for Achilles' hut and find him singing and playing the harp: "A beautiful thing it was, made by an artist, with a silver bridge and a clear lovely tone, part of the spoils of Thêbe."

> **COMMENT:** Achilles is playing and singing of the feats of heroes, appropriately enough. Thêbes had been sacked by Achilles, who had killed the king and his seven sons. The king's daughter was Andromache, and Chryseis had been seized in the raid. Note the intricate tying-in of the slightest detail in the whole vast legend, in this case touched off by the mention of the harp. Homer's audience would have a multifarious set of associations with which to tie in every detail.

Odysseus repeats Agamemnon's offer, using the very same words (but he does soften Agamemnon's harsh demands at the end of his speech). Achilles' reply is long and angry: "I hate that man like the gates of hell who says one thing and hides another thing in his heart. . . . This Agamemnon *lags* behind and takes it, distributes a few trifles and keeps the rest." (Note Homer's fondness for puns.) The upshot is that the wrathful Achilles (remember that the theme is his *wrath*) rejects the offer and reminds them that the Fates say he will live long if he returns home, and die if he stays.

> **COMMENT:** Achilles has replied, not only to Agamemnon's offer as stated by Odysseus, but also to what Odysseus left unstated—that Agamemnon still is haughty and unwilling to recognize the matter of Achilles' honor. The Achaeans had an "external" sense of honor: it depends upon what other people think of you, and not upon your own evaluation of yourself. What is vital is what *others* think of you as a public image.

Phoenix recalls how he used to cut Achilles' meat and hold his wine-cup: "How often you have wetted my tunic, spluttering out drops of wine like a naughty child!" Achilles remains adamant in spite of Phoenix' stirring appeal, by relating the tale of Meleager, the moral of which is *external honor*. (Achilles seems to promulgate an "internal" sense of honor at this point, a concept later taught by Socrates in the fifth century.) The bewildered embassy leaves, but not before hearing Achilles say that he will stay apart from the battle until the day Hector sets fire to their ships. They return with the bad news, and Diomedes feels that Achilles will be prouder than ever. They all go to bed in preparation for the battle to come.

THE *ILIAD*

BOOK X: THE DOLONEIA

DOLON CAPTURED AND KILLED: Agamemnon and Menelaus, unable to sleep, discuss sending someone out to spy on the Trojans. Agamemnon tells Menelaus to "call out wherever you go, and tell them to get up; but address them with proper politeness, name and surname for each, and don't be too proud. We must do the work of menials ourselves. Such indignity was ordained for us, it seems, by Zeus, on the day we were born."

> **COMMENT:** Notice Agamemnon's wry disgust at this menial function—the awaking of sleeping heroes. Even the delicate social amenity of addressing them by name and surname, a sign that the arouser is respectfully addressing his superiors, is observed!

Nestor arouses Diomedes by kicking him with his foot. Others are aroused among the heroes. Diomedes volunteers quickly, but Odysseus is among the last to do so (see Book VII where Odysseus is again the last; Odysseus is not a coward, but neither is he a fool). Naturally Diomedes chooses Odysseus, the wiliest of the Achaeans, to accompany him, and the two set off. Meanwhile in the Trojan camp Dolon, not a handsome man but swift-footed, is chosen as a spy to scout the Greek camp: "He was a poor creature to look at, that is true, but a quick runner. He was an only son with five sisters" (Homer never forgets the homely biographical details). The Greek spies allow Dolon to pass them in the darkness, "but when he had got as far away as the width of a day's work with mules—they are better than oxen to plow the deep furrow—," the two chase Dolon and capture him. The cowardly Trojan bleats out the details of the Trojan camp in the belief he will be spared, but instead the frowning Diomedes says, "No escape for you, Dolon, don't imagine such a thing, now you are in our hands, although we are much obliged to you for the information. If we set you free now and let you go, you will come another time to spy upon us, or to fight; but if we kill you while we have you, then you will not trouble the Achaians any more." (What beautiful, irrefragable logic!) Dolon is slain.

THE HORSES OF RHESUS: Odysseus and Diomedes, armed with Dolon's information, steal into the Trojan camp and find the white horses of Rhesus, the king of the Thracians. While Diomedes kills thirteen of the Thracians, including Rhesus himself, Odysseus unties the horses. The two of them now ride swiftly back to the spot where they had killed Dolon; they take his weapons and return to camp.

THE *ILIAD*

BOOK XI: THE ARISTEIA OF AGAMEMNON

AGAMEMNON ON THE WARPATH: At dawn, the third battle of the *Iliad* begins (it will last through Book XVIII). Only Eris, the goddess of strife, is present from among the immortal gods, since Zeus' orders had kept all other gods clear of the struggle. Agamemnon slays Bienor and his chariot driver and then kills Isus and Antiphus, the two sons of Priam; and after that slays Peisander and Hippolochus in spite of their plea for life:

> "With these words he struck Peisander on the chest with his spear and tumbled him out on his back. Hippolochus jumped down, and Agamemnon killed him there on the ground, and cut off his hands and head, and sent the body trundling along like a roller" (note the gory details and the exulting comic touch).

The Trojans are driven back to the gates of their city. This alarms the onlooking Zeus, who decides to intervene. Iris, his messenger, is sent to tell Hector to yield to Agamemnon until the king is hit with a spear or arrow. Now Agamemnon kills Iphidamas, a son of Antenor:

> "So Iphidamas (eye FID uh muss) fell, and slept as in hoops of steel, unhappy man! fell fighting for his people, far from his bride so newly wed, of whom he had small comfort—and what a world of bridal gifts he had given! a hundred cattle then and there, and a thousand promised, goats and sheep also, all those countless flocks!"

Coön, his brother, succeeds in piercing Agamemnon's arm before being slain. The wound forces Agamemnon to withdraw. Hector now assumes the offensive and kills many Greeks until he meets Odysseus and Diomedes. At this point Paris shoots Diomedes through the foot with an arrow. Paris' gloating is met with contempt: "Hide yourself and pull your bow!
> Come and steal a wife and go!
> Frizzle-head with pretty curls,
> You can make eyes at pretty girls!"

Diomedes challenges Paris to stand up and fight like a man: "When I shoot an arrow," says Diomedes, "it finds its mark." (The sight

of battle-scarred warriors hurling contempt in verse at each other
is not uncommon in Homer.)

Odysseus and Diomedes escape to their ships. Paris wounds Machaon, the physician to the Achaeans, whom Nestor removes from
the field. Now Aias is forced to retreat, much against his will:

> "since he feared greatly for the Achaian ships. You have seen
> a stubborn ass in a cornfield, who is too much for the boys.
> They may break many sticks on his back, but he goes on
> cropping the corn; they beat away with their sticks, but what
> is the strength of a child! They can hardly drive him out
> when he has eaten all he wants. So the crowds of Trojans
> hung upon the heels of mighty Aias."

ACHILLES TAKES NOTE: Achilles sends his friend Patroclus
(PAT roh cluss) to find out whether Machaon had been wounded.
Patroclus finds Nestor tending Machaon. By the telling of tales
of bravery and appealing to Patroclus' glorious ancestors, the long-
winded Nestor succeeds in stirring up in Patroclus the will to fight.
He stops on his way back to Achilles to help the wounded Euryp-
lus (you RIP ih luss), who tells Patroclus that the Achaeans
will be destroyed. Patroclus helps him to his hut and, taking the
arrow from his thigh, washes the wound.

THE *ILIAD*

BOOK XII: THE BATTLE BY THE WALL

THE GATES CRASHED: The Trojans on the offensive assail the wall built by the Greeks to defend their ships. Hector "like a tower" urges his men to leap the trench dug before the wall. Divided into five groups they proceed to cross the trench on foot. The very ships of the Greeks are threatened, their lifeline to home and supplies! A sign from Zeus is interpreted by Polydamus (po LID uh muss) as meaning that it would be wise for the Trojans to retreat. Hector rejects the advice and swears Polydamus to silence. Sarpedon and Glaucus advance towards the wall. Menestheus calls for help against the advancing Trojans, and Aias and Teucer arrive in time for Aias to kill Epicles with a rock:

> "A huge jagged stone, which lay on the top of the heap which was ready for use inside the breastwork. A man could not easily lift that stone with both hands, such as men are today, were he ever so strong; but Aias lifted it high and swung it, smashed the horned helmet and broke the bones of the man's head into a mess—the breath left his bones, and he took a header off the wall."

Glaucus is shot in the arm by Teucer's arrow. Finally, Hector lifts a huge boulder and tosses it against the gate, breaking it down. The first to rush through is Hector himself, who calls upon his men to follow. They climb over the wall and run in through the gate. The Damaans flee to their ships (the Danaans, the Achaeans = the Greek forces).

THE *ILIAD*

BOOK XIII: THE BATTLE BY THE SHIPS

POSEIDON HELPS: Zeus from Olympus turns from the battle scene and gazes upon distant peoples—Thracians, Mysians, Hippemolgoi, and Abioi.

> **COMMENT:** Homer interrupts the tense action with an abrupt contrast; he evokes strange images: the Hippemolgoi ("milkers of horses") and the Abioi are described as "most righteous of men." As the god turns to this unreal spectacle, there is stressed most poignantly the difference between the gods who cannot die and the suffering mortals who must.

Poseidon disobeys Zeus' orders and comes to the aid of the Achaeans. His bronze-hoofed horses with manes of gold draw his chariot over the waves (Poseidon is god of the seas), and the beasts of the sea rejoice at the sight of their master. He enters the Achaean camp in the form of the prophet Calchas. He fills the two Aiantes with the courage to resist the fierce Hector. Aias, the son of the Oileus, recognizes the god: "That was one of the gods of Olympos, in the shape of our diviner, telling us to fight! That was not Calchas our interpreter of birds. I knew him at once by the way his feet and legs moved from behind—the gods are easy to know!" Poseidon fills the Greeks with warlike zeal to resist. (His encouraging war speeches are like those delivered by generals before battle, a standard part of ancient warfare. These served as the subect of lyric poems, such as those by Tyrtaeus, a Spartan poet of the seventh century B.C. Homer incorporates various species of "the hortatory" in his poems.)

The Argives (Achaeans = Danaans = Argives = Greeks) rally.

Hector and Deiphobus (dee IFF oh busss), his brother, are stopped in their advance. Teucer the Greek slays Imbrius, the husband of an illegitimate daughter of Priam, but Hector prevents for the moment the stripping of his armor. The Aiantes bravely carry off Imbrius from the scene, while this is followed up by the Oilean Aias decapitating the corpse in his fury. (The battle takes on a more primitive savagery now that the Greeks are at bay.)

THE INDOMITABLE IDOMENEUS: Idomeneus is inspired, dons his armor and encounters his squire Meriones, who is returning to

39

replace a spear he has lost. Each boasts of his valor against the Trojans. Idomeneus offers a spear to Meriones to join him in an attempt for more glory on the battlefield. Zeus and Poseidon, in a kind of desperate tug-of-war, keep the battle uncertain, Zeus rooting for the Trojans and his brother Poseidon for the Danaans. The indomitable Idomeneus slays Othryoneus, who had fought for the hand of Priam's loveliest daughter, Cassandra. He kills Asius, and then Alcathous. Next he challenges Deiphobus, who receives help from Aeneas and others. Menelaus joins the fray and slays Peisander, accusing (after this) the Trojans of having broken the sacred laws of hospitality when they stole his wife.

COMMENT: Idomeneus is the appropriate hero for this bloody fight. He is an old man from an ancient kingdom, and his code demands a primitive fierceness, where virtue lies in fearlessly meeting one's fate. Note that he fights to kill and not for personal glory.

Hector seeks out the Trojan leaders for advice, and he learns of the rout of his left wing, for which he curses Paris; yet it is Paris and Hector who lead the next attack.

THE *ILIAD*

BOOK XIV: THE DECEIVING OF ZEUS

AGAMEMNON'S COUNSEL: Diomedes, Odysseus, and Agamemnon are all wounded, and use their spears as crutches. Nestor hurries to them to tell of the destruction of the wall by the Trojans. The despondent Agamemnon urges flight, since Zeus has given the palm to Hector and his Trojans, but Odysseus scolds him for his cowardice and tells him that even in flight they will lose. Diomedes, the youngest hero of the Greeks and Trojans both, boasts of his proud lineage, and urges continued fighting in spite of their wounds; thus they will inspire their troops to renewed effort. The kings accept his suggestion. Poseidon, in the guise of an old man, assures the kings of eventual victory; and speeding across the plain with the cry of nine or ten thousand warriors (one of the few instances of exaggeration in Homer), he rouses the spirit for battle in the ranks of the Achaeans.

HERA'S SEX TRICK: Hera, Zeus' wife, devises a plan to divert her husband's attention so that she, Poseidon, and others can come to the aid of the highly oppressed Greeks. She will seduce him. She bathes in ambrosia (divine liquid), dons a lovely robe woven by Athena herself; by lying to Aphrodite (the goddess of love) as to the aim of her mission, she obtains Aphrodite's "broidered strap with all the charms worked in it: there is love, there is desire, there is lovers' tender prattle, the cajolery which deceives the mind of the wisest." Tucking it into her bosom, Hera travels to Lemnos in Thrace where she finds Sleep, the brother of Death. Finally, she almost induces the fearful Sleep to work his powers over her husband by putting him to sleep after the sex trick. With the bribe of one of the younger Graces as a bride, Sleep consents but not before she swears the sacred oath: "Very well, swear me an oath by the inviolate water of Styx, touching mother earth with one hand and the glittering sea with the other; call to witness the gods below with Cronos; and swear on your honor that you will give me one of the young Graces." (Note that the wily Sleep insists on the most sacred of oaths.) They then travel to Gargarus, the highest peak of Mount Ida, where Zeus in the form of a songbird sits amid the branches. Upon seeing his lovely wife, he is filled with sexual desire, calling her the loveliest of his conquests! He urges her to a sexual bout immediately. His artful queen says, (the Greeks love the artful and the cunning):

41

"You dreadful creature! What a thing to say! You want to make love on the top of a mountain where anyone can see! What if one of the gods should see us asleep and go and tell tales to the whole family? I couldn't get up from the bed and go straight home. I should be ashamed."

Zeus, the Cloud gatherer, reassures her they will not be seen:

"As he spoke, he took his wife in his arms: and under them the earth divine made a bed of fresh new grass to grow, with dewy clover and crocus and hyacinth soft and thick, which raised them high above the ground. There they lay, and a beautiful golden cloud spread over them, from which fell drops of sparkling dew."

COMMENT: This is one of the most delightful episodes in the *Iliad*, and what a relief it is from all the blood-and-guts fighting. Note the cleverness of Hera's intricate strategy, her female womanliness, and her maidenly modesty, which remind us of some proper city woman. Remember that without the love-strap this would not have been possible. There is also somewhat of a domestic tragedy here—I think—the powerful charms of Aphrodite are necessary for a wife to seduce her own husband, or is Homer so universally wise even here? Note also that the forces of nature harmonize with the procreating gods.

ZEUS ASLEEP: Zeus now falls into a deep sleep, and Sleep then informs Poseidon that he can go on helping the Greeks unseen by Zeus. Poseidon advises the Greeks to pool their armor so that the best fighters may have the best weapons. (The transfer of armor in the midst of battle suggests a pooling of identities. At the moment of crisis, individuals melt into a common entity of the tribe.) Now Hector and Poseidon each heads an opposing army.

COMMENT: Poseidon clearly represents the elemental force of battle, with perhaps a suggestion that it is the sea at the backs of the Argives which drives them forward. We must understand Poseidon as symbolic of the sea and its might, and not as an actual fighting general of a force.

The battles, also, are won not by intellectual men of forethought and plan, but rather by elemental men who have al-almost descended to the level of inert matter, if passive, and to the level of blind force, if in momentum. The secret of the

Iliad lies in its similes, which compare fighters to fire, flood, wind, wild animals, trees, sand, or water—"to anything in nature that is set into motion by the violence of external forces." (See Simone Weil, *The Iliad or the Poem of Force.*)

Hector is knocked down by a huge boulder thrown by Aias. He is carried by his men to the river Xanthus (ZAN thuss) where he recovers and then again faints. King Peneleos slays Ilioneus, an only child: "Peneleos drew his sword and cut right through the neck; head and helmet fell to the ground with the spear still sticking in the eye. Then Peneleos held it up for the Trojans to see, like a poppyhead on a long stalk." He cries out for the wife and parents of the only child to lament for the lost son. The book closes with an enumeration of the dead.

THE *ILIAD*

BOOK XV: THE RENEWED OFFENSIVE

ZEUS AWAKENS: The Argives now chase the Trojans back beyond the trench and wall. Zeus awakes after the seduction only to see the Trojans being routed. He angrily threatens his wife, and orders Hera back to Olympus to send Iris and Apollo to his side:

> "I want to send Iris to tell Poseidon that he must stop meddling in the war and go home; and I want Apollo to breathe courage into Hector again, and make him forget the pain that torments him, and send him back to the battle. The Achaeans are to be turned again in headlong flight, and to fall back on the ships of Achilles; he is to put up his friend Patroclus; and Hector is to kill Patroclus under the walls of Ilios, after he has killed many other fine fellows, and among them Sarpedon my own son. Then Achilles in revenge for Patroclus is to kill Hector."

COMMENT: Note that throughout the *Iliad* the reader is never held in suspense as to what the future will hold. In a capsule here, for example, we foresee the entire course of the war. The suspense in Homer does not lie in the suspense of an unknown future action but in the minds and actions of the characters as the debate alternates between actions. Even though we know all along how the hero will decide, the suspense resides in the reality and humanity of the hero while faced with alternative actions.

Meanwhile, Zeus will give glory to the Trojans, in accordance with the promise he made to Thetis to honor Achilles. After Hera's message, Athena and Apollo fly to Zeus on Mount Ida. Iris delivers her message to the enraged Earth-shaker, who points out that he is Zeus' equal. (The three brothers divided sky, sea, and Hades among them: Zeus = sky; Poseidon = sea; Puluto (Hades) = Hades, or the regions below.)

Nevertheless, Poseidon leaves the battle. Next Zeus gives Apollo the *aegis* (the breastplate of Zeus and Athena in the center of which was the terrifying image of the Gorgon Medusa, a snake-haired woman's face that turned all to stone who dared look at it). Apollo is to terrify the leaders of the Achaeans with the aegis

44

(EE jiss), and is to inspire Hector with such boldness that he will reach the ships of the Danaans. The Danaans retreat in panic at the sight of the newly inspired Hector, but the Greek leaders hold their ground. With Apollo in the lead, the Trojans advance. Before Apollo's aegis the Danaans flee "like a herd of cattle or a great flock of sheep chased by a couple of wild beasts in the murk of night, with a sudden attack when the keeper is away, so fled the Achaeans in panic; for Apollo put fear into them and gave victory to Hector and his Trojans." The wall is smashed like so many sand castles.

> **COMMENT:** The transitory nature of man's works is most strikingly expressed in this simile. The destruction of the Achaean wall suggests the razing of the wall of Troy, which takes place after the poem's conclusion. One purpose of the *Iliad* is to show that man's importance lies not in the futile constructions of his hands, but in the process of struggle itself.

Now Zeus spurs Hector on to set the ships ablaze, using the Trojans to honor the wrathful Achilles. Aias, weary and under continual attack, slowly backs off, slaying twelve men, and ever exhorting the Argives to fight bravely, for there is no ally behind them, no room to retreat; the battle is life or death for the Achaean host.

THE *ILIAD*

BOOK XVI: THE PATROCLEIA

THE HEROIC DEATH OF PATROCLUS: The plight of his fel-
low-Greeks brings tears down Patroclus' cheeks. Achilles is deeply
grieved but frank:

> "My dear Patroclus, why are you crying like a baby? You
> might be some little girl running to her mother, and pulling
> at her apron, and keeping her from work, and blubbering
> and looking up and saying, Nurse me, mammy dear! That's
> what you look like, my dear man, crying like that. Have you
> some news for the men, or just for me, or is it a special mes-
> sage from home to you?"

(Note the irony and mockery—as if Achilles really did not know
why his dearest friend and boon-companion was weeping.) Patroclus reports the misery of the Argive army and the injuries of
the great Diomedes, Odysseus, Agamemnon, and Eurypylus. He
berates the vengeful, pitiless Achilles. He calls him the "child of
the sea and hard crags," (a pun: Thetis his mother is a sea-nymph,
and his father's name, Peleus, resembles Pelion, a rocky mountain
in Magnesia). Patroclus pleads at least for the loan of Achilles'
armor, so that the Trojans will take him for the mighty Achilles
and flee. Achilles recounts the public shame handed him over the
Briseis affair—"that girl my lord King Agamemnon tore from my
hands as if I were a foreigner without any rights (note that foreigners had no rights in Homer's day)." Yet Achilles lends the
famous armor and his fierce Myrmidons besides, savage warriors
indeed! Patroclus is to return to the hut after the Trojans are driven
back; under no circumstances is Patroclus to forge on beyond that
point!

COMMENT: This speech gives profound insight into Achilles'
problem. He has long desired to return to the side of his
comrades, to take his rightful place among the lords in the
great struggle and terminate his self-imposed excommunica-
tion. Yet he is still unable to act as a member of society, the
dynamic living force within him is yet in chains; his excuse
is his vow: Achilles has not yet learned to renounce absolutes.
One part of Achilles, however, does respond, his pity for the
Achaeans and his kindness. These qualities in Achilles are represented by Patroclus, who is always gentle. Patroclus goes to

war in Achilles' armor, and thus in Achilles' place. When Patroclus dies, all mercy will leave the heart of Achilles, who will emerge as pure violence and energy.

The Trojans ignite the ships, which arouses Achilles to action. Patroclus is armed in Achilles' armor, delivers a hortatory address to the Myrmidons, who swarm like wasps after their victims. Patroclus is mighty in his victories; Sarpedon, son of Zeus, decides to resist him, and even his father cannot deny his fate: Sarpedon is to die. While dying, Sarpedon calls on Glaucus to prevent the spoilation of the body, but the armor is saved by the Argives, and Zeus dispatches Apollo to bear away the body of Sarpedon into the hands of the twins, Sleep and Death, and thence to his homeland, Lycia.

> **COMMENT:** This close relationship between sleep and death, which we do not feel so strongly as the Greeks, has meaning: life is struggle and conflict, not passive existence. For Aristotle, a man asleep was neither good nor bad; he could be judged only by his actions, and not by his inherent moral disposition. Thus, sleep and death are alike to the Greeks.

Patroclus drives the Trojans to the very walls of Ilium! Even Apollo warns him repeatedly not to go on, for the conquest of Ilium is not to be his. The mighty Patroclus brings down nine more men in a vicious fray, but Apollo causes his armor to fall off and Patroclus is stabbed by Euphorbus' spear while Hector delivers the death stroke, (not too heroically it seems, for he was only the third to strike). Patroclus foretells Hector's death and perishes. (The words of dying men are prophetic for the Greeks.)

THE *ILIAD*

BOOK XVII: THE BATTLE OVER THE CORPSE

MENELAUS THE PROTECTOR: "Menelaus had not failed to mark the death of Patroclus. He came up at once and bestrode the body, like a cow standing over her calf, the first she ever bore, with plaintive lowing." After boasting of his valor and past mighty deeds, he fells Euphorbus who "fell with a dull thud in his rattling armour. . . . He lay like a tall stem of olive, which a man keeps in a private garden where plenty of water flows, growing fair and high . . . until suddenly a storm-wind roots it out of the trench and lays it along the ground. And so lay he, when Menelaus had killed him and stript his armour." When the enraged Hector storms at Menelaus he says to himself:

> "What shall I do! If I leave the spoils, and if I leave Patroclos, who lies here for my sake, not a Danaän but will hate the sight of me. If I stand and fight Hector and the Trojan army alone, to save my honour, I shall be surrounded. . . . No, no, all that is nonsense. When one fights a fellow that finds favour in the sight of God, he simply tempts providence and brings tribulations rolling upon himself. Then no Danaän will hate the sight of me, if he sees me retreat before Hector, because Hector has heaven to help him."

(Note that when insurmountable odds threaten, a hero can coolly debate the issue over his honor and take the wiser course—in this case retreat—without losing his honor.) Aias, son of Oileus, comes to his aid, as does Idomeneus and his squire, Meriones. The Trojans are put on the run, but Apollo intervenes by instilling Aeneas with valor.

COMMENT: The gods serve many functions in the *Iliad*. In their role of disguised assistants, however, it is clear that Homer is unwilling to stress their anthropomorphic intervention in human affairs. The "divine machinery" rather expresses "psychic intervention," "or inspiration outside or beyond the usual faculties or capacities of a human being. Professor E.R. Dodds in the first chapter of *The Greeks and the Irrational* (see Bibliography) suggests that "the inward monition, or the sudden unaccountable feeling of power, or the sudden unaccountable loss of judgment, is the germ out of which the divine machinery developed."

The earth around the corpse of Patroclus runs red with blood and a fog covers the scene. Neither side yields.

THE HORSES OF ACHILLES: At some distance the horses of Achilles weep with heads bowed over their dead driver Automedon. "They drooped their heads till they touched the ground, hot tears ran from their eyes and fell, as they mourned the driver whom they had loved and lost; their thick manes hung from the yoke-pad over both sides of the yoke."

> **COMMENT:** Herodotus, the great Greek historian, describes the ritual for the burial of Scythian ings in Book IV, chapters 71-72, of his famous *History.* Fifty horses are strangled and stuffed, and then mounted with bit and bridle, each with a dead youth upon it. This extravagant custom doubtless derives from a more simple procedure in which the horses of a prince served as his grave sign, and we may suppose that Homer's picture of Achilles' horses is borrowed from such a burial rite.

Athena inspires Menelaus and Apollo Hector, but Zeus with a thunderclap and brandishing his aegis, gives victory to the Trojans. The corpse, however, is slowly slipping into the hands of the Argive Greeks.

THE *ILIAD*

BOOK XVIII: ACHILLES REARMED

THE WRATH ENDED: Antilochus tells Achilles the baleful news, and Achilles sinks to the ground, pours dust and ashes about his head, lying in his hugeness upon the ground. And the hand-maidens of Achilles and Patroclus come out to mourn also.

COMMENT: The language describing Achilles lying in ashes resembles the language employed elsewhere in the *Iliad* to describe the dead heroes. The maidens who stand around Achilles and weep for him as well as Patroclus are comparable to the usual complement of lamenting women for a dead man. Homer thus incorporates a deliberate ambiguity into the scene, connecting Patroclus' death with the death of Achilles. That Antilochus holds Achilles' hands to prevent his suicide is adduced as a reason to suspect the line was added to the original *Iliad* by someone other than Homer, since "it introduces the idea of suicide, which is elsewhere unknown in the *Iliad*" (Walter Leaf). Suicide, however, is a dominant motif in the poem: Achilles will slay Hector, who is wearing Achilles' own armor, and with the knowledge that his own death must immediately follow upon Hector's. The suggestion of suicide is clearly appropriate here.

Thetis, Achilles' mother, hears his terrible cries, even from where she is sitting by her old father deep down in the sea. She shrieks, and all the Nerëid nymphs gathered about her in the deep sea: There came Glaucê and Thaleia and Cymodocê, Nesaia and Speio, Thoê and round-eyed Haliê, Cymothoê, and Actaia and Limnoraia . . . (These beautiful names are traditional; and the effect is a soft and soothing echo of legendary fairyland. The meaning matters little—but the sound is lovely.) She visits her son, who tells her the woeful tale of his squire's death. She again repeats he will die after Hector does.

Achilles quickly asks for death then, angry that he had not been able to defend his friend. "O that discord might utterly cease in heaven or earth! and anger, that makes even the prudent man take offence—anger that is far sweeter than trickling honey, and grows in men's hearts like smoke—just as I was made angry now by my lord King Agamemnon . . . May I bring sobs and groaning to some wives of Troy and Dardania, and tears to their tender cheeks, which they shall wipe away with both hands!"

COMMENT: Achilles denounces anger and yet speaks of it in loving terms—and instantly and *angrily* cries for revenge! Thus his humanity is endeared within our hearts.

Thetis promises to visit Hephaestus, god of crafts, and beg him to prepare armor for Achilles, which she will deliver on the morrow. Till then he must refrain from fighting. Unarmed, but with Athena's aegis blazing, he sets the Trojans in retreat while Patroclus' body is saved. Sunset gives respite in battle, while Polydamas, future-teller, advises retreat within the walls of Ilium. Hector advises otherwise (fatally), and his counsel of open combat is applauded.

THE SHIELD OF ACHILLES: Thetis finds Hephaestus, the ugly craftsman of the gods, in his brilliant palace: "She found him in a sweat, running about among his bellows, very busy." He agrees to forge immediately a shield and armor for her son. On the shield he carves the earth, the sky, the sea, the sun and moon, and the constellations. Then a warlike city and one at peace are represented, the peaceful one showing wedding processions and court trials. (Note that the Trojan War is being fought in order that the laws of marriage may be respected. War and peace are a necessary part of life in Homer.) Ploughing farmer, reaping laborers, vineyards, livestock, and dancers are shown; and encircling all is the river Ocean. Hephaestus completes the armor and hands it to Thetis.

THE *ILIAD*

BOOK XIX: APOLOGY AND PREPARATION

THE APOLOGY: At dawn the next morning Thetis delivers the armor to her son. He is both pleased and amazed at the splendid new armor. First, he summons all the Achaeans to council (the first council was called in Book I—that is by Achilles, when Agamemnon should have been the logical one. But this one is called for a peace-session). Agamemnon and his warriors are overjoyed, the king telling how he had been deceived by Atê (Folly). He offers Achilles great and varied gifts already listed in Book IX. The rest follow this by dining heavily in order to be ready for battle, but Achilles has vowed not to eat until Hector lies dead at his feet. The wise Odysseus advises a full stomach before battle.

> **COMMENT:** Here especially Achilles is disassociated from the living. Later he will be sustained on nectar and ambrosia, the food of the immortals, which also is used in the *Iliad* to preserve the bodies of Patroclus and Hector. Note also that Achilles, unlike Hector in the previous book, yields to the counsel of the wiser man.

All is forgiven, Achilles laying the blame on Folly, and the gifts are brought to his tent, among them the unsullied Briseis. She laments over the body of Patroclus, for he had been kind and had promised to make her Achilles' wife.

THE PREPARATION FOR BATTLE: Zeus sends Athena to distil nectar and ambrosia in the veins of Achilles so that he may not feel hunger or thirst. The men gather like snowflakes in preparation for battle. His divine horses are hitched to his chariot, and Xanthus, one of the immortal team, makes answer, for Hera puts voice into his mouth:

> "Sure enough we will save you yet this time, mighty Achilles. But the day of your death is near. We are not to blame, but a great god and compelling fate."

Homer generally avoids the supernatural, but here the animal speech is a startling and effective prelude to the last battle.

Achilles admits his fate, but he must fight to the death.

THE *ILIAD*

BOOK XX: THE BATTLE, ACHILLES, AND THE GODS

THE GODS IN COUNCIL: Zeus on Olympus bids Themis, goddess of order and custom, to summon the gods to council. He tells them that Achilles must not win too soon, contrary to destiny. He therefore will permit the gods to enter the combat, taking any side they choose. (*Pro-Greek* = Hera, Athena, Poseidon, Hermes, Hephaestus; *Pro-Trojan* = Ares, Apollo, Artemis, Leto—mother of Artemis and Apollo, and Aphrodite plus the god of the Xanthus River.) Poseidon *vs.* Apollo, Athena *vs.* Ares, Hera *vs.* Artemis, Hermes *vs.* Leto, and Hephaistus *vs.* Xanthus is how they are ranged on the battlefield.

> **COMMENT:** A battle of the gods, or *theomachy*, which is an element in many mythological traditions, is here suggested to magnify the importance of the return of Achilles. The actual *theomachy* is postponed to the following book, where Homer employs what was very probably an ancient epic theme to express the sheer energy of war and to relate human events to cosmic struggles.

Aeneas, in spite of past warnings, resolves to fight Achilles, especially since Apollo is giving him spirit. The Trojans have by and large only the most inconsequential immortals to protect them in battle. The gods, covered by a thick mist, watch the battle, especially that between Achilles and Aeneas.

> **COMMENT:** In Book XIII there is a suggestion that Aeneas bears ill-will towards King Priam. Aeneas generally is unenthusiastic for combat and must be exhorted. Note, moreover, that Achilles in his wrath is yet reluctant to engage Aeneas; and Poseidon, below, takes pity on this son of Aphrodite, though the sea-god is an implacable enemy of the Trojans. A dynastic conflict has been presumed by some scholars to have occurred between Hector and Aeneas.
>
> In addition Roman mythology held that Aeneas was the ancestor of the Romans, presumably drawing upon this passage in the effort to link their past with the great cultural heritage of the Greeks.

Just in time, the god Poseidon carries Aeneas from the battle, leaving Achilles thunderstruck. Achilles rages into the thick of the fighting killing Iphition, Polydorus, the youngest son of Priam. About to charge Hector, Apollo wraps him in a mist and carries him from the scene. Thrice Achilles vainly stabs. The fourth time, like a man possessed, he lunges, hurls an acid insult at Hector, and slays many Trojans, including Tros, who first seeks mercy by supplication, clutching the knees of Achilles. Like a fire Achilles continues to rage:

> "On went Achilles: as a devouring conflagration rages through the valleys of a parched mountain height, and the thick forest blazes, while the wind rolls the flames to all sides in riotous confusion, so he stormed over the field like a fury, driving all before him, and killing until the earth was a river of blood. . . . On went Achilles, with spatters of gore upon his invincible hands."

COMMENT: Homer's similes are never arbitrary. Hector was compared to fire when he was about to ignite the Achaean ships. Here Achilles is likened to flame in anticipation of the symbolic battle between Hephaestus and Xanthus in the next book.

THE *ILIAD*

BOOK XXI: THE BATTLE BY THE RIVER

WATER AND FIRE: Achilles forces many Trojans to leap into the river (the Xanthus; ZAN thuss). Again Achilles is compared to fire; and armed only with his sword he leaps into the river, slaughtering as he goes until the river runs scarlet with the blood of the dead. He captures twelve Trojans alive, whom he sends back to camp to be sacrificed at the funeral pyre of Patroclus. After a piteous plea to be spared, Achilles slays Lycaon, telling him to be resigned to Fate, just as Achilles himself is.

> **COMMENT:** Note Achilles' assertion that since the death of Patroclus, all kindness has been driven from his heart; thus we have a merciless Achilles, but one who speaks not in derision but solemnly: Achilles has chosen death by his decision to remain at Troy and slay Hector, death by the arrow of Paris. Lycaon, the disarmed suppliant, can appeal to Achilles only on the ground of their common humanity. Achilles replies on the same grounds, and Lycaon accepts the argument.

Lycaon's body is thrown into the river for fish to feed upon. The river-god Xanthus is on the side of the Trojans and inspires Asteropaeus, grandson of the river Axius. Achilles slays him, shouting that he is descended from the thunderbolt-wielder himself, Zeus (note the fire imagery again). Then Xanthus complains that his streams are clogged with dead bodies. He tells Achilles to finish his slaughter on the plain. Achilles leaps into the river, which surges up and spouts out all the slain, protecting the still-living Trojans. He is powerless against the river, which pursues him across the plain. (He seems about to meet an ignominious death; Homer is reminding us that this hero is mortal. Note how the gods take him by the hands like a helpless child). The river Simois helps Xanthus, but Hephaestus kindles the plain, devouring the corpses in flame, then turns upon the river, heating it to boiling. Hera, in answer to the river's pleas, checks her son, but not before the river renounces all aid to the Trojans.

> **COMMENT:** Note that the battle of the river-god and the fire god does not transgress the laws of nature. We can conceive of a river choked with bodies rising above its banks, as well as a blaze which checks the river's flood. Conceived as a contest of antagonistic deities, however, these forces of nature

emphasize the magnitude of human warfare, and focus attention on the blind energy of man which war releases.

THE GODS BATTLE: The other gods are aroused to action. Ares lands a blow on Athena, who then drops him with a boulder on the neck. The redoubtable Athena next bangs Aphrodite on her chest, while she mocks both Ares and Aphrodite. Hera boxes the insolent Artemis on the ears, and the girl flees in tears. Only Apollo is left to stand with the Trojans, since all the other gods have returned by now to Olympus. Agenor, brave but foolish, is saved from death at Achilles' hands by Apollo (with the mist-trick again!), and by leading Achilles away from the walls of Troy, the Trojans are permitted to return safely to their city.

THE *ILIAD*

BOOK XXII: THE DEATH OF HECTOR

HECTOR FLEES: Hector alone remains outside the Scaean (SEE uhn) gates of Ilium. Achilles returns after vainly trying to chase the fleeing Apollo. Hector's father Priam begs him to come within the walls so as not to meet his death at Achilles' hands. He begs Hector to take pity on his family—

> "To perish in my old age, after I have lived to see many troubles, seen my sons destroyed and daughters dragged into slavery, my house ransacked, little children dashed on the ground in fury, my sons' wives dragged away by Achaean hands. . . . But a hoary head, and a white beard, and nakedness violated by dogs, when an old man is killed, there is the most pitiable sight that mortal eyes can see."

COMMENT: Homer imparts human will to the guardians of destiny, while binding them by the firm laws of fate. Thus destiny is at once blind and full of meaning. *Cf.* Book I, line 5.

Achilles approaches Hector, preventing him from using the wall as a rear-protector. As in a dream they run, the one pursuing but unable to catch up, the other fleeing yet incapable of escaping. Zeus weighs portions of death in his golden scales; Hector's is heavier, at which point the god Apollo abandons Hector forever, while Athena does not desert Achilles (deserting gods are symbolic of those destinies life transmits to one—the gods are not to blame for this). Athena takes on the form of Hector's brother, Deiphobus, and urges him to fight. The sight of his brave brother impels Hector to make his stand (note the goddess' deception here). After having run three times around the walls of Troy, he tells Achilles he will fight, providing their bodies are not defiled. Achilles rejects the provision. Spears are thrown and miss. Hector calls for another spear from his brother; it is at this point he realizes Athena's trick. Still he will die courageously with a final act of valor: "Yet I pray that I may die not without a blow, not inglorious. First may I do some notable thing that shall be remembered in generations to come." (Note the wish to be remembered as brave, a hero's chief hope.) Achilles spears Hector who has charged with drawn sword upon him. Hector is stabbed in the throat. With his dying breath Hector begs Achilles to accept ransom and return his body for cremation and burial, but he is savagely turned down, even with cannibalistic threats (perhaps a reflection of primitive death rites, in which the body of the deceased was consumed by his king. *Cf.* Herodotus, Book III, Chapter 38, for example.) The dying man predicts Achilles' death and dies:

> ". . . the shadow of death encompassed him; and his soul left the body and went down to Hades, bewailing his fate, bidding a last farewell to manhood and lusty strength."

Achilles strips the armor, his own by the way, which had been formerly seized from the corpse of Patroclus. Achilles fastens thongs through holes pierced in Hector's ankles, and ties the corpse to his chariot so that the head hangs behind in the dust. The body is dragged around the walls three times, while Hector's parents and Trojans lament.

HECTOR'S WIFE: Andromache, Hector's wife, summons a bath for Hector in her house, for she is still in ignorance of his fate. When she hears the mourning from the wall, she suspects the truth, and races madly to the edge of the city, where she sees Hector being dragged toward the beach. She swoons. When she revives, she cries that she and Hector share one fate. She is left a widow, their son Astyanax without a protector:

> "But now he will have plenty to suffer since his father is gone— my Astyanax as they all call him in this city, because you alone saved their gates and walls. And now you are in the enemy camp, far from your father and mother . . . naked, although there is nice soft linen in your house made by your own women."

She wept while she spoke, and the women lamented with her.

THE *ILIAD*

BOOK XXIII: THE FUNERAL GAMES

THE GHOST OF PATROCLUS: The Trojans mourn Hector while the Achaeans lament the death of Patroclus, and the sand grows wet with tears. After the lament there is bathing and funeral feasting except for Achilles, who continues to moan and lament. Finally asleep, Achilles is visited in his dream by the ghost of Patroclus: the ghost tells him to bury the corpse straightaway so that the soul may be free to enter the shades of the dead. The spirit foretells the death of Achilles and begs that their bones may lie in the same golden urn given to Achilles by his mother Thetis. Achilles replies that he will do so, "But come nearer; for one short moment let us lay our arms about each other and console ourselves with lamentation!" Achilles awakes in wonder that the soul survives in Hades, though with no real life or substance (some anthropologists find in dreams the source of belief in ghosts and the afterlife).

THE FUNERAL OF PATROCLUS: Wood is piled on the beach to prepare for the cremation. The body is wrapped in animal fat; four horses, two dogs belonging to Patroclus, and the twelve captured Trojan youths are added to the flames while Achilles wails like a father over a dead son. Later the flames are doused in wine and the bones are collected; a slight mound is prepared for Achilles, awaiting the day of Achilles' own funeral.

THE FUNERAL GAMES: The first contest is the chariot race. Nestor gives his son Antilochus some pointers on winning—that skill is more important than fast horses. Idomeneus sees Diomedes in the lead and announces that some mishap must have befallen Eumelus, one of the contestants. Aias, son of Oileus, a partisan of Eumelus, berates Idomeneus for empty talk. Achilles intervenes to stop the quarrel. (Aias has an unpleasant character. A Greek epic poem describes Aias' dragging Cassandra, daughter of Priam, away as she clutched the Palladium, a statue of Athena. Some say he even had raped her.)

Diomedes is the winner, then Antilochus, then Menelaus, then Meriones, and Eumelus last. A dispute arises between Menelaus and Antilochus over prizes.

> **COMMENT:**   The funeral games provide a striking contrast to the rest of the *Iliad*. Here the contests are supervised fairly

by Achilles, arguments mediated by reason. The dispute between Menelaus and Antilochus is in a sense a peaceful reflection of the quarrel between Agamemnon and Achilles which motivates the poem. Here Antilochus yields to his superior with good grace, and Agamemnon's brother shows proper regal detachment and royal pardon.

Next comes the boxing contest; leather straps are used for gloves. Epeius wins over Eryalus. Aias, son of Telamon, and Odysseus compete for the wrestling prize, and before Odysseus can fell Aias a third time, Achilles interrupts the battles and offers equal gifts to both.

COMMENT: Aias' defeat may again be proleptic (anticipatory) suggestion of the contest for the arms of Achilles, where Odysseus is granted the armor of the dead hero; Aias commits suicide in his rage at the alleged treachery of Achilles. Here the contest is peacefully resolved, as was Menelaus' argument with Antilochus.

In the following footrace, Odysseus wins over Aias, son of Oileus (see above commentary), even though Odysseus is middle-aged and Aias youthful. Polypoetes wins the shot-put (the prize a precious lump of iron, an indication of the culture values). Meriones defeats Teucer in the archery contest, and Agamemnon is awarded the spear-throwing prize in a no-contest.

THE *ILIAD*

BOOK XXIV: THE RANSOMING OF HECTOR

HECTOR DESECRATED: The inconsolable Achilles drags the body of Hector thrice around the tomb of Patroclus, but Apollo protects it from defilement.

THE GODS INTERVENE: The gods take pity on Hector, but not Poseidon, nor Athena and Hera, who remember the judgment of Paris. Apollo defends the pious Hector and condemns the pitiless Achilles, who is without shame before mankind. Achilles is offending the gods with his excessive wrath. Iris is sent to the sea's bottom to summon Thetis. Zeus tells her to relate to her son his displeasure while he sends Iris to suggest that Priam bear ransom to Achilles for the corpse of Hector. (Achilles as a mortal should accept objective necessity and not allow his subjective passions to dominate life in the real world. Unending wrath is for the gods only.)

FATHER AND MOTHER: Iris finds Priam rolling in dung, with the whole city in lamentation; she delivers her message, and the father consults with his wife Hecuba, who says,

> "O misery! where are your wits flown? Once you were famous for good sense throughout your kingdom and even in foreign lands! . . . If he sets eyes on you—if he gets hold of you— that is a faithless man, a cannibal! He'll never pity, he'll never have mercy!"

Priam nevertheless obeys the god-sent messenger. He draws from his treasure chests elaborate gifts of clothes, linen, gold, tripods, cauldrons. Leaving, he chides his nine remaining sons for frivolity, cowardice, and dishonesty. His mule wagon is loaded with gifts for Achilles. Hermes is sent by Zeus to escort Priam unharmed through the Achaean camp.

> **COMMENT:** The god Hermes is not only guide and messenger but *psychopomp*, "escorter of souls" who led the spirits of the dead to the underworld. The magic wand here is most appropriate. Note that the Trojans have just mourned Priam as if he were on his way to death, the pervasive atmosphere of the last book.

Hermes charms into sleep the guards of the Argive camp, and the

three men, Hermes, Idaeus (i DEE us), and Priam reach Achilles'
hut. Priam enters alone to find Achilles with his two squires, Automedon and Alcimus. Priam embraces the knees of Achilles, an attitude of supplication, and kisses his hands. Then Priam makes his
prayer:

> "Remember your own father, most noble prince Achilles, an
> old man like me near the end of his days. . . . But *he* indeed,
> so long as he hears that you still live, is glad at heart and hopes
> every day that he will see his well-loved son return home from
> Troy. Fifty I had when the men of Achaia came; nineteen
> borne to me of one womb, the others of women in my house-
> hold . . . and my only one, who by himself was our safeguard,
> that one you killed the other day fighting for his country,
> Hector . . ." As he said it, he lifted his hand to the face of
> Achilles, and the heart of Achilles ached with anguish at the
> thought of the father. . . . So the two thought of their dead
> and wept, one for his Hector while he crouched before the feet
> of Achilles, and Achilles for his own father and then for
> Patroclus."

Achilles is highly moved, and himself places the body on a bier,
and with his friends lays it on the wagon. He addresses the dead
Patroclus, begging that he be not angry, for the ransom he has
accepted is worthy, and Patroclus will get a fair share of it. (Note
that the *Iliad* opened with an unsuccessful effort at ransom, that
midway (Book IX) Achilles refuses a huge ransom, and here
ransom is finally accepted: Achilles learns that men must relent
in the face of proper recompense.) They dine together, and Achilles
accedes to Priam's request for a twelve-day burial truce. Priam returns to Troy with the body of his son. Hecuba and Andromache
mourn, Hector's wife predicting the fall of Troy and the death of
Astyanax. Lastly, Helen leads the funeral chant recalling her fondness for the dead Hector. Priam announces the truce to the Trojans
and the burial rites are consummated. The epic tale, certainly one
of the greatest in the world, ends. (Note: All direct quotations
taken from W.H.D. Rouse's translation published by Mentor
paperbacks.)

GREEK EPIC: THE ODYSSEY

HOMER'S ODYSSEY

INTRODUCTION

See GREEK EPIC: INTRODUCTION for a detailed introduction to Homer's *Iliad* and *Odyssey*, as well as for information on all related material such as background, milieu, history of the Greeks, literary forms, etc.

THE PLOT OPENS: The *Odyssey* begins *in medias res* like all true epics, which is to say in the midst of the story. Only in Book IX is there a "flashback" by Odysseus in which the reader is informed of what had happened previous to the opening of the epic.

The *Odyssey* begins with the Olympian gods listening to Athena's plea for their aid in bidding the goddess Calypso to allow Odysseus to leave her enchanted island. After ten years of wandering Odysseus has been stranded on Ogygia, an island in the Mediterranean, and the home of the nymph Calypso.

As for his wife Penelope, after ten years of waiting, she is still cleverly keeping the insistent suitors at bay. Their young son Telemachus is now a young man, impatient to know the whereabouts of his 10-year-absent father, Odysseus.

ODYSSEUS' GENEALOGY

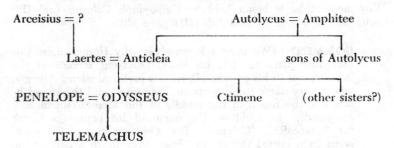

THE ODYSSEY

BOOK I: THE SITUATION IN ITHACA

INVOCATION AND THEME: The invocation to the muse of epic poetry. Homer pretends the muse is speaking through him. (*Cf.* Book XXII, 347, Phemius the bard's statement, "I am self-taught; a god caused all sorts of songs to be in me.") Phemius and Homer see no contradiction in crediting their self-taught skill to the gods. Homer, in this invocation, is really asking that his memory not fail him.

> **COMMENT:** "This is the story of a man, one who was never at a loss. He had traveled far in the world, after the sack of Troy . . . he endured many troubles and hardships in the struggle to save his own life and to bring back his men safe to their homes. . . ." The first adjective to be applied to Odysseus (oh DISS seeoos) is significant. The Greek word *polytropus* can mean either "much-traveled" or "crafty." In this context both meanings are implied and both contained in the word "adventurous."

CALYPSO'S ISLE: After the invocation we learn of Odysseus' present condition. He alone, of all the Greek chieftains who had fought in Troy, has not yet reached home. He had angered Poseidon, the god of the sea, and it was the sea god who had caused the long delay in reaching home. Ten years have passed since the fall of Troy, but *Odysseus* is still far from Ithaca. At this moment he is being held by the nymph *Calypso* (cal IPP soh) on the isle of *Ogygia* (oh GIH ghee ah).

> **COMMENT:** We must ask ourselves why Homer chose this particular place to start his story. Odysseus is now at the lowest point in his travels. He is on a mythical island, Ogygia, whose very name came to mean "primitive" and the island itself is to be found in the middle of the Mediterranean Sea, supposedly. In addition, the name of his captor is Greek for "concealer" (Calypso). The *Odyssey* traces Odysseus' steps from unreal Ogygia to Ithaca, very much a part of the real world.

MOUNT OLYMPUS: At the home of the gods on the mountaintop of Olympus we meet *Athena*, Odysseus' patron among the gods.

She takes advantage of Poseidon's temporary absence from Olympus to bring up the topic of Odysseus.

COMMENT: In her plea in behalf of Odysseus, Athena makes a punning reference to Odysseus' name. When she asks why Zeus hurts Odysseus so much, she uses the verb *odyssomai,* "to cause pain to." Such puns are common in Homer and always carry more than a comic intention. Homer is a lover of the language.

Athena suggests that *Zeus,* the king of the gods, send Hermes (HER meez) the messenger of the gods, to tell Calypso to release her favorite Odysseus, and that she herself be allowed to journey to Ithaca in order to raise the spirits of Odysseus' son, Telemachus, and to send him to Pylos so that he might obtain news of his father's whereabouts.

MENTES AND TELEMACHUS: *Athena* in the form of a pirate chieftain, *Mentes* (MEN teez), travels to Ithaca and enters the main hall of Odysseus' home where the suitors and *Telemachus* (tell EM uh kuss) are dining. We learn that all the men of Ithaca who were too young to journey to Troy have now grown up and are all courting Odysseus' wife, Penelope. (Odysseus' wealth stays with his wife, should she marry one of the suitors.) Athena urges Telemachus to call an Assembly of the suitors for the next day and there to tell them to return to their own homes. She also suggests that he leave Ithaca to seek news of his father's whereabouts. Pylos, Nestor's kingdom, and then Sparta, the home of Menelaus and Helen, would be his first stops. Athena tells a long tale of Orestes, (this to inspire Telemachus to action) who had been a man of action in the avenging of his father's death. *Phemius,* a bard like Homer himself, recites tales of Troy, and *Penelope* (pen ELL oh pee) enters to scold the bard; but her son rebukes her and then boldly calls an Assembly for the next day. Here is a new and brave Telemachus, who now goes to his bedroom accompanied by the faithful nurse Eurycleia (your ih KLEE uh).

THE ODYSSEY

BOOK II: THE ASSEMBLY IN ITHACA

THE ASSEMBLY: We learn that this is the first Assembly to be held in Ithaca since Odysseus had left for Troy.

> **COMMENT:** Telemachus is now a man, stepping rightly into his mighty father's shoes: "He sat in his father's seat, and the old men yielded to him." While Telemachus is gaining a new awareness, his country is regaining an old awareness in holding its Assembly. Assemblies, where all the male citizens gather to discuss and decide upon matters of policy, are the mark of a civilized people. When, for example, Homer wants to characterize the race of the Cyclopes as primitive, he says that they have no "counsel-bearing assemblies" (*Cf.* Book IX, 112), or when he wants to describe the over-civilized Phaeacians (*Cf.* Books VII and VIII) he shows them constantly holding assemblies.

Telemachus delivers a moving speech, listing all the injustices and misfortunes that have befallen him and his household: not only is his father gone (and presumed dead), but the younger lords are consuming his father's livestocks and making themselves unbearable. At the finish of his speech he bursts into tears (tear-shedding is copious in the *Odyssey*, but is never to be taken as a sign of weakness or effeminacy). Antinous (an TIN ooh uhs), a suitor, tries to lay the blame on Penelope. She had promised to wed one of the suitors as soon as she finished a shroud she was weaving for her father-in-law, Laertes. But, Antinous complains, she unwove at night what she had woven during the day; she was thus able to keep the suitors at bay for three years, until they discovered her trick and forced her to finish the shroud in a hurry. The suitors will not leave until she makes a decision for one of them as her husband. Telemachus asks to be allowed to visit Pylos and Sparta for news of his father; if he is found to have died, he will give his mother in marriage to one of the suitors. *Mentor*, an older man, arises and blames the other old men for allowing the disgraceful conduct of the suitors to continue. The suitors reply by returning to the house of Odysseus to consume and revel some more.

> **COMMENT:** By telling us that the suitors went to Odysseus' house, and contrasting them with the law-abiding elders who went to their own homes, Homer dramatically reinforces what

we already know—that the first of the two purposes of the Assembly has failed. Telemachus has not convinced them to leave. In other words, Telemachus, who has certainly grown up, is still not a man equal to his own father, who would (and does in Book XXII) rid the suitors with dispatch.

TELEMACHUS LEAVES: By the sea shore Athena as *Mentor* praises Telemachus for his powers in debate, telling him to forget the suitors for the present and to prepare for his journey. Thus encouraged, he returns home to dine with the suitors as usual. Then he leaves the main hall and asks Eurycleia to prepare wine and food for the journey in spite of her warnings at his leaving the suitors alone. Next, Athena, disguised as Telemachus himself, picks out twenty men for the crew, instructing them to be ready for evening. She then causes the suitors to fall into a heavy sleep. Appearing once more in Mentor's form, she tells Telemachus that the ship is ready. Telemachus and his men leave Ithaca under cover of darkness and sail through the night.

THE ODYSSEY

BOOK III: NESTOR THE HOST

NESTOR RECITES: Telemachus and his crew arrive at Pylos, where Athena, who has accompanied Telemachus, gently reproaches him for being the last to leave the ship:

"Telemachus, there is no need to be shy, not a bit. You know why you have come on this voyage: to ask news of your father, how he died, and where he was buried. Come along, then, straight to Nestor." Note, by the way, that the Greeks (and most ancient peoples) burned the inedible portions in their religious sacrifices and saved the edible parts (in a most sensible way) for their own stomachs!

Following custom, Nestor waits for his guests to finish dining before asking them their identities. Telemachus then inquires whether Nestor has knowledge of Odysseus. The reply is typically long-winded and rambling; here is a portion of interest:

"Nine long years we were busy, scheming and plotting and planning in every possible way, and only just managed it, thanks be to God! All that time no one came near Odysseus in resource, for that grand man was first by a long way in all plots and plans and schemes, your father, I say, if you are really his son—if! you amaze me, young man: when I hear you speak, I might be hearing him, you could not imagine a young man *could* speak so like him!" (Note the ever-cautious and comic uncertainty as to Telemachus' parentage followed by the tactful flattery. The Greeks take nothing for granted—not even birth certificates!)

Naturally, Nestor has no real information about Odysseus' whereabouts; but he is filled with rambling reminiscenses of the Trojan War. When Telemachus grows pessimistic as to divine help, Athena says: "Telemachus, what words you have let slip between your teeth! It is easy for God to bring a man safely home if it be his will, even from a long way off." It is better, she says, to undergo many hardships to get home safely than to arrive home quickly only to be murdered by your own wife, as had happened to King Agamemnon.

NESTOR'S TALES: Nestor tells the tale of Agamemnon's death, the wanderings of Menelaus, who, it seems, has had to wander for many years before reaching home. In that time, he lost a part of his crew and traveled to many lands, including Egypt.

TELEMACHUS DEPARTS: Nestor and Telemachus now go to the palace, where a bed is prepared for Telemachus; here is the pre-ritual:

> "Meanwhile Telemachus had been bathed by Polycasta, the youngest daughter of Nestor Neleïadês. And when she had bathed him and rubbed him with olive oil, she gave him a wrap and a tunic to wear; then he stept out of the tub, as handsome as a young god (the height of Greek comparative beauty)."

The next day Nestor calls together all his sons, announcing that he will pay homage to Athena by offering her the gilded horns of a young cow. After Nestor's commands are carried out, Telemachus and Peisistratus (py ZISS truh tuss), the son of Nestor, depart from sandy Pylos. The journey takes two days, and they spend the first night at the house of Diocles, in Pherae. By travelling all the next day, they reach Sparta, the kingdom of Menelaus, at nightfall.

THE ODYSSEY

BOOK IV: MENELAUS THE HOST

MUTUAL REMINISCENCE: Telemachus and Peisistratus visit Menelaus, where they dine heartily. They are amazed at the display of wealth in the palace.

> **COMMENT:** Menelaus, like Agememnon, is presented to us for comparison with Odysseus. His great wealth is the first example of his current happiness, which plays an important part in his character. We have already seen what has happened to the king of the Greeks, Agamemnon, when he arrived home. We must keep the three heroes' home-arrivals in mind at all times, but naturally the climactic homecoming is that of Odysseus.

When Menelaus in a long speech mentions his father's name, Telemachus breaks into tears just as Helen, Menelaus' wife, enters the room with her attendants. She recognizes the boy immediately, although she has never seen him before.

> "Now the young man could not restrain himself: tears dropt from his eyes to the ground as he heard his father's name, and he held up the purple robe before his eyes with both hands."

(Note how Helen's character is revealed objectively—in word and action—without explanatory comment by Homer; this objective vision is characteristic of the best writers, even today.) In exchanging gossip and memories, the entire group weeps: "This made them all seek relief in tears. Argive Helen (her husband's kingdom = Argos) wept. Helen the daughter of Zeus; Telemachus wept, and King Menelaus; tears also were in the eyes of Nestor's son." (The luxury of weeping cannot be denied the Greeks; the entire epic is suffused with this pathetic quality, and yet somehow it is natural and unsentimental.) Helen then narrates one of Odysseus' exploits in the Trojan War, in which she reveals her feelings:

> "For I was already longing to come home again, and I mourned the infatuation which Aphrodite brought upon me; when she carried me away from my native land, and parted me from my daughter and my home and husband, although there was no fault in him either of mind or body."

(Note that the blame is laid upon the head of the goddess of love; note too the pains she goes to in absolving herself and her husband. Blaming the gods for every thought and deed is typically Homeric, but beneath lies a subtle psychology which is explanation enough.) Menelaus too has a story about Odysseus. When the Greek warriors were hidden in the Trojan horse, Helen, who had learned of the plan from Odysseus, approached the horse and whispered to the men inside, assuming in turn the voices of several of their wives. Some of the men inside the horse were taken in by this impersonation and would have leaped out, thereby giving away the Greek's scheme for subverting Troy, had not Odysseus held them back. After the finish of anecdotes, they retire for the night.

MORE STORIES: The next morning, Menelaus tells of his stay in Egypt. With the help of a goddess, Menelaus captured the Old Man of the Sea (Proteus), who is forced to reveal his prophetic knowledge of the fates of Aias, of Locris, Agamemnon, and Odysseus, who was at this very moment in the power of Calypso. Menelaus' own fate is that he will be sent to the Greek paradise (Elysian Fields, where there is no snow or rainfall).

> **COMMENT:**   In other words, Menelaus will become immortal and without cares—the same condition that Odysseus will be offered by Calypso in the next book. Odysseus, however, is too much a part of the real world ever to accept such a choice.

BACK IN ITHACA: The herald Medon overhears the suitors' plot to kill Telemachus and informs Penelope, who weeps and prays before going to bed. As the book closes, the suitors establish their ambush and await Telemachus' homecoming. (Books I-IV = *Telemachy*, "maturity and father search"; but the scene is also set for Odysseus' homecoming, a real world in contrast to the forthcoming fairyland travels; note also that somehow Odysseus has been the absent center of interest in these four books.)

THE ODYSSEY

BOOK V: CALYPSO AND INO

HERMES ON ERRAND: On Olympus, Athena reminds Zeus of her favorite Odysseus still becalmed with the goddess Calypso. Hermes is sent to tell Calypso to release our hero.

> **COMMENT:** This second Assembly seems to ignore the first. There too Athena had made a similar request. Homer evidently has nodded, or else he duplicated the episode in order that it should not conflict with Telemachus' search.

Hermes, the messenger of the gods, bearing his magic wand (*caduceus* = kah DEW suhss), which has the power both to cause sleep and wakefulness, travels to Calypso's isle, Ogygia, where the trees are tall and stately, the birds predatory or nocturnal (land of immortality ruled by a death goddess; life should involve struggle and the knowledge of one's own mortality). Hermes enters Calypso's cave: "Over the gaping mouth of the cave trailed a luxuriant grapevine, with clusters of ripe fruit; and four rills of clear water ran in a row close together, winding over the ground. Beyond were soft meadows thick with violets and wild celery. That was a sight to gladden the gods." After receiving the command from Hermes, she approaches the weeping Odysseus:

> "She found him sitting upon the shore. The tears were never dry in his eyes; life with its sweetness was slowly trickling away. He cared for her no longer; at night he was forced to sleep by her side in the cave, although the love was all on her part, and he spent the days sitting upon the rocks or the sands, staring at the barren sea and sorrowing."

But after hearing he is to leave on a mere raft, his caution returns: "I should not care to embark on a raft without your good will: not unless you could bring yourself to swear a solemn oath that you will not work some secret mischief against me." The goddess smiles and strokes him with her hand: "Ah, you are a wicked man! always wide awake! or you would never have thought of such a thing." She swears the most solemn of oaths that she will practice no trickery, and they go in to dine. Like all women, she mentions her own beauty as surpassing that of Penelope. The hero "knew what to say to that, and he answered at once: "Gracious goddess, don't be cross with me! I know all that as well as you do. My wife

is nothing compared to you for beauty, I can see that for myself."
(Such tact is incomparable; it is the delicate insights into human
nature like this that make Homer great.)

THE DEPARTURE: A raft is built, and on the fifth day he sails
with supplies furnished by the goddess. On the eighteenth day
he sights Scheria (SKEER ee uh), the home of the Phaeacians.
But Poseidon, his indomitable enemy, whips up a fierce storm.

COMMENT: Homer says that Poseidon concealed the earth
and the sea with a cover of clouds. The Greek word for "concealed = *calypsai* has the same stem as Calypso, whose name
means "concealer." This pun reinforces the idea that Odysseus
is undergoing perhaps a rebirth as he leaves Ogygia, the
primeval isle in the middle of the sea.

Fortunately, the goddess Leucothea or Ino (AY noh) takes pity:
"Poor Odysseus! You're odd-I-see, true to your name. (Note the
pun!) Why does Poseidon Earth-shaker knock you about in this
monstrous way, and persecute you so much?" She hands him a
veil which will save him from drowning; she tells him to throw
it back into the sea once he reaches land. "Then the goddess gave
him the veil, and dived back herself into the sea, like a great shear-
water (a powerful diving bird), and the dark waves covered her."
The ever-cautious and wily Odysseus will not trust the veil until the
raft is smashed to pieces. After swimming for two days, he sights
Scheria on the dawn of the third, but the coast is rocky and the
surf vicious; nevertheless he succeeds in clasping tightly onto a
projecting rock (the battle with nature is unique in Greek literature!), and he finally makes shore. He tosses the veil back into the
sea (wise Odysseus!) and falls exhausted to sleep.

THE ODYSSEY

BOOK VI: NAUSICAA

NAUSICAA'S DREAM: Athena now comes to Alcinous' daughter, the princess Nausicaa (naw ZEE khy uh), in a dream, and puts the idea into her head to wash the family clothes. Nobody, says Athena, wants to marry a girl who always has heaps of dirty laundry.

> **COMMENT:** Nausicaa is the typical princess of fairy tales. And, in many ways, Odysseus is the typical stranger who arrives in the princess' land, demonstrates his prowess, and (if this were a true fairy tale) marries the princess. Much of the dialogue in the sixth book should be read with an awareness of how Homer is playing with the typical fairy tale and using it for his own ends.

THE NAKED HERO: Nausicaa obeys and asks her father for a wagon and mules to carry the clothes to the river:

> "Daddy dear, couldn't you let me have a good big cart with plenty of room? because I want to take our best clothes to the river and give them a wash; they are all lying in a dirty heap!"

Nausicaa and her maids take the clothes to the river and wash them in a running stream, after which they picnic and play games, one of which is tossing a ball around. They awaken Odysseus with their shrieks, and, naked and salt-encrusted, he steps forth:

> "What a vision they saw! Something filthy and caked in sea-salt which fairly terrified them: away they scampered in all directions to hide behind hillocks of sand. Only the young princess stood her ground; for Athena took all fear away. So she halted and stood firm; and Odysseus was uncertain what to do. Should he throw his arms round her knees, and crave mercy of the lovely girl? or should he stand where he was, and ask her politely to give him some clothes, and to tell him the way to the city?"

He thinks the matter over carefully and decides to address her while kneeling: "I kneel to thee, Queen!—Art thou goddess? Are you mortal? If you are a goddess, one of those who rule the broad heavens, I would liken you most to Artemis, the daughter of Zeus Almighty, so tall and beautiful and fair." He then congratulates her parents on having such a graceful daughter, but (he continues cleverly, knowing just as Athena did, how a young girl's thoughts revolve around marriage) "happiest of all is he who will be your husband" (a masterpiece of clever tact and graceful flattery!). All this has the desired effect on the princess: she offers him clothing and aid. The maids return, but the modest hero refuses their services in bathing: "Just stand a little way off, good maids, while I wash the salt off my shoulders by myself, and give them a rub with the oil: it is long since my skin knew what oil feels like. I will not wash before you, for I am too shy to show myself naked before a lot of pretty girls." When he reappears, Nausicaa looks at him with undisguised admiration, saying to her maids that she hopes for just such a husband as this godlike stranger.

TO THE PALACE: The modest and careful Nausicaa does not want Odysseus to be seen entering the town with her, for this would start unpleasant rumors: "Indeed, I should not approve of any girl who did such a thing, flying in the face of her friends, with father and mother to teach her better, if she has anything to do with men before it comes to marriage open and above-board." Once in the palace he is to approach her mother and ask her for help in returning to his home. (Perhaps Phaeacia is matriarchal, since the father is not the one to go to for aid first.) The book ends as Nausicaa goes off to the city, leaving Odysseus behind in a grove dedicated to Athena.

THE *ODYSSEY*

BOOK VII: THE PALACE OF ALCINOUS

THE HOSTS: Athena covers Odysseus with a thick mist so that unseen he might pass through the streets without a fight, since the Phaeacians are mildly hostile to strangers. Athena repeats Nausicaa's directions: he is to pass by the king (Alcinous = al SIN ooh us) and supplicate the queen (Arete = uh REE tee). As he enters the house, Odysseus marvels at the splendor and wealth of the palace.

> **COMMENT:** The bronze walls, gold doors, and statuary suggest the splendor of the palaces that have been unearthed in Crete. It is therefore thought by some that Homer imagined Scheria (SKEER ee uh) to be located there. Others, including the ancient Greek historian Thucydides, thought Scheria is to be equated with Corfu, an Ionian island.

The palace has fifty maids who can weave cleverly; fruits, vegetables, and grapes for wine are in bountiful supply.

> **COMMENT:** The Phaeacians, living in this fertile paradise, beset by no enemy, are as much a part of fairyland as Calypso's isle. They, like most of the peoples we shall meet in the course of Odysseus' adventures, are presented to us for contrast with Ithaca. The Phaeacians represent civilization carried to the extreme, where all conflict and hard labor has been eliminated.

Odysseus enters and passing by Alcinous he clasps Arete's knees:

"Arete, daughter of divine Rhexenor! I come in my distress, a suppliant to your husband and to your knees. Yes, and to these who sit at meat; may the gods grant them to be happy while they live, and may each have children to inherit his wealth and the honorable place which the people has given him. Now I beseech you to send me home to my native land without delay, for I have long suffered tribulation far from my friends."

(Note the tact, the good wishes for happiness and children before the plea for aid is made.) Odysseus is seated at the royal table and royally fed. Alcinous compares Odysseus to a god, perhaps in the hope that Odysseus, when he denies that he is a god, will reveal his true identity. But Odysseus is too wily to be so tricked: he says that he is not built like a god. (Note how quickly Odysseus gains command of the situation, for the Phaeacians, unaccustomed to wile and strife, are like children when compared to the worldly Odysseus.) Odysseus answers Arete's questions as to where he had obtained his garment (one she had woven herself), and also tells her of Nausicaa's kindness. So charmed is Alcinous by his guest that he declares nothing would please him more than to have Odysseus remain in his court as his son-in-law. But if this cannot be, he will have Odysseus taken to his home, no matter how far away. With his usual diplomacy, Odysseus mentions nothing in his reply to Alcinous' suggestion that he marry Nausicaa; he does react favorably to the idea that he leave for home the next day (in point of fact he leaves two days later). Arete, like the good hostess she is, had, during the conversation, given orders that a bed be prepared for Odysseus. The book ends as all present go to bed.

THE ODYSSEY

BOOK VII: PHAEACIAN SPORTS

THE CHALLENGE: The next morning Demodocus (dee MOH doh cus), the court bard, who is blind, sings a tale of the Trojan War: the story of the quarrel between Odysseus and Achilles.

> **COMMENT:** There have been two conflicting reasons given for the cause of the quarrel: 1. Achilles was annoyed that he was not invited to a dinner, and 2. Achilles and Odysseus were debating the best method of overthrowing Troy. But the actual story of the quarrel matters not so much as the fact that when Odysseus finally identifies himself, he will be known to the Phaeacians. Note also that Demodocus is blind, just as Homer was supposedly reported to be.

Odysseus starts weeping as he hears again of his now dead comrades:

> "But Odysseus when he heard it caught up his purple robe in his hands, and drew it down over his head, hiding his face; for he was ashamed to let the company see the tears in his eyes."

The king, unaware of the sources of our hero's grief, tactfully suggests that the games begin. The catalogue of the names of the participating athletes follows, names reflecting dependence on the sea for livelihood. There is running, wrestling, jumping, discus-throwing, and boxing. These include all the standard Greek sports. When Odysseus refuses to participate, he is insulted by Euryalus (you REE uh lus), who calls him a mere merchant out to make money.

> **COMMENT:** This illustrates quite clearly the typical Greek disregard for people who earn their living by buying and selling.

Odysseus replies to the insult:

> "So you are as handsome as God could make a man, but your mind is empty. You have made me angry by your bad manners. I am no duffer in sports, as you say, but I think I was among the first while I could trust in my youth and my hands. Now

I am tired and worn out with perils in battle and perils of the sea. Well, never mind that; I will try my hand. You have cut me to the quick, and I cannot sit still any longer." Odysseus then picks up the weight and throws it farther than any of the others, and then proceeds to challenge all comers.

Alcinous apologizes for the insult:

"The truth is, we are not first-rate boxers or wrestlers, but we are fine oarsmen and the best of seamen; our delight is in feasting, in music, and dancing, plenty of clean linen, a warm bath, and bed!"

DEMODOCUS SINGS: Demodocus ends the embarrassment by singing of the seduction of Aphrodite, Hephaestus' wife, by Ares; how Hephaestus, the god of fire and crafts, when he learned of Aphrodite's unfaithfulness devised a trap over his bed. The next time Ares and Aphrodite lay together in the bed, the nets fell over them, locking the naked couple in a tight embrace. Hephaestus called all the other gods to witness the ludicrous sight (the goddesses were too modest to come, says Homer), and there is uproarious laughter. (This is one of the most vivid and entertaining stories in the whole of the Odyssey: the reader should not miss it!) Later Odysseus is plied with numerous gifts, including a bronze sword from the shamefaced Euryalus. His tactful and wise speech to the admiring Nausicaa follows. During the meal Odysseus offers Demodocus a cut of meat from the main table, "for in every nation of mankind upon the earth minstrels have honour and respect, since the Muse has taught them their songs, and she loves them, one and all (of a kind of Homeric self-tribute!)" He sings of the fall of Troy, which causes Odysseus to weep in reminiscence. At this point Alcinous asks his identity.

THE ODYSSEY

BOOK IX: THE LOTUS-EATERS AND THE CYCLOPES

THE CICONES OF THRACE: Odysseus identifies himself and his homeland in reply to Alcinous' question as to his identity:

> "My home is Ithaca, that bright conspicuous isle, with Mount Neriton rising clear out of the quivering forests. Round it lie many islands clustering close, Dulichion and Samê and woody Zacynthos. . . . It is rough, but a nurse of good lads; I tell you there is no sweeter sight any man can see than his own country." (An affecting, simple and homely tribute to one's country, one of the best in literature.)

Odysseus begins a narrative of his adventures, which will continue for the next four books up to the point where we met him on Calypso's isle in Book V. (Like most epics, Homer's begins *in medias res*—in the middle of the tale—and by use of flashback technique recites what had happened previously.) He tells of his first adventure after leaving Troy with his men. He and his men sack the Cicones (see KOH neez), allies of the Trojans. (Piracy was an accepted occupation among the sea-faring Greeks, and Odysseus proved no exception.) The Greeks are driven off from the land losing seventy men in the struggle.

THE LOTUS EATERS: Still attempting to reach home, Odysseus and his crew fall upon the land of the Lotus-eaters (a race of people, perhaps located in North Africa—if anywhere):

> "Nine days after that I was beaten about on the sea by foul winds, and on the tenth day we made land in the country of the lotus-eaters, who get their food from flowers (not the lotus grass, but perhaps a berry or date or poppy-pod)."

The food of the lotus acts like a "super-tranquilizer." Once having eaten the plant, one loses all thoughts of returning home. Two of the crew are dragged forcibly into the boat by Odysseus after they have eaten of the lotus. Orders are given to set sail as soon as possible so that no others could eat of the drugging plant. (More than the Phaeacians even, this is a land without strife and struggle, which makes the inhabitants inhuman, strife and conflict being that which develops man's inner humanity.)

THE CYCLOPES: After leaving lotus-land, they sail until they fall upon the land of the Cyclopes (sy KLOH peez *or* SY klops). These are rustic, one-eyed barbarians who neither cultivate crops nor have any body of laws, and no assemblies (whose decisions the anarchic Cyclopes wouldn't obey anyway, unlike the lethargic Lotus-eaters who would be too indolent to attend them, and unlike the over-civilized Phoenecians who attend them too often!). Each family of the Cyclopes lives alone. The first day on the land they kill and feast on wild goat and wine. On the next, while exploring the land, they discover (they = Odysseus and twelve companions) a cave surrounded by pens of sheep and goats, containing plentiful cheeses. Odysseus insists on staying and waiting for the owner (that ever-active and often dangerous curiosity of his again!) rather than stealing off with stolen animals and food before the owner arrives. At last the Cyclops comes bringing his flocks with him, but not before blocking the entrance with a huge boulder ("not two and twenty good carts with four wheels apiece could have lifted it from off the ground, such was the size of the precipitous rock which he planted in front of the entrance": Rouse—page 105—notes that this item might be a parody of the common phrase in Homer of how "two good men" could not have lifted a certain stone; so with "precipitous rock," used for cliffs and mountains). Cyclops inhospitably asks just who they are (note the omitted ritual of dining first with the guests), and Odysseus replies they are Greeks who had fought in the Trojan War, wisely not revealing his name nor the location of his ship. Polyphemus (POL ih FEE muss, the name of the Cyclops), without preliminaries, grabs two men and dines on them. The next morning two more are eaten before Polyphemus goes off to work, carefully replacing the boulder. Odysseus, the clever, hits on a plan: He has his men cut and sharpen a wooden stick which Polyphemus had left behind. When the giant returns that evening, Odysseus gives him strong wine, which he had brought with him. While the Cyclops is tipsy from the wine, Odysseus tells him that his name is really No-Man. At this point when Polyphemus falls down into a deep sleep, they quickly heat the sharpened pole to a fiery red and ram it directly into the single eye (the Cyclopes, supposedly, are one-eyed giants, the eye being located directly in the middle of the forehead):

> "The men took hold of the stake, and thrust the sharp point into his eye; and I leaned hard on it from above, and turned it round and round. As a man bores a ship's timber with an auger, while others at the lower part keep turning it with

a strap which they hold at each end, and round and round it runs: so we held the fire-sharpened pole and turned it, and the blood bubbled about its hot point. The fumes singed eyelids and eyelashes all about as the eyeball burnt and the roots crackled in the fire. As a smith plunges an axe or an adze in cold water, for that makes the strength of steel (steel was unknown to Homer, really a form of iron), and it hisses loud when he tempers it, so his eye sizzled about the pole of olive-wood."

Poor Polyphemus roars for aid from his comrades, but when asked who was afflicting him, he replies that No-Man was killing him, at which point his neighbors leave in disgust. Another cunning device of Odysseus obtains egress from the cave. The men tie themselves to the undersides of the huge sheep and are let out undetected by Polyphemus himself. Exulting in his cleverness, Odysseus could not resist shouting out his real name to Polyphemus, who was staggering about on the shore. The giant begs his father, Poseidon, god of the sea, to afflict Odysseus (which prayer is only too well answered as we shall see). The giant pelts huge rocks at them, just missing the boats as they escape. Again our heroes are on their way.

THE ODYSSEY

BOOK X: THE WINDS, THE MIDNIGHT SUN, AND CIRCE

AEOLUS, THE GOD OF THE WINDS: They next reach the floating island of Aeolia (ee OH lee uh), the home of Aeolus (EE oh lus), the god who was given command over all the winds. Odysseus stays with him as an honored guest for a month, and as a parting present is given a leather bag that held captive all the destructive winds which might impede their progress to Ithaca. After ten days they sight Ithaca, at which point Odysseus falls asleep, and the curious and greedy crew, believing gifts were contained in the leather bag, open it only to set free the destructive winds. They are straightaway blown back to Aeolia, where he is refused aid— Aeolus feeling that the gods were against Odysseus.

THE LAESTRYGONIANS: Without the aid of winds the crew is forced to row six weary days until they reach the harbor of the Laestrygonians (lice tree GOH nee uhnz). Three men are sent ahead to investigate and are met by the king's daughter, who directs them to her father's house. They meet the gigantic queen and king who are cannibals; one of the men is caught, the rest escaping to their ships. But the cannibals pelt the ships with huge boulders, and men are harpooned and taken home to be eaten.

> **COMMENT:** Just as Odysseus' crew and Penelope's suitors are equated by their regard for cattle, so they are equated by the fact that both groups of men are compared to fish; the crew here, the suitors in Book XXII. This is no coincidence, nor is it a coincidence that both animals, cattle and fish, are typically thought of as travelling in groups. Thus the comparisons we have been making between groups and between individuals serves to enable us to make a higher comparison and one more important to the meaning of the *Odyssey*: a comparison between man as an individual and man as a member of the community. This is elaborated upon in the Introduction.

Odysseus, whose ship is outside the harbor, sees that he can do nothing for his men trapped within. He sails away on his one remaining ship.

> **COMMENT:** In the cannibal-giant country the "nights are so short that the shepherd driving his flock out meets the shep-

herd driving his flock in." This tale is very likely some travel-
er's yarn from the northern latitudes. Hence, the land of the
midnight sun. Later writers placed the land in Sicily, south of
Mount Aetna.

CIRCE: With his one remaining ship he reaches the island of
Aeaea (ee EE ah), near the Italian coast, supposedly. Odysseus
splits his men into two parties, assigning the command of the
second group to Eurylochus (you RILL oh kuss), and it is the
latter group who discovers Circe's house:

> "They found in a dell the house of Circe, well built with
> shaped stones, and set in a clearing. All round it were wolves
> and lions of the mountains, really men whom she had be-
> witched by giving them poisonous drugs. They did not at-
> tack the men, but jumped up fawning on them and wagging
> their long tails, just like a lot of dogs playing about their
> master when he comes out after dinner, because they know
> he has always something nice for them in his pocket. So these
> wolves and lions with their sharp claws played about and
> pawed my men, who were frightened out of their wits by the
> terrible creatures." (It's metaphors or similes like the ones
> above that serve to make Homer the greatest of writers!)

All but Eurylochus greedily eat the food offered them by the witch
Circe (SIR see), the lovely enchantress. Mixed with the food is
a drug that turns the men into swine. Eurylochus relates the episode
to his master, who, while on his way to the witch's house meets
Hermes, who gives him directions on how to cope with the beautiful goddess:

> "As soon as Circe gives you a tap with her long rod, draw
> your sword at once and rush upon her as if you meant to kill
> her. She will be terrified, and will invite you to lie with her.
> Do not refuse, for you want her to free your companions and
> to entertain you; but tell her to swear the most solemn oath
> of the blessed gods that she will never attempt any other
> evil against you, or else when you are stript she may unman
> you and make you a weakling."

Odysseus did as Hermes directed him, not forgetting the charmed
flower that would offset Circe's magic: "The root was black, but
the flower was milk-white. The gods call it moly." Circe is in his
power now, and all the animals are returned to their human forms.

After feasting, Odysseus is invited to put away his sword in its sheath and lie down with her in bed. All stay for a year, feasting every day, but once again all are eager to return home. Circe tells Odysseus that in order to reach home he would first have to visit Hades, the home of the god of the underworld, where the ghosts of the dead dwell. There he is to speak to the prophet Teiresias, who will tell him all he needs to know about getting home. In the bustle of leaving they are unaware that one of their number, Elpenor (ell PEE nor), had fallen from the roof of Circe's house and was killed. The men are heartbroken at the thought of delay but comply with Odysseus' orders to sail for the entrance of the underworld first.

COMMENT: An interesting episode is the encounter between Odysseus and the suspicious Eurylochus, who disbelieves his master's words: "When I [i.e., Odysseus] heard this, I thought for a moment that I would draw my sword and cut off his head, and let it roll on the ground, for all he was my near relation. But the others held me back, and did their best to soften me." (There are times when Odysseus' anger is hot and quick, like that of Achilles.)

THE *ODYSSEY*

BOOK XI: THE LAND OF THE DEAD

ELPENOR AND TEIRESIAS: The crew and Odysseus finally reach the place Circe had described for them, the so-called end of the world (the Atlantic Ocean for the Greeks); here is the entrance to Hades. Following Circe's instructions, Odysseus digs a trench and makes the correct prayers and libations to the dead.

> **COMMENT:** The action of opening a trench for the dead seems to imply the burial of the dead—a custom practiced by the Myceneans (see Introduction), but not by anyone else among the Greeks, who practiced cremation. This is an example of poetical but not archeological sense in Homer.

Then the souls of the dead came crowding from Erebos (Hades):

> "Young men and brides, old men who had suffered much, and tender maidens to whom sorrow was a new thing; others killed in battle, warriors clad in bloodstained armour. All this crowd gathered about the pit from every side, with a dreadful great noise, which made me pale with fear."

They are eager to drink the blood Odysseus had spilled, the first soul reaching him being that of Elpenor, who had fallen from Circe's roof. He pleads with Odysseus to return to Aeaea and cremate his dead body so that he can properly enter the ranks of the dead. This Odysseus promises to do. The next ghost is that of his mother Anticleia (an tih KLEE uh), but he refuses her blood (giving her the power to speak) until he has spoken with Teiresias (Elpenor still had the power of speech because he had not yet been cremated). Teiresias, after strengthening himself with some blood from the pit, tells Odysseus about the islands of Helios and its sacred cattle, which are not to be harmed in any way. He then tells Odysseus about the suitors in his home and that he must slay them. (This event occurs three years after the Trojan War, when the suitors had not yet started their wooing; but even Homer nods once in a while. But a seer like Teiresias can see into the future also.) After slaying the suitors he (bearing an oar) is to travel until he is so far away from the sea that no one will recognize the oar for what it is. Then he should offer sacrifices to Poseidon and return home. A quiet death will then be asured him:

"Death shall come to you from the sea, death ever so peaceful shall take you off when comfortable old age shall be your only burden, and your people shall be happy round you."

ANTICLEIA: After his mother (the next ghost to accost him) has drunk the speech-enabling blood, she speaks of her own death:

"And this is how I sickened and died . . . it was no disease that made me pine away: but I missed you so much, and your clever wit and your gay merry ways, and life was sweet no longer, so I died."

When Odysseus hears this he longs to throw his arms round her neck, but every time he tries to embrace her the ghost slips through his arms like a shadow or a dream. She assures him Penelope is still faithful, and that his son is happy in Ithaca, but his father is grieving for his son's return still.

EPICASTE (or Jocasta): The tragic mother of Oedipus who wedded her own son (unknowingly) and begat children by him arrives next. She tells how she took her life by hanging after discovering her horrible incest (see the great play by Sophocles entitled *Oedipus Rex* for details of that famous story). Then comes Nestor's mother Chloris; Leda, the mother of Helen of Troy and Clytemnestra; Iphimedia; Phaedra; Procris; Ariadne; Meara; Clymene, and Eriphyle.

AGAMEMNON: Agamemnon's ghost relates his own death and counsels Odysseus not to trust anyone, and to sail secretly into his home port.

ACHILLES: Achilles' retort is famous:

"Don't bepraise death to me, Odysseus. I would rather be plowman to a yeoman farmer on a small holding than lord paramount in the kingdom of the dead."

Odysseus gives Achilles news of his son Neoptolemus:

"When we held a council of war, he was always the first to speak, and always found the right thing to say. Only Nestor and I were superior. When we met our enemies in battle, he did not lag among the crowd or in the scrimmage, but showed himself well in front, the bravest of the brave: many a man he killed in fair fight." (Such a son would be a great consolation to the mighty Achilles.)

AIAS (EYE uhs): Aias is still angry at Odysseus for having won Achilles' armor after he had died. Odysseus begs that he be forgiven, but Aias turns silently away:

"He replied not a word, but moved away into Erebos after the other ghosts of the dead. Then in spite of all, he should have spoken to me, or I to him; but I wished to see the souls of the others who were dead."

COMMENT: Aias' silence has been called a "silence more sublime than speech" by Longinus, a great Greek critic. Achilles, after hearing of his son's valor in battle, also expresses his fetlings in a most subtle way: "When I told him this, the ghost of clean-heeled Achilles marched away with long steps over the meadow of asphodel, proud to hear how his son had made his mark."

Next comes Minos, the judge of the dead, dispensing his decisions: on Orion, the hunter whose form became a constellation; on Tityos, who was punished by having his liver constantly consumed by vultures (also known as Prometheus); on Tantalus, the great-grandfather of Agamemnon, who was tantalized with food and water while kept hungry and thirsty; on Sisyphus, who never can reach the top of the hill up which he is rolling his giant boulder; and finally Heracles (Hercules), the mighty hunter. At last, Odysseus departs for other shores.

THE *ODYSSEY*

BOOK XII: SIRENS; SCYLLA AND CHARYBDIS

THE SIRENS: First, Odysseus returns to Aeaea to cremate Elpenor's body as he had promised. Later Circe foretells and forewarns Odysseus about the dangers of the Sirens, and the disasters facing one who sails too near to Scylla and Charybdis, and again repeats her warning about doing harm to the cattle of Helios. They set sail for home once more.

THE SIRENS: As they approach the Sirens, Odysseus plugs up the ears of his crew members, has himself tied to the mast with open ears so that he might enjoy the music of the sirens but is yet restrained from leaping into their arms.

> **COMMENT:**   Observe that the lure of the Sirens is not in their beauty, as is usually thought, but in the lyric quality of their song: "The Sirens bewitch every one who comes near them. If any man draws near in his innocence and listens to their voice, he never sees home again, never again will wife and little children run to greet him with joy; but the Sirens bewitch him with their melodious song. There in a meadow they sit, and all round is a great heap of bones, mouldering bodies and withering skins."

SCYLLA AND CHARYBDIS: At the narrow straits (of Messina, Sicily?) is found the monster Scylla (SILL uh)—perhaps a giant squid in reality—who sticks out her six long necks down to water level and grabs six of the crew for her meal. (Note that Odysseus cleverly avoids telling his crew that six of them were to be seized by Scylla, as predicted by Circe.) So Scylla obtains her toll as they pass her by.

THE ISLAND OF HELIOS: The crew, exhausted from travel, thirsty and hungry, insist on beaching at the island of the sun in spite of Odysseus' reluctance. They promise solemnly not to harm the cattle of Helios, the sun god.

Unfortunately, they are becalmed on the island for an entire month, at which time their food runs out. While Odysseus is at his prayers, Eurylochus (remember him from Book X?) suggests they kill some of Helios' cattle, which they proceed to do. The furious Odysseus discovers the betrayal of his trust. The empty cow-hides begin to crawl along the ground, and the cuts of meat begin to moo. Nevertheless the men go on eating. A week later they are able to sail away, but when they are in open water, Zeus (as penalty for eating the cattle) sets up a hurricane that breaks the boat in two and drowns all but Odysseus, who manages to make a crude raft from the wreckage of the boat. The storm almost sends him again into the arms of Scylla and Charybdis, had he not grabbed hold of a fig tree growing from the face of a cliff (Charybdis = whirlpool). After nine days of paddling his tiny raft, he comes to Calypso's island, where we first met Odysseus in Book V; and it was at that point Homer chose to begin his story of the adventures of Odysseus—*in medias res*. (This is the end of his long recital to the people of Phaeacia, the breathless and wonderful story of his marvelous adventures on the high seas.)

THE *ODYSSEY*

BOOK XIII: ITHACA AT LAST:

THE LANDING: Odysseus has just finished his long tale, leaving a long silence in the hall, which Alcinous breaks by suggesting that, in addition to the gifts they have already given him, they give him a tripod and a cauldron. The nobles will be repaid afterwards by asking the people of Phaeacia to pay for the gifts given to Odysseus.

> **COMMENT:** Here we see how serious the business of "gifts" is. In a world without national states, travelers were dependent upon the hospitality of the people with whom they stayed. Gifts were exchanged as a means of payment. These gifts were usually objects made of metal, rarely used, but rather kept to be given away. Anyone who gave a gift expected one in return. In other words, the gift-giving procedure was so established that Alcinous was (in our terms) asking his people to pay a tax to pay a state function.

In his farewell speech, Odysseus thanks them for their gifts and kind prayers; he prays that the gods will bring no evil to them. When they reach the boat, the young nobles do all the work, leaving Odysseus idle. (Observe carefully how Homer shows us a people who do everything to please; yet they are harshly treated by the gods, as we shall soon see.)

ITHACA AT LAST: The boat beaches in a calm inlet in Ithaca, at the head of which are an olive tree and a cave. Odysseus, who has fallen into a deep slep during the journey and has not yet reawakened, is lifted gently and placed, still wrapped in the linen they had covered him with, by the olive tree. Next to him they lay the precious gifts and then make their departure.

> **COMMENT:** This is the second time the olive tree has been mentioned in the *Odyssey*. The first occurred at the end of Book V, where Odysseus, who had just dragged himself onto the Phaeacian shore, covered himself with leaves beneath two olive trees, whose leaves formed a protective covering. The leaves are said to conceal his body, and the word for *conceal* has the same root as Calypso's name. Here, too, the olive tree is associated with a deep sleep, "death-like." The cave is the equivalent of the protective covering of the

91

olive tree, both of which can be taken (by modern symbolists) as womb-symbols, emphasizing, at strategic points in the poem, the theme of rebirth. The more anti-Freudian, scholarly-minded need not take this comment too seriously!

POSEIDON'S VENGEANCE: Meanwhile, Poseidon begs Zeus to punish the Phaeacians for their aid to the cursed Odysseus. So the Phaeacian ship is turned to stone just as it re-enters its own harbor. Alcinous, a witness of the transformation, suggests that they promise never to receive strangers again, and that they sacrifice twelve bulls to the sea-god. Nevertheless, they find they have been severely punished: a ship turned to stone, and their city surrounded with a ring of high mountains, forever cutting them off from the sea, their only source of livelihood. We never learn how successful they are in their prayers, for just at this moment the scene switches back to Ithaca.

ATHENA ENTERS: Odysseus awakens, not recognizing his own country. He thinks the Phaeacians have abandoned him in some strange land and counts his gifts to see if any have been stolen! (This seems petty when we see the fate the Phaeacians have undergone.) Athena in disguise, after playing tease for a while, finally informs him he is home. He tells the unrecognized Athena the first of his lying tales, which amuses and delights his protectress. After revealing herself, she disguises him as a beggar, and the climax of the tale now begins.

THE ODYSSEY

BOOK XIV: ODYSSEUS AND EUMAEUS

EUMAEUS: Odysseus, disguised as a beggar, enters the hut of Eumaeus (you MAY us), the swineherd, who is found sitting in front of the pigsty, cutting on leather. He greets the stranger kindly, grieving over not being able to do better for his guest. Odysseus is invited in, seated, given food, while the swineherd grumbles about the suitors and the pretty cause of the Trojan War, Helen of Troy. If only Odysseus were here, he says, he wouldn't have to work any longer (a loyal, hard-working servant who doesn't hesitate to complain about his condition—a fine minor character). Odysseus asks questions about his master and promises the swineherd that his master will soon be present once more in Ithaca. As for liars, Odysseus will have nothing to do with them! (A fine joke—no one has the fine art of lying so well developed as Odysseus himself.) With the meal over, Odysseus regales the swineherd with a splendidly complex and fascinating tale about his origins and travels. Eumaeus is moved by the story, but refuses to believe the one bit of truth in it—that Odysseus is still alive! Eumaeus once more prepares some pork for his guest:

> "The bread was taken round by Mesaulios—a slave whom the swineherd had bought [piracy and the buying and selling of slaves was common then—even among servants to the nobility like Eumaeus]. He got him from the Taphians and paid out of his own savings."

Odysseus is chilly now, but rather than ask for a cloak he tells a lying tale about how Odysseus was cold for lack of one during an escapade in the Trojan War (the patriotic war!). Eumaeus is wise enough to realize that his guest is hinting for the loan of a cloak or blanket. The beggar is given a blanket as cover while the swineherd spends the night protecting the swine from dogs and thieves (what a sense of duty to master!). And so to bed.

THE ODYSSEY

BOOK XV: THE RETURN OF TELEMACHUS

THE JOURNEY HOME: That same night Athena goes to Sparta to urge Telemachus to return home: "Don't dally in this valley, Telemachus, I tell thee! Remember your estates and the bullies in your house!" (The words for *fighting man* and *loafing man* and *feckless man* have enough similarities in Greek for Homer to play off at this point a scintillating pun!) She informs him the suitors are waiting for him in ambush, so that in order to arrive safely he must sneak into Ithaca and stay at Eumaeus' hut until he can safely enter the town. With Peisistratus, Nestor's son, they travel the entire day, reaching Pylos at nightfall of the second day. Telemachus, remembers Nestor's long speeches: "Nestoridês (*i.e.*, son of Nestor), old fellow, will you do something for me? Say yes! . . . leave me here, or the old gentleman will delay me out of pure good nature, but I simply must hurry on." He takes on board a certain Theoclymenus, a noble youth, who demands to know Telemachus' own pedigree before entering the ship (these people are very conscious of class, status, and family as is only too obvious). When all is in readiness, they set sail for Ithaca, the suitors still waiting in ambush. Later in this book we learn that Telemachus arrives safely in Ithaca without having encountered the ambushing suitors.

WITH EUMAEUS AGAIN: Odysseus is testing the swineherd's hospitality still. He wants to go to town to get a job as a servant of Penelope's. Eumaeus is dismayed: the beggar runs the risk of getting beaten by one of the drunken suitors; and secondly, they prefer pretty young boys as servants rather than old beggars:

> "Their servants are not a bit like thee. Young men, drest up fair and smart, sleek heads and pretty faces, that's what their servants be." (Is this a hint at homosexual activity among the suitors? Most scholars think not.)

Odysseus agrees to stay until Telemachus' arrival. We learn from their conversation that Odysseus has a sister, perhaps more than one. Her name is Ctimene, and she lives with her husband in Samos.

> **COMMENT:** According to some Greek writers, her husband was Eurylochus, the most outspoken member of Odysseus' crew (remember the Circe episode?).

We learn further that the faithful swineherd is of noble blood (recall that in Homer's time a nobleman was anyone who owned his own house and land). When just a baby Eumaeus was kidnapped (a popular activity then) from his parents by a maid who ran off with traders:

> "In a twink she picks up three cups, hides 'em in her bosom and carries them out; I followed like a little innocent. . . . Six days and six nights we sailed; when the seventh day came, Artemis Archeress (goddess of hunting, virginity, chastity) shot the wench, and down she went plump into the bilge like a sea-diver."

BACK TO TELEMACHUS: As they talk, Telemachus and his crew land in Ithaca. He suggests that Theoclymenus, his passenger, stay with Eurymachus, one of the suitors. Then a hawk carrying a dove flies by, an act interpreted by Theoclymenus as a good omen—that Telemachus will win over the suitors ("bird-reading" was a common way of interpreting the wills of gods). This omen pleases Telemachus, who now suggests that Theoclymenus stay with his friend and crew member, Peiraeus.

THE ODYSSEY

BOOK XVI: FATHER AND SON

TELEMACHUS AND EUMAEUS: Odysseus and Eumaeus are eating breakfast when Telemachus arrives. Eumaeus, overjoyed at the sight of him, upsets his bowl in his haste to embrace the young lad:

> "As a father fondles the son whom he dearly loves, when he returns from a far country after ten long years, his only son well-beloved for whose sake he has suffered much, so the faithful swineherd threw his arms round the noble boy, and kissed him all over as one come back from the dead: then sobbing for joy he spoke from the bottom of his heart."

Odysseus, true to his role of beggar, rises to give his son a place at the table. Respecting the apparent age of this old beggar, Telemachus politely refuses to take his seat. Eumaeus gives the details of the beggar's supposed origins and travels and suggests that Telemachus take him home. As in the case of Theoclymenus, the boy admits his shame at bringing a stranger into his disturbed home.

> **COMMENT:** In other words, Telemachus seems to have given up the position he had gained when he left Ithaca in Book II. There, he for the first time began to order the suitors about. Now he does not consider himself to be the master of his own house.

Telemachus sends the swineherd to tell his mother that he is back in Ithaca.

THE TRANSFORMATION AND CONFRONTATION: Athena calls Odysseus outside and advises him to now reveal his identity so that the two of them may plan together to rid the palace of suitors. Odysseus, without his disguise, re-enters the hut, stunning Telemachus with his dazzling manliness. His son can hardly believe his eyes:

> ". . . he kissed his son, and let the tears run freely down his cheeks; until that hour he had always held them back. . . . He sat down, and Telemachus threw his arms round his noble father and burst into tears. They sat sobbing and shaking in the relief from that long strain, like a pair of sea-eagles

robbed of their young before they are feathered, who quiver and shake as they utter shrill cries."

After this, Odysseus learns that there are 108 suitors in his house, but Odysseus is confident since they have Zeus and Athena on their side, and that makes all the difference. (Naturally the gods would gravely disapprove of the suitors; Athena herself is the goddess of domesticity and virtue in the home—among other things.) They plan to enter the hall with the father again disguised as a beggar. Then they plan to gather all the weapons that are lying about the room, leaving weapons only for the two of them. No one must know that Odysseus is back, not even his wife.

THE SUITORS: The suitors are angry at Telemachus' escape. Antinous suggests that, if they are successfully to settle the matter of Penelope, they must either slay the son and divide the property among themselves, or they must go each to his own home and court Penelope in the accepted manner. At this point Penelope appears, for she has heard of the attempted ambush of her son, and has descended to denounce the rapacious suitors, Antinous in particular, as cowards and double-dealers. Eurymachus denies her charges, but all the while he is plotting the boy's murder. Penelope returns to her room and cries herself to sleep. And so to bed. (A quite common book ending in Homer—everyone goes into a honey-lidded, sweet sleep—sleep that knits up the ravelled sleeve of care.)

THE *ODYSSEY*

BOOK XVII: ODYSSEUS RETURNS HOME

TELEMACHUS REPORTS TO HIS MOTHER: At dawn Telemachus announces that he is returning to the palace, and upon entering the house he is greeted by the old nurse Eurycleia, and then by his mother; naturally there is much weeping over the boy. Later Theoclymenus and Peiraeus join Telemachus in breakfast, and during the meal he briefs his mother on what had happened on his trip abroad; but true to his promise says nothing of his father's return. Theoclymenus, however, says that all the signs point to Odysseus' return, and that he is in all probability in Ithaca now. Penelope hopes that what he says is true.

MELANTHIUS: Odysseus and Eumaeus take a walk to town, Odysseus still leaning on his cane and using the beggar disguise. On their way they meet Melanthius, a goatherd, who is bringing two of his flock to the suitors for slaughter. Unlike the faithful swineherd, Melanthius has been only too anxious to please the suitors. He especially hates Eumaeus (note the purposeful contrast Homer draws between the two characters), whom he berates:

> "Here's a procession! Rags in the rear, and tatters in the van! It's always like to like, as the proverb says. Where did you pick up this dirty pig, you dirty pig-man? The beggar, this nuisance, this spoil-sport? He'll stand and rub shoulders on many a door-post, begging for scraps—he's not the sort that goes begging for my lord's guest-gifts (not a gentleman who would receive a grand parting gift. From the base man's point of view that is only another kind of beggar)."

As Melanthius passes them by, he gives Odysseus a kick that nearly knocks him on the road. Odysseus "thought for a moment he would kill the man with a blow of his staff, or lift him by the waist and dash his head on the ground; yet he controlled himself and bore it. (Note the mighty anger and yet the control; the vengeance will be swift and terrible!) Melanthius continues serenely on his way, scornful of Eumaeus' childing.

ARGUS: In the palace courtyard Odysseus notices his dog Argus ("Flash" in Greek). This old dog recognizes his master, but is too weak to approach him; he can only wag his tail and droop his ears, after which he dies. Odysseus is deeply moved.

ANTINOUS AND THE BEGGAR: Once inside Odysseus starts begging food from the suitors, among whom is to be found Melanthius, who tells the suitors that Eumaeus had brought this beggar into town. Antinous, annoyed at Eumaeus, insults him, but the swineherd is stoutly defended by Telemachus. At this point the suitor picks up his footstool to threaten Odysseus. Odysseus launches into his third lying tale, telling of his noble heritage and how he had never refused anything to a beggar in his house: "Upon my word, your heart's not like your looks! You wouldn't give a grain of salt to your own housekeeper out of the pantry, if you sit by another man's table, and can't let yourself stretch out a hand and give me a bit of bread. There's plenty here!" Antinous is stung and flings a footstool at Odysseus, hitting him squarely in the shoulder. Odysseus stands up to the blow (there will be two more times when he will be struck with objects thrown by suitors: in Book XVIII and again in Book XX), and states his hope that Antinous will never live to reach his wedding day.

> **COMMENT:** The statement is ironical, for not only is it Odysseus himself who makes sure that Antinous never lives to reach his wedding day, but it is this "wedding day", *i.e.*, Antinous' hoped-for wedding with Penelope, that is the cause of his death. That is, if he had not planned on marrying her, he would not have been killed.

Penelope requests Odysseus' presence, but Odysseus replies that he will see her in the evening. This he does so as not to raise suspicions.

THE ODYSSEY

BOOK XVIII: ODYSSEUS AND IRUS

THE GENTLE BLOW: While Odysseus is waiting for the suitors' departure so that he can visit Penelope unseen, a beggar enters the palace in search of food (he is nicknamed Irus, meaning "talker"; he evidently delivers messages for people). He immediately starts insulting Odysseus:

> "Get away from the door, greybeard, unless you want to be dragged out by the leg! Don't you see how they are all squinting at me and telling me to drag you out? . . . Up with you, before it comes to a beating!"

Odysseus, frowning:

> "Don't say too much about fists, or you may make me angry. I am an old man, but I might colour your face and chest with ruby red."

The suitors urge a fight, but Irus, glimpsing the stalwart thighs of his opponent, is quaking in his boots. He faces Odysseus and is laid low by one smashing blow to the neck:

> "Odysseus struck the man's neck under the ear and broke his jawbone; the red blood gushed out of his mouth, and he fell in the dust bleating, and gnashed his teeth, drumming with his heels on the ground."

Odysseus drags him out by the leg into the courtyard:

> "Sit there now, and keep off the pigs and dogs. Don't set up to be Monarch of all the Beggars, you miserable wretch, or a worse thing may come upon you" [note the lack of pity or sentimentality in the Homeric hero].

Odysseus is congratulated by the suitors and offered bread by Amphinomus (am FIN uh mus), the same one who in Book XVI opposed the other suitors in the plot against Telemachus' murder. Odysseus tries, without revealing his identity, to warn Amphinomus on the impending slaughter, but Amphinomus does nothing to avoid his own death.

100

THE BEAUTIFUL PENELOPE: Penelope, after some divine cosmeticizing by Athena, enters the hall where the suitors are congregated, and causes a stir. She goes straight up to her son and chides him for allowing mistreatment of a guest. Her son admits he shouldn't have allowed the fight.

> **COMMENT:** Notice, now that his father is present, Telemachus is here much more polite to his mother than in Book I, where he almost rudely refused to listen to her request that Phemius, the bard, stop singing about Troy.

Eurymachus breaks in, praising Penelope's great beauty, but she bewails the fact that her choice for a husband is limited to such a cheaply vulgar crowd of youngsters. Stung at the word *cheap* they immediately send for gifts of clothes and jewelry to impress her with their generosity.

ODYSSEUS SCOLDS A MAID: When darkness comes, the maids scurry about the palace, lighting the torches for the suitors. This infuriates Odysseus, who feels they should be helping the mistress of the palace. Melantho, the sister of the evil goatherd Melanthius, laughs at Odysseus' offer of help; she, like the rest of the servants, prefers serving the suitors to helping her mistress. Odysseus' threat to tell Telemachus finally chases them back to Penelope. Eurymachus pokes fun at Odysseus' baldness (Athena had given him a shiny baldness) and offers him a job as a serf.

> **COMMENT:** The serf was the lowest person in the social hierarchy of free men in that period. When in Book XI Achilles says that he would rather be a serf on earth than a king of the underworld, he meant the worst position on earth was better than the highest after death. Obviously then the offer is an insult to a free beggar.

Odysseus replies: "Eurymachus, I should be glad if you and I could have a match in the springtime, when the long days come round. In the hayfield . . . give me a well-curved scythe and you take another . . ." The farmer's challenge is followed by a footstool hurled at our hero (the second assault), which misses. Telemachus angrily orders all the suitors from his home, and (oddly) they depart.

THE ODYSSEY

BOOK XIX: ODYSSEUS AND THE OLD NURSE

THE ARMS REMOVAL: Odysseus tells his son to go and lie down: "Leave me alone here, for I want to tease the maids and your mother a little more, and she will ask me everything amid showers of tears." He reminds Telemachus of the excuse he is to have ready, should the suitors notice what he is doing: that the arms are smudged from smoke and, in addition, that a suitor might kill someone with one of the swords the next time he becomes drunk. So father and son begin to clear the house of arms. Melantho, the servant, again insults Odysseus for being a tramp. Odysseus angrily says there is more than one kind of tramp. Penelope too is angry at Melantho for her insults; she invites Odysseus to sit at her feet and tell her of his past; but he refuses politely, saying he gets too sad when he reminisces.

PENELOPE'S TALE: Penelope tells her own hard-luck story: how she kept off the suitors by claiming that she was weaving a funeral shroud for her father-in-law and could not accept any offers of marriage until she had completed the weaving. How each night she would undo what she had completed during the day; in this way she foiled the suitors for three years, almost four. Naturally they had caught on.

ODYSSEUS' FIFTH LYING TALE: At her second request for the story of his life, Odysseus complies by telling how as a Cretan he had entertained Odysseus in his home; this part brings tears to his wife's cheeks; she is convinced that his accurate knowledge of her husband's habits and clothes is indeed indicative of the beggar's probity. He finally promises her that Odysseus will be home before the end of the year.

EURYCLEIA KNOWS: While washing Odysseus' legs (at his own behest), Eurycleia sees a scar on his leg obtained in her master's youth—now she knows the beggar is her master.

> **COMMENT:** Precisely at this point, before we can learn the consequences of Eurycleia's recognition, Homer enters into a long explanation of how Odysseus had received the wound which caused his scar. Some scholars claim that this digression arises from Homer's desire to give the history of every object he mentions; but this cannot be the whole answer.

102

What is more to the point is that Homer uses this method to stress the importance of the object. If he ever gives the history of a weapon, it is for the reason that this weapon is soon to play a decisive role in the future action. Homer describes in detail the construction of the raft which took Odysseus away from Calypso's island, not out of any desire to let us know as much as he can tell us, but because he wants us to know that this voyage will be an important one. Now that Homer has interrupted the action to tell in great detail the history of the scar, we should examine this history carefully to see what it is about this scar that Homer considers so important.

THE SCAR STORY: Homer tells us that Odysseus received the wound on a boar hunt during a visit to his grandfather Autolycus, who had named his grandson *Odysseus* from the Greek word *odyssomai* meaning "to cause pain to someone" (the English word "anodyne," a pain-reliever, is from the same stem). On the boar hunt Odysseus was gored on his thigh by a surprise attack by a boar, which Odysseus then killed with his spear.

> **COMMENT:** Odysseus both *gives* and *receives* pain; he has both an active and passive nature. He either gives out pain to others or suffers pain in return. Note how he has pained his mother, his wife, and his dog for example.

THE DECISION OF PENELOPE: Eurycleia promises not to tell anyone she knows who the beggar is. Penelope tells him of the myth of the two gates through which all dreams come—the ivory gate for false dreams and the one of horn for dreams of truth. She is sure that her dream (she had dreamed an eagle had slain some geese) had issued from the gates of ivory.

> **COMMENT:** Bird omens are very important signs of things to come, much like tea-leaf reading today. Dream interpretation then was a highly advanced art. The theory was that when the conscious mind was asleep, the various forces of night, demons and gods, could more subtly work their charms and reveal their intents to you. Hence the extreme importance of dreams for knowing the intent of the gods. Here for example, the interpretation is that Odysseus will come (the eagle) and slay all the suitors (the geese).

She is prompted to let a contest decide who shall become her husband. The next day, she says, she will test the suitors' skill in archery. Odysseus encourages her in this enterprise and promises her that her husband will be there. And so to bed.

THE ODYSSEY

BOOK XX: THINGS TO COME

THAT NIGHT: As Odysseus prepares his bed, a party of maids passes by. The sight of these girls who have become the mistresses of the suitors infuriates him:

> "He felt as fierce as a bitch standing over her litter of pups, snarling and growling at someone she does not know, and ready to fight; so his heart growled in him at their shameless ways. For a while he did not know whether to kill them all, or to let them go for the last dalliance of their lives" [each was the mistress of a suitor and spent the night with him].

Athena appears to him as a young girl and assures him she will help him and to have faith in her. Penelope awakens in tears. The image of Odysseus had appeared in her dream.

DAWN: Odysseus awakes and asks Zeus for a sign that he will succeed in his goal; Zeus obliges him with a thunderclap.

COMMENT: This day is the last day for the suitors; it is also the most completely described day in the *Odyssey*, filling out Books XX, XXI, and XXII.

Eumaeus arrives with three pigs to be consumed in the oncoming feast, planned when Penelope announces her choice of a husband. Again Melanthius, the evil goatherd, insults the internally furious Odysseus. Philoetius (fy LOH tee us), a cowherd, arriving soon after, proves that he, unlike the goatherd, is loyal and friendly. He, too, can be trusted to help in the fight to come.

CTESIPPUS (stee SIP us): The scene shifts to the main hall where the suitors are interrupted by an omen: an eagle passes overhead holding a dove in its claws. Amphinomus interprets the omen as an evil one for the suitors. Drunken brawls arise during the feasting, and Ctesippus, a sarcastic suitor, offers a gift, a cow's hoof, to the beggar by tossing it at his head. Odysseus ducks it, smiling nastily, and his son again denounces the suitors. They laugh so lustily at Telemachus that in their hysteria they think they see blood all over the food—a bad omen. Unheeding, they proceed again to insult Odysseus.

THE *ODYSSEY*

BOOK XXI: THE BOW CONTEST

TELEMACHUS TRIES: Penelope, carrying out the plan she had outlined to Odysseus in Book XIX, goes to fetch Odysseus' bow from the storeroom, at which point we are given its biography by Homer. Then Penelope:

> "sat down and laid it across her knees, weeping bitterly as she handled her husband's bow. But after she had enjoyed a good cry, she descended to the boisterous company in the great hall, holding in her hand the bow and the quiver with its arrows of sorrow."

Telemachus is happy now that the end is near, and prepares the hall for the contest. Digging a trench in the dirt floor, he places the handles of twelve axes in a straight line so that the holes through which the axeheads were fastened are aligned. The aim of the contest is to shoot an arrow through all twelve holes. Telemachus attempts the formidable task of stringing his father's mighty bow and fails; but he would have succeeded on the fourth try had not Odysseus signaled him to cease (an unusual twist in the mythic stereotype—the son usually surpasses his father in the last, mighty contest). The son sees the nod and pretends to have failed, offering the yet unstrung bow to the suitors. The effeminate Leodes tries and fails; Antinous mocks him, ever true to his sneering character.

THE FAITHFUL SERVANTS: In the courtyard where he cannot be overheard, Odysseus reveals himself to the faithful servants (by showing his scar) Eumaeus and Philoetius, and asks their aid: Eumaeus is to give the bow to Odysseus when he asks for it, and he is to see to it that the maids stay in their rooms. Philoetius is to close the door to the courtyard to foil escape.

THE WINNER: Odysseus re-enters the hall in time to see Eurymachus attempting the bow.

> **COMMENT:** Note how Homer, by taking us outside for a few minutes, has avoided having to describe the failure of all the suitors between Leodes and Eurymachus. Observe also how much faith Odysseus has in the inability of the suitors to string the bow—so much faith that he dares to leave the hall while they are trying.

Eurymachus says:

"Upon my word, I am sorry for myself and for everyone! It is not so much the wedding, though I am sorry enough about that; there are plenty of women to be had in Ithaca and elsewhere. But to think that we can be so much weaker than Prince Odysseus, that we can't bend his bow! That will be no credit to us in future generations!"

When Antinous is about to ask a postponement of the contest, Odysseus is allowed to try at Penelope's insistence. Eumaeus carries the bow to Odysseus, and then tells Eurycleia to keep the maids in their rooms, while Philoetius carries out his orders by locking the courtyard door. The beggar Odysseus expertly handles the bow, strings it easily, his strength striking the suitors with amazement. A clap of thunder is heard, and at that point Oydsseus, without seeming to aim, shoots an arrow straight through the holes of all twelve axe handles. Telemachus runs to his side. The massacre is about to begin!

THE ODYSSEY

BOOK XXII: THE MASSACRE

EURYMACHUS THE FIRST: Odysseus tears off his clothes and leaps onto the threshold of the main entrance of the hall. He is exultant now as he shouts, "This contest is over now—but there's another target I'd like to hit."

> **COMMENT:** The rage in Odysseus' heart is better indicated by this savage war-cry: "Dogs! you thought I would never come back from Troy, so you have been carving up my substance, forcing the women to lie with you, courting my wife before I was dead, not fearing the gods who rule the broad heavens, nor the execration of man which follows you for ever. And now the cords of death are made fast about you all!"

The first arrow is sent through Antinous' neck just as he reaches for a cup of wine. The suitors, still unknowing in their recognition, threaten to kill the careless archer for his accidental shot. They turn pale after his speech (see above), and the ever-smooth Eurymachus tries to put all the blame on Antinous, even offering a bribe, which is spurned. The suitors rush at Odysseus with drawn swords (these had not been removed, but they have no armor); Eurymachus is shot through the breast; Amphimedon is killed by Telemachus' spear; Odysseus continues the slaughter with bow and arrow. Melanthius is able to bring some armor for the remaining suitors, but when dashing out for more weapons he is overpowered and then hanged from the ceiling with a rope pulled by the loyal Philoetius and Eumaeus. He is left there dangling from his middle until the end of the fighting, when he is promptly dispatched. Athena (as Mentor) joins in the fighting: "At that moment Athena lifted her man-shattering aegis-cape (remember the gorgon's head!) and held it against them from on high: they fell into a panic and scampered along the hall like a herd of cows."

She spurs Odysseus on to finish the slaughter, then leaves without really having taken an active role in the fighting. Odysseus and his companions dodge spears and kill four more suitors. Both Telemachus and Eumaeus are slightly hurt, but go on fighting. Leodes begs for mercy since he had acted as priest and had not molested any of the maids; but the merciless Odysseus cuts him down also.

PHEMIUS: Now Phemius, the minstrel, pleads for his life:

> "Spare me, Odysseus, I pray! Have mercy upon me! You will
> be sorry afterwards if you kill a singer like me, one who can
> sing before god and man! I am self-taught, but God has plant-
> ed all manner of songs in my mind. I am fit to sing before you
> as before God; then do not be eager to cut my throat!"

He explains he had never sung for them voluntarily: he had been
forced to sing for the suitors. Telemachus speaks up for Phemius
and also for Medon, the herald. These two non-traitors are spared,
but all the suitors are by now killed.

> **COMMENT:**   The suitors, like Odysseus' crew in Book X,
> who were killed by the Laestrygonians, are compared to fish.
> Odysseus, on the other hand is now, as before, described as
> a raging lion.

Eurycleia points out twelve maids who had adopted shameful ways.
Odysseus has them remove the bodies and clean the hall, which
is splattered with blood and gore. After that, Telemachus takes
them outside and hangs them all by the neck:

> "They were strung up with their heads in a row—a pitiable
> death to die, no lover's bed indeed! They looked like a lot of
> thrushes or doves caught in a net when they come to roost in
> the bushes. Their feet jerked for a little while, but not long."

Melanthius' nose, ears, and cods (testicles), are cut off and
thrown to the dogs to eat raw; then hands and feet are cut off to
vent their fury. The massacre is over!

THE ODYSSEY

BOOK XXIII: HUSBAND AND WIFE

THE DOUBTFUL WIFE: Eurycleia happily climbs up the stairs to tell her mistress that her husband is home and that the suitors are all slain. Naturally Penelope is full of wonder.

> **COMMENT:** Penelope hesitates to accept the truth, much as she would like to. By asking what Odysseus has done, she keeps his presence hypothetical.

Even the mention of the scar does not convince the wife; it might be some clever god who took on the beggar disguise and slew the suitors. Face to face with the beggar, she can only stare at his face, then at his rags:

> "He was sitting against a pillar looking down, and wondering whether his brave wife would speak to him when she saw him. But she sat silent a long time as if struck dumb. Again and again she turned her eager eyes and looked hard at his face."

Telemachus is impatient with his cautious mother. She replies that she is still not sure that he is her husband and that she will test him when they are alone.

THE TEST: After bathing and dressing in fine clothes, the two are face to face. *The test*: Penelope asks Eurycleia to move her bed, which Odysseus himself had built from a living oak tree so that it could never be moved. Her husband bursts into a rage (neatly falling into the trap, or is it *out* of the trap?):

> "Wife, that has cut me to the heart! Who has moved my bed? That would be a difficult job for the best workman, unless God himself should come down and move it."

Penelope was conquered; she could hold out no longer when Odysseus told the secret she knew so well. She burst into tears and ran straight to him, throwing her arms about his neck. She kissed his head, and cried:

> "Don't be cross with me, my husband, you were always a most understanding man! My heart has been frozen all this time with a fear that some one would come and deceive me with

a false tale; there are so many imposters. . . . You have convinced your hard-hearted wife!"

Odysseus was even more deeply moved, and:

"his tears ran as he held her in his arms (this is his second flow of recognition tears; the first was with his son), the wife of his heart, so faithful and wise. She felt like a shipwrecked mariner, when the stout ship has been driven before the storm and smashed by the heavy waves, but a few have escaped by swimming. How glad they are to see land at last. . . . So glad was Penelope to see her husband at last; she held her white arms close round his neck, and could not let him go."

COMMENT: One of the most affecting and famous recognition scenes in all literature. What makes the scene especially effective is the distrust and caution of the wife herself—mistrusting even the well-known scar!

THE FOLLOW-UP: Odysseus confides in his wife that Teiresias (Book XI) had instructed him to travel inland with an oar on his shoulder until someone should mistake it as a fan for winnowing wheat. He is then to plant the oar in the earth, sacrifice a bull, a ram, and a boar to Poseidon, and return home, where, after many years, he will meet a peaceful death. The happy couple then go to bed together where he delights her with tales (truthful ones), and then "these two enjoyed at last the blessing of love."

COMMENT: There are some who think the epic ends at this point, but this is wrong: there are some loose ends such as Laertes and the relatives of the suitors.

THE ODYSSEY

BOOK XXIV: FATHER AND SON; HOW IT ALL ENDS

HADES: The scene is Hades where Hermes, the traditional guide of the dead, is leading the souls of the dead suitors to Hades. On the way they pass such Trojan heroes as Agamemnon and Achilles (see Book XI). There is much reminiscing.

> **COMMENT:** This bit of small talk makes us realize what a romance the *Odyssey* is. Achilles and Agamemnon lived as heroes, but they are dead now. Unlike the dead in Hades, Odysseus has had the best of all possible experiences as a soldier, adventurer, and lover—and that supreme jewel—a faithful wife to come home to.

Achilles recognizes Amphimedon, who relates in great detail of the years of wooing, the shroud-trick, the return of the beggar, Odysseus, and the massacre. (We must remember that Homer constantly repeats the same stories for his audiences, since his songs were sung and recited orally over periods of several days and even weeks. Such oral reminders are vital to the success of long recited works. Besides, who could resist the special joy that comes with a repeated tale cast in a slightly different light?) Agamemnon praises the faithful Penelope and groans over his own faithless wife Clytemnestra.

FATHER AND SON: Odysseus reaches his father's farm, where he finds the ragged and woebegone Laertes. Posing as a stranger, the son asks about Odysseus, a question which brings tears to his father's eyes. Finally, he reveals all that has happened, even showing the boar wound, and telling him the exact number of fruit trees he had planted with his father many years ago:

> "Thirteen pear trees you gave me and ten apples, forty figs, rows of vines you promised, fifty of them . . . with grapes of all sorts . . . heavy in the season of the year!"

"The old man's knees crumpled under him, and his heart melted, as he heard the signs recounted which he knew so well; he laid his arms about his son's neck, and Odysseus held him fainting." Quickly Laertes (lay AIR teez) warns him of the relatives and friends of the suitors who seek revenge. They return to the house to dine in happiness with Telemachus.

THE END: The news of the massacre leaks out and an assembly is hastily called. Medon and the bard Phemius are there. Medon, the herald, tells the assembly that Odysseus was helped by a god in the form of Mentor. The gods seem to be on his side. Yet the relatives and friends of the suitors arm for battle, even reaching Laertes' farm. Athena has time to rush to Odysseus' side, again in the form of Mentor. Eupeithes, a suitor relative, is slain by the spear of old Laertes, now glad to see son and grandson lusting for battle. Just as Odysseus and Telemachus are ready to slay the entire array of relatives and friends of the suitors, Athena calls a halt to the fighting:

"Stay your hands from battle, men of Ithaca, be reconciled and let bloodshed cease!"

Pale as death they drop their weapons and turn back homewards, "for they did not wish to die." A sharp command stops the warlike Odysseus in his tracks, and he too obeys the stern Athena, "gladly with all his heart." There is peace in Ithaca at last.

COMMENT: This last picture of Odysseus, almost crazed with his lust to kill, is truly exciting. It is to be compared with the first time we saw him on Calypso's island, where he sat crying on the seashore, eager to be home once more. He is home now, back in the real world, and it is everything he has longed for. (Note: All quotations from W.H.D. Rouse's translations in Mentor paperback.)

END

GREEK LYRIC POETRY:

INTRODUCTION

WHAT DOES LYRIC POETRY MEAN?

Lyric in the days of ancient Greece meant poems which are to be sung, accompanied by the music of the lyre (a harplike, stringed instrument). The poems dealt with the poet's *personal sentiments* or *feelings;* such poems were carefully distinguished from the other two main forms of poetry: *epic* and *dramatic.* Later the lyre accompaniment was dropped.

HOW DOES LYRIC POETRY DIFFER FROM THE EPIC POETRY OF HOMER, FOR EXAMPLE?

Epic poetry is written almost always in dactylic hexameter; almost always recited in accompaniment to the harp; epic poetry is long (24 books in Homer's *Iliad*), and the feelings are not the intensely personal ones of the lyric poet, but rather the communally objective ones of a whole society. In other words, the author's personality is kept out of the verse as much as possible—strictly objective narrative; epic poetry harks back to the past, and existed well before drama, history, or philosophy.

WHEN DID LYRIC POETRY FLOURISH?

The greatest writers of lyric poetry wrote between the eighth and fifth centuries before Christ.

WHAT IS ELEGIAC POETRY?

Elegiac poetry is like lyric except that originally the flute was used for accompaniment:

1. The meter was *dactylic hexameter,* alternated with pentameters.

2. Every two lines rhymed—*couplets.*

3. *Elegiac couplets* were largely of the reflective type rather than passionately lyrical—used as epitaphs on tombstones, to celebrate military matters, to express political ideas, and to utter sentiments during banqueting or mourning.

113

4. They are often *gnomic,* pithy and axiomatic sayings.

WHAT IS IAMBIC POETRY?

Iambic poetry uses iambic meter: alternate short and long syllables (∪ – ∪ – ∪ –), usually three such to a line.

Iambic poetry was recited generally in a satiric vein and was most often directed at individuals.

WHAT IS MELIC POETRY?

1. It is pure lyric poetry accompanied by the seven-stringed lyre; it was written to be sung.

2. The *Ode* (= song in Greek) reached its highest expression in the poetry of Pindar, ca. 522-448 B.C.

WHAT IS MONODIC AND CHORAL LYRIC?

1. *Monodic lyric* is lyric sung by the poet, generally to his friends, the poet himself being both the composer of the words and the music.

2. *Choral lyric* was that poetry which was both sung and danced by a chorus, the poet composing the words, music, and the choreography. Some types of choral lyric are
a. hymns
b. marriage songs (*epithalamia*)
c. victory songs (*epinicia*)
d. dirges and hymns

WHAT IS GREEK METER?

Greek meter is "quantitative," that is, the length of time necessary for the pronouncing of each *syllable* was either long (–) or short (∪); a short syllable took about half the time to utter as did a long one. Here are the main patterns of rhythm (meter) in Greek verse:

Dactyl: – ∪ ∪
Spondee: – –
Iamb: ∪ –
Anapest: ∪ ∪ –
Trochee: – ∪
Tribrach: ∪ ∪ ∪
Cretic: – ∪ –
Bacchius: ∪ – –

Dactylic hexameter means six dactyls to a verse. Pentameter, trimeter etc. (five, three to a verse etc.). Iambic pentameter = five *iambs* to a line. Epic verse was in dactylic hexameter.

GREEK LYRIC POETRY: ARCHILOCHUS

ARCHILOCHUS OF PAROS (earlier 7th century B.C.)

LIFE: Archilochus (ar KILL oh kuss) is considered only second to Homer among the Ionian poets. He was the son of a slave woman and an aristocrat. At one time he was a mercenary soldier; at another he fell in love with Neobule, the daughter of Lycambes, who forbade the marriage. Tradition has it that the poet avenged himself with such savage satiric attacks (in iambic verse) that both father and daughter hanged themselves. The poet is said to have died on the battlefield.

CONTRIBUTION: He is regarded as the inventor of *iambics* (see Int.). He wrote witty, frank verse on the subject of his own sorrow, anger, and love. He also wrote elegies (poems lamenting death). "His iambic poems show a great variety of talent, mockery, enthusiasm, melancholy, and a mordant wit . . . 'scorpion-tongued' " (*Oxf. Comp.*). "And Archilochus' thorny blossoms, in their tangle thicket growing,/Bitter as the spindrift that drives across the seas (Meleager)."

POEMS: *"The Better Part of Valour"*:
"Some Thracian now goes strutting with a shield I left behind me,
Under a bush—a peerless shield—regretfully.
However—I came home living. Plague take it!
I will find me
Another one hereafter—and just as good to me." (Lucas)

COMMENT: Here are a few lines on his famous shield poem; he says it was right to throw it away in the midst of battle because in that way he saved his life. Note the opposite of the heroic ideal as seen in Homer, where honor is all. Archilochus' frank mockery is balm for one too much steeped in Homer!

"Too Versatile" (elegiac satiric couplet in iambs):
"Many a trick the wise fox knows;
But the hedgehog has *one*, worth a lot of those." (Lucas)

We have only fragments of this great poet who could be violent and passionate, tender and graceful, bitter and cynical.

GREEK LYRIC POETRY: ALCAEUS

ALCAEUS OF LESBOS (born ca. 620 B.C.)

LIFE: Alcaeus (al SEE us) was a Greek poet who flourished in Mytilene in Lesbos around the early sixth century. He too fought in battle and threw away his shield (see Archilochus), and lived to write a poem about it. He was an aristocrat driven into fifteen years exile by his political enemies. Eventually he was allowed to return home.

CONTRIBUTION:

1. His lyrics are the prototype of Sappho's, his contemporary, who also had been driven into exile.

2. Fragments of his hymns, political songs, drinking songs, and love songs survive.

3. Very likely the inventor of the Alcaic verse, a metrical form popular with later classical poets.

4. Very much admired by Horace (later Roman poet), who imitated his style and meter.

5. His style is forceful, simple, serious and frank; often however he can show virulent hate.

POEMS:

1. He condemns the Lesbians for their indifference to a tyrant. He sneers at the tyrant (Pittacus) for his low birth, and poetically attempts to stir up rebellion.

2. The heroic code of the aristocrat: Alcaeus asks for excellence in manliness, courage, and virtue.

3. Drinking songs: among his best lyrics; how brief is human life; "seize the moment," make the most of youth and life, for both are short and subject to decay. This became a most popular theme with the later poets like Horace; the verse is polished, elegant, and serious: there is an awareness of the limitations of the human condition.

"The Footsteps of Spring" (extract):
"The flowery spring—I heard her, coming upon her way.
A bowl of honey-sweet wine! And mix it fast as ye may."
(Lucas)

Wine is the cure-all of all ills; keep the cups full to the brim;
There is no return from the underworld, once Death comes.

GREEK LYRIC POETRY: SAPPHO

SAPPHO OF LESBOS (born c. 610 B.C.)

LIFE: Sappho (SAFF oh) probably lived in Mytilene, in Lesbos, where she spent her entire life. One of her brothers, Charaxus, fell in love with an Egyptian courtesan and purchased her freedom at an extremely high price. Sappho had a daughter named Cleïs, and a husband named Cercolas or Cercylas. She was a contemporary of Alcaeus, both sharing the palm of supremacy in Aeolian lyric poetry. She possibly was the teacher of a literary coterie of women, who loved her most affectionately. She too (like Alcaeus) was exiled for a time by the tyrant Pittacus. There is no evidence that she threw herself from a cliff out of love for a beautiful youth named Phaon, who had rejected her advances.

CONTRIBUTIONS:

1. We have two odes and a number of fragments surviving.

2. She used a wide variety of styles and meters.

3. She used the non-literary language of the day.

4. Her work and style is very intimate and personal, filled with melodious grace.

5. Her love poetry is splendid in its expression of longing that is too intense to have any joy in it; "too serious to allow room for metaphor and imaginative ornament." (Gilbert Murray) Simple language, immediate emotion, are the soul of her verse.

POEMS:

1. "Some say the fairest thing on the black earth is a troop of horsemen, others a band of foot-soldiers, others a squadron of ships. But I say the fairest thing is the beloved."

2. "Like the sweet apple reddening on the highest limb, upon the tallest twig—which the pluckers somehow forgot,—forgot it not, no, but got it not, for none could get it till now."

    COMMENT: The simple directness, the easy colloquial style, the bareness of imagery, the intense feeling, the art

119

that conceals the art (like Emily Dickinson)—all this truly makes her "The Tenth Huse," as she was called by the Greeks.

3. *"To Aphrodite"*: "Do not now with frenzy and desperation/ Utterly crush me. . . . 'Tell me what it is, then, that most thou cravest,/Heart so full of madness?—Who *is* it, Sappho, Passion must awake to desire and love thee?/ Who is it wrongs thee?/ . . . Though she scorn thy presents, herself shall bring them; though she love thee not, yet she soon shall love thee!—Yea, though she would not.'" (Diehl, I, p. 325)

> **COMMENT:** Tradition makes Sappho small, dark, and not very beautiful. Her possible homosexuality has about the same basis for truth as has that supposedly of Shakespeare's as expressed in his sonnets. But there is no doubt that her passion for other women was expressed more intensely than for men; nevertheless we must remember that in some Greek communities, feelings of this type were both honorable and acceptable. Note how the dense terse style yields a subtle simplicity. Most translators find her impossible to translate because of these qualities.

4. *"Forsaken"*:
"Moon's set, and Pleiads;
Midnight goes by;
The hours pass onward;
Lonely I lie." (Diehl I, p. 368)

5. *"Lost Heart"*:
"I cannot, sweetest mother,
My loom I cannot mind;
Delicate Aphrodite
With longing leaves me blind." (Diehl I, p. 325)

> **COMMENT:** No. 4 above, even in translation, is one of the most haunting lyrics in the literature. It defies analysis. No. 5 above almost aches with passionate longing, and yet the language is so utterly simple.

6. *"Lost Maidenhead"*:
"As the hyacinth high on the mountains under the shepherds' tread
Lies trampled, and to earthward bows down its purple head. . . ." (Diehl, *Ibid.*)

GREEK LYRIC POETRY: ANACREON

ANACREON OF TEOS (c. 570–c. 485 B. C.)

LIFE: Anacreon (ah NAK ree on) was a Greek lyric poet born in Teos, Asia Minor. He too supposedly "lost" his shield in battle. He was a court poet, a favorite of Polycrates of Samos and Hipparchus of Athens. The myth that he choked on a grape seed and died is a good indication of his love of the *dolce vita*. Only fragments of his work remain.

CONTRIBUTIONS:

1. Writer of short, witty, graceful, facile lyrics.

2. Has become the model for such epicurean (i.e., "love the good life now, for tomorrow we may die" school) poets as La Fontaine and Robert Herrick. He reflects the height of Ionian decadence.

3. The old energy and fight are gone—only languor and rosebuds remain.

4. His gracefully frivolous poetry reflects his own life—a period of eighty-five years of luxury, wine, and women.

POEMS:

1. *"The Coy Mistress"*:
   "Thracian filly, why are you so heartless? Why do you look at me so shyly, with your sidelong glances? Why do you always hold me at a distance, like a fool without a brain in use? Yes, I could slam a bridle on you very well, no matter how you should prance. . . . You have yet to find the master who will curb and ride you."

   COMMENT: The poetry is simple, graceful; without passion, somewhat cynical, and even lecherous. Good Cavalier and Restoration stuff!

2. *"War's Folly"*:
   "Timocritus fought well enough. This is his grave./For Ares spares the coward—but not the brave."

Followers of Anacreon are often called "anacreontics."

GREEK LYRIC POETRY: PINDAR

PINDAR OF THEBES (ca. 522-448 B.C.)

LIFE: Pindar (PIN dahr) was born near Thebes in Boeotia of an aristocratic family, who traced their supposed origins to Aegeus (ancient king of Athens). Highly talented in music (flute and lyre) and in the training of choruses, he had by the age of twenty achieved a high reputation as a lyric poet. Tradition has it that a certain Corinna told him to stop studding his poems with too much mythological ornamentation. He wrote for many of the wealthiest and most aristocratic families, in such places as Rhodes, Tenedos, Athens (his special love), Macedon, and Sicily. He ardently supported the orthodox traditional religion. A true Dorian aristocrat, proud of his blue blood as well as of his undoubted genius, he felt himself descended from the heroic greats like Heracles.

CONTRIBUTIONS:

1. Purely a poet, he commemorates an earlier period.

2. He wrote widely in many modes and styles including hymns, paeans, choral lyrics, processional songs, *encomia* (odes of praise), *scolia* (festive banquet songs), *dirges* (songs with flute and choral dancing), and *epinicia* (victory odes) in honor of athletic heroes.

3. Forty-four victory odes to the winners of Olympian, Pythian, Nemean, and Isthmian games survive.

4. Believed implicitly in Greek mythology, even changing some of the more cannibalistic stories to suit his taste.

5. He called Odysseus "a supple liar" who owed his reputation to Homer. He was especially fond of Ajax and his descendants, among whom he considered himself. (He disliked Odysseus' treatment of his beloved Ajax.)

6. He wrote in the dialect of Ionia in an almost archaic style, rich in complex and difficult imagery.

7. So great was his reputation that Alexander the Great, a hun-

dred years later, spared his house when he sacked Thebes!

POEMS:

1. *Pindaric Ode* = three stanzas (*strophe, antistrophe, epode*). Strophe and antistrophe (an TISS tro fee) = same in meter and music, the chorus being in two parts. The *epodes* are sung and performed (danced) by the entire chorus; the music and meter of the epodes are similar. The *ode* often contains a *prelude* (the poet's subjective and personal remarks concerning the victor in the game); next comes the *myth* of gods or heroes or both, and finally an *epilogue* containing moral commentary, maxims. The stylistic effect is like a mighty organ—dazzling and majestic, the metaphors brilliant and complex, the transitions and associations swift and subtle.

SUMMARY OF POEMS:

Olympian I. "For Hiero of Syracuse":
Hiero was the victor in a horse race (376 B.C.). He was the tyrant (benevolent despot) of Syracuse in the sophisticated and wealthy Sicily. Pindar mentions Pherenicus, the great and beautiful horse, who ran the race; the horse is famous in Elis, the land of Pelops (son of Tantalus and Dione), who won the beautiful Hippodamia in a chariot race against her father, Oenamaus. Tantalus served Pelops to the gods at a feast, but all except Demeter rejected the flesh. Clotho restored Pelops to life and Demeter replaced the shoulder she had consumed with one of ivory. Pindar, disliking the cannibalism, changes the myth, calling the cannibalistic section a lie invented by Pelops' enemies. Poseidon took his beloved Pelops to Olympus with him. When Pelops returned to earth, it was then he won his race against Hippodamia's father. He thus became the model for all Olympic victors. He weds Hippodamia, who bore him six mighty sons, and to this day the Olympic games are conducted near his tomb. Finally, Pindar speaks again of Hiero's glory, voicing hope he will soon win the four-horse chariot race. He then will again sing his praises of the tyrant (there are no bad associations in this word).

Olympian II. "For Theron of Acragas":

A victory ode for the winner in a chariot race in 476 B.C.

a. What god, what great hero of the past, what man should I sing the praises of?

b. I will sing the praises of Zeus, of Heracles, the first to establish the Olympic games; and I will sing of Theron, the present triumphant winner of the chariot race; his ancestors ruled over Sicily.

c. May Zeus grant good luck to his family, which can trace its ancestry back to Cadmus. Cadmus' daughters suffered greatly, but were rewarded for their suffering; Semele, even though struck by Zeus' thunderbolt, gave birth to the god Dionysus. Laius, though slain by his own son Oedipus, left mighty descendants such as Polyneices, the son of Oedipus. Even though Polyneices was slain by his brother, he left a great and noble son, Thersander.

d. Thus Theron's noble ancestors have won Olympic games, and he nobly continues the tradition.

e. Virtue and riches give birth to honor and, after death, the virtuous and wealthy will join the great heroes like Achilles and Cadmus in the Isles of the Blessed.

f. I myself have many a mighty "arrow" to shoot forth, which only the wise will understand. A real poet has nature for his teacher, and Pindar himself is an eagle, and his rivals in poetry mere crows. My praises of Theron will win over the envious ones.

Olympian III. "For Theron of Acragas":

For the same victor in the same race as in Olympian II.

a. I ask for the goodwill of Castor and Pollux, and Helen, their sister (Helen of Troy), while I sing of the glory of Theron.

b. I am inspired by the Muse to invent a new kind of poetry, with music in the Dorian measure, to be accompanied by the lyre and flute.

c. The town of Pisa (in Elis) orders me to sing, for it is the city sends out songs in praise of athletes who are winners of the victory wreath of olive leaves.

d. It was Heracles who got the olive from the Hyperborean and brought it to Olympia. Now the great god is at the festival, along with Castor and Pollux, who are in charge. This is Theron's reward for victory!

GREEK TRAGEDY: INTRODUCTION

THE STORIES:

The subjects of Greek tragedy are generally chosen from Greek legend and legendary history.

1. The field of fiction and contemporary history were avoided as subjects fit for tragedy. Aeschylus' *Persians* is an exception, since it does deal with contemporary events.

2. The audience was quite well acquainted with the legends of their native land; hence, they knew beforehand the outcome of the plot. Suspense was not a primary part of Greek tragedy.

THE THEATER:

The theater held about 20,000 spectators, who attended the tragic performances from dawn to nightfall.

1. Three poets competed (selected from a larger number), each presenting four plays.

2. In the front row on seats of marble sat priests and important politicians.

3. Just beyond the priests and politicians was a circular "orchestra" or "dancing place," in the center of which stood the altar of Dionysus, the god of wine and of the vegetation; a fit god for the late March season, the time when the tragedies were presented.

4. Behind the altar was a long stage, low and narrow, which was backed by buildings serving as a greenroom. On the wooden wall of the buildings there would be a painted representation of a palace or temple—or whatever might be the setting of the play.

THE ACTORS:

1. There are never more than three actors on the stage at any time.

2. They wore a *cothurnus* or *buskin* (six-inch high wooden soles), and padded chest garments, in order to give an effect of height and power. On their heads were linen masks, with wide mouths,

a great cone-shaped projection above, and highly exaggerated features.

3. The actors moved on the stage, supplemented by 15 other persons called a *chorus,* who performed dances and various complex movements in the orchestra, singing at diverse intervals of the drama (choral songs). Through their leader they sometimes engaged in dialogue with the actors.

THE PLAY:

1. There was no curtain; breaks in the dramatic action were filled with *choric songs.*

2. The speeches of the actors were much longer than those we are accustomed to; often the dialogue took on a peculiar form called *stichomythia,* single-line dialogue exchanges between two speakers.

3. There was invariably a Messenger's speech, which was almost always quite lengthy, its purpose being to narrate the *catastrophe,* the climactic incident that was never performed on stage.

4. The scenery was starkly simple. If it was necessary to show characters within a house or palace in a state of sleep or death, they were rolled out on a trolley platform (*eccyclema*).

The whole play seemed to be an odd mixture of play and opera in a rather crude form. The first tragedy was followed by two other tragedies, and then, more oddly still, the fourth play was a *"satyric"* drama, usually a comic play with satyrs, or wild men of the woods, functioning as the chorus. Originally, the four plays (by the same author) dealt with different stages of the same story: later, though, the subjects of the different plays might have no connection in theme or subject.

ORIGIN OF TRAGEDY:

Among the most important religious celebrations among the Greeks were those in honor of Dionysus, the god of vegetation and wine.

1. The Greek drama was in actuality a religious service honoring Dionysus; it was his altar that stood in the front-row center of the

theater, and it was in his honor that both tragedy and comedy was celebrated.

a. The first stage of the Dionysiac ritual was a song called a *dithyramb,* sung by farmers, later by a chorus of fifty performers. Out of such crude origins was the greatest of dramas born!

b. In the intervals of the dithyrambic song, at first, the leader told a story about Dionysus in recitative. This is the germ of Greek tragedy—the *choric song* became the *choruses* of Greek tragedy; and the rest of the play was an extension of the leader's recitative.

c. At first the chorus took up almost the entire ritual, but as the recitative enlarged, two actors took part in it instead of one; and finally a third speaker was added—giving us the three actors.

d. The chorus, too, diminished: from 50 to 12, finally staying at 15 in number. In the late plays of Euripides the chorus may be cut to only a few, the songs becoming nothing but musical, irrelevant interludes!

The masks were survivals of the old religious ritual in which the players appeared as gods. The "satyric" drama was the tag end of the riotous religious wine festivals. From Aeschylus' early *Suppliant Women* to Euripides' *Bacchae* we see that the drama in ancient Greece developed such principles as Unity of Action, Development to a Climax, power and realism of Tragic Character etc.—elements common to the stage ever since, but which the Greeks had to learn and develop by themselves.

ACTING:

There are two differences between modern and ancient Greek acting:

1. In Greece the voice was the actor's chief instrument; declamation was a fine and highly developed art—an art virtually unknown to present-day actors; hence the failure to do justice to revivals of Greek tragedy!

2. Gestures were heavy, slow, solemn in Greek drama; modern acting utilizes gestures of quick and rapid movement, many of considerable subtlety. Greek gestures were, on the other hand, sculptured and statuesque, due to the heavy soles (buskins) and highly padded garments and masks.

A REVIEW:

1. Greek tragedy has a tendency to describe events, rather than to show them on the stage.

2. It contains long speeches of reflection and argumentative statements of the performer's point of view.

3. The construction of Greek Tragedy is simple and less complex than ours; it has very little or no comic relief, and no under- or sub-plots.

4. The choric songs are long, often lyric interludes; but they comprise more than mere music; for example, as in a Wagnerian opera, they sound the leit-motifs of the play, or they may yield atmosphere, or summary, or exposition, or mood etc.

5. As for the rather fantastic and bloody legends about gods and humans, I quote Matthew Arnold:

> "The poet has in the first place to select an excellent action; and what actions are the most excellent? Those, certainly, which most powerfully appeal to the great primary human affections; to those elementary feelings which subsist permanently in the race, and which are independent of time. Those feelings are permanent and the same; that which interests them is permanent and the same also. The modernness or antiquity of an action, therefore, has nothing to do with its fitness for poetical representation; this depends upon its inherent qualities. To the elementary part of our nature, to our passions, that which is great and passionate is eternally interesting; and interesting solely in proportion to its greatness and to its passion."

Greek Tragedy fulfills Arnold's requirements completely!

GREEK TRAGEDY: AESCHYLUS

LIFE: Aeschylus (ESS kuh luss) was born in 525 B.C. and lived to be 69 years old. He is the earliest and first of the three major Greek writers of tragedy (the other two are Sophocles and Euriides.) Aeschylus' family belonged to the old Athenian nobility, and as part of his duties as a citizen, he fought in at least two of the battles in which the Greeks defeated the Persians: Marathon (490 B.C.) and Salamis. His birthplace was Eleusis, where he probably became early acquainted with the processions and ceremonies associated with the famous shrine of Demeter there. He began writing at an early age, his first play being acted in 499, when he was 26. He is reputed to have written over 80 plays, of which only seven have survived.

CONTRIBUTIONS: Aeschylus is famous as the creator of a theatrical tradition which has continued to the present day.

1. He changed the dramatic tradition he inherited from what it was, essentially a choral song, into a performance by individual actors.

   a. He should probably be credited with increasing the length of the dialogue passages at the expense of the choral lyrics.

   b. He introduced a second actor on the stage.

   c. He probably wrote the first trilogy or group of three plays based on a single story.

2. Such innovations indicate the first steps of the characteristic development of western drama towards a more realistic representation of life. In his early *Suppliants,* for example, King Pelasgus is little more than a stock heroic figure of a good king; in the later *Agamemnon* even the minor figure of the Watchman is individualized. By modern standards, of course, the plays of Aeschylus would hardly be called realistic; the quality exists as a change from earlier drama, but is embryonic in comparison with plays by Aeschylus' immediate successors.

AESCHYLUS

PROMETHEUS BOUND (date?)

BACKGROUND: Greek mythology, like other mythologies, explains the origins of gods, man, the physical universe, and the customs of mankind in a series of stories which are rarely complete or consistent. The Greek dramatists based their plots on myths handed down through successive generations, and because the myths were inconsistent, the dramatists felt free to choose versions appropriate to their dramatic purposes. Aeschylus, in *Prometheus Bound,* represents the personality of Zeus as he imagined it to have been when Zeus first seized power. In other plays, Aeschylus attributes a completely different personality to Zeus. According to the Greek myths, the first god was Uranus, who had a group of sons called the Titans. These sons, led by Cronos, overthrew their father and established Cronos as their king. Eventually one of Cronos' sons, Zeus, planned a revolt. One of the Titans, Prometheus, had been told by his mother that the Titans could not win by brute force alone; they must use guile. Cronos refused to listen to this advice, and Prometheus decided to join Zeus and his group, known as the Olympians, who then defeated the Titans. After being made king of Olympus, Zeus decided to destroy mankind, of whose mortality the gods were contemptuous, and create a new race; Prometheus, being "philanthropic," opposed this plan, and Zeus punished him by chaining him to a rock.

CHARACTERS

FORCE, POWER: servants of Zeus whose names summarize their characteristics. Power speaks, but Force does not.

SEPHAESTUS (see FESS tuss): son of Zeus; god of fire and of the forge. He was the metal-worker of the gods, and is also regarded as the god of handicrafts.

PROMETHEUS (pro MEE thoos): a Titan who had sided with the Olympians in revolt against the other Titans.

OCEANUS (oh SEE uh nuss): a Titan who was god of the sea before Poseidon.

IO (EYE oh): a human Zeus fell in love with and who was changed into a heifer when Zeus' wife, Hera, became jealous.

HERMES (HER meez): a god who was messenger of the Olympians.

CHORUS (oh SEE uh nidz): the daughters of Oceanus, known as the Oceanids.

SETTING: A desolate part of the Caucasus Mountains in Scythia, the area between the Black Sea and the Caspian Sea in the southwestern part of what is now Russia.

PROLOGUE (lines 1-127): *Power* says that he has come with *Force* and *Hephaestus* to this desolate part of Scythia to chain Prometheus to a rock, this being Prometheus' punishment for stealing fire and giving it to human beings.

Hephaestus is reluctant to punish another god, but he is too afraid of Zeus to disobey. He has an imaginative mind and vividly describes the pain Prometheus will suffer while chained to the rock and exposed to the burning sun and violent mountain storms.

Power believes it to be futile for Hephaestus to worry about what is inevitable, and tells him to get on with his business. Hephaestus wields his hammer, and Power urges him to hit harder and make the bonds tighter. The climax of the scene occurs when a wedge is driven through Prometheus' chest.

Hephaestus leaves, and Power taunts Prometheus, insolently asking how the humans he helped can help him now. Prometheus, alone, asks the natural forces around him to behold what he, a god himself, has to suffer at the hands of other gods. Able to foresee the future, he knows how great his suffering will be. He points out that his only sin was helping mankind.

> **COMMENT:** The rugged and isolated Caucasus Mountains were deemed then to be near the ends of the earth. The setting emphasizes Prometheus' isolation. Force and Power are essentially abstractions symbolizing qualities inherent in their names. Hephaestus (Vulcan in Roman myth), surprisingly, does not resent the theft of his fire: he reflects rather a conflict between his liking for Prometheus and his fear of King Zeus. Note that only Io is human in this play—all others are divine characters, but their motivation, their personalities are reflections of universal human characteristics.

Power insists that Prometheus "must pay the price of such a

sin to the gods, that he may be taught to submit to the rule of
Zeus, and give up his notions of helping men." He is impatient at the delay, the show of "empty pity" by *Hephaestus,*
since there is no one except Zeus who has freedom." Power
is savage and barbaric: "Now the unfeeling tooth of a spike of
adamant! Use all your strength and nail it right through his
breast! ... The gods who called you 'Forethought' gave you
a false name. You need forethought ("prometheus" means
forethought in Greek) yourself if you would find a way to
break out into freedom from this work of art."

Prometheus when alone, calls upon the "heavenly air, and
breezes swift upon the wing, fountains of rivers and innumerable laughter of the waves of the sea, and earth, mother of all,
and you, all-seeing circle of the sun, I call, see what I suffer,
a god at the hand of gods. ... For I am he who sought the
stolen fount of fire, stored in a stalk, which proved to be the
teacher of all kind of craft to mortals and their great resource.
This was the sin for which I pay the punishment nailed hard
and fast in chains beneath the open sky!"

PARODOS (128-192): In a winged chariot, the *Chorus of
Oceanids* enter; they have come from their cave in the sea to pro-
fess friendship and sympathy. A group of charming young girls,
they tell *Prometheus* they came as soon as they could get their
father's permission—they did not even have time to put their sandals
on. They are shocked because Zeus has rejected the great laws of
the past and made up his own laws.

Prometheus wishes his punishment had condemned him to Tartarus
(usually thought of as being even lower than Hades), where he
would have been hidden from anyone who would gloat over his
pain. The Chorus says Zeus will be a tyrant until he either satisfies
his desire for cruelty or is overthrown.

Prometheus hints that Zeus will indeed be overthrown; he knows
what action of Zeus will cause his fall, but Zeus can learn the
secret only by freeing Prometheus.

COMMENT: Prometheus' secret is that if Zeus consummates
his passion for Thetis, she will bear him a son (Heracles)
who will overthrow him. Hints of this secret appear throughout the play and give some suspense to the lack of action.
Prometheus symbolizes knowledge and *Zeus* symbolizes force.
Knowledge will eventually require force to compromise, as

we shall see. On another level, the crucified Titan symbolizes disinterested action directed towards helping others, hence his affinity with Jesus. Fire is Prometheus' gift to man, the symbol of practical knowledge. In Athens the worship of Prometheus was closely associated with the worship of Hephaestus. This may explain Hephaestus' sympathy in the prologue.

The *Chorus* complains of the new rulers who now hold power in Olympus "and in new-fangled law Zeus blindly lords it. Titanic powers of old can now be seen no more." Prometheus boldly asserts he "shall never shrink from his terrible threats and reveal it (the secret), till he has loosed me from these cruel chains, and is willing to pay recompense for my shame." The frightened girls, shocked at his boldness, reply that his "speech's freedom goes too far. A piercing fear is stirring up my heart, and for your fortune terror fills me."

FIRST EPISODE (193-396): *Prometheus* satisfies the *Chorus'* curiosity by telling them the story of the events leading to his punishment: a group of gods revolted to drive Cronos, king of the Titans, from his throne and establish Zeus in his place as king of the Olympians. Prometheus sided at first with the Titans and proposed a crafty scheme for attaining victory; but they despised the use of craft, believing they could win by force alone. Prometheus then offered help to Zeus, who consequently won the battle. Once king, Zeus gave various powers and privileges to those who had aided him; but he decided to destroy human beings and create a new race. Only Prometheus defied Zeus in this latter plan; his defiance angered Zeus and brought about Prometheus' punishment. The Chorus ask whether he did anything else to anger Zeus; he replies that he gave two gifts to man: blind hope, so man could forget the inevitability of his own death, and fire.

Oceanus enters, borne on a winged sea-monster. Preoccupied with himself, he first talks about his long trip.

Prometheus wonders how he had ever found courage to leave his safe home in the ocean.

Oceanus offers the kind of advice one might expect from a timid person interested mainly in self-preservation. He wants Prometheus to show humility and to conform to the new ways, to stop speaking angry and defiant words to Zeus, and to plan a way to get released from the rock. Oceanus offers to intercede with Zeus to get Prometheus freed, but Prometheus warns him that this will only make Zeus angry with him too.

FIRST STASIMON (397-435): The *Chorus* lament the sufferings of Prometheus and compare them to the sufferings of another Titan (Atlas) who bears on his back the pillar supporting the skies.

> **COMMENT:** *Oceanus* is a comic figure, absurdly inadequate in the role of mediator between two such mighty opposites. Timid, cowardly, and good-natured, he serves tyranny differently, but just as usefully, as do Force, Power, and later, Hermes. Oceanus' timidity and self-interest contrast sharply with *Prometheus'* boldness and mighty self-sacrificing courage.
>
> *Oceanus* wishes to give the best advice he can: "Recognize your own weakness, learn to adapt your ways to new ways. . . . You must lie low and check the pride of your language . . . the reward of empty language is always punishment." He adds that the safest "thing is to be wise and not thought wise. . . . My four-foot flyer with his wings brushes the smooth paths of the air, and he will, I know, be happy to bend his knee again in the familiar stable."

SECOND EPISODE (436-525): *Prometheus* tells the *Chorus* what gifts he has bestowed on mankind: the use of the mind and the arts of building; of telling the seasons of the year apart; of using numbers and the alphabet; of history; of domesticating wild animals; of building ships; of medicine; of foretelling the future, and of the use of metals.

The Chorus tell Prometheus he has gone beyond all limits of expediency in helping mankind; he has neglected himself. Prometheus, in a dialogue with the Chorus, explains the idea of Necessity, or Destiny, a higher law than any Zeus can establish. Referring again to his secret, Prometheus implies that the rule of Zeus will not last forever.

SECOND STASIMON (526-560): The *Chorus* say they hope Zeus will never be angry with any of them. Prometheus' love of mankind, they say again, showed no moderation. Why, they wonder, did he ever bother to help such weak beings, creatures who live such a short life? Like many laments, this one ends by a recall of happier days: the Oceanids recall the bridal song they sang when Prometheus wed their sister Hesione.

COMMENT: Many mythologies, describing the early conditions of man, show early man as a kind of noble savage who
later falls into corruption and decline. Aeschylus describes
primitive man here as an unenlightened brute sorely in need
of Prometheus' gifts to raise him above the animal condition.
The *Chorus,* insofar as they represent a norm of conduct,
are here warning *Prometheus* against the sin of *hybris,* lack
of moderation.

Prometheus tells how man mingled all "things aimlessly,
never aware of houses, brick-built and warm, or the art of
wood-work. They lived in burrows, like the light and nimble
ants down in the deep sunless recesses of their caves . . .
without intelligence, till I revealed to them the risings of the
stars and settings . . . until I showed them the ingredients of
soothing medicines. . . . I gave all arts and sciences to men."
The *Chorus* blames him for having "no fear of Zeus, but
following the way of a private judgment, you give honour in
excess to mortal men."

THIRD EPISODE (561-886): *Io,* transformed in part to a heifer,
and pursued by the ghost of Argus in the form of a stinging fly (a
gadfly), runs onto the stage. The insect has her in a state of distraction: she asks where she is, why she has suffered so much, and
what man is chained to the rock. She piteously begs to be swal-
lowed up by the earth.

Prometheus answers some of her questions; she then wants to
know what is in store for her in the future. He is about to tell her
when the *Chorus,* their curiosity aroused, ask her to tell the story
of her past.

Io's adventures began when she was a young girl living in her
father's house. She had visions in which voices said that Zeus had
fallen in love with her and that she should go into the fields alone
and meet him. She reported these visions to her father, who consulted the oracle and was told to drive her away from home. After
Io was driven out, Hera, Zeus' wife, jealous of Io as a rival for
her husband's love, caused her to grow and take on the shape of a
cow, then sending the gadfly to drive her from place to place.

With interruptions and questions from Io and the Chorus, Prome-
theus tells Io's future. Among other events, she will cross the
Bosphorus, thus giving it its name (the crossing of the heifer =
Bosphorus). Near the mouth of the Nile, Zeus will finally grant

her peace and restore her natural shape. After this meeting with him, she will bear a child, and from the line of this child, thirteen generations later, will be born Hercules (Heracles), who will free Prometheus. To show that his prediction of the future will come true, Prometheus tells of events from her past that Io had never revealed. The gadfly begins biting her again, and she flees from the scene.

THIRD STASIMON 887-907): The *Chorus* react to Io's story by praying that a god will never fall in love with any of them; they prefer marriages between equals. They admit however that if Zeus were to fall in love with them, they would be powerless to resist him.

> **COMMENT:** The *Chorus* admits that wisdom, if defined as being some compromise between extremes, cannot be easily or automatically attained.
>
> *Io* is the most pathetic victim of Zeus because she had done nothing at all. Prometheus openly defied Zeus, but Io is simply victimized. Further, she has not the strength to fight back: she has not even the comfort Prometheus derives from withholding his terrible secret. This scene (Third Episode) makes Zeus appear to be an absolutely malicious tyrant, and makes the idea of tyranny in human government appear to be monstrous. The audience is receiving by example a lesson in politics.
>
> *Io* tells of the visions "haunting my virgin bed night after night, and speaking kindly in my ears with smooth words saying: 'O most fortunate maiden, why keep so long your maidenhood, when you might make the greatest match (note the seductive ways of the mighty Zeus!)? Zeus is on fire with a shaft of longing for you!' "
>
> *Prometheus* foretells in splendid geographical detail of "the Gorgon lowlands of Kisthene. Here there dwell the children of Phorkis, three old unmarried hags, swan-shaped, and having a single eye between them, and a single tooth. . . . And near to them are dwelling their three winged sisters, the Gorgons with their snaky hair, hated by men, for no mortal can see them and not cease to breathe." And he tells of Heracles, "a child, bold, famous for the bow, and he it is who will free me from suffering."

EXODOS: (908-1093):   *Prometheus* tells the *Chorus* that Cronos, when he was overthrown, cursed Zeus. Prometheus foretells that Zeus will be hurled from his throne unless he discovers the secret. The Chorus says this is wishful thinking.

Hermes enters with a message: Zeus demands to know the secret of his downfall. Prometheus, who despises Hermes, calls him a slave, saying that Zeus must release him before he will reveal the secret. Zeus has anticipated this defiance, Hermes says, and a violent storm will smash the mountains and bury Prometheus. Centuries later he will emerge to the surface of the earth, and an eagle will punctually every day tear out his liver and eat it. This torture will continue until some god willingly gives up his immortality and goes to Tartarus (lower than Hades where the Titans are confined) as a substitute for Prometheus.

Prometheus says that Zeus can do his worst; while he may have to suffer, he cannot be destroyed.

Hermes calls him delirious, warning the Chorus to leave before the arrival of the great storm. They reply that they will suffer with Prometheus rather than to join with traitors. Telling the Chorus that whatever may happen to them is their own fault, Hermes leaves. Prometheus describes the beginning of a violent storm. He concludes the play with a simple and powerful request that Earth and Air behold what wrongs he is undergoing.

> **COMMENT:**   The other two plays of this trilogy, *Prometheus Unbound* and *Prometheus the Fire-Bringer,* have not survived; hence, we do not know what ideas Aeschylus would have associated with the final release of Prometheus. It seems likely, however, on the basis of outside evidence, that some compromise would have been effected between him and Zeus. In other accounts of the myth, Zeus is not overthrown; moreover, he probably learns that a successful ruler must eventually acquire the virtues of justice and benevolence to soften unmitigated tyranny.
>
> Hermes' threat contains the last of three references made in the play as to the way in which Prometheus will be finally freed. The first reference is to the secret Prometheus mentions several times regarding a woman who will bear a child by Zeus, a child who will effect the overthrow of his own father. This story of the secret is associated with Prometheus, probably for

the first time by Aeschylus. The usual version is that *Hercules* will ultimately free Prometheus by killing the eagle eating his liver: this version is referred to by Prometheus in the third episode of the play. Hermes' threat seems to set an impossible condition: that a god be willing to surrender his immortality and go to Tartarus. However, Chiron, a centaur (a mythological half-man, half-horse), incurably wounded by Hercules' arrow, desired to surrender his immortality rather than suffer forever.

Hermes ridicules Prometheus for his "self-conceit . . . no doubt it is better to be a menial to this rock than to be a trusted messenger of father Zeus . . . you do not yet know how to behave wisely . . . stubbornness, in a mind whose thoughts have gone astray, has in its simple self less strength than anything."

Prometheus defies the servile and slimy Hermes: "And so let all his burning flame be hurled at me . . . thunders let him confound and mingle everything. . . . None of all this will bend me so that I will tell! . . . Let a blast blow to make earth's depths totter down to their roots! . . . Zeus cannot any way put me to death! . . . O my glorious mother, O Heaven with circle of light that is common to everyone, you see me and see this injustice."

INTERPRETATION:
PROMETHEUS BOUND, QUESTIONS AND ANSWERS

What does Prometheus mean in Greek, and what is the significance of the name?

ANSWER: Prometheus means "forethought" in Greek, and signifies that he differed from his brother Titans in realizing that intelligence, and not the brute force of tyranny, was to be the underlying rule of the universe.

In what way is Prometheus the champion of man?

ANSWER: Although Zeus had wished to wipe man from the face of the earth and create another race, it was the Titan Prometheus who saved mankind from that fate; in addition, he initiated man into all the arts and sciences, which form the very fabric of civilization itself. In order to raise man from a state of animal existence, he stole the fire of the Olympian gods and gave this supreme gift to man himself.

Does Prometheus Bound *glorify the revolutionary hero as in* Shelley's Prometheus Unbound?

ANSWER: No, decidedly not, for there were *three* plays in the cycle, and *Prometheus Bound* is the sole survivor in the trilogy. To seize the theme of the first play as Aeschylus' overall theme would be unfair. In fact, we do know that in some way there was a reconciliation between the two adamantine foes, Zeus and Prometheus. The best guess is that Zeus grew wiser, became less dictatorial, and that Prometheus softened his flaming defiance.

Is Prometheus then the perfect hero?

ANSWER: No, he is not because the Greeks knew that an outstanding fact in life was *"necessity"*—something that does not always accord with our concept of human justice. The processes of life are often inhumane—and not to realize this is a form of unforgivable pride (*hybris*). The answer seems to lie in a faith that ultimately injustice will have been justified.

AESCHYLUS

AGAMEMNON (458 B.C.)

BACKGROUND: The *Oresteia* comprises three plays: the *Aga-memnon*, the *Choephoroe*, and the *Eumenides*. The name "Oresteia" derives from "Orestes," the name of Agamemnon's son, who is the chief character of the second and third plays. Although the action of each play forms a separate dramatic unit, the full significance of the trilogy is not apparent until the end. The *Oresteia* is the only complete trilogy of Greek plays that has come down to us.

Atreus, King of Argos, had a long-standing quarrel with his younger brother Thyestes, who had seduced Atreus' wife Aerope. Thyestes went into exile, but Atreus lured him back with a promise of forgiveness. At a welcoming banquet, Atreus sought revenge by serving the bodies of Thyestes' two sons to him in a stew. After Thyestes had partaken, the boys' heads were brought in on a platter to show Thyestes what he had just eaten. Before again going into exile, Thyestes laid a curse on the entire house of Atreus.

Before marrying Atreus, Aerope had been married to Plisthenes, Atreus' son. By him she had become the mother of Agamemnon and Menelaus, who were raised by Atreus, and were generally considered to be his children. Agamemnon and Menelaus married sisters: Clytemnestra and Helen. Helen, reputed to be the most beautiful woman in the world, was seduced by Paris (Alexander) and carried off to Troy. To get her back, Agamemnon rallied the Greek princes to attack Troy. The war which followed lasted ten years. The *Aga-memnon* opens just before the return of Agamemnon to his home in Argos.

CHARACTERS

WATCHMAN: given no name, he appears only in the prologue.

CLYTEMNESTRA: the wife of King Agamemnon.

HERALD: a messenger who brings a first-hand account of events immediately succeeding the Trojan War.

AGAMEMNON: king of Argos and chief leader of the Greek forces who had fought in the Trojan War.

CASSANDRA (kuh SAND ruh): daughter of Priam, king of Troy.

When the spoils were divided after the Trojan War, she was given to Agamemnon as a war prize.

AEGISTHUS (ee JISS thooss): son of Thyestes by his own daughter, Pelopia. During Agamemnon's absence, he had become the lover of Queen Clytemnestra.

CHORUS: composed of elderly citizens of Argos.

SETTING: in front of the palace of King Agamemnon in Argos (a kingdom in the northeastern part of the Greek Peloponnesus).

PROLOGUE (lines 1-39): A *Watchman*, alone on the roof of Agamemnon's palace, tells how he is tired of watching for a beacon light, which will signify the end of the Trojan War and the imminent return of King Agamemnon. Agamemnon's wife, Clytemnestra, who has ruled in his absence, has the strong character of a man, but the Watchman does not praise her. He is frightened and unhappy: some dishonor has recently come upon the house. When the Watchman sees the beacon, he has a moment's joyful anticipation of Agamemnon's return; then he becomes gloomy again and says that though the walls might speak if they had a voice, he intends to be quiet about what has been happening. He goes out to tell Clytemnestra that the beacon has been lighted; the ten years of waiting are over.

PARODOS (40-104): The *Chorus* of elderly citizens say that ten years have passed since Agamemnon and Menelaus had left to attack Troy in Asia Minor. They won the war because Paris had taken Helen while a guest in Menelaus' house. This sin against the laws of hospitality angered Zeus, who helped the Greeks to win. Describing themselves, the members of the Chorus say that they were too old to have fought in the war.

> **COMMENT:** The audience knew their heritage of myths as well as many Christians know their *New Testament*. What the Watchman was so mysteriously referring to was that Aegisthus had become Clytemnestra's lover; they also knew that Aegisthus, as Thyestes' son, is seeking revenge upon Agamemnon, son of Atreus, and that the king will be murdered when he returns. This knowledge gives a double meaning to almost everything said by the characters, who do not know what is going to happen (i.e., *dramatic irony*). In the prologue, for example, the audience knows that misfortune will befall Aga-

memnon, and that the hopes for happiness expressed by the Watchman will have been disappointed.

The *Chorus* act as dispassionate commentators on the actions of the younger, more hot-blooded central characters. No action, the Chorus imply, is single in itself, and it constantly refers to the past, which is still working itself out in the present; and to the future, which reveals the results of deeds done in the present; and to the gods, who watch and judge. Its feeling that man is being trapped and confined by the uncontrollable and unknowable is characteristic of much tragedy.

Watchman: ". . . this watch, a year's length now, spending my nights like a dog, watching on my elbow on the roof. . . . And may it be when he (i.e. Agamemnon) comes . . . that I grasp his hand in my hand. As to the rest, I am silent. A great ox, as they say, stands on my tongue."

FIRST STASIMON (105-257): *Clytemnestra* enters and the *Chorus* ask her why she has ordered so many sacrifices made on the altars. Before she answers, a pair of eagles has attacked and torn open a rabbit. The prophet Calchas (KAL kuss) had said that the eagles represented Agamemnon and Menelaus; the rabbit, Troy. Calchas had warned, however, that Artemis (AHR tem iss), goddess of the hunt, was angry with Zeus for sending the eagles to kill the rabbit, and might exact vengeance by demanding a sacrifice from Agamemnon. In a meditative interlude, the Chorus contemplate the violence and subsequent pain for mankind which seem to accompany Zeus' intervention in human affairs; Zeus, they say, has ordained that wisdom can come to man only through suffering.

Resuming their story, the Chorus tell how, when adverse winds kept the Greek fleet at Aulis on its way to Troy, Calchas explained to the leaders that Artemis was offended and would not grant favorable winds until Agamemnon's daughter, Iphigenia (iff ihj in EYE uh), should be made a human sacrifice on Artemis' altar. Torn between loyalty to his companions and love for his daughter, Agamemnon decided to sacrifice her. The Chorus says they disapprove of Agamemnon's choice; they condemn the soldier's lust for a war fought on behalf of a false woman. They movingly describe the pitiful scene of the sacrifice, the gag placed in Iphigenia's mouth so she could not speak a curse, and the beseeching look in her eyes.

FIRST EPISODE (258-354): The *Chorus* again ask *Clytemnestra* to reveal the reason for the sacrifices. She tells them the Greeks have defeated the Trojans and explains the way beacon fires had passed the news from one hilltop to another.

She vividly describes the unhappiness of the Trojans as she imagines it to have been when the Greeks moved into Troy to loot and to divide the spoils of war. She ends on a warning note, expressing a hope that the Greeks not anger the gods by destroying any of the gods' temples there.

> **COMMENT:** The choice *Agamemnon* had to make was be-
> tween conflicting loyalties, and either alternative would have
> brought him misfortune:
>
> 1. On one level of reading Agamemnon is an individual suf-
>   fering the consequences of the old curse on his family, a
>   curse "inherited" by his son later in the trilogy.
>
> 2. On another level, Agamemnon is a symbol of all mankind,
>   and Aeschylus' tragic view of life suggests that man's
>   choices in life are limited to evil alternatives, and that suf-
>   fering is the necessary consequences of all actions.
>
> It should be noted, however, that Agamemnon is not simply
> a passive victim of a family curse. The *Chorus* say he fought
> an unjust war; the sacrifice therefore was unjust too. In this
> way, the matter focuses on Agamemnon's character: he was a
> soldier whose loyalty to his army transcended his loyalty to his
> family.
>
> *First Stasimon*: Chorus says it was Zeus who "made this valid
> law—'That men must learn by suffering.' Drop by drop is sleep
> upon the heart falls the laborious memory of pain. Against
> one's will comes wisdom; . . . To learn by suffering is the
> equation of Justice; the Future is known when it comes, let
> it go till then. To know in advance is to sorrow in advance."
>
> *First Episode*: Clytemnestra describes the beacons vividly as
> "the strapping flame, not yet enfeebled, leapt over the plain of
> Asopus like a blazing moon and woke on the crags of Cithaeron
> another relay in the chain of fire."

SECOND STASIMON (355-474): The *Chorus* address Zeus and attribute the Greek victory to his desire to punish the Trojans. They say great daring will always be punished; the sin of Paris brought the destruction of Troy. The dowry of Helen was death. When she left the house of Menelaus, the prophets foresaw calamity, and the horrors of war fulfilled their prophecies. The Greeks suffered too; their young men returned home as ashes in urns. The populace hated this war fought over a woman and believed that the house of Atreus would be punished for excessive wealth, excessive daring, and for excessive loss of life in battle.

SECOND EPISODE (475-680): The *Chorus* begin to doubt the truth of the beacon's signal. Perhaps, they say, Clytemnestra was carried away by her feminine desire to believe what she wants to hear. Confirmation of the beacon's message comes with a *Herald* who enters with a first-hand account of the war's end.

More than a mere reporter of news, the Herald first expresses his personal happiness at being home again. He praises Agamemnon and casually mentions the destruction of the temples in Troy. His account of the war is not a tale of heroism, but one of discomfort, pain, and death.

The Chorus say they have longed for the soldiers to return home because there are troubles at home only they can solve. *Clytemnestra* then taunts the Chorus for having doubted the message of the beacon. Pride and strength are evident in her disdain for men who doubted her word. Playing the role of a faithful wife, she makes elaborate plans for Agamemnon's reception and sends him a message praising her own faithfulness.

Answering the questions of the Chorus the Herald tells of a violent storm that separated the returning ships and says that the fate of Menelaus is unknown.

COMMENT: *Second Stasimon*: Clearly expressed here is the important Greek concept of *hybris* or excess in behavior. Called variously "the middle way" and "the golden mean," this attitude condemned the sins of exceeding the bounds of normalcy in human action: for example, it was *hybris* to be excessively brave (rashness) and *hybris* to display excessive fear (cowardice); the "mean" behavior was best. Note the critical attitude towards the Trojan War, far different from that of the *Iliad* more than two centuries earlier. The different attitudes demonstrate the transformation of values which occurs as a civilization develops. As the *Chorus* say: "When men are puffed up unduly and their houses are stuffed with riches, measure (the mean) is the best." Of war they say it is a "changer of bodies . . . stowing a man's worth of ashes in an easily handled jar. . . . Over-great glory is a sore burden. The high peak is blasted by the eyes of Zeus."

Episode Two: The Herald in his tale of destroyed temples inadvertently brings more evidence against Agamemnon. The brief and defiant appearance of his wife, who lies in the face of the Chorus, increases her stature, if not her integrity, and makes her a worthy opponent of Agamemnon. The *Herald* recites a common Greek idea: "Yet who except the gods is free from pain the whole duration of life?" His description of the horrors of war is fiercely realistic: "If I were to tell of our labors, our hard lodging, the sleeping on crowded decks, the scanty blankets, tossing and groaning, rations that never reached us . . . continuous drizzle from the sky, dews from the marshes, rotting our clothes, filling our hair with lice . . . or of the heat when the sea slackened at noon waveless and dozing in a depressed calm—." Of a wreck at sea he says he saw "the Aegean sea flowering with corpses of Greek men."

THIRD STASIMON (681-781): The *Chorus* say that the name of Helen means death; it is an appropriate name for one who caused the death of ships, of cities, and of men. There is a saying, the Chorus say, that wealth causes suffering; but they state the only cause of suffering to be committing of evil acts. Excessive pride and daring (*hybris*) lead to disaster: it is to just men with simple hearts that the blessing of happiness comes—the strength of gold and the false face of flattery will not give it. (Note the inconsistency here: they say wealth does not *necessarily* make men evil; they also say that justice shuns wealth.)

THIRD EPISODE (782-974): *Agamemnon* enters in a chariot, with *Cassandra* beside him. The *Chorus* try to find a greeting neither excessive nor inadequate. They frankly tell him they opposed the Trojan War, but they are also happy he has come home.

They say he will quickly find out who has governed well, and who badly, during his absence.

Agamemnon says he must first visit the temples and thank the gods for victory. Then he will assemble the citizens and, with them, judge any who have done evil.

Clytemnestra vividly describes the sufferings a faithful wife undergoes when she must live with daily rumors of her husband's death, sufferings which, she says, had driven her to attempt suicide many times.

These same rumors have, she also says, led her to send their son Orestes away, lest the people rebel and kill him. She orders her servants to spread rich purple tapestries on the ground so that Agamemnon's feet may not touch the common earth, but he refuses—such pomp, he says, should only be reserved for the gods. Clytemnestra then masks her formidable strength with feminine wiles and wheedles him into walking on the purple tapestries just to please her.

Agamemnon removes his sandals before walking on the tapestries, hoping no god will be offended; Clytemnestra proudly says that she would have trampled on many such tapestries if it had been necessary to bring her husband home alive. Before going into the house with Clytemnestra, Agamemnon requests that Cassandra be treated kindly (a superb example of dramatic irony, since the audience is quite aware of what is to come).

FOURTH STASIMON (975-1033): The *Chorus,* happy that Agamemnon has returned, yet is fearful of misfortune.

> **COMMENT:** *Third Episode:* The *Chorus* greet Agamemnon in this wise: "Come then my King, stormer of Troy, offspring of Atreus; how shall I hail you, how give you honor, neither overshooting nor falling short of the measure of homage?" Even the great king made mistakes when he "marshalled the troops for Helen's sake; I will not hide it; made a harsh and ugly picture, holding badly the tiller of reason, paying with the death of men ransom for a willing whore."
>
> Agamemnon is greeted by his *wife* with magnificent lies: "For me the outrushing wells of weeping are dried up, there is no drop left in them. . . . I have been waked by the thin whizz of a buzzing gnat, seeing more horrors fasten on you than could take place in the mere time of my dream." *Agamemnon's* reply is a plea: "—do not by women's methods make me effeminate nor in barbarian fashion gape ground-grovelling acclamations at me. . . . It is the gods should be honored in this way . . . and not to think unwisely is the greatest gift of God. Call happy only him who has ended his life in sweet prosperity."

FOURTH EPISODE (1034-1071): *Clytemnestra* comes out of the house and politely asks Cassandra to enter, but receiving no answer, she angrily goes inside again.

Cassandra, in a prophetic frenzy, calls upon Apollo, saying that now he has destroyed her utterly. She recalls the old curse on the house of the Atridae (children of Atreus), and how the children were killed and served up to their father; then she prophesies that Clytemnestra will murder Agamemnon. The *Chorus* say they want no prophets in their city: divination brings no good to men.

Cassandra says her prophetic gift was given her by Apollo, who had fallen in love with her. When she rebuffed his advances, he decreed that no one should ever believe her prophecies. Thus, when she foretells the murder of Agamemnon, the Chorus refuse to understand her.

She tears off the flowers she has been wearing and casts away her prophetic staff. Knowing that she will be killed too, she offers as a hope for the future that someone will come to avenge her by slaying Clytemnestra (this will happen in the next play of the trilogy, *The Choephoroe*). As she enters the house, *Agamemnon's* voice is heard from within, crying out that he has been stabbed. The *Chorus* run about in distraction, suggesting various courses of action.

> **COMMENT:** *Fourth Episode:* The distracted *Cassandra* knowing she is going to certain death when she enters the palace cries out, "Apollo! Apollo! God of the Ways! My destroyer! Destroyed again—and this time utterly! . . . Look! They are these. These wailing, these children, butchery of children; roasted flesh, a father sitting to dinner (she raves over the Thyestes banquet)." She envisions the murder of the king: "The bull—Keep him clear of the cow. Caught with a trick, the black horn's point, she strikes. He falls; lies in the water. Murder; a trick in a bath. I tell what I see!"
>
> *Agamemnon* from within (i.e., offstage) cries out, "Oh! I am struck a mortal blow—within! . . . Again—the second blow—I am struck again." (The comments of the twelve old men of the Chorus during and immediately after the murder are almost comic).

EXODOS (1406-1673): The palace doors open, revealing the bodies of Agamemnon and Cassandra.

Clytemnestra, standing over them in triumph, says she had lied to spring her trap, but now can speak the truth. She exultantly describes the net she had woven to trap Agamemnon, and the three blows she had struck to kill him; for a long time she had desired to feel his blood spatter over her.

The *Chorus* say she will be banished from the city for murder. She points out in reply that Agamemnon was not banished for the slaying of her daughter, and enumerates her reasons for considering the murder of her husband justified: it was a sacrifice to Artemis, against whom Agamemnon had sinned; it was her revenge upon him for bringing Cassandra to her house; it was a fulfillment of the curse on the house of Atreus.

Aegisthus, Clytemnestra's lover, comes out of the palace. He too desired Agamemnon's death: it had been Agamemnon's father who had killed the two sons of his own father, Thyestes.

The *Chorus* however merely despise Aegisthus for having relied on Clytemnestra to effect his revenge.

Aegisthus threatens them, but Clytemnestra speaks, calmly and authoritatively, saying that the two of them will be strong enough to control the townspeople and that there is no reason to quarrel now.

> **COMMENT:** *Exodos*: In this concluding scene the pride, defiance, and self-confidence of *Clytemnestra* are effectively heightened by contrast with the short-tempered hysteria of Aegisthus. It seems apparent that by himself, Aegisthus could never have brought about his revenge upon King Agamemnon.
>
> *Clytemnestra* describes her murder: "I cast about him a vicious wealth of raiment and struck him twice and with two groans he loosed his limbs beneath him, and upon him fallen I dealt him the third blow . . . and with that he spits his life out where he lies, and smartly spouting blood he sprays me with the somber drizzle of bloody dew and I rejoice no less than in God's gift of rain; the crops are glad when the ear of corn gives birth. . . . The man who outraged me lies here, the darling of each courtesan at Troy."

INTERPRETATION: *AGAMEMNON*, QUESTIONS AND ANSWERS

Why does Clytemnestra kill Agamemnon?

ANSWER: Clytemnestra wanted revenge upon Agamemnon because he had sacrificed their daughter, Iphigenia, to Artemis so that the Greek ships would have a favorable wind when they sailed against Troy. She also objected to his bringing his mistress Cassandra back home with him. A motive that is not explicit in the play is that she put herself in a dangerous position when she took Aegisthus as her lover while her husband was at war. He would probably have discovered the adultery and punished her.

What attitude toward the Trojan War is expressed in the play?

ANSWER: The Trojan War is condemned by the Watchman because the city has fallen on evil times during Agamemnon's absence. Clytemnestra objects to the sacrifice of her daughter Iphigenia. The Chorus express the greatest dislike of the war, attacking it as a gratuitous waste of human life in a worthless cause: the return of an adulteress, Helen.

What is the general significance of Agamemnon's death?

ANSWER: Although killed by his wife, the death of Agamemnon has more significance than it would have if it were only the revenge of Clytemnestra. Agamemnon is guilty of the sin of *hybris*, excessive daring and pride. The specific acts which demonstrate this sin are his sacrifice of his daughter, his destruction of the Trojan temples, his desire for greatness, and his walking on the crimson (purple) carpet spread out by his wife.

What are the distinctive features of Aeschylus' plays?

ANSWER: Simple plots without suspense; much spectacle and grandeur; high moral and religious themes; poor motivation of actors' movements. *Chief theme*: Man is weak and the gods make him suffer to gain knowledge of his own nature.

AESCHYLUS

CHOEPHOROE (LIBATION BEARERS)

BACKGROUND: The events in the *Choephoroe* occur about seven years after those in the Agamemnon. Clytemnestra and Aegisthus still rule Argos; Electra, daughter of Clytemnestra and Agamemnon, has been raised to young womanhood in the household; her brother Orestes, sent away before Agamemnon had returned to Argos, is about to return as the play begins. Apollo has ordered Orestes to avenge his father's death.

CHARACTERS

ORESTES: son of Agamemnon and Clytemnestra, away from home with his friend, Pylades, since his childhood.

CHORUS: slave women brought back from Troy by Agamemnon.

ELECTRA: daughter of Agamemnon and Clytemnestra, sister of Orestes.

NURSE: cared for Orestes when he was a baby.

CLYTEMNESTRA: wife of Agamemnon who, during his absence in Troy, took Aegisthus as a lover, and with his aid killed Agamemnon upon the king's return to his native Argos.

AEGISTHUS: lover of Clytemnestra. Son of Thyestes and a cousin of Agamemnon.

PYLADES (PILL uh deez): friend of Orestes.

SETTING: The first part of the play is set before the tomb of Agamemnon; the second part before Agamemnon's palace.

SUMMARY: *Orestes* lays two locks of his hair on the tomb of his father, Agamemnon. Seeing Electra and the Chorus approach the tomb, Orestes and *Pylades* withdraw.

The *Chorus* reveal that Clytemnestra, because of frightening dreams, has sent them to pour a libation on her husband's tomb. The offering is designed to prevent one crime from bringing about another.

Electra, who is offering the libation, prays for revenge against her mother and Aegisthus. She complains that she and her brother have been kept from their rightful place in the kingdom and must live in poverty. She notices the two locks of hair and knows from their color and from the fact no one else could have left them there, that they are her brother's. She then sees a footprint, fits her own foot into it, and declares that Orestes has been there in person.

Orestes comes forward and identifies himself by showing Electra a robe she had woven years earlier. Orestes says he is seeking revenge at the express command of Apollo. He also advances his personal reasons for revenge: love for his father, desire to possess his father's wealth, and outrage that Argos should be ruled by a woman and her lover. Orestes asks why Clytemnestra, of all people, had sent the libation. The *Chorus* reply that she dreamed she had given birth to a serpent which she nursed, and which drew forth a blood-clot with its milk. Orestes interprets the dream by saying he is the serpent, and the blood-clot a symbol of his mother's death.

The setting for the rest of the play is now in front of the palace. Orestes and *Pylades,* disguised as travellers, ask for a night's lodging. *Clytemnestra* courteously welcomes them. Orestes says they are travelers and that a stranger had told them to give the message, "Orestes is no more." Clytemnestra loudly laments the death of her son before the strangers.

The *Nurse* tells the Chorus Clytemnestra was glad to hear the news of her son's death, but the nurse's grief is genuine. The hatred of the Chorus for Clytemnestra and Aegisthus reaches a frenzied pitch. They hope that Orestes will not weaken when his mother cries for mercy, and they pray that the old family curse will then die.

An *Attendant* rushes out saying that Aegisthus has been killed. Clytemnestra appears and calls for the axe she had used to kill Agamemnon. Orestes comes out of the palace carrying a blood-covered sword—his mother begs for mercy. He returns for advice to his friend Pylades, who reminds him of Apollo's orders. Clytemnestra pleads Agamemnon's lewdness in bringing a mistress with him and vows revenge through the hounds of hell if Orestes kills her. She pleads in vain; he drives her into the house and murders his own mother!

The central doors of the palace open, revealing the bodies of Clytemnestra and Aegisthus. Orestes justifies his murders, citing reasons given earlier to his sister. Struck by visions, he thinks he recognizes the hounds of hell, his mother's threatened avengers. When Orestes runs from the stage to seek refuge at Apollo's shrine, the *Chorus* point out that madness is the last, inevitable stage in the progress of the house of Atreus toward its doom.

AESCHYLUS

EUMENIDES (KINDLY ONES)

BACKGROUND: Orestes has fled to the temple of Apollo at Delphi to seek protection from the avenging Furies stirred up by his mother after he had murdered her. Only a few days have elapsed since the closing scene of the *Choephoroe*.

CHARACTERS

PRIESTESS: in charge of the temple of Apollo.

APOLLO: god of prophecy, frequently represented in his role as god of the sun.

ORESTES: son of Agamemnon, King of Argos, and his wife, Clytemnestra.

THE GHOST OF CLYTEMNESTRA: seeking revenge on her son, who has murdered her.

CHORUS: a band of supernatural creatures, the Furies (Erinyes), deities who bring revenge, especially for the murder of blood kindred, appear as women wearing horrible masks.

ATHENA: daughter of Zeus, born by springing from his forehead. Her chief attributes are power and wisdom. She was regarded also as the protector of the state.

ATTENDANTS OF ATHENA

TWELVE ATHENIAN CITIZENS: chosen as jurors for the trial of Orestes.

SETTING: This is one of the few Greek plays in which the Chorus goes off the stage entirely, and in which there is a complete change of scene. The first part of the play is set before the temple of Apollo at Delphi, the second, apparently, on the Areopagus (Ares' Hill) in Athens.

The *Priestess of Apollo* issues from the temple in great fear; she has seen Orestes crouching at the altar, bloody sword in hand. Near him are the monstrous Furies, sound asleep.

Apollo and *Hermes* appear. *Apollo* speaks to Orestes, promising to protect him from the Furies. He tells Orestes to go to Athens, Athena's city, where he will find justice.

The *Ghost of Clytemnestra* appears and, in a rage, denounces the Furies for letting Orestes escape. Only slowly do they awaken from their deep sleep.

The *Furies* lament the escape of Orestes, accusing Apollo of having wronged them. They say the younger gods, such as Apollo, have no respect for the ancient divinities and their laws.

Apollo orders the Furies out of his temple, but they swear never to cease from their pursuit.

The scene shifts to Athens, before the temple of Athena.

The *Chorus* enter pursuing Orestes like a pack of bloodhounds. Orestes says that the bloodstain on his hands disappeared after he had visited Apollo's shrine, and that therefore the gods have absolved him of guilt.

Athena enters and charges the Furies as being interested more in the forms of justice than in its substance. After hearing Orestes' story however, she says she is not able to decide the issue herself; both he and the Furies have rights she cannot abrogate with her decision alone. She announces that she will choose a panel of the truest men in Athens to listen to the case and decide upon its merits.

The Furies during the trial question Orestes, who admits that he did indeed kill his mother. Orestes asks them why they did not try to avenge the death of Agamemnon. Apollo as a witness for Orestes defends him and attacks the Furies. Athena turns the case over to the *Jury*, formally establishing the court of the Areopagus (air ee OP ih guss)—to endure forever. A jury tie is announced, but is broken by Athena's vote for the defendant. Orestes is free and absolved of guilt.

The Furies are promised a special shrine and worship as the Kindly Ones (*Eumenides*) by the people. The Eumenides are to dispense favors instead of misfortune. Athena leads them in a joyful procession to their new home in a cave.

INTERPRETATION OF THE TRILOGY, (AGAMEMNON, CHOEPHOROE, EUMENIDES): THE ORESTEIA: QUESTIONS AND ANSWERS

What is the importance of the Oresteia *in the history of drama?*

ANSWER: The *Oreiesta* is the only Greek trilogy to have survived in its entirety. Furthermore, being written on a theme also treated by Sophocles and Euripides, it served as a basis for plays of theirs which were "answers" to Euripides' plays on the same theme.

What theme carries through the whole of the Oresteia?

ANSWER: The relationship between an individual and his past, as well as his future. The particular form of this theme is that the sins of the fathers are visited upon the heads of their children.

What is the theme of the Choephoroe?

ANSWER: The main theme is the punishment of Clytemnestra, whose motivation is subtly changed from what it had been in the *Agamemnon*. Here she appears more culpable because emphasis is on her lust in taking a lover while her husband is away. The play is *not* an argument for matricide.

What are the Eumenides?

ANSWER: The Eumenides are a band of Avenging Deities. They are represented as women who are extremely ugly and frightening. The name "Eumenides" is a euphemism (the substitution of a gentler term for a more harsh one) meaning "kindly ones." It was originally used because people dreaded to call them by their real name, *Erinyes* (ee RIN uh eez). In the play the *Eumenides*, they are given the attributes of *kindly ones* because of Athena's efforts after the trial of Orestes.

What is peculiar about the structure of the Eumenides?

ANSWER: The play at the beginning is about the attempt of Clytemnestra's Ghost to punish her son for having murdered her. The focus is on Orestes' flight. The end of the play, however, is entirely concerned with the establishment of the *Areopagus*, the court on Ares' Hill in Athens. Orestes completely disappears at the play's close.

What does the Oresteia *say about Justice?*

ANSWER: The "eye for an eye" primitive codes of justice based on family honor and vengeance must be supplanted by a more civilized code based on civil law. Individual codes of justice are too anarchic and uncivilized for a mighty center of thought like Athens. In addition, there must be a clear distinction made between involuntary and premeditated murder. Any committer of a crime *must* suffer for his deed—a supreme law of justice. On the other hand, wisdom comes through suffering only.

What is hybris?

ANSWER: *Hybris* is overweening pride and arrogance that generally accompanies prosperity. In such cases there comes inevitable retribution through the righteous anger of the gods (*Nemesis*).

How is the more civilized code of justice reflected in the gods?

ANSWER: Zeus is no longer the merciless and bloody tyrant of old—he has a benevolent aspect, and such gods as Apollo and Athena, symbolizing light and reason, subdue the more terrible forces of darkness (*Erinyes* or Furies).

List Aeschylus' main contributions to thought.

1. The *lex talonis* ("an eye for an eye") must yield to trial by jury, and state law.

2. Wisdom arrives only through suffering.

3. Life is filled with sorrow, a tragic span on earth.

4. Man is basically a weak and limited being who therefore must submit to the wiser guidance of the gods and the state.

5. *Ethical monotheism* is better than tribal superstition with its familial gods of individual force and vengeance.

6. No man can escape personal responsibility for sin, since he will inevitably face retribution.

7. Moderation is far better than excessive pride and self-will.

GREEK TRAGEDY: SOPHOCLES

LIFE (497-405 B.C.): Sophocles (SOFF oh Kleez) was born around 497 B.C. at Colonus, which is the site for one of his greatest plays, *Oedipus at Colonus.*

He was the son of an armor manufacturer called Sophillus, who saw to it that his promising son got the best of the traditional education in such things as music, dancing, and gymnastics. In 480 B.C. Sophocles himself led the chorus in the victory song and dance after the defeat of Xerxes in the battle of Salamis.

He was handsome, tactful, gracious, musically skilled—all in addition to being a dramatic genius, the author of some of the greatest tragedies in the western world.

He often was chosen to public office, such as general (*strategus*), commissioner on the Constitution of Athens in 413 B.C.

In his first competition for the tragic prize (at the age of twenty-seven), he defeated the great Aeschylus! His career was astonishingly successful and prolific, and public recognition was generous.

Yet in spite of his extraordinarily successful career as a dramatist and artist, in spite of a life that seems unusually tranquil and blessed, he wrote with acute insight about suffering and conflict amongst men. No man could write of human suffering and anguish with such conviction and fervor who has not suffered at some time in his own life; it is a cliché to regard his career as totally peaceful.

There is an interesting story that his son brought him to court on the charge of senility (the father then being ninety), and that the aged father proved his vigor of mind by reading the choral ode on Colonus from his own *Oedipus at Colonus*—needless to say, his son lost the case.

Only seven tragedies remain out of a life *corpus* of about 130 plays.

The seven extant tragedies are the following:

AJAX (c. 444 B.C.)
ANTIGONE (c. 442)
OEDIPUS THE KING (c. 430)
ELECTRA (c. 418)

THE WOMEN OF TRACHIS (c. 413)
PHILOCTETES (409)
OEDIPUS AT COLONUS (401 B.C., produced after his death)

SOPHOCLES' INNOVATIONS IN TRAGEDY:

1. The introduction of the third actor, a speaking actor.

2. A wider and more complex use of scenery than Aeschylus.

3. Chorus increased in number from twelve to fifteen.

4. Developed the single play as distinguished from a play as part of a trilogy or tetrology.

HIS UNIVERSALITY:

1. His characters are at once individuals and universal types.

2. His themes are profoundly personal and individual, and at the same time widely universal.

3. He is unsurpassed in his dramatizations of man's search for the truth about himself, and the suffering he must undergo in the realization of that truth.

4. His characters have great dignity, suffer great pain, come to great rewards when they are faced with the truths about themselves. In other words, truth is its own reward when man is blind about his own nature.

5. One realizes after reading his plays that self-restraint, temperance in all things, and a sense of balance (*sophrosyne*) are the only personal characteristics that can make life endurable, steady, and whole.

SOPHOCLES

AJAX (c. 447 B.C.)

BACKGROUND: After Achilles dies in combat, there is a great competition for his magical mighty arms. Two of the chief competitors are Ajax and Odysseus; the leaders of the Greek troops (mainly Agamemnon and his brother Menelaus) award the arms to Odysseus. The highly insulted Ajax, the mightiest living Greek warrior, plans to murder the Greek leaders, Agamemnon and Menelaus at night, but Athena afflicts him with madness (Ajax in his pride had once refused her aid in battle). In his mad delusion he slays the sheep and cattle of the Greeks, thinking them to be the Greek leaders.

SETTING:

1. The Greek camp at Troy.

2. Then, on the seashore.

CHARACTERS

AJAX: the great warrior gone mad.

EURYSACES (you RISS uh keez): his son.

TECMESSA: Ajax' concubine, and mother of Eurysaces.

TEUCER: Ajax' half brother.

ATHENA: goddess of Athens, of wisdom, of battle.

MESSENGER: who announces attack on Teucer.

ODYSSEUS: the winner in the arms competition, the most cunning of the Greeks.

AGAMEMNON: king of the Greeks.

MENELAUS: his brother, husband of Helen.

CHORUS: fifteen seamen of Salamis.

159

SUMMARY: *Athena* meets *Odysseus* outside the tent of Ajax. She relates how she had afflicted Ajax with delusionary madness, which had inspired him to mistake sheep and cattle for the Greek leaders he had wished to murder. He had slaughtered many animals, and had captured many others and brought them to his tent for the purpose of later torturing them.

Athena summons *Ajax* from within the tent. He boasts in his madness of having killed the Greek leaders and captured Odysseus. Athena, after Ajax re-enters his tent, tells Odysseus to note the power of the gods. Odysseus expresses pity for Ajax.

The *Chorus of Seamen* of Salamis sing of Ajax' shameful deeds and call for punishment by the gods.

Tecmessa, Ajax' concubine, recites how she saw Ajax slay the animals. She tells how his fit of madness is now over. Ajax appears filled with despair and calls for his son and his half brother; he is tortured by the laughter of the Greeks at his mad actions. He is dishonored and scorned, wretched beyond imagination. There is only one way out—suicide.

Tecmessa pleads with him, citing how the Greeks will make slaves of her and his son. His *child* is brought in, and there is a touching farewell scene.

The Chorus express sympathy for Ajax, who appears now as if no longer intending suicide, since Tecmessa had dissuaded him from the act. He plans to ask Athena for forgiveness.

A *Messenger* relates how the Greeks have attacked and insulted Teucer as the relative of the mad Ajax.

The scene is the seashore now: Ajax is alone and asks *Hermes* to conduct him swiftly to Hades; he begs the Furies to punish the Greek leaders. He bids life, light, country, Salamis, Athens, and Troy farewell. Then he kills himself by falling on his sword.

Tecmessa finds the body and joins in lament with the Chorus of Seamen.

Teucer then enters and hears the tragic story of his half brother. He bids Tecmessa to bring Ajax's son to him quickly, away from the Greeks. He laments over his beloved brother's suicide.

Menelaus and then *Agamemnon* enter, only to forbid the burial of the corpse (thus it would never find peace in the world of the dead in Hades), and to leave the corpse for the dogs and vultures. Teucer nobly defies them, speaking of Ajax' great deeds on the battlefield in the Grecian cause, his unimpeachable loyalty to the Greeks, and his magnificent courage. Odysseus enters and admits that Ajax was the greatest after Achilles, and in spite of their being enemies, he respects the mighty warrior. Odysseus then persuades King Agamemnon to permit the proper burial of the body.

INTERPRETATION: *AJAX*, QUESTIONS AND ANSWERS

Name a critical difficulty with this play.

ANSWER: Ajax kills himself a little over halfway through the play. The remainder of the play is at loose ends, not vital to the story. The interest is seemingly gone. There is too much attention devoted to Ajax' burial. The play seemingly lacks unity. We are reminded of Shakespeare's *Julius Caesar,* where Caesar himself dies at about the middle of the play.

Discuss the character of Ajax.

ANSWER: Ajax has committed a horrible and silly crime for which, even though sane later, he is not the least sorry. He regrets only that he failed to kill the Greek leaders. His vanity is great: he can see no reason why he should not have won over Odysseus. He is always wrong in his estimate of Odysseus, a person of low acumen. He is guilty of pride and insolence towards a goddess, Athena. Notwithstanding all this, he is a great soldier, noble and daring of spirit, a character who utters great poetry. What he lacks is intellectual and moral wisdom, *phronesis.*

SOPHOCLES

ANTIGONE (c. 441 B.C.)

BACKGROUND: A father, Oedipus, before he dies lays a curse on his two sons, Polyneices and Eteocles, foretelling that both would die in a duel. In a quarrel over the throne Eteocles, the younger brother, sends Polyneices into exile. Eteocles is now king of Thebes. The older brother persuades his father-in-law to wage war on Thebes. Adrastus, king of Argos (the father-in-law), leads the expedition, with Polyneices and six other warriors making up a unit of generals known as the *Seven Against Thebes*. In a duel the brothers kill each other. Their mother's brother, Creon, now becomes king of Thebes. He orders the burial of Eteocles with full honors, but for the corpse of Polyneices no burial at all—and hence no peace for the soul of Polyneices in the underworld.

CHARACTERS

ANTIGONE (an TIGG oh nee): daughter of Oedipus and Creon's niece.

ISMENE (izz MEE nee): her sister.

CREON: king of Thebes, brother of Oedipus, uncle to Antigone and Ismene.

GUARD: a simple soldier of Creon.

CHORUS: made up of fifteen Theban elderly citizens.

HAEMON (HEE mon): son of Creon, fiancé of Antigone.

TEIRESIAS (ty REE see uss): blind soothsayer of Thebes.

MESSENGER: who relates Antigone's death and Haemon's suicide.

EURYDICE (you RID uh see): wife of Creon.

SETTING: Before the palace of the king in Thebes.

PROLOGUE (lines 1-99): *Antigone* and her sister *Ismene* are discussing their uncle's (Creon's) edict: Eteocles is to be buried with full honors, but the rebellious brother, Polyneices, is to be refused burial, to be left on the plain subject to the depredations of wild dogs and vultures. Creon's edict also states that anyone caught violating his edict will be put to death by stoning.

Antigone tells her sister that she will not obey the edict; that she will not let her brother lie unburied; that not only is this a family responsibility, it is one required by the gods themselves. The laws of the gods demand loyalty to kin and immediate burial after death, so that the ghost may live on in untroubled peace in the Underworld. Man's laws, says Antigone, are not superior to the laws of the gods themselves.

Ismene (less passionate, more gentle than her sister), on the other hand, accepts the edict; she cannot and will not defy the laws of the State, although she too suffers pain at the desecration of her brother's corpse.

Antigone vehemently (almost savagely) replies that then she will do it alone: she will place soil upon her brother (a symbol that the body is duly and properly buried according to Greek religious rites). The sisters exit.

PARODOS (100-162): The *Chorus of Theban Elders* make their entrance and sing an ode dealing with the battle of the *Seven Against Thebes* (See Background). Polyneices was guilty of treason and *hybris* (pride); he deserved his fate.

FIRST EPISODE (163-331): *Creon,* king of Thebes, enters accompanied by two attendants. He tells the *Chorus* that he believes in the supremacy of the law of the State; that the highest loyalty expressible is that of loyalty and love of country.

Creon gives the details of his new edict; that anyone caught violating it will be promptly executed; moreover, he has placed guards around the corpse to prevent its burial by anyone.

A guard enters now to relate (hesitatingly; he is rather simple-minded) that someone has succeeded in placing earth upon the corpse. The *Leader of the Chorus* opines that the decree violator may have been a god.

Creon is furious at the violation of his edict and threatens to have the guard tortured and put to death unless he finds the culprit who dared disobey his decree.

FIRST STASIMON (332-383):   The *Chorus* are left alone on the stage to sing a marvelous ode on man:

1. Man is the greatest and most marvelous miracle on earth.

2. Man has conquered all the earth, all the seas; he has conquered and tamed the wild beasts of the world.

3. Man has marvelous powers of thought and speech—*yet* in spite of his might, his conquests, and his powers, he too is subject to Death; Death the conqueror of all. Moreover, his cunning and shrewdness can wreak havoc if used in unrighteous ways—especially when used to defy or undermine the laws of the State. When the laws of the land are cherished and the gods are properly worshipped, the State will flourish—but not otherwise.

> **COMMENT:** *Prologue*: *Antigone* is a fiercely loyal family girl; above all things is love, fidelity, and loyalty to the obligations of family—of loyalty and duty to brother in this case. To her gentle and law-respecting sister, Ismene, she reveals her plan to bury the corpse of Polyneices: "Now you know!—and now you will show whether you are nobly bred, or the unworthy daughter of a noble line." The wise *Ismene* replies that "it is foolish to be too zealous even in a good cause" (here is the case for moderation, so dear to the Greek heart). Antigone is intense and passionate, almost hot-headed. She denounces her sister for not joining in her crime: "I will condemn you more if you are silent than if you proclaim my deed to all."
>
> *Parodos*: "And a thing abhorred by Zeus is the boastful tongue of the haughty."
>
> *First Episode*: The Guard enters somewhat comically: "My mind was telling me two different things. 'Fool,' it said to me, 'why do you go where you are sure to be condemned?'" Torn between two feelings he "came on slowly and unwillingly, making a short road long . . . bad news is nothing to be in a hurry about." This delay of vital news drives *Creon* almost in a frenzy of anxious worry: "Tell it, man, will you?—tell it and be off." In his anger Creon accuses the guard of complicity in the crime. Creon, like Antigone, is also emotional and hot-headed.

First Stasimon: "Wonders are many in the world, and the wonder of all is man. . . . Only against Death man arms himself in vain. . . . Yet in his rashness often he scorns the ways that are good—." The rash temper is the "flaw" (*harmartia*) in Creon's temper as it is in Antigone's.

SECOND EPISODE (384-581):   The *Guard* comes in with *Antigone* under arrest. She has been caught pouring soil over her brother's corpse, giving it the rites of burial a second time.

The news that his niece is responsible astounds Creon. Antigone defends herself saying that the higher laws of the gods supersede the laws of a mere king.

Ismene enters and loyally offers to share Antigone's punishment, but the fierce Antigone spurns her offer. Ismene asks her uncle if he really intends to execute his niece because of her act, her niece Antigone who is the fiancée of his own son Haemon.

Creon is adamant: Antigone must die.

SECOND STASIMON (582-630):   The *Chorus of Theban Elders* sings an ode about how family curses have doomed great houses such as the family of Labdacus (the origin of Oepidus, Antigone etc.) There is suffering and sorrow passed down from father to children. They sing of man, who when he exceeds the mean of normal conduct in such matters as love and hate will inevitably suffer for his excess.

THIRD EPISODE (631-780):   *Haemon* now enters; he attempts to dissuade his father from enforcing his harsh decree against Antigone, who is Haemon's betrothed. He declares that she has done a glorious thing. Haemon loves his father, he says calmly, but the people agree with Haemon: Antigone must not be executed! In contrast to Haemon's quiet appeal, his father's ire increases in its vehemence. Creon is the senior and the wiser in these matters, says the king; sons do not tell their fathers what to do.

Haemon loses his calm and rushes off the stage. He calls his father unjust, says that he will never see him again.

Creon tells the Chorus he intends to imprison Antigone in a cave until she is dead—entombed alive! (This is a sudden change from the original decree that stated death by stoning would be the method of execution.)

THIRD STASIMON (781-882):   *Antigone* issues from the palace. Creon's *soldiers* are attending her on her way to death. She and the *Chorus* engage in a beautiful and lyric dialogue: she bewails the fact that she has had no husband, no children; only Hades will be her marriage mate. Nevertheless, she proudly states that gladly would she yield life for parents or brother but never for her own husband or child. The Chorus sympathize but warn her about the dangers of *hybris* and stubborn pride.

> **COMMENT:**   *Second Episode*:   The *Guard's* description is realistic: "Then we sat us down on the brow of the hill to windward, so that the smell from him would not strike us. . . . It is good to escape danger one's self, but hard to bring trouble to one's friends. However, nothing counts with me so much as my own safety." *Antigone*'s passionate plea on the higher law of the gods is stirring: "Yes, for it was not Zeus made such a law; such is not the Justice of the gods. Nor did I think that your decrees had so much force, that a mortal could over- ride the unwritten and unchanging statutes of heaven."

> *Second Stasimon*: The *Chorus* utter some common Sophoclean concepts: "Evil strikes at it (i.e., the ill-fated house) down the generations, wave after wave, like seas that batter a head- land. . . . O Zeus, how vain is the mortal will that opposes the Will Immortal. . . . Wise was he who said that ancient saying: 'Whom the gods bewilder, at last takes evil for virtue' . . . And let no man lament if his lot is humble—no great things come to mortals without a curse."

> **COMMENT:**   *Episode Three*:   *Creon* especially detests dis- obedience, calling it the "worst of evils. It desolates house- holds; it ruins cities; it throws the ranks of allies into con- fusion and rout. . . . Therefore we must uphold the cause of order; and certainly we must not let a woman defy us." *Hae- mon's* plea tells his father some home truths: "The people dare not say to your face what would displease you; but I can hear the things murmured in the dark, and the whole city weeps for this maiden. . . . For the man who thinks he is the only wise man always proves hollow when we sound him . . . the stubborn are torn up and perish, root and branch."

> *Third Stasimon*: Most interesting is the following of *Antigone's*

declarations: "Not for my children, if I had been a mother, nor for my husband, if his dead body were rotting before me, would I have chosen to suffer like this in violent defiance of the citizens. . . . If my husband had died, there would have been another man for me; I could have had a child from another husband. . . . But with my mother and father both hidden away in Hades, no other brother could ever have come into being for me" (some translators omit this passage, finding its sophism too crude and unnatural; others justify its inclusion as being true to character).

FOURTH EPISODE (883-943): *Creon* enters to make sure she is quickly led to her death, which is that of being entombed in a cave alive and there abandoned! This mode of official murder will thus leave Creon's hands unstained of blood; he will not have murdered her directly, as he says. Antigone bids the citizens a touching farewell but not before she had staunchly defended her act of treason.

FOURTH STASIMON (944-987): The *Chorus* relates tales of other imprisoned people such as Danaë "young and wistful, taken away from the sunlight. . . . Dread indeed are the Fates, their ways mysterious: neither by wealth nor war—neither by hiding . . . shall man evade them."

FIFTH EPISODE (988-1114): *Teiresias*, led by a boy, appears before the King and the Chorus of Elders. He denounces Creon for leaving the body of Polyneices unburied, and for burying Antigone alive: "Think then on these things, my son. All men are liable to err; but he shows wisdom and earns blessings who heals the ills his errors caused, being not too stubborn; too stiff a will is folly." The angry *Creon* accuses the holy prophet of collusion with Antigone's sympathizers in order to get her released: "So, hoary prophet, the wisest come to a shameful fall when they clothe shameful counsels in fair words to earn a bribe." *Teiresias* predicts that the "dread Erinyes, . . . lie now in wait for you, preparing a vengeance equal to your guilt [someone in his family will soon die]." Teiresias is then led away.

The *Leader of the Chorus* advises Creon to heed good counsel, and *Creon* changes his mind. "It is hard to do—to retreat from a firm stand—but I yield. . . . We must not wage a vain war with Fate. . . . My heart misgives me, it is best to keep the established laws, even to life's end." Creon and his servants rush off to free Antigone from her vault.

FIFTH STASIMON (1115-1152): The *Chorus* sings of the "god of many names, fruit of the daughter of Cadmus [Dionysus]," of the "joys of his fruit [the grape-vine]," of the dance of the Corycian nymphs "besides Castalia's stream," of "Thebes, where your mother conceived amid lightning, first among cities. . . ."

EXODOS (1153-1353): A *Messenger* appears from the direction of the vault where Antigone lies entombed. He tells of the suicide of Antigone's fiancé, Haemon, and of Antigone herself "hanging by the neck, her scarf of fine linen twisted into a cruel noose. And there too we saw Haemon—his arms about her waist, while he cried out upon the loss of his bride. . . . Then that maddened boy, torn between grief and rage and penitence, straightway leaned upon his sword, and drove it half its length into his side. . . . Corpse enfolding corpse they lie; he has won his bride." After this terrible news, *Eurydice* silently goes into the house, the Chorus finding her silence ominous. The Messenger enters the house, and at this point *Creon* enters accompanying the dead body of his son, Haemon, on a bier carried by attendants. His sorrow is tragic: "Woe for the sins of a darkened soul, the sins of a stubborn pride that played with death! . . . I have learned the bitter lesson. . . . Alas, man's labors come but to foolish ends!" Then the doors of the King's house are opened, and the corpse of Creon's wife is disclosed; she had killed herself by stabbing when she heard the news of her son's suicide. Creon's last words are "Lead me away, I pray you; a rash, foolish man, who has slain you, O my son, unwittingly, and you too, my wife—unhappy that I am! Where can I find comfort, where can I turn my gaze?" The "moral" is the final comment of the Chorus:

> "If any man would be happy, and not broken by Fate, wisdom is the thing he should seek, for happiness hides there."

COMMENT: So ends one of the greatest tragedies ever written. Its basic theme is that suffering is inescapable for man no matter how he directs his life, since a wise and balanced life in a world of conflicting loyalties and desires is impossible.

INTERPRETATION: *ANTIGONE*, QUESTIONS AND ANSWERS

What is the abstract conflict in law in Antigone?

ANSWER: The abstract conflict in law is that between a) *"divine" law*, upheld by Antigone (the gods demand burial for peace of the soul or ghost), and b) *man-made law,* upheld by Creon (treason to the State must not go unpunished; it is one of the most heinous of crimes against the citizens of a State).

Briefly, what is Aristotle's tragic flaw (harmartia) *theory?*

ANSWER: Tragic flaw (*harmartia*) is that excess in behavior which leads to a character's downfall. In Creon it is his pride and stubborn unwillingness to yield.

Is Antigone's character flawed in any way?

ANSWER: Opinion is divided:

1. The answer is *no!* She has none but the noblest motives for her deeds. "Hers is a supreme, completely voluntary courage which chooses the right and makes no compromise with reality; in fact, for her the true reality consists simply in the execution of her duty according to ancient Greek conventions: the burial of her brother." (L.R. Lind, translator of *Antigone*)

2. The answer is *yes!* She seems to go deliberately out of her way in her attempts to seek martyrdom. Moreover, she seems as stubborn and disregardful of consequences as the king, her uncle.

What is Creon's hybris *(fatal excess of behavior)?*

ANSWER: His *hybris* was his fatal unwillingness to change his stubborn course of action regarding Antigone's burial of her brother. He does eventually change his mind, but by then it is too late.

What does Antigone symbolize to most of us today?

ANSWER: She is the symbol of unyielding resistance to implacable tyranny, perhaps even in her own day, since the tyrant, both in name and symbol, struck terror in the breasts of most fifth-century Greeks.

Contrast love and hate as expressed in the play.

ANSWER: Creon applies the *letter of the law,* which kills, and the *spirit of divine law,* which gives life. Love must inevitably win over unyielding hate. Compassion, moderation and sympathy are among the highest of virtues.

What is the core of Sophocles' philosophy as revealed in this play?

ANSWER: The core of his philosophy, says Kitto, is that "virtue alone cannot assure happiness nor wickedness alone explain disaster." In addition, any house laboring under a curse must suffer, the innocent along with the guilty.

What is a clearly dominant theme in the play?

ANSWER: The gods will bring retribution upon anyone who wrongs the dead. In the play Creon has clearly offended the gods by his refusal to give proper burial, and for that he must suffer.

Discuss the structure of the play.

ANSWER: We can list some of the elements of structure:

1. Antigone, in spite of her importance as a character, disappears from the stage before the play is two-thirds completed. Some justify this by saying that this is done to concentrate on the true protagonist of the play, Creon, who, despite the title, is the real "hero" of the drama.

2. We see a series of inevitable and dramatically convincing blunders committed by Creon as he blindly and inexorably seals his own doom. The last scene when he turns from his son's corpse to that of his wife is deeply affecting.

SOPHOCLES

OEDIPUS THE KING (c. 430 B.C.)

BACKGROUND: Laius (LAY yuhss), king of Thebes, kidnaps a son of Pelops called Chrysippus.

The oracle at Delphi informs him that some day he will be killed by his own son.

To prevent this from happening, Laius pierces and ties together the feet of his infant son and abandons him on Mount Cithaeron. But the shepherd who had been ordered to abandon the child takes pity on him and gives him to a shepherd from Corinth.

The infant is taken to the king of Corinth, who brings him up as his own son under the name of Oedipus (*oedipus* = swollen foot).

The oracle at Delphi tells the young man Oedipus that one day he will kill his father (named Polybus) and marry his own mother!

Oedipus, in order to avoid his fate, leaves his supposed parents and travels to Thebes. On his way there, his chariot is met by another coming in the opposite direction from Thebes. This is at a spot where three roads meet. Oedipus and the man (really his father Laius) in the other chariot quarrel, and the hot-tempered Oedipus unknowingly slays his own father, thus fulfilling the oracle in half its prediction. He arrives at Thebes and meets a monster called the Sphinx (half woman, half lion). She kills all who cannot solve her difficult and puzzling riddle. It is this monster who daily plagues Thebes. The wise Oedipus solves the riddle: What walks on four legs in the morning, two at noon, and on three legs in the evening? Answer: *"man"*—first as *infant* on all fours, then as *man* on two legs, and lastly as an *old man* leaning on a staff. The outsmarted monster commits suicide by hurling herself from a rock.

Oedipus is received as a great hero who has saved Thebes from destruction by the Sphinx. He weds the widow (his own mother), of Laius, unaware of their relationship, and they have two sons and two daughters.

CHARACTERS

OEDIPUS (EDD ih puss): king of Thebes.

JOCASTA: his wife, queen of Thebes.

CREON: Jocasta's brother and Oedipus' uncle.

TEIRESIAS (ty REE see uss): a blind soothsayer.

PRIEST.

MESSENGER FROM CORINTH.

SECOND MESSENGER.

SHEPHERD: servant of Laius, father of Oedipus.

CHORUS OF THEBAN ELDERS.

(silent) ANTIGONE and ISMENE, daughters of King Oedipus.

SETTING: Before the palace of the king of Thebes (THEEBZ). Oedipus is king, happily married with four children. Thebes has recently been afflicted by a plague that threatens to destroy the city.

PROLOGUE (lines 1-150):   The play opens with *King Oedipus* speaking to the *citizens* of Thebes, who are headed by a Priest of Zeus. They are begging him for help in ending this devastating plague that is destroying Thebes. Oedipus had helped them by ridding the country of the depredations of the Sphynx; he must try again to help them now.

Oedipus shows grief for the terrible results of the plague (the land, women, and animals are all barren, for example). He tells them he has done something already: he has sent his brother-in-law Creon to consult the oracle of Apollo to find out the cause for the plague.

Creon returns and tells Oedipus that the plague was and is caused by the presence of a murderer in Thebes, the murderer of their former king, Laius. When that murderer is found and punished, Apollo says, then the plague will come to an end.

Oedipus wants to know why the murderer wasn't found long ago, since the murder had occurred many years ago.

Creon replies that the confusion caused by the Sphynx prevented a full search; he does add that there had been a witness to the murder of Laius: he had said that the murder had been committed by a group of thieves. King Oedipus, confident and assured, swears that just as he had solved the riddle of the Sphynx many years ago, so he will solve the riddle of the murderer of King Laius.

PARODOS (151-215): The *Chorus of Theban Elders* pray to Zeus, Apollo of Delos, undying Athene, Artemis and others for help against the plague: "Unnumbered of the city die. Unpitied babies bearing death lie unmoaned on the ground."

FIRST EPISODE (216-242): *Oedipus* issues an edict: anyone who knows anything at all about the circumstances of Laius' murder must come forth at once and tell all. If the killer confesses, he will be spared by being sent into exile. "I charge that none who dwell within this land, whereof I hold the power and the throne, give this man shelter whoever he may be. . . . I further pray, that, if at my own hearth he dwells known to me in my own home, I may suffer myself the curse I just now uttered."

> **COMMENT:** This is one of many examples of Sophoclean *dramatic irony* in this play. Here, for example, Oedipus swears a terrible curse on the murderer, unaware that he himself is that man! Dramatic irony always involves an added meaning to a situation of which the character himself is unaware. Watch for them in this play; they are supremely effective.

The blind soothsayer, *Teiresias,* now enters led by a boy. Immediately *Oedipus* demands that he reveal the name of the murderer of the former king of Thebes so that the curse of the plague will be lifted from the city.

The prophet pretends ignorance, which at once sends Oedipus into a rage: "I am so angry. Know that you seem to me creator of the deed and worker too in all, short of slaughter; if you were not blind, I would say this crime was your work alone!"

Under the smarts of this charge, the angry prophet blurts out that Oedipus himself is the murderer of Laius!

Again Oedipus, in his blind fury, angrily acuses Teiresias of complicity in a plot (with Creon) to overthrow him, "a crooked swindler who has got his eyes on gain alone, but in his art is blind." Oedipus goes on to declare that the prophet was not even able to solve the riddle of the Sphinx!

The *Chorus,* as usual, deplores the display of anger on both sides; "Such is not our need, but to find out how best we shall discharge Apollo's orders."

In a ringing and angry prophecy the soothsayer predicts Oedipus will be an exile, blind, "and there shall be no harbour for your cry . . . there shall never be a mortal man eradicated more wretchedly than you." But the unhearing Oedipus pays his words little heed.

FIRST STASIMON (463-511):   The *Elders* are apprehensive about the predictions of Teiresias, yet remain loyal to their king. They cannot believe that their saviour from the Sphinx could possibly be the sought-for murderer.

SECOND EPISODE (512-862):   *Creon* enters only to be faced with the charge of plotting treason, *Oedipus* even going so far as accusing him of plotting against his life.

Creon defends himself against the unjust accusations from the hot-tempered Oedipus. Creon says, "I am prudent yet, no lover of such plots, nor would I ever endure others' treason." The *Chorus* speaks well of his rationality and calm defense; they say, "A cautious man would say he has spoken well. O king, the quick to think are never sure."

Jocasta now enters when she hears the raised and angry voices. She tries to calm her husband and her brother, who by now is himself angry. Oedipus orders Creon to leave; *Creon* leaves, saying, "I am on my way. You know me not, but these men (the Elders of Thebes) see me just."

Oedipus replies to his wife's questions as to the cause of the dispute by telling her that her brother Creon had used Teiresias as his tool in order to charge Oedipus with the killing of Laius.

Jocasta replies that the people know little about prophecies. She relates the story of Laius' avoiding the prophecy by abandoning his male child on Mount Cithaeron. She tells how her husband was killed where the three roads meet, the deed committed by robbers. Obviously then, Oedipus could not have been the murderer. The three roads' reference rings a bell in Oedipus' memory, and he is disturbed, especially since the time of Laius' murder coincided with his own arrival at the three-road intersection. (Note the dramatic irony of Jocasta's intention of reassuring her husband; instead of assurance, Oedipus is afflicted with doubt.) Oedipus feels now that he indeed might have been the slayer of Laius.

Jocasta goes on to tell that a servant had escaped from the robbers who had killed Laius. This servant, upon finding Oedipus ruling as king in Laius' place, had asked to be allowed to work as a shepherd far away from Thebes.

Oedipus is more than ever disturbed: he tells Jocasta about his mother and father in Corinth, of the Delphic Oracle, of his leaving town, his encountering the stranger where the three roads meet, and of his killing him in a dispute over the right of way. Now he fears that he had killed Laius.

There is one hope left that Oedipus might not be the killer of Laius: Jocasta had told him that a large group of thieves had participated in the slaying. *Oedipus,* in a feverish search for the truth (even though the Chorus and others had told him repeatedly to leave well enough alone—to let sleeping dogs lie), bids his wife to send for the servant who had successfully escaped from the robbers. Surely "if he still says the selfsame number, I could not have killed him, since one man does not equal many men. But if he speaks of a single lonely traveller, the scale of guilt now clearly falls to me." They both enter the palace.

> **COMMENT:** As Oedipus desperately searches for the iden-tity of the killer of Laius, the net of Fate is inexorably closed around him. The *Chorus* at one point cries, "Enough, enough! When the land is pained, it seemed to us at this point we should stop."

> Ironically again, at the end of the scene, Jocasta reassures him again that the oracle is not to be trusted.

SECOND STASIMON (863-910): The *Chorus* sings an ode: "Pride breeds the tyrant . . . it hurls to a dire fate where no foot-hold is found. Men who are haughty in word and deed with no fear of the Right, with no piety for the gods (as in the case of Oedipus) . . . may evil doom seize him for his ill-fated pride. . . . Men now hold light the fading oracles . . . and nowhere is Apollo clearly honored; things divine are going down to ruin." Although the Chorus do not mean anyone in particular, the ode clearly points to Oedipus himself as the man guilty of pride and impiety, and hot-tempered disrespect at the cost of reason.

THIRD EPISODE (911-1185):   *Jocasta* enters and prays to Apollo.

Then a *Messenger* from Corinth enters with good news while she is praying: Polybus, king of Corinth and the supposed father of Oedipus, is dead; moreover, the people of Cornith wish his son to be the new king.

Oedipus enters and hears the "good" news and both he and Jocasta are joyous in their relief: since his father is dead, they no longer need fear the oracle that states he is to kill his father. But there is still the matter of the oracle's prophecy that he will marry his mother.

At this point the Messenger, in an (ironic and unintentional) attempt to reassure them on that score relates a bit of past history: he tells Oedipus that he is not really the child of King Polybus and his wife Merope. Indeed, it was the Messenger himself that had found the foot-bound baby on the slopes of Mount Cithaeron; he had given the abandoned child to the childless King of Corinth, who had brought up Oedipus as his own son.

By now *Jocasta* realizes that her own husband was that very child that she and Laius had tied and abandoned on Mount Cithaeron! She pleads with her husband to not brood in vain on what has just been said: "Don't, by the gods, investigate this more if you care for your own life. I am sick enough," but *Oedipus* is steelily determined to pursue the truth, come what may: "Let whatever will break forth. I plan to see the seed of my descent, however small." He believes that she has warned him out of fear that he will discover that he is of humble origins.

Jocasta rushes into the palace crying, "Alas, alas, hapless man. I have this alone to tell you, and nothing else forevermore!"

The proud *Oedipus* calls himself the "son of Fortune, giver of the good . . . nor shall I cease to search out my descent."

The *Chorus* is delighted to find that Oedipus is a native of Thebes; they echo Oedipus' own proud joy of possession. They sing of his possible divine origins from Hermes or Bacchus (note the irony even in the joy of the Chorus). Now the *shepherd* for whom Oedipus has sent is brought in. He had worked for Laius; haltingly and unwillingly he reveals that Oedipus is indeed the son of Laius. He confesses the truth—that he was told to expose the child of Laius and Jocasta on the mountain, but he was seized with pity and gave the infant to another shepherd, the very shepherd who came from Corinth bearing the information that Polybus was dead. "If you are he whom this man speaks of, you were born curst by fate."

At this fateful news, terrible and tragic *Oedipus* cries out:

> "O light, for the last time now I look upon you;
> I am shown to be born from those I ought not to have been.
> I married the woman I should not have married,
> I killed the man whom I should not have killed."

Oedipus gives a wretched cry of woe and rushes into the palace with horror in his eyes.

THIRD STASIMON (1186-1222): The *Chorus* sings a tragic ode (note contrast with second Stasimon) warning others of the fate of Oedipus. They indicate sorrow for the woebegone man. "All seeing Time has discovered all. . . . Alas, child of Laius, would I had never seen you."

EXODOS (1223-1530): A *Messenger* issues from the palace relating that Jocasta has just committed suicide after moaning, "the bed on which by double curse she bore husband to husband, children to child." Then he tells how Oedipus with a horrible shout leaped within, after wrenching the double doors from their sockets, and "there beheld his wife hung by her neck from twisted cords, swinging to and fro. . . . He tore the golden brooch pins from her clothes, and raised them up, and struck his own eyeballs, shouting such words as these:

> " 'No more shall you
> Behold the evils I have suffered and done.'
> . . . Moaning such cries, not once but many times
> he raised and struck his eyes. The bloody pupils
> bedewed his beard. The gore oozed not in drops,
> but poured in a black shower, a hail of blood."

Oedipus now issues from the palace and bewails the tragic workings of fate. He has murdered his father, bred children with his own mother, "And if there is any evil older than evil left, it is the lot of Oedipus."

The *Chorus* and *Oedipus* sing alternately of his tragic sorrows and horrible sufferings. (These lines are known as the *kommos*—lines of song indicating woe and suffering on the part of the protagonist

—usually in alternating stanzas with the Chorus.) *Creon* now enters (he is the new king), and Oedipus asks for exile from the land; but Creon says that he must first discover Apollo's will in the matter.

Antigone and *Ismene* are brought out on stage. Oedipus hugs them weeping: "Your father's eyes, once bright, to see like this. . . . Who then will wed you?"

Creon will not let the daughters accompany their father into exile, and the play ends with the *Chorus* asking, "What citizen on his [Oedipus"] lot did with envy gaze? See to how great a surge of dread fate he has come! So I would say a mortal man, while he is watching to see the final day, can have no happiness till he pass the bound of life, nor be relieved of pain." In other words, "Judge no man happy until his whole life has been lived."

INTERPRETATION:
OEDIPUS THE KING, QUESTIONS AND ANSWERS

What did Aristotle think of this play?

ANSWER: He mentioned it eleven times in his famous piece of literary criticism, the *Poetics*. He thought it was the well-nigh perfect tragedy. He especially found its recognition scenes admirable, its sudden reversals of fortune stunning, and its plot most perfectly accomplished and constructed. Jean Cocteau found the plot so perfectly and mechanically engineered that he called his adaptation of it *The Infernal Machine*.

What does Oedipus the King say about the place of Fate and Free Will in man's life?

ANSWER: Most students finish this play with the idea that *Fate* to the Greeks was an irrevocable, pre-determined fore-ordained scheme of life laid down for all men by the gods. In such a world there can be no *free will*, no choice between alternatives, no say as to one's future. Oedipus' tragic life seems to have been unalterably determined for him by the oracles of the gods. Free will, if it exists at all is an illusion. More than that, the more man tries to lay out a path different than that fixed by Destiny, the more man is sure to follow that path.

But all this is a misreading of the play and a misunderstanding of Greek character and will. Oedipus does follow a predetermined path, but he follows it because there is that in his nature that wills it. He fled his foster-parents without first making a thorough inquiry into his birth; he felt intellectually challenged enough to demonstrate his intelligence by solving the riddle of the Sphinx; he chose to marry a woman old enough to be his mother. He allows his passions and quick temper to rule his better instincts: he denounces the high priest as a traitor; he accuses his brother-in-law of treachery; he fiercely and doggedly pursues the truth at his own cost and that of the people nearest and dearest to him. He displays impiety towards the gods, hot anger towards the well-intentioned, and intellectual inquiry beyond the bounds of reason: all these are summed up in his *hybris*, his lack of common sense or well-rounded wisdom.

As for Fate, that is only a term for the way life turns out for all men, not how all was predetermined from the beginning. Vengeance for our deeds implies free will to act in the manner which called for retribution.

"Even if everything is determined, we have no way of knowing what the total pattern is, so we must act on our own best judgment; free will is, therefore, a necessary illusion. Apparently wise men attain some insight into this pattern (or are given it by the gods), but all of us have the freedom to disregard such insight, follow our own desires, and suffer the consequences (Walter Agard)." In fact, there can be no real *human suffering* if there is no free will. Indeed, the characters of Sophocles' plays have more free will than that of most other characters in Greek drama.

What is Sophocles' view of human suffering then?

ANSWER:

Bowra: "The central idea of a Sophoclean tragedy is that through suffering a man learns to be modest before the gods."

Sheppard: "His Oedipus stands for human suffering, and he neither attempts, like Aeschylus, to justify the evil nor presumes, like Euripides, to deny its divine origin."

Zimmern: "Sophocles' difficulty is the problem of suffering as Aeschylus' is the problem of sin."

Lind: "All Oedipus had to do to avoid his fate, if he had made the attempt to do so, was not to run away from Corinth, not to take the road to Thebes, not to kill an old man on that road even in self-defense, and certainly not to answer the riddle of the Sphinx."

Discuss dramatic irony in the play.

ANSWER: The lines of this play are filled with a peculiar kind of double meaning known by the critics as *dramatic irony*. There is a constant wide gap between the one meaning of which the audience is aware and the other known only to the players; and it is the emotional surge between the awarenesses of these two meanings that give the play such awful force and such tremendous emotional impact:

1. Oedipus is blindest when he calls the soothsayer blind.

2. Oedipus is cursing himself when he thinks he is cursing the slayer of Laius.

3. Oedipus can answer the impossible Sphinx-riddle, but has no answer to the riddle of his own existence.

4. Every attempt to help his subjects of Thebes only serves to bring more harm upon himself.

5. Every attempt he makes to avert danger only serves to bring it nearer.

What is the chief imagery-pattern throughout?

ANSWER: Throughout the play the one pattern that is outstanding is that of *sight* and *blindness*, of *light* and *darkness*.

What is one of the most horrible scenes in all literature?

ANSWER: The scene of the blinded Oedipus with dark blood streaming from his pin-stabbed eyes: "Not Dante's Ugolino gnawing his child's skull in the dungeon, Lear mad on the heath, Marlowe's Barabas in his cauldron, the handmaidens hanging from the rafters in *Odyssey*, or Ganelon drawn apart by horses in the *Song of Roland*," exceeds in horror this scene of the King of Thebes blinded when he sees all! (Kilto)

Discuss another major theme—the "free spirit of inquiry"—in this play.

ANSWER: The free spirit of inquiry (*historia*) attains tragic heights in this play: while pursuing truth to its farthest reaches, Oedipus glimpses the face of truth through a glass darkly, but it is truth—face to face. The result of such knowledge is blindness and exile. In a later play we shall see that it also brings Oedipus immortality (*Oedipus at Colonus*). The play is really the archetypal play for all heroes who venture on quests in search of themselves.

What about the Oedipus Complex?

ANSWER: Freud used the term loosely without much reference to this play, which is the source of the expression. For Freud all male children are instinctively and sexually desirous of possessing their mothers, as well as instinctively desirous of wishing to slay their fathers as rivals for the mothers' affection. One can see immediately that such a situation has little foundation in Sophocles' play: Oedipus has no such instincts, and such a concept would have horrified Sophocles most of all. Indeed, the concept of blind fate operates most exclusively in the Freudian concept, much more so than among the Greeks.

List some of the main ideas to be found in the play.

ANSWER:

1. Suffering only can bring man knowledge and awareness.

2. Man is individually and solely responsible for his own behavior.

3. To set human reason above strict obedience to the gods is an act of pride (*hybris*), which will lead to retribution (*ate*) at the hands of the gods.

4. Fate for man contains within it a myriad complex of ironies.

5. The tragic and fateful consequences to man for a display of excessive pride.

How heroic is Oedipus in his struggle to attain self-knowledge?

ANSWER: He is magnificently heroic, more so than most men: in his quest for self-knowledge Oedipus uncovers and discovers qualities within himself of which he had been unaware—such as a profound capacity for intellectual honesty, so much so that it overcomes and subdues his overweening pride that had formerly inhibited his honesty. In addition, he exhibits a capacity and power for endurance that raises him to supreme heights.

What was Aristotle's definition of a tragic hero?

ANSWER: Aristotle's definition of a tragic hero was based largely upon his reading of *Oedipus the King*: tragedy deals with a man of high estate, but no saint, who suffers a downfall, not through depravity or vice, but from some aspect of human weakness. The tragic hero must be:

1. Of high rank in life so that his fall assumes greatness.

2. He must be essentially a good man in order to win the sympathy of the onlookers.

3. He must be hurt enough so that the onlookers are instilled with pity and fear, the pity arising from the unjust treatment accorded the hero.

Were the dice of destiny loaded against Oedipus?

ANSWER: It seems so; his blind rashness was not excessive enough for the fate accorded him. Certainly, such rashness and anger as he displayed were not beyond the norms of humanity. In a sense the gods were obviously not just to Oedipus: his incest was innocent, his murder of his father performed in ignorance and self-defense. Even his suspicions of Teiresias were not abnormal—the Delphic oracle could at times be corrupted.

SOPHOCLES

ELECTRA (ca. 418-414 B.C.)

BACKGROUND: Sophocles initiates some changes on the mythical background of the House of Atreus:

1. Agamemnon is murdered by his wife Clytemnestra and her lover Aegisthus. Then Electra, the daughter of Agamemnon and Clytemnestra, sends her brother Orestes to the town of Phocis in order to save him from harm at the hands of his mother and her lover. Accompanying Orestes in refuge is a loyal old servant.

2. Clytemnestra weds her lover Aegisthus; they rule Mycenae most despotically, all the while subjecting Electra to the most humiliating mistreatment for her unswerving loyalty to the memory of her dead father.

3. The woebegone and despairing Electra prays daily that her brother will return and avenge the death of their father.

4. Orestes in Phocis has been ordered by the oracle at Delphi (Apollo) to wreak vengeance upon his mother and her lover for the murder of his father.

5. Orestes obeys the oracle, and the play opens with his arrival in Mycenae with the loyal old servant who had accompanied him when he had fled Mycenae before. With Orestes is his close friend Pylades.

SETTING: Before the palace of Clytemnestra at Mycenae.

CHARACTERS

ELECTRA (ee LEK truh): daughter of the murdered King Agamemnon and his wife Clytemnestra.

CHRYSOTHEMIS (kriss SAW them iss): Electra's sister.

CLYTEMNESTRA (kly tem NESS truh): slayer of her husband Agamemnon and now living with her lover Aegisthus.

ORESTES (oh RESS teez): long-absent brother of Electra.

AEGISTHUS (ee JISS thooss): the usurper-king of Argos, and Clytemnestra's consort, who abetted in the murder.

PYLADES (PILL uh deez): son of Strophius of Phocis, Orestes' cousin and loyal companion.

OLD MAN: attendant of Orestes.

CHORUS: Mycenaean (my sin EE uhn) women.

SUMMARY:　*Orestes, Pylades,* and the *Paedogogus* (old servant) enter the town of Mycenae. Orestes tells his old servant to enter the palace and spread the lie that he has hurried from Phocis to Mycenae to tell of the news of Orestes' death.

Meanwhile, Orestes and Pylades go to Agamemnon's grave to pay their respects. They plan to display an urn which they will claim contains the ashes of the cremated Orestes. The three leave the stage.

Electra now enters alone and she bewails her miserable life at the palace and her murdered and unavenged father. The *Chorus of Mycenaean Women* join in her lamentations. They caution her to be more calm in her display of grief, and to be less recklessly rebellious in the face of her mother and Aegisthus.

Electra cannot be calm or temperate. She bitterly and violently hates both her mother and Aegisthus. Moreover, she is resentful of their mistreatment of her.

Chrysothemis, Electra's sister, enters, and there is an argument over Electra's behavior. Chrysothemis recommends obedience to the rulers in spite of the two sisters' common hatred of the usurpers (this recalls a similar scene between Antigone and Ismene in Sophocles' *Antigone*). Electra berates her sister for her meekness and compromise with evil.

Chrysothemis relates how her mother had a dream about her dead husband which terrified her; and how she had sent Chrysothemis with propitiatory libations to be poured on Agamemnon's tomb. Electra persuades her sister to replace their mother's offerings with locks of their own hair upon their dead father's tomb.

Chrysothemis leaves and the Chorus tell how Justice will yet triumph in the House of Atreus.

Clytemnestra enters, scolds Electra for her abuse of her mother and Aegisthus; she justifies her murder of Agamemnon by telling how he had cruelly sacrificed their daughter Iphigenia in the cause of the Trojan War. (Sophocles justifies Agamemnon's slaying of Iphigenia much more sympathetically than does Aeschylus in the *Oresteia*.) Electra still continues to denounce her mother, who threatens her with harm. The old *servant* of Orestes enters and announces Orestes' death.

Electra wails in great grief, but her mother simply inquires after more details. Clytemnestra pretends sorrow at the news, but internally she gloats over the news. Clytemnestra and the old servant enter the palace.

Chrysothemis enters and relates how she had found a lock of hair on the tomb belonging to her brother. She is certain he is here in Mycenae, but Electra tells her the news of Orestes' death. When Chrysothemis refuses to join her in killing their mother and her lover, Electra resolves to accomplish the vengeance herself now that her brother is dead.

Orestes and *Pylades* enter, bearing the so-called ashes of the dead Orestes. Orestes reveals his true identity to his weeping sister and they wildly express their joy at the mutual recognition of brother and sister. The old man tells them to enter the palace now and do their deed—while Clytemnestra is alone. They all enter the palace. Electra appears and informs the Chorus that Orestes and Pylades are about to murder Clytemnestra, who is heard shrieking and begging for mercy. Orestes and Pylades enter and relate how they had killed Clytemnestra, but quickly scamper within at the arrival of *Aegisthus*. After Aegisthus recognizes the dead corpse of his wife, Orestes orders him to enter the palace to be killed on the same spot where Agamemnon had been murdered.

The *Chorus* express their joy at the vengeance of Orestes, who declares the woes of the House of Atreus at an end.

INTERPRETATION: *ELECTRA*, QUESTIONS AND ANSWERS

What was the focus of each of the playwrights who have treated this subject?

ANSWER: All three dramatists (Aeschylus, Sophocles, Euripides) have written plays about Orestes and Electra:

1. Sophocles in this play indicates sympathy with Orestes and his sister; their murder of Clytemnestra was a just vengeance, and approved by the gods.

2. Aeschylus focuses on Orestes and the great moral predicament, resolved later by compromise in the *Eumenides*.

3. Euripides concentrates on the psychology of Orestes and Electra, the resultant portrait being none too flattering.

What is the role of Chrysothemis?

ANSWER: Her role is to debate the issue with her sister Electra. They represent opposing points of view in relation to the problem of reacting to evil: Electra is defiant, rebellious, reckless and foolhardy; Chrysothemis, on the other hand, also condemns evil and tyranny, but she cautions obedience and submission, avoidance of reckless behavior. It is Sophocles' tactic to create characters to represent single, clear points of view: there are no Hamlets in Greek drama until Euripides.

How are Aegisthus and Clytemnestra portrayed?

ANSWER: They are portrayed as immersed in evil and deserving of death for their evil ways. They are both adulterers and murderers of King Agamemnon—more than that, they are also usurpers. Sophocles shows his approval of Orestes' and Electra's deeds by the comments of the Chorus, who say that the two have acted under the nodding approval of Justice and the gods. Electra is a true heroine in contrast to the evil rulers: she is noble, principled, fiercely clinging to her sense of justice and right.

GREEK TRAGEDY: SOPHOCLES

PHILOCTETES (409 B.C.)

BACKGROUND: When the Greek fleet stopped on its way to Troy at the island of Lemnos in order to take on fresh water, Philoctetes was bitten by a snake. Soon the wound festered and stank continuously, whereupon the Greeks decide to leave Philoctetes on Lemnos with his bow and arrows, which had been given him by the great Heracles.

The prophecy was that Troy could not be won without the bow and arrow of Philoctetes, and accordingly Odysseus and Neoptolemus (Diomedes in the epic version) are sent to bring back Philoctetes with his bow and arrows. Their orders are to obtain the weapons and their owner by hook or crook, fair means or foul.

SETTING: The desert island of Lemnos off Greece in the Aegean sea. Philoctetes had been abandoned on the island for ten years.

CHARACTERS

ODYSSEUS (oh DISS ooz): King of Ithaca, the most cunning of the Greek leaders.

NEOPTOLEMUS (NEE op TALL ee muhss): son of Achilles, sent along with Odysseus to obtain Philoctetes and his weapons.

PHILOCTETES (fill ok TEE teez): son of Poeas and owner of the bow and arrows of Heracles.

SAILOR: disguised as a Merchant Captain.

HERACLES: son of Zeus and Alcmene of Thebes.

SAILORS: as Chorus from the crew of Neoptolemus.

MATE: of the ship.

SUMMARY: *Odysseus, Neoptolemus,* and *Chorus of Greek sailors* enter and approach the cave that has served as Philoctetes' home for ten years. Neoptolemus sees rags stained from Philoctetes' snake-bite wound lying to dry in the sun.

Odysseus tells Neoptolemus how he must use trickery in order to get Philoctetes to accompany them back to Troy. Neoptolemus reluctantly accepts Odysseus' plan.

Philoctetes enters and Neoptolemus introduces himself as the son of Achilles, even pretending he is unaware of Philoctetes' name. Philoctetes tells his own story, begging the gods to avenge the crime done against him by the Greek leaders, especially Agamemnon, Menelaus, and Odysseus. Neoptolemus expresses sympathy, pretending that he too is angry with the Greeks for having awarded his father's arms to Odysseus. Neoptolemus promises to take Philoctetes back to his homeland in Greece, which is not far from Neoptolemus' own home in Oeta.

Two sailors enter, one in the disguise of a Merchant Captain. The Captain has been sent by Odysseus to "warn" Neoptolemus that the Greek leaders are coming to force Neoptolemus and Odysseus to accompany them to Troy. Philoctetes declares he will never go to Troy, and urges Neoptolemus to get ready to sail for Greece— not Troy! Philoctetes gives his famous bow to Neoptolemus to hold and examine. They enter the cave.

Philoctetes cries out in pain over his stinking and festering wound that he has endured for ten years. While Philoctetes sleeps, Neoptolemus refuses to run off with the bow and arrows. Ashamed, he reveals the plot to Philoctetes. Odysseus enters and threatens force, but Philoctetes would rather die than go to Troy. Odysseus and Neoptolemus leave Philoctetes, taking the bow with them. Soon Neoptolemus returns to atone for his trickery and to return the bow. Odysseus departs, threatening to bring back a band of men.

Neoptolemus argues that it is in Philoctetes' self interest to go to Troy: his wound will heal and he will do great deeds on the battlefield. Philoctetes refuses, preferring his pain and his hate of the Greeks; Neoptolemus gives in and agrees to take Philoctetes to his home in Greece.

Just as they are about to leave Lemnos, the mighty god Heracles suddenly appears (does he symbolize the heroic nature of Philoctetes?), and orders Philoctetes to turn back and go to Troy. Heracles predicts that with his mighty bow he will kill Paris and help to bring about the fall of Troy itself. Philoctetes gladly promises to obey; he bids farewell to Lemnos, a place he had fallen in love with, the scene of ten years of suffering.

INTERPRETATION: *PHILOLTETES*, QUESTIONS AND ANSWERS

How do most critics regard the central problem of this play?

ANSWER: They regard the play as representing the conflict between the demands of the individual and the demands of society. Edmund Wilson (*The Wound and the Bow*) finds the two chief symbols to be the artist's fraility and his power: society must accept the artist's weaknesses and disabilities as well as his talents.

What makes for the unusual and attractive atmosphere of the play?

ANSWER:

1. The Chorus of old Greek sailors.

2. The sea-coast setting, and the cave of Philoctetes.

3. Philoctetes' lyric, final farewell to his beloved island of Lemnos.

4. The happy ending.

What is the central ethical purpose of the play?

ANSWER: Its central ethical purpose is to disclose the villainy of Odysseus to Neoptolemus and to indicate its effect upon him. The play is not a true tragedy in the Aristotelian sense; rather it is a kind of morality play in realistic form. Neoptolemus is tempted to cooperate with the evil Odysseus, but his better nature wins out: he will not win glory at the expense of the wretched Philoctetes. Finally, the *deus ex machina* (Heracles) solves his ethical problem.

SOPHOCLES

OEDIPUS AT COLONUS (c. 409 B.C.)

BACKGROUND: See *Oedipus the King* Background. After Oedipus has blinded himself for having committed incest and parricide, he is allowed to stay in Thebes until Creon and the others decide that his presence constitutes a desecration and pollution of the city. They order him to leave. His sons Polyneices and Eteocles do nothing to help him remain; but his two daughters, Ismene and Antigone, do care for him. Antigone accompanies him in his wanderings.

Meanwhile, in a struggle over power, Eteocles, with Creon's help, banishes his brother Polyneices who flees to Argos, where he marries the daughter to the king (Adrastus). He persuades the king to wage war on Thebes.

During this time Oedipus and Antigone have arrived at the grove of the *Eumenides* (the Kindly Goddesses) at Colonus, a small suburb near Athens.

SETTING: Colonus, before the grove of the Kindly Goddesses.

CHARACTERS

OEDIPUS (EE dih puss): exiled King of Thebes.

ANTIGONE (an TIG oh nee): his daughter.

ISMENE (iz MEE nee): his daughter.

CITIZEN: of Colonus.

THESEUS (THEE sooz): King of Athens.

CREON: uncle to Oedipus, former king of Thebes after Oedipus' self-imposed blindness.

MESSENGER

CHORUS: of Elderly Citizens of Colonus.

SUMMARY: The old and blind *Oedipus* enters, led by his daughter *Antigone*. They are at the grove of the Kindly Goddesses. A stranger enters and tells Oedipus to leave the grove.

Oedipus now realizes that he has reached the very place that the gods have arranged for the scene of his death. Oedipus tells the stranger to tell his king (Theseus) that the land that shows him hospitality will be blessed by the gods. *The prophecy*: the land that banishes him will be cursed; the land that buries him will be blessed.

The *Chorus* berates Oedipus for his hideous past, but Antigone defends her father eloquently. Oedipus too defends himself, saying that his deeds of incest and parricide were done in complete ignorance and innocence. The Chorus is visibly affected by their appeals; but they say the decision is up to the king.

Ismene enters and relates that Polyneices and the Argive troops are about to attack Thebes. Creon now needs Oedipus near Thebes, for the oracles declare only his presence can save the city from capture by Polyneices.

Oedipus complains of his neglectful and greedy sons; he hopes that the gods will allow neither to rule Thebes; as for himself—he will never return to Thebes!

Under the Chorus' direction Oedipus performs rites of atonement to the Kindly Goddesses (*Eumenides*) since he has trespassed in their sacred grove.

Theseus enters. He treats Oedipus kindly and with cordial welcome, calling him a citizen of Athens.

The *Chorus* sings an ode of beautiful praise to their city.

Creon now enters and tries to persuade his brother-in-law to return to Thebes—but Oedipus angrily rejects his offer.

Creon says that Ismene is his prisoner, and he now seizes Antigone and leaves for Thebes.

Theseus enters and pursues Creon's men, soon returning with the two daughters.

Polyneices enters and beseeches his father's aid; but Oedipus violently turns him down, ordering him to leave, adding a curse that one day he will die at the hands of his own kin and he (Polyneices) will in turn slay Eteocles, his brother.

Polyneices bids his sister a sad farewell and leaves to meet his doom (he will be slain by his brother, who in turn will be slain by him as foretold by Oedipus).

Theseus enters, and Oedipus conducts him to a secret place where Oedipus will die in peace. This place will forever be a sacred defense against Athens' enemies.

A *Messenger* announces Oedipus' death: only Theseus knows how and where he has died. He relates that the death was a peaceful and gentle one—a mysterious transition from life into death.

The daughters enter weeping and are comforted by the Chorus; they are told that they may not approach the sacred place of the scene of their father's death—it is forbidden for any mortal to know the secret place. Antigone and Ismene now decide to return to their native Thebes.

INTERPRETATION: *OEDIPUS AT COLONUS,* QUESTIONS AND ANSWERS

When was this play written and produced?

ANSWER: It was written when Sophocles was about ninety— just before his death. The play was produced posthumously in 401 B.C. Sparta at about this time had decisively shattered the Athenian forces in battle.

Is there civic progaganda in the play?

ANSWER: Indeed there is: the play is quite patriotic in its fervid belief in Athens as the city of refuge, hospitality, and kindliness. Athens is idealized and placed under the divine guard of the gods.

What does the play teach essentially?

ANSWER:

1. How a great hero like Oedipus, despite his faults and inadvertent sins, is raised to divine immortality by the gods.

2. True piety is help to your fellow-man. The gods who incarnate Oedipus are reconciled. Suffering and adversity have their divine plan.

GREEK TRAGEDY: EURIPIDES

LIFE (480-406 B.C.): Euripides (you RIP ih deez) is, along with Aeschylus and Sophocles one of the three greatest Greek writers of tragedy. He was the son of Mnesarchus, a middle-class landholder. His mother Cleito, a noblewoman, and he were very close (but see the attacks upon her by the comic poet Aristophanes, who called her a greengrocer of bad vegetables). He was an excellent athlete and a good soldier. He studied under Anaxagoras (who was banished from Athens for impiety), and later, under the Sophists, Prodicus and Protagoras. Socrates was a lifelong friend of his, and it is said that Socrates saw only the plays of his friend Euripides on the stage. Sophism preached rationalism in religion and life; and its stress was intellectual—hence the stress on intellectualism in his plays.

He married once only and had three sons; in his adult life he lived apart from society at Salamis; and from his cave overlooking the sea, he wrote his great plays.

About 408 B.C., at the age of seventy-two, he went into voluntary exile because:

1. he had opposed the war party in its battles against the Spartans—the Peloponnesian War;

2. he was unorthodox in his religious beliefs;

3. he was suspected of being immoral in character and deed because of subversive speeches made by certain characters in his plays.

He spent his last days at the court of King Archelaus of Macedonia, in talented and artistic company. The king refused to ship his remains back to his home city of Athens.

Out of a possible 92 plays he had won only four times in the contests. His *Cyclops* is the only complete satyr play to have survived from ancient Greece. (Satyr plays dealt with grotesque portions of ancient legends; the chorus dressed to resemble satyrs, the language and gestures were often obscene in character. They were usually performed after a course of three tragedies had been performed.)

Eighteen of his plays survive in addition to his *Cyclops*:

Alcestis, 438 B.C.
Medea, 431 B.C.
Hippolytus, 428 B.C.
Trojan Women, 415 B.C.
Helen, 412 B.C.
Orestes, 408 B.C.
Iphigenia at Aulis, 405 B.C.
Bacchae, 405 B.C.
Andromache, 426 B.C.
Hecuba, c. 425 B.C.
Mad Hercules c. 422 B.C.
Suppliants, 421 B.C.
Ion, c. 417 B.C.
Iphigenia in Tauris c. 413 B.C.
Electra, 413 B.C.
Phoenician Women, c. 410 B.C.

CHARACTERISTICS OF EURIPIDES:

1. He preferred situations showing violent stress; his characters are generally gripped by violent passions in which they are torn by conflicting desires.

2. He drew scenes of ordinary life much more realistically than any other of his contemporary dramatists.

3. He questioned the orthodox beliefs in religion, morality, and politics. His views often scandalized the public.

4. There is much variety of mood in his plays.

5. He admired the heroic in man; he loved the beautiful things in nature.

6. He was especially keen in his knowledge of women.

EURIPIDES

ALCESTIS (438 B.C.)

BACKGROUND: Admetus in Greek mythology is the son of Pheres and king of Pherae in Thessaly. Zeus kills Asclepius for restoring Hippolytus to life. Apollo, the father of Asclepius, takes vengeance on the Cyclopes (who forged the thunderbolts with which Zeus had slain his son), and slays them. To expiate his crime Apollo is made to serve as a serf under Admetus, who treated his royal serf most gently. Out of gratitude, Apollo cajoled the Fates into granting Admetus longer life (he had been due for an early death). The Fates consented, with the proviso that at the hour chosen for his death he obtain a substitute ready to die in his place. Now the fateful day of his death has arrived, and only Admetus' wife, Alcestis, is willing to offer herself as his substitute in death.

SETTING: At Pherae, outside the palace of Admetus, king of Thessaly.

CHARACTERS

APOLLO: the god of sunlight.

DEATH.

CHORUS: Old Men of Pherae.

ALCESTIS (al SESS tiss): the queen, wife of Admetus.

ADMETUS (ad MEE tuhss): king of Thessaly.

EUMELUS (you MEE luhss): their child.

HERACLES (HAIR uh kleez): the heroic savior.

PHERES (FEER eez): father of Admetus.

A MAN SERVANT.

SUMMARY

PROLOGUE (lines 1-76): *Apollo* issues from the palace and relates the background given above. Already Alcestis is in the process of death. *Death* enters with a sword in his hand; he scolds Apollo for having cheated him of Admetus. After an exchange with Death (some of it in jest), attempting to persuade him not to take Alcestis (the attempt is unsuccessful), Apollo declares that a man shall "be a guest in the house of Admetus, and by force shall he tear this woman from you!" Apollo goes out, with Death gazing at him in scorn. Death enters the palace by the open main door with sword in hand to shear a lock of the victim's hair, a symbolic sign of death.

PARODOS (77-140):   The *Chorus* of old men sing a lament over the imminent death of Alcestis: "Ah! to roll back the wave of our woe, O Healer, Appear!" They go on to sing her praises.

FIRST EPISODE (141-434):   A *handmaiden* of Alcestis tells the *Chorus* that her mistress has already donned her robes of death, has prayed for her children, and has said goodbye to her husband:

> "O my marriage-bed, wherein I loosed my virgin girdle to him for whom I die! Farewell! I have no hatred for you. Only me you lose. Because I held faith to you and to my lord—I must die. Another woman shall possess you, not more chaste indeed than I, more fortunate perhaps."

The Chorus laments at Alcestis' woe.

Admetus enters with his wife, *Alcestis,* who is borne on a litter; their two children trail the litter.

> **COMMENT:**   Why on earth is Alcestis taken outside the palace to die? One reason is supplied by her opening words of delirium: "Sun, and you, light of day, Vast whirlings of swift cloud! O Earth, O roof-tree of my home, Bridal-bed of my country, Iolcus!"

Admetus begs her not to leave him, but she reminds him of the gift of life he has as a result of her death, a gift not even his parents would give up for their son's sake.

She begs him never to place another woman over their children, to which Admetus fervidly consents: "And since I held you living as my wife, so, when dead, you only shall be called my wife. . . . O my wife, not for one year but all my days, abhorring the woman who bore me, hating my father—for they loved me in words, not deeds. But you—to save my life you give the dearest thing you have!" Never shall the children have a stepmother, never shall he forget his beloved Alcestis! His wife bids him a touching farewell and dies. All mourn, and Admetus swears to eternal fidelity. Her body is borne back into the palace with Admetus and his children following.

FIRST STASIMON (435-476): The *Chorus* sing an ode in honor of Alcestis: "Far, far off is the best of women borne beyond the flood of Acheron in the two-oared boat! . . . But you, in your lively youth, died for him, and are gone from the light!"

SECOND EPISODE (477-577): *Heracles* enters clad in his usual lion skin and carrying his usual club; he is black-bearded and of gigantic strength. He is on one of his many labors (the fetching of the mares of Diomedes).

Admetus enters dressed in mourning and welcomes Heracles to his home. He does not mention the death of his wife, but manages to hint at someone (vaguely) who had died. On Heracles' offer to leave, Admetus insists that he stay, assuring that Heracles will be put up in a part of the palace where he will not hear the sound of lamentation. Heracles is led off to his quarters by attendants.

SECOND STASIMON (578-605): The *Chorus* sing the praises of the house of Admetus, where there is a bountiful lord, "ever open to many guests. . . . Even today he opened his house and received a guest, though his eyelids were wet with tears wept by the corpse of a dear bedfellow dead in the house."

THIRD EPISODE (606-861): *Admetus* enters leading the funeral procession of his wife. His father *Pheres* is berated by the son: "I am not your begotten son; or you surpass all men in cowardice, for, being at the very verge and end of life, you had neither courage nor will to die for your son." Pheres replies that

> "it is not a law of our ancestors or of Hellas that the fathers should die for the children! . . . You love to look upon the light of day—do you think your father hates it? I tell myself that we are a long time underground and that life is short, but sweet."

Admetus sends his father away, disowning him, and proceeds to lead the funeral procession to the funeral pyre.

A *servant* enters and tells about their strange guest: instead of mourning, he is thoroughly drunk on wine, crowning "his head with myrtle sprays, howling discordant songs."

Heracles reels on stage and scolds them all for their sad looks:

> "You see before you a man who is your Lord's friend, and you greet him with a gloomy, frowning face, because of your zeal about a strange woman's death. (Drinks) Come here, and let me make you a little wiser!"

At last a servant reveals to Heracles the fact that it is the wife of his host for whom they are mourning.

Heracles throws down his winecup and wine-skin, and tears off the wreath. He will rescue Alcestis from her existence in the underworld. He will go there and wrest her from the arms of black Death himself:

> "I shall watch for Death, the black-robed Lord of the Dead, and I know I shall find him near the tomb, drinking the blood of the sacrifices."

Heracles leaves on his promised mission to bring Alcestis back from the world of the dead.

KOMMOS (862-1007): *Admetus* and the *Chorus* exchange in song alternate strains of grief. Admetus bewails his loss: "But I, I who should have died, I have escaped my fate, only to drag out a wretched life." He covers his head and crouches in abject misery on the steps of his palace. The Chorus ask that Alcestis' memory be blessed: "She died for her lord; a blessed spirit is she now."

EXODOS (1008-1164): *Heracles* enters leading a veiled *woman*. He tells *Admetus* he has won her as a prize in a wrestling match. He offers his prize to Admetus as a gift, but Admetus, aware of his promise to his dying wife, declines: he will take no woman into his home! He begs Heracles to take this veiled woman away (she strongly resembles his own wife).

Heracles tells him that time will heal his grief; that one must not mourn forever. Finally, after much protesting, Admetus accepts the hand of the veiled figure, saying, "O King, you force me to this against my will." At this point Heracles takes off the veil and reveals Alcestis herself. Admetus is thunderstruck, thinking it a phantom, but soon takes her in his arms.

Heracles tells him how he had hid by her tomb and leaped upon Death, defeating him in the match.

ADMETUS: "But why is she speechless?"

HERACLES: "You may not hear her voice until she is purified from her consecration to the Lower Gods, and until the third dawn has risen. Lead her in."

Admetus announces a feast of joy as Heracles proceeds on his mission to capture the wild mares of Diomedes.

INTERPRETATION: *ALCESTIS*, QUESTIONS AND ANSWERS

Why is this play so unlike the typical Greek tragedy?

ANSWER: Because it was presented in place of the satyr play, which usually followed as the fourth play after a cycle of three tragedies. This is why there are both comic and tragic elements in this play.

What makes its theme unique in Greek tragedy?

ANSWER: The unique theme concerns self-sacrifice by a noble and more-than-loving wife who is nevertheless shown as all too human in her fear of death.

What is D. L. Drew's theory as to the identity of the veiled woman?

ANSWER: That she is really the corpse of Alcestis—not a living woman!

Review Admetus' sacred promises to his dying wife.

ANSWER:

1. That he would mourn her forever after her death.

2. That he would never marry another woman.

3. That he would no longer entertain his friends with wine and song in his home.

4. That he would have a statue of her permanently lying by his side in his marriage bed.

Obviously, most of the vows are soon broken!

Why did the deceived Heracles fetch Alcestis from Hades?

ANSWER:

1. Drew states that after having been deceived by his host, Heracles returned with a dead woman on stage whom he at first urges Admetus to keep until he returns from his ninth labor. At last, after Admetus' rather insincere protests, she is accepted. "Thus in a blood-curdling 150 lines at the end of the play, the dead wife of Admetus returns—to take him with her to the grave; a fit repayment for his treacherous and abominable behavior." (Drew)

2. The critic, Verrall, explains her silence as that of a trance instead of death itself; and that Heracles was indeed restoring the live wife to Admetus' bosom.

3. The silence of the veiled woman can easily be explained as it is in the play: on the basis of purification rites: that she is indeed the wife—alive—of Admetus, and that Heracles was truly grateful for the hospitality shown him by Admetus who tried to spare him the sad details of his wife's death; that Heracles need have felt no resentment at Admetus' deception, which was played in a good cause—that of exaggerated hospitality—for which the gods reward Admetus with his wife returned to life. Iolcus was famous for its hospitality.

What makes it possibly a chthonic myth, so regarded by K. O. Mueller?

ANSWER: Mueller saw the play as a chthonic myth—that is, an identification of underground gods with human beings:

1. Admetus = originally Pluto, god of the underworld, and

2. Alcestis = Persephone, his wife. After slaying the Python, Apollo was forced to serve under Pluto in Hades for a short while. By localizing the tale in Thessaly, Pluto becomes Admetus and Persephone his wife.

What are the comic elements in the play?

ANSWER:

1. The treatment of Death in the first scene.

2. The comic quarrel between Admetus and his father Pheres.

3. The drunkenness of Heracles and his comic surprise upon learning the truth.

Is Alcestis a favorite with artists?

ANSWER: Yes, indeed: see H. W. Hayley's text (1898), which lists all such representations in art. The theme was a favorite with the Etruscans, the Greeks, and the Romans. See also Robert Browning's *Balaustion's Adventure,* an adaptation of *Alcestis.*

GREEK TRAGEDY: EURIPIDES

MEDEA (431 B.C.)

BACKGROUND: Jason arrives in Colchis on the Black Sea in far off Crimea. He and the Greek heroes with him are searching for the fabulous Golden Fleece. With the help of Medea, the king's daughter, who was master of the arts of magic and enchantment, he secures the Fleece. Medea is passionately in love with Jason and does everything within her power to aid him in his dangerous mission. Medea is forced to flee the country with Jason, with her father in hot pursuit. To save her lover from capture, she slays her own brother and throws pieces of his body into the sea, where they are picked up by the grieving father. The delay saves Jason and his crew. Jason lives with Medea for some time in his homeland of Iolcus, but they are forced to flee after she kills Jason's wicked and treacherous uncle. Banished from Iolcus, Jason and Medea are given sanctuary in Corinth.

Here they raise two sons in the space of ten years, dwelling together in peace.

Then Creon, King of Corinth, offers the hand of his daughter in marriage to Jason. The husband of Medea consents to the match in spite of his foreign wife. Jason is now named as the successor to the throne in Corinth.

SETTING: In front of Medea's house in Corinth, about fifty miles west of Athens.

CHARACTERS

NURSE: to Medea; now her confidential handmaiden.

TUTOR: cares for Medea's children.

MEDEA (mee DEE uh): wife of Jason, who has deserted her for the daughter of King Creon.

CHORUS: women of Corinth.

CREON: king of Corinth.

JASON: husband of Medea, now son-in-law to King Creon.

AEGEUS (EE joos): king of Athens, offers refuge to Medea.

MESSENGER: brings news from the palace of Creon.

TWO CHILDREN: sons of Jason and Medea.

SUMMARY

PROLOGUE (lines 1-130): The *Nurse* comes out of the house and laments that Jason and the Argonauts have ever set out in quest of the Golden Fleece—then Medea would never have fallen in love with Jason, never would have tricked the daughters of Pelias into slaying their father, and never would have come to live in Corinth, where Jason has betrayed her and their children for King Creon's daughter.

The Nurse knows Medea's moods well and is afraid she will kill her two sons, or even kill Jason and his bride. The *Tutor* enters with the two children and asks the Nurse why she has left Medea alone.

Her grief, the Nurse replies, was unbearable, and she had to come outside and proclaim it aloud to the heavens.

> **COMMENT:** Euripides is always at great pains to motivate the exits and entrances of his characters; here he even explains the presence of the Nurse in what could have been left as the usual expository prologue of Greek tragedy.

The *Tutor* says that even worse misfortunes are in store for Medea: Creon plans to banish her and her two children.

The Nurse finds it shocking that Jason would permit such treatment of his own sons. She warns the Tutor to keep the children away from their mother because she is in a dangerous mood.

From inside the house comes Medea's voice, cursing Jason and the children.

That Medea should make the children suffer for their father's crime, the Nurse attributes to the nature of people in high places; unaccustomed to obedience and the suffering it imposes, they do not know how to suffer—when fortune turns against them, they strike back in every way they can. She recommends moderation as the only way to avoid misfortune.

PARODOS (131-213):   The *Chorus of Corinthian Women* enter, having heard the lamentations of Medea. They are curious to know what misfortune has befallen a house they have come to love.

Medea, offstage, cries out for her own death, and then for the death of Jason and his bride.

The Chorus ask the *Nurse* to bring her outside, hoping they can console her.

The Nurse offers to try, but sardonically adds that mankind has foolishly invented music and songs for banquets, where they are not needed, but can find no music to allay grief.

FIRST EPISODE (214-409):   *Medea,* completely self-possessed, emerges from the house. She proposes to justify herself, knowing the reputation people get by remaining silent. She appeals to the *Chorus* as women, who know the difficulties of a woman's lot: they must buy a husband at great price, and yet find they have set a tyrant over themselves; they cannot obtain divorces; they must adjust to new ways of living, having almost to be prophets to guess what will please husbands; they have to give birth to children, something far more painful than the wars men complain about. From the Chorus she begs one boon—silence, should she find some plan to avenge herself with.

Creon, King of Corinth, enters and tells Medea that she and her children have been banished from the city. He knows her reputation as a sorceress and has heard of her threats; he fears especially for his daughter.

Medea pleads for a 24-hour delay so she can find some place to go, and arrange some support for her two children.

Creon reluctantly grants her request, but acknowledges that he is probably making a mistake.

After he leaves, Medea tells the Chorus that she had fawned upon him only to gain time enough to effect her revenge. She vows to kill Jason, Creon, and his daughter. She ponders various methods and her means of escape after the crime; should worse come to worst, she vows to kill them with a sword and take her chances on escaping.

FIRST STASIMON (410-445):   The *Chorus* say that the way of the world is being reversed; that women are finally coming into their own; no longer will they be slandered for their faithlessness. Jason's behavior proves that the old oaths are honored no longer by men.

SECOND EPISODE (446-626):   *Jason* enters and *Medea* comes out of the house.

He accuses her of causing her own banishment by threatening Creon's family, and he wants to make some financial arrangements for her exile.

Medea says his coming to see her proves that he has reached the lowest possible condition: he no longer feels shame. She recites the crimes she had committed to help him, crimes which have cut her off from any possibility of obtaining refuge with her family. He does not even have the excuse that she has not borne him children, to justify his new marriage with Creon's daughter.

Jason maintains that she overrates her help to him and underrates the blessing he bestowed by bringing her to such a civilized country as Greece. He is remarrying, he says, to gain wealth and power for her and for their children—not because he does not love her or because he loves the princess.

She answers him by saying that had he really put the interests of his family first, he would have consulted her first, and not made a secret match. She refuses his help and tells him to go: he has left his new bride alone too long.

SECOND STASIMON (627-662):   The *Chorus* say that love, when too powerful, brings misfortune; they hope to love moderately. Contemplating Medea, they hope that they will never find themselves away from friends and family, in a foreign land.

THIRD EPISODE (663-823):   *Aegeus*, King of Athens, enters. He is on his way to Athens, having gone to consult the oracle of Apollo to discover why he remains childless. After telling Aegeus her troubles, *Medea* promises to cure his childlessness by her magic if he will give her refuge in Athens.

He promises, with the qualification that she will have to get to Athens by herself; taking her might antagonize his friends in Corinth.

Not satisfied with a promise, Medea makes him swear an oath never to surrender her to her enemies. After he leaves, she tells the *Chorus* that she now has a real chance of success. She confides her plan of revenge to them: she will send for Jason and sweetly beg that he keep the children. They will take a robe and a headdress as gifts for the king's daughter; wearing them, she, and anyone who touches her, will die. Medea plans then to kill her own children, leaving Jason childless. The Chorus try, but fail, to dissuade her. She sends the Nurse to summon Jason.

THIRD STASIMON (824-865): The *Chorus* sing of the blessed city of Athens; but how will such a murderess as Medea be received there? ow is it possible that a mother could be so hard-hearted and cruel to her own children?

FOURTH EPISODE (866-975): *Jason* enters to confront a *Medea* feigning humility and regret for her earlier anger. She says she should have encouraged his new marriage and hopes that they can now be reconciled. He is glad she is finally being sensible. She asks him to keep the children in Corinth.

He promises to do so, thinking he can probably persuade his new wife, at least. He goes out with the children, who carry the robe and golden headdress for his bride.

FOURTH STASIMON (976-1001): The *Chorus* show pity for the children and Jason's bride; they sympathize with Jason, and even with Medea!

FIFTH EPISODE (1002-1250): The *Tutor* enters with Medea's children. The request has been granted, and the children may stay. The Tutor is dumbfounded by the moans with which *Medea* receives the news.

Left alone with the *children*, Medea decides to spare their lives; then she changes her mind. Torn by conflict between love for them and desire for revenge, she sends them into the house, then calls them back again to be fondled. She says she now understands the terrible nature of the deed she is about to perform, but she will not turn back. Her passion, she says, is stronger than her reason.

FIFTH STASIMON (1251-1292): The *Chorus* say that, though women, they are not incapable of wisdom, and assert that childless people are happiest. Children may grow up to be blessings or curses and, even if they turn out well, they may die, and what misfortune is worse than that?

EXODOS (1293-1419): A *Messenger* comes from the palace to warn *Medea* to flee; the princess and Creon have been killed by her magic. She is exultant and tells him not to talk so fast; she wants to hear every detail of their suffering.

When the children arrived, he relates, the household was happy to see the quarrel between Jason and Medea ended. Although the princess was displeased to see the children, she changed when she saw their gifts. Putting them on, she walked to the mirror. The garments burst into flames and she sank to the ground; the servants ran in distraction through the house. Creon came in to find his daughter dead and throwing himself on her body, was immediately engulfed by the flames, unable to pull away.

Medea goes into the house to kill her children immediately lest someone come from the palace to kill them. Cries are heard from within the house and the Chorus lament the murder, saying that only one other woman, the mad Ino, ever killed her own children.

Jason comes looking for the children, afraid someone from the palace will seek vengeance on him and them.

The *Chorus* tell him they are dead, and he rushes into the doors of his house.

Medea appears above the house in a chariot drawn by dragons; the bodies of her children are beside her. She taunts Jason, saying he will never be able to reach her.

He reproaches himself for not having realized what a monster she was after seeing the first crimes she had committed for his sake.

Medea is triumphant; she knows she has touched his heart at last. His love, she tells him, was too feeble: this is his punishment.

He begs to be allowed to bury his children, to at least be permitted to touch or kiss them.

Medea refuses to give him any comfort whátsoever, and flies away in her chariot.

INTERPRETATION: *MEDEA*, QUESTIONS AND ANSWERS

What is the meaning of the dragon-drawn chariot?

ANSWER: It is a device similar to the *deus ex machina* (the sudden appearance of a god to resolve a difficulty far too complex for human solution) which Euripides is so fond of in many of his plays. Supernatural intrusions are not uncommon in Euripides, in this case the magic fiery garments.

What is the theme of Medea?

ANSWER: The theme is revenge, a common one in Greek tragedy. An important subsidiary theme is the power of passion to override the rational mind of an individual. A third theme is what might be called the feminist argument for equal rights. Medea explicitly appeals to the Chorus of Corinthian Women on the grounds that women have an inferior place and limited rights in society, and they sympathetically second her arguments. It is worth noting that although the Chorus question Medea's excessive passion and her head-strong upper-class actions, they never question her feminist arguments.

Does Medea have an internal conflict between emotions of a mother's love for her children and her uncontrollable and malignant desire to wreak revenge upon her husband?

ANSWER: Yes. In a sense, the whole conflict of the play is within Medea herself. Her love of her children makes her sympathetic, human, tragic—but her love for Jason turned to humiliation, and desire for vengeance for his desertion touch her deepest and strongest feelings.

Is Euripides fond of argumentative rhetoric?

ANSWER: Yes, indeed; in the second episode the speeches of Jason and Medea are of nearly identical length, and the arguments of one are answered by the other, as if in a formal debate. The Chorus accuse Jason of using a specious art, and he clearly loses the debate. His arguments, however, have served to delineate further his character, revealing his ambition for wealth and power, and his cowardliness.

Is the choral ode in the third stasimon unmotivated and irrelevant?

ANSWER: This celebrated choral ode in praise of Athens, and the scene with Aegeus that precedes it, have been criticized as unmotivated and irrelevant to the play. Yet Aegeus' unhappiness about his childlessness illustrates the effect Medea's revenge will have upon Jason, who will lose both his children and his bride; a refuge is offered to Medea, who throughout the play is a victim of isolation and loneliness; and the choral ode provides the only opportunity in the play for someone who knows Medea's plan to try to deter her.

Discuss the play in terms of cultural suspicion of foreigners.

ANSWER: Medea is a passionate oriental from a culture that is unsophisticated, plunged in magic and superstition. The clash of civilized Corinth with alien Colchis results in tragedy: "Never the twain shall meet?"

GREEK TRAGEDY: EURIPIDES

HIPPOLYTUS (428 B.C.)

BACKGROUND: King Theseus once had attacked the Amazons and carried off their queen, Antiope, by whom he later had an illegitimate son named Hippolytus. Later Theseus married Phaedra, who became his queen in Troezen.

CHARACTERS

APHRODITE: goddess of love, enemy of Artemis; she seeks revenge on Hippolytus for his dedication to Artemis.

ARTEMIS: goddess of chastity and of the hunt; enemy of Aphrodite, she defends Hippolytus.

THESEUS (THEE sooz): king of Troezen, father of Hippolytus.

PHAEDRA (FEE druh): wife of Theseus, stepmother of Hippolytus.

HIPPOLYTUS (hih POLL ih tuhss): son of Theseus and Antiope, dedicated to chastity.

ATTENDANTS: companions of Hippolytus.

CHORUS: women of Troezen.

NURSE: companion of Phaedra.

MESSENGER.

SETTING: In front of the palace of King Theseus in Troezen (a city on the coast of the Saronic Gulf, about forty miles east of Argos). A statue of Artemis is on one side of the stage and a statue of Aphrodite on the other.

SUMMARY: *Aphrodite* enters and swears she will punish Hippolytus for showing contempt for her by dedicating himself solely to the chaste goddess Artemis. Hippolytus has forgotten the importance of balance: it is wrong to dedicate oneself entirely to any one god or goddess. This day there will be vengeance frought on Hippolytus, say Aphrodite; she leaves.

Hippolytus enters with his huntsmen *friends,* and the first thing he does is to sing the glories of Artemis. He leaves. Hippolytus' *servant* prays that his master's extremism may be forgiven. The servant leaves.

A *Chorus* of Troezenian ladies enters and speaks of unhappy Phaedra who seems very ill, with no wish to live.

Phaedra approaches with her *nurse* and *handmaidens.* She reveals her deep sorrow and unhappiness. Phaedra recalls the unhappy history of her own family—of her mother, Pasiphaë, who copulated with a bull; of her sister Ariadne, who betrayed her father and country out of love for Theseus. Finally, Phaedra reveals that she is violently in love with her stepson Hippolytus.

The Nurse and Chorus are horrified at the news of her incestuous love for her stepson.

Phaedra says she would rather die than shame her husband. The Nurse then broaches other suggestions, since death is a serious thing. Everyone must give way to the power of Aphrodite, who has Phaedra in her grip right now. Even the gods are under her sway. Therefore it is right that Phaedra accept the sway of Aphrodite, since it is the will of a powerful god.

Phaedra instantly rejects the Nurse's unethical suggestions; her practical reasoning Phaedra finds abhorrent. Honor is more important than life, but the Nurse says otherwise.

The Chorus sings of the great power of love and the great grief it can bring.

From within the palace we hear the voice of Hippolytus. He is furious with the nurse for suggesting he have a love affair with his stepmother, that he betray his father. Had not the Nurse sworn him to secrecy, he would tell his father immediately! Hippolytus (who has been on stage for some time) leaves.

Phaedra enters and declares she wishes to die, but will not leave this life dishonoring her sons or Theseus. At the same time she must punish Hippolytus for neglecting Aphrodite—all the gods must be paid their just respects. She leaves. A cry is heard from within the palace. *Theseus* enters and orders the doors to his palace opened—revealing his wife hanging from a lintel.

Theseus mourns: what, how, and why did she do such a thing? He sees a note written in his wife's hand: she accuses Hippolytus of having raped her. In a rage, Theseus prays that one of the three wishes granted him by Poseidon be fulfilled that day: he asks for the death of his son Hippolytus!

Hippolytus returns and is accused of raping his own stepmother. Theseus banishes his son.

The son's answers to his father's charges is more formal argument than passionate denial; he pleads his religious dedication to chastity, his straightforward manner, his lack of ambition for the throne, and Phaedra's plain appearance. Theseus is not swayed and reaffirms the banishment.

A *Messenger* recounts the presumed death of Hippolytus: when, near the beach, a huge bull rose from the waves and frightened the horses and upset the chariot. Entangled in the reins, Hippolytus was dragged among the rocks.

The father thanks the gods for securing the death of his son. The Chorus sing of the power of Aphrodite, who maddens her victims. The goddess *Artemis* appears, wanting to know why the father is joyous at the news of his son's death; why he listened to a charge that was not clearly proved true. She reveals that Aphrodite filled his wife with incestuous love; that Hippolytus was innocent and true to his oath to the Nurse. Theseus is guilty of false accusation and hasty judgment.

Hippolytus, mortally injured, is helped in; he asks only for death and release from pain. Artemis promises to wreak revenge upon Aphrodite, but henceforth all girls about to be married in Troezen will cut off their hair as an offering to him. She asks for mutual forgiveness and vanishes. Son absolves father of murder and Hippolytus dies.

INTERPRETATION: *HIPPOLYTUS*, QUESTIONS AND ANSWERS

How do you account for Hippolytus' lack of passion in his arguments?

ANSWER: His lack of passion can partly be attributed to Euripides' characteristic use of formal argument in his plays; it is also perhaps appropriate to Hippolytus' character.

The serious regard Greek society held for oaths explains why Hippolytus does not defend himself by repeating what the Nurse had told him, not that his father would believe him. He would have believed the Chorus, but they too respect their oath of silence. Of course, had they broken the oath, Theseus would learn they had lied to him earlier, when they said they did not know what had happened. Theseus might therefore refuse to believe their altered story and subsequent action would remain the same. After the false accusation by Phaedra and the violent reaction of Theseus, Hippolytus has the audience's sympathy.

Discuss the use of the deus ex machina *in this play.*

ANSWER: The device of the *deus ex machina* is used at both the beginning and end of *Hippolytus*, framing as it were, the actions of men within the confines of the wills of the gods. This, apart from its general religious overtones, is especially apt in a play celebrating the establishment of the Troezenian cult honoring Hippolytus. The play gives the vividness of drama to the practices of religion, much in the manner of the stories in the Bible or the medieval mystery plays.

What is Aphrodite's function in the Prologue?

ANSWER: This extremely detailed description of what will happen in the play is probably intended to do more than give dramatic irony to succeeding scenes. It has been conjectured that Euripides' earlier play on this subject was criticized on the grounds that Phaedra's passion for Hippolytus was distasteful to the audience. In this version, by making Aphrodite the instigator who takes total responsibility, Euripides makes Phaedra an unwilling instrument of Aphrodite's revenge. It also keeps the focus of the play firmly on Hippolytus; later dramatists made Phaedra the main character—in fact, used her name for the title. On a symbolic level, Aphrodite represents the natural force of love; Hippolytus, in denying this force, is a puritan guilty of one-sided excessive zeal.

Is Hippolytus guilty of hybris?

ANSWER: Yes. Hippolytus' pride in his chastity is evident in his scornful treatment of the goddess Aphrodite. As a representative of adolescent fanaticism, Hippolytus is perhaps unrivalled in dramatic literature. Although emphasis has been placed on his alleged priggishness, much can also be said about qualities which make him appealing to the audience, even before their sympathy is aroused by the unjust accusation later in the play. Dedication to chastity (as a principle of life) has a long history in civilization; in association with Hippolytus' youth, handsomeness, and almost excessive vitality, it is shorn of its drearier associations. Further, the existence of Artemis as goddess of chastity postulates at least the theory of dedication to her worship. Of course, the Greek virtue of the "golden mean" or moderation in all things, would recommend the avoidance of either extreme.

What is the Nurse like?

ANSWER: Throughout the play, the Nurse provides an effective contrast to Phaedra. Being a servant, she can be represented as crude, practical, insensitive, and complaining. The contrast is so great that it frequently approaches comedy. The effect on the stage would depend on the way the actor played the role. She is an example of a stock stage character which finds its culmination in the Nurse in Shakespeare's *Romeo and Juliet*.

GREEK TRAGEDY: EURIPIDES

TROJAN WOMEN (415 B.C.)

BACKGROUND: The *Trojan Women* is one of the greatest anti-war plays ever written. Written in the midst of the Peloponnesian War (431-404 B.C.), and presented the year after Athens had captured the neutral island of Melos, killed all its surviving men and sold the women and children into slavery, this play reflects Euripides' disillusionment with the idea of a just and noble Athenian democracy. The ruling faction which instigated the attack on Melos was still in power when the play was presented—was, in fact, about to embark on an attack against Sicily where the entire Athenian force was to be destroyed. Public sentiment at the time may explain why the tetralogy in which the play appeared received only second place in the competition of 415.

The first two plays of the tetralogy were the *Alexander* and the *Palamedes;* the fourth was a satyric drama, *Sisyphus*. These plays have not survived, but the stories they told and some of Euripides' attitudes are known. The *Alexander* is concerned with the early life of Paris (also called Alexander). Before his birth, his mother, Queen Hecuba of Troy, dreamed that she had given birth to a firebrand whose flames destroyed the city. Paris was therefore left exposed so that he should perish; but he was found and reared by shepherds and grew up to win athletic contests held by his father, King Priam, in Paris' "memory." After the victory he was recognized and accepted as a son by Priam, despite the dire warnings of his sister, the prophetess Cassandra, who said he would cause the destruction of Troy.

The *Palamedes* tells of one of the Greek leaders (Palamedes) who sailed to Troy. He revealed that Odysseus was pretending to be mad so that he could dodge the draft. In revenge, Odysseus planted a forged letter from Priam in Palamedes' tent. Accused of treachery, Palamedes was found guilty and stoned to death.

CHARACTERS

POSEIDON: god of the sea.

ATHENA: goddess of war and wisdom, patroness of Athens.

HECUBA: Queen of Troy, wife of Priam, mother of Hector, Paris and Cassandra.

CASSANDRA: prophetess doomed never to be believed. Daughter of Hecuba and Priam.

ANDROMACHE: wife of Hector, a prince of Troy killed by Achilles.

HELEN: wife of King Menelaus of Sparta, carried off to Troy by Paris.

TALTHYBIUS: a herald of the Greeks.

MENELAUS: king of Sparta, brother of Agamemnon, leader of the Greek forces.

CHORUS: captured Trojan women, young and old, married and single.

SOLDIERS.

SETTING: The *Trojan Women* takes place just after the successful stratagem of the Trojan Horse, through which, after ten years of siege, Troy finally falls to the Greeks. The scene is the battlefield a few days after the fall of Troy. Behind are the partly destroyed walls of Troy. To the right and left are huts in which live the captive women set aside for the Greek leaders.

SUMMARY

PROLOGUE (Lines 1-152):   The god *Poseidon* appears before the walls. He declares that he and Apollo had built Troy and he still loves the city. Its king lies unburied now, its gold is being carried to Greek ships, and its holy places defiled with blood. The Greek soldiers are restlessly waiting for a favorable wind. He calls particular attention to Hecuba, who lies before him in the dust, her sons and husband slain, her daughter Polyxena recently sacrificed at the demand of Achilles' spirit, and her daughter Cassandra given to Agamemnon.

The goddess, *Athena*, enters. She favored the Greeks to win, but is angry because one of them has attempted to rape Cassandra while she had clung to Athena's altar. To gain her revenge, Athena has asked that thunder and lightning, wind and hail, strike the ships. She wants Poseidon to make the seas wild. He promises that as soon as the last ship has left the land his full fury will strike.

Hecuba, who has been sleeping on the ground, awakens. She laments her woes: no longer is she among the lords of Troy. City, wealth, social position, and most of her family have been lost— nothing is left her but to endure. She gazes at the Greek ships and deplores the great disasters they have brought, all for the sake of the evil and adulterous Helen. She calls to the other women to come out and sing with her as they had in Troy—but now with songs of woe.

PARODOS (153-234): Singing alternate verses, *Hecuba* and the *Chorus* of Trojan women speak of the Greeks preparing to sail, of being separated from one another, of their slavery, and of the cities to which they may be taken.

FIRST EPISODE (235-510): The Greek herald, *Talthybius,* enters and tells the women that lots have been cast, and they have been assigned to various Greek leaders: Cassandra is to be Agamemnon's concubine; about the fate of Polyxena the herald is vague, saying only that she is to "watch Achilles' tomb"; Andromache, the widow of Hector, is to go to Neoptolemus, son of Achilles; *Hecuba* herself to Odysseus. She laments her fate at the hands of the lying Odysseus.

Talthybius has just ordered his men to bring out the women when he sees flames inside the hut. He believes the women are trying to avoid slavery by killing themselves; but Hecuba tells him that what he sees is only Cassandra's torch. Carrying a torch, *Cassandra* comes out of the hut. She sings to Hymen, the god of marriage, of her joy in being chosen for a king's bed; she compares her mother's weeping to her own joy and invites her mother to laugh and join her dance. Hecuba recalls her plans for Cassandra's marriage day—how different from the present! She takes the torch from her daughter, remarking that all her griefs have not changed her frenzies: she still lacks wisdom. The other women, she says, should answer Cassandra's bridal song with tears. Cassandra insists there will be joy in her marriage: the axe is waiting which shall kill her and Agamemnon, and lead eventually to matricide. Even now, Cassandra says, the Trojans are happier than the Greeks. Why did the Greeks die? For one woman's beauty—no one had attacked *their* towns. They died in a foreign land, many fathered children at home whom they had never seen, and their graves lie unmourned.

The Trojans, on the other hand, have died gloriously in the defense of their country; they fought near their homes and were buried on their own soil. War is an evil, but there is triumph for those who fight well for just causes. Only those who die in sin have cause for lamentation. Talthybius bids Cassandra walk quietly by his side and lets Hecuba know that someone will come to take her to Odysseus. After Cassandra leaves, Hecuba falls to the ground, where she lies, bewailing the futility of her life.

FIRST STASIMON (511-576): The women of the *Chorus* sing of the golden Trojan Horse, dragged into the city as a gift for Athena. The plain where the Greeks had camped lay silent that night, and in Troy a celebration began to mark the end of the war. At night the Greeks came out of the horse and defeated the city.

SECOND EPISODE (577-798): *Andromache* enters, carrying her child. She is riding a chariot piled with loot which is on its way to the Greeks. On arrival, she will become the concubine of Neoptolemus, son of Achilles, her husband's killer. In a lament, she tells *Hecuba* of a new misfortune: Polyxena has been offered up as a sacrifice to Achilles' spirit.

Hecuba tells her daughter to honor her new lord and raise her child among his father's enemies—for someday Troy may be rebuilt.

Talthybius returns and tells Andromache that the Greeks have ordered her son, Astyanax, killed: he is to be thrown from the walls of Troy. Odysseus had said that the son of Hector may become a danger to the Greeks when he will have grown up.

Talthybius gently and reluctantly takes the child from Hecuba and goes toward Troy. Andromache is set on the chariot again and driven towards the ships.

SECOND STASIMON (799-859): The *Chorus* sing that this is not the first time Troy has been taken. Long ago, in the time of Priam's father, King Laomedon, Hercales and Telamon had defeated the city. Yet the gods did not always hate Troy, and so, they sing about Ganymede and Tithonus.

THIRD EPISODE (860-1059): *King Menelaus* enters and declares it is indeed a beautiful day on which he can get back the woman stolen from him. Then he suddenly checks himself, saying that he had come to Troy not to regain Helen, his wife, but to punish the thief who had stolen her—Paris. He has decided not to kill his wife, but to carry her home and punish her there.

Hecuba praises the god who is bringing justice, and she warns Menelaus not to be snared by Helen's beauty.

Helen proudly issues from the hut, calmly asking whether she is to live or die. If she is to die, she wants only to be allowed to speak first. She tells the story of Paris: how he could have been killed at birth because of the prophecy that he should bring about the destruction of Troy. When he judged Aphrodite (Venus) more beautiful than Athena (Minerva) or Hera (Juno), Aphrodite fulfilled her promise to give him the most beautiful woman in the world—Helen. She is thus only a victim of the gods. When Paris came to visit Menelaus, he came with the goddess' assistance. Nor did it help matters for Menelaus to sail for Crete and leave them alone! Surely this was all Aphrodite's fault; Menelaus should punish *her*—Aphrodite! Helen says she tried several times to lower herself from the Trojan walls after Paris was killed, but the Trojans always caught her and pulled her back.

Hecuba replies that the judgment story is nonsense. The truth is that Helen fell in love with the handsome Paris. In Troy she always cagily praised the side who happened to be winning on that day. And as for her escape attempts, Hecuba asks, why had she never heard of them before? Who did catch her? Had Helen any shame at all she should have committed suicide; she certainly would not be appearing well groomed and proud now—she would be crawling.

Menelaus orders Helen to walk before him towards the Greeks. There are many there who would gladly kill her. Helen kneels before her husband and embraces him; Menelaus weakens and tells the soldiers to escort her to the ship. Hecuba warns him that, as he loved her once, he will love her again. He makes no promise on this score, but says he will sail on a different ship from that of Helen's.

THIRD STASIMON (1060-1122): The *Chorus* sing to Zeus about the Trojan woes. They hope for death soon; that the proud Helen will never see her home.

EXODOS (1123-1332): *Talthybius* comes back from Troy carrying the dead body of Andromache's son *Astyanax*. The mother has sailed with Neoptolemus already but has requested that her son be buried with the shield of his father Hector. Talthybius leaves the body with *Hecuba* and goes out to dig the grave.

Hecuba decries the fear that led the Greeks to kill the boy. She laments the youth and love he will never know, and remembers the nights he had slept with her.

The women of the *Chorus* join in her grief while she prepares the body for burial.

Hecuba rises from her task and says that she has just had a vision of the hand of God; and that there was nothing in it but a rod of affliction; prayer and sacrifice are all in vain. She bids the women take the child's body to his grave.

Talthybius returns and orders the *soldiers* to set fire to what remains of Troy.

Hecuba tries to run into the flames and die within the burning city, but the soldiers restrain her.

Talthybius has said that the last ships are waiting—with a great crash the towers collapse, and the women are led away.

INTERPRETATION: *TROJAN WOMEN*, QUESTIONS AND ANSWERS

Briefly, what is the theme of the Trojan Women?

ANSWER: The theme displays the suffering brought about by war; the play indicates in many ways the stupidity, futility, and utter barbarism attendant upon war.

Who else wrote a play with the same title?

ANSWER: Secena the Philosopher (c. 4 B.C.-65 A.D.) based his play on that of Euripides, combining it with the sacrifice of Polyxena (that episode taken from Euripides' *Hecuba*). It is the best of Seneca's tragedies, containing deep pathos and suffering.

What is the tragic irony of the play?

ANSWER: The tragic irony of the play is that the Trojan women (Hecuba, Andromache etc.) display great courage, pride, and dignity—qualities now lost to their Greek captors. The old Homeric valor is not displayed by the soldiers in this play; indeed, the only heroism of the genuine kind is that displayed by the widows and mothers of the conquered Trojans.

What are some of the deeds that brought about the many misfortunes which plagued the Greeks after the Trojan War, such as in the wanderings of Odysseus and the murder of Agamemnon?

ANSWER: The attempted rape of Cassandra while she clung to Athena's altar is an example of such a deed. See the Prologue, where the divine origin of some of the misdeeds is given in detail.

Where is there a fierce travesty of a marriage hymn?

ANSWER: In the First Episode, where Cassandra issues from the hut carrying a marriage torch. The torch was a symbol of the god of marriage; her wild exultation provides a startling contrast with that which follows.

What does Cassandra prophesy concerning the house of Atreus?

ANSWER: Agamemnon's wife will slay her husband; his son will slay his own father. See Aeschylus' *Oresteia*.

How have the Greek leaders committed hybris?

ANSWER: *Hybris* (excessive pride) meant that one exceeded the norm of human conduct couched in cautious wisdom and piety.

As Poseidon and Athena had made clear in the Prologue, even those gods who favored the Greeks during the Trojan War have turned against them now. The episode with Cassandra is merely the first delineation of several Greek outrages recited in this play (the murder of Astyanax, for example). Thus, while we see the Trojans suffering, we see the Greeks sinning: our sympathy is with the Trojans, our fear is for the Greeks in the commission of their *hybris*-like acts.

Why do not the choral odes in the Stasima comment on the action of the preceding episode?

ANSWER: The women of the Chorus make no such comments, not because they are insensitive to the misfortunes of individuals but because they are, in a way, protagonists. The individuals who appear in the separate episodes of the play do indeed suffer, but they represent only a part of the whole. The women of the Chorus are preoccupied with the fall of an entire city; they call attention to a multiplicity of unfortunate fates.

Does this play follow a conventional plot?

ANSWER: No. As becomes clear by the end of the Second Episode, there is no conventional "plot" developed. The sequence of scenes, rather than being based on an order of events, contain an ever-increasing intensity of pathos. The structure of the play is episodic (i.e., scenes follow each other like beads on a string).

What scene would carry great interest for moderns?

ANSWER: Helen's justification for her adultery in the Third Episode. She blames Paris, then Aphrodite, and then her husband (for leaving them alone together). She pleads her many attempts to escape. Is she sincere?

GREEK TRAGEDY: EURIPIDES

ELECTRA (ca. 413 B.C.)

BACKGROUND: *Electra* dramatizes the same events as do Aeschylus *Choephoroe* and Sophocles' *Electra*. Aeschylus' version was the second part of a trilogy which had profound religious significance. Euripides emphasizes the psychological states of his characters. In some respects, Euripides is "correcting" Aeschylus' moral view. Whether this play was written before or after Sophocles' version has never been proved, but much evidence indicates that it was written before, and that Sophocles' *Electra* is a dramatic reply to Euripides.

When King Agamemnon returned to his home in Argos after the end of the Trojan War, he brought with him as a concubine, Cassandra, a Trojan princess. Clytemnestra, Agamemnon's wife, had taken Aegisthus as a lover during her husband's absence. The day Agamemnon returned, he was murdered by Clytemnestra and her lover (see Aeschylus' *Agamemnon*). The *Electra* begins several years later.

CHARACTERS

CLYTEMNESTRA: widow of King Agamemnon.

ELECTRA: daughter of Agamemnon and Clytemnestra.

PEASANT: husband of Electra.

ORESTES: brother of Electra.

PYLADES: friend of Orestes.

CHORUS: country women.

OLD MAN: former servant of Agamemnon.

MESSENGER.

THE DIOSCURI (digh oh SKEW ree): Castor and Polydeuces (pohl ih DEW seez), brothers of Clytemnestra and Helen; they joined the immortals after their death; they appear in the *Electra* as the *deus ex machina*.

SETTING: In front of the hut of the Peasant, located on the borders of Argolis, a peninsula in the northeast of the Peloponnesus.

SUMMARY: The *Peasant* tells the history of the house of Atreus. He tells how Aegisthus married Clytemnestra after the two of them had murdered Agamemnon; they now rule Argos. Orestes, Agamemnon's son, was sent away for safety by a friend of Agamemnon's to Phocis, about ninety miles north. Electra, Orestes' sister, was kept at home and all offers of marriage were refused for her by Aegisthus, who was afraid a son of hers might avenge Agamemnon's murder. His fears reached such a pitch that he finally decided to kill her; but her mother managed to save her life by agreeing to her marriage with a peasant, since a low-born son could make no claim. Aegisthus also offered a reward to anyone who would kill Orestes. The Peasant says his family is noble enough but they are poor. Because he regards Electra to be far above him in station, the peasant has never asked for his rights as a husband.

Electra issues from the hut, her head shaved, and dressed in rags; she is carrying a water pitcher. She performs these menial tasks to remind the gods of Aegisthus' insults. Her *husband* hates to see so high-born a lady do such work; in turn, she has great respect for his kindness, wanting to help him as much as she can. Electra goes to the spring and her husband to the fields.

A moment later *Orestes* and *Pylades* (PILL uh deez) enter. They have come from Phocis to avenge Agamemnon's murder. The night before Orestes left a lock of his hair and made an offering on his father's tomb and is now seeking Electra. When he sees her returning with water, he thinks she is a servant and approaches to make inquiries. As *Electra* comes in, she sings of the death of Agamemnon, of the unknown fate of her brother, and of the cruelty of her mother and her husband Aegisthus.

Orestes and Pylades approach the *women* of the town. Orestes reveals that her brother is living.

Electra relates her own history and comments kindly on her respectful husband. She is willing to help Orestes kill their mother. She wonders why Orestes has not yet returned for vengeance.

The Peasant invites Orestes into the hut, and Orestes comments that a man is proved in nobility only through action. Electra orders her husband to have Agamemnon's foster father bring in more food. He will want to see the strangers too, for he had saved Orestes years before and will enjoy news about him.

The *Old Man,* who had been Agamemnon's foster father, and who had taken Orestes to Phocis, enters laden with food. Having stopped at the tomb and seen the hair and sacrifice there, he suggests that Orestes had left them; for no one else would have been so reverent.

Electra replies that such "clues" mean nothing: a man's hair would be different from hers; and why should her brave brother return by stealth? She also denies the Old Man's suggestions that Orestes could have left the footprint, or that he might still have some article of clothing she would recognize.

When Orestes and Pylades come out of the hut, the Old Man recognizes Orestes by a scar on his forehead. Electra and Orestes embrace, and the Chorus say that now her turn has arrived for victory.

Orestes asks whether he has any friends left who can help. The Old Man tells him he will not only have to act alone, but that he will never succeed if he tries to kill Aegisthus and Clytemnestra inside the palace. However, Aegisthus is preparing oxen for a sacrifice at his estate. There, Orestes will be invited to the feast and can kill him at the first opportunity.

Later, loud cries are heard in the distance, and Electra comes out of the hut. A *Messenger* brings the news that Aegisthus is dead. He relates how after graciously welcoming Orestes and Pylades to his feast, he had attached no significance to their refusal to purify themselves after they explained they had already done so. While Aegisthus was examining the sacrifice, Orestes killed him from behind with a meat cleaver, severing his spine. The Chorus and Electra joyfully celebrate the death of Aegisthus.

Orestes and Pylades are welcomed by Electra as they enter with the body of *Aegisthus.* Electra turns disdainfully away from the body, and Orestes has it carried into the hut so Clytemnestra will not see it.

When they see *Clytemnestra* approaching in her chariot, Orestes doubts that he can kill his mother; he says the oracle of Apollo was foolish in ordering him to murder.

Electra urges him on, taunts him with unmanly timidity, tells him men cannot be wiser than the gods.

Orestes goes into the hut as Clytemnestra enters, surrounded by attendants. Clytemnestra justifies her murder of her husband.

At the invitation of Clytemnestra. Electra voices her grievances: Clytemnestra, she says, is famous for her unfaithfulness—she never wanted her husband back home. Also, why has she cut off Electra and Orestes from their patrimony?

Clytemnestra promises to oppress her no longer; she goes inside the hut to perform sacrifices. Electra says, ironically, she will make a fitting sacrifice indeed!

Cries are heard from Clytemnestra; Electra and Orestes issue from the hut spattered with blood. The bodies of both Clytemnestra and Aegisthus are brought out, and Orestes laments the punishment he will suffer for these murders.

Electra too laments her misfortunes to come, but Orestes charges her with changing like the wind because it had been she who had urged the foul deed.

From above, the *Dioscuri* appear as the *deus ex machina*. They say Clytemnestra has been justly punished, but that they were wrong to kill her. They imply that Apollo was wrong to order her death, yet declare they will not speak against the great god. They reveal that Electra is to marry Pylades; Orestes, who is to go into exile, will be pursued by the Furies and driven mad. He is to go to the statue of Athena in Athens; a trial will be held on the Hill of Ares, and the precedent will be established that if tie votes are rendered by the Jury, the accused will be acquitted and absolved of his crimes. The citizens are to bury Aegisthus, and Menelaus and Helen are to bury Clytemnestra. The Dioscuri also reveal that Helen was never at Troy; only a phantom was seduced by Paris. The real Helen was safely in Egypt (See Euripides' *Helen*).

Orestes and Electra bid each other a tender farewell and the Dioscuri vanish, but not before warning against doing injustice.

INTERPRETATION: *ELECTRA*, QUESTIONS AND ANSWERS

Sophocles has written on the same theme in a play with the same title: what are some of the differences of plot in this play?

ANSWER: Some of the differences are

1. Aegisthus has married Electra to a humble peasant so that no son of hers will menace the throne.

2. The peasant is a gentle and fine character, who respects Electra for her nobility and sad life.

3. Electra accepts part of the responsibility for the murder of Clytemnestra.

4. Euripides' play is a study in depth of the characters of Orestes and Electra.

What are some of the better translations of this play?

ANSWER: R.C. Jebb's in 1904; Francis Fergusson's in 1938, and H. D. F. Kitto's in 1962.

Is there an implied criticism of Aeschylus' similar recognition scene in the Libation Bearers?

ANSWER: Yes, in the scene where there is much criticism from Electra of the old servant's evidence that Orestes has returned in person, i.e., the hair, the footprints, the clothing. Aeschylus was careless about his evidence for recognition.

Why are the Dioscuri brought in as deus ex machina?

ANSWER:

1. They without doubt represent Euripides' own point of view on certain thorny problems coming to a head by the time the play is about to end.

2. Obviously, they can look over the situation with strict objectivity and calmness, certainly much more so than the protagonists.

3. They reveal the tremendous complexity of conflict lying within the breasts of not only Orestes and his sister but in all criminals.

4. Although Clytemnestra is guilty, vengeance is clearly not the solution. Vengeance merely leads to more crime and renewed feelings of guilt.

What is Sophocles' attitude towards the slaying of Clytemnestra?

ANSWER: Sophocles in his *Electra* seems to say that the murder of the mother was a justifiable act. Orestes has done rightfully and dutifully the act of a good son. Sophocles agrees with Homer (the *Odyssey*) in his similarity of approach to Orestes. In addition, Electra in Sophocles' play is most prominent as a character, over-shadowing all others. Sophocles stresses her deep suffering and her almost insane obsession for vengeance.

What do Aeschylus and Euripides find more of interest?

ANSWER: They are more interested in the nature and extent of the workings of justice; and the great and terrible price man must pay to be able to glimpse even a little bit of its true nature. In both authors we find Orestes and Electra torn between love and hate, vengeance feelings and guilt over such vengeful acts; but they learn through pain and experience that the old "eye for an eye" code of blood-vengeance is no longer in the interests of society, justice, or the gods.

Why has this play been called more a melodrama than a tragedy?

ANSWER: The violent actions, the starkly melodramatic scenes, and the sensational blood and guilt scenes. In addition the *exodos* or last scene ties up loose ends by narrating what will happen; and the ending is, ultimately, happy.

Is there some criticism of the institution of the Apollonian oracle?

ANSWER: Yes, but the criticism is not systematically developed.

Discuss Euripides' treatment of Orestes in this play.

ANSWER: Orestes delays inordinately long (a Hamlet?), presumably out of caution or fear, to reveal his identity; he leaves the planning of the murders to the Old Man and Electra. He is not a coward, but he does show much irresolution—a marked contrast to Electra.

GREEK TRAGEDY: EURIPIDES

BACCHAE (405? B.C.)

BACKGROUND: After Euripides' death, the *Bacchae* was produced at Athens by his son. Dionysus' coming to Greece from the Orient was a frequent theme in Greek poetry and art, and a number of lost plays dealt with the subject. This play was widely read, admired, and quoted by classical Latin writers. Dionysus (also called Bacchus) was the god of fertility and wine, and his worship followed the introduction of grape-growing into Greece. Festivals celebrating Dionysus became wild and orgiastic; he may be taken as a symbol of the intoxicating power of nature. The *Bacchae* dramatizes the establishment of Dionysus and his cult in Greece, as well as the effects of the cult and the attitudes of its detractors.

King Cadmus, who had founded Thebes, had a daughter, Semele, loved by Zeus. She was tricked by the jealous Hera, Zeus' wife, into asking Zeus to appear before her in the same form in which he appeared before Hera. Zeus had promised earlier to grant Semele a wish, so he reluctantly appeared as the god of thunder. The lightning which accompanied him killed her, and she was prematurely delivered of a child by Zeus. Zeus sewed the child into his thigh, thus preserving him until his maturity. The child was Dionysus. In his travels he taught the cultivation of the vine.

CHARACTERS

DIONYSUS (DIGH oh NIGH suhss): god of wine, son of Zeus and the Theban princess Semele; he has arrived in Greece to spread his worship.

CADMUS: former king of Thebes, father of Semele.

PENTHEUS: grandson of Cadmus, now king of Thebes.

AGAVE (uh GAY vee): daughter of Cadmus, mother of King Pentheus.

TEIRESIAS: an aged prophet of Thebes.

CHORUS: Bacchantes, followers of Dionysus who have come with him from the East.

SOLDIERS.

MESSENGERS.

SETTING: Before the palace of Pentheus, king of Thebes. Nearby is the tomb of Semele.

PROLOGUE (lines 1-63): The god *Dionysus* announces that he has come to Thebes (where his mother was killed) in the form of a man. He has seen his mother's tomb, where the fire ignited at the time of his mother's death still smoulders; he approves of Cadmus' making a sanctuary there. His purpose is to call Greece to his worship, for, despite his success in the East, from which he has just come, the Greeks are unbelievers. Some even call Semele a wanton who claimed Zeus was the father of her child to hide her shame; they say the lightning was Zeus' punishment. To teach the unbelievers a lesson, Dionysus has sent his spirit upon the women of the town; they have left their homes and run to the mountain sides in ecstatic frenzy. He is especially angry with King Pentheus, an outspoken sceptic; he and his people must be taught the god's power:

> "Pentheus wars against my godhead and he outlaws me by force, and as for prayers, not a word for me in them! And for that reason I'll display myself a god to him and all the Thebans."

Should the townspeople attack the worshippers who have come with him, he will appear as a god and lead his "army" against them.

PARODOS (64-168): The *Chorus,* devotees of Dionysus, enter. They wear the "uniform" of the cult: a fawn skin over white robes. Many carry the *thyrsus,* a staff with a pine cone on the end; their heads are decked with ivy. Some carry musical instruments. They praise Dionysus joyfully, telling of his birth, and calling upon others to join them.

FIRST EPISODE (169-369): The aged prophet *Teiresias* enters, wearing the garb of the Dionysian cult. He has come to celebrate the rites with the retired old *King Cadmus.* Both are conscious of their great age and feeble condition, especially inappropriate to the rather energetic Dionysiac rites; but both feel rejuvenated enough to look forward to the ceremonies. They are the only two men in Thebes preparing for the rites, and both agree that no god's worship should be ignored, even if old men are required to attend wild dances.

King Pentheus approaches and they draw to one side. Pentheus is furious about the new religion, calling Dionysus

"a juggler, a magician out of Lydia, with golden ringlets on his sweetly scented head, a fresh complexion, eyes with Aphrodite's charms, who under cover of some shouting ceremonies spends days and nights consorting with the younger girls . . . the girlish stranger who has introduced corruption for our women and defiles our beds."

Pentheus orders his men to destroy the rock-seat where the ceremonies are held, and to find the effeminate-looking stranger who is leading them.

Teiresias warns Pentheus against arrogance and pride, and the two old men, supporting one another, go off to worship Dionysus. They will pray that Pentheus not be punished, the city not destroyed.

FIRST STASIMON (370-432): The *Chorus* sing praises of life's material pleasures; they sing the praises of wine, women, and song; they call glorious the humble and simple pleasures of the common man.

SECOND EPISODE (433-518): A *soldier* reports that Dionysus surrendered with so charming a grace that he had to apologize for arresting him. He also reports that the prison doors opened of their own accord; the worshippers captured earlier have returned to the mountainsides. *Pentheus* taunts *Dionysus* about his fair skin and long curls, and tries unsuccessfully to elicit secret details of the rites. Despite the warnings of Dionysus that sacred objects are being profaned, Pentheus has some of Dionysus' hair cut off, takes his *thyrsus,* and has him bound.

Ordered imprisoned, Dionysus says he can release himself whenever he chooses. The Dionysian maidens of the *Chorus* Pentheus takes as slaves to work in his house or be sold into slavery. Dionysus again warns him he will pay for denying the wine god.

SECOND STASIMON (519-575): The *Chorus* sing of the emotional joys and beauties to be found in a life close to nature. At the end there is an earthquake.

THIRD EPISODE (576-861): *Dionysus*, unbound, comes out of the palace alone. Inside, he says, Pentheus has been sent visions: he has seen a bull ready for the offering and bound it; then he ran about for water when the flame rose above Semele's tomb; then stabbed an image of Dionysus in the prison—and finally Pentheus fell exhausted.

Dionysus hears footsteps in the hall, and Pentheus emerges, unchastened: he orders the guards to bar the gates. Before his order is carried out, a panting *Messenger* arrives from the mountain, where he has seen the townswomen.

The Messenger goes on to tell how at dawn he saw three groups, one led by Pentheus' mother, Agave, sleeping on the mountainside— and no evidence of wine, music, and lovemaking, as Pentheus had expected. When they awoke they dressed in fawn skins with live snakes for belts; food and drink sprang miraculously from rocks and the ground. Shepherds, seeing them, decided to capture Agave to gain the king's favor. When she passed by them in the ceremony, they tried to catch her, but she called to the others, who chased the men and then attacked the cattle, tearing them apart and throwing the pieces around until the trees dripped blood. They then destroyed a village, the spears of the townspeople not deterring them. The Messenger recommends that Pentheus accept the new god. In a rage, *Pentheus* calls his *soldiers* together to attack the women. Dionysus warns him not to—even offering to bring the women to the palace. Pentheus suspects a trick and sets off to attack them. With the same mildness that has marked his appearance throughout the play, which is physically represented by an appearance Pentheus called effeminate, Dionysus asks Pentheus if he would like to watch the women at their worship.

Pentheus will have to dress as a woman for Dionysus to protect him from the worshippers; and only after much indecision about such a disguise, does he decide to go.

He is assured by Dionysus that he can get through the streets unseen.

While Pentheus is in the palace dressing, Dionysus assures the *Chorus* that Pentheus will now be punished. Praying, he asks that Pentheus' reason be darkened so he will dress as a woman—in the Dionysian garb he so despised—that he will be laughed at in the streets, detected in the ceremony, and killed.

THIRD STASIMON (862-911):   The *Chorus* sing of peace and of the eternal love beauty inspires. Those who fail to understand this and who strive in pride beyond their limits are ruthlessly punished. Those who know that merely to live is happiness, are in heaven.

FOURTH EPISODE (912-976):   Pentheus comes out dressed as a woman. He is in a strangely exalted state. With Dionysus helping him, he arranges his dress and worries about his hair with female finickiness. But he is not converted, and looks forward to destroying the group with his clever disguise.

FOURTH STASIMON (977-1023):   The *Chorus* look forward to the discovery and punishment of Pentheus. Knowledge, they say, is good to seek, but the world also has a spirit of mystery which is not to be denied.

EXODOS (1024-1392):   A *Messenger* rushes in with the news that King Pentheus is dead. He had been with the group which went to the mountain, where they had hidden to watch the women in orgy.

Pentheus wanted a better view, so Dionysus bent a tall pine tree over, and it carried the king to where he could see and be seen. The Messenger goes on to relate how Dionysus called the women, who then tried to stone the king; but he was too high up.

Then they all gripped the tree and tore it down. Agave stood over her son; he removed his headdress and begged for mercy. She, slave to a Dionysiac frenzy, did not recognize him, and, with her foot on his side, tugged at his arm and pulled it off. His aunt, Ino, pulled off his other arm; and soon women were running around with various pieces of his body.

The *Chorus* sing of the triumph over Pentheus, but when *Agave* comes in they are horrified to see her carrying *Pentheus' head*. Agave thinks she is carrying the head of a lion, and shouts for Cadmus and Pentheus to come out and see what the women have caught with their own hands.

Cadmus comes from the mountain, with men carrying the pieces of Pentheus' body. Agave brags to him of her trophy and shows him the head. Cadmus tries to bring her back to her senses; she slowly comes out of the frenzy with no knowledge of the events which have occurred since Dionysus had put the spell on all the women of Thebes.

Cadmus laments over the body of Pentheus, praising him as a just man, quick to attack dishonor. (A page of the only surviving manuscript is missing at this point.)

Dionysus appears as a *deus ex machina* and tells Cadmus of his future wanderings as punishment for not accepting Dionysus. He and Agave acknowledge their sin and beg forgiveness, but Dionysus remains adamant.

INTERPRETATION: *BACCHAE*, QUESTIONS AND ANSWERS

What is Euripides saying about the more primitive natural emotions in all men?

ANSWER: He is saying that they are to be recognized and given expression; if they are scorned and overlooked, they will assert themselves in powerful and destructive ways. On the other hand, Euripides is saying that an overstress on the primitive emotions can be just as disastrous—the *golden mean* is best.

What is Euripides saying about suffering in life?

ANSWER: Pentheus' attitude of cold reason and unemotional logic is extreme, as is Agave's fanatical and passionate addiction to a religion of unreason, instinct, and supernaturalism—the Apollonian versus the Dionysiac attitudes in life. There must be a median, a compromise struck between these two attitudes for man to avoid acute suffering in life.

What essentially religious rite does the drama dramatize?

ANSWER: The *Bacchae* dramatizes the establishment of Dionysus and his cult in Greece (Thebes), as well as showing the effects of the cult and the attitudes of its detractors.

In what way does the prologue here differ, say, from that of Euripides' Hippolytus?

ANSWER: Unlike the god whose speech opens the *Hippolytus*, Dionysus does not reveal the action of the play. He makes clear, however, that Pentheus must make a decision, and that punishment of the wrong decision will be severe.

In what way does the Chorus in the Parodos revert to the older Aeschylean dramatic structure?

ANSWER: The Parodos has one of the longest series of choral lyrics in Euripides' plays. The Chorus has here an integral part in the plot as well as lengthy lyrics, both occurring rarely in the "typical" Euripidean play.

What would have been the audience's reaction to Pentheus' decision to combat Dionysus' cult?

ANSWER: They would have felt fear, for his conduct here was irrational. The parting words of Teiresias show that the wrath might be expected as the natural consequence of ignoring any god. The Athenians, after all, had an altar dedicated to the "unknown god" in case their pantheon had made any inadvertent omissions.

What scene dramatizes most effectively Pentheus' sin of hybris?

ANSWER: It would be difficult to point out a more effective dramatization of the sin of *hybris* than Pentheus' refusal to accept the miracles of the never-dying fire at Semele's tomb, and the freeing of the women from prison. When he denies the god himself and outrages his person, he approaches the very image of Sin personified. Euripides' careful preparation in the earlier scenes renders this superb encounter effective.

In brief, state specifically the "flaws" in Pentheus' character.

ANSWER: Pentheus' opposition to Dionysus and the new religion grows as the play progresses. The more evidence he sees of divine origin, the more devoted he becomes to his original error. Yet he is no melodramatic villain. He is normally, as Cadmus says later, a well-meaning man; but he lacks imagination and, of course, humility. In addition, there is something of the peeping Tom, the voyeur, the prurient fascination with sex behind the upright facade Pentheus displays. His decision to dress as a woman is intended to be taken as an indication of his moral debasement.

GREEK COMEDY: INTRODUCTION

DIONYSUS RITES: At the great festival of Dionysus in early April, both comedy and tragedy were performed. Comedy is a lineal descendant of a harvest festival, the grape and wine rites of joy, song, and dance—and revelry, sexual and otherwise! Buffoonery, scurrilous humor, rollicking satire of social and personal foibles—the whole mixed with the worship of the god of vegetation and the vine—Dionysus. Basically, then, comedy was born in fertility rites. What is astounding is that such wild revelry and rites became the seeds of the greatest comedy of the Western world!

FACTS OF GREEK COMEDY:

1. Three poets competed, but with only one comedy each.

2. Three actors only were featured; they wore comically grotesque masks, padded garments, and often wore a leather phallus, a sure sign of the fertility origins of Greek comedy.

3. The meters were treated much more loosely than the choric songs of tragedy.

4. The action was mostly confined to the first half of the play; at about the middle of the play the Chorus came forward and delivered a speech known as the *Parabasis* (*coming forward* in Greek). The Parabasis generally aired the views of the author himself.

5. Then followed an episodic and loosely connected series of scenes continuing to the end of the play.

6. Generally, the choruses were disguised as animals such as frogs, goats, storks, and wasps.

7. The chief feature of Greek comedy was its wild buffoonery, its license of tongue, its profanity, its lechery, and its free-swinging satire of any institution and person, usually a living contemporary of the author! No one was spared—not even the gods!

8. The Chorus numbered 24.

STRUCTURE OF GREEK COMEDY:

1. PROLOGUE: the leading character dreams up some "happy idea," such as Lysistrata's sex strike idea to put an end to the war quickly (see Aristophanes' *Lysistrata*).

2. PARODOS: the chorus enters the stage.

3. AGON: this is a comically dramatized debate between the inventor of the "happy idea" and the hater of the happy idea. The hater ("villain") is always put to rout by the triumphant principal.

4. PARABASIS: The Chorus comes forward to address the audience directly. Usually the author's views are aired, his speech not being necessarily relevant to the play's subject.

5. EPISODES: These are the series of episodic scenes in which the "happy idea" is put into action.

NOTE: Modern comedy owes very little to old Greek comedy (such as those of Aristophanes).

New Comedy (so called by the Greeks) sprang up in the fourth century B.C. It was a comedy of manners with its subjects taken from everyday life.

1. The greatest proponent of New Comedy was *Menander* (343-291 B.C.)

2. Latin literature imitated the New Comedy (*Plautus* and *Terence*), which in turn influenced Shakespeare, Molière, Congreve, Sheridan, Wilde, Shaw, etc.

3. Its virtues were naturalness, mastery of plot-making and character, an exquisite style.

4. Its characters were middle-class, and the plots dealt with love intrigue and comic slaves.

5. There was little or nothing Aristophanic about them—alas!

GREEK COMEDY: ARISTOPHANES

LIFE (c. 450 B.C.—c. 385 B.C.)

Aristophanes (air iss TOFF uh neez) was an Athenian who wrote comedies that are considered among the greatest ever written. He was a staunch conservative, believing that the values of the past, the days of old, the rural virtues were the best. Consequently he attacked new-fangled ideas in education, in philosophy, in contemporary tragedy (Euripides), and with consummate vigor ridiculed political demagoguery and corruption.

His *Frogs* is the play containing criticism of the tragedies of both Aeschylus and Euripides, the earliest extant example of literary criticism.

The following are some of the characteristics of his comedies:

1. Great wealth of vivid, imaginative poetry.

2. Vibrant, fresh, and engaging wit.

3. Satire which strikes home with pungency and acridity.

4. Poetry of consummate lyric quality, perhaps only bettered by the comedies of Shakespeare.

5. A great sense of the comic—slapstick, buffoonery, jokes, cracks, burlesque, extravaganza, straight and funny man comic routines, wild farce, strip tease, and outright bawdry.

Gilbert Murray (*The Literature of Ancient Greece*) said of Aristophanes that his most characteristic quality, "perhaps, is his combination of the wildest and broadest farce on the one hand, with the most exquisite lyric beauty on the other."

Only eleven of his large output of comedies survive:

The Acharnians (425 B.C.)　　*Lysistrata* (411 B.C.)
The Knights (424 B.C.)　　*The Thesmophoriazusae*
The Clouds (423 B.C.)　　　(411 B.C.)
The Wasps (422 B.C.)　　*The Frogs* (405 B.C.)
The Peace (421 B.C.)　　*The Ecclesiazusae* (391 B.C.)
The Birds (414 B.C.)　　*The Plutus* (388 B.C.)

GREEK COMEDY: ARISTOPHANES

CLOUDS (423 B.C.)

CHARACTERS

STREPSIADES (strep SIGH uh deez): old man whose son has gotten him in debt.

PHIDIPPIDES (figh DIP uh deez): his son who spends his father's money on chariot racing.

SOCRATES: philosopher who runs a school called "The Thoughtery."

DISCIPLES OF SOCRATES: students in the school of Socrates.

JUST DISCOURSE: personification, who argues for "old fashioned" standards.

UNJUST DISCOURSE: personification, who argues for "modern" standards.

PASIAS: a money-lender, who comes to collect from Strepsiades.

ANYNIAS: another money-lender.

CHORUS OF CLOUDS.

SETTING

SETTING: Two houses are shown, that of Strepsiades and that of Socrates.

PROLOGUE (lines 1-262): A cranky old man, *Strepsiades,* lies in bed worrying about the money his son spends on horses. He holds his city-bred wife responsible for his son's extravagance because she was extravagant, and she wanted their son to be named Phidippides (a made-up name incongruously combining the ideas of "thrifty" and "horses"). He suddenly has a *bright idea* and wakes up his *son:* he will enroll the young man in The Thoughtery, where he can learn to win lawsuits, regardless of whether they are just or not. Phidippides refuses because he would lose his sun tan in school, so Strepsiades decides to go himself.

At the door of the school, *Strepsiades* hears obscene stories from a *disciple* about Socrates' genius, and is delighted with his cleverness. Inside, he meets *Socrates*, suspended in a basket in mid-air, the better "to study higher things." The old man learns that elevated thoughts require elevation by basket in the more rarefied atmosphere of the "clouds." Strepsiades informs the philosopher that he wishes to learn the oily art of slippery speech so that he can avoid the payment of his debts.

PARODOS (263-509): While *Socrates* invokes the Clouds to come, *Strepsiades* covers his head to keep dry. The *Chorus* of Clouds enter, and Strepsiades wonders why they look like people. They are the goddesses of the lazy; they teach "high" thoughts, trickery, boasting, and lying. They are the only goddesses and cause everything: Zeus does not exist. They promise to teach him great eloquence, and are pleased with his modesty when he settles for being able to win lawsuits. To consider his fitness for admission, Socrates takes him into "The Thoughtery" for an examination.

FIRST PARABASIS (510-626): The *Chorus* then directly address the audience, praising them, the play they are watching (which they call Aristophanes' best play), and the skill of the playwright. They tell the audience to worship the clouds, and they attack the politician, Cleon.

EPISODES (627-888): *Socrates* and *Strepsiades* come out, the latter with a bed. The course is to include music and poetry, but Strepsiades is interested only in money. He utterly fails to understand the gender of nouns. He is told to lie on the bed and think, but all his remarks are about the bedbugs. Given up as a complete moron with a bad memory, he goes home to persuade his *son* to attend The Thoughtery. He tries unsuccessfully to teach him some scraps he remembers from his own experience, finally leaving him in the school, even though Phidippides warns him he will regret it.

FIRST AGON (889-1112): *Just* and *Unjust Discourse* come out to teach *Phidippides*. They are quarreling violently, and the *Chorus* separate them, ordering each to speak in turn. Just Discourse praises the old days of justice and modesty when parents were respected and lewdness avoided. Men were healthy then, and honorable. Unjust Discourse indicates the ways to confute the laws by triumphing with weak arguments. How can adultery be enjoyed if the guilty cannot defend themselves? Unjust Discourse wins the argument and takes out Phidippides to educate him.

SECOND AGON (1321-1452): *Phidippides* defends Euripides' audience, threatening to punish them with drought if this play does not win the prize.

EPISODE (1131-1320): Several days have passed, and *Strepsiades* comes back with a present for *Socrates*. Phidippides has been a great success, and when he comes out demonstrates that he can argue as glibly as the Sophists. *Pasias*, the money-lender, arrives to collect a debt, but Strepsiades refuses to pay because the man makes a mistake in the gender of nouns. He also refuses to pay the next money-lender, *Anynias,* arguing that if the sea does not get any fuller with the rivers pouring in, money shouldn't grow either.

The *Chorus* have no sooner said the old man will be punished for refusing to pay his debts, when his son drives him out of the house, beating him.

SECOND AGON (321-1452): *Phidippides* defends Euripides as the greatest of poets, but his *father* calls Euripides immoral. The son justifies beating his father because the old man is now in his second childhood, and it is lawful for children to be beaten. Moreover, says the son, he can also prove that it is just and lawful to beat one's mother.

EXODOS (1453-1510): *Strepsiades* appeals to the *Chorus* to defend him, but they say he deserves his punishment for trying to cheat his creditors. Furious, Strepsiades gets a torch and sets fire to The Thoughtery!

INTERPRETATION: *CLOUDS,* QUESTIONS AND ANSWERS

What are the two principal butts of Aristophanes' satire in this play?

ANSWER: The two butts of his satire are:

1. The great philosopher Socrates, who is caricatured as a farcical idealist and a corrupter of youth through his teaching of sophistic argument, such as "How to make the worse appear the better reason."

2. The New Education as promulgated by the Sophists; and the new methods of scientific research, which the author considers destructive of the old-time values in ethics and religion.

Does the Socrates in this play resemble the actual one?

ANSWER: The Socrates lampooned in this play bears little resemblance to the original, except that both were philosophers. The philosopher of the play is a composite of those teachers called the Sophists, notorious for their clever, specious arguments.

Is there an attack on the "egg-head" intellectuals?

ANSWER: Yes They make themseves ridicuous with their cloud-borne theories, and they make even worse citizens.

Why did Aristophanes pillory the intellectuals of his day?

ANSWER: He hated the intellectuals, because in teaching the young students of Athens to criticize, they were in effect educating a younger generation to be sceptical, shallow-minded, irreverent, glib of tongue and weak of mind—intellectual play boys.

E.g.: *Student*: "Which theory did he sanction; that the gnats hummed through their mouth, or backwards, through the tail?"

Strep: "Aye, and what said your Master (Socrates) of the gnat?"

Student: "He answered thus: the entrail of the gnat is small: and through this narrow pipe the wind rushes with violence straight towards the tail; there, close against the pipe, the hollow rump receives the wind, and whistles to the blast."

What type of conservative was Aristophanes? A reactionary?

ANSWER: He belongs to those who are conservative, not because they do not understand and sympathize with the new, but because they find distasteful the fakery, asininity, hoopla, humbuggery, and extravagancies that generally accompany it. Such conservatives find that most new criticism and reform upset the stability of the old ways, finally leaving things much the same as before.

Was Aristophanes ignorant of the new science and philosophy?

ANSWER: Indeed not. The Clouds show a deep knowledge of both. In addition, we know that Aristophanes had met and discussed ideas with Socrates over the dinner meal, as Plato's *Symposium* indicates.

What does the speech of Just Discourse *reveal about some of the things Aristophanes loved?*

ANSWER: He loved fine, strapping healthy young men; he loved the great old days of the Marathon—with their genial, jovial, robust characters, their love of drink and the good wielding of arms. Most of all he loved the farm and country life, with its Greek simplicity and homely love of neighbor.

GREEK COMEDY: ARISTOPHANES

FROGS (405 B.C.)

CHARACTERS

DIONYSUS: god of fertility and wine, disguises himself as Heracles to get Euripides back from Hades.

XANTHIAS (Zan thee uhs): his slave.

AESCHYLUS and
EURIPIDES: tragic poets in Hades; they argue the merits of their works.

HERACLES: famous hero of the "twelve labors" who, as one of the labors, brought back Cerberus from Hades.

HADES: king of the underworld, which is also called Hades.

AEACUS (EE uh kuss): a judge of the dead.

CORPSE: on way to his funeral; refuses to carry Dionysus' luggage.

LANDLADY: of an inn in Hades to whom Heracles owed money.

PLATHANE: her servant.

CHORUS OF FROGS: they sing a rowing song when Dionysus crosses the River Styx.

CHORUS OF INITIATED: initiates into the Eleusinian mysteries —serves for episodes in Hades.

CHARON: the ferryman of the River Styx in the Underworld.

SETTING: Before the house of Heracles; next to it is the house of Hades.

SUMMARY

PROLOGUE (lines 1-208): The god *Dionysus* enters incongruously wearing the lion-skin and carrying the club of Heracles over the yellow tunic of tragedy. With him is his servant *Xanthias,* riding a donkey carrying an enormous load of baggage.

They knock at the door of Heracles' house, where, to *Heracles'*
great amusement, Dionysus asks directions for getting to Hades.
He has developed a great craving to have Euripides on earth
again; he consults Heracles because only he has been there and
back. The three short ways to Hades Heracles suggests are three
different forms of suicide. He tries to frighten him off by emphasizing the horrors to be encountered. Dionysus goes to Hades, however, after first trying to get a dead man in a funeral to help with
the luggage—but the fee is too large.

At the river Styx, *Charon*, the ferryman, refuses to carry the
servant, and Xanthias has to walk around the edge. Dionysus is
made to row.

FIRST PARADOS (209-270): While *Dionysus* rows, the *Chorus* of
Frogs set the rhythm, using the refrain, *coax, coax, coax, brekeke-
kex coax.*

EPISODE (271-353): On the other side, *Xanthias* rejoins his
master, and they both are terrified by the monsters of Hades.
The frightened *Dionysus* seeks protection from the priest sitting
in the place of honor in the audience. Hearing music approaching,
master and slave crouch down to watch.

SECOND PARODOS (354-459): The *Chorus* of Initiates in the
Eleusinian mysteries enter. (The Initiates were a Dionysian cult
which promised a happy life in Hades to its members.) They sing
to Dionysus, dance, and make satirical thrusts at corrupt persons
and practices in contemporary Athens. *Dionysus* and *Xanthias* join
the dance and find out from the Chorus where Hades' palace is.

EPISODE (460-673): The door of Hades' palace is opened by
Aeacus, a judge of the dead. *Dionysus* announces himself as
Heracles, and Aeacus threatens him with torture at the hands of
monsters of Hades for the theft of Cerberus. *Xanthias* chides him
for cowardice, and Dionysus says that if Xanthias wants to be a
hero, he can put on Heracles' costume. He does so, and Dionysus
becomes the servant. The *maids* of Persephone (Hades' wife)
come out and invite "Heracles" to a feast.

Dionysus demands his costume back; a *landlady* and her *servant*
then threaten Dionysus with lawsuits because Heracles had left

a huge bill at her inn when he was in Hades. Dionysus gives his costume back to Xanthias again. Aeacus returns with *two servants*. Dionysus reveals his true identity, but since doubt remains as to which is the god and which is the slave, both are whipped to find the actual truth. An immortal presumably feels no pain, and both try not to cry out, but do so nevertheless. Aeacus decides to take them in to Hades, saying he can tell which is the god.

PARABASIS (674-737): The *Chorus* render high praise to Athenian citizens and attacks a contemporary politician named Cleophon. Next they attack Cligenes. The song ends with praise for the old-time citizens and their families as distinguished from the newer "climbers." Unqualified persons are being raised to high political position.

EPISODE (738-894):   *Xanthias* and *Aeacus* come out of the house, now good friends. They discuss the difficulties and pleasures of being servants. From inside comes the noise of a quarrel: Aeacus explains that Aeschylus and Euripides are arguing about the first place in Hades. Aeschylus had held it until the time of Euripides' death, but now the criminals have so loudly applauded Euripides' argumentative skill that he is claiming the prize. To settle the dispute, *Hades* has ordained a trial in which each poet will argue his case—*Dionysus* is to be the judge.

When the disputants issue from the house, still railing at one another, Dionysus tries to quiet them and urges each to pray. The *Chorus* look forward to an exciting battle.

AGON (895-1499):   *Euripides* begins by attacking Aeschylus:

1. his characters on stage have long silences;
2. his choral passages are interminable;
3. he uses long words and bombastic language;
4. he uses obscure allusions.

He goes on to say that in his own plays everything is made clear in the prologue and that

1. he uses realistic characters;
2. he has taught men to examine all questions and to speak their minds freely.

Aeschylus replies that Euripides' "realistic" characters are immoral and set bad examples. He justifies his own use of highly poetic language by holding it appropriate to lofty subject matter. The duty of a poet, says Aeschylus, is, after all, to teach—and anyone who teaches the speechmaking arts to everyone invites civil disobedience.

Each poet then quotes lines from his plays, the opponent then attacking the statement. In the famous "oil-can" passage which follows, Euripides' Prologues are made to appear repetitious and monotonous when Aeschylus shows that the phrase "found his oil-can gone" will complete the second half of many lines.

Euripides retaliates by showing that Aeschylus' choral odes monotonously repeat the same rhythm.

Aeschylus criticizes Euripides' songs by pointing out the cheap effects and the triviality of content combined with a high tragic style.

Dionysus calls for a set of balances, and each poet places one of his verses on each side.

Aeschylus always wins, for his "heavier" content lowers his side of the balance.

Hades comes out to ask who has won, but Dionysus has been unable to decide. He finally asks each poet how he would save Athens. Euripides, in general terms, recommends recalling the exiled rulers and throwing out those in power.

Aeschylus recommends building a large navy.

Dionysus decides in Aeschylus' favor; when Euripides recalls Dionysus' oath to take back Euripides, he is quoted the line from his own *Hippolytus*, "only my tongue swore."

EXODOS (1500-1533): Hades bids farewell to Aeschylus, giving him swords and poison to use for sending certain Athenians to Hades. Aeschylus says that Sophocles should occupy his throne in Hades—by no means should Euripides be allowed that honor. The *Chorus* wish him a good trip.

INTERPRETATION: FROGS, QUESTIONS AND ANSWERS

Who is the first of all literary critics?

ANSWER: Aristophanes—and a brilliant one! He has an intimate knowledge of the works and personalities of the two authors he criticizes, Aeschylus and Euripides.

Is there a political theme?

ANSWER: Yes. Aristophanes asks for political unity in a strife-torn Athens. In addition, he asks for the recall of certain political exiles. Remember that this play was written during the bitter war between Athens and Sparta.

Does Aristophanes' literary conservatism show?

ANSWER: Yes. Aristophanes prefers Aeschylus' highly ethical and religious themes over Euripides' mordant realism and scepticism.

Exactly when was the play written and presented and what was the political situation of the time?

ANSWER: The play was presented in the year of the defeat of Athens at sea by Spartan forces (405 B.C.); and the year before Lysander, the Spartan commander, tore down the very walls of Athens. The play would seem to be justified in its denunciation of the corruption and incompetence among Athenian leaders of the day.

Why have puritan-minded people preferred this play to all others of Aristophanes?

ANSWER: It is the one most free of bawdry and scabrous comment—hence atypical of the author. The subject of the play is almost entirely literary, and, astonishingly for Aristophanes, there are very few passages that would arouse the antipathy of the puritan-minded—hence the popularity of the play in college and high school anthologies.

What are the actual dramatic demerits of this play?

ANSWER:

1. It is poorly constructed.

2. It is impoverished in humor and wit.

3. The solemn manner coupled with the thinnest of spirit is atypical and poor Aristophanes.

Did Aristophanes actually attack Euripides as a dramatist?

ANSWER: Yes, but not as an individual. The satire on Euripides' use of excessive pathos and ingenious intellectualism is harmless enough, and a popular subject for satire. In addition, Euripides' dramatic experiments easily lend themselves to gibes and ridicule. But never is Euripides accused of cowardice, venality, sycophancy, pederasty; nor does Aristophanes ever dream that Euripides is not at least the third greatest poet of the stage. Not counting Aeschylus and Sophocles, none of the numerous *other* tragic poets of the time were to be even remotely compared with Euripides! Finally, if we are to assume that Dionysus is speaking for the author himself in the decision-weighing scene, we must see that Dionysus had no easy time of it: Aeschylus wins by a hair because his plays evoke in the author a great nostalgia for the heroic past.

What did the famous Greek scholar (Gilbert Murray) discover about Aeschylus' criticism that many Euripidean lines in the Prologues can be finished in the last half by tacking on a single phrase—"found his oil-can gone" (lekythion apólese).

ANSWER: He found that "all three tragedians have such passages in the opening of about half their extant plays, and the 'monotony,' if such it be, belongs rather to the style of the tragic prologue than to Euripides."

GREEK COMEDY: ARISTOPHANES

LYSISTRATA (411 B.C.)

CHARACTERS

LYSISTRATA: an Athenian housewife, (liz iss STRAH tah).

CLEONICE: friend to Lysistrata, (klee oh NIGH kee).

MYRRHINE: Athenian housewife, (meer EE nee).

LAMPITO: a Spartan girl.

MAGISTRATES: Athenians.

CINESIAS: Myrrhine's husband.

CHILD OF CINESIAS.

HERALD OF THE LACEDAEMONIANS.

ENVOYS OF THE LACEDAEMONIANS.

AN ATHENIAN CITIZEN.

CHORUS OF OLD MEN: Athenians; actually a semi-chorus.

CHORUS OF WOMEN: Athenians; really a semi-chorus.

SETTING: Athens, just beneath the Acropolis, before Lysistrata's house. Later the scene is before the entrance of the Acropolis.

SUMMARY

PROLOGUE (lines 1-253): *Lysistrata* is pacing up and down before the door of her house. She is filled with great excitement and great annoyance. She has laid her plans carefully, and the moment to strike is imminent: she has sent some Athenian women to seize the Acropolis (public citadel and location of temples and treasury; the buildings are located on the flat surface of a high hill). In addition, she is impatiently awaiting women representatives of other Grecian states who have agreed to meet her here at this very time.

Her plan: the women of Greece are to force their husbands to lay down their arms and cease fighting their stupid war against each other (Athens versus Sparta principally); if their husbands refuse, their wives will refuse to give their men any sexual satisfaction whatsoever! *Cleonice* and *Myrrhine* arrive; and then the athletic *Lampito* from Sparta and others.

After the women have been informed of the plan, there is raised a chorus of objections; but the loyal support of Lampito brings them around. They swear an awful oath of female celibacy over a bowl of wine (in Aristophanes, women find wine irresistible).

There is heard a great commotion offstage; this signifies that the Acropolis has been captured; the revolt is now in full swing!

PARADOS (254-386): The scene shifts to the entrance of the Acropolis; a group of *old men,* who make up one half of the Chorus, enter slowly and painfully up the steep hill; they are carrying sticks and logs and pots of fire, and intend to chase the women from the citadel with smoke. The other Chorus, made up of *women,* appear on the scene armed with pots of water. The inevitable happens: the old men are thoroughly doused with water, and their pots of fire are put out.

PRO-AGON (387-475): A *Magistrate* arrives accompanied by four Scythian *policemen.* He orders his officers to break down the gates and arrest the leader of the insurrection—*Lysistrata,* who issues from the Acropolis voluntarily. But as she is about to be taken, her *comrades* attack the police so fiercely that they retire in fear and great defecation!

AGON (476-613): Now the *Magistrate* offers to debate the issue and is eloquently attacked by *Lysistrata,* who gives a moving statement of her plan and intended actions. The *police* are unmoved however, and so the *women* convert words into deeds: they douse the Magistrate with water, attiring him like a corpse on a funeral bier. He leaves in a towering rage, vowing to tell his fellow magistrates how ignominiously he has been treated. The victorious women return within the gates of the Acropolis.

PARABASIS (614-705): The two *Choruses* engage in a verbal battle of the sexes. The Women (they are as old as the men) stridently boast of how the state is served through the children they offer to it. The old men object to the interference of women in men's affairs.

FIRST EPISODE (706-780): Several days elapse, and now we see *Lysistrata* before the Acropolis in a deeply anxious and disillusioned mood. The initial enthusiasm of her *followers* has cooled, and there is muttering and signs of defection in the female ranks. They miss their men and the sexual joys of the marriage bed. Excuses for desertion now unfold:

1. There is wool at home to be spread.

2. There is flax to be stripped.

3. The hooting of the sacred Acropolis owls is unbearable.

4. One woman pretends pregnancy by slipping a helmet under her robe: she must get to town immediately to seek the aid of a midwife!

The revolution seems to be dissolving into anarchy, but by some means Lysistrata temporarily holds them together.

FIRST STASIMON (781-828): Again a battle of the sexes with the two *Choruses* shouting verbal abuse at each other.

SECOND EPISODE (829-1013): Now *Cinesias,* the husband of one of Lysistrata's high command, named Myrrhine, enters. He is wretched from lack of sexual satisfaction, his household is in a mess. He is accompanied by their *baby* with the hope that its presence will lure his wife to his bedside.

The obedient *Myrrhine* carries out her orders (from Lysistrata) with fiendish perfection. She deliberately tantalizes her husband with continuous sexual allurements so that the poor deprived fellow is writhing in swollen agony (the scene is one of the most sexually comic in all drama). She finally leaves her husband in a state of utter misery and runs back into the Acropolis.

Now a *Herald* of the Spartans (Lacedaemonians) arrives; and his state of erection leaves no doubt that the Spartans are in as woeful a state as the Athenians. "Are you a man or a Priapus (a god of fertility usually in an enormous state of erection)?" asks the Athenian official who meets him, "or is that a lance you're hiding under your clothes?"

SECOND STASIMON (1014-1071): The *Chorus* of Old Men and Old Women reconcile and make peace.

THIRD EPISODE (1072-1188):   The Spartan *Envoys* arrive and make a bid for peace; even at the cost of laying down their arms and ending the war between Athens and Sparta.

Lysistrata appears and gives a stirring speech on the joys of peace, but the men's minds are on other things; they quickly agree to a peace; and the play ends with all entering the Acropolis to make their sacrifices to the gods.

THIRD STASIMON (1189-1215):   The Chorus, no longer divided, sing an ode of joy.

EXODOS (1216-1321):   There is a joyous banquet to celebrate the peace declaration. There is complete harmony and joyous celebrations between the *Spartans* and their erstwhile enemies, the *Athenians*. There is much singing of folk songs and dancing the national dances of the respective countries. The play ends with all leaving for their domiciles amidst more singing and dancing.

INTERPRETATION: *LYSISTRATA*, QUESTIONS AND ANSWERS

What is the serious plea underneath the farce and buffoonery of this raucous play?

ANSWER: Aristophanes is pleading for an end to the debilitating and futile war with Sparta, giving a picture of what joys would follow such a peace. Obviously, the means to securing such a peace is utopian and visionary. Moreover, there is a plea for all the various tribes and states to get together and act in unity towards common goals—Panhellenism.

In what other plays did Aristophanes give the important roles to women besides this one?

ANSWER: The *Ecclesiazusae* and the *Thesmophoriazusae*. Aristophanes was wise enough to realize that human sexual phenomena provide the richest material for comedy.

What other two plays of Aristophanes deal with the peace theme?

ANSWER: The *Acharnians* and *Peace*, but unlike the war during the time when the other two plays had been written, things had gone so badly for the Athenians in 411 B.C. that they had their backs to the wall. The *Lysistrata* is pure fantasy produced at a time when a realizable peace with Sparta would have been impossible. Hence, the pacifism of *Lysistrata* is pure fantasy and is as divorced from reality as was Aristophanes in the *Birds*.

What is the popularity of this play since the time of Aristophanes?

ANSWER: Its popularity has far outstripped that of any other old comedy and rivals the popularity and influence of the new comedy. Christian prudery has more or less successfully opposed the production of this play, among the wittiest ever written, but in spite of censorship it has kept itself vigorously alive in print; in recent times the play has enjoyed a renewed popularity on the stage.

What are the themes of Aristophanes' other plays besides those covered in this book?

ANSWER:

1. The *Acharnians* (425) is a frontal attack on the Athenian war-mongering party.

2. The *Peace* (421) shows the hero flying to heaven on an enormous beetle in order to seek an end to the war.

3. The *Knights* (424) bitterly and personally attacks Cleon, a demagogue who succeeded Pericles as the democratic leader in Athens.

4. The *Thesmophoriazusae* is a play in which the women of Athens put the poet on trial for casting slanders on the female sex.

5. The *Wasps,* in which fun is made of the Athenian love of suing in court.

6. The *Ecclesiazusae* (392) mocks certain utopian schemes for the betterment of society; one such scheme being Plato's community of wives mentioned in his *Republic*.

7. The *Birds* (414), in which birds rule men in a play of pure comic fantasy.

8. *Plutus* (388), his last extant play, shows the blind god of Wealth no longer blind, the result being that the good are made rich and the bad made poor—and the amazing consequences thereon.

*As a comic writer what are some of the forms of comedy in which
Aristophanes excels?*

ANSWER: Aristophanes utilizes all comic forms and devices which
excite to laughter; and in all he is superb: parody, farce, burlesque,
word-play, the witty retort, the blackout turn, the physical joke
in pantomine (i.e., sight gag), etc.

GREEK HISTORY: INTRODUCTION

ORIGINS: History writing began in Ionia in the sixth and fifth centuries B.C.

1. Prose was first used in the writing of history. The subject matter usually dealt with ancient legends, genealogies of aristocratic families; and some early histories even dealt with scientific subjects.

2. History was retarded for many years by its use of poetry as its medium, and its tendency to look upon ancient legend and myth as fact. In addition, there was a lack of a written record of past events, a lack of good communication between the city-states, and a religion that hampered rational, historical thinking.

3. The writing of history was encouraged by the Greek spirit of rationalism, unique to Greece alone. Especially in Ionia there developed a spirit of rationalism and scientific inquiry that is conducive to the writing of good history.

   a. The rapidly spreading colonization of the Mediterranean was highly conducive to historical thought.

   b. The highly volatile commercial activity was vital to the historical process.

   c. The Persian Wars gave rise to a vast interest in modern history.

   d. The scepticism of the Sophists aided historical outlook, as did their artistic prose.

PREDECESSORS OF HERODOTUS: Hecataeus of Miletus and Hellanicus of Lesbos. Both lived in the latter half of the fifth century; they laid the foundations of historical writing; but in the main they were principally geographers.

GREEK HISTORY: HERODOTUS

LIFE (484 B.C.-420(?) B.C.)

Little is known about the life of the man who wrote of the struggle between the small Greek city-states and the ponderous Persian Empire. The "Father of History," as Herodotus has come to be known, was born in Halicarnassus, a town located in southwestern Asia Minor, probably in 484 B.C. The coast of Asia Minor was at the time a center of Greek civilization called Ionia, an area in which Herodotus received a sound Greek education. He belonged to the Dorian branch of the Greek family.

Herodotus traveled extensively. He was forced to seek refuge at Samos, an island in the southeastern Aegean Sea; it was there that he learned the Ionic dialect in which his work was written. Other trips took him to Greece, Egypt, Scythia, and Libya, among other places. About 443 B.C. he joined Athenian pioneers and migrated to Thruii in southern Italy. He is supposed to have died there in the 420's B.C.

BACKGROUND TO HERODOTUS: Despite the fact that Herodotus spent most of his time within the orbit of the Greek world, he also came into contact with Persian culture because his native city had been under Persian control during the early years of his life. Although Herodotus was not familiar with the language of the conquerors, there were opportunities to learn about their laws, their religion, and their humanity. It was also through Persian influence that the Eastern style of telling stories, which lends such a delightful quality to the *Histories*, was absorbed by Herodotus. Acquaintance with Greek and Persian cultures made him aware of the merits of both, and the enemies of Greece are treated with fairness.

HIS WORK: The *Histories* tell about the great war between Greece and Persia. Herodotus attempts to answer the question of *why* the two peoples came into conflict. In doing this, he felt it necessary to tell not only the tale of the war itself, but also the history, culture, customs, and religion of the countries mentioned in his work. It is for this reason that the classic is entitled *Histories* (i.e., *investigations*, as the Greeks used the word), and not merely "A History of the Persian Wars."

Since he was writing for a Greek audience, it was essential to dwell

257

on the more unfamiliar aspects of Persian history. In gathering material, Herodotus visited such Persian provinces as Egypt, Syria and Lydia (the Kingdom of Lydia, before its conquest by Persia, comprised about half of the territory of present-day Turkey), collected stories from the priests and wrote of his own observations. In many cases his writings are our only sources of information for these ancient countries. Of course Herodotus had to include the histories of the Greek states which participated in the war. He did this, telling the fables and legends of both large and small nations.

THREE-PART DIVISION OF THE HISTORIES: The *Histories* divide naturally into three parts.

Part One: Composed of Books I through IV; this section is concerned primarily with the history of the provinces of the Persian Empire.

Part Two: Consists of Book V and part of Book VI, telling about the immediate causes of the war: Persian expansion into Greece and the revolt of the Ionian cities against their Persian rulers.

Part Three: The warfare between the Greeks and Persians is the subject of the rest of the work. Book IX ends rather abruptly, suggesting that Herodotus was still working on it when he died.

ITS VALUE: Although the book is a masterpiece of literary art and is still read today, the accuracy of Herodotus has always been called into question:

1. his recounting of fables and legends,
2. his belief in supernatural influences,
3. some very obvious inaccuracies—

all have led many prominent authors to believe that he was worthless as an historical observer. (Indeed, "Father of History" was not his only title, for at one time he was also given the name, "Father of Lies.")

This attitude has changed in recent times, however, for archaeological findings tend largely to confirm his facts. Even when he tells stories and fables, Herodotus frequently informs the reader that they are legends, and he gives his opinions as to whether or not he thinks they are true; on the other hand, he did believe in oracles, though not blindly.

As for his probable inaccuracies—for example, the gross exaggeration of the number of Persian troops invading Greece—are concerned, they are minor.

On the whole, the *Histories* give a comprehensive view of the life of many ancient nations, as well as telling of the heroism of both Greeks and Persians in their bitter battles. In the clash between East and West, Herodotus felt that he had to portray each of the conflicting cultures as completely as possible, and this he did to the best of his ability.

HERODOTUS

THE HISTORIES: SUMMARY

THE PERSIAN WARS: *BRIEF SKETCH*

CAUSES: The immediate cause of the Persian Wars was the unwillingness of the Greeks to be absorbed into the Persian Empire. A collision between the peoples involved occurred in the year 546 B.C. when the great king of the Persians, *Cyrus,* toppled the Kingdom of Lydia and overthrew *Croesus,* its Hellenistic (i.e. Greek oriented) monarch. Croesus had already conquered the Greek cities of Asia Minor, but he was a lenient ruler and allowed the cities to practically govern themselves, provided they paid him tribute. When Cyrus gained control of Lydia, the Greek cities asked the same privileges of him as they had enjoyed under Croesus. The Persian king refused, and the cities revolted; Cyrus curbed that rebellion and added Greece to an empire which extended from Asia Minor to India.

Some years after the death of Cyrus, a lieutenant of Darius I, *Megabazus,* crossed into Europe and took parts of Thrace (northern Greece), including some Athenian possessions. In response to an Athenian protest, the Persians ordered Athens to restore *Hippias,* a former tyrant, to power. When the order was refused, it was understood that a conflict was unavoidable.

THE IONIAN REVOLT: *Darius* could not march against Athens immediately, however. In the year 499 the Ionian cities which had been conquered by Cyrus revolted and asked their Greek brethren for aid. Athens, soon to be the major sea power, and the city of Tretria, responded by sending ships to Asia Minor. A combined Greek expedition was formed which took Sardis, the capital of the Lydian province, and burned it. The Greeks were forced to retreat by the Persians, who then resumed the offensive. Miletus, a center of Greek learning and civilization, and once the first city of the Greek intellectual world, was finally taken and utterly destroyed. By 493 B.C. the revolt of the Ionian cities had been completely crushed.

THE WARS: By now it was clear to the Persians that their next task was to defeat the European Greeks, especially the Athenians and the Spartans. *Darius* sent a fleet and an army to Greece under the command of *Mardonius,* his son-in-law. The army managed to cross into Europe and to take several northern Greek cities, but the fleet was destroyed in an attempt to round Mt. Athos, northeast of Greece, in 492 B.C. Mardonius returned home as a result of this disaster.

MARATHON: *Darius* had not abandoned his plan to punish the city-states for their aid to the Asiatic Greeks, however. In 490 B.C. another Persian army and fleet appeared in Greece, this time under the command of Darius himself. The Great King was able to take and destroy Eretria, Athens' partner in the raid on Sardis. When Athenians and Persians met in the famous Battle of Marathon, the result was a complete victory for the Athenians. After the battle, the Persian fleet sailed to Athens in the hope that it would find the city unguarded. The Greek troops who had fought at Marathon, however, reached Athens before the fleet, and the Persians sailed home.

THERMOPYLAE (thurhr MOP ih lee): The crushing defeat dealt Darius at Marathon encouraged revolt among the subject nationalities of the Persian Empire. It therefore became a necessity to subdue the Greeks, and the next attempt was made under *Xerxes* (ZURK seez), son of Darius, in 480 B.C. Xerxes gathered all the forces of the Empire available and marched towards Greece with an enormous army. Several Greek city-states submitted to him without struggle, but a combined force under Spartan command—Sparta was the major Greek land power—met him at Thermopylae in central Greece. The larger Persian army overcame stubborn Greek resistance and gained the victory: the road to Athens was open.

SALAMIS: When *Xerxes* and his victorious Persians entered Athens, they encountered little opposition, for the city's inhabitants had been evacuated to the nearby island of Salamis. The sea battle which ensued ended in a complete victory for the Greeks as the Persian fleet was destroyed with heavy loss of life—the Persian sailors did not know how to swim. After this defeat, Xerxes left for home, leaving an army in Greece under *Mardonius*.

PLATAEA AND MYCALE: The next year, 479 B.C. was an eventful one: after spring had come, *Mardonius* ventured out with his army and met the Greeks at Plataea. The number of soldiers opposing each other was approximately equal. Plataea resulted in another overwhelming defeat for the Persians as their commander was killed and the army practically destroyed. What remained of the invading force hastily retreated to Asia: the Persian attempt to conquer Greece had completely failed. The year did not end before another resounding victory had been won, however; for the Greeks now assumed the offensive. A combined Greek fleet converged upon Mycale in Asia Minor, landed a force, defeated the Persians, and burned what warships it found there. Only relatively minor skirmishes were fought between the two combatants after the battles of Plataea and Mycale.

It is at this point that the Book IX (the last one) closes.

THE HISTORIES: *DETAILED SUMMARY*

BOOK I *(TO CLIO, THE MUSE OF HISTORY)*

PURPOSE: The first Book deals mainly with the early history of Lydia and Persia and with the peoples with whom these nations came into contact. It opens with the avowal of Herodotus that his work will seek the causes of enmity between the Greeks and Persians and will record the accomplishments of both Greeks and barbarians.

Conflict between Greeks and Asians is traced back to legendary times. The Trojan War was the first act of aggression by Greeks against Asia, because hitherto, warfare between the two worlds had been confined to raiding each other for wives. When Helen, wife of the Greek King Menelaus, was stolen, however, the Greeks gathered an army and destroyed the Asian city of Troy. This seemed the height of foolishness to the Persians.

THE STORY OF CROESUS: After indicating that he is skeptical concerning these legendary origins of the hostility between the two peoples, Herodotus goes on to describe events nearer to his own time, and he begins with *Croesus*, the last king of independent Lydia. Croesus was the fifth descendant of Gyges, the first king of the Mermnad family. Gyges had usurped the throne by murdering the king and marrying the queen; and the vengeance of the gods was promised for the fifth of his line to sin on the throne—Croesus. Yet it did not seem as if the prophesy would come true because Croesus was not only fabulously rich, but he had also waged a successful campaign against the cities of the Asiatic Greeks. Croesus confined himself to subduing the mainland cities, however, since he dared not meet the fleets of the Greeks who lived on the islands off the coast of Asia Minor.

SOLON AND CROESUS: *Croesus* felt himself to be the happiest of men because of his riches and his conquests, but forebodings of his future fate were to be seen.

Solon, an Athenian lawgiver who went into voluntary exile, visited the capital city of Sardis and came to see Croesus. Hearing that Solon was wise, Croesus decided to test him by asking who was "the most enviable of men." Croesus fully expected that he would be named. He was dismayed when Solon answered that "Tellus, the Athenian" was because he had many children and grandchildren and had died honorably. Not content, Croesus asked who came second to Tellus. Solon replied that surely Cleobis and Biton did because they were virtuous and had died a good death. When Croesus protested, Solon told him that although the king had riches and was fortunate at the moment, a judgment could not be made upon his happiness until the type of death Croesus had met became known. Solon, the wise man of Athens, was dismissed by the Lydian king as an ignorant man.

CYRUS AND CROESUS: Two years after the death of his son, *Croesus* became suspicious of the growing power of *Cyrus,* king of the neighboring Persians. Despite the fact that Cyrus had given no provocation, Croesus began to plan a war against him. His first move was an attempt to win the favor of the gods by sending gifts to the shrine of Apollo at Delphi, and by offering sacrifices. Then he put a number of questions to the oracles (which were supposed to tell the future): What would happen if he should start a war with Persia? When the reply informed him that *if he began a war he would put an end to a great empire,* Croesus advanced against the Persians. The empire about to come to an end was Croesus' own! An indecisive battle was fought in Persian territory, after which Croesus retired to his capital, disbanded the army and called on his Spartan and Egyptian allies to send him aid within five months, for he thought that Cyrus would not dare attack him. This view proved false. Cyrus marched on Sardis and took it before any help could reach Croesus. Thus fell the mighty empire of Croesus: he had fulfilled the fate from which even the god Apollo—so the oracle said—had been powerless to save him.

HISTORY OF CYRUS: *Cyrus* was the first Persian king. He achieved power by leading a revolt of his people against his maternal grandfather, *Astyages.*

Before the accession of Cyrus, the Persians were subject to a people known as the Medes. When Cyrus was born, Astyages—fearing a possible rival in the boy because his father was a Persian—

ordered his grandson killed by his lieutenant, *Harpagus*. Wishing to insure himself in case of a change in regime, Harpagus ordered one of the king's herdsmen to commit the murder. The herdsman gave in to the pleas of his wife to substitute their stillborn son for the future king and to raise the baby as their own. After a number of years the true story of how Cyrus had been saved became known. Astyages, no longer fearing him, restored him to his parents, but resolved to punish Harpagus for his disobedience. The *son* of Harpagus was invited to the king's palace, killed, cooked, and served to his father at a royal banquet. Harpagus was revenged some years later when he advised Cyrus to lead a revolt of the Persians. Astyages appointed Harpagus the commander of his armies in order to crush the rebellion, and was betrayed. Astyages ended his days as a prisoner of his grandson.

CYRUS AND THE RIVER GYNDES: The successes *Cyrus* had achieved gave him a trait in common with Croesus—pride. On his march to Babylon, one of his sacred horses had drowned while attempting to cross the river Gyndes. The Persian king became so furious that he vowed to punish the river by making it impotent. This he did by employing his army in digging three hundred and sixty channels and allowing the river to disperse itself into them. The Persian army spent a whole summer in performing this task!

CYRUS AND TOMYRIS: *Cyrus* met his end when he began a war with the Massagetae, a people who inhabited what is now part of south central Russia.

Tomyris, the queen of the Massagetae, attempted to dissuade Cyrus from war, but he refused. When it was certain that a conflict was near, Tomyris proposed that the armies should be allowed to meet either in her territory or within the limits of the Empire. *Croesus,* whose life had been spared by Cyrus, convinced the Persian monarch to enter the realm of Tomyris, telling him of a scheme to win the battle by guile.

The plan worked, but the queen hastily gathered another army and promised Cyrus his fill of blood. When the armies came together in a battle which was judged by Herodotus to be "the hardest that was ever fought between barbarians," the Persians were defeated and Cyrus was killed.

CUSTOMS OF THESE PEOPLES: It is with this battle between the Massagetae and the Persians that the first Book ends. Throughout his narration of intrigues and battles, however, Herodotus frequently pauses to tell about the customs of the countries under examination:

1. Speaking about Lydia, for example, he mentions that their customs resemble those of the Greeks. The Lydians were also the first people, so far as is known, to use coins.

2. The Persians, on the other hand, were unlike the Greeks in their customs:

     a. Persian religion did not conceive of the gods as having a nature like that of man, as Greek religion did. For this reason they did not have altars or images.

     b. When sacrificing, the Persian had to pray, not only for himself, but for all his countrymen and for his king.

3. Persian education was also unlike the Greek. A son was not admitted into his father's presence until he was five years old. From that age until he was twenty, the young Persian lad was instructed in three things: how to ride a horse, how to shoot a bow, and to tell the truth.

BABYLONIAN CUSTOMS: The Babylonians, on the other hand, had customs worthy of note in regard to marriage:

1. All marriageable women were sold to the highest bidder, and the bidding began with the most beautiful girl. What was received for the most beautiful girls was used to provide a dowry for the ones who were not so beautiful, thus making them more desirable. This custom, however, was discontinued when the Persians conquered Babylon.

2. Another custom which was considered wise by Herodotus was that of taking a sick man to the market place; there passers-by who had had similar afflictions, or who knew of a cure, could give advice and comfort to the sufferer.

3. Herodotus also reports a custom among the Babylonians which he labels "infamous." The women of Babylon, at least once in their lives, had to go to the temple of Aphrodite (or Mylitta, the goddess of love) and offer themselves to the first man who threw a coin of whatever value into her lap. A woman could not leave her place at the temple until she had been chosen by

a stranger; so some women spent as many as three or four years fulfilling this obligation.

AN UNUSUAL CUSTOM OF THE MASSAGETAE: The Massagetae, the people who had defeated Cyrus, also had a noteworthy custom: when a man became quite old, all his relatives gathered in order that they might kill him ceremoniously and eat his flesh. This was considered by them to be the happiest possible death.

HERODOTUS

THE HISTORIES: SUMMARY (BOOK II)

BOOK II (TO EUTERPE, MUSE OF FLUTE-PLAYING)

PURPOSE OF BOOK II: Among the many provinces of the mighty Persian Empire was the ancient land of Egypt. Herodotus visited the country and was impressed with its wonders, especially with the magnificent achievements of the pharaohs. The second Book of the *Histories* is devoted to a description of Egypt—its topography, customs, religion and history—before the successful Persian invasion. Besides giving an eyewitness account of Egypt as it was in his own day, the historian repeated stories relating to Egyptian history as they were told to him by the priests who believed them to be true.

RELIGION AND CUSTOMS: The Egyptians were a polytheistic people. Many of their gods and rites bore similarities to Greek gods and practices; Herodotus was of the opinion that his country-men had been influenced by the Egyptians, rather than *vice versa*. An Egyptian god named Heracles, for instance, was one of the oldest deities known. Nothing, however, could be heard about the Greek hero Heracles in Egypt. The conclusion therefore was that Greeks had taken the name of Heracles from the Egyptians.

Nor was the story that the Egyptians had attempted to sacrifice the Greek Heracles a credible one, for the Egyptians were allowed to kill only pigs (which were considered unclean) and cattle with certain markings. Many animals were sacred to the natives, cows being the most holy; but cats and rams, as well as others, were also revered. The people had a high regard for animals in general, vows being taken and money being set aside for their care. The Egyptian counterpart of Zeus, Ammon, was even represented as a ram because it was said that he once appeared to Heracles dressed in the head and fleece of a newly killed ram.

EGYPTIANS AND THEIR DEAD: Among the notable customs of the Egyptians was the practice of embalming their dead. There were several ways—depending upon price—in which this was done.

1. The most expensive procedure involved drawing out the brain and the intestines from the corpse and then filling the abdomen

with various spices. After being buried in saltpeter for 70 days, the body was wrapped in fine linen and coated with a gum.

2. In less expensive treatments, the brain and intestines were drawn out. The mummy was usually put in a case and kept in the home.

THEIR AWARENESS OF DEATH: The Egyptians were constantly aware of death. At higher-class banquets, wooden corpses in coffins were sometimes shown to the guests; they were then told to enjoy themselves, for they would one day be like the images. Egyptians did, however, believe in an immortal soul. Herodotus relates that they thought that after one's death, the soul entered the body of an animal which was just being born. When that animal died, it would enter the body of another, and so on until it had inhabited the bodies of all types of creatures. (Perhaps this accounted for the respect the Egyptians had for animals.) After 3000 years, the Egyptians maintained, the soul again entered the body of a human.

AMASIS: It was under *Amasis* (Ahmose) that Egypt led a successful army revolt against *Apries*. It was under Amasis that Egypt reached its highest degree of prosperity. Although Amasis was supposed to have led a riotous personal life, his character was amply demonstrated when he sent gifts to only those oracles which had called him a thief, while to those which deemed him an honest man, he gave nothing and openly called them false. This king was also friendly to the Greeks, giving them the city of Naucratis in which to trade with Egyptians.

HERODOTUS

THE HISTORIES: SUMMARY (BOOK III)

BOOK III (TO THALIA, MUSE OF COMEDY)

Herodotus tells how Cambyses, the son of Cyrus, added Egypt
to his empire, how the Ethiopian campaign ended in disaster; and
how Cambyses finally went mad and died; a recounting of the death
is interesting:

THE DEATH OF CAMBYSES: The death of *Cambyses* seemed to
have been in divine retribution for his sins. His troubles began
when a herald arrived from his capital city of Susa proclaiming
that the Persians should now obey *Smerdis*, brother of the king.
When Cambyses heard the news, he was stunned, for he had
secretly ordered his brother's death.

Upon further investigation he learned that the imposter was a man
of the Magian tribe of the Medes whose true name was also
Smerdis. (The Magians were the priestly tribe of the Medes.)
Learning that this Smerdis was a priest, Cambyses suddenly understood the meaning of the dream which had led him to have
his brother murdered: the one in which a messenger proclaimed
that Smerdis sat on the throne with his head reaching toward the
sky. Lamenting his haste in having his brother killed, Cambyses
rode out against the usurper. On his way, however, his sword ac-
cidentally pierced his thigh. Knowing he was dying a slow death,
Cambyses called in his Persians, told them about his brother and
the imposter and set a curse on them if they did not win the throne
back from the Medes. Soon after, he died of the wound, which was
said by Herodotus to be in the same place where the king had
struck the Egyptian calf-god, Apis.

Through trickery *Darius* became the king of Persia. Herodotus
describes the empire and the great extent of his wealth; the book
ends with the quelling of a Babylonian revolt.

HERODOTUS

THE HISTORIES: SUMMARY (BOOK IV)

BOOK IV (TO MELPOMENE, THE MUSE OF TRAGEDY)

INTRODUCTION: Darius decided to attack the Scythians (who inhabited what is now part of Rumania and southwestern Russia) before he invaded Greece. He did this an an attempt to secure his flank for the time when a war with the Greeks would begin. Darius' ostensible reason for attacking the Scythians, however, was an historical one: some years before, they had invaded, toppled and ruled over the Medean Empire (the immediate predecessor of the Persian Empire) for a period of 28 years. Thus it was with revenge in their hearts that the Persians undertook the Scythian campaign.

CUSTOMS: Herodotus describes the land of the Scythians; their geography, cultural, social, and military ways. Such details are cited as the burial of their monarch, when his stomach was first opened and filled with spices; the corpse was then carried through his domains in a wagon, so that it might be seen by all Scythians before burial. He was then buried in a barrow along with one of his concubines, his cook, cup-bearer, groom, squire and messenger, all of whom were first strangled. A great mound of earth was then heaped upon the grave. Before a year was out, fifty of the finest horses and fifty of the king's servants were also strangled. The dead horses were set upon stakes so as to surround the grave, and each of the servants was mounted on a horse and made to remain upright by means of a stake driven through his body. A circle of corpses was thus made to guard the mound before the burial was considered complete.

INVASION AND WITHDRAWAL: After a long campaign, *Darius* withdrew without being able to conquer the Scythians. The book ends with an account of his campaigns in Cyrene and Libya.

HERODOTUS

THE HISTORIES: SUMMARY (BOOK V)

BOOK V (TO TERPSICHORE, THE MUSE OF DANCING)

Book V describes the Persian victory over the Thracians. Then
follows an acount of the Persian negotiations with the Macedonians.
Ionian rebellion against Persian rule (499 B.C.) is then recounted,
followed by a digression on Athens and Sparta. The Ionians were
aided in their rebellion by the Athenians and Eretrians, and even
joined in the burning of Sardis. The Book ends with a quelling
of the Ionian rebellion by their rulers, the Persians.

HERODOTUS

THE HISTORIES: SUMMARY (BOOK VI)

BOOK VI (TO ERATO, THE MUSE OF THE LYRE)

Although the Ionian revolt continued for a number of years after the burning of Sardis, its days were clearly numbered. The Persians made slow headway against the rebels, but the progress was steady. Unable to obtain any substantial Spartan or Athenian aid, the Greek cities of Asia Minor (Ionians) were fighting a doomed battle, for they could not hope to match the resources which were at the disposal of the Persian Empire. Finally, the Ionians were decisively defeated after the destruction of the splendid town of Miletus.

DIGRESSION: *Miltiades the Elder* ruled the Chersonese. After the Persian army scored their victory in Ionia, the *younger Miltiades* returned to Athens. In 492 B.C. Darius' son-in-law (*Mardonius*) attempted to conquer Athens and Eretria for the help they had rendered the Ionians. Mardonius did conquer Thasos and Macedonia, but a violent sea storm destroyed his entire fleet, putting an abrupt end to his intended invasion of Athens and Eretria. Herodotus follows with another digression on the cultural, social, and political history of Sparta. Then follows a description of the war between Athens and Aegina (another Grecian city).

THE PERSIAN ATTACK: Darius would not accept the Athenian and Spartan refusal to submit to him, nor had he forgotten that Athens and Eretria had helped the Ionians burn Sardis. Since the northerly route taken by Mardonius had proved unfeasible because of Mount Athos, *Datis,* a nephew of Darius ordered his maritime dominions to build ships for him, and by the time 600 were ready, he was set to launch the invasion: it was going to be seaborne.

ERETRIA LOST: The Persian fleet assembled at Samos and sailed westward. When it reached Naxos, it landed troops and took the city which the Persians had been unable to conquer before the Ionian revolt began. Continuing on its westward course, the Persian force spared the sacred island of Delos (where Apollo and Artemis were supposed to have been born), but stopped at other islands and forced men into their army by holding their children hostage.

It was plain after some time that the Persians were going to besiege

Eretria before making for Athens. The Athenians attempted to help Eretria by sending 4000 soldiers who had been placed as armed colonists on Euboea, but the Eretrians sent them back to Athens. They did this because treachery on the part of some Eretrians was expected. This, in fact, came to pass on the seventh day of the Persian siege when the city was betrayed from within.

MARATHON: After they had sacked Eretria, the Persians landed at Marathon, a site north of Athens which they thought suitable for cavalry action. *Hippias,* who hoped to return to Athens by the force of Persian arms, guided them to the spot. The Persians expected the Athenians to await them behind the walls of their city as the Eretrians had done, but the Athenian soldiers were rushed to Marathon when word came that the enemy had landed there. Before opposing forces joined in battle, the generals sent a runner (*Pheidippides*) to secure aid from Sparta. The Spartans, however, told the messenger that they could not come because of a religious ceremony: they would help when the moon was full. Although the Spartans could not bring aid, help came from Plataea, a city which was under the protection of Athens. The force was small, but it was appreciated.

THE DISPUTE OVER STRATEGY: A difference of opinion as to whether a battle should be fought at all soon split the ten generals (each representing a different tribe of troops). Five commanders thought that the Athenians were too few to confront such a large enemy force alone. The other five were for attacking immediately.

Miltiades was the leader of those who wanted to engage the Persians. He had been a tyrant in the Chersonese, the peninsula which forms the northern shore of the Hellespont, and had served with Darius in the Scythian campaign. His familiarity with Persian tactics made him a particularly fit commander to oppose them. He spoke to *Callimachus* (the war leader whose vote was to break the deadlock) and convinced him to declare for battle.

THE BATTLE: Although the other generals had abdicated their right of command to *Miltiades* (mill TIGH uh deez), he waited until his turn to command the army arrived. The Athenians and Plataeans were then ordered to make their line as long as the enemy's. Both wings were made strong and as a result of this maneuver the center of the Athenian line was weak because it was thin at that point.

The fight began when Greek heavy-armed troops attacked the

Persians at a run and routed them on both wings. The Athenian line was broken at the center, but this did not help the Persians because the Greeks closed both wings in upon the center and drove the remaining Persian soldiers back to their ships. It was a complete victory for the Athenians and Plataeans: Persian tactics, hitherto irresistible, had been successfully countered by Miltiades. More than 6400 Persians were killed, while Greek losses were only 192.

The Persian fleet, which was manned mostly by Phoenicians, did not sail home after the battle, but immediately made for Athens in an effort to reach the unguarded city before the Greeks had a chance to return. The move was a failure, for the troops which had fought at Marathon returned and occupied defensive positions before the Persians arrived. No landing was attempted, and the fleet sailed for home.

THE MISFORTUNES: The Athenians were jubilant after they had won the Battle of Marathon. They quickly voted ships and money to *Miltiades,* the hero of Marathon, when he promised to lead them to a (unnamed) place where riches could be obtained at almost no cost to the state. It turned out that Miltiades landed the force at Paros, an island in the Cyclades group famed for its marble. (This incident showed that Athens already had ideas of expansion which were to cause conflict with Sparta at a later time.) The attempt to conquer Paros failed and Miltiades himself was wounded.

When Miltiades returned to Athens, he was brought to trial for his life because he had abused the trust of the people. The court decided not to vote a death sentence because of the many services he had performed for the state; but it fined him heavily instead. Miltiades soon died of his wound and the fine was paid by his son *Cimon.* At this point Book VI ends.

HERODOTUS

THE HISTORIES: SUMMARY (BOOK VII)

THE ACCESSION OF XERXES: *Darius* became furious when news reached him of Marathon, and he swore that he would have vengeance. Every nation subject to the Persian Empire was ordered to begin vigorous preparations for war against Greece. These continued for the next three years, as both army and navy were brought to the peak of readiness. In the fourth year after Marathon, however, a revolt against Persia erupted in Egypt. When an expedition was finally ready to set out against both Greece and Egypt, Darius suddenly died. *Xerxes,* the eldest son born to him during his reign, ascended to the throne. He quickly suppressed the Egyptian rebellion.

PREPARATIONS FOR WAR: First the Persians built a bridge over the Hellespont; then they proceeded to dig a canal through Mount Athos. Next they set out to attack Greece, which meant *all* of Greece—not merely Athens.

It was Athens who led the defense. *Themistocles* (the Athenian leader) advocated a rapid naval build-up and defense by sea. There was an unsuccessful attempt to unify the Grecian states. Soon the Persians conquered Thessaly, who later even gave assistance to their conquerors.

THE BATTLE OF THERMOPYLAE (thuhr MOP ih lee): When the huge Persian army came to the pass at Thermopylae, it found about 5000 Greeks ready to dispute the passage into southern Greece. Of these soldiers, only 300 were Spartans, for the Lacedaemonians were celebrating a religious festival (the same one they had celebrated during the Battle of Marathon) and would allow only an advance guard to proceed to the pass. More troops were to follow later.

When the two armies engaged, the Persians were surprised at the fight displayed by the small Greek force which was commanded by *Leonidas,* a Spartan king. For three days the Greeks repulsed attacks by the Persians. The pass being defended was narrow, and Persian numbers could not be brought to bear; even the elite Immortals of the Persians were roughly handled by the Greeks.

THE TRAITOR EPHIALTES: *Xerxes* was at a loss as to how to force the passage when a Greek named *Ephialtes* came to him and offered to tell of a path which could be used to encircle the defending force. Ephialtes—he stands strongly condemned by Herodotus—then consented to guide the Persions to the path. A thousand troops guarded the path, but when they saw the enemy come upon them, they fled for cover and prepared to make a stand. The Persians and their betrayer-guide however were not interested in them, and they moved towards the main force, ignoring the defenders.

THE BREAKTHROUGH: When word of the Persian breakthrough reached *Leonidas,* he realized that the situation was hopeless and he dismissed all his troops except the Thebans, whose loyalty was suspect. The Spartans, along with seven hundred Thespian soldiers who had refused to leave, made preparations for a last stand. Leonidas remembered that an oracle had forewarned that either Sparta or one of its kings would be destroyed by the Persians. When Leonidas saw that he was trapped, the truth of the oracle dawned upon him. Either he or Sparta would have to perish; so he chose not to escape.

The Spartans and Thespians resisted stubbornly before they were overwhelmed, and many heroic deeds are recorded by Herodotus. All the defenders were killed. The exasperation which the Greeks had caused *Xerxes* was shown by the way he had Leonidas' head cut off and his body impaled. The action was out of character for the Persians, since Herodotus states that they honored the fallen brave of the enemy. End of Book VII.

HERODOTUS

THE HISTORIES: SUMMARY (BOOK VIII)

BOOK VIII (TO URANIA, MUSE OF ASTRONOMY)

SALAMIS: The Persian fleet followed the Greek retreat south from Artemisium, and the Greek fleet stationed its fleet in the Bay of Salamis near Athens. Then the Persians put Attica to ruins, occupied Athens, and destroyed the Acropolis. At Phalerum the Persian fleet prepared for an engagement with the enemy fleet in the Bay of Salamis. It turned out that *Themistocles'* estimates had been correct. The Persians could not make use of their numbers in the straits, and the heavier Greek ships were able to ram them at close quarters. The battle resulted in a complete victory for the Greeks, although the Persian force, the bulk of whose ships were manned by Phoenicians, Egyptians, and Ionians, fought well. On the Greek side, it was agreed that the Aeginetan sailors gave the best account of themselves. The Athenians came second in valor, and the Corinthians—hated and much maligned by the Athenians—also fought valiantly.

RESULTS OF THE BATTLE: The far-reaching results of the Battle of Salamis (480 B.C.) were not at first discerned by the Greeks. Defeated at sea, the Great King ran the risk of being cut off from his kingdom and of having his supply routes interrupted. Although disguising his intentions, Xerxes decided to withdraw, leaving *Mardonius* with 300,000 troops in Greece. (The figure is that mentioned by Herodotus, but about 80,000 would be more appropriate.) *Xerxes'* ostensible objective in invading Greece (punishing Athens for the raid on Sardis) had been achieved, and so he felt he could retire without too much loss of prestige. Some Persian troops remained at Sardis, but the mass of the Persian fleet withdrew to Asia.

A REJECTED ALLIANCE: Mardonius attempted to induce the Athenians to ally themselves with the Persians; they even sent a spokesman to Athens, but the offer was rejected. End of Book VIII.

HERODOTUS

THE HISTORIES: SUMMARY (BOOK IX)

VICTORY AT PLATAEA (479 B.C.): When Mardonius reached the region of Boeotia, he had a wooden fort built between Plataea and Thebes. This was to serve as a base and place of refuge if the forthcoming battle with the Greeks did not go well for the Persians. It was learned at a banquet held at the city of Thebes (favorable to the Persians) that some Persians had a premonition that they were foredoomed. Perhaps there was a loss of confidence among the Persian leaders and low morale among the soldiers. In conformity with his plan of attack, Mardonius unleashed his horsemen on the Greeks. The cavalry made the Greek position so untenable that a decision to retreat to more favorable ground was taken. The withdrawal was attempted under the cover of night, but the morning found the parts of the Greek army separated from each other because the center had panicked. When Mardonius heard that the Greeks were pulling back, he thought they were in headlong retreat and immediately led his whole army across the Aesopus for the chase.

THE GREEK VICTORY: The Persians were too eager for victory: their advance was disordered. Greeks and Persians were soon fighting at close quarters, a factor which gave the skilled *hoplites* (heavy infantry) the advantage because the Persians wore no armor and could not make use of their cavalry. The Greeks however had by no means an easy time of it, for the Persians fought stubbornly while Mardonius was alive. When he was killed, the Persians fled. The retreat soon became a rout, and soon the whole Persian force was fleeing.

MYCALE (479 B.C.): The Greek fleet also scored a great victory over the Persian fleet at Mycale on the coast of Asia Minor opposite Samos. By the end of the year the Greeks had also conquered Sestus, a heavily fortified town. The Persian governor was crucified by the Greeks for his desecration of a Greek shrine. End of Book IX and end of *The Histories*.

THE HISTORIES

INTERPRETATION, *HISTORIES*, QUESTIONS AND ANSWERS

What was Herodotus' approach to history?

ANSWER: Herodotus cannot be said to have had any definite approach to history in the modern sense. He was not, for example, a "scientific" historian or an economic determinist. He did not propound any one definite thesis in his work; but his masterpiece has a theme: *the Persian Wars*.

In expounding this theme, Herodotus touches upon many subjects. In order to determine why Greece and Persia fought each other, he felt it necessary to examine the Persian Empire as thoroughly as possible; and in so doing he described the life of the different peoples of the various provinces. By fulfilling this obligation, he became an historian of politics and of military affairs and in a sense is what we would now call an anthropologist.

The stories which he delighted in telling (and they are in the tragic and epic tradition of his time) not only give an insight into the culture of those about whom the story is being told, but also tell something about his own Greek world. Herodotus' approach to history, then, was to tell all he knew about the life of the peoples and persons he was describing, considering nothing irrelevant.

Are most of the stories Herodotus relates literally true?

ANSWER: No.

What was the most important probable cause of the wars between Persia and Greece?

ANSWER: Despite the ostensible reason the Persian monarchs gave for their invasion—that Athens had to be punished for its intervention in the Ionian revolt—the two antagonists were bound to conflict because the Persian Empire was steadily expanding westwards.

How does Herodotus contrast Sparta and Athens?

ANSWER: Herodotus spent time in Athens and was pro-Athenian himself, so that Sparta appears in a poor light. Sparta is portrayed as having a conservative and narrow policy, while Athens is shown as having had marvelous foresight, herself the very spirit of the resistance to Persia.

The Spartans, for example, are shown delaying at Marathon, Thermopylae (the force under Leonidas was an advance-guard) and Plataea because of religious festivals. The Athenians, on the other hand, who received most of the credit for Marathon and Salamis, were the first to breach the wall at Plataea, and fought best at Mycale. The Spartans also sailed home after Mycale, leaving the Athenians to carry on the crusade against the Persians. (Many of these stories, however, are a reflection of Herodotus' sources and of the political conditions existing during his own time.)

If Herodotus' object was to write a history of the Persian Wars, why did he include the first six books which do not deal with the subject?

ANSWER: In addition to describing the fighting, Herodotus also wanted to investigate the causes of the war. In order to do this, he felt he had to describe the differences between Persians and Greeks. It is this purpose which the first six Books serve.

How does Herodotus show his preference for the hard fact as against revered authority?

ANSWER: Homer and Hesiod, the great and revered ancient authorities, had declared there was a great river Ocean encircling the earth, but Herodotus says,

> "I smile at those who with no sure knowledge to guide them describe the ocean flowing around a perfectly circular earth."

He in his matter-of-fact way states that even the holy-of-holies, the Greek Delphic oracle, could be bribed to give a decision favorable to the briber; today this would be like accusing the Pope of taking bribes to color his papal decisions as the Vicar of Christ on earth! "When an authority, no matter how traditionally sacrosanct, came into conflict with a fact," the Greeks preferred the fact. They had no inclination to protect "sound doctrine taught of old." (Edith Hamilton, *The Greek Way*, p. 117.)

Was Herodotus free of prejudice?

ANSWER: Yes, as much as was possible for that time of the fifth century before Christ:

1. He did not have the typical Greek contempt for foreigners, known in Greek as "barbarians."

2. He saw and admired whatever he saw that was worthy of ad-

miration—whether among the Egyptians, Phoenicians or even in uncivilized Scythia and Libya. "All men, if asked to choose the best way of ordering life would choose their own," says Herodotus, to whom custom determined the ways of all men on earth, however odd.

What was the nature of Herodotus' scepticism?

ANSWER: It was a gentle scepticism which involved neither judgment nor condemnation. Man's weakness and fallibility merely aroused his sympathy, and although his heroes are rather imperfectly great and his villains never absolutely villainous, he looks on both with impartial and dispassionate interest.

What things were of interest to Herodotus?

ANSWER: It seems that everything everywhere concerning the world of humankind was of deep interest to him. For example:

1. How homely girls in Illyria get husbands.
2. How the lake dwellers keep their children from falling into the water.
3. What Egyptian mosquito nets are like.
4. How the Arabians cut their hair.
5. How the Scythians milk their mares.
6. How the streets of Babylon are laid out.

GREEK HISTORY: THUCYDIDES

THE PELOPONNESIAN WAR

BACKGROUND

THE PERSIAN WAR: In 493 B.C. the Persian War, one of the most decisive in world history, was begun between the large and powerful Persian Empire and the Greek city states. Had Persia won, it is quite possible that western civilization would never have developed, and in its place, a semi-oriental despotism would have controlled the world. But the Greeks, led by the democratic city-state of Athens, won the war, thus preserving their remarkable civilization, not the least of whose accomplishments was the idea of democracy.

THE DELIAN LEAGUE: Athens was the leader of the Delian League, an organization formed during the war as a defensive alliance against Persia. The League was not dissolved after the war, for the Greeks feared that Persia might rise up once more.

In time, Athens transformed this alliance of equals into a vehicle for her own aggrandizement, in particular using its funds for her own interests. Within a few decades, Greece was once more threatened with conquest. Whereas the Persians were foreigners who attempted to conquer Greece and subjugate it to a tyranny, Athens was a fellow-member of the civilization which spoke in terms of sharing its knowledge and accomplishments with less fortunate cities. Nevertheless, this was imperialism, and the other members of the Delian League began to break away from Athens, turning to Sparta, a powerful state which was not a member of the League.

DIFFERENCES BETWEEN ATHENS AND SPARTA:

Athens	*Sparta*
1. Racial stock Ionian.	1. Racial stock Dorian.
2. Democratic sea power.	2. Oligarchic land power.
3. High culture and learning.	3. Inferior culture and learning.
4. Willing to take risks.	4. Conservative in all things.

Thus, although they had a common heritage and had fought together against Persia, the two states had long-standing differences.

THE IMMEDIATE CAUSES OF THE WAR: By the middle of the fifth century B.C. Athenian imperialism had reached serious proportions. Potidaea, a colony of the Dorian city of Corinth and an unwilling member of the Athenian empire, refused to allow Athens to interfere in her internal affairs.

In addition, Corinth's colony of Corcyra had founded a colony of its own, Epidamnus.

When Corinth and Corcyra disputed the status of the colony, Athens took Corcyra's side, further alienating the Corinthians.

Finally, Athens issued the Megaran decrees, which ruined the rich carrying trade of the Dorian colony of Megara.

These, then, were the underlying and immediate causes of the war.

LIFE OF THUCYDIDES (470? B.C.—400? B.C.)

EARLY LIFE: Thucydides' early life went almost unrecorded. It is believed that he studied philosophy under Anaxagoras, a dualist who was later expelled from Athens for his views on religion. There is a story of Thucydides' bursting into tears of joy on hearing Herodotus, the "Father of History" read his works. Later on Herodotus congratulated Olorus, Thucydides' father, on the fine literary taste of the son.

LATER LIFE: Thucydides was a general in the early part of the Peloponnesian War. He failed to relieve the Athenian forces at Amphipolis in time to prevent their falling to the Spartan commander, Brasidas; and for this he was exiled from Athens for twenty years. He went to his family estates in Thrace, observing the rest of the war from a distance. After the war, Thucydides returned to Athens, where he died around 400 B.C.

THE FIRST "SCIENTIFIC HISTORIAN":   Thucydides visited almost every theater of the war, and to a great extent relied upon his own observations in his work. In addition, he looked through documents, spoke to eyewitnesses whenever possible, and verified his material with individuals involved in the conflict. In short, he is considered the first "scientific historian." Some writers believe Thucydides was attempting to do for history what Socrates was doing for philosophy—to view it with rationalistic objectivity.

THUCYDIDES THE SOPHIST: Thucydides was a Sophist, a member of a group whose beliefs were diametrically opposed to those of Socrates on many issues. He believed that there were no absolute truths and, as the greatest Sophist of them all, Protagoras said, "man is the measure of all things." It was this relativism which led to his attempts at detachment; which in turn resulted in an apparent willingness to criticize Athens, his native city, which he admired. In all probability, his exile (perhaps at the hands of Cleon, who is an "anti-hero" in the book) added to this somewhat.

HISTORY AND DRAMA: Like most educated Greeks of his day, Thucydides was strongly interested in and influenced by the drama, for he wrote in a style resembling that of the tragedy. In Greek tragedies the sin of pride (*hybris*) is followed by an act or acts of folly, and then by punishment (*nemesis*). Thus, in the Peloponnesian War, the Athenians were defeated because of sins committed during the fighting.

THE MECHANISTIC VIEW OF HISTORY: In this, we can see that Thucydides had a mechanistic view of history; there is little room for free will in his philosophy. When faced with similar problems, he believed, all men will react in similar ways. Nor does Thucydides believe the gods can interfere in human affairs. Like all Sophists, he did not think that one had to bring in the deities to explain human affairs. As one author wrote, "Properly to appreciate Thucydides, one may contrast the *History of the Peloponnesian War* with the Book of Kings (in the Bible). Each book records how catastrophe overwhelmed a city, and each book attempts to explain why. Chronologically, the two books were separated by only two hundred years, but in attitude they are light-years apart." (H. B. Parkes, *Gods and Men,* 1959, 218)

HISTORY AS LESSON: Believing as he did that humans act the same in similar circumstances, Thucydides thought his history of the war could be read with profit by future generations, and the lessons of the war could be applied to prevent future conflicts.

Thus, Thucydides wrote his book as a lesson in morality as well as a history. As such, it often presents facts as fitted into preconceived patterns, a method which today's historians try to avoid.

In addition, he tended to stress political and military events, almost completely ignoring economic and social factors. Still, Thucydides is generally regarded as one of the greatest historians of all times.

BOOK ONE: CHAPTER 1

SEA-POWER: Thucydides tells us that he began to write his book at the beginning of the war, for he knew even then that it would be the most important event in Greek history.

In the early period, there was no unity on the peninsula. This unity came with the Trojan War, in which for the first time, the city-states acted together. This war was decided by sea power, which Thucydides believed was the most important source of Greece's strength. After the war, those cities with large armies declined, while those with important navies became more powerful. At this time the old hereditary monarchies began to give way to tyrannies resting on wealth and naval strength.

THE TWO RIVAL BLOCS: The city-states united once again during the Persian Wars, after which two rival blocs appeared. The Athenian group was based on naval power, while the Lacedaemons (Spartans) headed a military confederation. "Athens imposed contributions in money on all but Chios and Lesbos." Conflicts arose between the Athenian and Spartan states, the underlying cause being the growth of Athens' power and Sparta's fear of encirclement.

CHAPTER 2

THE FIRST CLASH: The immediate cause of the war was Athens' attempt to intervene in a conflict between the city-states of Corinth and Corcyra. The Corcyraeans (see map) asked Athens for help, and were promised a defensive alliance from the Athenian Assembly. Since Corinth was allied with Sparta, the groundwork for an Athenian-Spartan war was laid.

Next followed two incidents which heightened tensions. An Athenian-Corcyraean naval force clashed with one from Corinth (located on the isthmus commanding the land-route between Central Greece and Peloponnese, giving access to two seas). Athens said her action was purely defensive, but Corinth claimed it constituted aggression, and broke a truce which formerly had existed.

THE SECOND CLASH: The second incident involved the Athenian attempt to prevent a revolt in Potidaea (a town on the Macedonian peninsula). Sparta promised the Potidaeans assistance, and armed with this backing, Potidaea and other states revolted against Athens. The Peloponnesian League, headed by Sparta, sent aid. The Athenians, led by Callias and Phormio, blockaded Potidaea and routed her allies, including Corinth.

CHAPTER 3

THE LEAGUE MEETS: Corinth called a meeting of the Peloponnesian League at Sparta to discuss Athenian provocations. The Corinthian envoys spoke, telling the Spartans they were too conservative and hesitant. Their isolation prevented them from realizing that dynamic Athens was in the process of taking over all Greece.

Athens was weak but acted strong; while Sparta, though strong, behaved as though it were weak.

The Athenians, in response to this, observed that their leadership was deserved, owing to their actions in the Persian Wars. "That empire we acquired by no violent means, but because you were unwilling to prosecute to its conclusion the war against the barbarian, and because the allies attached themselves to us and spontaneously asked us to assume the command."

Then King Archidamus of Sparta expressed his belief that Spartan caution was well advised, and proclaimed his opposition to war. But Sthenlaidas, and Ephor (one of five magistrates exercising control over the kings), spoke for war, and the Assembly followed him rather than the king.

CHAPTER 4

ATHENIAN EXPANSIONISM: Thucydides begins this chapter by recounting the expansionist activities of Athens after the Persian Wars. The Spartans were disturbed at the construction of a wall around Athens and the growth of Athenian naval power. But Themistocles, the Athenian leader, was able to still their fears.

The Athenians fortified their port of Piraeus and constructed a new harbor, both of which acts were viewed with suspicion by other city-states.

At the same time the Spartan commander, Pausanias, conducted raids against Cyprus and Byzantius, which struck fear into the hearts of other Greek states. They appealed to Athens for leadership, and were accepted, thus forming the basis for the Athenian empire.

During the next few years, Athens continued to expand, Spartan mistrust grew, and the allies of each power clashed.

CHAPTER 5

THE ORACLE SPEAKS: Wishing to discover their chances of success against the Athenians, the Spartans went to Delphi to consult the Oracle, who answered "that if they put their whole strength into the war, victory would be theirs, and the promise that he himself would be with them, whether invoked or uninvoked."

THE SECOND CONGRESS AT LACEDAEMON: Then the Spartans called a second Congress at Lacedaemon and put the question of war or peace before their allies. The Corinthians spoke, urging war due to Athenian provocations, and observing that the strength of the League was such that victory would surely be theirs. Then embassies were sent to Athens "in order to obtain as good a pretext for war as possible." The Spartans tried to turn the Athenians against Pericles, their leader, but failed.

Then Thucydides digresses, and tells of the treachery of Pausanias of Sparta and Themistocles of Athens, both of whom die.

THE BOLD PERICLES REPLIES: In taking up the story once more, Thucydides relates the demands made by Sparta upon Athens, which amounted to a breakup of the Athenian empire.

Pericles urged the Athenians to refuse all the demands and not yield an inch. If war comes, he said, the Athenians, through their naval power, would be able to take care of themselves easily. He would be willing to free Athens' allies if Sparta would do the same with theirs, and then be willing to arbitrate the dispute.

Still, Pericles maintained his bold line at the end of his speech:

> "It must be thoroughly understood that war is a necessity; but that the more ready we are to accept it, the less will be the ardour of our opponents, and that out of the greatest dangers communities and individuals acquire the greatest glories."

The Assembly took his advice, making war inevitable.

THE PELOPONNESIAN WAR: BOOK II

CHAPTER 6

THE WAR BEGINS: When Thebes (Thebes and Plataea were located in Boeotia, northwest of Athens), an ally of Sparta, attacked Plataea, an ally of Athens, in the spring of 431 B.C., the war may be said to have begun.

The Thebans were repulsed, and prisoners were taken. Athens sent reinforcements to Plataea, and prepared for war.

Sparta ordered her allies to build up their military and naval forces. Both sides were eager for war:

> "Zeal is always at its height at the commencement of an undertaking; and on this particular occasion Peloponnesia and Athens were both full of young men whose inexperience made them eager to take up arms, while the rest of Hellas stood straining with excitement at the conflict of its leading cities."

THE MARCH ON ATHENS: After the Plataean incident, the Spartans organized their allies for an expedition against Athens.

Archidamus, leader of the Spartans, made a speech in which he told his officers of his tactics and strategy.

The Athenian leader, Pericles—a friend of Archidamus—though his present foe—organized the Athenian force for the defense. Realizing that the walls of Athens were impregnable, he commanded the people of the outlying districts to gather within the city. Although it was difficult to leave their homes, the citizens listened to their leader, and Athens was flooded with humanity.

THE COUNTERATTACK: Archidamus then marched on Athens, and was criticized for hesitating before attacking the town of Aenoe. This delay gave the Athenians needed time to organize their defenses. The attack on Aenoe failed, and Archidamus was obliged to bypass it and head for Athens instead.

He tried to lure Pericles out of the city in order to engage in open combat, but the Athenians, safe where they were, refused to budge. Instead, a fleet of 100 ships was sent to ravage the enemy's cities. Thucydides then describes the activities of the fleet, showing how, with Athens under siege, the Athenians were able to seize the advantage in the first years of the fighting. In addition to these attacks, Pericles sent a force to Megara (on the Bay of Salamis, directly west of Athens) and ravaged the territory of that ally of Sparta.

PERICLES' FUNERAL ORATION: At this point, Thucydides writes of the funeral of those Athenians who fell at the first clashes of the war. After describing the methods by which the Athenians care for their dead, he has Pericles deliver a funeral oration over their bodies. Pericles' eulogy is the most famous part of the book, and one of the greatest statements on the meaning of democracy and freedom ever made:

a. At first he speaks of the history of Athens, the sources of its greatness and power. All know the history of the city, so Pericles does not go into it in detail.

b. Instead, he analyzes the past to find what made Athens great, so that its citizens can appreciate their heritage and foreigners may copy:

"Its administration favors the many instead of the few; that is why it is called a democracy. If we look to the laws, they afford equal justice to all in their private differences; if to social standing, advancement in public life falls to reputation for capacity, class considerations not being allowed to interfere with merit; nor again does poverty bar the way, if a man is able to serve the state, he is not hindered by the obscurity of his condition."

c. Pericles notes that Athens has not any secrets; it is an "open society." He is convinced of the superiority of Athens' ways, and feels that those who come to conquer will stay to learn. "In short, I say that as a city we are the school of Greece."

d. At this point, Pericles turns to the dead. They gave their lives for freedom, he says, knowing full well what they were dying for:

"For it is not the miserable that would most justly be unsparing of their lives; these have nothing to hope for: it is rather they to whom continued life may bring reverses as yet unknown, and to whom a fall, if it came, would be most tremendous in its consequences. And surely, to a man of spirit, the degradation of cowardice must be immeasurably more grievous than the unfelt death which strikes him in the midst of his strength and patriotism!"

For these reasons, Pericles does not attempt to console the parents of the dead; their honor is so great that such consolation would be unnecessary.

CHAPTER 7

THE PLAGUE: The funeral ended the first year of the war. Archidamus, apparently giving up his attempt to take Athens itself, laid the countryside waste.

More deadly than the Spartans, however, was a mysterious plague, greater than any in the past. Thucydides thought it came from Egypt, but was not sure. In any case, it is Piraeus' first, and from there spread out to Athens proper. Thucydides describes the symptoms:

"Violent heats in the head and redness and inflammation in the eyes, the inward parts, such as the throat or tongue, becoming bloody and emitting an unnatural and foul breath."

The plague demoralized the Athenians, and led to a disintegration of national sentiment.

PERICLES' SPEECH IN DEFENSE OF HIS POLICY: The victories overseas did not add to Pericles' popularity. The plague and the Spartan depredations continued to demoralize the Athenians, and they blamed their difficulties on their leaders, especially Pericles. Feeling obliged to defend his course of action, Pericles delivered a speech to the population:

"A man may be personally ever so well off, and yet if his country be ruined he must be ruined with it; whereas a flourishing commonwealth always affords chances of salvation to unfortunate individuals."

He urged the Athenions to seek a greater identification with the city and realize that if it fell, they fell with it. The choice was between "submission with loss of independence and danger with the hope of preserving that independence." Freedom brings dangers and responsibilities, but it is well worth the risks.

The Athenians were reminded of their greatness, and were urged to remember their past glories in the moment of despair:

"For the judgment of mankind is as relentless to the weakness that falls short of a recognized renown, as it is jealous of the arrogance that aspires higher than its due."

Then Pericles reviewed the strategy of the war:

1. Despite all appearances of Spartan victory, the war was going well.
2. Athens was holding fast, and the Spartan homeland was being destroyed.
3. Athens' true possessions lie in its spirit, and not in farms. The farms could be rebuilt, but if the spirit is broken, then Athens would surely be defeated.
4. He urges the Athenians not to send heralds to Sparta to bid for peace, for such a peace would destroy the state.

Pericles convinces the Athenians to continue the war, but many still oppose him. As a result, he is fined. Not long after, however, he is re-elected general. Thucydides, a strong supporter of Pericles writes:

"For as long as he was the head of the state during the peace, he pursued a moderate and conservative policy; and in his time its greatness was at its height. When the war broke out, he also seems to have rightly gauged the power of his country."

In addition, Pericles knows the temper of the city; he is a politician as well as a statesman; he has the knack of bringing out the best in the Athenian spirit. Thucydides intimates that Pericles was the only invaluable man the city had.

THE DEATH OF PERICLES: Pericles died of the plague shortly thereafter (430 B.C.); and with his death the city began to stray from his moderate course of action. Pericles was able to maintain the empire, but he did not try to enlarge it through conquests. His successors were not so moderate in their approach. This new ruthlessness can be seen when, shortly after Pericles' death, envoys from the Peloponnesian League were put to death.

CHAPTER 8

THE MODERATE ARCHIDAMUS: In the summer of 429 B.C. the Peloponnesians mounted still another attack on Athens, once again being led by Archidamus. He headed in the direction of Plataea, but before he could reach the city, envoys came to meet with the Spartans. Archidamus offered to return their farms to them after the war was over. For the time being, he would have to occupy them. If the Plataeans resisted, however, he would have to lay the land waste. After consulting with the Athenians, Plataea decided to resist. After appealing to the gods to witness his good faith, Archidamus began the siege of Plataea.

THE SPARTAN COMMANDER: The Spartan commander speaks to his men on the question of their position. He says that they are braver than the Athenians, who nonetheless excel in science. Still, bravery is better than science, and will win the next encounter.

PHORMIO'S SPEECH: Thucydides then writes of Phormio's speech to his men, in which the Athenian tells them not to fear the numerical superiority of the Spartans. They had defeated the enemy once, and they would do so again.

In a speech somewhat reminiscent of those of Pericles, he tells them that their unity and belief in themselves will give them strength against the enemy, which is divided and at odds with one another. Phormio concludes by saying,

> "And may I remind you once more that you have defeated most of them already; and beaten men do not face a danger twice with the same determination."

The Spartans attempt to seize the port of Piraeus but are forced to withdraw, and conditions settle down to normal once more.

THE REST OF 429 B.C.: For the rest of the year each side makes forays against the other, but none is decisive. End of Book Two.

THE PELOPONNESIAN WAR: BOOK THREE

CHAPTER 9

SUMMER OF 428 B.C.: Archidamus attacks Athens once more and destroys the area; they then withdraw.

THE DEFECTON OF LESBOS: Archidamus' attack moves the citizens of Lesbos (island near north Asia Minor) to revolt against Athens. Lesbos had wanted to withdraw from the Athenian empire previously, but held back because the Spartans would not offer her protection.

When news of Lesbos' disalliance reaches Athens, troops are sent and the revolt is suppressed.

CLEON: The demagogue Cleon proposes to destroy the entire people of Mitylene in Lesbos. He first begins his speech with an attempt to replace the Athenian Constitution by majority voice votes of the popular Assembly:

> "I have often before now been convinced that a democracy is incapable of empire, and never more so than by your present change of mind in the matter of Mitylene."

He implies and later states that he would gladly choose a strong Athenian empire over a strong Athenian democracy. The Mitylenians revolted, and must be made to suffer, both for their sins and as an example to those who might think of revolt in the future. One may be able to maintain democracy at home and yet forget about it in dealings with foreign states. Such must be the course of Athens. He then implies that those who disagree with him in this are traitors. Destroy your enemy, he says, before they can destroy you, and any means employed are good so long as they work. Nevertheless, Cleon lost the vote. Cleon's followers did win a victory, however. Some Mitylenian ambassadors were executed. Mitylene's walls were leveled, and her ships confiscated. In addition, much of her territory was taken and distributed to Athenians.

CHAPTER 10

CIVIL WARS: Thucydides contrasts the fates of Mitylene and Plataea, showing the effects of Athenian democratic sentiments in saving the former and Spartan lack of morality in destroying the latter.

Corcyra was torn by a civil war between her two chief parties—the oligarchic, representing the wealthy, and the democratic. The Spartans gave assistance to the oligarchs, and the Athenians helped the democrats. Similar scenes were being enacted in a great many of the Greek city-states. These civil wars brought out all the base instincts in man. "Frantic violence became the attribute of manliness," says Thucydides. It was his belief that war destroys morality and honor.

CHAPTER 11

MELOS: Demosthenes attacked Melos (Aegean island) in 426 B.C. when that city refused to become part of the Athenian alliance. Then Demosthenes was persuaded by the Messenians to attack their enemy Aetolia, which was almost defenseless. At first he met with nothing but success, but then the Aetolians counterattacked and stopped the Athenian army. A second Aetolian attack sent the Athenians flying and forced them to seek a truce, which was granted.

DELOS: Athenian soldiers took Delos, and proceeded to "purify" it. All those who were about to die, and mothers ready to bear children, would have to do so elsewhere. Then the Athenians celebrated the ancient Delian games.

Other battles followed, closing the sixth year (426 B.C.) of the war. End of Book Three.

THE PELOPONNESIAN WAR: BOOK FOUR

CHAPTERS 12-14

Book Four covers the years from 425-323 B.C. in which the following events are recounted:

1. The Athenians defeat the Spartans at Sphacteria, an island near Pylos, in 425 B.C. The Spartans seek peace, but the Athenian demands are to them far too demanding.

2. There are more Athenian conquests.

3. Despite these conquests, Brasidas, a great Spartan general, himself scores some brilliant successes.

4. The Athenians and Spartans agree to a truce for one year (423-422 B.C.), and agree to return all prisoners. End of Book Four.

THE PELOPONNESIAN WAR: BOOK FIVE

CHAPTERS 15-16

In 422 B.C. fighting begins again.

AMPHIPOLIS: Cleon was brash, and expected no major difficulties in the taking of Amphipolis. As soon as Brasidas saw this, he moved his force into the city, and awaited the Athenian attack. He had more troops than Cleon, but the Athenian force represented the flower of that city's youth. After showing the Athenians how many men he had, Brasidas resolved to attempt once more the stratagem of a surprise attack which had worked so well in the past. But Cleon noticed the preparations, and all seemed lost for Brasidas. Cleon sounds a retreat, preferring to await the coming of reserves before engaging in battle. Before this could be done, however, Brasidas attacks, kills Cleon, and all but completely destroys the Athenian force. There is a major loss for Sparta, since Brasidas himself dies in the battle. He is buried with full honors, and Amphipolis considers him one of the founders of the city.

THE TRUCE: In the tenth year of the war (421 B.C.) Athens and Sparta strike a truce, agreeing to an alliance of fifty years' duration. The truce is good for the next seven years, although in reality hostile acts were constantly in progress.

THE WAR PARTY: In both Sparta and Athens ruthless, warmongering parties clamored for a renewal of the war.

CHAPTER 17

MELOS: Alcibiades sets sail for Argos in the summer of 417 B.C. and seizes the remainder of the pro-Spartan faction. The Athenians also make an expedition against Melos, a Spartan colony. Melos was neutral at first, but when Athens attacks the city, its citizens show great hostility. The Athenians take up positions around the town and led by Cleomedes and Tisias, they meet with the Melians.

The Athenians and Melian envoys meet to discuss the situation. The Athenians speak first, stating that they prefer secret meetings, for open ones lead to interruptions on the part of the people, who want to know all sorts of irrelevant things. They want no speechmaking, but only an accord. The Melians respond, protesting that the Athenians are acting as judges while they are actually only participants in the discussion. We will be brief, say the Athenians. We defeated the Persians, thus demonstrating our right to rule. Your arguments for neutrality are unacceptable. "The strong do what they can and the weak suffer what they must." As for the prospect of neutrals joining with Sparta as a result of the Melian episode, the Athenians reject this argument.

THE TRAGEDY OF MELOS: Submit, say the Athenians, and do not feel that by accepting us you are committing a dishonorable act. It is not disgraceful to surrender to the most powerful state in all Greece.

With this the Athenians withdraw, and the Melians are left to consider their fate.

After a short deliberation, the Melians tell the Athenians that they have decided not to surrender. To do so would be dishonorable. They make a last plea for neutrality in the war.

The Athenians refuse to consider neutrality, and attack Melos. After a long siege, the city surrenders. The men are put to death, while the women and children of Melos are sold into slavery. Then Athenian colonizers are sent to take over the city. End of Book Five.

THE PELOPONNESIAN WAR: BOOK SIX

CHAPTER 18

ASSEMBLY VOTES ON SICILY: In 415 B.C. the Athenian Assembly votes to send Alcibiades to Sicily to lead an expeditionary force to take Sicily, endanger the Peloponnesian allies, and cut Sparta from aid. Nicias, leader of the peace party, was also chosen as a commander, much against his will. He charges Alcibiades with ambition, egotism, and arrogance; the major reasons for their going to Sicily are all to be found in Alcibiades' vast ambition, and not his interest in the future of Athens. Then Alcibiades replies to the charges:

1. He has the right to command armies.

2. Sicily is peopled "by motley rabbles . . . without any feeling of patriotism . . . why worry about such a mob?"

3. Nothing is so fatal as inaction; the empire that does not expand will perish.

4. We must attack Sicily!

In spite of Nicias' objections, the Assembly supports Alcibiades. Athens wants the expedition to Sicily; they vote large appropriations and give a completely free hand to the generals.

THE MUTILATED HERMAE: The expedition was about to leave, when it was discovered that the Stone Hermae (religious symbols of fertility and prosperity) had been mutilated:

> "It was thought to be ominous for the expedition, and part of a conspiracy to bring about a revolution and to upset the democracy."

Alcibiades had been implicated in such actions during one of his drunken revels, and was charged with acts of impiety. He offered to stand trial, protested his innocence, and offered to die if found guilty. His enemies withdraw and Alcibiades is permitted to sail with the Sicilian fleet.

CHAPTER 19

THE SICILIAN ASSEMBLY: Reports of the expedition reach the principal city of Sicily, Syracuse, and an assembly is called to discuss the problems caused by the Athenian expedition to Sicily. Hermocrates is the first to speak:

1. The Athenians say they want to aid the Egestaeans, but actually, they are out to conquer Sicily, and above all Syracuse.

2. Sicily is well armed and will inflict severe casualities on the invaders.

3. The Athenian defeat of the Persians was due mainly to accidents and pure luck.

4. Prepare for the attack and get Sparta and Corinth for allies.

Few actually believed the Greeks would attack; and thus Hermocrates' speech fell on many deaf ears.

ATHENAGORAS SPEAKS: Athenagoras treats the reports of Athens' expedition with scorn. Why should Athens desire a Sicilian campaign? He launches into a defense of democracy, and rebukes the oligarchs, who are inciting the people, in a vain hope of seizing still more power.

THE EXPEDITION: By the time the fleet reaches Sicily, it is clear that there are fundamental differences of opinion between Alcibiades, Nicias, and Lamachus, the third general of the expedition. After speaking his peace, Lamachus agrees to back Alcibiades' proposal, thus outvoting Nicias. While the army moves to Catana, a nearby spot, word comes from Camarina that if they went to the town, it would go over to the Athenian side. Since Camarina was near Syracuse, the fleet set sail at once. When it arrives, however, the Camarinaeans refuse them and the fleet withdraws. Fresh evidence has arisen as to Alcibiades' guilt in the Hermae matter, but Alcibiades flees and offers his services to Sparta. Alcibiades is then tried in absentia, and sentenced to death.

CHAPTER 20

ALCIBIADES BETRAYS: Nicias and Lamachus divided their forces after Alcibiades left, and now following Nicias' suggestion, sail for Selinus and Egesta; the expedition is conducted with timidity, and the rest of the summer sees only brief and inconclusive skirmishes. When the people of Syracuse appeal to Sparta for aid, Alcibiades persuades the Spartans to consent. Alcibiades also induces the Spartans to use Decelia (near Athens) as a fortress. During the summer of 414 B.C. the Athenian army in Sicily is reinforced.

THE SURPRISE MARCH: The Syracusans learn of Athenian reinforcements, and put off their attack accordingly. But Hermocrates selects a small group for a surprise march on the Athenian position. The Syracusan attack, which takes place at Epipolae, is a failure, and on the following day an Athenian force begins the attack on Syracuse itself.

NICIAS: Both sides begin to construct walls and fortifications outside the city. The Athenians are able to capture some Syracusan positions in the early fighting, although the Syracusans kill Lamachus, the Athenian general, in battle. Nicias, then in sole command, presses the attack to the point where the Syracusans begin proposing terms of peace. But any chance of an Athenian victory of major proportions is lost when Nicias, sick at the time, commits a series of blunders. The most important of these is the permitting of Peloponnesian ships, led by Gylippus, to land in Sicily with reinforcements.

> "Nicias heard of his approach, but, like the Thurians, despised the scanty number of his ships, and set down piracy as the only probable object of the voyage, and so took no precautions for the present."

About the same time, the Spartans invade Argos and lay waste the countryside. An Athenian force relieves the Argives, thus breaking their treaty with Sparta. In the past, Athenian aid had been indirect; now, for the first time since the truce, Athenian fights Spartan once again. End of Book Six.

THE PELOPONNESIAN WAR: BOOK SEVEN

CHAPTER 21

NICIAS' LETTER: Nicias sends envoys to Athens for reinforcements. The envoys reach Athens in the winter of 414 B.C. and deliver Nicias' letter to the Assembly. The letter opens with a statement regarding the past accomplishments of the army. Nicias observes that he had won many battles, until the coming of Gylippus' superior force. Even then, the Athenians won the first encounter, but were soon forced to take defensive positions. Now he was pinned in, while the enemy prepares to attack by sea. The Athenian fleet is in sad shape, and in no condition to resist. Nicias asks for more troops. If they are not sent, then he asks permission to return. In addition, he would like to be relieved of his command, for he suffers from a disease of the kidneys.

THE ASSEMBLY ACTS: The Athenians are not ready to abandon the Syracusan positions. They vote overwhelmingly for large reinforcements, naming Menander and Euthydemus as temporary generals to fill the places of Nicias' dead colleagues. The permanent colleagues, Demosthenes and Eurymedon, are to be sent along with the new army. The Athenians also vote for a new fleet, which will be sent to the Peloponnesian area to prevent a Corinthian or Spartan force from reinforcing Gylippus.

THE SECOND FRONT: Meanwhile, the Spartans plan an invasion of Athens, in the hope of weakening that city by the presentation of a two-front war.

The invasion force, led by Agis, set off in the spring of 413 B.C. Decelea, a town some thirteen miles from Athens, is taken and fortified. At the same time, a second force, this one of Sparta and her allies and led by Eccritus, sets out for Sicily.

DEFEAT AT SEA: The Athenians are not idle in this period. They send Charicles, at the head of a fleet of thirty ships, to the Peloponnesian area, and further instruct him to call on Argos for reinforcements. At the same time Demosthenes takes his large force to Sicily.

Gylippus decides that the best way to stop the Athenians would be on the sea. He is supported in this by Hermocrates, who says that the Syracusans should not be fearful of Athens' supposed prowess on the sea, since this reputation is largely undeserved. The first attacks are unsuccessful but the skirmishes continue. Finally, the Athenians are defeated.

THE THRACIAN SWORDSMEN: Meanwhile, Demosthenes is on his way to Sicily with the reinforcements. In addition, a large force of Thracian swordsmen arrives at Athens. They are sent home, however, since the city did not want to pay their salaries. On the way home, the Thracians, who are semi-barbarians, take the town of Mycalessus, destroy it, and ruthlessly butcher its inhabitants. In particular, they kill the children at a boys' school.

News of the massacre reaches Thebes, which quickly outfits a force to overtake the Thracians and disperse them. This is done, and the Thracians themselves are butchered without mercy.

DESMOSTHENES' DEFEAT AT SEA: Meanwhile, Demothenes continues on his way to Sicily, word of his advance preceding him. Some Sicilian cities, which had previously been neutral, join Syracuse at this juncture, in fear of the Athenian invaders. As Demosthenes draws nearer, the Syracusans fortify themselves, in addition making some structural changes in their warships. Rams are added to the ships so as to enable them to crush the Athenian force.

The changes prove successful. Together with the superior tactics of Gylippus, the rams are able to defeat the Athenian force. This victory leads the Syracusans to believe that they will have no trouble in conquering Demosthenes' army once it lands.

CHAPTER 22

DEFEAT AGAIN: Demosthenes is convinced that the dallying tactics of Nicias had been wrong, and immediately prepares to attack. At first he lays the surrounding area waste; then he tries to take some of the Syracusan fortifications, but fails. Next, he attacks nearby Epipolae, but is repulsed by Gylippus and the Syracusans, who are aided by darkness and disorder.

The defenders gain confidence with their victory, and send to other cities for aid in completely expelling Demosthenes and his army.

The Athenians are disgusted with the defeat, and at the same time have to fight a small epidemic which has broken out among the troops.

NICIAS CHANGES HIS MIND: Demosthenes urges a withdrawal, but Nicias, previously in favor of such a move, changes his mind and argues for remaining. The Athenians will win, he said, if they can continue the siege. Moreover, there is a peace party in Syracuse which may come to their aid. To return would be dishonor; and Nicias feels that death is better than that. Eurymedon agrees with him, and the Athenians do not withdraw.

CHAPTER 23

THE SURRENDER OF DEMOSTHENES: Nicias is defeated in battle to the point where he must try to comfort his shattered forces. Men have been saved from worse situations, he says. He is physically sick as well as emotionally spent, but still, he has hope. You must be braver now than at any time in the past, he concludes.

But his entreaties are all but useless; the navy, which has refused to sail out, is miserably defeated. The wary Syracusans had blocked the roads so that escape via land routes is veritably impossible.

The Syracusan cavalry harasses them whenever they move, while the supply of food grows shorter and shorter. The Athenians finally give the Syracusans the slip, but the forces of Nicias and Demosthenes become separated. Demosthenes is quickly surrounded by Gylippus, and after a brief skirmish, is obliged to surrender his 6,000 troops.

NICIAS SURRENDERS: Nicias offers to pay the Syracusans and Gylippus a large amount of money, equal to what they had spent on the war if they would only allow his army to leave. This offer is rejected, Gylippus attacking fiercely. The slaughter is almost indescribable.

Finally, Nicias has to surrender. He turns himself over to Gylippus, whom he trusts more than he did the Syracusans. Gylippus had hoped to take both Nicias and Demosthenes back to Sparta, where they would participate in his victory parade. But the Syracusans get at them, and they are butchered along with other Athenians.

CONCLUSION: "This was the greatest Hellenic achievement of any in this war, or in my opinion, in Hellenic history; at once most glorious to the victors, and most calamitous to the conquered. They were beaten at all points and altogether; all that they suffered was great; they were destroyed, as the saying is, with a total destruction, their fleet, their army—everything was destroyed, and few of the men returned home!" End of Book Seven.

THE PELOPONNESIAN WAR: BOOK EIGHT

CHAPTER 24

AFTERMATH: The Spartans are overjoyed at their victory; a few years before they had feared for their very existence; now they plan to take over all Greece. Under Agis, who was king at the time, they gather a large force for the campaign. Meanwhile, the Athenians are not idle: they too organize an impressive force. The Athenians meet a fleet returning from the Sicilian expedition and after a brief battle, defeat it. Thus, the tide seems to be turning in the direction of Athens once more. Popular revolts in Samos and Lesbos bring over those cities to the Athenian side. For the rest of the year 412 B.C. the battles seesaw back and forth. Another Peloponnesian fleet is sent to Athens, while an Athenian force besieges Chios. In addition some Spartans become appalled at the Persian treaty of alliance (with Sparta) and demand its revocation.

CHAPTER 25

DEMOCRACY AND THE LOSS OF VIRTUE: There are two oligarchical conspiracies to overthrow the government. Those responsible for the banishment of Alcibiades are assassinated, along with others of the democratic camp. The Council is terrorized by the oligarchs:

"Fear, and the sight of the numbers of the conspirators, closed the mouths of the rest; or, if any ventured to rise in opposition, he was presently put to death in some convenient way, and there was neither search for the murderers nor justice to be had against them if suspected; but the people remained motionless, being so thoroughly cowed that men thought themselves lucky to escape violence, even when they held their tongues. An exaggerated belief in the numbers of the conspirators demoralized the people, rendered helpless by the magnitude of the city, and by their lack of intelligence with each other, and being without means of finding out what those numbers really were." (This is one of the most famous passages in the work. Thucydides reiterates his basic belief that democracies are never destroyed by external challenges, but rather commit suicide through a loss of virtue on the part of its citizens. Even after the Sicilian expedition, Sparta could not conquer Athens. But now Athens destroys herself.)

PISANDER: At this point, a force led by Pisander, an ally of Alcibiades, arrives in Athens and assembles the people. First, through a series of ruses, they destroy the existing government. They meet with no opposition.

Next, they move that all power be placed in a Council of 400, to be dominated by the oligarchs. Then a wave of violence begins, during which enemies of the new oligarchy are murdered (compare with Hitler in 1933).

CHAPTER 26

ALCIBIADES AGAIN: Alcibiades is called and made general of the Athenian army. At this point he does Athens a great service. He insists that the "Four Hundred" be dismissed and a new government take its place. Shortly thereafter the government falls, to be replaced by one which comprises the 5,000 wealthiest citizens of the city, who form a government—a compromise between oligarchy and democracy. The battles teeter for a while after this, with neither side in ascendancy.

411 B.C., THE 21st YEAR OF THE WAR: The next battle takes place in the Hellespont, where Spartan and Athenian fleets clash in combat. The Athenians win this engagement and force the Spartans to flee. On hearing of this, Tissaphernes sets out for the Hellespont with his fleet and troops.

At this point Thucydides writes:

> "When the winter after this summer is over, the twenty-first year of the war will be completed."

This marks the end of his history.

INTERPRETATION: *THUCYDIDES*, QUESTIONS AND ANSWERS

What was the conclusion of the Peloponnesian War from the point where Thucydides cuts it off?

ANSWER: Alcibiades still heads the Athenian army. In 410 B.C. the democracy is restored, while Sparta foments revolt among the allies of Athens. In that same year Alcibiades almost completely destroys the Spartan fleet in the battle of Cyzicus. Once more Athens is in control of the situation. A peace based upon the *status quo* is offered to Athens, but the radicals in that city, led by Cleophon, reject it. Lysander defeats Alcibiades in 407 B.C., and 404 B.C. the Athenian fleet is almost wiped out by the Spartan Lysander near Aegospotami; this disaster breaks the Athenian spirit. Lysander lays down his terms:

1. The walls of Athens are to be torn down.

2. Her overseas' possessions are taken from her.

3. The Athenian fleet is reduced to twelve ships.

From 404 to 371 B.C. Sparta is the most powerful Greek state.

Identify the leading figures of the war.

ANSWER:

1. ALCIBIADES—An Athenian commander who showed great brilliance and audacity. He later deserted to Sparta, and aided that state in its defeat of Athens. Alcibiades plotted to gain control of Athens and hoped to become tyrant of that city.

2. ALCIDAS—A Spartan commander involved in several of the early battles of the war. He fought at Mitylene, and had several victories before fleeing.

3. ARCHIDAMUS—A Spartan commander early in the war. He led the first attacks on Athens, despite his friendship with Pericles. Later Archidamus captured Plataea. He was responsible for winning Lesbos for the Spartan cause.

4. BRASIDAS—One of the most brilliant and forceful leaders in the history. A Spartan general, he took Megara, Thrace, and other areas in the north. Brasidas subdued Amphipolis and nearly choked the Athenian economy. He was killed near Amphipolis by Cleon's army.

5. DEMOSTHENES—An Athenian commander who attacked Aetolia and failed to take the city. A later expedition under his

command captured Delos. He was commander with Cleon during an attack on Pylos, and afterwards he tried to stir up revolts in Boeotia. Together with Nicias, he led the Athenians in the ill-fated Sicilian campaign, during which he died.

6. GYLIPPUS—The brilliant Spartan commander who led the victors in the Sicilian campaign.

7. HERMOCRATES—An important leader of Syracuse, who was instrumental in the defeat of Athens in the Sicilian campaign.

8. NICIAS—A head of the war party in Athens after the death of Cleon. Nicias was Cleon's major enemy, as both tried to take power in the city. He was rather a poor general, who was known for his vacillations. Nicias was in charge of the Sicilian campaign, and he died after Athens' defeat.

9. PERICLES—An Athenian leader during the early part of the war, and the closest to a "hero" in the book. He was a moderate. He believed that Athens should defend herself through sea power and guard against those who would destroy democracy by arguing that war calls for stricter forms of government. Before this, he led an attack on Corinth, and took Cythera.

10. PHORMIO—An Athenian commander who defeated a Spartan fleet near Acarnania.

11. THUCYDIDES—The author of the history who was a general in the Peloponnesian War. He was general during the attack on Amphipolis, and arrived too late to save the main force. He was later exiled.

12. TISSAPHERNES—The Persian leader who subsidized Sparta in the last years of the fighting, and who became a leader of the anti-Athenian alliance.

13. XENOPHON—An Athenian commander who captured Potidaea in the early part of the war, and who was later defeated at Chalcidice. Xenophon was an historian and wrote of Socrates. It is from his works that we can construct the later history of the war.

How does Thucydides compare with Herodotus as an historian?

ANSWER:

1. Herodotus' area of history was a vast one, whereas Thucydides subject was concentrated mainly on a small area.

2. Herodotus lived some time after the events he narrates, whereas Thucydides was involved in the very events he is relating.

3. Herodotus was the pioneer and innovator whose errors as an historian were to help Thucydides, who avoided them.

4. Herodotus' knowledge of military matters is slight, but that of Thucydides indicates profound knowledge and experience in things military.

5. Herodotus writes a history that ambles erratically without much regard for chronology and time factors, but Thucydides is careful to keep his chronology accurate.

6. Herodotus' style is clear, colloquial, easy-going, often naive and uncritical in his outlook; the style of Thucydides is carefully measured and rhetorical, often leaning to abstraction and economy. Thucydides' critical outlook is open-eyed, an unceasing search for the truth of the matter—the whole dyed with typical Sophistic scepticism.

7. Herodotus loves digressions which are folksy and casual, full of human interest; whereas Thucydides digresses seldom, and then always to prove a point.

8. In Herodotus' work the gods intervene in human affairs, while they do not in the Peloponnesian War.

9. Cause and effect are not clear at times in Herodotus, and although his speeches are often fabricated as are those of Thucydides, they are not nearly so accurate.

10. Despite his pro-Greek biases, Herodotus does try to be impartial, as does Thucydides.

11. Herodotus realized the importance of social and economic factors in history far more than Thucydides.

What is the "lesson" of the Peloponnesian War?

ANSWER: Thucydides tried to show us that the greatest dangers to democratic states are internal rather than external. Athens is strong only so long as she believes in herself, has a moral code which most citizens accept, and is led by moderate men like Pericles. Although suffering military defeats and plague in the early years of the war, she is able to survive due to internal unity.

After the death of Pericles and with the coming to power of Cleon, these conditions change. In her treatment of both friends and allies, Athens begins to abandon her previous beliefs. This is most vividly shown in the case of Melos. After this Athens has a series of victories but, due to the sin of *hybris* (pride), is doomed to defeat.

What is the difference between Thucydides and modern historians?

ANSWER: Although known as an historian, Thucydides is actually more in the tradition of teachers of morality.

He apparently began his work in the belief that there were patterns of behavior which emerged during the war, and that they would be repeated in the future.

Most modern historians shy away from this method and philosophy, although they will admit that at times they cannot avoid the sweeping generalization, the moral lesson, the construction of a structure which ignores or plays down some events while magnifying others. They do this in an apologetic way, however, and excuse themselves by observing that they were human after as well as before they became historians.

What was Secretary of State George C. Marshall's opinion of Thucydides?

ANSWER: The Secretary said,

> "I doubt seriously whether a man can think with full wisdom and with deep convictions regarding certain of the basic international issues today who has not at least reviewed in his mind the period of the Peloponnesian War and the fall of Athens."

And most of our knowledge of this period comes from Thucydides. Like it or not, we see the war through his eyes.

If Thucydides did not complete his book, how do we know about the ending of the war?

ANSWER: Xenophon of Athens, also a general in the Peloponnesian War (who was banished from Athens and wrote under Spartan patronage), wrote of the war in the Hellenica. He picks up where Thucydides left off, and describes how Athens fell. Then he goes on to show the failures of Sparta in creating an empire, the rise and fall of Thebes. Unlike Thucydides, Xenophon was not a Sophist, but rather a friend of Socrates.

What was Thucydides conception of history?

ANSWER:

1. Thucydides was a mechanist in that he believed that when faced with similar problems, similar people will react in similar fashions.

2. Individuals do not believe this (in No. 1 above), and attempt to exert their free will in order to change the world.

3. This is vanity, he says, for although one may change immediate situations, the end-products of large-scale enterprises are the results of mechanical forces present in nature and in man.

4. The gods play no role in man's historical development.

5. Rather, it is what today we call "human nature" that determines actions. Thus, Thucydides may be viewed as a predecessor of Freud and the social Darwinists of the late nineteenth century. Thucydides does not attempt to offer a complete psychological portrait of men like Pericles and Cleon, or Alcibiades and Nicias; but the psychologically oriented student can see that the faint glimmerings of that discipline can be found in *The Peloponnesian War* of Thucydides.

GREEK PHILOSOPHY: INTRODUCTION

PREFACE: Before the Greeks came into the Mediterranean world, man was primarily oriented toward death and built his monuments in honor of death:

1. The ziggurats of Babylon and the pyramids of Egypt testify to the hold of death upon these early civilizations.

2. Life on earth was dominated by spirits, devils, gods, etc. who caused all illnesses, natural phenomena, events. Every move on earth was at some god's whim.

To the Greeks, however, life was the most significant fact in the world; and human life was the greatest wonder on earth.

1. The Greeks were the first people to play. Their famous Olympic Games are witness to their boundless enthusiasm for living.

2. Their art speaks of the pleasure they derived from the form of the human body.

3. The Greeks were also the first philosophers. Man was a miracle above the other creatures because he possessed what they called *logos* (*logos* in Greek means a word by which a thought is expressed. It can also mean the thought itself, or *reason*.).

4. The Greeks were the first people to say that the world was knowable, because they believed in man's powers of reason. They had no idea of changing their own life or the world around them through the knowledge acquired by reason. The world was something to be understood and admired as it was.

5. Through understanding the nature of the universe and the nature of man, a Greek believed he had the key to understanding man's own place in the scheme of things.

THE NATURAL PHILOSOPHERS: Some six centures before Christ, on the island of Miletus in the Aegean Sea, a man called *Thales* asked a question: "What is the world made of?" He had looked around himself and saw a world where things were changing all the time. The tide came in and went out. A tree grew where a seed had been. He thought there must be something unchanging and permanent beneath all the change. Beneath the world of life and death there must be some basic substance which explains and makes possible everything else.

Instead of turning to religion, Thales tried to give a scientific explanation:

1. He said the first substance was water.

2. *Anaximander* (his pupil) said that the first substance was a lump of matter which had no form or shape, or definite character of any kind. He called this first matter *"The Unlimited."*

   a. Its chief characteristic was that it was always in motion. How did our world evolve from this shapeless lump?

   b. Anaximander's theory was that the world is a battlefield where opposites are constantly fighting each other, encroaching on one another.

      (1) At some time in the past, while basic matter was whirling through space, four basic opposites—*hot* and *cold,* and *wet* and *dry*—separated themselves out. The cold and wet went into the center of the whirling mass to become earth. The hot and dry moved toward the edge and formed rings of fire around the earth.

      (2) The mist rising from the earth prevented the rings of fire from being seen on the earth. Man could only see the flames peeping through the fog in the forms of the sun, the moon, and the stars.

      (3) Before man appeared, the heat dried up the wet to form land. Life was the result of the action of heat on moisture.

      (4) Life first appeared in the ocean. Eventually man evolved from fish that took to dry land.

This theory may well be considered a precursor to Darwin's account of evolution.

ANAXIMENES: Another pupil of Thales named *Anaximenes* held that the world was not made of either water or indefinite matter.

1. It was made of *air*.

   a. Seeing how air condensed to form rain, he said that the earth and ocean were formed that way.

   b. The wet fell toward the center, while the purer air remained in the heavens.

Like the other early philosophers, Anaximenes believed that the universe was alive in the same way that man is alive. He accounted for man's particular form of life (the life of reason) by saying that the soul of man was formed from the very pure air which had remained at the farthest edge of the universe.

THE SOURCE OF MOTION: One problem which these early philosophers faced was why the first substance of the universe, be it water, matter or air, formed the world at all.

What first set things in motion?

1. Since they thought all matter was alive, they said that the first substance was *self-moving*.

2. Not only did it cause motion in other things, it was the cause of its own motion. It *produced* life and was life at the same time. Because it moved itself, they said it was divine.

THE IONIAN SCHOOL: *Thales* was the first of what is called the Ionian School of philosophers. In classical times the school was famous as one which sought scientific answers to questions about nature. Because the school was mainly concerned with observing nature, its followers were called *phusikoi* or natural philosophers. *Phusis* is the Greek word for nature, from which is derived our word physics.

HERACLITUS: Later philosophers continued the Ionian tradition. Following in the steps of Anaximander, a thinker from the city of Ephesus in Asia Minor by the name of *Heraclitus* held (in the fifth century B.C.) that the world was the scene of the conflict of opposites.

1. He too was impressed by the instability and changing character of the physical world.

2. But he disagreed with Anaximander's view that the strife which characterizes the world is something disorderly or unjust:

"Strife," he said, "is the justice of the world."

The existence of this conflict of opposing forces, in his view, is essential to the existence of the *One,* or *God.*

1. In accordance with this attitude, he held that "everlasting *fire,*" not air, or water, or the unlimited, is the essence of all things, because it exhibits the most continuous state of tension.

2. "All things are in *flux,*" he said. Being the most fluctuating of all things, fire is therefore the essential reality of the universe.

3. Heraclitus explained change by saying that it is the upward and downward path of fire by virtue of which the universe came into being.

4. The relative stability of the world, he said, is due to different "measures" of the everlasting fire, some being kindled (burning upward) and some burning out (going downward) in more or less equal proportions.

5. The balance between the upward and downward paths of the different "measures" of fire, forms what Heraclitus called the *"hidden attunement"* of the universe. This is an attunement of opposite tensions, he said, "like that of a bow and a lyre."

Thus, Heraclitus saw the harmony of the world as the resolution of many diverse tensions in the unity of the one Reality, which is fire. This concept of unity in diversity, of the One as Many, is Heraclitus' most significant contribution to philosophy. He himself felt that his special "Word," or message, to mankind was the knowledge that "all things are one."

IMPORTANCE OF REASON: A second aspect of Heraclitus' philosophy is his idea of the One, or God as an all-ordering Reason, a Universal Law present in all things.

1. This view led him to emphasize the value of man's *reason,* which he considered the fiery element in man and thus a moment of *Universal Reason.*

2. In his "Word" he urged men to live by reason.

He was one of the first philosophers to suggest that we cannot wholly rely on our powers of observation.

1. Our senses often play tricks on us.

2. Only by trying to see the world from the viewpoint of Universal Reason, he said, can man understand the hidden laws of the universe that "all things are one," and that "War . . . is the father . . . of all things."

PYTHAGORAS AND THE PYTHAGOREANS: A second school which greatly influenced the course of Greek philosophy, and particularly Aristotle's famous teacher, Plato, was the school of Pythagoras of Samos, another island in the Aegean Sea. Little is known about the life of the school's founder. It seems that Pythagoras left his native Samos about 530 B.C. and settled in Croton, a Greek colony in southern Italy. There he founded a religious brotherhood.

1. Legend says that Pythagoras performed many miracles.

2. He was also very much interested in mathematics, and seems to have been the first man to treat mathematics as a science.

3. One of his contributions to mathematics is known to us today as the *Pythagorean Formula*:

   "The square of the hypotenuse of a right triangle is equal to the sum of the squares of the two sides."

4. The importance he gave to numbers was upheld by his followers, many of whom thought numbers were divine.

PYTHAGOREAN PHILOSOPHY:

1. First, Pythagoras believed in the *transmigration* of souls. Each soul comes from God, in whose image it is made, and to whom it will at last return when it has been cleansed of sin. Until that time, each soul enters into the body of a plant or animal, stays there until it dies, and then enters another body, and then another.

2. Next, if God and the human soul have similar natures, then the structure of man and the structure of the universe must be based on the same principle. The human *soul* is the cause of order in man, as God is the cause of order in the universe.

3. The human soul, which makes man one complete being, is finite; it has a definite form. The One which unifies the world must

likewise be definite, i.e., finite and limited, else its form could not be reproduced in miniature in the soul of man. This view of the relation between God and man made the Pythagoreans identify order, goodness, and beauty with the idea of Limit or *Form*, and disorder and evil with the Unlimited or *Formless*. Their word for universe was *kosmos* which itself means order or arrangement.

4. The similarity between the whole and its parts can be expressed in terms of some proportion supposed to exist between the whole and its part, and the part and *its* parts. One result of Pythagoras' interest in proportion was the numerical ratios in the musical octave (2:1), the fifth (3:2), and the fourth (4:3) in the musical scale. As the musical scale is defined and limited by these numerical ratios, so every whole is made by the action of *Limit* (order) upon the *Unlimited*. The correct proportion between the whole and its parts was the cause of beauty in the object, and was called *harmony*, meaning perfect arrangement. Aristotle in his *Metaphysics* attacks the later Pythagorean idea that numerical ratios can be the cause of anything.

NUMBER IS THE FIRST SUBSTANCE OF THE UNIVERSE: The realization that all things are numerable, and can be related to each other in a numerical proportion is one factor which led the Pythagoreans to their emphasis on the value of *number* in explaining the world order.

1. If musical harmony is dependent on number, world harmony must also be dependent on number, they thought. Most probably they assumed that the conflict of opposites in the world (which the natural philosophers had observed) could be resolved in terms of number.

2. If, as they thought, *Limit* is what gives *Form* to the *Unlimited* and can be expressed in a numerical proportion, number must obviously play a significant role in the world.

Such thinking contributed to the Pythagorean position that all things are numbers. But to understand this theory better, we must also look at their view of numbers.

1. Most scholars agree that the Pythagoreans thought of numbers *spatially*. For example, in their view *one* is the point; *two* is the line; *three* is the surface; and *four* is the solid. To say that all things are numbers is thus another way of saying that everything

that exists consists of points, or units in space, which taken together make a number.

2. In making number the first substance of the world, the Pythagoreans most likely transferred these mathematical conceptions to material reality. Consequently, they said that points, lines, and surfaces are the real units from which all bodies in the world are made.

3. Every material body, in fact, is a solid (i.e., it is an expression of the number *four*).

It is difficult to say which aspect of Pythagorean science most influenced the theory that basic reality is number: their research into the nature of musical sound, or their geometrical view of numbers.

That their theory was taken seriously is evident from the fact that Aristotle devotes a good part of his work on the nature of being to the refutation of the idea that mathematical concepts have a concrete, substantial existence.

THE IDENTITY OF HARMONY WITH GOOD ORDER: The identity of *harmony* with *good order* was the main contribution to Greek philosophy by the Pythagoreans. They approached all things with the purpose of finding the right relation between the whole or the *One,* and its parts (the *Many*).

1. Medicine, for instance, was the science which brought about harmony, or the good ordering, of the parts or vital fluids of the body. Pythagoras' view that health was the right harmony of the body became the ideal of Greek medicine.

2. One of the problems of this distinction between the whole and its parts, and the One and the Many (a problem Heraclitus did not have) is that Pythagoras could find no way of explaining how the Many could have come from the One. The question of *unity* and *diversity* plays a large part in Aristotle's own philosophy.

MATTER AND FORM: The difference between the Ionian School and the so-called Italian School (because Pythagoreans clustered in Sicily) of Pythagoras lay in their different approaches. The *Ionians* asked, "What is the world made of?" The *Pythagoreans* asked, "What is its structure?"

1. Thus, the Ionians said the basic world substance was some kind of self-moving matter;

2. The Pythagoreans saw number or form as the first principle.

Both schools were led to make a definite distinction between matter and form. Aristotle inherited the problem of the relation between matter and form. His solution forms the key to his philosophy.

In thinking of matter and form we must not make the mistake of thinking that form simply means the *shape* of an object; and that matter means the *stuff* from which the object is made. To think in this way would be to misunderstand the problems the Greek philosophers were trying to solve.

1. The Greek word for *form* comes from a verb which can mean both *to see* and *to know*. The form of anything was that which is knowable about it. When you wanted to say what was knowable about an object you gave its *logos* or definition. But no object is the same as its definition.

2. The Greek philosopers were trying to find some way of making their system of language fit the structure of thought to reflect accurately the nature of reality.

3. The early Ionian philosophers thought the problem was relatively simple. Just divide up the natural world into its elements, and you will have found the nature of reality.

4. By the time of Heraclitus, men were thinking that the question was more difficult. Perhaps our senses cannot be trusted to tell us about reality.

5. Only the way we think can give us any information about the nature of things. The Pythagoreans thought things were best understood through their intelligible structure. They said that what could be known about an object was what you could say about it in numbers.

PARMENIDES' "IT IS":   The real break between language and thought on the one hand, and the sensible world on the other, came with a pupil of the Pythagoreans named *Parmenides* (c. 540-470 B.C.). Parmenides was particularly impressed with the vital contrast which existed between *being* and *non-being*.

The basic tenet of his philosophy reveals his fundamental approach to the problem of being:

1. "It (i.e., being)" he said, "*is*." Non-being is not and cannot be thought." In other words, man cannot think something which does not exist. He cannot think non-being.

2. This means that whatever I say, or whatever I think *is*, it exists.

3. Reality is not primarily what can be experienced by the senses. It is what you *think* it is, as stated in language.

4. For reasons which follow, the sensible world, the world which is familiar to all of us, is not, in Parmenides' view, the real world at all.

The result of this theory was to divide philosophy henceforth into two camps.

1. Some said that all sensible things were *thought*.

2. Others held that all thought was *sensible things*.

No one could say that the sensible world and the world of thought were one world any longer. *Reason* and *sense* had split the world in two.

BEING IS ONE, ETERNAL, AND UNCHANGING: It would be a mistake to believe that Parmenides' important distinctions between *reason* and *sense*, and *truth* and *appearance* made him an idealist. His notion of being was not an abstract concept. He thought of being as a space-filling mass. Being is the full, he said; non-being is therefore empty space. From this basic idea he derived his other theories of being.

1. Being always *is*. It cannot have a beginning nor cease to be, because it cannot come from non-being.

3. Being is *unchanging* and *unmoving*. The identity of the verbs "to because it is everywhere the same. Since being is, there is nothing that exists which can divide it.

3. Being is *unchanging* and *unmoving*. The fact that the verb "to be" and "to exist" (the distinction between the two meanings

had not yet been made clear) supported Parmenides' argument that there can be no change and no motion.

"To change" means that something becomes what it is not. Since "to be" meant "to exist" for Parmenides, he said that it was impossible for something which is (i.e., exists) to become what it is not (i.e., not to exist).

Similarly, being is unmoving; "to move" means that something moves into a space where something is not (i.e., does not exist). But being is the full. Therefore, empty space, or a space where nothing is (a space of non-being) logically cannot exist.

TRUTH AND APPEARANCE: Parmenides was the first to make the distinction noted above between truth and appearance. It is clear that the type of being which he describes is one that is completely foreign to that which experience shows us.

Parmenides held that only that perception is true which shows us an unchanging being. Since our senses tell us of a world of change and decay (i.e., of non-being in his view), Parmenides said that they are the cause of intellectual error. They only show us what *appears* to exist. They tell us nothing about the one, indivisible, unchanging *reality*. The only way, he said, we can know the nature of reality is through the structure of thought.

SAVING THE SENSIBLE WORLD, EMPEDOCLES: Parmenides' theory of the unreality of change could not long go unchallenged. The philosophers who came after him were left with the problem of reconciling the unchanging world of being with the changing world in which we live, for no matter what anyone might say, common sense indicated that there was a world of change, and this world had to be real. One attempt to resolve the problem was made in the fifth century B.C. by a man named *Empedocles,* who came from the town of Akragas in Sicily.

1. Parmenides had reasoned that the world we can see and touch is unreal. But he had not said that matter was unreal.

2. Rather he had held that being was an indefinite, space-filling, unchanging, and eternal mass.

Empedocles tried to reconcile the world of change with unchanging being by saying that the world as we know it is composed of four basic material particles which are themselves unchanging and indestructible.

1. According to Empedocles, the four elements were *earth, air, fire,* and *water.*

2. As the father of the classification of the elements, Empedocles was the originator of the concept of element.

3. The objects of the physical world, he said, are made up of the haphazard combination of these four elements.

   a. Although the elements never change their nature, the different ways they can be combined result in the coming-into-being of different physical objects.

   b. Objects cease to be when the elements of which they are composed separate.

What causes the elements to combine and to separate? Since Parmenides had upset the notion that there could be a self-moving substance, Empedocles explained the phenomenon of change by returning to the concept of the conflict of opposites familiar to the Ionian philosophers and putting it in a new light.

1. Since motion cannot be caused by matter, Empedocles said that it was caused by two opposing forces acting upon matter from the outside.

2. These two forces are the forces of *love* and *hate;* that is, of attraction and repulsion. The balance between the two keeps the world stable.

ANAXAGORAS AND MIND: Empedocles posited two forces outside the world of the elements as the cause of motion. Despite their names of love and hate, he thought of these forces in physical and material terms.

It was the contribution of Anaxagoras of Clazomenae in Asia (born about 500 B.C.) to introduce the concept of *mind* as the cause of change and becoming.

1. He admitted that there was a difference between the sensible world and the world of thought.

2. But one was not more "real" than the other. The problem was simple:

   a. What was not matter was *mind*.

   b. The formation of the world was the imposition of *mind*, or order, upon the chaos of matter.

Although it is not clear whether Anaxagoras thought of mind as something essentially intellectual or essentially material, most scholars agree that he was feeling his way toward a theory of causation based on a purely intellectual principle. Thus, his theory is of great importance for the later philosophies of Plato and Aristotle, both of whom conceived of mind in non-material terms.

LEUCIPPUS AND DEMOCRITUS, THE ATOMISTS: A third philosophy to try and resolve the paradox of unchanging being and a changing world was that of a school which came to be called the *Atomists*. This school was the most radical of all.

1. It agreed with Parmenides that the sensible world was not the real world.

2. But if you divide the world into its smallest indivisible parts, you will reach reality, they thought.

The best-known philosophers of the school were Leucippus of Miletus, who lived around 435 B.C., and Democritus of Abdera, a village in Thrace in what is today northern Greece (460-370 B.C.).

1. Both these men took the Parmenidean idea of the One, which was the unity and reality of the universe, and gave all its characteristics to many little "ones," which they said composed the material world.

2. *Atom* means in Greek "that which cannot be broken up." Like the element of Empedocles, it was limited, eternal, and unchangeable. It differed from Empedocles' element in that there were many more atoms. The Atomists considered them more fundamental than the elements. Many atoms, for example, composed the element of water.

3. Democritus was faced with the problem of how these tiny particles could move in space.

   a. Taking a great leap forward, he said that empty space (Parmenides' non-being) really existed. He conceived of the atoms as tiny particles moving in infinite empty space, as dust particles move in a ray of sunshine.

b. The chance combination of these particles occurred when one atom moved from its course and bumped into another one.

Aristotle blamed the Atomists for not giving any reason why the atoms should move, and he is partly right. The Atomists returned to the Ionian idea of a self-moving substance, saying that due to their varying sizes and weights, the atoms are in a state of rotary motion for all eternity.

SECONDARY AND PRIMARY QUALITIES OF ATOMS: The Atomists made the distinction between those qualities belonging to the combinations of the atoms themselves, and those which *appear* to belong to them because of the way in which they are perceived.

1. The Atomists thus maintained Parmenides' distinction between truth and appearance.

2. Primary qualities, they said, belong to physical objects; these are such qualities as size and shape.

3. Secondary qualities are merely qualities which convention and custom say belong to objects. These are qualities such as color, taste (bitter, sweet), temperature (hot, cold) and so on.

The primary qualities are fixed in the atom; secondary qualities are relative and depend upon the perceiver. What might taste *sweet* to me, for example, might taste *bitter* to you. Everyone does not see the same hue of blue when he looks at an autumn sky.

The Atomists thought that such things as sweetness and color merely express the way a particular object affects the perceiver. A rose does not really have a sweet smell. It just *seems* to smell sweet.

THE STUDY OF MAN—THE SOPHISTS: While philosophers were arguing about the nature of reality, a number of teachers were traveling all over Greece claiming that they could teach anyone all there was to know about man. These teachers were called *Sophists*. The word comes from the Greek word, *sophia*, meaning wisdom. The wisdom of the Sophists was not connected with such questions as "What is reality?" The Sophists were more practical: They were interested in human nature and man's actions in the world. They appeared in the Greek world in the fourth century B.C. at a time when Athens was engaged in a life-and-death struggle with Sparta. Unrest was in the air. Long established values were being questioned; the whole city-state system was being subjected to intense study. For the first time, morals and ethics came to the forefront as subjects of scientific investigation.

1. The Sophists claimed they could teach a man to be a good speaker, a good ruler, a good anything.

2. But they were openly sceptical that anything like real goodness actually existed.

"What is truth? What is justice? What is man? Why should we obey?" they asked. The world is changing all around us. Our own faculties of sense and smell have been shown to be useless in telling us what the world really is. What is bitter to one man is sweet to the next. Obviously, then, what is just to one man must be unjust to the next.

1. There are no objective standards or values.

2. It all depends on the way you look at things, on your class position in society.

3. *Man is the measure of all things,"* they said.

THE SOPHISTS SHOULD BE CALLED THE FIRST SOCIOLOGISTS: Athens had become the center of a wealthy empire to which people from all over the known world came. It was also the port from which many Greeks set sail to colonize new lands around the Mediterranean Sea. There was growing contact between different civilizations. The great Greek historian, Herodotus, had traveled far and wide and had returned to write of the various customs he had seen in his travels. The Sophists shared his appreciation of foreign cultures. They concluded that every system had its own kind of justice. What the Athenians called law was a product of their traditions. Values and moral codes varied from culture to culture.

NATURE AND CONVENTION: In their questioning of cultural and political values, the Sophists brought a new problem into the world.

1. If all law is based on man-made tradition, what is the relation between law and the nature of man?

2. The Sophist put the two ideas of *phusis* (nature) and *nomos* (convention or tradition) in opposition to each other.

3. Some of them were the first of a long line of thinkers to hold that civilization had corrupted the nature of man.

   a. All men are naturally equal.

   b. Society creates injustice by making some men slaves and other men despots.

Other Sophists took the opposite view.

1. Nature means the survival of the fittest, they said.

2. Civilization only tries to soften the struggle to which man by nature is fitted by making laws.

3. Real justice is the *rule of the stronger*.

4. The conventional justice of a given society is simply the means whereby those who are unfitted to survive *can* survive.

Whatever their approach, the Sophists were essentially relativists in political science. There is no best state. One society is as good as another society. Differences in constitutions depend upon variables, such as geographic location, or the idea of justice which a particular society has.

THE BAD NAME OF THE SOPHISTS: It is not surprising that the Athenian government did not welcome the activities of the Sophists in its war-torn city.

1. The Sophists were accused of corrupting the values of Athenian youth,

2. of mocking the religion of Athens, and

3. of undermining the morals of the city!

Governments and people are inclined to be much less tolerant of new ideas in a moment of crisis; and the Sophists earned a very bad name. Some of them were banished from the city (banishment being a traditional Athenian punishment for political offenders) for their "dangerous" teachings.

The reader should not conclude, however, that the Sophists were a destructive element in Greek society as a whole. The great philosophers among them, such as Protagoras and Gorgias, were truly an educative force, helping to broaden the outlook of the average Greek citizen. Although many men in Athens thought the Sophists had gone too far in their new ideas, there was only one man who took up their challenge—Socrates. No other teacher created such a deep impression upon his followers; yet he did not write a single word. He is the only man who was ever condemned to death by the citizens of Athens because of what he believed. Although the great Greek historian, Xenophon, and others wrote about him, our most interesting source of information about Socrates comes from his famous pupil, Plato.

PLATO

INTRODUCTION

HISTORICAL BACKGROUND

PLATO AND THE WAR: Plato was born in 428 or 427 B.C. and died about the age of eighty in 348 or 347 B.C. His life, therefore, spanned the two greatest centuries of Greek civilization. Although he was little more than a youth when the war ended, the Peloponnesian struggle and the changes it produced in Athens were to become the single most decisive factor in determining the course of his later life.

ATHENS AND HER CONFEDERACY: The Peloponnesian War was essentially a power struggle between the two giants of the Greek world, Athens and Sparta. Since the defeat of the Persians in 480 B.C., Athens had benefited tremendously from the war-time alliance created to defend Greece from the barbarian invader. Because Athens had spearheaded that campaign, she emerged from the war with a large number of smaller cities and islands "affiliated" with her for mutual defense.

THE ATHENIAN EMPIRE: The confederacy was voluntary at first; the aim was to preserve Greece from reconquest by the barbarians; and to ravage the lands of Persia when possible. A treasury was set up on the island of Delos to which the other states contributed. Gradually, however, it grew to become something quite different; when the island of Naxos wished to withdraw, Athens compelled it to remain within the alliance by means of blockade. And another city, Carystus, a non-member, was compelled to join.

The treasury was moved to Athens a bit later, and a certain part employed for the beautification of the city; *the confederacy had become an empire.*

ATHENS VS. SPARTA: The now-subjugated states grew increasingly restless, of course, and Sparta saw her chance for power in their dissatisfaction.

Finally, in 431 B.C. Athens and Sparta came to blows. The war lasted for 27 years, until Athens was defeated at Aegospotami in 404 B.C.; yet the moral and spiritual decline of Athens proved in the final analysis to be far more damaging than her military defeat.

DEGENERATION OF ATHENS DURING WAR: Although there was a respite of seven years, when only a sort of "cold war" was being waged, the long extended nature of the war took its toll of the Athenians.

Soon after war began, a plague broke out in Athens with devastating results; it seemed almost incurable, and a large percentage of Athenian citizens perished. Yet, according to Thucydides, the historian of the war, it produced an even more profound effect upon the moral tone of the city:

> "Men who had formerly hidden what they took pleasure in now grew bolder. . . . The pleasure of the moment and whatever assisted it took the place of honor. . . . No fear of gods or law of man deterred a criminal."

The city never fully recovered from the effects of this physical and moral degeneration. The latter part of the war was directed by ambitious politicians, who exerted a philosophy of power to inspire the war effort. There were revolutions within the city itself, as the democracy and the oligarchy (rule by the wealthy) fought for control; each time the power changed hands, atrocities were committed and more hatred arose between the classes. When the was finally ended in 404 B.C., the oligarchy ruled briefly, instituted a purge, and soon was replaced by the democratic faction in the city.

EVIL EFFECTS OF THE WAR: Some of the most distinguished of Athenians were caught up in the web of this war:

1. Thucydides, the historian, was exiled for "incompetence" as a general.

2. The orator Antiphon was executed for his part in the rule of the 400.

3. Andocides, another orator, was also forced to go abroad.

4. Lysias, the orator, lost his property, and saw his brother murdered.

DEATH OF SOCRATES: Yet, to Plato, the greatest tragedy of all was the execution of Socrates in 399 B.C., caused by the distrust and resentment of the democracy against the aristocratic class (from which Socrates drew many of his disciples), and the harmful effects, in the eyes of many, which the Sophists had caused among the younger generation.

Indeed, Anytus, one of the prosecutors of Socrates, was said to have been openly mocked by his son, who was a follower of Socrates; the questioning, which Socrates encouraged, seemed like unthinking recklessness to many.

Socrates, then, was executed; and Plato was filled with disgust for the democracy, just as he had become disillusioned earlier with the oligarchic group which had seized power.

EFFECTS OF POLITICAL TURMOIL ON PLATO: Plato himself tells of his feelings at this time in his life, revealing his concern, even then, with the problems of moral and political justice:

> "When I considered these things and the men in charge of public affairs, and made a closer study of law and custom as I grew older, it seemed even more difficult to govern a state rightly. . . . At the same time the whole fabric of law and custom was growing worse and worse at a troubling rate. As a result, although I had first been full of enthusiasm for a public career, when I saw all this happening, and everything falling to pieces, I was at last completely bewildered. I did not cease thinking how this situation might be changed, and, especially the whole organization of the state; yet all the time I was waiting for the right time to act." (*Seventh Letter.*)

This passage tells a good deal about the influences upon Plato's thought as a young man; the seeds which were later to sprout full-blown in the *Republic* can already be detected in his confusion and concern.

PLATO

LIFE AND WORKS (428/7-348/7 B.C.)

SOCRATES' INFLUENCE UPON PLATO: Plato was born into one of the more distinguished families of Athens, and, as a young man, was given all those advantages to which the upper class Athenian was accustomed.

This included, at the time of Plato's youth, association with Socrates, and exposure to his "Socratic Method," which usually resulted in the embarrassment and confusion of those who believed they were authorities on various subjects.

The magnetism of Socrates' personality attracted the most gifted of Athenian youth, including Alcibiades, the ill-starred general, and of course Plato.

In the "Apology," Socrates tells us that these young men were quick to imitate his method; and so the city was filled with young men questioning and confuting their elders.

SOCRATES' PERSONAL EMPIRE: There is a story told that Plato had completed a tragedy and was about to enter it in competition when he heard Socrates speak; as soon as he did, he cast his tragedy into the fire. True or not, Plato was deeply influenced, perhaps as much by Socrates' living example as by his "teaching."

He tells in his *Seventh Letter* how the leaders of the oligarchy tried unsuccessfully to implicate Socrates in their crimes, describing him as "my friend, a man then advanced in years—a man whom I would not hesitate to call the most just man then living."

EVIL OF THE OLIGARCHY: Plato also tells us that many of his own relatives were involved in this oligarchic reaction known as the rule of "The Thirty" (Critias, the leader, was his mother's cousin), and that he had actually been invited to take part. But he soon realized the evil of their régime: "These men made the former constitution seem like a paradise."

THE TRAVELS OF PLATO: Shortly after the execution of Socrates, Plato is believed to have left Athens and spent the next twenty years traveling among various peoples. His exact itinerary is not known; yet he seems to have visited Egypt, where the existence

328

of a small priestly class ruling an agricultural community made an impression upon him, which was later to bear fruit in the organizing of his *Republic.*

He also visited Sicily and Italy, becoming acquainted with the school founded by Pythagoras there. He seems to have borrowed certain Pythagorean elements for his own Utopia, and here again his acquaintance with a small group of men, dedicated to study and ruling in a life of simplicity, had its effects upon his later political writings.

THE GORGIAS: *The Gorgias,* probably written when Plato was about forty, is the earliest of Plato's major statements of political theory. Here, all the themes which had preoccupied him (and would continue to do so throughout his life) are first stated: the life of the philosopher vs. the life of the "rhetorician"; the meaning of justice; the right use of rhetoric, and the use and misuse of political power.

PLATO ENTERS PRACTICAL POLITICS: Yet Plato was not content merely to theorize; when an opportunity arrived to put his ideals into practice, and actually produce a "philosopher-king" he took advantage of it. He was ashamed, he tells us, to be thought of as a "theorist." His chance came in an invitation to the court of King Dionysius of Sicily, an absolute despot. He soon made the acquaintance of Dion, the king's brother-in-law, and believed that he possessed the necessary qualifications for his future "philosopher-king." Dion became his devoted disciple, and Plato was equally devoted: "He listened with keener attention than any young man I have ever met: and he decided to live in the future a different life . . . preferring virtue to pleasure and luxury."

FAILURE OF HIS DREAM: Yet Plato's training and indoctrination made the tyrant Dionysius suspicious, and he was soon compelled to leave. Plato made two more trips to Sicily, but fared no better. Both he and Dion were suspected of planning a revolution (which was probably true) and both fell into disfavor.

PLATO AND THE ACADEMY: Plato devoted the remainder of his life to his Academy, the first "university," and an influence throughout antiquity for centuries to come. The school was meant as a training area for philosophic statesmen, attracting from the neighboring states promising young men whom Plato trained in his "Art of Ruling." Here, too, he borrowed from the community founded by Pythagoras, which he had visited and learned from as a young man. Although disappointed in his hopes for his native city Athens, Plato could hope to spread the doctrines of the philosophic ruler throughout the then known world.

PLATO'S ATTITUDE TO HIS WRITING: Plato also wrote a good number of his dialogues during this period, in which the basic Socratic teaching, as developed further by himself, could become better known throughout the world, offering some sort of beacon light to surrounding communities.

As he himself points out in the "Phaedrus," however, Plato never imagined his writings to be any substitute for the personal training and moral development which he believed could only come from personal contact with his student. If there are any doubts about this fact, Plato makes it clear in a strong statement of his policy in the *Seventh Letter*:

> "One statement at least I can make regarding all those who have written or will write, claiming knowledge of the subjects I pursue—regardless of how they claim to have acquired it. . . . These writers, in my opinion, can have no real acquaintance with the subject. I have composed no work about it, nor will I ever do so in the future; there is no way of expressing it in words like other studies. Knowledge of it must come after a long period of . . . instruction . . . when, suddenly, like a blaze ignited by a leaping spark, it is kindled in soul, and immediately becomes self-sustaining."

This is what Plato had formerly tried to do in Sicily with Dion, and what he was now dedicating himself to doing in the Academy.

DEATH OF PLATO: The story is told that, at the age of eighty, Plato was invited to a wedding feast, and in the morning, when the hosts tried to awaken him after having fallen asleep in a chair, they found that he had died quietly during the night.

PLATO SURVIVES ENTIRE: Of all classical writers, Plato seems to be the only one who has survived complete into modern times; no commentators mention works of his which we do not possess; and indeed there are several imitations of his Socratic dialogues included in the Platonic corpus. Some of them seem to have been written more than a century or so later, and contain themes which were contemporary with these later writers, such as a dialogue concerning Stoic doctrines. The bulk of Plato's work is concerned with political and ethical theory; yet there are several which defy classification.

VARIOUS KINDS OF DIALOGUES:

1. One group can be called "The Socratic Dialogue," which keep generally to the same form. Socrates enters into discussion with someone who claims to have special knowledge (a poet, a prophet, a general), Socrates' role being limited to exposing their true ignorance of their position.

2. There are also the larger "political dialogues," some containing an elaborate setting (*Gorgias, Protagoras*), others which do not (*Statesman*); these deal with the basic Platonic problems mentioned earlier.

3. Still others of the larger ones deal with such varied matters as rhetoric (*Phaedrus*) and epistemology (study of knowledge) such as in his *Theatetus*.

4. *The Republic* is Plato's masterpiece, a work longer than all but the *Laws;* it deals with the fundamental question of the "just man" and the "just state," while containing Plato's views on various other matters within this central framework.

5. There are the four dialogues usually linked together as a "biography" of Socrates:

   a. The "Euthyphro."

   b. The "Apology."

   c. The "Crito."

   d. The "Phaedo."

Together they relate the last several weeks of his life.

6. And then there are dialogues difficult to classify:

   a. The "Symposium" (a dinner-party discussion of love).

   b. The "Menexenus" (a mock funeral speech).

   c. The "Timaeus" (a work of cosmology and theology).

7. Finally there is the enormous *Laws*, which in certain ways parallels the *Republic*, seeming to be Plato's "second thoughts" on the founding of the ideal state. Here, too, Plato founds a city, in great detail; but there seems to be a crabbed, pessimistic tone to the book, which marks it as a work of his old age. Compulsion seems to be the most characteristic quality of this "new" *Republic*.

PLATO

PLATO'S LITERARY CONTEMPORARIES

THE GOLDEN AGE ENDS: Some of the giants of Greek literature passed from the scene within a few years of the Athenian defeat in the Peloponnesian War. Thucydides, its historian, died several years before it ended, and the two tragedians, Sophocles and Euripedes, both died in 405 B.C.

ARISTOPHANES AND HIS COMEDIES: The chief respresentative of this "old order" to survive into the fourth century was *Aristophanes*. His earliest plays had been produced when Athens was still the undisputed leader of Hellas, its cultural resources even more impressive than its political power. Yet the two surviving plays which he wrote after the war are notable most for their falling-off of power; there is no longer the ·confident exuberance Aristophanes had possessed in the days of Athens' glory. Then, he had mocked even the political demagogue Cleon (*Knights*); but now he could only produce a tame allegory about the blindness of the god of Wealth, who regains his sight and rewards just men (*Plutus*). His other play of this period, *Women in Parliament* or *Ecclesiazusae*, discusses the possibility of a communistic state run entirely by women; the disillusionment and loss of spirit in this work are evident to anyone who has read the earlier plays.

XENOPHON, THE PUPIL OF SOCRATES: One of the chief prose writers of this century was *Xenophon*, and in many ways he presents an interesting contrast to Plato:

1. Both Plato and Xenophon were followers of Socrates.

2. Both of them respected him sufficiently to write works in which he was the chief character.

3. Xenophon too wrote an "Apology" and a "Symposium."

4. Xenophon wrote the "Memorabilia," a miscellaneous collection of tales and brief sketches of the master seen through the eyes of the author. Yet this Socrates is scarcely recognizable to the reader who is accustomed to the Platonic Socrates. In Xenophon, Socrates appears as a rather kindly gentleman with a practical bent; he is made to discuss such things as household

management. But there is nothing of the intense concern for knowledge and truth that marks the Socrates of Plato.

Although he was a member of Socrates' circle, Xenophon seems never to have fully appreciated the lessons his teacher was attempting to communicate, and so his Socrates is kindly and witty, but little more than that.

THE YOUNG POET AGATHON: The tragic poet *Agathon* inherited the prestige of the earlier tragedians; yet his poetry never seemed to rise above a certain prettiness and elegance of expression.

None of his plays has survived, which seems to express the judgment of the later generations upon his work. Both Aristophanes and Plato (in the "Symposium") wrote parodies of him and his work, and in both he appears to be a graceful and gifted person, but shallow.

ISOCRATES THE ORATOR: *Isocrates* is another intellectual of the fourth century who believed, like Plato, that he had a practical responsibility to influence Greek politics whenever possible.

1. Just as Plato pursued the dream of an ideal state, Isocrates was concerned with the unification of all Greece, which he could see was weakened and divided by the continual bickerings of the citizens.

2. At various times in his life he appealed to King Archidamus of Sparta, Philip of Macedon, and the city of Athens to intervene in this matter, and to unite all Greece.

3. In his "Panegyricus" he hails Athens as the cultural leader of the Greeks. She has made the word "Hellene" mean "not a race, but an attitude of mind."

PLATO

THE REPUBLIC: INTRODUCTION

Plato wrote a body of twenty-seven (more or less) works: the *Republic* is the twenty-third in the following list:

Alcibiades
Apology
Charmides
Cratylus
Critias
Crito
Euthydemus
Euthyphro
Gorgias
Hippias Minor
Ion
Laches
Laws
Letters
Lysis
Meno
Parmenides
Phaedo
Phaedrus
Philebus
Politicus
Protagoras
Republic
Sophist
Symposium
Theaetetus
Timaeus

THE DIALOGUE: All the above works are written in the form of philosophic dialogues with the exception of the "Letters" and the "Apology."

The *Platonic dialogue* is a dramatic work with a cast of two to as many as nine characters:

1. The main speaker is generally Socrates.

2. Socrates is generally speaking Plato's mind. He is his mouthpiece.

3. The dialogue is usually on some subject like justice, happiness, virtue, the ideal state, etc.

4. The "action" consists of the interplay of conversational dialogue between Socrates and the rest of the cast.

5. Generally, a Platonic dialogue begins with some character venturing an answer to some question of Socrates, which is then taken up by others; the play of question-answer under the direction of a skillful questioner whose main purpose is to let you discover your own ignorance, is known as "the Socratic Method."

6. The dialogues often contain myths which function as narrative illustrations, parable, and allegory.

7. The dialogues are written in a fluent and powerful prose, often by virtue of its eloquence and power soaring into pure poetry. Plato is not always serious: he has a sense of humor that is delightful.

8. Many of the characters actually come alive on the printed page through Plato's dramatic skill: in this sense the dialogues are genuine drama.

THE REPUBLIC: PLATO'S MASTERPIECE: *The Republic* is the best known work of Plato, and is usually regarded as his masterpiece; it also contains his major statements on politics and ethics.

A later and longer work, *The Laws*, considered the work of the "old" Plato, modifies these views somewhat, yet *The Republic* is generally regarded as representative of Plato's mature reflections on the subject of the "just" man and the "just" state. It contains, as well, his views on a variety of other subjects (including education, poetry, and women). Its very diversity, drawn together into a unified whole, makes it a remarkable work of literature, as well as of philosophy.

SUBJECT MATTER OF *THE REPUBLIC*:   The question is raised from time to time as to what *The Republic* is about: Is it primarily a treatise on ethics, or politics? As the Plato scholar, A. E. Taylor, points out, this question ignores the crucial point. To Plato, the two areas of *ethics* and *politics* are so closely related as to be indistinguishable from one another; the same basic law governs both the individual and the state (which is, Plato would hasten to add, "the individual writ large").

ITS CONCERN WITH "THE OTHER WORLD":   And yet, Plato does not focus his gaze only on this world:

1. There is an intensely other-worldly quality about it, which can easily enough be lost sight of in our agonizings about the details of his ideal Commonwealth.

2. The work begins and ends with explicit discussions of death, and the happiness or unhappiness which a man may merit.

3. The remark of Cephalus, about how, as a man grows older, he begins to grow more and more concerned with those stories of the "other world" which he had mocked as a young man with all his life before him, induces Socrates to raise the question of justice in this life, and its relation to that "other" life.

4. The work ends with Socrates' Myth of Er, which outlines the rewards and punishments accorded all men in the next life, depending upon their free choices made in this life.

5. Socrates concludes by encouraging the young man Glaucon to live his life wisely and well so that he will "fare well" in the next world.

THE IMPORTANCE OF JUSTICE: The problem of *justice*, then, and the *"just"* man becomes not just an exercise in abstract thinking or idle woolgathering, but a most practical search for what will most benefit a man. Socrates sometimes assumes a mock-serious tone in Plato's writings; yet we can be sure that he is in deadly earnest when he keeps impressing upon the two young men, Glaucon and Adeimantus, the difficulty and yet the necessity of this "search" for justice.

THE CHARACTERS

PLATO'S CHARACTERS: In choosing the dialogue form for the writing of his *Republic*, Plato set himself a formidable challenge, yet managing successfully to create several unforgettable characters.

SOCRATES: Chief among these is Socrates himself, of course; and in considering him we are faced with the perennial "Platonic

Question," i.e.: how much of the Socrates whom we know in the dialogues accurately represents the real, historical Socrates; and how much is he a result of Plato's intrusion of his own ideas and personality. It is generally agreed that the "Apology" of Plato is substantially the same as the one which Socrates actually delivered in court when he was on trial for his life. It is here we must look to find the most accurate portrayal of the man.

THE "HISTORICAL" VS. THE "PLATONIC" SOCRATES: The ironic one, the good humor, and the intense moral seriousness which we find there, are most marked in Book One of the *Republic*, which represents Socrates sparring verbally with a famous Sophist. He propounds no doctrine here; and denies that he "knows" anything which he could teach; he is only interested in pointing out the shallowness of a man's reasoning.

Once Socrates begins discussing justice in detail, however, the tone seems to change; and we are introduced to a man who has very definite and carefully thought-out ideas relating to a variety of subjects, although he keeps up the pretense throughout that he is just stumbling upon one after another of these insights—an absurd suggestion. Strangely, however, the particular personality traits usually thought to be Socrates' own (1. his sly, good humor; 2. his pretense at ignorance; 3. an almost mocking quality which shows itself)—these remain attached to Plato's literary Socrates.

The answer seems to be then that although the personality of Socrates is accurately represented throughout, the ideas and teachings are Plato's own, excepting only Book One.

THE "IRONY" OF PLATO: This "ironic" tone of Socrates is particularly marked in his long dialogue with Glaucon when planning their ideal state.

It is obvious that Socrates is developing the ideas and the argument almost completely by himself, with Glaucon serving as little more than a "yes-man"; yet he often defers to Glaucon as to a superior, asking "if this is what you mean." When Glaucon does not understand, Socrates immediately blames himself for explaining badly. (The "irony" of Socrates is really a transliteration of the Greek word *"eironia"* meaning "saying less than you know"; in this sense, we can see that it exactly fitted Socrates' attitude.)

POLEMARCHUS: Polemarchus plays a very minor role in *The Republic;* his chief contribution is a definition of justice borrowed second-hand from the poet Simonides. Socrates quickly shows him the inadequacy of his ready-made formula, by leading all of his arguments to absurd conclusions. The young man is represented as a model son, and decent; but unwilling to think hard about abstract problems.

CEPHALUS, THE OLD MAN: Cephalus is the father of Polemarchus, the young man who offers Socrates the invitation to his father's house. Plato depicts him expertly in a few sharp strokes. He is a good, reverent man (he has just come from having offered sacrifices) who represents "the decent average man" coming to the end of an honest life; his views of justice are typical of this sort of man as well. Cephalus is a witty conversationalist, who enjoys telling anecdotes, as old men will, about the famous men of his own generation. He is probably best characterized by his sound good sense, and his unsentimental attitude to old age—he makes the best of it. Although he disappears before the middle of Book One, he remains vividly in our memory.

THRASYMACHUS, THE SOPHIST: Thrasymachus suddenly bursts into the conversation unannounced and uninvited: this is most typical of the man himself. He is a brusque fellow who has radical views about the nature of law and society, and is eager to state them in no uncertain terms. The "pussy-footing" of Socrates and Polemarchus only disgusts him; when Socrates tries to establish his points by logic, he impatiently insists upon "facing facts," and looking at the world as it "really is." At one point, he insults Socrates by telling him that he needs a nurse to wipe his nose, since his talk is nothing but childish prattle.

Yet, as he begins to lose the argument, most of the bluster disappears, and he politely allows Socrates, towards the end, to lead the argument in whatever direction he desires (not always a wise move when dealing with Socrates). Although Thrasymachus was a professional Sophist, who was paid to teach others the art of argumentation, he seems to have been no match for Socrates.

GLAUCON: Glaucon is rather lighthearted and spirited. Adeimantus remarks that the "timocratic" man probably resembled his brother. He listens politely and tries to agree, if possible; yet if Socrates' ideas seem outlandish, he is quick to tell him so. When Socrates has described the simple life of his citizens, living on bread, meat and simple fruits, Glaucon complains to him that he is founding a community of pigs; as a child of the "affluent" society, he finds this "back to nature" ideal a bit hard to take. And like any student eager to please his teacher, Glaucon jumps in to suggest certainly astronomy, if any subject, "raises the mind upwards," only to find that, on the contrary, it leads the mind *downwards!*

ADEIMANTUS: Adeimantus and Glaucon are Plato's brothers. Adeimantus takes a much smaller part in the discussion. He stands out most vividly in his defense of injustice in Book II. He is indignant because his elders only praise justice for "practical" reasons, not for its own sake. Whether they are teachers, poets, or parents, they all believe that justice is just "good policy."

Adeimantus is something of an idealist, who pushes the argument to the extreme, and insists on knowing if justice is worthwhile, even if the just man is punished and reviled for his virtue. None of the "reasonable" clichés of the contented elder generation will satisfy him. Even the gods seem to wink at injustice, he complains. This disillusionment of the intense Adeimantus contrasts interestingly with the more outgoing Glaucon.

PLATO

THE REPUBLIC: BOOK ONE

SOCRATES VISITS CEPHALUS: The entire dialogue is narrated in the first person by Socrates:

Socrates relates that he was walking down to the Piraeus (the port of Athens) to attend the festival of the Goddess Bendis with the young man Glaucon. On his way back he is overtaken by Polemarchus, the son of Cephalus, who invites them to his father's house for the evening festival. Glaucon wants to go, and after the young men humorously threaten to take him by force, Socrates relents, and follows them to Cephalus' house. Back at the home of Cephalus, they find the old man seated and wearing a garland; he has just come from sacrificing. His sons, Lysias ("the Attic Orator"), and Euthydemus, as well as Polemarchus and Thrasymachus, the Sophist, are present.

CEPHALUS ON JUSTICE: *Cephalus* remarks that Socrates should visit him more often: as he gets older, he develops more of an interest in philosophy.

Socrates (represented as comparatively young) asks the old man if he finds old age painful.

Cephalus replies that many of his old friends regret no longer being young. They claim that they have lost both the pleasures of youth and the respect of the young. Yet not all old men feel this way: when the old poet Sophocles was asked whether he could still enjoy a woman, he answered, "I am only too glad to be free of that; it is like escaping from the hands of a raging madman."

Cephalus states that old age brings peace and contentment; a man's character is the important thing.

Socrates suggests that his wealth makes him content.

Cephalus answers with an anecdote:

> When the great politician, Themistocles, of Athens, was taunted by a man from Seriphus (a small Aegean island), who claimed he was famous because he came from Athens, The-

mistocles answered, "Of course I would not be famous, if I were born in Seriphus; but neither would you, even if you came from Athens."

Cephalus admits that a good man needs some wealth to be happy in old age; but wealth will never help the bad man. He explains that he is moderately wealthy; he believes that the greatest benefit of money is that when a man becomes old, he does not have to fear "that other world" and punishment after death, since he is able to pay back any debts, either to men or to the gods (by sacrifice).

Socrates wonders, however, whether "right conduct" can be defined merely as telling the truth, and paying back what is owed.

It would not be "right" to pay back a sword lent by a man who is mad, nor to tell him the truth.

Cephalus agrees, but "bequeaths the argument" to his son, since he must attend the sacrifice.

THE VIEWS OF POLEMARCHUS (pall ee MARK uhs): Polemarchus, who has "inherited" his father's argument, now quotes the poet Simonides that, "it is just to render to each man his due"; yet Polemarchus claims that to the enemy, "injury" is appropriate.

> "It seems then that Simonides was using words with a hidden meaning, as poets will."

Socrates remarks ironically that Polemarchus has said "his due" when he means "what is appropriate." Now Socrates asks him a series of questions about "when the just man is most useful"; by these questions Polemarchus is brought to agree that

> "Justice is never of any use in using things; it becomes useful when they are useless."

To this humorous conclusion, Socrates answers,

> "If so, my friend, then justice can hardly be a thing of much value."

He confuses the young man further, making him agree that justice is "a form of skill in cheating."

Polemarchus protests that "I have forgotten by now what I did mean."

Socrates points out that it is possible for a man to misjudge the character of another; he would be then doing ill to a good man. Is it ever right to harm any human being? To harm him means to make him less just; so, can the just man exercise his justice by making men unjust?

Polemarchus agrees that he cannot, and that it is never right to harm anyone.

THRASYMACHUS' VIEWS ON JUSTICE: Thrasymachus (threh SIM ih kuss), who had been trying to break into the conversation, now "reared back like a wild beast and sprang towards us, as if he would tear us to shreds." The Sophist complains that they are stupidly deferring to one another in their polite way: let Socrates answer questions for a change, and make a clear statement instead of vague generalities.

Thrasymachus offers his definition, that *justice is "the interest of the stronger";* but Socrates objects, declaring that since a wrestler is "stronger," and has an "interest" in beef, justice seems to be beef.

Thrasymachus, not amused, explains that in every state the rulers are the "strongest." Each ruler makes laws in his own interest; so *"justice" becomes what, in each case, is in the interest of the ruler.* (By this he is claiming that there is no intrinsic "right" or "wrong" common to all men; whatever a ruler decides to be right *is* right, and if another ruler decides it is wrong, *there*, it is wrong).

Socrates asks whether these rulers can err; if so, and if they make laws which are, mistakenly, *not* in their own interest, it seems that justice cannot be defined as "the interest of the stronger."

Thrasymachus explains that a ruler is not *really* a ruler at the time he is erring; a craftsman, when he is making a mistake in his craft, is no craftsman. He boasts that Socrates has not tricked him; he is no match for a good Sophist. But Socrates protests that he is "not mad enough to put a beard on a lion, or attempt to outwit a Thrasymachus."

Every art, says Socrates, has an "interest" which is the matter with which it is concerned; for example, the art of medicine is concerned with the care of the body. So every art *as* art is only concerned with its particular interest; a doctor, therefore, "acting in his capacity as doctor" is interested, not in making money, but in curing the patient's body. So a ruler also, acing as *ruler*, is only concerned with the good of the ruled, not his personal interest.

Thrasymachus asks Socrates if he has a nurse, since he runs about like a sniffing child who cannot recognize a shepherd or a sheep. In real life, a ruler treats his subjects like sheep, for the benefit he can get from them; the honest man is always cheated.

Whether running a business or paying taxes, the unjust man comes out ahead; and the man who is completely unjust, the despot, is rewarded with the greatest happiness.

Once a man holds all his citizens as slaves, he is called happy, and they bless his name.

(Thrasymachus now tries to leave, but the listeners insist he stay and defend his position.)

Socrates makes clear that, to him, *injustice can never be more profitable than justice*.

He again stresses his belief that each art is concerned with its own particular "interest"; medicine produces health, navigation produces safety at sea, and wage-earning wages.

All these craftsmen not only practice their various crafts, but practice "wage-earning" as well; and so, the wages do not come to a man from his particular art. A doctor practices both "the art of healing" *and* wage-earning.

To Socrates, the honest man assumes political power, not for selfish motives, but because he cannot find another as capable of doing the work.

The "penalty" for refusing to rule is to be ruled by a man worse than yourself; and it is this which motivates honest men in a state to assume political office.

Socrates now attacks the view of Thrasymachus that "a life of injustice is to be preferred to a life of justice"; the latter claims that justice is the mark of a good-natured simpleton, whereas injustice is "prudence."

Just as in music, Socrates explains, a musician tunes each string, and aims at a certain pitch which is absolutely right, the "limit" or "measure" for that string; in this way one can make an analogy with justice. To step beyond this "limit" throws the instrument out of tune, and makes one a bad musician.

In the same way, it is the just man who discovers and attains the "measure" in moral conduct. But the unjust man, who recognizes no limit but always grasps for more, shows no intelligence.

Socrates next attacks the belief that *injustice is a source of strength.*

He doubts that any state can do without justice when it is making use of its power.

He points out that robbers do not act unjustly among themselves when they are banded together in committing an injustice against others.

Injustice is always divisive, in a state, an army, or an individual.

The individual who is unable to act, and who is without determination because of injustice, certainly has not any strength.

IS THE LIFE OF JUSTICE THE BETTER LIFE?   Socrates now undertakes the central question of *"whether the life of justice is the better life."* They both agree that certain things have a function; forexample, a pruning knife for cutting; an eye for seeing.

Living seems to be above all the function of the soul. But if the particular virtue of the soul is lost (like sight lost by the eyes, for example), it cannot possibly work well. But they have agreed that *the virtue of the soul is justice,* the just man must live well, and the unjust, not.

Thrasymachus must answer to this "apparently, according to your argument."

Thrasymachus is beaten; he remarks that "since this is a feast day, this will be your share of the entertainment."

Socrates thanks him politely, and taunts him a bit by saying, "You have been so gentle with me since you regained your temper." Like a hungry guest, Socrates has been sampling "every new dish that comes around, before properly enjoying the one before," and never did get around to defining justice.

And on this inconclusive note, Book One ends.

INTERPRETATION OF BOOK ONE: QUESTIONS AND ANSWERS

What is the major significance of Book One?

ANSWER: It raises the question "What is justice?" or "How should a man govern his life?"

Name another contribution of this Book.

ANSWER: It denies that justice can be identified with business morality; that is, as Polemarchus attempts to define it, justice is "helping your friends and harming your enemies."

How does Socrates answer the very cogent argument expressed by Thrasymachus that "might makes right"?

ANSWER: In answering the arguments of Thrasymachus (and Polemarchus), Plato introduces several concepts which not only are used throughout the remainder of the books of the *Republic* but which are still influential in formulating ethical and political theories.

1. The first concept is that of a *universal* or *idea*.

   A universal is a form or model after which all of a class of existing things are patterned. For example, a man may be tall or short, belong to one of five races, have all his limbs or be missing some. There is, however, a sense in which, despite variations, we call every individual a man. Plato believes that we do so because they all partake of the *idea* of man; in the same way, Plato is saying that there is a sense in which all just acts partake of the idea of justice. Justice, whether in an act, a man, or a state, is one and the same thing. And to search for justice in a man's soul it will be appropriate to consider also a just state.

2. Plato hints at his own definition of justice when he tells us that justice is an art analogous to the craftsman's special skill.

   As the craftsman's special skill requires knowledge, so too will a man's ability to live a just life. This doctrine, then (*that being just or acting justly requires knowledge*) is fundamental to the entire *Republic*.

3. Still another concept that Plato introduces into the book is the concept of *function*. This concept later became the major argument for Aristotle's *Nichomachean Ethics*, and, through the influence of this work, found its way into most medieval ethical works.

Fundamentally, this concept asserts that *all things* (living and non-living) *have a particular work to perform* or function to fulfill. The satisfactory fulfillment of this work constitutes the virtue of the thing in question. The function of the eyes is to see; the *virtue* of the eyes is to see well; and if we can determine man's function, we then can determine his virtue.

The tentative answer offered in Book One is that the function *of man's soul is to live and its virtue is to live well.*

Is Socrates proven to be as skilled in argument as the Sophist?

ANSWER: This first book presents Socrates to us matched against a famous Sophist, who is presumably a master of argumentation. Although Socrates is profoundly different from these facile speakers, he proves himself just as skilled in argument and even in pseudo-argument. Certainly Thrasymachus is justified, at least once or twice, in complaining that Socrates is purposely trying to lead him astray.

PLATO

THE REPUBLIC: BOOK TWO

INTRODUCTION: Book I has ended with Socrates' admission to Thrasymachus that he "does not know what justice is"; yet the young men Glaucon and Adeimantus are not satisfied, and insist that Socrates pick up the question again, and show that *justice is good* "*for its own sake.*" This sincere request from them induces Socrates to become fully serious, and to begin his description of the ideal state, where justice should be found.

JUSTICE FOR ITS BENEFITS ONLY: Glaucon explains that the reason for his defense of injustice is this: all men who defend and praise justice never do it for the sake of justice itself—it is for the benefits it offers. "No one has proved that a soul can harbor no worse evil than injustice, no greater good than justice."

Adeimantus explains that "I personally believe that (these arguments) are a crude distortion of their real worth; but I have tried my best to speak as forcefully as I can, since I want to hear the other side from you."

Socrates is delighted with these speeches of the two brothers, believing that "there must be indeed some divine quality in your nature, if you can plead the cause of injustice so eloquently and still not be convinced yourselves that it is better than justice."

Socrates agrees to look into the real nature of justice.

THE REAL NATURE OF JUSTICE: Since justice says Socrates, can exist in a state as well as an individual, it would seem easier to look for justice there, where it is larger, and easier to make out.

States come into existence, Socrates believes, because no man is self-sufficient. We all have various needs. Each one helps the other to satisfy his needs, and when men have gathered together for this purpose, we call it a state.

THE STATE: Socrates will build his state from the beginning:

1. Such men as farmers, shoemakers, and weavers must be represented. Each of them agrees to care for a certain function for

all the others. The famer grows the food for all, as an example; each man is suited to a certain task, and works best at a single task. Yet, we will need more than four or five citizens, says Socrates.

2. Carpenters and smiths and other craftsmen will be needed in the state.

3. Cowherds and shepherds, too, as well as merchants who will import and export what the state needs, are a necessity.

4. And since there must be someone within the state to exchange goods for the citizens, the shopkeepers are necessary, as well as hired laborers.

Glaucon complains at this: Socrates seems to be founding a community of pigs; he appeals for the "ordinary comforts," dining from couches and eating sweets. Glaucon's state, then, seems to be of the luxurious kind.

Socrates comments that such a state is not healthy but suffering from an inflammation. These people will need couches and delicacies like perfumes, sweetmeats, etc.

For this kind of state a whole new troop of people, ministering to luxury, will be needed: artists and poets, actors, and those who make trinkets for women.

But with all of these, the country will become too small to contain them, so we will need a slice of our neighbor's territory; the result will be war.

An army, then, will be needed, and they must be specially chosen for this task. Warfare requires professionals who know their work.

THE GUARDIANS OF THE STATE: The best sort of men for guarding the state would resemble well-bred watch dogs. They would be keen in sighting an enemy, swift and strong. They must have a spirited disposition in times of danger, and yet be gentle with their own people.

PHILOSOPHIC WATCH DOGS: Dogs, says Socrates, are able to recognize some people as friends, and others as enemies;

in other words, they can "make distinctions," and it is this ability which marks the philosopher. Dogs, therefore, are "lovers of wisdom," or "philosophic."

The same will be true of these guardians, who will also be "philosophic"; it is important then, that their education be considered, though it might involve a bit of time.

"Come, then," says Socrates, "let us take our time, and educate our imaginary citizens." (Socrates' "philosophic dogs" shows his enjoyment of whimsical paradox.)

EDUCATION OF THE GUARDIANS: Long experience has shown that the traditional Greek style of education will serve our purposes in educating the Guardians.

It is a two-part system, designed for the cultivation of the mind and of the body. "We will begin with the mind," says Socrates.

1. In educating the young mind, we make use of tales, some of which are true, others fictitious. These "fictitious" tales are the sort we tell children which, although really make-believe, contain *some* portion of truth.

2. Since young minds are so easily impressed, and the beginning of an education so crucial, *it is important to censor the stories which children hear.* Homer and Hesiod, for example, contain stories which will have to be rejected; shameful tales like the punishment of Uranus by his son Cronos; and then, the punishment of Cronos by Zeus, *his* son. No child should be told that it is noble to punish his parents.

3. Poets will be given instructions on how to represent the gods. The nature of a god is good, Socrates says, and so is incapable of any evil. We must not blame the evils in life upon the gods. The poets must justify the gods on every occasion; if someone is punished in a poem or play, the poets will say that he deserved it, and was the better for being punished.

INTERPRETATION OF BOOK TWO: QUESTIONS AND ANSWERS

It is said that Glaucon's argument is one of the earliest statements of the "Social Contract" theory of government; is this true? Discuss.

ANSWER: It is true. Basically, this theory asserts that all the rules, social sanctions, and religious rituals rest finally on the consent of the ruled. This theory has been used to justify tyrannical governments as well as our own democracy. Glaucon uses this theory to explain why men practice morality at all. He attempts to argue that morality is not an intrinsic good (good in itself) but rather it is useful in preventing greater evil. Men are good only out of fear, and the wise man will be immoral when he is certain to escape detection. This theory reappears once again in the English philosopher Hobbes. *It is Socrates' task to justify morality and justice in the soul without reference to any reward.*

What is Socrates' answer to Glaucon?

ANSWER: Socrates (really Plato) attempts to find justice in the soul as it would be "writ large," that is, in the context of a just society. He first rules out any need to explain the origin of society in terms of Social Contract by showing that man is by nature not self-sufficient, and so *naturally* seeks society.

Man's state of dependency is fundamental to Plato's first level of justice. No man can do all tasks equally well. The division of labor and specialization which results is a form of justice working on the lowest level, and each level of society corresponds to a level of the human soul.

What is the second level of the state?

ANSWER: It is the Guardian class, whose task is to defend the state. Their virtue is courage. They take orders from the highest level.

Is education of primary importance in the state?

ANSWER: Yes. Education is the path to knowledge, which plays such an important role in the acquiring of justice.

Why did Plato advocate censorship?

ANSWER: He advocated censorship because he believed that if a man cannot attain true knowledge, he can at least hold good opinions. In his proposals for censoring Greek poetry, Plato stressed two points which revolutionized Western theology:

1. First, he defined the gods in terms of goodness.

2. Second, it follows that it no longer makes sense to talk of the gods as sinning, since good can not be the cause of evil. The vexing problem of the origin of evil in the world is thus raised, and Plato must supply a solution for this too.

Is Plato the first to criticize the morality of some Greek myths?

ANSWER: No. Xenophanes, an Ionian thinker of the sixth century, wrote that "Homer and Hesiod adorned the gods with all that is shameful and scandalous in man: stealing, adultery, and mutual deceit."

Would Plato, if alive today, censor books, television, etc.?

ANSWER: Adeimantus claims that one of the chief reasons for turning to unjust habits of mind, among young men, is the continual stream of stories they hear from the poets, offering bad advice about justice, and claiming that the gods can be bribed. Plato feels that they have a bad effect on young men's minds that is not sufficiently realized.

PLATO

THE REPUBLIC: BOOK THREE

THE RIGHT STORIES: Socrates goes on to say that children in this Commonwealth must also learn to be brave. Thus the stories they hear must not make them afraid of death. In addition, the world after death must be spoken of in attractive terms.

The following scenes in Homer would be barred:

1. Achilles and Patroclus lamenting their fate in the underworld. (Plato refers in one case to Achilles' remark in Hades that he would rather be the poorest serf on earth than the king of all the dead.)

2. Hades must not be described in frightening terms such as "the hateful Styx," etc.

3. Achilles, lamenting his friend Patroclus, and Priam lamenting his son Hector, would be barred because such scenes suggest that death offers terrors.

4. Since the citizens must not be too uncontrolled in their laughter, Homer's lines about "the unquenchable laughter" of the gods must also be deleted.

STYLE IN ART: In Socrates' Commonwealth, the simple style only will be allowed. If some "brilliant" poet appears, who can imitate anything in his poetry, and gives the masses great pleasure, Socrates decides that "we shall crown him with strips of wool, anoint his head with myrrh, and conduct him to the borders of the country"; he cannot remain in the Commonwealth, since he does not accept the established law of specialties.

Socrates next discusses the "modes" (musical scales) and "rhythms" in Greek poetry and music:

1. In the Dorian and Phrygian modes there is to be found musical keys and rhythms suggesting bravery, temperance and self-control of a man at peace; these will be kept. Most "sophisticated instruments like the flute will be unnecessary for our simple music; only the lyre and pipe will remain."

2. Our Guardians, says Socrates, cannot grow up in a "foul" pasture where they are corrupted daily by poisonous weeds. They must have a wholesome climate where they may see examples of good order and nobility from childhood on. This rhythm and harmony will sink into their souls, and they will easily learn to scorn the ugly and honor the beautiful, whether in art or in life.

3. If a man is exposed to the beauty of music, at first the high-spirited part of his nature is tempered, like iron that is heated to soften it; but if he continues too long, he will end, like the iron, in being melted away.

On the other hand, if a man dedicates himself to physical things only, he is at first energetic and confident. But if he refuses to cultivate his mind, he finally becomes dulled and a hater of reason and balance, and tries to gain his ends by violence, like a brute beast.

STANDARDS OF SELECTION: Socrate now determines which of the Guardians are to be rulers, and which to become the obeyers.

1. The men chosen to be the Rulers must act only for the good of the Commonwealth, and think only of *its* interest, not their own.

2. They must be continually watched to see that they do not give up this conviction, either by *theft, violence,* or *bewitchment.*
   a. Loss by theft = a Guardian forgetting, being argued out of, or being deceived out of principle Number 1 above.
   b. Loss by violence = a Guardian yielding his conviction of principle Number 1 above through pain, suffering or toil.

THE FICTION: Socrates proposes a convenient "fiction" for the citizens: They will believe that all education they were receiving, or *seemed* to be receiving, was really only an illusion, a dream. They were actually inside the earth, being molded with their equipment, and when they were complete, they sprang out of the earth into daylight. So, they must consider the earth is their mother, and defend her from attack, and that all other citizens are their brothers. Now the following combinations resulted:

1. In creating some of the citizens the god used gold as part of the mixture; these are fitted to be the Rulers of the Commonwealth.

2. Others are a mixture of silver—the Auxiliaries.

3. The rest are the farmers and craftsmen, composed of iron and brass.

Although "gold" parents will usually produce "gold" children, and so similarly the others, there will occasionally be silver or bronze children from gold parents, and other "mutations" will occur also. *It is most important that these children be returned to their natural grouping*:

1. If gold or silver children are born to bronze parents, they will be raised to their appropriate state.

2. And if a bronze child is born to a golden parent, he will be reduced to a bronze grouping.

THE GUARDIANS AND PROPERTY: First, then, says Socrates, they must not possess any private property, beyond the barest necessities. They will receive their food, just enough for the year, from the other citizens as the payment for their guardianship. They cannot possess, or even touch silver or gold. Otherwise, if they came to own private property, they would turn to their own possessions, and become tyrants instead of allies.

INTERPRETATION OF BOOK THREE: QUESTIONS AND ANSWERS

Is Plato proposing some sort of caste system in this Book?

ANSWER: No. In a caste system one may, by certain actions, be rejected by the caste into which he is born, but he cannot on his own merits rise to a higher caste. In Plato's Commonwealth, while the importance of heredity is understood, the importance of environment is not overlooked. All of the citizens start with the same education, and their education becomes specialized *according to their ability* only after tests have shown to which class they really belong.

Does not Plato's Commonwealth suggest the communist or socialist state?

ANSWER: In part, but this is essentially a misconception. It arises from the following facts:

1. The lowest level of society is identified with the working class of our society. Actually, the lowest level of society in Plato's

state is composed of most of the citizens, with only a small percentage who rule and enforce the laws. (Doctors as well as farmers fall into the third class.)

2. Plato asserts that money *might* corrupt the Guardians in the carrying out of their duties. While all citizens in a socialistic state would possess no private property, in Plato's Commonwealth the prohibition on acquiring private wealth applies only to the Guardians.

How are the Guardians kept happy in Plato's Commonwealth without incitements to financial reward?

ANSWER: They will be happy in their work, not because of financial reward, but because people are happy when they are given the opportunity to exercise their *natural* gifts. People working below the level of their ability need extrinsic rewards (rewards outside their work). Plato believes that the rewards of justice in the state or soul are *intrinsic*.

PLATO

THE REPUBLIC: BOOK FOUR

WAR WITHOUT MONEY: Adeimantus interrupts with a practical question: how will this state be able to conduct war without money, especially if their enemy is rich and powerful?

Socrates declares that it is easier to deal with two of them; just as a boxer in good condition might overcome two heavy enemies who cannot box, so their state might be a match for more than two. They will send a notice to one of the two enemy countries, explaining that they cannot possess wealth: "But you are permitted to join with us, and you may have the booty of the other country."

Any nation would gladly join them. Even if one state possesses all the wealth, it should not be called "one state," but *many states,* or at least two; the rich and the poor. If they make alliances with one faction against the other, they will have no problem of maintaining their freedom.

NEW FASHIONS OF MUSIC: Socrates states that the Guardians must be especially careful of music! New songs may be written, but the style of music must remain unchanged.

New styles in music could endanger the whole fabric of society. This lawless spirit can creep into a society unnoticed, and, proceeding slowly with gathering force, it ends by overthrowing the entire structure of public life.

THE FOUR CARDINAL VIRTUES: Socrates states that the state, to be a good one, must contain the four "cardinal virtues" of *wisdom, bravery, temperance,* and *justice:*

1. The first quality the state should possess is wisdom. Yet there will be many kinds of *knowledge* in the state, such as knowledge of carpentry and crop raising; but the kind of knowledge which is used to care for the state well, possessed by the Rulers, is what makes the state wise. Yet, although the Rulers are the smallest group in the state, in numbers, the wisdom of the whole will reside in this smallest part.

2. When we speak of "courage" we think of the group which takes

the field and fights in defense; but, also, *to have courage* means preserving the right convictions about what is to be feared, regardless of pain or pleasure, desire or fear.

3. *Temperance,* the third virtue we are considering, seems like a kind of harmony or concord, says Socrates. People use the expression "master of oneself"; and this seems to mean that there are two parts within the soul of every man, the better and the worse. A man is "master of himself" when the better part has the worse part under control. The great mass of unruly passions will be found in women, children, and inferior men. Only a few, the moderate, controlled Rulers, are "masters of themselves." In the same way the Commonwealth will be temperate, with the better part in control of the worse.

4. Suddenly Socrates exclaims that he is "on the right track": it has been under their noses all this time. They have been saying all along that everyone should perform the duty to which his nature best suits him: *this "minding of one's business" is the same thing as justice.*

THE THREE ELEMENTS OF THE SOUL: Socrates adds that there are three distinct elements in the soul, just as in the state; the soul, too, has its workers, Auxiliaries, and Rulers. Now that it is agreed that the same three elements exist both in a state and in an individual soul, Socrates decides that "a man is just in the same way that a state is just."

The reason will rule with wisdom like the Guardians. The "spirited element" will act as its ally, like the Auxiliaries. They will be brought into harmony by that form of education which has been described, and stand guard over the appetites (corresponding to the craftsmen).

The four cardinal virtues of *bravery, wisdom, temperance,* and *justice* will be present in this soul, too, as it is in the state.

Justice, then, in the individual man, means that *each element of his nature is performing its proper function,* just as each group in the state performs its proper function. The just man has brought each element into harmony with the others, like the order of notes in a musical scale.

INJUSTICE—PROFITABLE?   Injustice, then, says Socrates, must be a kind of civil rebellion among the three elements, when one part rebels, claiming a supremacy to which it has no right. It is a kind of *disease* in the soul.

The question remains then, says Socrates, which is more profitable: to be just, regardless of opinion, or the opposite.

Glaucon answers that it is ridiculous to ask the question now, since we have discovered the nature of justice.

INTERPRETATION OF BOOK FOUR: QUESTIONS AND ANSWERS

What was the proof of Socrates that Glaucon found acceptable?

ANSWER: Glaucon found that Socrates had successfully proved the problem posed to Socrates at the beginning of Book II, to show that *justice is worth practicing for its "own sake"*; but Socrates will continue to discuss his imaginary state: having found justice in his state, he will turn soon to the matter of unjust states.

What are the four cardinal virtues of Plato?

ANSWER: Wisdom, courage, temperance, and justice.

Which class is in possession of the virtue of wisdom?

ANSWER: The Rulers.

What is the distinction Socrates draws between wisdom and right belief?

ANSWER: Right belief might be found also in the Guardian class but could not be called knowledge because knowledge demands not only the right answer but the justification for calling something a right answer.

Which class possesses courage?

ANSWER: Courage is found in the Guardian class. According to Socrates, courage is the ability to distinguish real evil from apparent evil and to fear only the former.

Which level is in possession of temperance?

ANSWER: Temperance, the third virtue, is not peculiar to the lowest level: it is a virtue of all the levels of society. It consists in the subordination of lower levels to the highest and the rule by the highest based on the support of these lower levels.

Justice, the remaining virtue, is the performing of one's function. True?

ANSWER: Yes, but the implications of this statement are, of course, enlarged; it no longer simply applies to division of labor.

What purpose does Plato have in mind in his discussion of the place of justice in the state?

ANSWER: It serves the purpose of locating justice in the soul. Plato now attempts to prove that his analogy has been correct and that the soul has three parts. He does this by appealing to the *Law of Contradiction*, which states that two contradictory traits cannot exist in one thing at the same time. (The law has been attributed to Aristotle, but it was first formulated by Plato.)

What are the three parts of the soul?

ANSWER:

1. The *reasoning* element.

2. The *appetite*.

3. The *spirited*, or indignant element.

In what condition is the soul said to be just?

ANSWER: Justice in the soul consists of an equilibrium among the three elements of reason, appetite, and spirit.

To what may the unjust soul be analogous?

ANSWER: The unjust soul is analogous to a diseased body, so obviously, since we value health for its own sake, we should value justice for itself.

PLATO

THE REPUBLIC: BOOK FIVE

ALL THINGS IN COMMON?   Adeimantus complains to Socrates that, although he mentioned earlier that "friends have all things in common," even with respect to women and children, he never explained himself.

Socrates takes up this issue, although he had been prepared to talk about unjust states. First he will discuss this matter of the so-called different natures of men and women.

MEN AND WOMEN—DIFFERENT?   Socrates asks whether we keep female dogs indoors, good only for bearing and feeding puppies; or do we use them in all ways the same as the males, except that the females are treated as weaker. If the latter is true, then women should be treated in the same way in our state, and receive the same education. He adds that the only difference common to all men and all women is that the male begets and the female brings forth children; aside from this, the women seem to be just as able to become good Guardians as the men. It is the present-day customs of how to treat women which are unnatural.

1. First, then, both men and women of the same natural capacity will be chosen as future Guardians, and live in the same dwellings, sharing the same common tables.

2. Also, a "fixed" lottery will be held for the pairing off of couples so that the superior males are certain of mating with the superior females.

3. When children are born, they will be brought to another part of the city to be reared by nurses, who will do the hard work, releasing these "working mothers" for their duties as female Guardians.

MINE? YOURS?   The greatest evil for a state is whatever tends to divide it, while the good is that which unites it and makes it one. Here, says Socrates, the citizens are united by sharing the same pleasures and pains, and divided when words such as "mine" and "not mine" are applied to different things by each person. Here, everyone is called a brother or sister, father or mother. So, all citizens will use the word "mine" with the same meaning; since they do not own private property, they will not drag off goods to a private home, but share all in common.

THE LOVERS OF WISDOM: Socrates attempts to define for Glaucon who these *"lovers of wisdom"* will be who are fitted to rule. He declares that a man deserves to be called "a lover" only if he loves the thing as a whole, not only in parts.

The only man who deserves the name of philosopher is he who desires *all* wisdom; he must have a taste for all sorts of knowledge.

A dreamer mistakes the semblance for reality itself; the real philosopher, however, in recognizing beauty itself, is certainly wide awake.

Socrates points out that whatever is perfectly real is perfectly knowable, and what is perfectly unreal (i.e., non-existent) is completely unknowable.

There is an intermediate state between knowledge and absence of knowledge.

1. It both "is" and "is not"; i.e., it stands part-way between the two; this he calls "belief."

2. *The "real" is the proper object of knowledge.*

3. "Belief" is more obscure than knowledge, but not so dark as ignorance. This appears to be, Socrates claims, the many things which men call beautiful, or ugly, etc. They are beautiful or ugly only to a certain degree, and in a way, things which we call "beautiful" are both beautiful and ugly.

These, then, seem to be the object of "belief," since they lie in the "twilight" between knowledge and ignorance. The ordinary man, who can only experience the many individual beautiful things, but has no awareness of beauty, can only be called "a lover of belief" and not "a lover of wisdom" (philosopher).

INTERPRETATION OF BOOK FIVE:
QUESTIONS AND ANSWERS

To what aspect in man is the philosopher analogous?

ANSWER: To the rational aspect of his soul.

What is Socrates' reply to the question whether the ideal Commonwealth could ever exist in reality?

ANSWER: Socrates replied that if philosophers were kings, such a state might be possible.

Discuss Plato's distinction between "Forms" and "Beliefs."

ANSWER: Most people are lovers of *appearances* whereas the philosopher loves what is *real*. The distinction between the apparent and the real relates again to Plato's theory of Forms.

These Forms are eternal and unchanging, while the objects of belief continually change and shift. Although most men accept the objects of belief as "really real," the philosopher knows better. To him, only the Forms are real, and anything below them on the scale of reality is bound to appear illusory and insignificant in comparison.

There is a further distinction between knowledge and belief, in addition to the type of objects studied. Belief can be either true or false, but knowledge can only be true. The conclusion which Plato draws is this: the same thing cannot be both the object of belief and of knowledge. We cannot, at the same time, both *believe* and *know* something.

Discuss the use of transitions in Plato's works.

ANSWER: The transitions (as in this Book V) come from "within the dialogue," from the personalities of the characters themselves. Here, it is Glaucon becoming a little impatient with Socrates for lingering over details.

PLATO

THE REPUBLIC: BOOK SIX

CHOOSING THE GUARDIANS: When we choose our Guardians, says Socrates, there will be no question as to which group will become the Rulers. Our Guardians cannot be blind; and this is exactly the condition of those who are cut off from any "knowledge" of the ideas.

There will be other qualifications, however:

1. He must be of quick memory.

2. He must be magnanimous and gracious.

3. He must be a friend of truth, justice, courage, and temperance.

THE WORTHLESS PHILOSOPHERS: Socrates now undertakes to show why the majority of those in the state who practice philosophy are worthless:

1. The type of man who would make the ideal philosopher is very rare; yet, his very remarkable qualities, courage, etc. tend to draw him from philosophy.

2. It is the best minds which are also capable of the greatest evil; evil is a worse enemy to the good man than to the mediocre one.

3. If early training is bad, the most promising men become most evil; and although many would blame bad training upon the traveling Sophists, the crowd itself is the greatest Sophist. The wild demonstrations occurring in the Assembly, or law courts, or theater makes a deep impression on men: they offer a much more influential "teaching" than any school of Sophists.

4. The young gifted man who has the natural ability to become a philosopher will be noticed, even as a boy, as possessing outstanding qualities. His friends and other citizens will fawn upon him, hoping to gain his help. And he himself will have a considerable opinion of himself. But if someone comes and quietly tells him that he really has no true understanding, and must humbly work to discover it, he will find it hard to listen. The

evil influences about him will struggle to make him theirs, flattering and persuading him.

5. As for the few noble souls, the philosophers who deserve the title, once they have witnessed the madness of the people, and realize that there are no allies to prevent the just man from escaping destruction if he holds out against folly—these men see the foolishness of entering public life, and so they are silent and go their own way, like a traveller who takes refuge in the storm under a protecting wall.

PHILOSOPHY AND POLITICAL POWER: If philosophy is ever to be wedded to political power, young men must be trained in a very different fashion to take control. Instead of giving up philosophy almost as soon as they grow up, and later, as they mature, their intellectual training should grow more intense. Finally, as old men, they may dedicate themselves completely to philosophy. *This true philosopher has his eyes fixed on the true reality,* and, contemplating this unchanging harmony, he will reproduce it within his own soul. And, if given the opportunity, he will fashion the entire state and public life in the perfect order which is a reflection of this unchanging and eternal harmony.

THE QUALIFIED GUARDIAN: The number of men qualified to become Guardians is extremely small, Socrates points out; and in addition he must have the stamina to follow "the highest form of knowledge."

THE GOOD: Socrates declares that the highest object of knowledge is the nature of the Good, from which everything that is good derives its value. Some people claim that "the Good" is pleasure, and others knowledge, but these latter are reduced, finally, to explaining this by "knowledge of the Good"; both agree that this is absurd.

Glaucon finally insists that Socrates himself explain what "the Good" means, but Socrates is insistent in declaring that he cannot answer this, and decides that instead, he will picture "the off-spring of the Good," the thing most resembling it.

THE "OFFSPRING OF THE GOOD":

1. Whoever designed the eyes, says Socrates, was quite generous in his use of materials; the eyes alone, of all the senses, need a "third thing" to be used. Although a man may have sight, and

the objects are visible, unless he has this "third thing" (light), he cannot see.

2. The Sun, then, supplies the eye with the power to see; it is the cause of vision. And it stands in the visible world in the same relation as the Good in the invisible world. When the soul gazes upon an object "lighted" by truth and reality, it gains understanding; but when it looks to the twilight world of passing things, it has only opinions and beliefs which pass away.

DIAGRAM OF THE "DIVIDED LINE": Socrates now establishes two orders of things, the first of which is ruled over by the Good, in the intelligible world, and the other by the sun in the visible world. He now imagines a line divided into two unequal parts, one representing the intelligible, the other the visible world; then each is again divided, to represent degrees of clearness within each world.

1. The first and lowest segment represents images, such things as shadows and water reflections.

2. The second segment above it represents actual things, living creatures, and, generally speaking, the actual world we live in. Both of these segments belong to the visible world, while the first segment is a reflection of, a "likeness" of the things in the actual world.

3. In the upper half of this "divided line," we find the third segment, which Socrates must describe at greater length. The example he gives is that of the various figures and angles which students postulate in mathematics; they are accepted as "given" without being questioned, yet they are also a kind of "image" of things in the fourth class. In other words, when students discuss a square or a diagonal which they have drawn, they are really discussing The Square, and The Diagonal, which belong to the Fourth Segment.

4. These diagrams are really "images" of the ideal Forms in class four, just as a shadow was an "image" of the actual world, in the lower half. On the other hand, these "mathematical objects" in class three can themselves have images in the lower half of the divided line, and are therefore more "real" than the "shadows and reflections" below them. Now, in the fourth and final segment, Socrates classes "everything that unaided reason under-

stands by the use of dialectic," and here its assumptions are treated not as "first principles" (as are the mathematical objects in segment three), but as hypotheses, by means of which the philosopher mounts all the way to the first principle of all, making use only of Forms, and never any sensible (perceived by the senses) object.

Socrates now assigns a state of mind to each of the four segments; these four terms: 1. Segment = *conjecture;* Segment 2 = *belief;* Segment 3 = *thinking;* Segment 4 = *knowledge.*

INTERPRETATION OF BOOK SIX: QUESTIONS AND ANSWERS

What are the two most striking analogies introduced in this Book?

ANSWER: Book VI introduces two striking analogies:

1. The first is the analogy between the universal of the Good and the sun. Our ability to see depends not only on our eyes and the objects we view with our eyes, but also on light from the sun. Without the light of the sun we would still *be in darkness* (blind).

   Now the rational part of our soul is like the eye, since it can be turned from ignorance to knowledge of the real by the force of the Good. Good is a universal, and also a force. It can give the soul the power to understand, and lead us from the darkness of ignorance to the light of knowledge. *The ultimate goal of all education is knowledge of the Good.*

2. The second striking analogy is that of the *divided line*: this line is not only meant to symbolize the hierarchy of knowledge, but it also represents a line of education. We start at the lowest point and, hopefully, we eventually reach knowledge of the Good.

Idea of the Good	Intellectual World	D. Knowledge	(Universals, the Good)
		C. Thinking	(Mathematical Objects)
Sun	Visible World	B. Belief	(Appearances)
		A. Conjecture	(Images)

Please explain the chart pictured above—if you can.

ANSWER: The value of the line from A to B is less than that from C to D. This inequality is intended to symbolize the fact that the lower world has a lesser degree of reality than the world of ideas. Only through education can we leave this world of lesser reality and approach the Good.

Throughout the *Republic,* Plato emphasizes that knowledge is necessary for justice and that education is a moral necessity.

Did Plato ever in his own life try training a philosopher-king?

ANSWER: Yes. Plato went to the court of King Dionysius I, and began teaching philosophy to the king's brothre-in-law, Dion. Both Dion and Plato, however, fell under the king's suspicion and pupil and teacher were separated.

What does Plato mean by calling the people Sophists?

ANSWER: Plato insists that, whatever harm the philosophic school of Sophists does, this cannot be compared with the lack of self-control and general irresponsibility of the Athenian citizens in Assembly and in courts; this kind of behavior exerts a much worse influence upon young men than did the Sophists' teachings, and deserves to be called "The Greatest Sophist" of all.

PLATO

THE REPUBLIC: BOOK SEVEN

ALLEGORY OF THE CAVE: To illustrate these (in Book VI) varying degrees of reality, Plato now presents his "*allegory of the cave.*" Socrates now imagines a group of men living deep underground in a cave, with an opening leading upward to the light. They have been chained here since childhood, and can only look forward at the wall before them, since the chains prevent them from looking towards the light.

There is a fire burning behind them, and between them and the fire is built a parapet, with people behind it holding up puppets such as women, men or animals.

All that the chained prisoners can see are the shadows of the puppets cast upon the wall by the burning fire behind them.

They can speak to each other only of the shadows on the wall, and any sounds behind them would seem to come from the shadows themselves; in every way, then, they believe these shadows to be the only reality.

THE FREED PRISONER: Socrates now imagines that one of these prisoners is freed and turned to face the light. At first he would be dazzled, and the less real objects (on the wall) would seem more real to him than the actual objects themselves (women, men, animals, etc.) And if he were forced to leave the cave and enter the upper world, he would at first be dazzled by the brightness of the sun. Yet slowly he would grow accustomed to its brightness, and realize that the sun was the real cause of all he saw. Thinking back upon his friends in the cave, he would pity them for their ignorance, and prefer, like Achilles, to "be the poorest hired servant on earth" rather than return to the cave.

Yet if he did return, his eyes would no longer be accustomed to the dark, and his friends would mock him, saying that the only benefit he had received was to ruin his vision.

THE MEANING OF THE PARABLE: Socrates says that each element in this parable has a meaning:

1. The prison dwelling represents the world of the ordinary man, who sees only with his eyes.

2. The ascent to the Sun symbolizes the journey of the soul to the region of the intellectual world.

3. The last thing to be perceived in the world of knowledge is the *Form of Goodness;* once that is known, we realize that this is the cause of all good and right things.

4. Those men who have actually seen the sun will be reluctant to return to the darkness of the cave, where they will probably be mocked by those who cannot really see. Just as the body of the prisoner was turned so that the eye could see light, so also education must attempt to turn the soul away from this changing world to the unchanging reality of the Good.

5. It is up to the founders of the Commonwealth to compel the most noble natures to turn towards the vision of the Good; and once they have seen this, they must be induced to return again to the cave for the good of their fellow-citizens.

The earlier principle that this must be done for the good of the state as a whole will apply here. Although it might seem "a worse life" for the philosophers themselves, they should return nonetheless, and take their turn in governing. They alone will recognize, in the darkness, every image for what it really is, since their vision is a thousand times better.

Only when the Rulers can have a better life than they actually do by ruling, will the state be well-governed; then they will rule, not for the love of power or money, but as a duty owed to the other citizens.

THE WAY UP: Socrates says that the Rulers must turn their Guardians from night to daylight by teaching them true wisdom.

1. This cannot be learned either by gymnastics or by poetry and music; but the "universally useful" art, mathematics, might be the solution to the way up. Most men learn to calculate, but the Guardians must master the art, not for practical, everyday reasons, but so as to raise their mind above material objects and learn to comprehend "pure numbers" theory.

2. Next, Socrates proposes a study of geometry for the Guardians.

    Glaucon agrees, since it will be useful "for pitching a camp or for occupying a position."

    Socrates adds that a much more thorough study of geometry must be taught, for, apart from practical purposes, it will aid in understanding the "Ideal Forms." Solid geometry should be studied too.

THE STUDY OF ASTRONOMY: Glaucon now attempts to score a point or two by praising the study of astronomy, but not because it is useful.

Socrates disagrees; he notes slyly that astronomy only turns the mind's eye *downwards,* not upwards as Glaucon contends. The reason is, of course, that the objects of astronomy, like the stars and the planets, are material, and a part of the visible world. The study of harmonics will be treated in the same way as that of astronomy: useful for leading the mind to that higher region. Yet the students of harmony concern themselves about trivial matters such as chords, ignoring the really essential concern in that discipline. Socrates now turns to that knowledge for which all these studies will be useful preparations: Just as the prisoner from the cave saw each of the things in the upper world, one by one, and ended by catching sight of the sun itself, so too the Guardians, will follow this kind of journey. They will climb upward *by the use of reason "unaided by the senses"* to the essential reality of each thing, and finally to the nature of the Good itself. And this journey upwards Socrates calls *"Dialectic."*

THE CURRICULUM IN SPECIFICS:

1. Up until the age of 18, the young men and women shall be educated in literature, mathematics, poetry. The lessons should be made as much like play as possible.

2. Then they must receive two or three years of the necessary physical training, during which nothing else can be done. Their time will be completely occupied. The best among them will then be chosen as future potential Rulers, and given courses which will link together and unify all their previous studies.

3. From 30 to 35 they will study Dialectic, and this will be accompanied by considerable stress placed upon moral questions. Only

then will they be introduced to rigid argumentation, since they will then possess the necessary maturity to use it correctly, the aim being always to discover the truth.

4. From the ages of 35 to 50 they will gain practical experience in public service so that they may not fall behind the other citizens in experience; this will serve as a further test for the potential Rulers.

5. Finally, at the age of 50, the best among them, will attain that vision of the Good towards which their education was directed. They will then pass their time in study, and in governing, but considering this latter task not the great delight in which it is considered by despots, but as a troublesome task (since they have grasped a higher and better kind of reality).

A "DAY-DREAM"?   Socrates now considers his dictum about the possibilities of bringing his "daydream" into reality. A genuine philosopher must gain power in the state; and, after sending all citizens over ten years outside the country, he will raise the children who remain in the style of education which he and Glaucon have been developing for five and one-half books.

INTERPRETATION OF BOOK SEVEN: QUESTIONS AND ANSWERS

In Plato's "Myth of the Cave," what is the symbolic meaning of the blinding effect of too sudden exposure to light?

ANSWER: The symbolic meaning is that Plato is warning against introducing untrained minds into the study of moral problems; to guard against this, Plato outlines a course of study which will ultimately lead to study of moral problems.

Why the rather naive faith in the study of geometry?

ANSWER: If we keep in mind that Plato defines knowledge in terms of atemporal facts, we can best understand his emphasis on the mathematical sciences.

The Greeks believed that with the formulation of geometry they had at last found a field of endeavor not dependent upon sense experience.

This belief in the certainty of *a priori* knowledge (knowledge by logical deduction) is found in the writings of most great *rationalist* philosophers such as Descartes, Spinoza and Leibnitz.

Does Plato believe that knowledge can be obtained via the senses?

ANSWER: No. Plato repeatedly denies that one can obtain knowledge through sense experience. His student, Aristotle, disagreed with him, asserting that knowledge comes through the senses. This is the historical basis of the still raging conflict between *empiricists* (knowledge comes through the empirical or observable world of sense experience) and *rationalists* (knowledge comes through reason and is hindered in its progress by sense experience).

Who poked fun at Socrates as the chief Sophist who ran a school for youths on how to make the worse appear the better reason?

ANSWER: Aristophanes, the comic dramatist, in his *Clouds*.

PLATO

THE REPUBLIC: BOOK EIGHT

INTRODUCTION: Having finished with his description of this ideal state, and the training necessary for its Guardians, Plato now turns to the project begun, but interrupted by Adeimantus in Book V: his delineation of the four types of "imperfect states," and the corresponding characters representative of each type. There are four main types, although variations on these appear from time to time:

1. Timocracy

2. Oligarchy

3. Democracy

4. Despotism

In each of these, a particular type of character predominates.

TIMOCRACY: First there will exist that golden era of the Commonwealth as already described by Socrates. Sometime, no matter how wise the Rulers, they will misjudge the times for mating and birth so that the classes of "gold," "silver," and "brass" will be mixed. When these children become Guardians, there will be a pulling in different directions, but eventually they will come to a compromise. The land will be distributed among the highest classes; the lowest class will be enslaved. The people will devote themselves to war.

Although authority will be respected, and the common meals and physical training maintained, the rulers in this "timocracy" will tend to be high-spirited men, better suited for war than to peace.

And since they will cherish a secret love for gold and silver, hoarding it in their private homes, it is obvious that this state is a mixture of good and evil elements: *ambition* and *a passion to excel*, are the distinctive qualities of a timocracy.

OLIGARCHY (PLUTOCRACY): The next form of government, says Socrates, is *oligarchy*, which is based on a property qualification: only the rich may hold office, wealth being considered the ultimate end in life. The rivalry for gaining riches, which was kept hidden at first (in the timocratic man), increases, money becoming more important as virtue becomes less. The rich man is admired and placed in office, and the poor man excluded.

The state now becomes divided in two: that of the rich and poor; wars cannot be fought, since the rulers fear weapons in the hands of the poor, an omnipresent threat of revolution.

The youth will value wealth above everything else, assuming a *money-loving* spirit. Only when he is certain of being undetected will his low qualities show themselves.

DEMOCRACY: Socrates now takes up the next step in this progressive decay from the golden ideals of the Commonwealth. Since the ruling class in an oligarchy is concerned only with wealth, they will not pass the necessary laws restraining young men from ruining themselves by extravagance. Instead, they will encourage this lack of self-control, lending them money, with the view to gaining their property. The following events will occur:

1. The young men will lose their property, becoming idle and dangerous "drones" (hive bees who do no labor), while the members of the oligarchy will be blind to any dangers, growing fat and lazy.

2. When these flabby rulers and the lean young drones get together, perhaps at some festival or a campaign, the poor man will take note of the degeneracy of the wealthy man and think: "Men like these are rich because we are cowards"; when he meets his friends, word will get around that "these men are at our mercy."

In a precarious situation like this, there is likely to be civil war at any time. When the poor men win, a democracy is established.

3. The particular quality of a democracy is *uncontrolled freedom*. Everyone is allowed to do just as he likes.

4. There is a greater variety of individuals here, so, "it may be the finest of all," with its differing sorts of characters. It is the best place to find a constitution, Socrates sneers, since it is so free that it contains a sample of every kind.

5. There is in a democracy "a pleasant kind of anarchy with plenty of variety."

6. Now the citizen spends all his time and money in satisfying both the necessary and unnecessary pleasures. He shuts the gates of appetite against truth, which counsels moderation, and insists that all the appetites must be satisfied.

THE FALL OF DEMOCRACIES: In this democracy, destruction comes through another kind of "greed"—*a greed for freedom*. This is praised, to the neglect of everything else; and the rulers begin treating the subjects as masters, while the rulers themselves act like subjects. Everything is turned upside-down by this passion for freedom:

> "The horses and donkeys adopt the habit of walking down the street with the greatest freedom, and bumping into any they meet who does not get out of their way."

Yet, as in many other things, this excessive freedom produces an equally violent reaction: excessive subjection under a despot.

THE THREE DEMOCRATIC CLASSES: Socrates lists three classes in his democracy:

1. The *drones*, who in this sort of government provide all the leaders, while the other drones sit around on the benches humming their applause.

2. Then there is a group of *businessmen*, quietly making money, whom the drones attack in the Assembly to gain wealth; in self-defense the businessmen form a conservative political party.

3. The *people* put forth *their* candidate, a single, powerful figure who eventually becomes the despot. The owner of property flees in fear, leaving the despot in complete mastery of the state.

DESPOTISM: In the beginning of the despot's rule, he will be gracious and pleasant, with a smile for all.

1. He will tend to make many political promises, and to bring about certain needed reforms.

2. Yet, after a while, he will stir up wars, to keep the mind of the people off revolution; and to stress the need of the people for him.

3. As he does away with his enemies, critics of his rule will arise even within his own circle, and he will be forced to plot against the best men in his court; leaving him, finally, with only worthless, foreign flatterers.

INTERPRETATION OF BOOK EIGHT:
QUESTIONS AND ANSWERS

How do political theorists view Plato's discussion of the breakdown of the ideal state?

ANSWER: They view it as an important contribution to political theory. Although its value in this area is unquestioned, it is also intended as a study of ethics in the individual.

What was the cause of the breakdown in the Commonwealth?

ANSWER: The breakdown came through the loss of equilibrium among the parts of society.

What leads to timocracy?

ANSWER: When *ambition* becomes master instead of servant of reason, corruption follows, and this leads to timocracy.

What leads to oligarchy?

ANSWER: When *money* is accumulated and become a qualification for holding office, the state becomes further corrupted to oligarchy.

What leads to democracy?

ANSWER: When any man, regardless of aptitude, may rule, we have democracy. *Greed for freedom* is its greatest vice.

Briefly compare a democracy and a republic like that of the United States.

ANSWER: The democracy described by Plato is not like the government of the United States, which has a representative form of government. In the United States everyone has the right to choose his leaders; but these leaders are still selected from chosen political "specialists." In the democracy described by Plato, *all* the citizens could vote in the Assembly, often producing chaos.

What is the final form of the breakdown in the ideal state?

ANSWER: The final form of the breakdown of the ideal state is the despotic government. In its cruelest form, one despot is in complete control of the rest of the state. All citizens become his *slaves.*

In what way does this Book treat of injustice?

ANSWER: The Book is a picture of injustice "writ large," and is intended to convince readers of the intrinsic value of justice. No one wants to live in these deteriorated states; and since the deterioration came about through injustice, justice is once again vindicated. The analogy must once again be brought back to the individual. In his final breakdown, the despotic man is a slave to his appetites, which rule him tyrannically.

CHART

I. TIMOCRACY   = AMBITION, Appetite dominates Reason.
II. OLIGARCHY = WEALTH, Appetite dominates Reason.
III. DEMOCRACY = ANARCHIC, Appetite FOR FREEDOM
                 dominates Reason.
IV. DESPOTISM = ALL APPETITE, complete subjugation of
                 Reason.

PLATO

THE REPUBLIC: BOOK NINE

THE UNJUST MAN: The unjust man, says Socrates, does not live a happy life as does the just person. The unjust man is not truly free since he is dominated by his own appetites and emotions; moreover, he lacks that internal harmony and balance under the rule of reason which makes for the good life. His appetites and desires are constantly clamoring for satisfaction; yet he is never satisfied, a slave to his own passions. Thus it is that the happiest man is master of his passions and appetites; master of himself in other words, one who lives the just and good life.

THREE TYPES OF MEN: Just as there are three parts in the soul of man, so too, there are three types of men, each of whom represent one function:

1. The man of business is a projection of the "appetite within the soul."

2. The ambitious man represents the "spirited part."

3. The philosopher personifies the third part of the soul, the "knowledge-seeking" part.

Each of these men, if asked, would claim that his own life was the most pleasant and the best; whose judgment shall we trust? We shall trust the philosopher because he has the most profound knowledge and the broadest range of experience as well as the deepest insight into the worth of all kinds of life.

IS WRONGDOING PROFITABLE? Finally, Socrates answers the objection that wrongdoing is profitable if a man is unjust but has a reputation for justice.

Socrates claims that this can best be done by comparing the soul to one of those famous monsters in legends, like the Chimaera, or Scylla, which possessed the form of several beasts combined into one person.

This first animal will be surrounded by many heads of both wild and tame beasts, which can be changed at will. To this, Socrates

379

adds a lion, and a man; the three forms are somehow joined into a single beast. Finally, it will have an outer appearance like the man, a single human being.

TAMING THE BEAST: Now to say that wrongdoing is profitable means that the composite beast and lion are fed, but the human part starved.

The first two drag the man about, giving him no peace; but to declare that justice is profitable means, on the contrary, that the man is in complete mastery: he tames the many-headed beast and gains the lion as his ally. From every point of view therefore, *justice is always more profitable than injustice.*

INTERPRETATION OF BOOK NINE: QUESTIONS AND ANSWERS

What is Plato's purpose in writing Book IX?

ANSWER: In Book IX Plato contrasts the perfectly just man (the philosopher-king) with the perfectly unjust man (the despot), in order to finally discredit the argument of Thrasymachus set forth in Book I. It is important to realize that Book IX is sufficient to answer Thrasymachus: *justice is an intrinsic good,* and any mention of afterlife (Book X) is *not necessary* to support justice.

In what sense is the despot not free?

ANSWER: The despot cannot be said to be free because he is incapable of doing what is reasonable; he is not *free* to act according to reason. The despot cannot be called rich either, because no man whose desires are insatiable can be called rich. Finally, he can never be secure. As a despot, he is the enemy of the whole of mankind, and so must be haunted by fear.

In what sense does the philosopher king enjoy more pleasure than the despot?

ANSWER: The philosopher-king has more pleasure than the despot.

1. The despot cannot experience the pleasures of the soul found on all three levels. He can only experience the lowest pleasure, that of satisfaction of appetite.

2. But besides the appetitic pleasure, the philosopher king experiences the gratification of the second level, and best of all, the fulfillment of the reasoning element of his soul.

What is the difference between the illusory and genuine pleasures?

ANSWER: Plato distinguishes between *illusory pleasure,* which is all that the despot can know (immediate, sensual pleasures of the appetite), and the *genuine pleasure* of the philosopher-king.

All of the despot's pleasure lies in the realm of the transient world of appearances, but the philosopher-king experiences pleasure beyond the bounds of time. The despot may feed his body, but the philosopher feeds his mind with real, unchanging knowledge of the Good.

What is the serious note in Socrates' jest that the life of the despot is exactly 729 times more unhappy than the "kingly" man (in the ideal state)?

ANSWER: The serious note is that a tremendous gulf separates the two in actual life.

PLATO

THE REPUBLIC: BOOK TEN

ONE FORM ONLY: Socrates notes that there is only one **Form** or Idea for each thing, such as there is only one Form or Idea for Bed or Table as distinguished from the many actual beds and tables existing in material shapes in our homes, restaurants, hotels, etc. It would take a very remarkable craftsman to create all sorts of craftwork, since a craftsman usually only produces a few things, always keeping his mind directed toward the Form (or Idea) of what he is making (a table, for example). Yet, in a certain sense, says Socrates, any man could do this, simply by holding up a mirror to what he wanted to produce; he would not be producing the actual thing reflected in his mirror, but only its appearance or image.

THREE KINDS OF "BED" THEN: There are three kinds of "bed" then:

1. The Form (or Idea within our minds) of Bed, produced by the god.

2. The actual, visible bed, produced by the craftsman.

3. The painting of the bed produced by the artist.

Yet, the artist has used the actual bed of the craftsman as his model, and so has begun with a somewhat "distorted" model for his painting; this artist only produces the appearance of truth, and therefore can only grasp a small part of the object: he is a long way from reality, notes Socrates.

What people fail to see is that the poets and painters have only reproduced appearances *three times removed from reality;* yet, if they have a real mastery of their art or craft we shall admit them into the Commonwealth, says Socrates.

According to Socrates, then, *poetry* (in drama, poems, etc.) *is only written to please the ignorant multitude,* and is a form of play not to be taken seriously.

THE PART OF REASON IN THE SOUL: Things do not always appear as they actually are; a stick looks bent when part is in the water, etc.; and it is this illusion of appearances that the dramatists take advantage of in scene-painting, for example. Yet, just as we have scales and measures to aid us in correcting this illusion, so too there is a part of the soul which helps us in judging correctly; yet this reasonable part of the soul finds itself in conflict with the part that most readily responds to art and poetry. Appealing to the lower instincts of the soul (passion, emotion), the dramatist, poet, or painter is acclaimed by the mob. There is no room for this sort of poet or artist, who is plotting to undermine reason, in the well-ordered state.

Only poetry which praises the gods and good men will be acceptable (this bars Homer's works, for example).

THE SOUL IS IMMORTAL: Socrates now declares that the greatest prize of all awarded for virtue has not yet been discussed: the immortal and imperishable soul.

Glaucon looks at Socrates with amazement.

Socrates sets out to prove the existence of man's immortal soul:

1. *Each thing has its particular good,* and particular evil as well: The evil for a body is disease; for timber, rot, and for iron, rust.

2. Each of these evils is directed to corrupting, and finally destroying its object; but if it can be shown that the particular evil of something cannot destroy it, then clearly that thing is indestructible. The particular evil of the soul is vice of various sorts. But none of these vices can completely destroy it; it may be harmed, perhaps, but no vice completely corrupts the soul so that it is separated from the body. On the other hand, the body *is* completely destroyed by its particular evil—disease, and as a result dies.

The soul, then, must exist forever, and must be immortal.

THE SOUL A PRISONER WITHIN A CORRUPT BODY: Yet to really understand the nature of the soul, we must see her purified of all the grime and corruption of the body, and be apart from it. Then we would truly understand the soul when she is raised out of the bodily sea in which she is sunk, encrusted with rock and shell and sealed within the body.

REWARDS AFTER DEATH: THE MYTH OF ER: Yet the rewards are much greater after death, and to illustrate this, Socrates begins to tell to Glaucon *"the Myth of Er."*

> "He was a noble man, a native of Pamphylia, who was killed in battle. Ten days later, his body remained undecayed, and when they tried to bury him, he came back to life and told of what he had seen in the other world."

THE VISION OF ER:

1. The souls after death take a long trip until they find two openings in the earth, and a similar two openings in heaven.

2. At that spot, a judgment on their destination is made, and some are sent into the earth opening and some to the heaven openings.

3. Souls are pouring in a constant stream to this place from both heaven and earth. They had been for a thousand years resident in either heaven or earth, and had been rewarded or punished for their corruption and sinful deeds while alive on earth, once every century.

4. Now, gathered together in a meadow, the souls are ready to be reincarnated into another form. But there are some incurable sinners who can never be purified by punishment and shall remain forever in darkest Hades (Tartarus), where they are put to eternal torture for their sins.

5. The souls now take a journey and finally reach the three Fates—Clotho, Lachesis, and Atropos.

6. The souls are told they have a free choice of new lives before them, but the responsibility of their individual choices lies with the chooser. Neither the gods nor Chance is to be made responsible for their choices.

7. Oddly, the choices of the various souls very often are based on their experiences in the souls' previous lives:

   a. Orpheus chose the life of a swan. Why? He intensely disliked women (women had torn him to pieces in his previous life).

b. Ajax selected the lot of an animal too—a lion, since he had been treated unjustly as a man on earth.

c. Agamemnon chose the eagle, Thersites the monkey (he loved idle chattering), and Odysseus chose the life of a person living in quiet obscurity, since he, a prominent leader, had lived a life of many sorrows while journeying homewards.

8. Now the souls gathered together in the Plain of Lethe (*Lethe* means "forgetfulness"), where each of them was commanded to drink from the River of Forgetfulness so that they would be able to remember nothing. At midnight they rose up to the sky, like shooting stars, to be born again; only Er was not permitted to drink, and when he awoke, he found himself on the funeral pyre.

THE MEANING OF THE MYTH OF ER: Socrates explains to Glaucon the meaning of the Myth of Er:

> "So, Glaucon, the tale was saved from being lost; and if we listen, it may save us, and all will be well when we cross the river of Lethe."

If Glaucon will believe that the soul is immortal, he will always pursue justice with wisdom so that not only in this life,

> "but also on the thousand-year journey of which I told you, all may be well with us."

INTERPRETATION OF BOOK TEN: QUESTIONS AND ANSWERS

What two main themes did Plato cover in this book?

ANSWER: He covered the following two themes:

1. That *Justice is an intrinsic good.*

2. The rewards of justice both in this world and the next. First, however, he must demonstrate the immortality of the soul.

In what other work of Plato's is there proof of the soul's immortality?

ANSWER: In his *Phaedo.* After the final proof in the *Phaedo,* Plato admits that his belief in immortality rests finally on faith: he was aware of the inadequacies in his proofs.

What is the proof for the soul's immortality offered in Book Ten of the Republic?

ANSWER: The proof offered in the *Republic* is based on the theory of *function* first mentioned in Book I.

The perfect functioning of a thing is its virtue.

As each thing has its unique virtue, so does it also have a unique evil. The evil of something is that which tends to destroy it. The evil of the soul is vice, yet vice does not actually destroy the soul; it is not a cause of death.

If the specific evil of the soul does not destroy it, the soul must be immortal; and the extinction of the body, which is not an evil of the soul, will certainly not harm the soul.

What is Plato's attempt at an answer to the problem of evil in this life?

ANSWER: Why do the righteous suffer and the evil go unpunished? Plato frames his solution in terms of the *Theory of Reincarnation*: any suffering of the righteous is due to offenses in a previous life for which he is atoning in this life.

Is there a stress on the theory of knowledge in the Myth of Er?

ANSWER: Yes. The Myth of Er once again stresses Plato's Theory of Knowledge. Even in the afterlife, knowledge of the genuine Good, as opposed to the *seeming* good, will prevent choice of an unwise life in successive reincarnations.

Mention some parallels to the Myth of Er.

ANSWER: Certain of the details of this myth can be found in other classical authors, including the *Sixth Book* of the *Aeneid*. They seem to trace back to a common source in the Orphic Mysteries.

Virgil especially (who wrote several centuries later than Plato) has several parallels, including a description of the punishments of the wicked, a flowery meadow, and the stream of Lethe. And of course there is Dante's *Divine Comedy*, which owes a good deal to Virgil and, by indirection, to Plato.

How close is Plato's view of the soul to that of the Christian theologian?

ANSWER: There is a certain similarity: in both, the soul is considered to be shackled within the body, and "encrusted over" with the evils of the body. Only after death is the soul liberated from these lower elements. Plato's ideas had a great influence upon Christianity several centuries later.

Is Plato correct in his charge that the dramatists appealed to the lower passions unswayed by reason?

ANSWER: Yes, in part. The weeping and lamenting which Plato condemns seems to have been particularly favored by Greek audiences. Certainly, the tragedians seemed to make full use of their choruses in this respect. Euripides seems to have been the most skillful at eliciting tears (so says Aristophanes).

PLATO

SYMPOSIUM

INTRODUCTION: The *Symposium* is one of the most justly famous of Plato's works; the subject matter is irresistible: a sophisticated Athenian dinner party at the height of the Periclean Age. Both Aristophanes (the comic dramatist) and Alcibiades (an Athenian general) were at the height of their respective careers.

This was all to change a few months later when the famous Athenian armada, under Alcibiades and others, sailed to Sicily and was completely destroyed.

Yet at this "symposium" there is nothing but the spirit of confidence and exuberance to be found among the famous guests.

THE GUESTS: Phaedrus, Pausanias, Alcibiades, Eryximachus (a physician), Aristophanes (the comic poet), Agathon (the tragic poet), and finally Socrates.

The dialogue is repeated, as told to him, by Apollodorus (a friend of Socrates), who had heard the conversation from Aristodemus, a disciple of Socrates.

One result of this indirect-report method is that we are able to see Socrates as others see him, as he really is, rather than through his own eyes (as when he is the narrator). Ordinarily Socrates plays down his own role when he himself is the narrator.

SUMMARY OF THE SYMPOSIUM

THE MEETING: Socrates is met by his friend Aristodemus "spruced up" and heading for a dinner party given in honor of Agathon, the tragic poet, who has just won his first victory at the tragedy contest.

Socrates invites him along too, but becomes preoccupied with a thought before reaching the house, and leaves Aristodemus to enter alone. When the situation is explained, no one pays much attention; it is "just like Socrates."

THE PARTY: When he finally arrives, Agathon asks for the benefit of "that wise thought which came to you in the portico"; Socrates only wishes that wisdom could be transmitted by touch. Then "how greatly I would value the right to recline by your side!"

After dinner, there is general agreement that instead of drinking or flute-playing (they will let the flute-girl "go and play by herself"), they will undertake a conversation on some subject.

Eryximachus suggests promptly that each one "make a speech in honor of love"; no one, in his view, has ever praised it sufficiently, although he has ever heard speeches "on the usefulness of salt" (probably by a Sophist).

PHAEDRUS ON LOVE: Phaedrus begins with his praise of Eros, which to him represents sexual passion, especially between males. He calls love "a mighty god, . . . especially remarkable in his birth," and proceeds to trace the genealogy of the god. (This is a commonplace of speeches in praise of famous men.)

1. Love is the greatest incentive to men in battle (he is speaking of homosexual love throughout), and if a state could be established, made only of lovers, "when fighting at each other's side, though only a few, they would conquer the world."

2. Love has always impelled lovers to die for their beloved:

   a. Alcestis gloriously died for love of her husband. (Euripides, in his *Alcestis*, wonders what sort of man would let his wife die in his place.)

   b. And Achilles slew Hector (in the *Iliad*) enraged by the death of his beloved (male) Patroclus.

PAUSANIAS ON LOVE: Pausanias next rises to speak. He is not satisfied with the speech of Phaedrus, and explains that love should not be praised in such an undiscriminating fashion since "there is more than one kind of love." This "common Aphrodite" (the Greek goddess of love; Eros was her son) is known by the more common sort of men, who experience love with women as often as men; they are only concerned with the body. The "heavenly Aphrodite" on the other hand is born of nobility. Those who experience this kind turn to the male lover, and are attracted by the more courageous and intelligent young men. These lovers treat the "beloved" with consideration, and remain faithful to them.

PAUSANIAS' TRUE LOVE: Customs relating to homosexuality differ throughout Greece, says Pausanias:

1. In Athens, custom is more divided than in Elis (where it is frankly favored by law). Everyone sympathizes with the lover, and yet the young man is carefully watched and protected. This custom is meant to encourage the "true" lover, and discourage the base.

2. The true love is love of the soul as well, and will persist in an enduring relationship; as for the other, "when the bloom of youth is over . . . he takes wing and flies away." The "true lovers" associate with each other with a view to the improvement of the soul.

ENTER ARISTOPHANES: This speech is followed by the Greek words *"Pausanias pausamenou"* a play on words perhaps best translated "Pausanias now came to a pause." It seems to herald the appearance of Aristophanes, but it seems also that he has the hiccoughs. He advises the physician Eryximachus either to cure his hiccoughs, or to take his place. The doctor tells him to hold his breath, gargle with water, and tickle his nose—a "sure" cure. Then the physician takes up the theme of the evening, in the place of Aristophanes.

ERYXIMACHUS ON LOVE: Pausanias has correctly distinguished between two kinds of love, says Eryximachus, but this "double love" exists not only among men, but in all living creatures.

1. There is within the human body, the "love of the healthy" and the "love of the diseased." The first must be encouraged and the second discouraged; and this is the art of the physician exactly.

2. The physician must know how to reconcile these contrasting elements in the human body. All of nature is made up of contrasting elements, the hot and the cold, the moist and the dry. Just as a good climate is a harmony between moistness and dryness, so the doctor tries to reconcile warring elements in the body, and produce harmony here too.

ARISTOPHANES ON LOVE: (It is the turn of Aristophanes next; he chooses a fantastic theme with a Rabelaisian twist: the origin of the various forms of love.)

Aristophanes is by now cured of his hiccoughs. He wonders if the harmony of the body has a fondness of such noises and ticklings, since "as soon as I employed the sneezing, I was cured." After this joke, Aristophanes begins with a description of the "original man."

ARISTOPHANES' STORY OF THE "ORIGINAL MAN":   Aristophanes relates how there were originally three sexes, not two: man, woman, and a combination of the two.

1. Man was then round, having a double body attached back-to-back, with two heads, two sets of arms and legs, and all other organs doubled. "He could walk upright as men do now, backwards or forwards as he desired, and he could roll over and over at a terrific rate, turning on his four hands and four feet like tumblers . . . spinning with his legs in the air; this was when he wanted to run fast."

2. Since they were powerful and ambitious, they decided to attack the gods.

Zeus was puzzled as to how they should be punished. If he destroyed them with thunderbolts, he would lose their sacrifices to the gods; so he finally decided to cut them in two. That way, their strength would be weakened, and there would be twice as many sacrifices. (And if they became insolent again, Zeus threatened to split them once again, and let them hop about on one leg.)

3. Apollo was assigned the task of smoothing off the rough edges, once they were divided in two.

But now the divided halves began wandering about in search of their "other half" (this is Aristophanes' explanation of the phenomenon known as "falling in love").

a. The all-male type sought out only males; the all-female only other females, and the combination of male and female sought a member of the opposite sex: thus Aristophanes accounts for both homosexual and heterosexual love. "And when one of them meets his other half, the actual half of his former self . . . the pair is lost in amazement of love and friendship . . . and the "mysterious longing" of men, which they do not understand, to be always together.

b. (There is a change of tone, and Aristophanes seems to speak seriously.) If every man found his true love, "then our race would be happy"; the next-best thing would be to "find an agreeable love."

AGATHON ON LOVE: Agathon calls love "the youngest of the gods"; he sends courtesy; he is the parent of delicacy, luxury, desire; the glory of gods and men; the best and brightest leader; and this speech, "according to my ability, I dedicate to the god."

SOCRATES HIMSELF BEGINS ON LOVE: Socrates is timid about speaking after such a "lovely" speech. "I am especially struck with the beauty of the final words; who could listen to them without amazement?" (Socrates can be cutting enough at times.) From what he had heard, it *appears* that they desire to *appear* to praise love, not actually to do so.

Socrates asks "to praise love" in his own style, and, of course, immediately begins asking Agathon questions. Socrates asks if love is not always love of *something*, a desire for what one does not have; so love is desire for something lacking. It is love *of the beautiful*, which is the same as the good. Now Socrates retells the teachings of a wise woman called Diotima, who once instructed him in the knowledge of love.

DIOTIMA ON LOVE: According to Diotima, love is not fair, but it is not evil and foul either; it lies somewhere in between the two. And love is not a god, nor is it a mortal either; it is again a "mean" between the two.

1. Love is the child of Plenty and Poverty, and (like its parents) is always poor, without shoes or home, always wandering about.

2. He is alive sometimes, at other times dead, then returning to life; and as a lover of wisdom, he is half way between wisdom and ignorance, not *being* wisdom, but desiring it.

3. Love is not only a love of beauty, however, but of sexual generation, too, since this is a kind of eternity and immortality. Human natures try as far as possible to share in the immortal; this is achieved through generation, and offspring produced.

4. The love of immortality also can be seen in ambition, for which men will perform all sorts of difficult tasks. The poets and the lawgivers have "children," too, in their poetry and law codes; and these are even finer than human children, since they last forever.

5. The man who would learn the secrets of love should begin with human forms, and proceed from this (seeing its inadequacy) to the love of the mind. He will then proceed to the laws, and the sciences, until he finally reaches the single "universal"—the science of beauty in every place. His aim then is a gradual mounting up to the highest and best, the true reality, which is *Beauty and Goodness*.

ALCIBIADES ENTERS DRUNK: Just as the audience is about to congratulate Socrates on his speech, there is a great knocking at the door outside. "They heard the voice of Alcibiades ringing out in the courtyard, 'Where is Agathon? Lead me to Agathon.'"

He is led in, supported by a flute-girl, and crowned with ivy and violets. "Will you receive a very drunken man as a companion in your celebrations?" He has come to crown Agathon for his victory, and so they insist that he remain. After he has settled into a couch, he insists on praising, not love, but Socrates himself!

ALCIBIADES ON SOCRATES: Alcibiades begins by comparing Socrates' appearance to that of Silenus, the satyr (a goat-man).

In fact, he is like the flute-player satyr, Marsyas, with even more seductive melodies, and, if Alcibiades did not shut his ears, Socrates would completely convince him.

> "He makes me admit that I should not live as I do, neglecting the good of my soul, and caring about Athenian politics. . . . He is the only person who has ever made me ashamed."

Alcibiades proceeds to relate his two attempts to seduce Socrates, and explains how, after openly speaking his mind, Socrates politely refused his advances.

He also tells of Socrates' bravery in battle; how he even rescued Alcibiades in battle, refusing any "decorations" offered him. He possessed even then his usual habit of standing transfixed in thought: one day, he stood for a whole day pondering some thought. Some Ionian soldiers near him dragged out their blankets all night long to watch this strange man.

"When Alcibiades had ended, there was a laugh at his openness of speech, since he seemed still to be in love with Socrates." Socrates himself brushes away the compliments; the party begins all over again, with a few (such as the pedantic physician) departing.

THE PARTY AT MORN: In the morning, the only ones left are Socrates, Aristophanes, and Agathon, who is forcing the two dramatists to admit that a true artist of tragedy can also produce a comedy. The drowsy listeners agree without much argument.

INTERPRETATION: *SYMPOSIUM*, QUESTIONS AND ANSWERS

What tragic touch is implied in the Alcibiades' episode?

ANSWER: Alcibiades, who delivers the eulogy on Socrates, is, of all those assembled at the party, the man who best understands what Socrates stood for. Yet, for all his brilliant talent and understanding, he was unable to live the life depicted by Socrates in his discourse on love. One is forced to wonder if the vision offered by Socrates can be attained by all men or must it be left to one who is "half man, half god."

What is the underlying approach in Socrates' discussion of love?

ANSWER: In Socrates' discussion of love, his task is not merely to praise love, as those who preceded him had done, but to tell the truth about it. He gathers together the concepts used by the others, giving them new meanings and clarifying their insights.

Love is indeed a search for that which we lack, but he is not referring to our missing half. Socrates explains the search for beauty in much the same manner he did in the *divided line* of the *Republic* (which see). In fact, this is his strongest assertion: that it is not the world's appearances which are important but the world of ideas, which is eternally and unchangeably real.

The steps he outlines are the following:

1. From *appearances* (the love of physical beauty)

2. to *belief* (love of unseen beauty in the soul)

3. to *thought* (love of beautiful ideas)

4. to *knowledge* (love of beauty itself).

Essentially, what was the subject of Phaedrus' speech?

ANSWER: The speech of Phaedrus was little more than a glorification of sexual passion, and not too brilliant a one at that.

Why is Eryximachus' speech largely an irrelevant one?

ANSWER: The speech, of course, is not really about "love," as such, at all. Eryximachus is stressing the cosmic significance of "opposites," health and disease, good and bad, using love and medicine as examples. There is a certain humor in his use of technical jargon, and in his fondness for seeing everything in terms of the medical arts.

Is Socrates all-Silenus?

ANSWER: No. He resembles Silenus externally (ugly), yet within there are golden statues, i.e., a purity of soul.

Identify Alcibiades and discuss the purpose served by showing him drunk.

ANSWER: Alcibiades, of course, was the brilliant Athenian general who had deserted to Sparta; but he had numerous other faults; he was a follower of Socrates, and an admirer, yet he never "reformed," as he explains here. Plato presents Alcibiades drunk, where he does not have his usual control over his speech, thus admitting his inner feelings and a secret sense of shame.

In what way does Diotima's description echo the progress of the Guardians in The Republic?

ANSWER: There is great similarity between Diotima's picture of a gradual "mounting up" to Beauty, and the progress of the Guardians to the Forms of Goodness, etc., in *The Republic*: each presents a set of steps leading to a higher reality.

PLATO

THE APOLOGY

INTRODUCTION: *The Apology* of Plato is unique for several reasons:

1. Unlike all his other works, it is not a dialogue at all, but a set of defense speeches spoken by Socrates at his trial in 399 B.C.

2. Moreover, we are certain that it is quite similar to the speech which Socrates actually delivered; that is, Plato has only "touched up" the speech of his master.

3. Then again it provides us with most of the historical information we have about the trial and death of this great philosopher.

Socrates was charged by his accusers, Anytus (a politician of the "new" democracy), the poet Meletus, and the rhetorician Lycon, with having:

1. "introduced new gods,"

2. and "corrupted the young."

Yet these charges were merely useful pretexts for bringing him to trial; he had been a "suspicious character" for many years in the city of Athens because of his public discussions and questioning of other citizens. He had long ago gained a reputation (as he himself tells us in his defense) for being "a wise man, who searched into the heavens above, and looked down into the earth below, and made the worse appear the better cause."

A good share of this prejudice grew up because the people of Athens had never distinguished between the work of Socrates and that of the "Sophists."

These men were famous orators who visited Athens, accepting students for pay (the first "university tuition"), teaching them to speak on either side of a question (Cf. our present-day college debating teams). They were taught not to argue fairly but to win their argument by any means possible. These Sophists were distrusted and resented by ordinary citizens, and Socrates seemed to them "just another Sophist." Aristophanes, the Athenian drama-

tist, in his comedy *The Clouds* presents Socrates in just this way—
as the teacher of a Sophist school, and many people took at face
value what was a comic exaggeration.

One more reason for the violent prejudice of the Athenians is that
Socrates was intimate with the oligarchy, who had plotted to overthrow their democracy in the past. There is no evidence that Socrates was in any way implicated, but his pupil Plato, for example,
had relatives who were members of the democracy-hating oligarchy.

The Apology of Socrates (and here we must remember that "Apology" is meant in the Greek sense of "a defense speech"—Socrates
is certainly not apologizing for anything!) is really a set of three
speeches delivered in the same day.

1. The first part is Socrates' *defense of himself* and his way of life,

2. and the second part was *delivered after he was found guilty* by
   a small margin, but was allowed by Athenian law to suggest
   his own punishment to the jury.

3. The third part (after he had been assigned the death penalty)
   is an *address to his enemies* (first) and then to his friends, explaining to each of them the results of his decision, and its
   effect upon them, the city, and upon Socrates himself.

The Apology of Socrates has been described by A. E. Taylor, the
great Plato scholar, as "the life of a martyr of the best type, as seen
from within by the martyr himself."

SUMMARY

NOT A SOPHIST: Socrates speaks: My slanderers have called me
an evil-doer, a strange person who has taught his strange doctrines
to others. You have all seen the comedy of Aristophanes (*The
Clouds*) in which a man named Socrates walks on air and talks a
lot of nonsense about physical sciences—yet anyone sitting beside
you will tell you that I never discuss such things (there is a pause,
where, apparently, his friends support the truth of what he says).
Nor do I accept money for teaching; the young men flock to
Gorgias, and Hippias, and Prodicus, however, and are delighted to
pay them for their teaching.

I once asked my friend Callias whom he would put in charge of
his sons, to teach them human excellence; if they were calves, he

would probably hire a horse trainer or farmer. He named Evenus, who charges five minae. His price is quite reasonable, I answered, if he really has wisdom; if I were he, I would be very conceited.

ON HIS WISDOM: And yet, one of you might say, "Still, Socrates, there must be something strange about, if we consider your reputation." Well, I suppose, then, it is because I possess a certain kind of wisdom, the only sort a human can have (he will explain this "wisdom" later).

> "The oracle at Delphi once told my friend Chaerephon that there was no man wiser than myself; yet I know I am not wise. I wondered what Apollo meant, since gods do not lie; so I decided to find someone wiser than myself, and prove the god wrong. I first went to a politician, generally considered wise; yet I found that he was not really wise, but only thought he was. When I pointed this out to him, he became my enemy; and I told myself, 'Neither of us really knows anything really fine or good.' But I am better off than he is: for he knows nothing, and thinks he knows; but I know nothing and realize this fact. I suppose then I have a slight advantage. Next, I went to poets, to prove I was more ignorant than they. I brought them some of their own poetry, yet they could not explain it. Then I realized that poets write their poetry through inspiration; they are like soothsayers who do not know the meaning of what they say. Yet because they were poets, they believed they were wise in many other matters. I visited the artisans, and found that they really did know things of which I was ignorant; but they too thought they were wise in other matters. The truth is, Athenians, that only God is wise; and what I think the Oracle at Delphi meant was that 'He is wisest who realizes, like Socrates, that he possesses no wisdom.'"

Many of the young Athenian men follow me about, listening to me examining people who appear to be wise; and they do it themselves, and call me a misleader of youth; they accuse me of the usual crimes; of teaching what is up in the clouds, etc. So men like Meletus, a poet, and Anytus, a politician, and Lycon, a rhetorician, hold against me a grudge, for exposing their pretense.

A CORRUPTER OF YOUTH? Now I shall turn to the second class of accusers, headed by Meletus (this second class is the group of men who have actually brought Socrates to trial). Their indictment says that Socrates is an evildoer who corrupts the youth; and that he does not believe in the gods of the city, but worships strange gods. But Meletus is the real evildoer, Athenians, since he pretends to be zealous, and really doesn't care.

MELETUS TO THE STAND: At this point Socrates calls Meletus to the stand, and "cross-examines" him. The scene begins with Socrates saying, "Tell me, Meletus, who improves the youth?" (Meletus names, first the judges, and finally everyone in the city but Socrates). Socrates says, "I am very unfortunate, if you are right." But in the case of horses, we see that only a very few can improve, or train horses, that is, the trainers; so, Socrates implies, in the same way, only a very few men can improve youth.

NOT A BELIEVER IN THE GODS OF THE CITY? Next, I will answer your charge that I do not believe in the gods of the city. (Meletus charges him, upon questioning, with being a complete atheist.) You must believe the judge is ignorant, for you to be accusing me of believing the sun is stone, for example; everyone knows these are the beliefs of Anaxagoras.

Next, I will show that Meletus contradicts himself: Did anyone ever believe in flute-playing, but not in flutes, or in horsemanship but not in horses. Well, in your indictment, you swear that I believe in new divine and spiritual agencies: Doesn't this also mean I believe in demi-gods? And what else are demi-gods, but the sons of gods; that is, if demi-gods exist, then their fathers, the gods, must exist too.

I WILL NEVER STOP: And if you tell me, "Socrates, we will let you go this time; but upon one condition, that you are not to question and speculate any more, and that if you are caught doing so again, you shall die," I will answer that, though I respect you, I honor the God more, and will never cease questioning and discussing with other men. And if I find they do not know what they claim to know, I will reproach them; and I will never stop telling men that they should care most of all about improving their soul— not money or property.

THE CONSEQUENCES: In addition, if you kill a man like myself, citizens, you are harming yourselves more than me. Nothing can injure me, for a bad man is not able to injure a man better than himself; and although Anytus can exile or kill me, the evil he does —unjustly taking a life—will harm him much more. I am a gift of God to you, a sort of gadfly (if you will pardon the expression) meant to keep the City alert; the City is a great stallion, sluggish because of its great size. It will be difficult to find another like me, even if I annoy you at times. And because of my mission, I have neglected my own affairs, and advised you patiently all these years.

"THE SIGN": You might wonder, Athenians, why I go about in private advising others, but do not take an active part in politics.

You have heard me speak of "the sign" or oracle that comes to me from time to time; it sometimes forbids me (but never commands me) when I am about to do something. It is a kind of voice which I have known from childhood. And this deters me from being a politician. If I had taken part in politics, I would have died long ago (a field full of traps for the participant).

TEARS FOR THE COURT: One more thing; there are probably some of you wondering why I do not bring my children and my relatives into court, to beg the judges with many tears; for this is done in far less serious cases by many of you. You may resent my actions, and vote against me as a result.

I do have three young sons, yet I will not bring them here to beg you; I think it would be shameful of me to act in this way. Since I have a reputation for wisdom (whether it is true or not) I will not stain it, as I have seen some famous and respected citizens do, by acting in this ridiculous way; a stranger would say that we Athenians were no better than women.

Besides, a judge should not make a gift of justice. He has sworn to judge according to the laws, not according to his whim. It would be wrong of me to try to persuade you to disobey your vows to the gods; that would be real atheism on my part. But I do believe in gods, and I trust my case to you and them.

(This marks the end of Socrates' first speech, his defense of himself proper.)

SECOND SPEECH BEFORE THE COURT

INTRODUCTION: Socrates was found guilty by his jury, and, according to Athenian law, both he and his accuser are permitted to propose a punishment; the jury would decide between the two. Socrates considers several possible ones, finally deciding upon a fine of thirty minae.

A STATE HERO: Now what sort of return shall we give a man who has never cared about the ordinary concerns, money, military office, etc., but who has urged his friends to be concerned with their own virtue and wisdom first of all? What is more suitable for a poor man, and a benefactor than maintenance in the Prytaneum (a public building where outstanding people were entertained at public expense, often ambassadors, generals, and winners in the Olympic games)? For he deserves it much more than any winner in the Olympic games. To be fair, I would suggest maintenance in the Prytaneum as a just return.

THE FINE: I have never wronged anyone, and do not deserve to be punished; if I had more time, I might convince you of this. Shall I suggest prison, or a fine, or exile? If you suggest that I go into exile and keep silent, I will tell you that this would be disobedience to the God, since my mission is to discuss and question; "the unexamined life is not worth living for man."

Still, I will suggest a fine of thirty minae (about $3,500 in present money), and my friends present here (including Plato) will be my security.

THIRD SPEECH BEFORE THE COURT

INTRODUCTION: Between the second and third speech, Socrates was condemned to death. In this speech, he addressed both his friends and his enemies in turn. In tone, it is most serious of all; and many of the ideas are developed at greater length in Plato's *Phaedo,* an account of the last day of Socrates.

I DID NOT FLATTER: Do not think I was condemned because I did not know what to say to defend myself. On the contrary, it was what I left undone that has condemned me, since I did not flatter or plead. A man should not use every way possible to escape death, either in court, or in war. . . . "The difficulty, friends, is not to avoid death, but to avoid unrighteousness, for that runs faster than death."

"My 'sign' has not opposed me during all this trial, nor during my speeches: I conclude, then, that what has happened is good, and that death is no evil. If it is like sleep, then it will doubtless be a gain, since most men pass few of their days in the same peace that they find in sleep, not even the Great King (the king of Persia, who was considered to have the greatest of power and happiness, since he was an absolute monarch).

"No evil can come to a good man. The gods do not neglect them. I ask my condemners, however, to treat my sons as they have treated me. And if they seem ever to care more for anything other than virtue, reprove them as I have reproved you.

"The hour of departure has arrived, and we go our ways—I to die, and you to live. Which is better God only knows."

INTERPRETATION: *APOLOGY,* QUESTIONS AND ANSWERS

Discuss Socrates' defense speech (the first half only) as to his attitude towards the court.

ANSWER: To fully understand the *Apology,* it is important to realize that the first half of Socrates' defense contains elements of whimsy. Socrates is aware that the charges against him are difficult to refute, and that he is defending himself against "trumped-up" charges.

Socrates does stress, however, in the first part of his defense, his views concerning the use of oratory. His accusers may have been fine rhetoricians, but the purpose of oratory is to *tell the truth.* (Socrates repeatedly makes this point in his dialogues.) So, despite his homely language, he is really the better orator because his only concern is a simple narration of the truth.

What is Socrates' attitude towards his "oracle"?

ANSWER: Socrates' description of the Delphic Oracle is not the major statement of his mission. But when he is speaking of his divine mission, imposed by the God, he becomes intensely serious. He genuinely believes in the divinity of his philosophical mission. A refusal to fulfill this task would constitute impiety.

His task is not to out-run death but to escape evil. Throughout Socrates' final statement, he emphasizes that the only real evil is moral evil. His belief in an afterlife is not the basis of his morality; nevertheless he does seem to believe in an afterlife, and his mention of it here is consistent with his later discussion of it in the *Phaedo.*

What kind of verbal comparisons was Socrates noted for?

ANSWER: Socrates was famous for his common, homely comparisons, in discussions of philosophy. In *The Clouds,* for example, Aristophanes shows him comparing the intellect to watercress. At one point in his early defense he compares the educating of children to the training of livestock.

What was the "Scripture" most often quoted to bolster his (Socrates') arguments?

ANSWER: Socrates quotes from Homer's *Iliad* to make his points about "choosing danger." This device was quite common among all Greeks after the time of Homer. All sorts of arguments or actions were defended by citation of passages from the *Iliad* or the *Odyssey;* Homer was the "Greek Bible," and the Greeks too "quoted Scripture" to win their arguments.

Socrates is inflexible in his refusal to bend before the jury in order to make a better case for himself. What was the usual situation of this sort?

ANSWER: In Athens it was quite common for defendants to flatter, beg and plead with the jury (with the artful use of oratory and rhetoric) for acquittal. Aristophanes wrote a comedy which satirizes the Athenian mob, who loved to sit in on jury duty; the play is the *Wasps,* so entitled because of the touchy and irritable nature of the Athenians.

What insect has been made famous by Socrates in his defense speech and has become a part of a proverbial expression?

ANSWER: Socrates says, "I am a gift of God to you (the citizens of Athens), *a sort of gadfly* (if you will pardon the expression) meant to keep the City alert." The expression has come to mean one who is persistent and galling to others because he persecutes his victims like a gadfly (a horsefly) in order to make them aware of the truth.

What is this "sign" so sacred to Socrates?

ANSWER: It seems to have been a kind of guiding voice, a "conscience" which Socrates obeyed from childhood.

PLATO

CRITO

INTRODUCTION: At the opening of the *Crito,* Socrates is waiting in his cell, soon to be executed (after being found guilty of "impiety") and sentenced to death by drinking a cup of poison hemlock. According to Athenian law, no citizen could be legally executed until the "sacred ship" had departed on its annual voyage to Delos and returned.

(According to legend, King Minos of Delos used to demand live sacrifices of young men and women for the monstrous Minotaur which he kept imprisoned on his island; Theseus slew the monster; this "sacred" ship commemorated the event.)

Crito, Socrates' friend, has come to take advantage of this delay, and offers to help Socrates escape. He has money enough, and friends, inside and outside of Athens, who will assist Socrates in escaping from this unjust sentence. The dialogue deals with Socrates' answer to these offers of help, and with his explanation of why he willingly chooses to undergo death rather than live through flight.

CRITO'S ARGUMENTS FOR FLIGHT: Crito offers a variety of arguments, not all of them completely disinterested.

1. People will criticize him and his friends, thinking that they would not help him; what could be worse than this, "that I be thought to value money more than the life of a friend."

2. Then again, "The opinion of the ordinary man must be regarded"; they are capable of great harm to a man (a fact which Socrates is quite aware of).

3. If Socrates is concerned that his friends will be blackmailed, well, these too can be bought off; besides, his foreign friends could help him without fear of punishment.

4. Finally, he has a responsibility to his family, which he is choosing to abandon by not escaping. His children must be educated, and "if they do not suffer the usual fate of orphans, it will be no thanks to you."

SOCRATES' REPLY TO CRITO: Socrates answers by acknowledging the concern and zeal of his friend. Nevertheless, "I am and have always been one of those souls who must be guided by reason"; now that misfortune has befallen him, he cannot reject his own teachings. Socrates used to insist that the opinions of some men, wise men, ought to be respected, and those of others, the unwise, should be rightfully rejected.

Now, has this sort of argument come to be "just talk for its own sake?" This is childish nonsense.

IS HARM TO OTHERS GOOD?   Socrates now raises the question which he resolved for Glaucon in the *Republic*: whether a man should ever harm another, even if he is harmed by that man first.

Crito agrees with him, that it is never right under any circumstances to harm another. (This doctrine was startlingly new to the Greek mind, which was accustomed to accepting without question the maxim that "a man should do good to his friends, and harm to his enemies.")

Socrates now applies this principle to his own particular case: Is he wronging anyone in escaping prison against the will of Athens; is he abandoning his just principles? "If individuals decide to trample upon the laws, no state can exist for long." Can Socrates defend himself, and, more important, justify himself, by answering, "Yes, but the State has harmed me and delivered an unjust verdict?"

LOVE OF THE LAW: Yet, Socrates, above all men, should obey these laws (this is what the Laws themselves would utter if they could speak), since he seemed so fond of them. He almost never left the city, even to see the games, nor did he travel about as most men tend to do. "We (the Laws) were your special favorites, and you yielded to us."

CONCLUSION: If he acts as Crito bids, no one concerned with him will benefit. "Now you depart in innocence, a sufferer and not a doer of evil," the Laws will now say. Yet, if he insists upon returning evil for evil, "we will be angry with you while you live, and our brothers, the Laws in the world below, will receive you as an enemy." This is the music which Socrates hears murmuring in his ears, so insistently that "it prevents me from hearing any other voice."

Crito's only answer to the old man is, "I have nothing to say, Socrates."

Socrates then replies, "Leave me then, Crito, to fulfill the will of God, and to follow wherever he leads."

INTERPRETATION: *CRITO,* QUESTIONS AND ANSWERS

What is the distinction Socrates makes in giving his reason for not escaping?

ANSWER: Socrates' decision not to escape was based on a clear distinction: although he was innocent *morally,* he was *legally* guilty, since the court had decided he was. It is his duty as a citizen to submit to the legal verdict. If a private citizen defies the courts, he is, in effect, defying all law and order. A wrong decision by the courts is nonetheless a legal decision and hence binding.

In what way would Socrates be destroying himself symbolically should he attempt to escape?

ANSWER: Here it is important to keep in mind his life-long career in Athens. Socrates had devoted his entire life to solving ethical problems; his respect for law was well known. In a very real sense he would be destroying himself if he were to escape, since his escape would represent the negation of his entire essence.

Repeatedly, in the dialogues, it is emphasized that a wrong harms only the one who commits it. An unjust act hurts the doer, not the one who is subject to it. If the courts have made an unjust decision, they are the ones who are hurt, not Socrates, who will die for it. Death is not an evil, since the only genuine evil is moral evil.

How does the afterlife figure also in his decision?

ANSWER: Socrates believes in an afterlife.

If he dies now and appears before a tribunal which judges the death, he will appear an innocent man who has been wrongly sentenced to death.

But if he escapes, lives out his remaining few years, and then appears before this same tribunal, he will be deemed as one who has wronged the laws.

Then, what position is wholly consistent with Socrates' principles?

ANSWER: Socrates is not anxious to flee death: he is far more concerned with forcing the Athenians to face the moral issue of the murder of an innocent man.

His defense of the philosophic life demands that he live in a manner consistent with his principles, and the logical conclusion of this must be his willing acceptance of death.

PLATO

PHAEDO

INTRODUCTION: The *Phaedo* contains Plato's description of the final hours of Socrates, ending with the moving passage which gives an account of his actual execution (death by drinking a potion of poison hemlock). The Plato scholar A. E. Taylor considers this dialogue to be one of the four Platonic masterpieces in that form (i.e., dialogue).

It is essentially a conversation narrated by one of those present at the execution, Phaedo to his friend Echecrates. Phaedo names the various companions of Socrates present at the execution: (all of them Socrates' disciples.)

1. Apollodorus of Phalerum

2. Simmias of Thebes

3. Cebes of Thebes

Phaedo notes that Plato was not present since he was ill at the time.

Phaedo also mentions the strange mixture of pleasure and pain he had felt—pleasure at the oncoming discourse, and pain at the impending death of his master.

SOCRATES' DREAM: As they enter, they find Socrates just released from his chains, and Xanthippe, his wife, weeping. She is led away, lamenting.

Socrates explains why he has spent his days in prison setting Aesop's fable to verse; he had had a recurring dream, telling him to "make and cultivate music," and although this seemed to mean to him "pursue philosophy," he is now obeying the command of the God, if indeed the command was literally meant.

WHAT IS WRONG WITH SUICIDE?   Socrates is asked why suicide is considered wrong: why cannot man be his own benefactor through death?

He claims that man is a possession of the gods, and has no right to run away until the God summons him.

409

Simmias suggests that Socrates is perhaps too ready to "run away," but Socrates expresses his trust that he is going to gods who are wise and good.

THE DESIRE FOR DEATH: The true philosopher is always trying to die, so why should he avoid actual death?

1. *The senses are an impediment, and the soul is continually trying to break from its bonds,* to become independent of material things.

2. It is only the mind which reveals the existence of the pure Forms: Justice, Goodness, etc.

3. Purification is the release of the soul from the dross of the body: death is therefore desirable to the philosopher, since it effects this longed-for release.

THE IMMORTALITY OF THE SOUL: Cebes now raises the question of the immortality of the soul. Many fear that the soul is scattered, as by a wind, at death.

Socrates replies: Are not all opposite things generated out of their opposites?

What becomes less was once greater, and then became less; so with other things also.

This *"generation of opposites"* comes from an intermediate passage from one state to the other, like increasing, dividing, etc.

Now life is the opposite of death, and the intermediate passages are "the act of dying," and "the act of being born." If this "compensation" or "cycle" did not exist, eventually all things would turn to a state of death.

THE DOCTRINE OF RECOLLECTION: The doctrine of "recollection" would also support the theory of immortality.

Man seems to "recollect" things he has never actually seen in the real world; he can imagine a "square" which is only an imitation of the "Square" in the world of Forms (Ideas) by this recollection from an earlier life.

In other words, "recollection" implies an awareness in a former life, and so the soul must have existed before birth.

THE BODY AS EVIDENCE: Even the body offers evidence for the immortality of the soul. For if the body can remain a short while after death undecomposed, sometimes lasting forever, if it were embalmed as in Egypt, why should the soul not last for a much longer time, once freed from the chains of the body?

1. The purified soul mounts "into the company of the gods" as soon as it is released from the passions and weaknesses of the body; while the souls of the wicked are dragged into the world below, longing for the bodily needs which never leave them. They are finally imprisoned in another body, of an animal or bird, perhaps.

2. The philosopher then, as much as he can, attempts to remove himself from the demands of pleasures and pains, since each one is like "a nail which nails and rivets the soul to the body until she becomes like the body."

SOCRATES REFUTES SIMMIAS: Socrates now takes up the argument of Simmias:

1. They have agreed upon the theory of "recollection," that the soul has existed in an earlier state before the body. Yet harmony in a lyre (Simmias had said it existed *in* the lyre) comes last, after the wooden frame and the strings are joined together: it has not existed *before* the lyre; and so the analogy is not sound.

2. Also, there are degrees of harmony, i.e., some things are more carefully harmonized than others.

3. But souls do not possess different "degrees" of existence—each soul is just as much a soul as another. This too proves the analogy false.

IMMORTALITY, CONCLUDING PROOF: Socrates finally offers his concluding proof of immortality, making use of the theory of "Forms" (See the *Republic,* Book VI).

There are two kinds of opposites:

1. The first kind is actual, *real objects* in which the *opposites dwell,* such as "fire" or "snow."

2. The second kind are the *Forms of these opposites* (their abstract Idea-Essences), such as "heatness" and "coldness." Now the first kind, the material objects, generate each other, as Socrates has already explained, but the second kind are forever opposed, and can never co-exist.

Now if these opposites meet, such as "snow" and "fire" (and their Forms "coldness" and "'heatness'"), the material objects "yield" to one another, the cyclic "alternation of opposites" occurs, i.e., the snow would melt. But the Forms are always opposed, and so "coldness" would simply withdraw.

1. The Forms are always present in each of the objects which share in their quality.

    a. The soul seems to be one of these objects of the first kind; and life always accompanies it.

    b. And the soul, as well as its Form, is never compatible with death, but withdraws when death appears.

2. The soul is therefore immortal indeed!

HIS FAMILY: Socrates now goes to bathe, and the others are grieved: "He was like a father of whom we were being bereaved, and we were about to spend the rest of our lives as orphans." When he finally returns, Socrates spends a bit of time with his children and his wife, and then returns to his cell.

THE EXECUTION: The jailor enters, and begs forgiveness for being compelled to administer the poison. He calls Socrates "the noblest and gentlest and best who ever came to this place," and departs weeping.

Although his friends want to delay the execution, Socrates sees no reason in gaining just an hour or so more. The jailor offers the poisoned cup, and Socrates, offering a prayer to the gods, drains it.

When they all break into tears, Socrates chides his friends for their lack of control; after a while he reclines on his back as the poison takes its effect. Towards the very end he turns to Crito and asks him to pay a debt: one cock owed to Asclepius, and in a short while he is dead.

"Such was the end, Echecrates, of our friend; concerning whom I may honestly say that of all the men of his time whom I have known, he was the wisest and most just and best."

INTERPRETATION, *PHAEDO:* QUESTIONS AND ANSWERS

Are Socrates' arguments only made to provide proofs for immortality?

ANSWER: Socrates' proofs for the immortality of the soul must be understood in light of all his previous teachings. Socrates is not merely trying to postpone death. He is asserting that the soul is immortal because it is *divine.*

The care of the soul is man's foremost obligation, and so Socrates' proofs are intended not only to prove immortality but to further his moral teachings.

Why is Socrates' proof based on the soul's virtue the most important?

ANSWER: The most important proof offered by Socrates is that based on the *virtue* of the soul.

The soul is immortal *because* it can perceive and have a share in goodness, beauty, and truth.

These values are eternal and the mind's ability to have knowledge of these eternal values argues for its kinship to them, i.e., its immortality.

This proof for immortality is identical with the proof later used by Spinoza (1632-1677). It may be added that they both used proof for the same reason: their concern is not for immortality but for virtue.

Upon which ritual is Socrates' description of the afterlife partly based?

ANSWER: Socrates' description of the afterlife is based in part on the Orphic mysteries (i.e., rites in honor of Orpheus, the god of music). He tells his disciples that they need not accept his description as true, and that yet some of it *must* be true.

GREEK PHILOSOPHY: ARISTOTLE

LIFE (384-322 B.C.)

Aristotle was born in 384 B.C. in the Macedonian town of Stagira on the northeast coast of the peninsula of Chalcidice, or what is now called Thessalonika.

He was born at a time when the Greek city-state system was already in decline. Athens, the city where the Greek genius had flowered, had been conquered by the city of Sparta in 404 B.C.

During the years that followed, Greece was torn by the struggle for leadership between Sparta and the city of Thebes. Sparta was eventually defeated in 362 B.C. After her own defeat, Athens went through a period of dictatorship under a council known as the "Thirty."

With the victory of Thebes she became once more the champion of liberty in Greece. While the Greek city-states were gradually growing weaker, a new power was rising in the North, the kingdom of Macedonia.

Aristotle's father, Nicomachus, was the court doctor and friend of the king of Macedonia, Amyntas II. Amyntas' son, Philip II, reorganized and increased the power of the kingdom.

His son, Alexander, made the name of Macedonia famous in history by his lightning conquest of a huge empire stretching from Greece to the Indian Ocean. Aristotle himself probably spent his childhood at the Macedonian capital, Pella.

YOUTH: The young boy's interest in natural science came both through his race and his family.

Stagira was an Ionian colony and Aristotle was an Ionian Greek. It is no wonder he followed the great scientific tradition of his forefathers. His family was of noble origin with a tradition of medicine.

His father was a member of the Asklepiad family, which claimed to be descended from Asklepios, the Greek god-physician, who was said to be the son of Apollo and a mortal princess.

414

We are told that the family trained its sons in medicine. Probably Aristotle had some medical training and helped his father perform surgical operations.

His mother's family came from Chalcis in Euboea, where Aristotle was to spend his last days. Unfortunately, both parents died when Aristotle was quite young, and he was put under the guardianship of a Macedonian official, Proxenus.

COMMENT: It is important to note that all his life Aristotle enjoyed the protection of the Macedonian court, first under Philip II and later under Alexander. Perhaps this is one of the main reasons why Aristotle was able to exert such an influence over the intellectual world of his time.

PLATO'S ACADEMY: When he was eighteen, Aristotle entered Plato's Academy at Athens. He remained at the Academy until the philosopher's death in 347 B.C.

We know that the Academy was literally *the* center of learning for the Mediterranean world into which Aristotle was born. The fame of the Academy and that of its founder brought men from all over the world to discuss the urgent questions of the day.

We know these men visited the Academy because Plato mentions them in his dialogues, and even named some of them after the visitors.

1. One who was so honored was Theaetetus, a man who is said to have discovered solid geometry.

2. The astronomer, Eudoxus, came all the way from his home in Czyicus in Asia Minor in 367 B.C. to discuss astronomy with Plato.

3. In his dialogue named after the great sophist, Protagoras, Plato shows us his interest in the Sophist's view of life.

Then, too, Plato was a man who traveled far and wide. In the course of his travels, he had come in contact with the Pythagoreans in Sicily, and with the Sicilian medical school of Philistion. It was from the Pythagoreans that Plato got his interest in numbers, which was to lead him in his later life to suggest that numbers were the basic principle of all things.

In short, the Academy at Athens was truly cosmopolitan, reflecting the many influences of the travelers from abroad.

THE ACADEMY "METHOD": The second fact about Plato's Academy was his method of teaching through discussion. The Academy aimed to put Socrates' way of life and his method into practice. Abstract problems were discussed with an enthusiasm which might amaze a visitor from the modern world.

1. One effect of the dialectic method on Aristotle was to make him distinguish between that kind of knowledge which could be gained through discussion and that which could be acquired through observation and deduction.

2. Probably because there was so much discussion, Aristotle had a chance to learn and examine thoroughly all the theories of the earlier philosophers.

3. He also gained a respect for their wisdom, as his frequent references to the "opinions of the wise" shows.

4. Another effect of the discussion method was to make both Aristotle and his fellow students realize the value of definition and orderly thinking. An argument has no value unless you define your terms and argue in a systematic manner. At the time of Aristotle's entrance into the Academy, there is reason to believe that Plato was working on a standard formula of argument. In such an atmosphere, it is not surprising that Aristotle should have developed his own tools for argument.

When we wonder why Aristotle, for example, devotes two books of his *Metaphysics* to showing that neither the Ideas nor numbers can be called substances, we must remember the background of the Academy.

ARISTOTLE LEAVES THE ACADEMY: When Plato died in 347 B.C., his pupil, Speusippus, was elected to succeed him as head of the Academy. Apparently, there was a great deal of friction between Speusippus and Aristotle, who did not like Speusippus' interest in Plato's theory of numbers.

At the same time Aristotle's presence had become not welcome in Athens. The Greek Confederacy had fallen to pieces. It was not the moment for a man who was known to have connections in Macedonian court circles to be in democratic Athens.

Thus, for both personal and political reasons, Aristotle decided to accept the invitation of a fellow student, Hermeias, to live at his court at Assos, a town on the slopes of Mount Ida.

THE CIRCLE AT ASSOS: Aristotle never returned to the Academy. Apparently, Hermeias gave him a great deal of liberty in organizing the small group of Platonists he had gathered at his court. Aristotle quickly became the leader of the group, directing discussions and giving lectures. This small group was later to form the core of the school that Aristotle himself founded at Athens. While at Assos, Aristotle married Hermeias' niece, Pythias. She gave him one daughter whom he named after her mother.

TUTOR TO ALEXANDER: Aristotle, in 342 B.C., accepted an invitation from Philip II of Macedonia to become tutor to his son, Alexander. We know little about Aristotle's education of the prince. Judging from Aristotle's *Politics*, we can be sure that Aristotle thought the education of kings was very important. We know that he wrote one short work for his pupil on the subject of monarchy, and another on colonies.

It was the fashion of the time to hire philosophers to teach a king's sons. Plato had tried to teach the young tyrant of Sicily. Aristotle tried to teach Alexander, apparently with little success. Alexander was more inclined towards a life of action than a life of study.

When Philip died in 336, relations between Aristotle and his pupil had already become quite strained. When Alexander set off to conquer the world, Aristotle returned to his native town of Stagira.

THE LYCEUM: There has been some question as to why Aristotle did not return to the Academy. Speusippus had died, but the Academy had already elected one of Aristotle's old friends, Xenocrates, as head. It was obvious that the teacher of Alexander of world reputation could not accept a position lower than head of the Academy. It was fitting that he open his own school.

Since he was by this time the recognized leading philosopher and teacher of Greece, Aristotle immediately announced that he was the successor to Plato and his school, the successor to the Academy.

In a short time, the Lyceum had taken the place of the Academy, whose students were applying for admission. The solitary reign of the Academy was over.

HIS WORK AT THE ACADEMY: Aristotle's work at the Lyceum was the fruit of his years of research and analysis. During his years at Athens he seems to have written or revised most of his major writings. He completed the classification of the sciences, developed his own system of logic, and carried most of the sciences to a point which they had never reached before and were not to reach again for a long, long time. At the same time the influence of his ethical and political theories was being felt in Athens and throughout the Greek world.

1. Following in the Platonic tradition of learning by discussion, Aristotle seems to have written most of his works which have come down to us as lecture notes from which he talked to the students.

2. Apparently, Aristotle was an organizer. Study hours were not free but were planned at the Lyceum.

3. Tradition tells us that Aristotle gave his most serious lectures in the morning.

4. In the afternoon he spoke on more popular subjects, like rhetoric, in order to attract the crowds that came out from the city to hear him.

5. Like the Academy, Aristotle laid down the rules by which both students and teachers lived. These rules were to survive long after his death. Under Aristotle, Plato's idea of a common life shared by friends in search of wisdom became the basis of the first university of Europe.

THE PERIPATETICS: As was the case with Plato, it is impossible for us to realize the influence which Aristotle's teaching and personality had over his students.

Aristotle seemed to live his own teaching. His followers, called *Peripatetics* because they used to walk around the arcades of the Lyceum discussing philosophy, showed little influence of Aristotle's teaching. Once the man was gone, it seemed to be difficult to recapture the original meaning of his words.

It was not until the Middle Ages that Aristotle became alive again and spoke to the Schoolmen with the same energy he had put into his teaching at the Lyceum.

However, Aristotle's teaching at the Lyceum did not give rise to a new philosophy. Rather, it marked the final achievement of Greek philosophy. Perhaps there was nothing more to say.

EXILE: The death of Alexander in 323 shocked the entire Greek world. Once again Aristotle was *persona non grata* (unwanted) at Athens.

A charge of "impiety" was brought against him. Rather than have Athens "sin twice against philosophy" (Socrates had been accused of the same crime), Aristotle turned his school over to his old friend, Theophrastus (author of a celebrated book called *Characters*) and fled to his mother's home in Chalcis. He died in Chalcis from a stomach disease at the age of 64 in 320 B.C.

Aristotle must have been a lonely old man in the last years of his life. Exiled from the school to which he had given so much, he withdrew more and more into himself. In one of his last letters he writes that he had become more and more attracted by "the wonderland of myth."

BURIAL AND WILL: Aristotle was buried by the body of his wife, as he had requested in his will.

His daughter Pythias, his adopted son Neandor, his son by his mistress, Nicomachus, and his mistress all survived him. For each he had made special provision in his will. It is wonderful that Aristotle's will has come down to us, for it proves once more how very human he was:

1. He provided fully for his family.

2. He freed all his slaves.

3. Antipater (a close friend) was appointed executor of the estate to see that everything was properly carried out.

Always an organizer, Aristotle did not forget anything which might contribute to the welfare of those he loved after his death.

ARISTOTLE

THE WORKS

THE WORKS OF ARISTOTLE: Aristotle's known writings form such an impressive body of knowledge that it is hard to believe he wrote many more books than have come down to us. The entire complex of his works falls roughly into three parts.

THE FIRST GROUP OF WRITINGS: The works in this group are of a popular nature and were published by the philosopher himself. Unfortunately, only fragments of them survive. The titles of some of these dialogues show the direct influence of Plato.

THE SECOND GROUP OF WRITINGS: This group contains notes and collections of research material which were incorporated into the third group of works, the scientific writings. Again, all of this second group has been lost in the passage of history. Only one of the books written during this period of Aristotle's research has come down to us. This is the famous *Constitution of Athens*. It is possible to gain some idea of the wealth of material Aristotle must have collected on every kind of subject because the lists of works said to have been written by him which were drawn up in classical times contains some 200 titles!

THE THIRD GROUP: Almost all the writings of Aristotle which are familiar to us today fall under the third group of his works known as the scientific writings.

It is generally agreed that most of them were written as lecture material and notes for the use of his students, while he was teaching at the Lyceum in Athens. As we noted earlier, it was while he was at the Lyceum that Aristotle completed his classification of the sciences as we have them today.

He divides the entire field of science into three parts:

1. The theoretical sciences.

2. The practical sciences.

3. The productive sciences.

Today we divide Aristotle's scientific works into eight parts, each

420

with its own method of procedure. This division follows Aristotle's own system of breaking down the different sciences according to *what* each studied and *how* it studied that topic. The eight sciences are:

I. Logic

II. Physics

III. Metaphysics (i.e., after physics)

IV. Biology

V. Psychology

VI. Ethics

VII. Politics

VIII. Esthetics (science of art)

Aristotle's contribution to science becomes clear when we remember that he was the first person to make a systematic classification of the various disciplines of human knowledge. He was the first to realize that it was impossible to study anything without first knowing what it was you wanted to study and finding out the best method to study that particular subject.

1. LOGIC

The science of the *logos* is the science of definition and argument. Aristotle's logic is perhaps his greatest contribution to both science and philosophy. He himself did not consider logic a separate branch of study but thought of it as an *organon* or tool to right thinking. You cannot find out the truth unless you can reason from sound principles in a systematic fashion.

Aristotle's logical system is his answer to the problem of the relation of the structure of language to the process of thought and the nature of reality. His logical works fall into four parts:

1. *The Categories*

2. *On Interpretation*

These two deal with the nature of individual terms and simple statements. These are the raw materials of language.

3. *The Prior Analytics*

This work introduces the student to what Aristotle considered the essence of argument: proving that the individual fact is what it is because of why it is.

It is relating the definition of anything to its cause. This method of proof Aristotle called the *syllogism*. Now, all syllogisms, like all arguments, are not the same. They differ according to the nature of the principles on which your argument is based.

4. *The Posterior Analytics*

Here Aristotle tells us how to argue scientifically. He discusses how we can use the syllogism so as to be sure that the outcome of the argument will be the truth. If we want our result to be the truth, the grounds or principles of our argument must be both true and necessary. This means that they must be principles derived from our experience of the nature of things.

In the last group of the logical works, Aristotle turns to those kinds of arguments which do not satisfy the requirements of scientific reasoning.

5. *Topics*

In this work he discusses that form of argument which is based on the dialectic or conversation. The grounds of such an argument are principles derived from the nature of the thought-process that are not rooted in objective experience. They are thus essentially opinions, the opinions either of "the many" or "the wise."

6. *Sophistic Elenchi*

In this work Aristotle discusses arguments which are not really arguments at all. The Sophists made two kinds of mistakes, he says.

a. The first kind of mistake is that of language. They think they have a premise for an argument, where there are no grounds for it at all.

b. Second, they make mistakes in thinking. From a true premise they think they are arguing in a scientific fashion, but this is not really the case. It was Aristotle who gave the word *sophism* its meaning of a fallacious argument. A sophism is a trick used instead of a sound argument to prove the point you want to prove.

II. PHYSICS

Aristotle wrote many treatises on physics. It is important to remember that physics did not mean the same thing to the Greeks as it means to us today. *Physics* comes from the Greek word for nature. Thus, the best translation of Aristotle's well known work which has been called the *Physics* would be the *Study of Nature*. Aristotle's writings on physics contained his philosophy of nature and his observations of the natural world. Of Aristotle's writings on nature the best known to us are the

7. *Physics*

8. *On the Heavens*

9. *Of Generation*

10. *Corruption*

11. *Meteorologica*

The *Meteorologica* is his work on the influences of the four elements: fire, air, earth, and water upon the heavenly bodies. Aristotle was the first to separate the study of weather from astronomy. Much that he includes under meteorology is still part of that science.

III. METAPHYSICS

The third discipline in Aristotle's list of sciences is what Aristotle called first philosophy, or the science of being, but which is commonly called today metaphysics. Aristotle's work by that name contains his concept of the nature of being, and what it is *to be* essentially.

IV. BIOLOGY

The fourth discipline in Aristotle's list of sciences is biology, or the science of life. In many respects Aristotle did his best work in this science, as it was the phenomenon of life which interested him most.

The titles of his biological works show the range of the philosopher's interests in the world of living things.

12. *The Parts of Animals*

This work is an introduction to biology

13. *On the Motion of Animals*

This book is one which many scholars believe Aristotle did not write, but which recent research has put back on the list of Aristotle's writings.

14. *On the Origin of Animals*

15. *On the Generation of Animals*

Numbers 14 and 15 above are additional works on natural history.

Ancient lists of the philosopher's works contain many other titles, which are now considered to have been written by his pupils or friends.

V. PSYCHOLOGY

Despite the fact that Plato played a large role in the development of the concept of the soul, Aristotle still remains the founder of the fifth branch of science, psychology. He was the first to consider the problems of the human psyche as a separate discipline. His best known work in this field is

16. *On the Soul*

This work defines what a soul is, and then takes up the functions of the soul specifically related to man, such as sensing and knowing. His other works on the same subject have been collected into a book with the title

17. *Parva Naturalia*

This work discusses such topics as

Sense and the Sensible

Memory and Recollection

Sleeping and Waking

Dreams

Prophecy in Sleep

On the Length and Shortness of Life

On Youth and Old Age

On Life and Death

On Breath

VI. ETHICS

The sixth discipline in Aristotle's classification of the sciences is ethics.

Ethics belongs to the practical sciences, to that branch of knowledge which is concerned with human action. Three books on ethics which have been at various times attributed to Aristotle have come down to us:

18. *Eudemian Ethics*

19. *Nicomachean Ethics*

20. *Magna Moralia or Great Ethics*

Only numbers 18 and 19 were written by Aristotle. The oldest list of Aristotle's writings give only one book on ethics, entitled simply *Ethics*. Until recently scholars did not think that Aristotle wrote the *Eudemian Ethics*, but attributed the work to one of his pupils, Eudemus. At the present time it is generally believed that the titles, Eudemian and Nicomachean, refer to two of Aristotle's pupils who edited these "textbooks" on ethics. Some scholars, however, believe that Aristotle named the *Nichomachean Ethics* after his son, Nicomachus. The *Magna Moralia* was probably written by followers of the Peripatetic School in the early third century B.C. Of the two works by Aristotle, the *Eudemian Ethics* is considered to have been the earlier work. Some think it might have been written at Assos during 348 and 345 B.C. The *Nicomachean Ethics* contains Aristotle's mature thinking on the subject.

Although the study of ethics was already becoming a separate science when Aristotle first came to the Academy, it was he who separated the study of virtue from the study of knowledge definitively. The word "ethics" comes from the Greek word *ethos,* meaning primarily, custom or habit, and secondly, character. Ethics is the study of those habits which go to make a good character; it is the study of morals as they relate to the individual.

VII. POLITICS

The seventh science, politics, is the study of morals as a system of behavior in a society. The question in ethics is, "Is there a set of values by which the individual may act wisely and well?" The question in politics is: "Is there an integrated system of values as expressed in the power structure of a community which will enable society to live well?"

Politics is the ethics of the political system, and is discussed in Aristotle's work by that name, the

21. *Politics*

VIII. ESTHETICS

The last branch of Aristotle's scientific system is that of the productive sciences. Artistic creativity, or rather the nature of the art object, forms the subject matter of Aristotle's eighth discipline, esthetics. Under this heading come two works,

22. *On Rhetoric*

23. *Poetics*

The word *rhetoric* comes from the Greek word, *rhetor,* a public speaker. As its title suggests, the book teaches the would-be politician or lawyer the art of persuasion through words. As a creative science, its aim is to produce the emotion desired by the speaker in his audience, and to sway the listeners to his opinion. Its aim is not to teach man to speak the truth. This is the aim, properly speaking, of logic. Nevertheless, Aristotle considers a sound argument an essential part of the art of public speaking. The *Rhetoric* was widely read in classical times, but it has little relevance to present-day problems of speaking to a mass audience. Public speaking was very important in Athenian law courts. Naturally, there was a definite method of speaking with which citizens wanted to be familiar. Since every Athenian had the chance to become either the judge or lawyer for a case, it was in his interest to know the rules of the game.

If the *Rhetoric* has had little influence in modern times, the *Poetics* has inspired more criticism than any other of Aristotle's works. It is the first work that we have on the philosophy of art.

The five most influential works of Aristotle's entire output have been his *Physics, Metaphysics, Ethics, Politics,* and *Poetics.*

ARISTOTLE

PHYSICS: A SURVEY

DEFINITION OF NATURE: Aristotle nowhere tells us what he means exactly by nature, but the way in which he uses the word in the *Physics* suggests two basic meanings:

1. The Greek word, *phusis,* comes from the verb, *phuo,* meaning to grow, to produce, to generate. Our word, nature, comes from the Latin verb, *nator,* to be born.

   Nature, in English, suggests something fixed and given, a starting point. Human nature, for instance, is the sum total of qualities with which a man starts when he is born. It is what distinguishes him from the other creatures. Aristotle would agree with this view, but would improve upon it. Human nature sets man apart from the world about him, not only in the sense of identifying the characteristics common to man, but also in the sense of differentiating the principle of human behavior. The *phusis* of anything is its capacity to realize all that it can possibly be. It at once determines *what* anything will become and *how* it will realize that end. Nature, as something inside and present in a natural body, is, in Aristotle's view, that body's *principle of motion.*

2. The second way in which Aristotle uses the word *nature* refers to the *sum total of objects* which possess their own principle of motion. Man-made objects are thus excluded from the world of nature.

   a. The wood in the chair, for instance, is a part of nature, for it has the tendency to age and decay. The chair itself is not a part of nature. You can destroy the chair by taking off its legs, but the chair does not have any inherent tendency to undergo change.

   b. Aristotle excludes artificial objects from nature, but he definitely puts lifeless bodies in his natural world. Stones belong to nature, because they have a tendency to move downwards, for example. He argues that stones would not fall to the earth, if they did not possess the ability to do so. It is the nature of stones, in other words, to be subject to the law of gravity. The ability of chairs, on the other hand, to fall toward the earth is not part of the nature of chairs but a function of the matter from which chairs are made, namely, wood, marble, and stone.

MIND AND NATURE: Aristotle never satisfactorily solves the relation of mind to nature.

1. On the one hand, mind is not part of nature in the sense that mind is soon subject to change.

2. Mind, as we know it today, is the act of understanding; it is therefore an activity, not a process, as Aristotle states. One either knows or he does not know. There is no beginning, middle, and end of knowing. It is a single act which is outside time, space, and motion. For this reason, mind could be considered something divine. Aristotle's psychology and ethics illustrate the difficulty he had deciding just what mind is.

ORGANIZATION OF THE *PHYSICS*: The *Physics* was originally meant to be the first in a series of works dealing with the natural world.

Books 1 and 2:   These two books define the subject matter of natural science, and discuss the *archai* or first principles of that science. They contain an analysis and general definition of motion.

Books 3 to 8:   In these books Aristotle takes up the movement of natural things which are without life. He develops a general theory of motion.

Aristotle continues his discussion of nature in his *On the Heavens, On Generation and Corruption,* and the *Meteorologica.*

ARISTOTLE

THE *METAPHYSICS*: A SURVEY

INTRODUCTION: The *Metaphysics* is the most important of all Aristotle's philosophical works, for it contains the philosopher's theory of being.

At the same time it is the most difficult of Aristotle's books to comprehend. The great Arabian philosopher of the eleventh century A.D., Avicenna, is said to have read the work forty times without understanding a word.

Research has indicated that the book is a selection of notes, written during various periods of Aristotle's career. Most of Book Lambda, for example, seems to be an expression of Aristotle's early thinking when he was still very much under Plato's influence. Other parts are evidently the result of Aristotle's later reflections on the same subject. For this reason, the *Metaphysics* does not form one well-organized whole. Aristotle seems to have changed his opinion regarding many matters during the course of his intellectual development. In this work, he seems at different times to have held opposing views on the two most important questions in the book, namely, the nature of primary being, and the possibility of having scientific knowledge.

THE TITLE: The word *metaphysics* comes from the Greek words, *meta* meaning *after* and *phusika* meaning *physical things*.

Aristotle never called his science of being "metaphysics" or "after physical things." Scholars attribute this name to the editorial work of early commentators on Aristotle, and in particular to the work of a certain Andronicus of Rhodes (early first century B.C.) who is credited with having unearthed the manuscript. As Aristotle's treatise on the nature of being was customarily placed after his treatment of "physical things," it was referred to as "the metaphysics."

THE CHALLENGE OF PLATO: As for the theory of being, the biggest challenge confronting Aristotle was Plato's theory of Ideas.

1. Plato held that what a thing is, is essentially the idea of the thing. Houseness, the universal concept of a house, is what

makes a house really a house. The bricks and stones are of secondary importance in determining what makes a house "housy."

2. Aristotle cannot develop any theory of being without taking his great teacher's theory into serious consideration.

    a. He agrees with Plato that universals are objectively real (that is, that they are present in the natural world and not just abstractions in our minds).

    b. But he does not agree that universals exist *choristos* (or separated) from matter, as self-existing forms.

The *Metaphysics* consequently is concerned with the two problems as follows:

1. Do super-sensible forms really exist?

2. Is science, which has such forms as its subject matter, possible?

Later in his career, Aristotle changed the form of the questions, as he saw more clearly that the forms of physical bodies cannot exist apart from their matter.

The question, "Do universals exist as super-sensible forms?" became "What do we mean when we say, 'Something is'? What does it mean 'to be'?"

THE SIGNIFICANCE OF THE *METAPHYSICS*:   It is evident from the foregoing that the *Metaphysics* will present many problems to the reader. Scholars of every age have worked long and hard trying to resolve the apparent contradictions contained within the book. Their solutions form the basis of our Western concept of being.

The *Metaphysics* as a result plays an important role in the history of ideas. We are all heirs to Aristotle's concepts of actuality and potentiality; of the doctrine of immanent form; of his theory of being as activity, and his idea of the First Cause of the world, the Unmoved Mover.

ORGANIZATION OF THE *METAPHYSICS*:   The first three books are an introduction to the problem of metaphysics, or, as we would call it, philosophy.

1. In the first book, Aristotle states his view of the origin and development of thought and the place of theoretical knowledge in his philosophical system.

2. In the second book, Book Alpha the Less, Aristotle makes some remarks on the philosophical method of inquiry.

3. Book Beta lists the problems connected with philosophy in general. As elsewhere, Aristotle does not present these difficulties in a dogmatic fashion.

4. Books Gamma, Epsilon, Zeta, Eta, Theta, Iota, Mu, and Nu attempt to examine these problems in an effort to arrive at the truth in the "science of first philosophy," as Aristotle calls it. Books Mu and Nu contain some of the best criticism we have from classical times of the ideas of Plato and the Pythagoreans.

5. Book Lambda, one of the most controversial of the books, presents Aristotle's conflicting views on the First Unmoved Mover.

6. Book Delta, the fifth book, reviews Aristotle's system of terms as a preparation for a definition of being which follows in the next books.

7. Only Book Kappa, the eleventh book, cannot be fitted into the general pattern of the work easily. It repeats concepts already known to us in the *Physics* and other works. Its chief value is that it serves as a prologue to the theory of the Unmoved Mover in Book Lambda.

In trying to piece together the essential parts of Aristotle's metaphysics, the reader will find most of the material in six of the twelve books listed above, and should look at these most important books in detail: they are Books Gamma, Epsilon, Zeta, Eta, Theta, and Book Lambda.

BOOK NAMES: The names of the books in the *Metaphysics* follow the letters of the Greek alphabet: A, in Greek, is "Alpha," B is "Beta," etc. The first letter of the Greek word represents the letter in the alphabet.

THE MAIN CONCEPTS:

1. *Change and Permanence*

Aristotle says that there are two basic elements to be found in any and every possible natural event:

a. The first is that there is, and must be, something that stays the same but yet is, somehow in some way, subject to variation.

b. The second is that actual and genuine changes in quality do occur. For example, when a corn grain grows into a cornstalk plant, there must be some unchanging and permanent quality that has at one time the aspects we give to a corn grain, and later, those aspects we attribute to a corn plant.

This must be so or we could not use the term *change* to describe the relationship between the original state and the latter one. But, if there is some permanent quality, there must be another that is subject to change; there must be something that is different be-between the corn grain and the corn plant or there would be no real alteration.

2. *Matter and Form*

The two features, Aristotle says, are form and matter.

a. Matter in its pure state obviously would contain no characteristics at all, but matter is actually that which is subject to and capable of being *informed*—that is, capable of assuming different shapes (forms). The matter of the corn grain and corn plant contains the potentiality of receiving varied forms, of taking on one form at a time and another form at a later time. *Actuality* is that form taken on by an object at a particular moment.

b. Thus all objects contain a permanent nature even though they may take on different forms at different times. To comprehend fully any object one must understand it in terms of both its form and its matter, and in addition must understand the process by which it grows, changes, or moves—which is to say that it is replacing one form with that of another.

c. The object in its permanent state can never exist alone without taking on some kind of form.

d. Moreover, the object is in some state at all times and is ever in the process of attaining another state.

Thus, the *formal* (changing state) and the *material* (permanent state) aspect of any object are both at all times present and must always be the basis for any understanding of what is occurring.

ARISTOTLE

THE *ETHICS:* A SURVEY

INTRODUCTION: Ethics belongs to the second main classification of science in Aristotle's system, practical science:

The word *practical* is derived from the Greek *praxis*, meaning doing, or action.

Ethics belongs to that branch of philosophy which has to do with human action.

The word *ethics* comes from the Greek *ethos*, the primary meaning of which is custom, manners, habit. Aristotle uses the word chiefly in its secondary meaning of character, that which reveals what a man really is.

Aristotle thinks that to ask what a man really is, is not to ask whether he is intelligent or talented. Such qualities are accidental to what it means to be a man.

He thinks that a man reveals what he is through what he does, through how he performs his function of being a man. In the *Metaphysics*, Aristotle showed how the Good (that is, excellence) is the Final Cause of man, and how the will, informed by reason, provides the motivation for human progress toward self-perfection. He made it clear that the Good is the standard of measurement of all human action.

For this reason, any judgment of character must be made in terms of moral values.

Ethics, therefore, is the study of character, of the moral element in human nature. It is the study of action in terms of self-perfection.

PLATO'S APPROACH TO ETHICS: Plato was highly conscious of the moral aspect of human nature. In his more intuitive perception of the fundamental unity of human existence, he made no hard and fast distinction between the *morally good* and the *scientifically true.*

1. He considered the world of action and the world of knowledge interdependent. A man could only become good by knowing

435

the truth, and he could not know the truth without being good.

2. Plato believed that to know what something really *is*, is to understand its significance—to realize what its intrinsic value is in relation to us.

3. Consequently, he identified perfect truth with perfect value in his concept of the Ideal Good, as the light which makes the world intelligible.

4. Since the Ideal Good was a form which existed separately from matter, absolute value was an objective and unchanging standard. It was not a product of man's reasoning, nor dependent upon man's knowledge for its existence.

5. Plato taught that the discovery of the real meaning of things was not a simple intellectual exercise. Knowledge could only be acquired by experience, by leading a life whose actions were in harmony with the Ideal Good.

Something of Plato's idea of what "meaning" really means is found in our expression "true to life." When we say a picture is true to life, we are not merely making a factual observation. We are saying that somehow the painting has caught what is significant in life, in the sense of what we think has value for us in understanding what life is all about. Plato believed that knowing was the experience of the meaningful in terms of its value.

ARISTOTLE'S APPROACH TO ETHICS: Aristotle's approach to ethics is more analytical and consequently more practical than Plato's. Aristotle is the first philosopher to make the definitive distinction between the Science of the Good and the Science of the True.

1. He breaks up Plato's unity of knowing and acting into two independent philosophical categories:

   a. The theoretical sciences.

   b. The practical sciences.

Each of these has its own subject matter, and its own method. The theoretical sciences study what always, or usually, is. Their first principles are thus rooted in experience, or in reality. Consequently, the theoretical sciences can arrive at the truth. The practical sciences, however, have human action as their subject matter. This, we know, is unpredictable, for it concerns what sometimes is and what sometimes is not. Thus, there is no way we can discover sure and certain principles for these sciences; we are forced to base our study on opinion rather than on experience. There can be no absolute moral standard which will serve as the principle governing every action, because every action is individual and unique. For this reason, the good of any action is relative to the kind of action it is.

1. It follows that the practical sciences can never have as their goal absolute truth.

2. Their truth can only be relative. Because moral truth, consequently, is a lesser kind of truth than scientific truth, Aristotle subordinates the life of acting to the life of knowing. With Aristotle, ethics descends from the world of eternal being to the world of becoming.

ARISTOTLE'S WRITINGS ON ETHICS: Of the three works said to have been written by Aristotle, only one is generally said to have come from his pen.

1. This is the *Nicomachean Ethics*. Many scholars say that the

2. *Eudemean Ethics* is an earlier version of Aristotle's ethical theory, but since we are not completely sure, it seems more fitting to turn to the *Nicomachean Ethics* for an understanding of Aristotle's ethical system.

THE MAIN CONCEPTS IN GERM; HAPPINESS: Aristotle noticed that there are such things as "good lives" and "bad lives" amongst various people. In addition, he noticed that the common strain in the so-called "good lives" was the idea of *happiness*. Similarly, the so-called "bad lives" had a common strain referred to as "unhappy." *Hence*: the good life is a life of happiness.

Aristotle defines happiness as "an activity of the soul in accord with perfect virtue." By this he meant (possibly) that happiness is *not* static but an active state or condition.

1. But happiness is not the *goal* of the soul's activity, but rather it is a state that *accompanies* various activities.

2. In other words, it is the *way* a certain action is performed, such as eating, making love, etc. For example, the man who enjoys intellectual activities, making good friends, and engaging in healthful recreation and such activities is *not* accompanied regularly by depression and pessimism and anxiety—he then can be considered happy. In some such rough way as this can be expressed by Aristotle's definition of happiness as an activity of the soul in accord with virtue.

THE GOOD LIFE: For Aristotle the good life was a life of happiness. As for the way man ought to behave, his answer was equally simple: man should behave in such a way as to achieve happiness.

THE MEAN: *Mean* does not mean average. Being happy and living the good life means a life of following the "golden mean."

1. There are different ways to live correctly, each way dependent upon the individual.

2. What is good for one man may not be equally good for another.

3. The use of reason alone is not enough in determining the life of goodness and happiness.

4. What is needed above all is a life of experimentation, trial and error experiment for each individual in determining for himself the correct way of life.

Being happy, says Aristotle, is like being well-fed. "Well-fed" is a variable term for each individual depending upon his size, activity, metabolism, etc. The correct amount, after trial and error experimentation of food we should eat to be well-fed, is a "mean" between eating too much and too little. Again, we must remember that "mean" here does not mean "average."

1. Happiness: a state of happiness is reached in the moral sphere if one behaves according to his "mean" of moral behavior.

   a. For example, courage, liberality, wittiness, modesty, etc. are some of the qualities one should have in order to be happy. But all these "virtues" are virtues of the "mean" or moderation.

b. Courage = the "mean" between cowardice and rashness. Liberality = the "mean" prodigality and frugality. Pride = the "mean" between vanity and humility, etc.

2. Aristotle's "golden mean" involves the following then:

a. To obtain happiness men must act moderately (i.e., they must act in such a way as to reach a "mean" between the two extremes of behavior).

b. Remember the "mean" varies in each person.

DOCTRINE OF PLEASURE:

1. Pleasure is *not* entirely bad.

2. A certain amount of pleasure in one's life is vital to the achievement of happiness.

3. His famous epigram is memorable: "No man is happy on the (torture) rack."

ARISTOTLE

POLITICS: A SURVEY

POLITICS—THE STUDY OF THE STATE: We have seen in the *Ethics* how a man's character depends on the society in which he is brought up.

To learn how to act intelligently, one must live in a community which believes that it is important to act intelligently. In order to perform his function of living according to reason, a man must have a field of action in which to operate. This field is the state.

1. In the *Politics* Aristotle investigates "that larger science" of which ethics is a part.

2. The book is an investigation of government. It tells us what Aristotle thinks government is and what good government *should be.*

ORDER OF THE BOOKS: Like all the rest of Aristotle's books, the *Politics* is a collection of teaching notes, which Aristotle used while he was at the Lyceum.

For this reason it has come down to us in a confusing form, and there has been much speculation about the "early" or the "late" politics. None of the books seems to relate directly to the one which follows.

The work falls into four sections, corresponding to Aristotle's four causes.

1. In Book I he states the first principles and definition of the state. He then proceeds to examine the "out of what" the state comes, namely, the *material cause* of the state.

2. In Books II, III, IV, he deals with the structure of government, the *formal cause,* or the constitution of the state.

3. In Books V and VI Aristotle looks at the sources of change and stability in a given society, or the *efficient cause* of change in the state.

4. Finally, in Books VII and VIII Aristotle investigates the *final cause* of government. What should be the aim of good government?

ARISTOTLE

POETICS: SUMMARY

INTRODUCTION: Of the three works which Aristotle classifies under the productive sciences, two seem to the modern reader to belong unquestionably to the ancient world. These are the *Topics*, or "How to make a good argument," and the *Rhetoric*, or "How to give a good speech."

As the Greeks were a nation of inveterate talkers, it is not surprising that, with Aristotle, argument and speech-making should have come into their own as skills or arts which the lawyer and the office-holder must needs learn, if they are to be successful.

Interesting as these two works are, the careful distinctions and logical refinement which constitute their subject matter seem like an art from the ancient past, long forgotten, and of little practical use to us.

The third work of this group, the *Poetics*, however, enjoys a completely different status. Perhaps no other work of Aristotle's has had such an influence on subsequent generations of philosophers and artists as this one has had.

Although Aristotle never intended the *Poetics* to be a fully thought-out philosophy of art, it nevertheless was the first attempt in history to analyze the beautiful and the pleasing from the standpoint of the individual art work itself, free from ethical principles. The subject matter of the *Poetics* is self-evident: poetry, and the poetry of tragedy, in particular.

INFLUENCE OF PLATO'S ESTHETIC THEORY: In his treatment of art in the *Republic* and elsewhere, Plato demonstrated his keen awareness of the impact of a great art work upon its audience.

1. He thought a morally bad subject beautifully presented would encourage men actually to do bad deeds by virtue of art's power of appeal to the irrational part of man's soul.

2. To avoid this danger, Plato was in favor of controlling the production of art in his ideal State so that only those works

appeared which were morally uplifting, and helped the citizen to live a good life.

3. Precisely because art has such an emotional appeal, Plato thought it should be used as a tool to educate men.

4. The principal theme of his esthetics is that art should teach morality. This view of art as propaganda is held by the leaders of the Soviet Union today.

ARISTOTLE—ART FOR ART'S SAKE: In the *Poetics,* Aristotle considers the art-work as a work of art, not as an instrument of propaganda. In his usual fashion he sets out to discover what is the nature of art, and what good art really is. In so doing, he marks a major departure from his teacher.

1. His inquiry into the nature of poetry starts, not with a moral "ought," but with his customary observation of fact.

2. Art can assume different forms, he says. "Making" can be in the form of an epic, tragedy, comedy, poetry, music and dancing.

3. After defining each of these forms in turn, he proceeds to lay down rules for what he considers the best form of art, namely tragedy. But before he discusses any kind of poetry, he first has to determine the first principles of his science.

THE PRINCIPLES OF ART: Aristotle's famous first principle of poetry, and indeed of any art, is that "art is an imitation of nature." There has been perhaps more controversy over what Aristotle really meant by art being an "imitation" of nature than there has been over any other aspect of his philosophy.

1. Does he mean that art copies nature, for example? If so, then his theory can offer no explanation why we can make things which are not found in the world of nature.

2. Perhaps he means that the artist sits down at his easel and simply reproduces faithfully what he sees. Aristotle was too fine a thinker to propose a banal and crude "first principle" such as *that* given above, i.e., number 2.

ART THE COMPLETION OF NATURE: To understand what Aristotle's concept of art is, we must first know something about the Greek word for art, *techne,* from which comes the English words "technical," "technology," and "technique." As can be seen from the kind of words derived from it, *techne* does not refer to the fine arts at all. In fact, the Greeks had no word for fine art. *Techne* to them meant what it still does to us in its derivatives— a "skill," the "making" of a thing.

The world for them was divided into the world of nature and the world where things were made.

1. In the *Physics* Aristotle makes it plain that he thinks processes which seem unintelligible in the world of nature can be best illustrated by the world of making, or *techne.*

2. To demonstrate his definition of natural process, for instance, he turns to *techne* for an example of motion, the building of a house.

3. In his treatment of the Four Causes he again turns to *techne* for the example of the bronze which becomes a statue. Art, the process of human *making,* he believes, is similar to nature or the process of natural growth.

   a. Nature herself is an artist, he says, for it is obvious that every natural process is directed toward an end. Man begets man, for instance.

   b. Moreover, one process follows another to accomplish the final purpose of nature, whatever that may be.

   c. In this respect, art has a vital function to perform for it takes over where nature leaves off. Nature makes the acorn become an oak, but only art can make an oak become an oak table.

Thus, says Aristotle, in a famous passage in Book II of the *Physics,* "art brings to completion that which nature is unable to finish, and in this sense she imitates nature. If then, artificial processes are purposeful, natural ones are too."

SUMMARY OF THE *POETICS*

Aristotle opens the *Poetics* with the remark that in the world of making there are many kinds of imitation. There is music and the various kinds of poetry, for example. These differ in their imitation of nature in three ways:

1. The means (color of the voice).

2. The object, or what is imitated.

3. The manner of imitation.

I. THE MEANS OF ART IMITATION

Aristotle distinguishes three *means* in art imitation:

1. Rhythm.

2. Language.

3. Harmony or tune.

Music, for instance, uses rhythm and harmony. Dancing is rhythm without tune. Prose writing imitates by language alone. Epic and elegiac poetry imitate by the use of language and rhythm, which together constitute meter. Only lyric, tragic, and comic poetry utilize all three means: rhythm, language, and tune.

II. THE OBJECT OF IMITATION

What does art imitate? Aristotle rejects Plato's view that the artist imitates the shadowy unreal world of becoming (the world known to the senses), because it means that the artist copies a copy of reality which is knowable to the mind alone. Consequently he never imitates the truth.

1. Aristotle boldly states that art imitates "men in action." In his view art is primarily concerned with the character of men which, as we already know, Aristotle believes can only be known through action.

2. Art imitates the world of man's soul. It is thus an imitation of not the material world, as Plato had taught, but of the world of forms (for the soul is the form of a man) that is known by the mind.

3. Because art imitates the character of man, Aristotle believes the artist must represent men either better or worse than they really are. Comedy, for example, represents men as worse than they are; tragedy as better than they are.

III. MANNER OF IMITATION

The third difference in the way art imitates nature is in the kind *of imitation*. Aristotle does not make his meaning here quite clear. Sophocles, he says, in one sense is the same kind of imitator as Homer for both imitate ideal characters. In another sense, Sophocles is the same kind of imitator as the comic writer, Aristophanes, because both are dramatists writing "poems representing action." In general, it seems that Aristotle's distinction sets off dramatic from narrative writing.

THE ORIGIN OF POETRY: According to Aristotle, poetry has two causes which are found in the nature of man himself:

1. The first cause is man's instinct to imitate. It is by imitation, he says, that a child starts to learn, because he experiences a definite pleasure in the things imitated. This point is important. Aristotle is saying that we delight in the work of art, not only because of what it represents, but also because of the *way it is made*. This explains why things which we would not like to see in the real world, such as a murder, we enjoy seeing in a work of art. Aristotle says that we enjoy art objects because of the nature of the way we learn. The artist opens our eyes, and widens our perspective. When you look at a painting or go to a play, you take pleasure in recognizing your friends in the characters of the play because you have learned something new about them.

2. The second cause of poetry is man's natural instinct for tune and rhythm. We enjoy the appeal to the senses found in all art, whether it be color, music, or form.

   (In this connection, it is important to realize that Aristotle never underestimates the sensual aspect of art.)

DEVELOPMENT OF POETRY: From this beginning, poetry took two directions:

1. Some poets imitated the actions of good men and

2. some the actions of lesser men.

Homer is an example of the more serious poet, while satire represents the actions of lesser men. From these two types of poets came the tragic writer and the comic writer. In seeing in the history of poetry the progressive evolution of art forms, Aristotle makes it clear that he considers drama a more advanced form of poetry. Tragedy is thus a better means of imitating the actions of good men than the type of seriousness of the *Iliad* or the *Odyssey*. Aristotle even questions whether tragedy has reached its highest form or not.

EVOLUTION OF TRAGEDY:　Both tragedy and comedy started, as did the first poetry, by improvisation. Spoken parts were inserted into two old forms of religious choral singing:

1. the dithyramb

2. and the phallic hymn.

Aristotle traces the evolution of tragedy from the dithyramb to its "natural form."

1. The first great Greek tragic poet, Aeschylus, he tells us, introduced a second actor, and deepened the importance of the chorus, so that the dialogue became the most important part of the play.

2. The next tragic poet, Sophocles, increased the number of actors to three, and added scenery. Next, by lengthening the plot, he introduced the "grand manner" into tragedy which took the place of earlier forms of diction. In addition he made changes in meter. The trochaic meter (alternating strong and weak beats) gave way to iambic meter (alternating weak and strong beats). The last is, in Aristotle's opinion, the more proper conversational meter for dialogue. Finally, the play itself was lengthened into five episodes or scenes.

HISTORY OF COMEDY:　Although tragedy has a long history, comedy does not. Comedy, he believes, had already taken the form known in his day by the time it had reached that stage of its development when it could be called comic. He thinks that the idea of the comic plot came from Sicily, but says it was the Athenian, Crates, who had introduced the general formula for comedy familiar to him.

THE DIFFERENCE BETWEEN EPIC POETRY AND TRAGEDY: Epic poetry and tragedy are alike in that they both are "imitations of serious character in a high type of verse." They differ in many ways, however.

1. Epic poetry is written in only one meter and is narrative in form. An epic tells a story and does not enact it. Again, epic poetry has no time limit; the action of the epic can take place over several years or even centuries.

2. But the action of tragedy generally takes place within a single day. (In practice on the Greek stage, the action of tragedy held within the limits of one day, or even from sunrise to sundown.)

All the elements of epic poetry are found in tragedy, but not vice versa. Thus from the standpoint of technique as well as evolution, tragedy is a higher form of poetry. After these introductory comments, Aristotle turns to an analysis of tragedy. This discussion takes up the remainder of the *Poetics*, and in many respects, resembles a manual to the budding writer on how to write a good play.

I. THE DEFINITION OF TRAGEDY:

Having determined the first principles of *techne*, the nature of the species of poetry, and the differences between two very similar forms of poetry, the epic and tragedy, Aristotle is ready to say what tragedy is.

> "Tragedy is an imitation of an action which is serious, complete in itself, and of a certain magnitude, in language embellished with every kind of artistic ornament which is to be found separately in different parts of the play; in a dramatic not a narrative form; through pity and fear bringing about the purgation (*katharsis*) of these emotions."

What this definition means becomes more clear as we go further into the *Poetics*, but some things can be said about it now.

> **COMMENT:** Aristotle has already explained what he means by imitation. "Language embellished" denotes the poetic means of rhythm, language and tune. The "artistic ornament" found "separately" in the different parts of the play refers to the fact that in Greek drama some parts were spoken, some sung, and, frequently the choral odes were danced as well as sung.

II. OTHER CHARACTERISTICS:

Other characteristics which tragedy must have are

1. Scenery.

2. Song.

3. Diction, or the arrangement of words in meter.

4. Since tragedy is the imitation of an action, it concerns character "that by which we say a person has certain qualities."

5. Tragedy must have thought, i.e., it must deal with universal truths.

6. It must have plot, or an arrangement of events.

III. IMPORTANCE OF THE SIX PARTS:

Of the six parts of the tragedy, Aristotle considers *plot* the "soul of tragedy" because without plot, or ordered action, there can be no tragedy and there can be no character. Plot is the first principle of tragedy in that it contains the most powerful elements of emotional interest, namely what Aristotle calls "scenes of reversal" of the situation, and "recognition."

Character is second in importance to plot. It is important because it shows the moral purpose of the hero by revealing what kinds of things he chooses or avoids. Third in importance is *thought*, which Aristotle defines as "the ability to say what is possible and relevant in a given circumstance."

Diction comes fourth. Of the "embellishments," Aristotle considers *song* most important.

The sixth part, *spectacle,* has for Aristotle, the least artistic merit, although he agrees that it is important as an emotional appeal to the audience.

IV. TRAGEDY AS ACTION:

Returning to his definition, Aristotle discusses what he means when he says the action of tragedy must be complete, whole, and of a certain magnitude, or length.

1. To be complete, he says, tragedy must have a beginning, a middle, and an end. The beginning must be understandable and natural, while the middle and the end must follow logically from the beginning.

2. A whole implies structure, and order. This means that a plot must show some kind of inner cohesion, or fail to be a plot. The plot must be of a certain length. The Greeks understood beauty in terms of visual proportion. n their view, the beautiful is a formal arrangement of parts with a definite limit of size relative to our power of sight. For this reason, a small animal cannot be beautiful because the eye can see all of it in too short a space of time. A large animal cannot be beautiful for the eye cannot take it all in at once, and it loses its sense of the whole. What is the proper length for tragedy that will permit the mind to grasp it in the proper way? Aristotle says it is that length which can be properly taken in by the memory so that "the sequence of events, according to the law of probability, or necessity, will bring about a change from bad fortune to good, or from good fortune to bad." The proper length of tragedy is a mean relative to our mental capacities.

V. THE CHARACTERISTICS OF TRAGIC ACTION:

1. It follows from the foregoing that there can be only one complete action or plot to a tragedy. Aristotle insists that there cannot be several plots in the same play, because this would detract from the unity and power of the drama.

2. Each part of the plot must be necessary so that if one part is removed the whole will seem incomplete and out of proportion.

3. Perhaps the most interesting of all Aristotle's conditions for a good plot is that the action must not relate what actually *did* happen but what possibly *can* happen. The plot must have an inner continuity which must seem possible but should not have happened. Now poetry relates what may happen, i.e., how a certain type of person will react in a given situation. History is only of individual events, but *poetry is of universals.*

For this reason, Aristotle considers poetry superior to history.

Because it is of universals, tragedy, in his view, is by its very nature more scientific than history. Thus Aristotle does not believe that playwrights should stick to legend or historical incidents as their source of material. There is not any reason why the dramatist should not invent a plot of his own choosing.

VI. KATHARSIS:

Tragedy is an imitation, not of any action, but of a particular kind of action with a particular purpose in view. In his definition of tragedy, Aristotle says that it must inspire pity and fear. He considers the aim of tragedy the purgation of these two emotions or the "cancelling-out" of the one by the other. This result is what he calls *Katharsis*. The Greek word means "cleansing, or purging." Aristotle says that a katharsis of our emotions is brought about when there is an element of surprise in tragedy. Just what he means by katharsis no one really knows, and many learned books have been written on the subject. Scholars seem to fall roughly into two categories in the way they define *katharsis*.

1. One group holds that Aristotle understood *katharsis* as some kind of religious experience, similar to the purging of the soul of guilt, which took place in the Greek mystery religion, the Orphic mysteries.

2. More recent scholars tend to support a second view, that Aristotle considered *katharsis* primarily as a medical phenomenon. They argue that the word was first used in a medical context, and referred to the cleansing of the body of bad humors. Since the idea that tragedy was supposed to arouse pity and fear was a popular theory, no doubt *katharsis* meant something particular to the Greeks that we can only imagine.

3. *Katharsis*, as the aim of tragedy, is still a mystery for the scholar to solve.

VII. THE PARTS OF TRAGEDY:

From a consideration of tragedy as a whole, Aristotle turns to its parts. Of the six parts mentioned above, three are related to the "object of imitation," plot, character, and thought; and three to the "means of imitation," diction, song, and spectacle.

1. *Plot*: Aristotle says plots are either simple or complex.

a. A complex plot is one in which a change of fortune takes place;

b. A simple plot is one in which no change of fortune takes place.

The change of fortune, (wealth to poverty, ignorance to knowledge) is brought about in one of two ways:

a. The first is what Aristotle calls *reversal of fortune,* when the action of the tragedy takes the opposite course from the one it has been taking.

b. The second way is by *recognition,* which Aristotle defines as "a change from ignorance to knowledge, producing love or hate between the characters involved."

He gives many examples of these two means of changing the fortune of the tragic hero, and insists that both of these two means must come upon the viewer as a complete surprise if pity and fear are to be aroused. (Unfortunately, Aristotle does not explain how the events of a play can come as a surprise when the plot is already familiar to the audience through their acquaintance with their own legends and history.)

c. The third part of the plot is what Aristotle calls the *scene of suffering,* where death, murder or some painful event is enacted on the stage.

The perfect tragedy, to Aristotle, is the one which uses the complex plot.

The perfect change of fortune is the one in which "a man who is not very good and just, yet whose misfortune is brought about not by vice and wickedness but by some error or weakness" is the hero. For example, in the great Greek play by Sophocles, *Oedipus the King,* Oedipus' reversal of fortune is brought about because he thought he could, single-handedly, solve the problem of the plague which was raging in his city. In fact, he was the cause of the plague, yet unaware of that fact.

VIII. RELATION OF PITY AND FEAR TO PLOT—DISCOVERY:

Pity and fear can be aroused either through the spectacle attached

to the play or through the element of discovery in the action of
the play. Aristotle says the latter is the better way. Family situations are the source of actions which arouse most pity and fear,
in his opinion, as when a son kills a mother, a brother kills a sister,
or a wife her husband. Sometimes the murder is the result of
ignorance, as when Oedipus kills his father, and sometimes it occurs with the full knowledge of the hero, as when Medea kills her
children. Aristotle feels that pity and fear are better aroused when
the deed is done in ignorance, and the discovery, or realization of
what has been done, comes later.

IX. CHARACTER—THE IDEAL TRAGIC HERO:

The relation of character to plot in Aristotle's analysis of tragedy
is considered by most scholars to be the same as the relation of
matter to form. Character is plot which has not been made actual.
It is potentially plot. Plot is therefore character-in-action. You only
know what sort of person a man is when you see him act. His acts
reveal his character, the moral element in his soul, and, Aristotle
would say, actually *are* his character. The same is true of characters
in a play. There are four things at which the playwright must aim
in making a tragic character:

1. The hero must be good, regardless of his station in life.

2. Character must be suitable to the hero. Manly courage is not
   appropriate in a woman, for example.

3. Character must be true to life, and

4. character must be consistent. The hero must act and speak as
   he would be expected to act and speak. His actions must have
   an understandable motivation.

Aristotle makes three further distinctions:

1. The hero should be well known. The common man is not a
   proper subject for tragedy, says Aristotle (himself an aristocrat).
   One of his main objections to the Greek tragedian, Euripides,
   was that "he brought the common man onto the stage."

2. Second, in drawing character and plot, the poet should always
   try to make it sound possible. Aristotle was not in favor of *deus
   ex machina* scenes, of which Euripides was a master, where the

gods come onto the stage to unravel the tangled threads of the play's ending.

3. Finally, the character should be true to life, but yet more beautiful. The poet should ennoble the character of the hero, a point already made by Aristotle.

X. FORMS OF RECOGNITON:

In this section Aristotle considers different forms of recognition. As the discussion is rather technical, it is of little interest to the modern reader. Aristotle thinks the best recognition is that in which the discovery comes naturally and is as little contrived as possible. The key word is vividness, and Aristotle urged the poet to keep the scene he is writing at all times before his eyes.

XI. TECHNIQUES OF PLOT:

In writing a play it is well to plan the plot and the scenes beforehand. Every tragedy falls into two parts:

1. The *complication* leads up to the change of fortune.

2. The dénouement, or unraveling, of the threads of the plot, goes from the complication's point of change of fortune and proceeds to the end of the play.

Aristotle distinguishes four kinds of tragedy:

1. The simple.

2. The complex.

3. The ethical (where the motives are moral).

4. The pathetic (where the motives are passion or emotion). His last warning on plot writing is that the chorus, a typical feature of Greek tragedy, should also be considered as an actor.

XII. THOUGHT:

Since the essence of tragedy is the imitation of action, thought plays a very minor role in Aristotle's analysis. Because moral goodness and excellence of character are revealed in action, he believes that the emphasis in tragedy must be on the plot. Thought includes "every effect which has to be produced by speech," and he feels that this is a subject which is better left to the study of rhetoric. Speech is the proper object of rhetoric, whereas action is the object of tragedy.

XIII. DICTION:

Aristotle's discussion is a handbook of poetic diction. He has little sympathy for high-flown and obscure poetic language. The Greek concept of beauty was rooted in the ideas of limit, order, and form. Since order implied an intelligible arrangement of parts, beauty and clarity were almost interchangeable in the Greek mind. For this reason Aristotle believes that the duty of the poet is not to indulge in lavish phrases, but to say what he has to say clearly with an eye to proportion.

He sees the mark of genius in the poet's use of metaphor, because the poet's ability to get his meaning across depends upon his choice of similes. "To make a good metaphor," says Aristotle, "is to have an eye for similarities."

XIV. TRAGEDY IS BETTER THAN EPIC POETRY:

The comparison of the two forms of "seriousness and dignity" in poetry leads Aristotle quite naturally to ask which is the better form: epic poetry or poetic tragedy.

1. General opinion, he points out, holds that epic poetry is better because it appeals to a better type of audience. Tragedy is frequently overacted, and thus tends to appeal to a mass audience.

2. Despite this strong argument, Aristotle thinks that tragedy is the better art form.

Aristotle lists five reasons why he thinks tragedy is the superior art form:

1. Tragedy has all the poetic elements that an epic has, plus two more of its own, namely, music and spectacle.

2. It leaves a vivid impression when it is read as well as when it is performed.

3. As an art form, it is more concentrated, and its limits more defined. Aristotle believes that a more pleasurable effect is produced when an activity is concentrated than when it is spread out over a longer period of time.

4. Tragedy has a greater unity of action. One epic poem, for example, will furnish subjects for many tragedies.

5. Finally, tragedy fulfills its specific function better than epic poetry in bringing pleasure through *katharsis*.

END OF THE *POETICS*:   At the beginning of the *Poetics,* Artistotle mentions that he will later deal with the subjects of comedy, and other kinds of poetry. Unfortunately the *Poetics* ends with the discussion of epic tragedy. As it is the only work on aesthetics which Aristotle wrote, we shall never know his view on the remaining forms of poetry.

INTERPRETATION: *POETICS*, QUESTIONS AND ANSWERS

Why does Aristotle rank tragedy (and poetry in general) above history?

ANSWER: The modern mind may be surprised that Aristotle valued tragedy above history. In our day, the theater tends to be a source of amusement rather than of knowledge. Yet, Aristotle's view has much sense in it. As we have seen, he believes that knowledge of universals is the only knowledge possible. We can never know particulars, individually existing things and events, except as we can determine in what way they are similar to or different from, other existing things.

Tragedy shows us what is universal in human action and in human character. It thus enables us to interpret both personal actions and historical events correctly.

Because it is concerned with particulars, and therefore, the unknowable, history can only be understood in the light of philosophy and poetry. For this reason, Aristotle ranks history as a secondary subject. In so doing, he is simply stating a fact of which every writer of history is aware. It is not so much the events that are important, but the interpretation of them that counts in the determination of historical truth.

What does Aristotle mean by katharsis?

ANSWER:　See section VI above.

Discuss Aristotle's view of art as imitation.

ANSWER:　This topic may be considered under three topics, the first being

1. the way in which art imitates nature;

2. the second, the purpose of art; and the third,

3. the integrity of art.

The way art imitates nature: It is clear that Aristotle did not think that art imitated nature in the sense that it copied natural objects. If art were purely representative, it would be impossible for the artist to create non-representative forms. The best explanation of how Aristotle thought art imitated nature is to be found in the *Physics*.

In Book II he suggests that art imitates nature in that it imitates natural processes. The acorn becomes an oak in a way similar to the way in which bronze becomes a statue. But nature can only do natural things. Art takes over where nature leaves off. In this sense, Aristotle says that art "perfects or completes" nature. The acorn can become an oak tree, but the oak tree can never become a table of its own effort. Nevertheless, the process by which the acorn becomes an oak, and the oak becomes a table, both involve the same four elements of causation. There is the matter from which the finished product comes. There is the form which determines the kind of thing it is to be. There is the agent which brings the finished product into being; and there is the purpose or function for the sake of which the thing exists.

If art imitates nature, in the sense that it completes what nature by herself is unable to do, it is clear that art is never the same as nature. It exists independently of nature with a purpose of its own.

Poetry, for example, imitates language, but it is language arranged in a special way for a special effect, which sets it off from ordinary speech.

Tragedy, Aristotle tells us, imitates action, but it does not imitate ordinary action. The hero must be a man who is better both materially and spiritually than the average person, and the tragic plot must be built around him in such a way that it reveals his moral character.

Tragedy is not concerned with any kind of action, but with that kind of action which tells us something fundamental about human nature.

The purpose of all art is to give expression to the universal element in human life. Aristotle thinks that art, and especially its highest form, poetry, is concerned with the universal human condition.

To say that art is concerned with universals is not to say that art is science. In the opening chapter of the *Metaphysics*, Aristotle discusses the relation of art to science, and where art stands in the hierarchy of knowledge. The doctor who cures a disease because he understands that all persons afflicted with the same disease have been helped by a particular medicine, is an artist in relation to health. The scientist is the man who is concerned not with similarities but with universal principles of cause and effect. Art, according to Aristotle, is the result of our grasping those similarities in experience in view of which many separate experiences become a unified whole.

In the *Poetics* Aristotle "scientifically" analyzes what are the causes and effects of good tragedy, but his analysis does not make a tragedy. Tragedy is the imitation of an action. It imitates those similarities which are universal to all human behavior. But it does not say why this universality exists.

A final characteristic of art as the imitation of nature is that it is self-contained and complete in itself. For this reason, it must be judged by standards of beauty, that is, by esthetic criteria, which are peculiar to it alone.

In the *Poetics* Aristotle gives us his criteria for evaluating art, according to the three ways in which art can be said to imitate nature:

1. according to the means it uses,

2. according to the object, and

3. according to the method employed.

Esthetic values are essentially values relative to human demands. A true Greek, Aristotle bases his whole standard of beauty on a sense of proportion. Tragedy, for example, cannot be too short or too long. It must be just the length which will permit the memory to accept it in a single "glance." Art perfects nature, but it is a human perfection to be judged by human standards.

Aristotle views art as the imitation of nature, in that nature is the material cause of art, the starting-point for artistic creation, and because artistic making is fundamentally the same process as natural production.

Nevertheless, the finished art work is an independent being in its own right, whose purpose is to express what is universal in human behavior and attitudes. This means that it must be judged according to esthetic criteria which are suitable and applicable to art alone.

Are we to trust Aristotle's views on the origin and development of Greek drama?

ANSWER: In part only; recent research has made a great contribution to our knowledge of the field, a knowledge which both corrects and supplements Aristotle's views. See the Introduction to Tragedy above.

What are the two causes of poetry which are found in the nature of man himself?

ANSWER: The two causes are:
1. Man's instinct to imitate. It is by imitation that a child starts to learn because he experiences a definite pleasure in the things imitated. This point is important; we delight in the work of art not only because of what it represents, but also because of the *way it is made*. This explains why things which we would not like to see in the real world, such as a murder, we enjoy seeing in a work of art. We enjoy art objects because of the nature of the way we learn.

2. Man's natural instinct for tune and rhythm. We enjoy the appeal to the senses found in all art.

CHRONOLOGICAL TABLE OF ROMAN LITERATURE

	AUTHORS & WORKS
Dates	(*Names in Capitals Covered in this Book*)

B.C.

272	Theocritus in Sicily
254-184?	Birth of Plautus at Sarsina in Umbria
235	Performance of Naevius' (?-201) first play
234	Cato the Elder (234-149), *Treatise on Agriculture*
212	Plautus' first play: the *Menaechmi*
204?	Plautus' *Miles Gloriosus*
ca. 203	Birth of Polybius at Megalopolis
185?-159	Terence born in Africa
186	Plautus' latest comedies
180?-103	Lucilius born at Suessa Aurunca
168?	Cato composes his *De Agri Cultura*
166	Terence's *Andria* produced
149	Publication of Cato's *Origines*
131	Publication of the first books of Lucilius' *Satires*
106-43	CICERO (born at Arpium)
101-44	Caesar
ca. 90-80	Atellanae ('Punch-and-Judy') of Pomponius
65-8	HORACE. About 65-64, CATULLUS' poetry
60	CICERO'S *Catilinarian Orations* prepared for publication
54	LUCRETIUS' *De Rerum Natura*
54?-19	Tibullus
ca. 51	Caesar's *De Bello Gallico*
48	The Library of Alexander destroyed by fire
43-A.D. 17?	OVID
ca. 39	Publication of VIRGIL'S *Bucolics*
35/34	HORACE, *Satires*, Bk. 1
23	HORACE'S *Odes*, Bks. 1-3
21/20	HORACE, *Epistles*, Bk. 1
19	Deaths of VIRGIL and Tibullus
19	Publication of the *Aeneid*
4-A.D. 65	Seneca

A.D.

ca. 8	OVID'S *Metamorphoses* and *Fasti*
17	Death of Livy, who had composed 142 books of his *History of Rome*
ca. 17	OVID'S death in exile
23-79	Pliny the Elder

A.D.

35?-115?	Quintilian
44?-102?	Martial
ca. 45	Philosophical treatises of Seneca
46-120	Plutarch
54/56-120?	TACITUS
ca. 55	Persius' *Satires*. Petronius' (?-65) *Satyricon*
60-130/140	JUVENAL
62?-114?	Pliny the Younger
69	Pliny the Elder's *Natural History*
75?-160?	Suetonius
98	Martial's *Epigrams*
92-93	Quintilian's *Institutio Oratoria*
98	TACITUS' *Agricola* and *Germania*
ca. 116	TACITUS' *Annales*

LUCRETIUS

ON THE NATURE OF THINGS: SUMMARY

INTRODUCTION: Lucretius (Titus Lucretius Carus) was probably born in Rome in 99 B.C. and died c. 55 B.C. Lucretius came from an aristocratic and wealthy family. He was a friend of Gaius Memmius, governor of Bithynia, and it is to the governor that his great poem *On the Nature of Things* is addressed.

Much of our information about Lucretius comes from St. Jerome's translation into Latin of the *Chronicles* by Eusebius; much of what he says is uncertain and questionable. For example, Jerome states that Lucretius was driven mad after having taken a love potion. Nevertheless, there were times when Lucretius was not mad, and in these intervals he composed his great poem. Finally, Jerome says he committed suicide at the age of forty-four. All the foregoing statements of Jerome are doubtful and remain unsupported to this day.

THE POEM:

1. *On the Nature of Things (De Rerum Natura)* is one of the greatest poems ever written.

2. It is a philosophical and didactic poem reflecting the Epicurean positions on science and philosophy.

3. The poem was left unfinished.

4. Virgil admired and imitated Lucretius.

5. Cicero, Statius, and Ovid all mention him.

6. The Roman Empire and the Middle Ages found his Epicurean views (philosophical materialism) unbearable and consequently ignored his poem.

7. The Renaissance and Seventeenth Century took to Lucretius, both eras translating and imitating his poem.

   a. There are traces of Lucretius' influence in Milton's great epic, *Paradise Lost*.

461

b. Dryden found his theories hostile but admired his masculine temper, his fire, and the "torrent of his verse."

c. Tennyson's poem "Lucretius" is significant except for its too great dependence upon Jerome.

8. The poem is written in dactylic hexameters (one strong beat followed by two weak accents), and can be dated some time before 55 B.C.

9. The poem has been translated by John Dryden (1692), C. Bailey, H. A. J. Munro, W. E. Leonard, W. H. D. Rouse, Ronald Latham, and L. L. Johnson (1963).

BOOK I (MATTER AND SPACE)

INTRODUCTION:

1. *Lucretius begins with a prayer to Venus,* whom he sees as Nature's creative force. He begs her to inspire and guide him while he explains to mankind the nature of the universe.

Once he has revealed the facts of the scientific laws governing nature and man, human beings will then be freed of their irrational superstitions and fears.

Lucretius reveals his intense love of the natural world. How he loves the mother earth, the oceans, and all the living and breathing creatures inhabiting the earth!

2. *He exhorts Memmius* (Gaius Memmius, his friend) to hearken to his exposition of Epicureanism governed by "true reason."

3. *Praise of Epicurus*: Epicurus (fourth century B.C. Greek philosopher) was the first to give man relief from the dread superstitions and fears showered upon him by his irrational religion, which was succeeding in crushing man to the ground! It was Epicurus, who, with his scientific natural laws, revealed the myths any gods of religion as bogeys. Impious acts are the result of religious fears, such as Agamemnon's brutal slaying of his daughter Iphigenia in order to placate an angry goddess.

4. *Superstition's Cause and Cure*: Because men fear what shall come after death, they pay heed to religion. They are especially

afraid of punishment in the world after death. Knowledge about such matters will spread light over the dark ignorance surrounding such superstitions. All life issues from atomic action, and natural laws will inevitably reveal this.

SIX PRIMARY PROPOSITIONS:

1. *Nothing can ever issue from nothing*: nothing can be created from nothing; neither can nothing be reduced to nothing; this is the first law of the atomic theory of Epicurus.

2. *Nothing is ever annihilated.*

3. *Invisible particles make up matter*: these invisible particles are called *atoms*.

4. *The universe contains, besides matter, empty space, which is called vacuity.*

5. *The Universe = matter plus vacuity*—and nothing else whatsoever.

6. *Every single atom is indestructible!*

The six primary propositions discuss the process of change and the principle of continuity. For example, rain may disappear into the ground, yet rain contributes to the healthy growth of plants. All matter is constantly in a state of change, yet it makes up all life in all its forms. Atoms make up the smallest particles, they are invisible, they are solid, and they contain no void or vacuity within them. All things are made up of these atoms.

REFUTATION OF FALSE THEORIES:

1. *Heraclitus'* theory that all matter consists of a single element is false.

2. *Empedocles* is wrong in his belief that two (or four) separate elements make up everything that exists in the universe.

3. *Anaxagoras* is mistaken in his theory that the component parts of all things are of the very same nature as the thing itself.

TWO MORE PROPOSITIONS:

1. The Universe is boundless and infinite.

2. The Universe does not contain a center as such.

A WORD OF ENCOURAGEMENT:

> "If you take a little trouble, you will attain to a thorough understanding of these truths. For one thing will be illumined by another, and eyeless night will not rob you of your road till you have looked into the heart of nature's darkest mysteries. So surely will facts throw light upon facts."

BOOK II (MOVEMENTS AND SHAPES OF ATOMS)

INTRODUCTION: From a citadel, the philosopher surveys mankind in its struggles. Philosophy can give man shelter and protection from needless suffering. Men are blind to reality because of their false values; they strive for power and wealth instead of knowledge, which is the sole source of peace.

SIX PROPOSITIONS ON THE MOVEMENT OF ATOMS:

1. Atoms are constantly in movement.

2. They move faster than light itself! (Digression: the gods did not make the universe.)

3. Normally, all atoms move in a downward direction.

4. Once in a while they swerve ever so slightly from their vertical downward movement.

5. Atoms have never been any more or less congested than they are now.

6. Matter only seems static and immobile; this is a mere optical illusion.

The swerving of atoms is called *clinamen,* and in their collision with other atoms there is fusion to form living things. Proposition 5 above simply means that matter never increases or decreases. In addition, the endless variety found in nature is owing to the various sizes and shapes of atoms, although the extent in number of these sizes and shapes is limited. Incidentally, smooth atoms render pleasure to our senses, whereas rough atoms yield rough textures and bitter tastes. The same principle holds for other sensations.

SIX PROPOSITIONS ON ATOMIC SHAPE:

1. Properties of different objects are determined by differences in atomic sizes and shapes (see above).

2. The number of atomic shapes is limited but large.

3. The number of atoms with any *one* shape is limitless.

4. All visible objects are simply combinations or compounds of various kinds of atoms.

5. Only certain combinations of atoms can exist.

6. Atoms lack color, sound, heat, taste, and smell; they also lack sentience.

Nature is in a constant state of warfare—a war between creation and destruction. The cry of the new-born child mingles everyday with the wail of the funeral dirge. All things are made up of a variety of atoms, and the earth itself consists of the largest variety of these atoms; thus, the earth is rightfully termed the Mother of all the gods, animals, and men.

The gods do exist; they are immortal; but they dwell apart from man and his concerns and heed not his prayers.

The earth is without sensation (see Proposition 6); hence the phenomena of earth such as the sea, corn, wheat, and wine can be given god's names, but such names are merely symbolic and need give rise neither to fear nor awe. Atoms are solely responsible for the earth's qualities, and nothing else.

Although atoms are colorless (Proposition 6), color itself is a result of the combination, place, and movement of atoms. Atoms themselves are immortal, and when found in certain combinations, the result is life and feeling.

Death of a being does not destroy his atoms of matter but merely disperses them to form other combinations.

THREE GENERAL COROLLARIES:

1. Our world is simply one of an infinite number of worlds.

2. Nature regulates herself: the gods never interfere in her processes.

3. There was a beginning to the world, and there will be an end to it.

Infinite space exists; an infinite number of atoms exist; therefore, other worlds must exist (see Proposition 1). Note Lucretius' insistence that the gods are not concerned with the affairs of men. Proposition 3 above indicates that since all things undergo change and decay, the earth too will undergo destruction—even now it is in a condition of decay!

BOOK III (LIFE AND MIND)

INTRODUCTION: *Tribute to Philosophy*: Epicurean philosophy can offer man shelter and relief from unnecessary suffering and internal and external conflict. The real nature of the Universe was discovered by the great Epicurus, and by that discovery he has offered man hope. The root of all evil is the fear of death, and the fear of what follows death.

SEVEN PROPOSITIONS:

1. The mind is only one section of the body of man; it is not a harmony of the whole body; this is true of the *vital spirit*.

2. Lodged in man's breast is man's mind; his vital spirit is diffused throughout his body; both man's mind and his vital spirit make up a single corporeal substance.

3. This single, corporeal substance is made up of

   a. Wind.

   b. Air.

c. Heat.

d. Mobile fourth element, which is combined with the others in varying proportions

4. Life is dependent upon the joining of mind-spirit with the body.

5. The amount of the mind-spirit in the body is comparatively small.

6. Spirit is under the control of the mind.

7. Spirit and mind both were born, and both will perish.

Man's mind and spirit are really matter, a part of his body, just as man's eyes, feet, and hands are parts of his body (See 1 above).

Man's mind is located right in the middle of his breast; and his spirit (under the direction of his mind) is found everywhere in his body. The mind governs his spirit and the rest of his body. When the mind is affected profoundly, there is a response by the entire body (See 4, 5, 6, and 3 above). Both mind and spirit (spirit = soul) are composed of round, tiny atoms; the very rapid activity of man's mind is due to the movement of these tiny round atoms.

Man's mind and spirit were born when his body was born; and like the body, they shall suffer death: they are not immortal, as indicated in Proposition 7 above.

PROOFS OF THE MORTALITY OF MIND AND SOUL: The mind and soul are one; and since the soul is mortal like the mind, there will be no sensation—nothing after death. Therefore, there is no need to fear death! "If you have had contentment in life, why not withdraw like a well-fed guest from a banquet?" There is no Hell, no Tartarus below. The matter making up the dead body will be used to form other shapes and to create other things.

THE UNDERWORLD: Lucretius denounces the fairy tales about our suffering-to-come in the afterworld. The myths about suffering in Hades are merely symbolic representations of our suffering life here on earth! Fools on earth do indeed live a hell on earth! Only a knowledge of the nature of the universe and its laws can relieve man of his fears and fairly tales.

THE MORAL:

1. Mortality and its blessings.

2. Hell's pains are imaginary and merely symbolic of suffering on earth.

3. Happiness = a cheerful acceptance of man's universal lot as natural law decrees.

The moral propositions are discussed above.

BOOK IV (SENSATION AND SEX)

INTRODUCTION: Lucretius calls himself a pioneer; he recounts his vast enterprise in undertaking this poem. His primary aim is to teach and to please (entertain) at the same time:

> "I am blazing a trail through pathless tracts of the Muses' Pierian realm, where no foot has ever trod before. . . . My object has been to engage your mind with my verses while you gain insight into the nature of the universe."

THE NATURE OF VISION:

1. Visual images = thin films emanating from the surfaces of things and objects.

2. Some images are formed by the combining of films from different objects.

3. These films are emitted and travel very rapidly.

4. When these film-images strike the eye, there is an impact similar to the sense of touch.

5. How mirrors are able to reflect images.

6. Weaknesses and illusions of the vision of man.

7. Sensation is the only foundation possible for obtaining belief, and the weaknesses of vision cannot be used to give the lie to sensation.

THE OTHER SENSES: Hearing, taste, and smell comprise the other senses.

THOUGHT AND WILL:

1. Mental images are flimsier than visual images—only mind-atoms are moved by their impact.

2. When the mind pays special attention to an image, it is then perceived.

3. Our voluntary movements spring from the impact of images of the mind.

4. In sleep, images affect the mind in a certain way.

All knowledge and reason depend upon sense· perception. The human body was not made for a particular purpose; but rather the uses for the various parts of the human body were discovered by the humans themselves. Food and sleep is vital to man; dreams are nothing but the reflection of our everyday activities.

SEX:

1. Sex organs of man and how they are stimulated by images.

2. Our reason is disturbed by the effect of sexual stimuli.

3. There is mutual joy in sex.

4. We are faced with certain problems in the procreative process.

Lucretius advises men to avoid the pain and anguish of excessive sexual passion, which takes away a man's reason and judgment. The enthralled lover is only too often tricked and ensnared by a scheming woman, so much so that he looks upon her faults as virtues; soon he loses his dignity and reason because of his silly, high-powered infatuation. Women are very often false, but there are some who are capable of sincere love and deep feeling. Family characteristics (No. 4 above) can be passed down even from the great-grandfather. Some are faced with sterility in the procreative process.

BOOK V (COSMOLOGY AND SOCIOLOGY)

INTRODUCTION: Epicurus' services to mankind are far greater than those of Hercules. "Therefore that man has a better claim to be called a god whose gospel, broadcast through the length of empires, even now bringing soothing solace to minds of men."

Lucretius then summarizes Books I-IV and gives his outline for Book V. Epicurus has freed men from the dark shades of delusion. No good life is possible without the freedom of mind and spirit. Hence, Epicurus is more divine than many so-called divinities.

NATURE AND FORMATION OF THE WORLD:

1. The world began and it will have an end. The gods did not create the universe and are not even concerned with it at all.

2. The world was created by a conflux of atoms.

3. The nature of heavenly bodies—and their movement.

The gods had no hand in the creation of the universe and therefore are not to be celebrated and praised. The atoms, in their varied combinations and movements, are the source of the creation of the universe—and not the gods!

The elements are *earth, water, air, fire,* and they are subject to life and death—they are mortal; hence, *the universe itself is mortal!* The end of the world will come about as a result of the constant warfare among the four elements.

EMERGENCE OF LIFE:

1. The evolution of animals and plants.

2. Some types disappeared because of their unfitness.

Other types of animals and plants survived the struggle for life because of their superior equipment of strength and cunning. As for the fantastic monsters of myth and fable—that is all nonsense!

DEVELOPMENT OF HUMAN SOCIETY:

1. Primitive man.

2. The social contract.

3. The natural origin of language.

4. The discovery of fire.

5. Of property, law, and government.

6. Superstition—and how it was born in ignorance.

7. The discovery of metals; their use in war.

8. Of costume, agriculture, music, of changing fashions, the reckoning of time, etc.

9. The mother of all progress is experience.

Lucretius traces the development of mankind from his early cave-dwelling days to his present-day role as citizen in a highly developed society.

Next, Lucretius describes how language originated and grew; how fire was discovered; how cities were formed and organized; how law originated and developed.

Then Lucretius tells how man himself—with his growing wealth and power—can find happiness only by a simple way of living and a contented mind. The power- and position-hungry men are not really fulfilling their genuinely true needs and desires; their values are mistaken and false, and they will never achieve content, wisdom, or happiness.

He closes the Book with a discussion of the origin and development of different tools, arts, and crafts.

BOOK VI (METEOROLOGY AND GEOLOGY)

INTRODUCTION: Lucretius again lavishes high praise on Epicurus, the crowning glory of the city of Athens. Again he repeats that knowledge of nature aids in banishing superstition.

CELESTIAL PHENOMENA:

1. Thunder, lightning, and thunderbolts.

2. Waterspouts, clouds, rain, etc.

Lucretius gives a "scientific" explanation of various weather phenomena: thunder, lightning, clouds, storms, hurricanes, the rainbow, snow, etc.

He speaks of the nature of earthquakes and why the sea is always the same size; of volcanoes, and why the Nile floods regularly; why some places are fatal to birds; of the properties of magnets. Like Thucydides (who he is imitating) he gives an account of the Athenian plague in the fifth century.

INTERPRETATION: *ON THE NATURE OF THINGS,* QUESTIONS AND ANSWERS

What is the Latin for "On the Nature of Things?"

ANSWER: *De rerum natura,* the title of Lucretius famous poem in six books, written in the early first century B.C.

Why did Lucretius write this didactic poem?

ANSWER: He wrote it to expound the philosophy of Epicurus, which scientific exposition of the nature of the Universe would be so convincingly true that men's minds would be released from religious superstitions, fears, and myths.

Upon what single principle is the philosophy of Epicurus based?

ANSWER: Epicurean philosophy is based upon the single principle of the infallibility of the senses. Whatever information we receive through our senses is true and must be accepted. When they can give us no information, we are to maintain a view in agreement with the information that is given us by our senses. Our senses give us information only on the subjects of matter and motion; hence, we accept matter as the single reality, and in order that matter may have room to move, we accept the reality of empty space, which is to be thought of as limitless in extent.

What is the nature of Epicurus' atoms?

ANSWER: Our senses can not and do not inform us as to the nature of matter, but, from whatever information they can give us, we can suppose that matter is made up of *atoms.* We are at liberty then to adopt the explanation that matter is composed of these small, indivisible, eternal particles, round-shaped, solid and immortal. There are atoms of different sizes and shapes and weights, and their number is infinite within their quantity of different sizes and shapes. The entire universe, and all it contains, is built out of atoms.

How does Lucretius prove that man is mortal—and therefore subject to decay and death without afterlife?

ANSWER: He proves that man is mortal by first showing that the Universe is composed of atoms; then, if the Universe is composed of atoms and man is part of that Universe—why, then, he too, is composed of atoms. Therefore, like the world and all that is in it, man too is mortal. All things made of matter can be divided into the atoms of which they are composed, and things that are divisible cannot endure forever. When human beings die, their body of matter disintegrates into the atoms of which it is composed.

What happens to the atoms of our disintegrated bodies after death?

ANSWER: The atoms do not perish since they are solid and indivisible—and hence eternal. They merely become separated and may fuse together again to form new bodies.

What about man's immortal soul?

ANSWER: Our soul, like our bodies, is also made up of atoms, and therefore subject to decay and death, although the atoms of which the soul is made up can be used to fuse together to shape other souls.

Does Lucretius reject the idea of a future life? Discuss.

ANSWER: Since our souls do not survive death, Lucretius rejects the idea of a future life. We gain much in the loss of such a concept because we can free our minds of those fears of torture and punishment in the other world, which fears have been planted within us by religion. Certainly, such punishments are mere superstitions. Nor does the idea of death bring many any loss, since after death we can neither desire nor miss the good things of life. Death, therefore, is as nothing to us. When it exists, we cease to exist. The two cannot exist together.

What is Lucretius' attitude toward belief in the gods?

ANSWER: We need not fear the gods; fear of the gods is as futile and empty as fear of death and punishment in Hades. The gods *do* exist, true, but they dwell in the "interspaces" between the worlds, where their bodies are being constantly renewed by the atom streams in such a way that they are immortal. But the gods have absolutely no interest in man, and any attempt to win their favor by being devout and pious is futile. It is just as futile to believe they are angry at man's sinfulness and crimes. The gods live in peace and quiet, lost in the contemplation of their own joy and happiness.

Is Lucretius substituting a greater tyranny than belief in gods— that of scientific determinism? Discuss.

ANSWER: No, this is not true. Since our senses never deceive us, we feel free, and therefore we *are* free. In addition, we can see that this is even so in the world of atoms and empty space:

1. We can assume that within the atoms themselves there is a tendency to swerve, making their exact movements unpredictable.

2. It is this element which gives man *free will*, and explains the nature of *chance* in inorganic matter; this also accounts for the origin of different things, for it tells us how the atoms in space were able to collide in empty space, and through collision formed the universe.

Which way of life does Lucretius then advocate?

ANSWER: Man is free from determinism and the gods, and is now ready to establish the proper way of life.

1. Our feelings always tell us that pain is evil and pleasure is good.

2. We will therefore conduct our lives in such a way as to extract the maximum amount of pleasure from it.

3. But when seeking pleasure, we must not involve ourselves in pain, whenever possible. All over-indulgence will be avoided, since pain follows a superfluity of rich foods. We will eat plain

foods in quantity just large enough to satisfy our hunger and keep us healthy.

4. In all other things concerning the body, we will behave in the same way: absence of pain is more important to well-being than active pleasure.

5. We also desire peace of mind and soul, and therefore we will avoid all those situations in life which are most likely to disturb and destroy our peace of mind and soul. We will take no part in politics and we will not marry; but we will form friendships with persons like ourselves. Friendship is better than love in obtaining pleasure from life, for love binds us too closely to life.

6. We will study nature in order to free our minds of religious fears and superstitions. For by learning about the nature of the universe, we can attain *ataraxia,* which is the tranquility of soul and absence of mental pain, which will be a state of happiness.

What proof is omitted in Epicurus' theory?

ANSWER: Proof for the infallibility of sense perception, which is the fundamental concept in Epicureanism.

Does Lucretius meet the problem of evil directly and convincingly?

ANSWER: No. Lucretius does not meet the problems of real pain—evil in general—too convincingly.

Is Lucretius' poem "mere honey to sweeten bitter medicine?"

ANSWER: It is more than that. It is the greatest and most beautiful didactic poem in antiquity; some go so far as to say that it is the world's greatest masterpiece of poetic didacticism.

CATULLUS

INTRODUCTION: Gaius Valerius Catullus was a Roman poet born in the town of Verona around 84 B.C. His wealthy family was able to give him an excellent education.

At the age of 22 he left for Rome and joined there a group of influential political and social luminaries. For example, Julius Caesar himself was a good friend of Catullus' father. An interesting insight into Caesar's genial and friendly nature is seen at the continuation of that friendship despite some bitter attacks against Caesar in the poetry of young Catullus.

CLODIA (LESBIA): Apuleius says in his *Apologia* that the wife of Q. Caecilius Metellus (sister of Publius Clodius), whose name was Clodia, was the person whom Catullus calls Lesbia in his great and moving love poetry. To this day there are still some strong doubts that Clodia and Lesbia are the same, in spite of Apuleius' assertions.

Catullus' love poems tell us that there was first a period of happiness between Lesbia and himself, only to be followed soon after by his intense bitterness and despair at her rejection of his love and her infidelity.

Henceforth, the love poems indicate that his love has turned into an obsession for Lesbia; we see a continuing attempt of Catullus to free himself from this deep infatuation and despair.

BITHYNIA: In 57 B.C. Catullus went to Bithynia to join the staff of the Roman governor of that province, Gaius Memmius. On his way there he visited his brother's grave near Troy. The emotional grief of that visit is recorded in his lovely elegy Number 101. It was not long after his return to Rome that he died in 54 B.C. when he was about thirty years of age.

ESTIMATE OF CATULLUS:

1. Catullus is a highly personal poet, unlike most of the ancient poets. He is veritably unique in his deep personal kind of lyricism.

2. His poems to Lesbia show varying degrees of joy, sorrow, de-

light, and despair, although there is no way of knowing whether these moods are based on his actual experiences.

3. Catullus imitated the Greek poetess, Sappho, in style and meter, and, like her, he was able to speak sincerely of his powerful feelings.

4. Much of his poetry contains learned allusions, but they (through some mysterious alchemy) serve to *intensify* feeling and personal expression, not to destroy them.

5. Catullus transforms the popular light, sophisticated society verse (*vers de société*) of his time into the genuine stuff of poetry.

6. Most of the poems are short in length, but in a few lines Catullus is able to recreate the experience or feeling in a completely genuine and convincing manner.

7. He did write some longer poems:

   a. Two great marriage songs.

   b. An emotional poem on the story of Attis.

   c. A little epic (*epyllion*) on the marriage of Peleus and Thetis.

   d. A poem on the lock of Berenice (a translation of Callimachus' Greek poem).

HIS INFLUENCE: Catullus' love poetry is the greatest of its kind in the ancient world, and his influence is shown in the work of the Roman poets Tibullus, Propertius, Horace, and Ovid. Renaissance and seventeenth century poets (such as Ben Jonson and Robert Herrick) tried to imitate Catullus in English, but they were not able to discover the secret of Catullus' brilliant passion and intense spontaneity.

THE POEMS

1. Catullus' poems are in varied meters, from dactylic hexameter to galliambic.

2. He is popular in English translation, such authors as Hugh

Macnaghyen, F. W. Cornish, F. A. Wright, Horace Gregory, and Roy A. Swanson · trying (with more or less success) to capture the essence of the verse in their various renderings.

THE POEMS TO LESBIA: The Lesbia poems deal with the following:

1. His intense love for her.

2. His inability to forget and renounce his love.

3. His bitter anger at the news of her infidelity to him.

4. His determination to keep his sanity despite his profound infatuation and dark despair.

5. These poems contain deep, intense feeling, sincerity and immediacy, equalled only by Sappho herself.

LESBIA CYCLE:

Number 51: (Adapted from Sappho). In vivid detail Catullus describes how the presence of Lesbia affects him physically. The form is Sapphic and the feeling intensely personal. He adds a last stanza of warning:

"This languid madness destroys you, Catullus,
  Long day and night shall be desolate, broken,
  As long ago ancient kings and rich cities
  Fell into ruin."

                        (Horace Gregory)

        Catullus tells how his senses are "lost and confounded" at the "fall of her sweet laughter," and how his body sinks into "swift dissolution" when she rises before him.

Number 5: These are intensely passionate lines pleading with Lesbia that they go on living and loving—and to hell with the criticisms of other people:

"Let us live, O my Lesbia, and go on loving!
  As for gabble of graybeards, stern, reproving,
  Mark them down to a cent for all their scorning!"

                        (Asa M. Hughes)

Number 7: Catullus tells Lesbia that he will be satisfied with kisses as numberless as the sands of the desert and the stars in the sky. In this way no evil-minded on-looker will be able to count the number of the kisses and with his evil eye try to impair their bliss.

Number 3: Catullus' elegy on Lesbia's pet sparrow is charming and beautiful. Lesbia's favorite bird is dead and has passed the gloomy "bourne/From whence he never can return." Cursed be that devouring grave, for now Lesbia's eyes overflow, "Her swollen cheeks with weeping glow."

Number 43: Catullus addresses "Madame, whose nose is not of the smallest, whose foot is unshapely, whose fingers are too short, whose mouth is over-moist, whose speech is without elegance." He gives her greetings and wonders how she can be celebrated for her beauty. "Our Lesbia is compared with you? O stupid and undiscerning age!"

Number 8: Here his tone changes. Catullus writes as if he is being addressed by first his rational side, and then by his passionate side. He begs himself to stop being a fool, and to give up what has already been lost to him. "Don't trail her,/Don't eat yourself up alive, /Show some spunk, stand up and take it."

> So long, girl. Catullus can take it.
> He won't bother you, he won't be bothered:
> But you'll be, nights.
> What do you want to live for?
> Whom will you see?
> Who'll say you're pretty?
> Who'll give it to you now?
> Whose name will you have?
> Kiss what guy? bite whose lips?
> Come on, Catullus, you can take it."
>
> (Louis Zukofsky)

Number 72: Catullus tells how in the old days Lesbia would rather have him than Jove himself. "I loved you then as the man in the street loves his girl!" But now he understands her, for to him she has become an object of vice. Her desertion has increased his passion, yes, but he loves her "with less consideration."

Number 76:   Catullus prays that he may be rid of the "disease" of his love for Lesbia. He knows that it would be impossible for Lesbia to be faithful to him—all he wants is some peace of mind from this raging fever of love.

Number 85:   Catullus in two lines writes a uniquely bitter and beautiful poem—a poem of sharp anguish:
"At once I hate and love as well."
—"In heaven's name, Catullus, how?"
—"God knows! And yet I feel it now
Here in my heart: the whole of hell."
                              (M. H. Tattersall)

Number 11:   Furius and Aurelius, Catullus's comrades, are to take a little "bulletin" to his girl friend—brief but not sweet. "Let her live and thrive with her fornicators, Of whom she hugs three hundred in an evening, With no true love for any," leaving them exhausted. Anyway, she need not look for Catullus's love, since it has died through her own fault "like a tumbling flower at the edge of the field" after the passing scythe had clipped and abandoned it.

POEMS OF FRIENDSHIP: These poems are lighter in mood than the Lesbia poems, but they are full of warmth and sensitivity, the very qualities that made him so gullible a victim of the tricky Lesbia.

Number 13:   He invites his friend Fabullus to dinner at his house. He tells him to bring his own food, a fair girl, wine, and "merry laughter." Catullus' purse has gathered cobwebs, but he'll give his love to his friend, but what is even rarer, he'll give him an unguent, one whiff of which will cause Fabullus to turn straightaway into all nose!

Number 50:   Catullus addresses his friend Calvus. It tells of an evening they had spent together improvising different verses. Calvus has so inspired Catullus that he has written a poem as a result. Catullus begs his friend to read the poem immediately.

OCCASIONAL POEMS:

Number 101: This elegy to his dead brother is immensely and deeply personal. He bids farewell to his dead brother in the grave and accepts sadly the inevitability of Death, "and take into eternity my hail and my farewell."

Number 49: To Cicero, whom Catullus calls the most eloquent of all the Romans "past, present, or to be," Catullus sends thanks from the "poorest of bards" as Cicero is "first in eloquence divine."

EPITHALAMIA (MARRIAGE SONGS):

Number 61: Written to celebrate the marriage of Manlius Torquatus and Junia Aurunculeia. The speaker hails Hymen (the god of marriage): "O Hyménaean Hymen. O Hymen Hymenaéan!" Marriage with its joys and blisses is celebrated, the bride is praised for her beauty, the future children are envisioned ("I wish to see a small Torquatus stretching his little hands toward me out of his mother's lap, to see him sweetly smiling at his papa, his baby mouth falling open."). The poem (a long one) closes with the closing of the doors of the bridal room, and an urging for the two newlyweds to make the "most of your dear delight while you are young and still able."

Number 62: This is arranged for two choruses to be divided between young men and young women. The men celebrate the Evening Star (Hesperus) and marriage, while the young women fearfully sing of the loss of virginity.

LONG POEMS: (OCCASIONAL):

Number 63: The tragic story of Attis who had emasculated himself.

Number 64: The marriage of Peleus and Thetis; and the story within the story is that of Theseus and Ariadne.

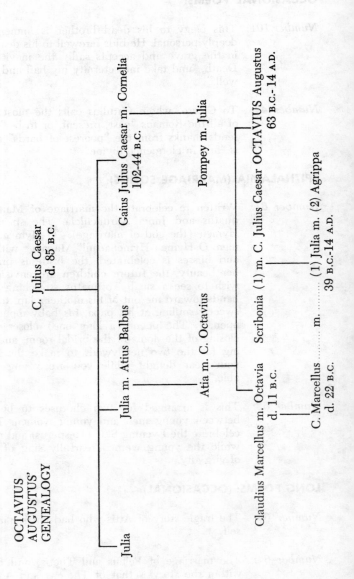

VIRGIL

AENEID

OCTAVIUS
AUGUSTUS'
GENEALOGY

C. Julius Caesar
d. 85 B.C.

Gaius Julius Caesar m. Cornelia
102-44 B.C.

Pompey m. Julia

Julia m. Atius Balbus

Atia m. C. Octavius

Scribonia (1) m. C. Julius Caesar OCTAVIUS Augustus
63 B.C.- 14 A.D.

Julia

Claudius Marcellus m. Octavia
d. 11 B.C.

(1) Julia m. (2) Agrippa
39 B.C.-14 A.D.

C. Marcellus .... m. .... m. ....
d. 22 B.C.

INTRODUCTION: The *Aeneid* is an epic. Webster's dictionary defines *epic* as follows:

> "A long narrative poem about the deeds of a traditional or historical hero or heroes of high station, such as the *Iliad* or *Odyssey*, with a background of warfare and the supernatural, a dignified style, and certain formal characteristics of structure (beginning in the middle of the story, catalogue passages, invocation of the muse, etc.)."

It is important to keep these points in mind in reading the *Aeneid*, but if we expect an exciting fulfillment of the first part of the definition, we shall be disappointed. The actual plot of the poem is weak. In fact, if the gods and goddesses did not interfere all the time, there would barely be any plot at all. Aeneas, the son of the goddess of love, Venus, and a prince of Troy, Anchises, escapes from the sack of Troy with a loyal group of fugitives. Their destination is Italy. They have a few insignificant adventures, mostly in the form of warnings about what to avoid.

They almost reach Italy but the queen of the gods, Juno, intervenes. She is angry that they have made the trip so easily, and sends a storm which drives them to Africa and the city of Carthage. There the hero meets the queen, Dido, makes love to her, and leaves her, because the king of the gods, Jupiter, tells him he must. He has a destiny: to found Rome. Aeneas obeys and sails for Italy. Dido leaps on her burning funeral pyre, and dies.

The hero, after a short stay in Sicily and a trip to the underworld, eventually arrives in Italy. There the natives are friendly until Juno stirs them up. The fortunes of the ensuing war ebb and flow, but finally Aeneas kills the enemy's champion. There the story ends.

Virgil wrote the *Aeneid* because he was obsessed with the idea of Rome's mission to the world. He wanted to create a work of art to rival the *Iliad* and *Odyssey* of Homer. He was a complex poet, taking as a skeleton the myth of Aeneas (which had existed in various forms for centuries) to convey the thoughts burning within him.

VIRGIL AND HOMER: It is impossible not to compare the *Aeneid* with Homer's two epics. In such a comparison, however, the Aeneid always seems to suffer. This is because so many people think that Virgil's poem tried to be a combination of Homer's two epics, and failed:

1. The hero, Aeneas, does not seem to be made of flesh and blood.

1. Homer's Achilles and Hector are flesh and blood.

2. When we read Homer there is tremendous excitement and thrills, especially on the field of Troy and on the voyages with Odysseus.

2. Aeneas, on the other hand, has really very few true adventures. He sails, he lands somewhere, and talks to someone who warns him about what will happen next. Except for his affair with Dido, and his trip to the underworld, his so-called adventures are quite uneventful.

3. In Homer, the characters are men.

3. In Virgil they are symbols first, and men only second.

This brings us to the important point. The two poets can be compared, as they have been for centuries, and always will be. But if we come to a conclusion which says that the *Iliad* is full of life and vigor and the *Aeneid* is slow and dull, we have totally missed the difference in the aims of the two poets:

1. Homer's main purpose is to tell a story.

1. Virgil's purpose is to show symbolically how Rome achieved her greatness.

2. Homer portrays true-to-life characters.

2. So does Virgil, but Virgil starts from the symbol and molds his characters to fit the symbol. Aeneas is symbolic both of the progress of Rome in history, and of Augustus' rise to the position of leader of the civilized world.

3. Homer's heroes are examples of certain types of human character; but he did not consciously intend to shape them into symbols.

3. Aeneas always acts fully aware of time past and time future, but hardly at all concerned with the present.

4. Achilles and Hector, notwithstanding a sense of tragedy hanging over them, are basically creatures of the present.

We could go on enumerating differences. The point is that because Virgil built his poem on a Greek model, using his own original conception of the symbolic aspects of human character and history, he was able to create a work which not only added hitherto unknown depths to the power of the Latin language, but which appeals to us now as it did to the men of the Renaissance, and always will to future generations.

THE COMPOSITIONS OF THE *AENEID*: Virgil might have begun a rough draft of his epic as early as 30 B.C. We have no way of knowing. But the rest of his life was occupied with the *Aeneid*. In 19 B.C. it was almost finished except for a few half lines and some passages he had not gone over.

That year he planned a trip to Greece and Asia Minor, where he intended to spend at least three years going over the work. He went as far as Athens where the emperor was staying on the last leg of his journey back to Rome. He persuaded Virgil to return to Italy with him. Before leaving Greece, Virgil fell ill. He lived only long enough to reach the Italian port of Brundisium.

His dying wish was to have the poem destroyed because of its poetic imperfections and inconsistencies in the plot. But Augustus ordered it published after Virgil's two literary executors had gone over it.

BRIEF BOOK-BY-BOOK SUMMARY: The poem consists of twelve books, the longest of which is 952 lines, the shortest, 705. The subjects of the books are as follows:

I. The invocation to the muse, the causes of Juno's anger, the wreck of Aeneas' fleet, and the arrival in Carthage where Aeneas meets Dido.

II. Aeneas' tale of the fall of Troy and his escape.

III. The tale of the adventures of the exiles on their voyage from Troy to Italy.

IV. The tragic love of Dido for Aeneas, the Trojan's departure from Africa, and Dido's death.

V. Festival of sports held in Sicily in honor of Aeneas' dead father, Anchises.

VI. Aeneas' visit to the prophetic Sibyl and his journey to the underworld.

VII. Landing in Latium in Italy, and Juno's rousing the native prince, Turnus, to fight the Trojans.

VIII. Aeneas' expedition up the Tiber to find allies in the war; his learning early Italian myths, and the start of the fighting while he is absent.

IX. Expedition of two Trojans, Nisus and Euryalus, to break through the enemy's camp to inform Aeneas of Turnus' attack; the burning of the Trojan ships, and Turnus' magnificent fighting.

X. The unproductive council of the gods; the return of Aeneas, and his search for Turnus whom Juno spirits away from the field of battle.

XI. Truce for both sides to bury their dead; the breaking of the treaty, and the renewal of fighting and the Trojans drive the enemy back within its own city walls.

XII. Encounter of the two champions, Aeneas and Turnus, and Turnus' death.

VIRGIL'S THREE CONCEPTS: Virgil manipulates these characters and events to portray symbolically the whole history of Rome. He sees this history as an incorporation of three separate concepts:

1. The presence of the divine in men because of their ability to think and create lawful society;

2. the idea of heroes with a destiny;

3. the world of historical people and events.

At times he treats these concepts individually; at times they are woven together. It is this unique three-way vision of the poet, this ability to see human character and history symbolically that enables Virgil to be ranked among the greatest poets of the world.

VIRGIL

AENEID: SUMMARY

BOOK I (THE TROJANS REACH CARTHAGE)

INTRODUCTION: The opening eleven lines of the *Aeneid* constitute a brief introduction, in the epic tradition of Homer.

1. Virgil announces that his story will concern the deeds and sufferings of a man (Aeneas, pronounced uh NEE uss) who is driven from Troy by destiny and a sense of divine duty.

2. Aeneas' task is to found the city of Rome, but he is being kept from fulfilling this duty by the anger of the queen of the gods, Juno, the wife of Jupiter.

3. Virgil appeals to the goddess of inspiration, the muse of poetry, to tell him the reasons for Juno's anger and to aid him in his great task of writing the poem.

THE CAUSE OF JUNO'S WRATH: Juno is the patron deity of Carthage, a city located on the coast of Africa. It was founded by settlers from two Phoenician cities in Syria, Tyre and Sidon. (Historically this event took place around 800 B.C.) Since Juno wants Carthage to rule the world, she decides to try keeping the Trojans from reaching their destined shore, Italy. If Rome is never founded, Juno thinks, then Carthage will have no rival; she has heard that if the city of Rome is built, descendants from that city will one day destroy her beloved Carthage.

1. The above is her first reason for her ire at the Trojans.

2. The second reason for her wrath is that she was not selected when the Trojan prince, Alexander (i.e., Paris in Greek), made the famous judgment as to which goddess was the most beautiful. The other two goddesses were Venus, the goddess of beauty and love, and Minerva, goddess of wisdom. Venus was chosen the beauty queen because she bribed Paris with a gift of the fairest mortal in the world, Helen. This choice is known as the "Judgment of Paris."

3. A third reason was that Trojans were descended from Jupiter, who was her husband, and another woman, a mortal.

4. A final reason for Juno's anger was that Ganymede, a member of the royal house of Troy, was selected as the cupbearer of the gods, replacing her daughter Hebe.

After enumerating these reasons for Juno's wrath, Virgil gives the reader a glimpse of the Trojan fleet sailing just beyond Sicily.

JUNO AND AEOLUS (EE oh luss):   We then go back to *Juno,* who decided to call a halt to their happiness. She goes to the king of the winds, *Aeolus,* to ask him to let loose the storm winds which he keeps chained in a cave. Juno is brooding all the while that she, the wife of Jupiter, should be allowed to cause storms if Minerva (Athena in Greek), who was only one of Jupiter's daughters, could cause them. To persuade him, Juno offers Aeolus a beautiful nymph (*Diaopea*). Aeolus consents, and strikes the mountain cave. The winds come shrieking out.

STORM AND LAND: *Aeolus* now releases the shrieking winds from the cave, and the resulting storm causes the destruction of Aeneas' fleet. Many ships of Aeneas' fleet are wrecked but the rest make for the nearest shore (Africa). At long last *Aeneas* and *his friends* reach land, though they do not know that the harbor they have come to is in Africa, quite close to Carthage.

VENUS AND JUPITER: Meanwhile, back among the gods, it is *Venus'* turn to get upset. Aeneas is her son, and it seems to her that *Jupiter* has gone back on his promise to help the Trojans. Tearfully she approaches the king of the gods and reminds him that the Trojans are his chosen people since they are to found the city of Rome. She reproaches him with the fact that another Trojan, Antenor, had found a refuge in the north of Italy, why should not Aeneas, who is his own grandson? Jupiter, smiling at her concern, comforts her with a prophecy of Rome's future greatness, and sends the messenger of the gods, *Mercury* (Hermes in Greek), to the Carthaginians. He persuades them to be hospitable to the Trojans.

DIDO'S STORY: The next morning *Aeneas* sets out to investigate his whereabouts and meets his mother (*Venus*) disguised as a huntress. He does not recognize her, though he is fairly sure she is not a mortal; upon asking her where he is, Venus tells him that he has landed in Africa near Carthage and that the queen of the country is Dido (DIGH doh). She then relates the story of Dido's flight from Tyre, the murder of her husband Sychaeus by her brother, and Dido's subsequent flight in secret. After Venus leaves, Aeneas realizes that she was Venus. He tries to keep her from going, but she vanishes after carefully veiling him and *Achates* (uh KAY teez) in an invisible cloud. Concealed in this manner, the two friends set out for Carthage.

CARTHAGE: *Aeneas* and his friend, *Achates,* still hidden in the cloud which Venus had thrown around them, make their way along a path until they finally reach Carthage. The *queen* proves to be a gracious host to a group of men who had made their way to Carthage, and Aeneas, observing this, bursts out of his enveloping cloud of invisibility, begs the gods to reward Dido, the first person to show any pity and love for the Trojans. Dido responds graciously by inviting them all to a banquet at the palace. Immediately Aeneas sends Achates back to the ship to get everyone who was left behind, and especially to fetch his son, Ascanius (ass KAN ee uhss).

THE FALSE ASCANIUS: But *Venus,* who has been keeping an eye on what has been going on and still worried that Juno may try some new trick, decides that, for the Trojans to be really safe, Dido must fall in love with Aeneas.

To accomplish this romance, she commands her son, *Cupid,* to assume the disguise of Ascanius (who is still a small boy); in the meantime she puts the real *Ascanius* to sleep. So *Achates* returns to the city, not with Ascanius, but with Cupid. The false Ascanius first embraces his "father" and then climbs on *Dido's* lap. Poor Dido hasn't a chance!

All during the banquet, and while the various Carthaginian *princes* are singing their ballads, she cannot take her eyes off Aeneas. Finally, she persuades him to tell the story of his adventures during the seven years from the fall of Troy until he landed on the shores of Africa. And with this forecast of the contents of Book II, the first book of the *Aeneid* comes to a close.

INTERPRETATION: *AENEID*, BOOK ONE, QUESTIONS AND ANSWERS

What do we learn of Aeneas' personality in this Book?

ANSWER: We get a good idea of the core of Aeneas' personality:

1. We learn that his personality is to grow and change with the development of the epic.

2. We learn of his sorrowful memory of the events in Troy and his yearning for the past.

3. We learn of his noble spirit looking forward to Rome, shown by his willingness to undergo all trials in order to fulfill the destiny set by the gods; and his human feeling for the sufferings of others.

What do we learn about Dido?

ANSWER: We learn a little about Dido's generosity and her impulsive actions of the heart.

Does Book I introduce the gods in various roles, and if so, what are their specific roles?

ANSWER: We are introduced to the various roles of the gods:

1. *Jupiter,* the unruffled dispenser of law and order.

2. *Juno,* the goddess with unruly emotions, jealousy, anger, passionate love for her chosen people, the Carthaginians.

3. *Venus,* the watchful mother and protectress of Aeneas.

4. *Neptune,* powerful, like his brother Jupiter, but not quite as serene; also on the side of the Trojans.

Which themes are revealed in this Book?

ANSWER: The themes revealed are the following:

1. The greatness and mission of Rome, symbolized by Aeneas, and given special emphasis by the fact that Rome is the last word in the first five introductory lines to the poem.

2. The contrast of violence with order, emotion with self-control, seen in the personalities of the gods and mortals, and even in nature itself.

3. The continuous awareness of the greatness of Homer; Virgil achieves this awareness by subtle references to the *Iliad* or

Odyssey, or by almost word-for-word translations. However, Virgil has a concept of the Homeric tradition which he develops with a more spiritual insight. For Homer's heroes are pretty much *men of the moment* who act as their natures make them, but Virgil's characters always carry with them a *sense of past and future,* acting from duty, the noblest of Roman virtues.

BOOK II (AENEAS' NARRATION—THE SACK OF TROY)

INTRODUCTION: The events of Books II and III are a flashback from Book I; in them Aeneas relates the tragedy of the fall of Troy (II) and the fortunes of the exiles on land and sea after they flee from Troy (III). At the end of the first book we left Aeneas (when the banquet was over) with an audience of Carthaginian nobles, waiting spellbound to hear his tale about the fall of Troy.

THE FALL OF TROY: *Aeneas* tells the tale of how the *Greeks* succeeded in opening the gates of Troy with their clever stratagem of the "wooden-horse trick." In spite of the priest *Laocoön's* warning ("I fear the Greeks, even when they bring gifts!"), the *Trojans* take in the horse as a good omen. Aeneas tells how the Greek *Sinon,* posing as pro-Trojan, persuades the Trojans to take the horse in. He goes on to relate how *two huge serpents* came from the sea and destroyed Laocoön and his *two young sons;* later he tells how the Trojans are led to discredit the truthful prophecies of the unfortunate *Cassandra.* Naturally enough the stratagem works, and in the middle of the night the Greeks, concealed within the wooden horse, issue out to open up the gates of Troy to the invading Greeks. Troy is put to torch and rapine. The king of Troy (*Priam*) and his *wife* are slain.

THE FLIGHT OF AENEAS: It was the horrible sight of Priam's death which brought *Aeneas* up short. He had been filled only with the rage to kill and to get even. But the violent death of the beloved king brought the image of Aeneas' own aged father to his mind. For the first time also he thought of his wife, Creusa, and their son Iulus (otherwise known as Ascanius). But amid all the flames and fighting, Aeneas, under divine protection, made his way safely back to his own home. At first his aged *father* refused to be rescued, claiming that he was too old and had lived long enough.

The whole household burst into tears trying to persuade Anchises, but to no avail. Finally Aeneas started to rush off into the fighting again, but *Creusa,* holding up the small son in her arms, begged him at least to let them die with him. But as she spoke a miraculous omen occurred: a tiny flame appeared over *Iulus'* head and set his hair on fire, and yet the holy flames did not burn him, although the anxious mother put them out as quickly as she could.

To the old father, Anchises, however, it was a sign. He resisted the entreaties of his son no longer. Two other omens followed: a thunderbolt and a shooting star. Without wasting any more time, Aeneas took his father on his shoulders and his son by the hand, while Creusa followed behind. Their destination was a small hill outside the city where an ancient temple of Ceres stood.

To prevent Aeneas' pollution of the sacred household images (since he had just come from battle) Anchises was to hold on to them. But the story was not to have such a happy ending. For Aeneas, hearing the sound of pursuing Greeks close at hand, took a few back alleys and shortcuts, arriving at Ceres' temple; but, alas, Creusa was no longer with them.

THE FATE OF CREUSA: Leaving his father and son at the temple, *Aeneas,* totally distraught, retraced his steps back to the burning city, calling loudly for Creusa. There was no answer. Suddenly *Creusa's ghost* appeared and told him it was not the will of the gods that she should go with him. He would find a royal wife in Hesperia (Italy) and a fortunate turn of events—even a kingdom. Her last words were to take care of their child. Aeneas tried to put his arms around her but she vanished; and so there was nothing else for him to do but to go back to his father and son and the other *Trojans* who had gathered with them. Thus Aeneas shouldered his burden of leadership, and the exiles departed.

INTERPRETATION: *AENEID*, BOOK II, QUESTIONS AND ANSWERS

Discuss the use of swift change of mood in the last passages of this book.

ANSWER: In the last passage we see one of Virgil's most important poetic effects, the swift change of mood. Up to the death of Priam we have been conscious only of the glory of war. Even the burning city is something splendid. But after the brutal slaying of the king of Troy, we become conscious only of the horror of war. It is this sense of horror that forces Aeneas to surrender himself to his destiny, which was first foretold him by Hector in the dream and later repeated by the ghost of his wife Creusa. Aeneas has thus changed from a Homeric hero living almost entirely in the present, to a Virgilian hero constantly aware both of past and future.

What are two important functions of Book II?

ANSWER: The two important functions are the following:

1. Virgil reveals his ability to create scenes that are immediately visible to the imagination of the reader. We are consistently aware of the turmoil of battle and the determination of the warriors.

2. The second function of the book is to make the reader realize what a horrible memory it is that Aeneas has to carry with him on his long journey to found a new city. The fierce heat of the flames, the screams, the lost wife, the king slaughtered in the still warm blood of his son—all these are ever present in Aeneas' mind. No wonder the process of forgetting takes so long! The ability to lay aside these memories, and his courage and dedication to go on to build a city with a mighty future, makes Aeneas a hero.

BOOK III (AENEAS' NARRATION CONTINUED—HIS TRAVELS)

INTRODUCTION: Book III continues the flashback begun in Book II. Aeneas is still relating the story of what had happened after the collapse of Troy.

POLYDORUS: By early summer *Aeneas* and the few *men* who had managed to escape the burning city had constructed a fleet. (In ancient times no one ever sailed directly across an open body of water if it were possible to sail close to the coast.) So the first place they landed at was Thrace, which had long been friendly to Troy. There Aeneas founded a city called Aeneadae. But as he was about to sacrifice to Venus (he was starting to pull up some saplings of myrtle to garland the altar) blood seemed to drip from the bark. Then came a moan and a voice asking why was he disturbing the grave of *Polydorus* (pall ih DORE uss), who had been sent by his father Priam (king of Troy) to the king of Thrace. When Agamemnon had conquered and the power of Troy was no longer great, the Thracian king had slain Polydorus. Because of such a dreadful omen, it was quite obvious to Aeneas that they could not stay where they were any longer. After performing new funeral rites to quiet the unhappy ghost, the Trojan exiles took to their ships again.

DELOS: The next shore they reached was the island of Delos, birthplace of Apollo and Diana. There the king, *Anius,* welcomed them. Here *Aeneas* sought the advice of Apollo's *oracle.* As was usual, the oracle's answer was not very clear: He has to seek out the land from which their race had originally sprung. *Anchises* assumed that this meant Crete because there was a Mount Ida on Crete as well as near Troy. Legend also said that Teucer, the founder of the Trojan race, came from Crete to Troy. Joyfully, the Trojans left Delos and with a following breeze they soon sighted the coast of Crete.

PERGAMUM: A second time they set to work to build a city. This time they named it Pergamum after the inner citadel of Troy. But misfortune was not far off. A dreadful disease attacked both men and crops, accompanied by a scorching drought. *Anchises* advised them to return to Delos and obtain another oracle.

THE STROPHADIC HARPIES: Again they set sail, and after a storm which lasted three days and nights they sighted land: the two islands of the Strophades in the Ionian Sea, west of Greece.

Bad luck was to be followed by worse, for these islands were inhabited by winged creatures with women's faces, known as Harpies. Whatever they touched became unclean. Thus, when *Aeneas* and his famished *followers* killed some of the goats and cattle they found feeding on the grass (they probably had little if anything to eat during the three-day storm and were ravenous) the *Harpies* swooped down contaminating everything, including the sacrifice on the altar. Hastily Aeneas told everyone to try and fight the winged things off. The hideous creatures flew away, but their leader, *Celaeno,* paused on a high cliff to curse them. She cried that they would reach Italy, but they would not build the walls of their city till hunger forced them to devour the very tables on which they ate. Everyone wanted to leave such a horrible place as quickly as possible, so they hastily got underway.

HELENUS: Next the *Trojans* reached Epirus, a place governed by *Helenus,* a Trojan, since the former ruler, the son of Achilles, had already been slain there. Although Hector's *widow* was now queen of the kingdom (originally she had been brought there as a captive), she still mourned for her brave husband, and in his name she gives the exiles a hearty welcome. Just before leaving, Helenus predicted that after many trials they would land in Italy at a spot where they would find a white sow suckling thirty young ones.

In addition he warns Aeneas about the dangers of Charybdis and Scylla, bidding Aeneas to be sure to visit the Cumaean Sibyl and ask for her help. After Helenus had given his advice, he heaped gifts on the travelers, while Andromache (Hector's former wife) gave a scarf of her own to Aeneas' son.

THE CYCLOPS: After narrowly avoiding the fateful whirlpool of *Charybdis,* they are faced with a new danger. They had landed on the coast of Sicily, which was the home of the Cyclops, huge one-eyed giants. Over the whole region towered the mighty volcano, Aetna. After hiding in the woods all night they were startled by the grotesque figure of a young man, all in tatters and wild-looking, who rushed toward them. Grovelling piteously he begged them to take him along. He, *Achaemenides* (ack ee MEEN uh deez), was one of Ulysses' companions who had been left behind when Ulysses had made his escape from the Cyclops, Polyphemus. For three months he had been living off berries and roots. Even if they were to kill him, it would still be better than being eaten by a Cyclops.

POLYPHEMUS: As he spoke, *Polyphemus* (a Cyclop) appeared in the distance. Even though he could not see the Trojans on the shore (Ulysses had put out his one eye), he heard the noise of the oars in the water. He headed for the sound and waded far out into the sea. When the fleet had got just out of reach, Polyphemus let out a roar of anger which summoned all the other *Cyclops* to the shore. They towered raging at the water's edge while the Trojans threw up all sail to escape.

ANCHISES' DEATH: This was their last adventure till they got to Drepanum on the western tip of Sicily because *Achaemenides* had been able to give them helpful information about the Sicilian coast. But *Aeneas* was not to leave Drepanum without suffering another sorrow—the loss of his father *Anchises*—for which he was completely unprepared. It was after leaving Drepanum that the storm arose (the point at which Virgil begins the tale in Book I) which drove them to the shores of Carthage. Aeneas finishes his story at last; the banquet and tale are over.

INTERPRETATION: *AENEID*, BOOK III, QUESTIONS AND ANSWERS

Why are the tales of Aeneas' travels somewhat of a disappointment to the reader?

ANSWER: Although the book is full of names, places, and events similar to those in Homer's *Odyssey*, it still lacks the vigorous flavor of adventure.

1. This is partly due to the fact that oracles always announce what is going to happen ahead of time so that there is little sense of suspense.

2. It is also due to the fact that the gods are removed from any direct action. True, Aeneas consults Apollo's oracle, sacrificing to both Jupiter and Juno; but these gods do not themselves have anything to do with what happens.

3. The apparent function of telling how Aeneas got from Troy to Carthage is the least important reason for the book. Virgil is really more concerned with unhappy recollections of the past (in the persons of Polydorus or Andromache, for instance) and the revelations concerning the future, which take place one after the other, rather than with the adventures themselves.

Why the stress on Homeric things?

ANSWER: The imitations of Homer are vital to Virgil's plan that the Roman tradition be said to have sprung as a direct offshoot of the great epic days of Homer and the heroes.

Identify the "lakes."

ANSWER: The "lakes" were the marshy area around Avernus in southern Italy; this area was thought to be where the entrance into the Lower World was to be found.

BOOK IV (THE TRAGEDY OF DIDO)

INTRODUCTION: We are now back to where we were in Book I; Queen *Dido* is suffering as only those wounded by love can suffer. To her sister *Anna,* Dido confesses that if she had not made up her mind to remain loyal to her long dead husband Sychaeus (sih KEE us), she would be more than willing to yield to this intense emotion she now feels.

THE CAVE: Anna, wanting her sister's happiness and also the welfare of Carthage, says that she thinks Dido has remained a widow long enough. Reminding Dido of the numerous enemies around Carthage, she subtly suggests that marriage with Aeneas would bring glory to the city. Still, Dido "burns" with love. She wanders around the city in a fog of unreality. Once while on a hunt with *Aeneas* and his *exiles* a storm arises in the forest. The rain and hail scatter the group all over the place, and "Dido and the Trojan leader arrive at the same cave" (all foretold by Venus). The only attendants at this sexual "wedding" are the forces of nature. For marriage torches there is only lightning. For the wedding hymn there is the wailing of wood nymphs (for thus Dido thinks of the moaning of the storm-tossed trees). In her mind she sees Juno and mother Earth as divine witnesses of the long-desired event.

RUMOR: To *Dido*, it is a wedding, but to the outside world it is a sin. The evil goddess, *Rumor*, takes care of that. Nothing in the world travels fast as Rumor with her countless eyes, ears and never-silent mouths. Her power is so great that she can strike terror into mighty cities. Sometimes her words are true, but just as often, they are false. Now gleefully she spreads the gossip: Dido and Aeneas are lovers!

MERCURY'S MISSION: When the story reaches *Iarbas,* Dido's rejected suitor, he becomes thoroughly upset. Raising his hands to his father, Jupiter Ammon, he complains that he has been dreadfully misused. It was he who gave Dido the parcel of ground on which to settle, and yet she could spurn him and open her arms to Aeneas. What sort of justice was this? *Jupiter* is moved and sends *Mercury* to do something about the situation. After all, Aeneas was not saved from burning Troy for the arms of a woman.

So Mercury is to remind Aeneas of his destiny and to tell him to set sail at once. And what does he find the great hero doing but building palaces and temples for Carthage! Mercury delivers the message: *Aeneas* is reminded of his duty and mission to found his new realm *in Italy*—not on the shores of Africa!

Aeneas prepares to obey. Slowly but surely all *Dido's* regal pride and self-respect leave her as she sees this energy which indicates that Aeneas is departing. Again and again she tries to get him to change his mind. Finally she goes to her *sister* to beg her to use her influence with him.

ANNA: But *Anna's* words cannot move the heroic greatness of *Aeneas,* anymore than the strong north winds, with all their buffet-

ing, can uproot a mighty oak tree. Still the hero has human qualities; for in spite of all, the scene, which could end with his appearing so cruel, ends with his weeping in sympathy with Anna.

THE PYRE: As *Dido* is tossing on her bed, racked with pain and
indecision, *Aeneas* is snatching his last night's rest on the poop
deck of his ship. Naturally he too dreams: a god, resembling
Mercury, appears, and warns him to set sail at once. Dido plans to
burn their ships before they can get away.

Without wasting a moment Aeneas rouses all his *men,* gives the
order to cut the cables; and they are away, churning up the waters.

When Dido looks out from the watchtower at the first streak of
dawn, she sees the sails white and full in the distance. Cursing herself for her inability to order the Trojans slain, her indecision when
she could have set fire to Aeneas' camp, she calls upon the gods to
hear her evil prophecy:

> "Aeneas will come to an untimely death and lie unburied in
> the sand, and never, never will there be any possibility of
> friendship between the nation that he should found and her
> own kingdom."

These words hurled at heaven bring an end to her irresolution.
She tells her old nurse, *Barce,* to fetch Anna and to make sure that
she is ritually cleansed for the ceremony of burning the great pyre.
The nurse leaves Dido and she, made strong at last with her
dreadful purpose, climbs the funeral pyre. Collapsing on the
bridal bed she reviews the past and begs to be released from her
woes. "I have lived," she says, "and accomplished the course of
life which fortune gave." Before any of the watchers realize what
is happening, she stabs herself and falls back in a faint.

DIDO'S DEATH: Loud wails fill the air. *Anna* comes running. Too
late it dawns on her why the pyre had been built. Scrambling up
she tries frantically to stem the flow of blood, while her robe turns
red. Three times Dido tries to rise up on her elbow. Finally, she
moans in pain, and Juno, pitying her, sends her messenger *Iris*
(the rainbow goddess) to release the soul from the tortured body.
Gently the goddess cuts a few golden hairs from the queen's head
to symbolize her sacrifice to the gods of the underworld. Dido
breathes her last.

INTERPRETATION: *AENEID*, BOOK IV, QUESTIONS AND ANSWERS

What did the storm of nature symbolize in Book I?

ANSWER: It symbolized the many storms in Rome's future, eventually subdued under Augustus, Virgil's great ruler.

How is Book IV a poetic continuity to the storm in Book I?

ANSWER: Book IV, showing poetic continuity to Book I, concerns the storm of man's greatest emotion, love. In this book Virgil is perhaps farthest from Homer. The theme of man attracted to women is barely suggested in Homer. Hector does bid a touching farewell to his wife. Achilles sulks because Agamemnon had stolen his captive princess. Odysseus leaves Calypso, Circe, and Nausicaa; but no tragedy is involved. It is Virgil who has the "humanity" to elevate the deserted woman to the position of a heroine of tragedy.

What is Virgil's conception of love in Book IV?

ANSWER: He conceives of it as a tragic force; and it is the poetry given this conception that aids in making Virgil a timeless poet. We see the suffering of Dido torn between the desires of the heart and the need for self-respect and greatness. We see Aeneas facing the forces of passion, bearing their pain, finally conquering them.

What double-conflict theme runs through the book?

ANSWER: The double conflict is

1. the historical one between Rome and Carthage, hinted at in Book I in the opposing goddesses, Venus and Juno;

2. and the human one. In the sense that Book IV stresses the struggle between the personal happiness and heroic glory, between passion and control, it can be thought of as the climax of the entire epic!

BOOK V (THE FUNERAL GAMES)

INTRODUCTION: Virgil is following Homeric tradition in his "field day" in Book V. In Homer there are funeral games in honor of Patroclus (*Iliad* XXIII, 262 f.). However, the boat race is original with Virgil, as is the later riding exhibition. All the sports have one thing in common: the man least expected to win, wins!

SICILY AGAIN: The flames of *Dido's* funeral pyre cause a glow to spread over the sky, which the fleeing *Trojans* cannot help but see. Everyone is filled with a sense of doom. To deepen their downcast spirits a storm comes up so that the chief helmsman, *Palinurus,* is unable to hold the course for Italy.

The head winds are too strong. He advises *Aeneas,* however, that they can bear off and make for Sicily, which is not too far distant. Aeneas gives his assent since the change of plan will enable him to visit his old friend Acestes. In addition, his father had died on Sicilian shores, so that the island is doubly dear to him.

Acestes, having seen the ships in the distance, is down on the shore to welcome the travelers when they land. The next morning Aeneas announces to everyone that it was a year ago that his father, Anchises, had died. In his honor he has decided to set the day apart for sacrificing and feasting. He also tells them that in nine days he will set up a great field day for sports. Nine days later the sun rises in a cloudless sky, and the Trojans and Sicilians gather together to take part in the sports.

THE GAMES AND RACES:

1. The first contest is a boat race which turns out to be dreadfully tense. *Cloanthus* pulls ahead and is proclaimed victor. Crowned with a green garland of bay leaves he receives his prize, a cloak of purple embroidered with gold. The other three captains get prizes too, so no one's feelings are hurt.

2. Now follow three traditional sports: racing, boxing, and archery. The foot race is exciting because two very close friends take part, *Nisus* and *Euryalus* (you REE uh luss). Nisus is far ahead when he slips on a spot where the heifers had been killed for the sacrifice. But though he cannot get up in time to keep the first place, he thinks of his friend who is third and manages to trip up the number two man, *Salius.* Euryalus wins, but Salius of course is angry at the foul play. To calm everyone, Aeneas gives him a lion's hide as a prize. Even Nisus gets a trophy, since Fortune was responsible for his fall. So he receives a shield Aeneas had captured from a Greek seven years before.

The first prize, a horse with all its trappings, seems hardly interesting at all.

3. The last scheduled event is a horse show put on by young Ascanius and his friends.

THE BURNING OF THE SHIPS: All of a sudden the happy events of the field day are interrupted by horrible news. The ships, hauled up on the beach, are burning. Not only that but the *women*, the very wives of the men participating in sports, had started the blaze. Of course, it is not completely their fault. Juno had sent her messenger Iris down to the women as they sat discontented by the deserted ships. *Iris*, posing as one of the wives, stirred them up to set the ships on fire. The *men* attempt to put the blaze out but succeed in saving only four of the whole fleet—and this possibly because of Jupiter's merciful sending of a rainstorm just in time to prevent utter annihilation of the entire fleet.

THE TROJAN COLONY: That night while *Aeneas* is weighing the pros and cons, his dead *father* appears in a vision. He tells Aeneas to follow the advice of Nautes and when he gets to the Italian shore near Avernus (where the ancients believed there was an entrance to the underworld), he was to let the Sibyl lead him to the lower regions where his father Anchises would be waiting for him. There he would see his entire future revealed to him.

So the next day everyone joins in marking out the site for the new Sicilian city of Acesta.

After nine days of feasting and sacrificing, the time for sad farewells is at hand. Those who chose to stay behind watch the oars of the ships they might have been on, as the small fleet pulls off into the distance.

PALINURUS: Meanwhile *Venus*, on her guard because of Juno's latest trick, goes to *Neptune* to get a guarantee from him that nothing will go wrong this time.

The king of the seas tells her she need not be afraid for her son any more. Only one man will die before the Trojans shall reach Avernus. Having said these words, he rides over the ocean, calming the heavy surf.

Aeneas gives the order to crowd on sail, and *Palinurus* sets the course for Italy.

Poor Palinurus! Though he was completely innocent of any wrong to the gods or to his friends, Neptune had set his eye on him. Disguising himself as one of the Trojans, he approaches the steersman and offers to relieve him at the helm. But Palinurus, loyal to Aeneas as always, refuses. The god has no other choice but to make him fall asleep. Moments later he falls overboard.

In spite of this calamity the ship seems to keep on her course for a few more hours as they make for the bay of Cumae (near modern Naples). When Aeneas finally realizes that the ship is drifting aimlessly, he takes over the helm himself, stunned by his dear friend's death by drowning.

INTERPRETATION: AENEID, BOOK V, QUESTIONS AND ANSWERS

Discuss briefly some of the more important significances of the games and sports field day.

ANSWER:

1. The descriptions of the various sports are really quite vivid, though in some places they tend to be too long. The reader does wonder, however, where such an enormous number of prizes came from, especially if he knows anything about the tiny size of ancient ships!

2. But it is important to notice the change that has taken place in Aeneas: he is the onlooker, the director, much more than the participant. Virgil calls him "father Aeneas" (*pater*), much more than he calls him "noble Aeneas" (*pius*).

What decisive moment has arrived in this book?

ANSWER: In the last passages of Book V Aeneas, after one last moment of irresolution, turns decisively to his divine task. Although it had been made quite clear in Book III by Helenus that his new home was to be Italy, Aeneas kept wanting to take the easier paths.

1. First it was Carthage;

2. then it was Sicily,

but always at the moment of greatest trial one of the gods comes to his aid, either by jogging his memory, or else by enlisting the forces of nature on his side.

What would you say is the purpose of Book V?

ANSWER: Although at times the reader feels that Virgil leans a little heavily on Homeric tradition when he inserts the descriptions of the funeral games, most of them are tense little dramas on their own plane. This is especially true of the boat race.

The whole book is necessary for understanding the growth of Aeneas' character. It also show's Virgil's belief that the *divine plays a crucial role in man's life.*

BOOK VI (VISIT TO THE UNDERWORLD)

THE SIBYL: At long last the Trojan *exiles* reach the shores of Italy. The eager adventurers leap ashore to explore, but *Aeneas* heads for the higher ground where there is the temple of Apollo. Nearby is the cave of the *Sibyl,* who is Apollo's prophetess.

HER PROPHECY: From her lips comes a gloomy prophecy:

1. For the Trojans more war, more bloodshed, and

2. Juno's continued hatred, all because of another foreign bride (the first was Helen stolen by Paris).

3. All these he must face more boldly than ever; but from a Greek city will come the first sign of safety.

THE GOLDEN BOUGH: *She* tells him that it is quite easy to get down to the underworld, but very few manage to make it up again, unless they are under the special protection of Jupiter. First he must find the golden branch which Proserpina, the queen of the lower regions, likes so much. If he finds it and can break it off easily, he will know fortune is with him. But he must bury the body of a friend who has died without his knowing it. Then he may try the road to the underworld.

Then he sees *two doves,* the messengers of his mother, Venus, and is filled with joy. They lead him to the mouth of the cave of Avernus, suddenly setting on a tree. There the gold branch shines out, as yellow mistletoe does in winter. Effortlessly Aeneas breaks it off and carries it to the Sibyl. When he has buried the body of his bugler, *Misenus,* who had previously drowned, Aeneas is free to make his way to the underworld.

THE UNDERWORLD: Into the dark, damp, smelly cave *Aeneas* goes. There he and the Sibyl perform ritual sacrifices to the gods of the lower regions. Then, as the sun rises, the earth rumbles with the threat of the volcano. The Sibyl shrieks at the Trojans to get out quickly. Aeneas she commands to unsheathe his sword and follow her. Down they go, through gloomy, ghostly passages. They come to the bank of the river Acheron.

CHARON: *Crowds* of men and women, boys and girls are standing at the river's edge, begging the hideous ferryman, *Charon* (CARE on), to take them across. Bewildered, *Aeneas* asks his *guide* what is happening. She tells him that all the people trying to get over the river are the unburied dead. Charon cannot take them across until they have been given a proper funeral, their ashes covered with earth. Only after they have wandered back and forth for a hundred years can Charon take them. Aeneas looks at them again with great pity.

Going farther, Aeneas finds several of his drowned companions, among them *Palinurus,* the faithful helmsman. He implores Aeneas to at least perform the ritual of throwing three handfuls of dirt on his corpse so that his spirit may have rest; or perhaps to take him back with him to the upper world. The Sibyl scolds him for trying to change the laws of heaven, but gives him one consolation. The people living along the coast, near where Palinurus' body was thought to have been washed up, will build his tomb and name the promontory after him.

DIDO: On the other side, the monster dog, *Cerberus* (SIR bur uss), snarls menacingly. To him the *Sibyl* throws a cake made of honey and sleep-inducing herbs. The dog promptly falls asleep while *Aeneas* enters the gate it had been guarding. The terrible wailing of new-born babies who had died almost at birth, the moaning of suicides and unhappy lovers, meet their ears. It is here that Aeneas comes upon angry *Dido.* He tries in vain to gain her understanding and forgiveness, for her grief is more than he can bear. His explanation (that it was the decree of the gods which had forced him to leave her) fails completely to soften her anger. Keeping her eyes on the ground and without changing her expression at all, she slowly walks away. The great hero can not keep back his tears.

THE ELYSIAN FIELDS: At long last the gruesome journey nears its end. The *hero* and his *guide* reach the archway that opens onto the Elysian fields. At the entrance Aeneas sprinkles his body with water for purification and plants the golden bough. Here is "the joyful land, the pleasant grassy spots, the happy abodes of the blessed groves." Tears spring to *Anchises'* eyes at the sight of his son Aeneas.

ANCHISES' PROPHECIES: *Anchises* leads his son to a rise of ground from which all the people waiting to go to earth can clearly be seen. Then, with ever-mounting pride he points out Aeneas' son, grandson, and descendants who will raise the glory of his line to the very stars.

1. Of those nearest in line to the front, the most famous is *Romulus,* who will found Rome.

2. Off to one side stands *Numa,* the second king of Rome, who will be the author of her religious customs.

3. Beyond him are the other kings: warring *Tullius,* boastful *Ancus Marcius,* and the three Etruscan kings, *Tarquin, Servius Tullius,* and *Tarquin the Proud.*

4. The heroes of the early Republic come next: *Brutus,* who will depose the last king of Rome, Tarquin the Proud, and many others.

5. Anchises traces down the centuries the men who are to make Rome great. There are also the men responsible for the terrible years of civil war and among them *Caesar* and *Pompey.*

6. In another group are those whose victories in war will help the spread of empire. With them are the great men who will defeat the power of Carthage. But at the end of the line there stands a soul greater than all the rest—

7. he is *Caesar Augustus.* Under him the long lost Golden Age will return again to Italy. The wonderful order of his rule will extend even to the stars! There is virtually no end to the glorious array of Rome's heroes.

And the blessings Rome will give to mankind cannot be matched. Others may create more life-like sculpture, may be more clever orators, or wiser astronomers—but "your destiny, oh Roman, is to govern the peoples of the world with order, to plant in them the habit of peace, to spare the conquered, and to crush the proud."

MARCELLUS: But *Anchises* has not quite finished naming the souls when *Aeneas* sees a young man of great beauty with melancholy eyes, and wonders who he is. He is the young *Marcellus* whom Augustus will adopt as his successor. All Rome will love him, but he will die prematurely at the age of twenty. His great promise will come to nothing. Never will there be a greater funeral, or such mourning.

Finally Aeneas takes his leave, his spirit fired with passion for renown. Through the gate of Sleep, which served for the passage of false dreams, the hero and the prophetess make their way. Soon Aeneas is back with his friends. The sail north to Latium is short. "Anchors are cast from the bows; the sterns rest upon the shore."

INTERPRETATION, *AENEID*, BOOK VI, QUESTIONS AND ANSWERS

How does Virgil feel about Rome's mission in the world.

ANSWER: Rome's mission in the world was almost a religion with Virgil. This creed is expressed in the stirring words toward the end of Anchises' speech: *order, peace, mercy, justice;* these were to be Rome's gifts to mankind. This magnificent revelation of Rome's destiny completely fills Aeneas. From this point on he consciously connects his mission with the future of Rome. The memory of his past fades before the hope of his future. The man has truly become the hero.

Compare Virgil's treatment of Aeneas' underworld visit to that of Odysseus in Homer's Odyssey (*Book XI*).

ANSWER:

1. Although there are many passages which are distinct echoes of Ulysses' experiences (such as when he tries to embrace the spirit of his mother, but she, like a shadow or dream, flits out of his grasp), the weird, solemn, and philosophic mood is wholly Virgilian. Ulysses meets heroes and talks to them, but he is neither affected nor changed by what he sees. Aeneas, on the other hand, cannot help feeling pity for the sufferings

of the unhappy souls he meets, and he changes from wavering and anxiety to a possession of heroic spiritual strength.

2. The whole narrative is interwoven with symbolism. The theme of the symbolism is the relation of the world of myth to the world of history.

   Both worlds are controlled by Jupiter, who represents order. Violators of world order suffer eternal punishment (such as the Titans who tried to overthrow Jupiter's rule).

   The theme of the interrelation of myth and history is not only a theme of Book VI but also a central idea of the whole *Aeneid*.

3. However, Virgil expresses it most clearly in the religious and philosophic atmosphere of this book. (It is possible that Virgil also thought of the journey through the underworld as symbolic of the tragedy of life.)

4. The next theme which transcends the simple narrative of the *Odyssey* is the glory of Rome, the theme with which the book closes. In the sense that the *Aeneid* is written to show the symbolic relation of history and myth to glorify Rome, Book VI contains the essence of the whole poem.

BOOK VII (WAR IN LATIUM)

LATIUM: *Aeneas* and his *crew* now set sail again, going past Circe's island, eventually ending up on the Tiber river itself, thanks to Neptune's favorable winds.

ERATO, THE MUSE: The muse Erato is invoked, and we are told of the history of the Latin peoples, a royal race who claim their descent from the god Saturn.

LATINUS: The land of the Latins is ruled by king *Latinus*. Both he and his wife, *Amata*, are getting old, and have no son to inherit the kingdom. Their only child is a girl, *Lavinia*, whose hand is sought in marriage by all the neighboring princes.

Of these the most renowned in valor and war-like deeds is *Turnus*, the young king of the Rutulians. The queen is anxious for Lavinia to marry this eligible suitor, but unfortunately there are numerous oracles and omens which seem to be against the union.

The *travelers* beach their ships and prepare something to eat. They make flat round cakes of cornmeal, on top of which they place the wild fruits they have gathered. It can hardly be called a banquet. In their hunger they eat the tasteless cakes too! All at once Iulus speaks up, almost without thinking: they are eating their own tables! An awed hush falls over everyone as they remember the Harpie's prophecy. Aeneas exclaims,

> "Hail, auspicious land!
> So long from Fate my due!
> All hail, ye Trojan deities,
> To Trojan fortunes true!
> At length we rest, no more to roam.
> Here is our country, here our home."

AMATA AND THE BRIDE: The Trojans discover the capital of the Latins and send to the king an *embassy* of a hundred men. Needless to say, the embassy is very kindly received by *Latinus* himself. Just in time it seems, for the king exclaims that the gods have told him to bestow his daughter to a man from a foreign land —and *Aeneas* is just that man! But Juno, the trouble-maker, works upon the feelings of Lavinia's mother, *Amata,* who promptly flees into the woods along with her *daughter.*

DISCORD: *Juno* then sends the Fury *Allecto* to Turnus' palace, where she appears to him in his dream, taunting him over the loss of Lavinia to a foreigner. The hot-tempered *Turnus* is stirred to war-like activity. All he needs is a pretext—and one is soon supplied.

THE WAR-STARTER: One of the Furies (*Allecto*) stirs *Iulus* (Ascanius) to chase and wound a pet stag belonging to a young shepherdess whose name is *Sylvia.* Her brothers attack the Trojan party with Iulus, who are forced to return the attack; and the war is begun, the peace is violated. As if this were not enough, Allecto hurries back to *Juno.* The goddess sees that Latinus is neutral in his sentiments and forces him to take an active part in the war. This is achieved by causing to open the gates of the temple of Janus (a sign of official declaration of war). All Italy blossoms with armed men.

THE WARRIOR CATALOGUE: The list of warriors is long and awesome. There is the Tuscan, *Mezentius* (the scorner of the gods), and his handsome son, *Lausus.* Next there is *Aventinus, s*on of Hercules, and the twins, *Catillus* and *Coras,* and many, many others.

At last *Turnus* appears, taller by a head than any of the other leaders. On his helmet is that most dreadful of fire-breathing beasts, a chimaera (lion-goat-dragon combination monster). His shield is emblazoned with a picture of Io being changed into a heifer. (Io was the daughter of Inachus, the first king of Argos. Jupiter loved her, but she was changed into a heifer because of Juno's jealousy.) Rank on rank of armed *infantry* follow him. Last of all, the warrior-maiden *Camilla* leads her troop of horse. As she goes by, the wives and mothers stare at her in amazement. Forward they all go to war. Turnus and his allies are ready for action.

INTERPRETATION: *AENEID*, BOOK VII, QUESTIONS AND ANSWERS

Why does Virgil give this catalogue of warriors?

ANSWER: He gives the listing for two reasons:

1. One is in deference to Homer's catalogue of ships (*Iliad*, Book II, 484 ff.).

2. The other is to give a feeling of buildup toward a frightful war. Juno, as always, stands as the symbol of the unleashed passion involved in battle. It is important to notice that most of the Italian allies are only half civilized, in contrast to the followers of Aeneas.

What do scholars mean when they term the first six books the "Odyssey half" and the last six books the "Iliad half"?

ANSWER: Book VII begins what is commonly termed the *Iliad half* of the *Aeneid*. The first six books are considered the *Odyssey half*. Virgil thought of it as parallel to Book I, but its development is directly reverse:

1. Book I proceeds out of the violent storm at sea to the peace of Dido's court.

2. Book VII progresses from the tranquil Tiber setting at sunrise to the tumult of war.

Allecto symbolizes the cruel power of the historical world as the storm is the cruel force of the natural world. The contrast between peace at the beginning and war at the end of the book is emphasized because of Virgil's own hatred of war, especially civil war. The whole of Book VII is permeated with the spirit of Allecto, the terrible personification of the unleashed passions of battle.

What are the two moods of Book VII?

ANSWER: The atmosphere of peace and friendship pervades every line of the beginning of the book. Virgil has taken great pains to create this tranquil mood to heighten the contrast with the warlike mood of the rest of the book.

BOOK VIII (THE FUTURE ROME)

KING EVANDER: *Aeneas* seeks an ally in the person of king *Evander* of Etruria, himself formerly a Greek. While on his way to the king's palace, Aeneas sees a white sow suckling her thirty young piglets. These pigs are then sacrificed to the gods as a sign that Aeneas understands that this will be the very site upon which Rome will be founded. The king without demur grants his gracious assistance in the war, the Etrurian contingent to be commanded by the king's son, Pallas.

Now follows a lavish description of the banquet in honor of Hercules. After the banquet, while Aeneas is asleep, *Venus* persuades *Vulcan* (the blacksmith of the Olympian gods, and Venus' husband) to forge a remarkable suit of armor for her son.

At dawn, all arise and are entertained with Evander's tales of Etrurian customs, while *Pallas* busies himself with the army preparations for battle.

THE ARMOR: *Venus* returns to earth to embrace her *son* and to bring him his newly-forged armor. Never has he seen such glorious armor—it is dazzling, bronze-shining, beautiful! He looks at the fabulous shield. With infinite pains Vulcan had hammered into its surface scenes of Rome's future:

1. His eyes pass over the picture of the wolf, which was to be the foster mother of the twins, Romulus and Remus.

2. Next in order is the story of the Sabine women, carried off to be Roman wives.

3. Then there is a picture of the king of the Sabines, Tatius, and Romulus, making peace.

4. Here Horatius at the bridge is trying to prevent the Etruscans under Lars Porsena from taking over Rome again.

5. Then there is Manlius keeping the Gauls from the Capitoline after the hissing of the sacred geese had awakened him.

6. There are scenes with Rome's enemies suffering in the under-world.

7. In the very center is portrayed the glorious playboy, Antony. In the scene, Augustus and his commander-in-chief, Agrippa, lead the fleet. Just beyond, the ships of Antony and Cleopatra can be seen, fleeing from the battle.

8. All the gods of war are present: Mars, Bellona, and Discord. Venus takes up arms against Minerva; the Egyptian god, Anubis (in his dog-form), attacks Roman Neptune. Pale Cleopatra and the weeping Nile-god are there, and finally Augustus Caesar himself, parading in triumph through the streets of Rome.

9. Then Augustus is seen consecrating all the temples, for his empire now extends to the farthest corners of their world.

Proudly Aeneas raises high (for all to see and admire) the magnificent shield of Rome's future glory!

INTERPRETATION: *AENEID*, BOOK VIII, QUESTIONS AND ANSWERS

What is symbolized by Aeneas' lifting high the shield?

ANSWER: This act symbolizes the fact that the hero has at last become mature enough to bear the destiny of Rome. The end of this book marks the end of the middle third of the poem. It closes with Aeneas lifting high the shield on which Roman history reaches its climax in the victory and triumph of Caesar Augustus, Virgil's contemporary and focus around whom circles the political propaganda of the *Aeneid*.

Contrast Homer and Virgil on shield descriptions.

ANSWER: The description of the shield, the high point to which the book has been leading, comes directly from Homer's description of Achilles' shield (*Iliad* XVIII, 478 ff.). But there the similarity ends. With Virgil every scene is prophetic of Rome's history, while Homer describes the varied occupations of daily life. This points up the differences between the two poets. One writes to glorify a nation, the other to glorify man.

What is the purpose of the Evander episode besides the obvious one of securing an ally?

ANSWER: The Evander episode symbolizes Aeneas' introduction to the customs and religious observances of Italy. It is only by leaving behind forever his Trojan ways that he can become a true ancestor of the Romans.

BOOK IX (SIEGE OF THE ROMANS)

THE SHIP-NYMPHS: War at last! While Aeneas is away, his enemies attack; for *Iris,* Juno's messanger, takes care to inform *Turnus* of the Trojan leader's absence. Then comes the call to arms. The followers of Turnus, inflamed by his fury, with one accord throw flaming pine torches at the unprotected fleet. The mother of Jupiter, *Cybele* (also known as Rhea), sees the smoke, and is alarmed. It was from her favorite mountain side that the pine timbers the Trojans used for their ships came. Surely Jupiter can do something to save her precious trees. Jupiter scolds her gently for trying to change fate, but then promises to change the ships into sea-nymphs. The *Rutulians* are terrified by this awesome change and their horses whinny in fright. Only Turnus is calm. Soon the twilight is pierced by a ring of light from a hundred circling camp fires. The first day of battle is over.

NISUS AND EURYALUS: The besieged *Trojans* are in serious difficulty and gladly accept the proposal of *Nisus* and *Euryalus* to sneak through the lines of the surrounding Rutulians and run for Aeneas to bring help to his besieged brothers.

They steal out of the Trojan camp by dark night, and while threading their way between the sleeping Rutulians, they slay many a foe. But a troop of 300 *horsemen* bear down upon the brave two as they seek to hide in the brush along the road. These warriors are arriving to give aid to Turnus; 300 against two are pretty frightful odds. Fear gets the better of wisdom, and the friends flee in opposite directions. Euryalus, being younger and less experienced, quickly loses his way, doubling back on his tracks without knowing it and is captured. Forming a prayer to Diana under his breath, Nisus dodges from bush to bush ever closer, until he comes upon *Vulcens,* just as he is ready to drive his sword home into Euryalus' body. Two others has Nisus already slain in his search for Vulcens. Now it is Vulcens' turn! As Euryalus rolls over, lifeless, Nisus plunges his sword right through the skull of his friend's slayer. Seconds later Nisus too is killed. The two, inseparable in life, are now together forever. *Turnus,* with the cruelty inspired by war, lifts high on sharp pikes the two heads of the reckless Trojans.

THE BATTLE: Now the piercing notes of battle trumpets rend the air as with ever-increasing force the *Rutulians* redouble the attack.

In front of another part of the wall parades an insolent upstart, *Numanus.* Giving himself airs because he has just married Turnus' younger sister, he shouts all kinds of jibes at *Ascanius:* he mocks him because of his style of clothes, hinting that he cannot be a man if he wears a helmet with ribbons on it, and purple embroidered gowns. Ascanius can stand it no longer, and vowing a steer to Jupiter once a year till death, if the king of the gods will guide his arrow, he takes aim and shoots the proud boaster through the head. Cheers go up from the ranks of the Trojans.

PANDARUS: A group of rash *Trojans* opens thee gates in order to do closer battle with the *Rutulians.* When Rutulians rush madly in, there is general carnage, especially since the war-god Mars is on the side of the Rutulians. Finally *Pandarus,* a tall man in his own right, ventures to take the mighty death-dealing *Turnus* on, only to have his skull split in half by the mighty Turnus. Turnus himself is surrounded by Trojans but escapes capture and sure death by a leap into the Tiber river, armor and all!

INTERPRETATION, *AENEID*, BOOK IX, QUESTIONS AND ANSWERS

In the last scenes of battle what is our impression of Turnus?

ANSWER: There is a horrible fascination in the bloody exploits of Turnus. Though he is the villain representing the demonic fury of battle and the cruelty of war, it is impossible not to admire him.

What are the chief and most pervasive similes in this book?

ANSWER: This is the book of thundering war in which Turnus is the star. It is also the book of wild animal similes: the lion, the wolf, the eagle.

What seems most uncharacteristic of Virgil in this book?

ANSWER: We may wonder how Virgil, a poet of pathos and insight, with seemingly tender sensibilities, could write such bloody battle scenes. And some critics may argue that the scenes lack the vitality and primitive power of Homer. They are still full of tremendous realism, symbolic of the bloodstained pages of Rome's history.

What is Virgil's purpose in showing the horrors of war?

ANSWER: By showing the horrors of war, Virgil makes the strength and glory of the peace which Rome finally brought to the world under Augustus, even greater.

What is the chief theme of the Nisus and Euryalus story?

ANSWER: The Nisus and Euryalus story is one of the most vivid in the entire *Aeneid;* and also one of the most romantic, in the sense that friendship is idealized and exalted at the expense of wisdom and prudence.

What is representative of Turnus, in contrast to Aeneas?

ANSWER: He is a hero no less than Aeneas, yet somehow doomed to tragedy. He represents passion in contrast to Aeneas' self-control in the last half of the Aeneid; in the first half Dido represented passion. But still Turnus possesses the most essential qualities of a hero: beauty, noble birth, youth, and courage. Before going into battle, he faithfully performs the rites due the gods. All this heightens the tragedy of his passionate fury, which is continually illustrated by comparisons with wild animals. And always he is the source of the destructive element with his army.

BOOK X (RELIEF AND BATTLE)

JUPITER'S DILEMMA: Meanwhile on Olympus *Jupiter* becomes very upset at the continued fighting and decides to call a council of the *gods;* for he had commanded that the Trojans and the Rutulians were to be friends. Unfortunately, like so many councils, it accomplishes little more than to give the rival parties a chance to quarrel in public. *Venus* naturally blames the war on Turnus, broadly hinting that Jupiter's wife has had a great deal to do with it. Still, if her grandson Ascanius is spared, she will be satisfied. *Juno* retorts that it isn't her fault if Aeneas attempts to marry someone else's promised bride (Lavinia). Nor was she to blame that the Trojan prince, Paris, carried off Sparta's princess, Helen. It wasn't her fault either that the Trojan war had started in the first place. All the rest of the gods take sides, and the dispute goes from bad to worse. Finally, in disgust, Jupiter throws up his hands, saying that he will take neither side. Whatever happens is in the hands of Fate.

THE BATTLE: Back among mortals, the battle rages fiercely, and the sorely tried *Trojans* begin to lose hope. But unknown to them help is at hand, for *Aeneas* approaches. With him is the small force of Evander and the huge *army* of his Etruscan allies. By daybreak they are in sight of the settlement. A shout of joy rises from the throats of the beleaguered Trojans. Their beloved leader has returned! Strengthened by fresh hope, they fight back fiercely.

HEROIC DEEDS: The heroes on the enemy's side are *Turnus,* of course, and then *Mezentius* and *Lausus*. Their equals on the Trojan side are *Aeneas, Pallas,* and *Iulus* respectively. Nevertheless, the redoubtable Turnus slays Aeneas' beloved Pallas.

TURNUS AND JUNO'S TRICK: News of Pallas' death drives *Aeneas* to his wildest deeds. Left and right he cuts the Rutulians down. Everywhere he looks for Turnus, but the latter is nowhere to be found. This is because Juno has sent *Turnus* on a wild-goose (really wild ghost) chase in order to remove him from meeting Aeneas.

MEZENTIUS: *Mezentius,* the deposed king of Etruria, is widely known for his cruelty. In the encounter between *Aeneas,* and the bloody Mezentius, the latter hurls his spear at Aeneas, but it glances off the hero's shield and kills another. Aeneas in his turn hurls his, and Mezentius is hit in the groin. The Trojan leader while pressing his attack, succeeds in burying his sword up to the hilt in the body of Mezentius' son, Lausus, who is fighting at his father's side. Wild with grief, the father crawls to his feet and manages to pull himself up onto his horse. As the horse paws nervously at the strangely unbalanced weight on his back, Mezentius talks encouragingly to the poor beast. Then charging back to the fight, he calls loudly for Aeneas: "I come, about to die, but first

I carry *these* as gifts." Javelin after javelin he hurls at the wary Aeneas, but his strength wanes while the spears bounce harmlessly off Aeneas' shield.

Finally, Aeneas, tired of waiting and turning round and round, strikes the horse a mighty blow on the head. Unsheathing his sword, Aeneas makes ready to finish off the Etruscan. Waiting only to hear his foe's last request that he be properly buried (this because his own people would refuse to do so), Aeneas plunges the sword through Mezentius' throat.

INTERPRETATION, *AENEID*, BOOK X, QUESTIONS AND ANSWERS

In what way could Fate be the true hero of Book X?

ANSWER: Fate could be the true hero of this book, for neither Jupiter's calm detachment, nor Juno's passionate partisanship can change the outcome of the war. Pallas and Lausus, the noblest of the young men on each side must die; and Juno's spiriting Turnus away has only put off the day of his death, as well she knows.

Describe a Homeric-like incident which has un-Homeric pathos in it.

ANSWER: For a brief period Aeneas is almost a Homeric hero, caught up in the present by the madness of war. But when, at the death of Lausus (Mezentius' son), he thinks of his own beloved son, his own destiny comes to mind, and he is filled with pity for the young life that is to know no future. Thus the book where Fate is the hero ends on a note of genuine pathos.

Contrast the natures of Mezentius and Aeneas during battle.

ANSWER: The passages describing Mezentius offer a splendid portrait, even though he is the hated tyrant of Etruria.

He is compared to a barren crag that resists all the buffets of the storms; to a wild boar which no one dare face; to a lion leaping on a stag; to a whirlwind, and to a giant.

In contrast to him is Aeneas, who seems to have lost the savage ways with which he had fought in the first part of Book X; a special such contrast is seen in his treatment of Lausus for whom he shows such deep compassion.

Describe Turnus' character as he appears in this book.

ANSWER: Turnus is not just a cruel killer; his heroic qualities show forth at their best when he refuses to rob the dead Pallas of more than his sword belt; and when despair comes upon him at the loss of his honor.

BOOK XI (COUNCIL AND BATTLE)

PALLAS' FUNERAL: Both sides have had enough of war. There are so many dead! *Envoys* from Turnus' camp come seeking a truce to bury their dead at the very moment when the Trojans are in the middle of the ceremony in honor of Pallas. Gladly *Aeneas* grants the twelve days truce they seek, and would willingly end the war if he could: it was not of his seeking.

EVANDER'S GRIEF: The news of his son's death reaches the ears of *Evander*. Rumor has flown on ahead; as the Trojans get closer to the city they see a long line of Evander's citizens, carrying flickering torches, winding out to meet them. Stumbling at the head of the group is the old king himself, his face streaked with the tears bewailing the cruelty of fate. He falls prostrate on the bier, moaning that life has no more meaning. All he wants are vengeance for his son Pallas and his own death.

All over the fields, smoke from the countless funeral pyres rises toward the sky. Latins, Rutulians, Trojans, made allies by death as they can not be in life, mourn their dead.

THE DISRUPTED COUNCIL: Into the midst of the Council, where there only seems to be disagreement, a *messenger* dashes to say that the Trojans are advancing with their Etruscan allies. This is the chance *Turnus* has been looking for. Ironically he asks the assembled group whether they are going to sit quietly talking peace while their city is being invaded by the enemy. In a flash the council chamber is empty.

CAMILLA: *Turnus*, glad for action at last, charges out the gate like a powerful stallion bursting from the imprisonment of his stall, who heads for the open pasture, neighing in wanton joy. The warrior maiden, *Camilla*, gallops to meet him, suggesting that he stay by the walls to guard the city while she and her Volscian *cavalry* engage the light-armed horse of Aeneas and the Etruscans. Turnus decides to let her face the cavalry while he goes to ambush the infantry as they come through a narrow pass. He is full of admiration for Camilla, as well he might be: she had been hardened to war from infancy. While an infant she was fed wild mare's milk, her first playthings being weapons of war.

CAMILLA IN BATTLE: The battle is on again. Into the heart of the fighting rides *Camilla*, one breast bare, wielding her battle-ax, and shooting arrows even in retreat. She is more than the equal of any Amazon, or even the most famous of Amazonian queens, Hippolyta. Many a Trojan bites the dust because of her faultless aim. As Camilla recklessly pursues a Trojan priest, the young Etruscan warrior *Arruns* stalks her stealthily, praying all the while to Apollo. Suddenly she raises her arm to throw the spear, but Arruns hurls his first, catching her unguarded with uplifted arm. And while the Etruscan, flushed with victory, loses his head and runs from the scene, the warrior maiden vainly tries to pull the spear out; but the barb has gone too deep. Just before she topples lifeless from her horse, she gasps out a last message to her *sister* to tell Turnus what has happened. He must return and defend Laurentum. With Camilla dead, the Latin cause is lost. A handmaid of the goddess Diana, *Opis*, slays Arruns in revenge for his slaying of the virginal devotee Camilla. Night falls, but not before *Aeneas* and his *troops* have entered the unguarded pass—the die is cast—the next sun will see a confrontation between Turnus and Aeneas.

INTERPRETATION: *AENEID*, BOOK XI, QUESTIONS AND ANSWERS

What does Camilla symbolize in the battle passages of this book?

ANSWER: In the battle passages Camilla seems to personify the bright aspect of war, even as Turnus symbolizes the crueler aspects. The description of Camilla and her cavalry is completely original with Virgil, considered by many to be his best battle scenes.

Discuss the tempo of action in this book.

ANSWER: This book leaves the reader almost breathless. It starts with the slow sad dignity of the funeral procession, and ends with the mad, headlong flight of the remnant of the Rutulian army and the massacre at the gates, while the Rutulians crowd upon one another in their panic to escape the Trojans.

Like a bright flash of light, Camilla appears in the last section, pointing up the way Virgil was torn between the tragic bitterness of war in real life, and the shining glamor of war as myth.

Where does Virgil show how he is affected by the savagery and bitterness of war?

ANSWER: The moving description of the funeral for Pallas in the first part of the book show how deeply Aeneas (and thus Virgil) was affected by the bitterness of war. Aeneas' sensitivity to tragedy at the beginning of the passage is in sharp contrast to Turnus' love of glory, whatever the cost.

Describe the "spear-cast" of Metabus.

ANSWER: When Camilla's father, Metabus, was driven by the enemy from his city, he took with him in his flight his baby daughter. Unable to swim the flooded river encumbered by the child, he tied her to the middle of his spear-shaft and hurled it across, plunging in and swimming over just in time to save her.

BOOK XII (THE DEATH OF TURNUS)

SINGLE COMBAT: *Turnus* now is the only hope. Only through him can Laurentum be saved. *Turnus'* wound still offers him great pain. He entreats king *Latinus,* with mounting impatience, to set up the agreement that he and Aeneas may contend for their countries' honor, and for victory, in single combat. But Latinus is still for appeasement.

AMATA AND LAVINIA: Turnus' loving *mother,* however, intrudes in an emotional outburst: he must not fight in single combat with the terrible Aeneas, for if he dies she will kill herself. Beautiful *Lavinia,* too, adds her tears to those of his mother. *Turnus* is appalled at the scene they are making. Tears are no fit accompaniment for a hero going into battle! Paying no heed to anyone, he summons his beautiful white horse, dons his armor, picks up the sword that Vulcan (the forge-god of Olympus) made for him, and seizes his spear, all with the grim frenzy with which a bull prepares to attack a tree trunk. At the same time *Aeneas* makes equal preparations, rejoicing in his heart that the war is to be settled by single combat.

THE COMPACT BROKEN: *One* of the Rutulians casts a spear at the opposite side, and a wild free-for-all begins. The hail of javelins, spears, and arrows is deadly. The solemn treaty, only minutes old, is worthless, king *Latinus* himself fleeing in despair. In the center of the chaos stands *Aeneas,* bare-headed, shouting, in the vain attempt to get himself heard; that they must remember the treaty contracting for single-combat only to settle the issue. But in a flash, an arrow from an unknown bow hits him in the knee. The hero becomes a martyr for the sake of law and order. With Venus' help, however, the wound is quickly healed. Aeneas now turns his energies to the walls and the high tower of Laurentum. Urging his soldiers on by the well-worn phrase that Jupiter is on their side; and determining to wait no longer for Turnus, he leads them with one accord in wedge formation up to the walls. Fires break out in a hundred different places at once. Scaling ladders are thrown up; the guards at the gates are cut down; clouds of smoke billow higher and higher. Poor queen *Amata* (Turnus' mother), thinking that the city is completely in the hands of her enemies and that Turnus is already dead, hangs herself in despair. The city resounds with the wailing of women.

JUPITER INTERVENES: *Jupiter* ceases to be a spectator; he forbids *Juno* (for her power is pitted against Fate) from meddling any more: "Is it not enough for you that you drove the Trojans over the sea, wrecked them on the shores of Carthage, and started this terrible war? What greater signs of power do you need, anyway?" Juno must admit that Jupiter is right. And seeing that Turnus and his side are doomed she asks that the two sides become united under the Latin name and that the descendants be Romans, possessing the primitive strength of Italy. Let the name of Troy fall into oblivion. Jupiter promises that this wish shall be fulfilled. Juno is content, her wrath appeased at last.

THE GREAT DUEL: Now the end is near and both champions know it. They taunt each other with angry words, but *Turnus* says that it is not *Aeneas* who terrifies him, but the gods, for Jupiter is his enemy. The full realization of the truth of these words seems almost to paralyze him. He picks up a huge stone to heave at Aeneas but the throw is wild and comes nowhere near the hero. Losing his senses he runs back and forth looking for a way to escape, while Aeneas, choosing the right moment, hurls his spear like a shot from a catapult. Its head sinks deep into Turnus' thigh, and he falls to the ground.

A mighty groan comes from the lips of the *Rutulians,* so loud that the whole hillside resounds with the echo. Not a sound comes from the *Trojan.* Turnus' last words are not a prayer for mercy but rather an admission of his guilt: "I have deserved this. You have conquered; Lavinia is your wife." With these words he repeats the terms of the treaty. Half-heartedly he pleads for his life, which Aeneas is ready to spare until he catches sight of the swordbelt of Pallas which Turnus has worn ever since he had killed the young man. Revenge and grief well up in the heart of Aeneas. Deep into the breast of his foe Aeneas plunges his sword and "with a groan, life fled to the underworld." End of the *Aeneid.*

INTERPRETATION: *AENEID,* BOOK XII, QUESTIONS AND ANSWERS

What are Virgil's three purposes in Book XII?

ANSWER: Book XII has three purposes:

1. *To complete the picture of Turnus' character.* This is accomplished by the many great similes used for comparative purposes: He is compared to a slightly wounded lion, ready to attack the hunters; then to a bellowing bull, charging a tree trunk (this indicates his nature is noble, but his fighting passion has robbed him of sanity); then to Mars, the very god of war himself, driving his wild, swift horses; then to a plunging landslide (this hints at defeat); lastly, to a stag in terror of hunting dogs and nets.

2. *To give a final understanding of Aeneas.* Aeneas in this book has become almost pure symbol, rather than a flesh-and-blood hero. Even in his similes, such as the one in which he is compared to a threatening storm, we do not see Aeneas the man so much as the psychological effects of his presence; and, above all, he is the personification of the *Roman concepts of justice and order.*

   a. In his speech establishing the treaty he promises to "spare the conquered," but when the truce is broken, he must destroy his enemy to fulfill the mission of crushing the proud.

b. For the sake of justice he is made a martyr, wounded by the unknown arrow, when he attempts to re-establish law and order. It is in this instance that he represents the Roman ideal of waging war only in self-defense. He no longer glories in fighting. It has become a bitter necessity, forced upon him by his obligation to avenge Pallas, which is for Aeneas a duty.

c. He personifies order and civilization also, when he and his disciplined troops attack Latinus' disorganized city.

d. At the end his tragic memory of Troy is gone forever. His personality has become so bound up with Rome's mission that he is the mythological symbol of glory.

3. *To emphasize the glory of Rome.* The triumph of Rome is seen in Aeneas' defeat of Turnus. Aeneas represents the high ideal of Rome's laws and ethics; while Turnus stands for the natural strength of primitive Italy. The terms of the treaty with Latinus —that both nations would live together as equals—and the last wish of Juno—that the Roman race become powerful because of Italian virtue—symbolically express what Virgil firmly believed: that the joining of these two forces, high ideals and primitive strength, in equal measure, is what produced the political and historical greatness of Rome.

HORACE

LIFE (65-8 B.C.)

Horace was born at Venosa (Venusia) in Apulia in 65 B.C. His father, formerly a slave but now a freedman, set out to give his gifted son an excellent (and aristocratic) education—succeeding admirably. Horace was never to forget that his father, though of humble origin, yet strove to give him the best.

PHILIPPI (42 B.C.): While continuing his education in Athens, he was persuaded by Brutus to join his army; unfortunately, the next big battle was the disastrous one at Philippi (32 B.C.), where Brutus' and Cassius' forces were destroyed by the army under Antony and Octavian. Both Brutus and Cassius were killed. Horace chose a less noble end and survived (he said once that he threw away his shield and ran for his life; but "shield-poems" were a vogue, and the story might be a deliberate stereotype).

THE CLERK: As a member of a defeated army, Horace discovered his lands confiscated and his beloved father dead. Happily, he managed to obtain a job as a petty financial clerk, which give him a humble kind of security. He was introduced to the millionaire aristocrat, Maecenas (my SEE nuss), who patronized artists most generously. Horace was given a farm (near Tibur) through the generosity of Maecenas (who also provided generously for Virgil; Virgil and Horace were by this time intimate friends). This patronage provided him with a more stable security than his clerical position, and it is at Tibur he remained, writing his exquisite verse and satires.

WORKS: In 35 B.C. *Satires, Book I;* 30 B.C. *Satires, Book II;* by 23 B.C. he had written three books of odes. The *Epistles* (letters) in 20 B.C.; the *Carmen Saeculare* in 17 B.C.; in 15 B.C. a fourth book of *Odes;* lastly the *Epistles (II).*

ESTIMATE:

1. The *Odes* are, next to the poetry of Virgil, the greatest achievement of the age of Augustus. The *Odes* are great lyric poetry, but unlike Catullus, his passions are less direct; indeed, they seem calmed and clarified by a precise and sophisticated mind at work. Some even think the *Odes* not to be genuine lyrics since the technique severely chastens the "high-flown" sentiments. But it was the self-same mastery of technique that made him so admired by the ancients, such as Quintilian, who called Horace the only poet of the Roman lyricists worth reading!

   a. The *Odes* sing of wine, nature, love; and the joys of wine and the good life.

   b. They sing of the transience of life; how one should seize upon the joys of life while he is still young—for who knows what death will bring?

   c. They sing of his patron Maecenas, of the Olympian gods, and of his emperor Augustus—and of Roman virtues in general.

   d. They sing of moderation in all things—how excess beyond the *golden mean* brings on sorrow and pain.

   e. He is brilliant in his use of quick transitions of thought; in his use of deliberate anti-climaxes; in the handling of mock-solemnity.

f. In poems dealing with love he is generally flippant and "genially hearty." The least serious of love poets.

g. He called himself the Roman Alcaeus—which he was—and like that great Greek lyricist, Horace celebrated the glories of Rome in lyrics of often great dignity and solemnity.

2. He is often said to have expressed the cliché and the common-place well—"what oft was thought but ne'er so well expressed." He could state general truths about life, art, and man with superb precision, accuracy, and subtlety. He is the sophisticated *social* poet of wit.

HORACE

ODES: COMMENT

INTRODUCTION: The *Carmina* (*Odes*) of Horace are in varied meters such as the alcaic and sapphic. He has been translated by many English writers, such as Connington (1870), Macnaghten (1927), Henze (1961), and Michie in 1963.

The *Odes* are in four books containing a total of 103 poems on the following subjects:

1. Politics and patriotism.

2. Drinking songs.

3. The poet's role in life.

4. On the voyages of his friends.

5. On the brevity of life—and on the urgency to *seize the day* (*carpe diem*) while young and vibrant.

6. On the best conduct—the *golden mean*—no excess in any pursuit, whether of wine or women, for the result is inevitably painful.

7. A few poems on love—treated wittily and lightly. His women are called Chloe and Lalage: ladies of beauty, wit, and charm—but little real life.

8. On achieving immortality by the writing of poetry that shall never leave the minds of men. In this category are some of his greatest lyrics.

9. On the inevitability of death; on the swiftness of time and the subtle approach of death. These are the best and most powerful of his odes.

The *Satires* (*Sermons*) are written in dactylic hexameter. The best translations are those of Fairclough in prose (1926), and Smith Bovie in verse (1959).

The *Satires* deal with the following subjects:

1. Man's behavior in society; the defense of his own poetry.

2. Country life is better than city; the *golden mean* is best. Sexual extremes are particularly satirized; the simple rural life is best; and best also are the simple pleasures.

ROMAN HISTORY: LIVY

LIFE 59 B.C.-A.D. 17

Titus Livius was a native of Padua (Roman Patavium). He is known as the greatest prose-writer of the Augustan age. At about the age of thirty, he began his great history of Rome "From the Foundation of the City." The history kept him busy for the rest of his life. The total number of books comes to 142! They relate the history of Rome from its founding to the death of the young prince, Drusus, in 9 B.C. Unfortunately, only 35 of the books survived entire:

1. Books 1-10 (survive); they contain a beautiful recapitulation of the various legends of Rome's founding.

2. Books 21-30 (survive); a brilliant description of the wars with Carthage; his fame was immediate after this.

ESTIMATE:

1. Not a very careful historian, since he is lax in his verification of details and in his odd acceptance of two conflicting authorities. Even a doubtful authority is used without any qualms! He left unused a vast treasure of research (inscriptions, etc.).

2. The history is a genuine work of art:

   a. The past comes to life with great vivacity and brilliance.

   b. His strokes are bold, his sweep broad, the detail vital. At a stroke he can bring to life the thoughts and character of a historical name, and bring instantly to the mind's eye a moment in time and place.

   c. The work is more than history—it is a poem in prose! It is a poetic epic on Rome's progress down the ages.

His glorification of the history of the Roman Republic and its virtues did for Rome what Virgil and Horace had accomplished in verse. Said Livy in his *History of Rome* (Preface to Book I), "There never was a nation whose history is richer in noble deeds, nor a community into which greed and luxury have made so late an entrance, or in which plain and thrifty living have been so long or so highly honoured."

LATIN POETRY: OVID

LIFE 43 B.C.-18 A.D.

Publius Ovidius Naso was born in Sulmo, east of Rome, the very year after Julius Caesar had died (43 B.C.). His mother was a noblewoman. His father had him educated to become a lawyer. But the young man preferred the emotional rather than the argumentative side of the study of rhetoric (essential to the study of law). Like Horace, he too studied at Athens, and indeed, he and Horace were friends. He had only seen Virgil, however. The fashionable Roman elite found his poetry exciting, and soon Ovid was well known. After two divorces, he struck gold with his third wife, who remained devoted and loyal during her husband's exile from Rome. Augustus had, by imperial edict, banished Ovid to Tomis on the western shores of the Black Sea.

WHY BANISHED? Ovid claims he was banished for having written a poem (without doubt his quite immoral "Ars Amatoria"—immoral even by today's standards!), and for having committed an "error." What that error was is a puzzle: Had he offended Augustus by connecting his name with the emperor's quite immoral and profligate daughter?

His *Tristia* is a collection of his poems written in exile. Therein he describes his tragic last night in Rome; the difficulties and hardships of his voyage to Tomis; and the dreadful years of overwhelming pain and boredom in his bleak land of exile. After ten years of exile, he was dead, never having succeeded in being recalled and forgiven by the emperor. It is interesting to note that the inhabitants of the land treated him kindly, thus winning Ovid's esteem.

THE WORKS: The *Amores, Heroides, Ars Amatoria* (Art of Love), *Remedia Amoris, Medicina Faciei, Medea* (a tragedy of which only two lines survive); all the foregoing published before A.D. 8; but by that date he had also completed (but not revised) his masterpiece, the *Metamorphoses*. In exile he finished his *Fasti* and wrote the *Tristia* (Poems of Sorrow), the *Epistulae Ex Ponto,* and the *Halieutica* (on fishing in the Black Sea); lastly, the *Ibis*.

ESTIMATE:

1. Ovid was an extremely skillful narrator who could combine that art with a scintillating and brilliant lyrical technique.

2. He was a careful and scrupulous craftsman in his art.

3. He was filled with high spirits and charming wit.

4. In his love poetry he treats passion with humor and lightness (as did Horace).

5. In his *Heroides* and his *Metamorphoses*, the heroes are not so much heroic as they are human and ordinary.

6. He is the master psychologist; very little of the human psyche escapes his sharp vision. No other poet could dig so deeply into the darkest recesses of the human mind—and do it with compelling pity and compassion at that! His wit, however subtle, is never deliberately cruel or barbaris. Ovid has that quality of sympathy for the feelings of others known as *empathy*.

7. Ovid is the keen observer of the world of man in all its infinite gyrations. One admires the constant *gusto* he feels for describing the human experience.

In the Epilogue to the *Metamorphoses* (met uh more FOH seez) he declares that his poetry will make him an immortal—and it did!

INFLUENCE: His influence was enormous: the Middle Ages doted on his works; and in the Renaissance, no other Latin poet had a greater influence than he. Spenser, Marlowe, Jonson, and, above all, Shakespeare were significantly influenced. Later, such poets as Dryden, Pope, Yeats, Joyce, Pound, and Eliot, and a host of others, felt his magic.

OVID

METAMORPHOSES

This poem is in fifteen books written in dactylic hexameter at around A.D. 8. The best Elizabethan translation is that of Arthur Golding's (very likely Shakespeare's main source for his myths), and the best prose translations are those of H. T. Riley (1869), Mary Innes (1955); the best in verse being those of Golding, Horace Gregory, and Rolfe Humphries.

COMMENT:

1. The *Metamorphoses* (met uh more FOH seez) is written in fifteen "books"—actually in total bulk equal to the size of the average paperback novel.

2. The theme is essentially the passions that rule all human beings; the subjects are the myths of the ancient world.

INTERPRETATION: *METAMORPHOSES,* QUESTIONS AND ANSWERS

What do the myths deal with?

ANSWER: They deal mainly with changes of human beings into animal, vegetable, or mineral states. For example, the climax of most of the tales is the change from the human state into a flower, a star, a tree, an animal, or a rock. The physical transformation almost always proceeds realistically and logically; very often the natural flora or fauna of the countryside are accounted for in this way.

With which myth does Ovid begin?

ANSWER: He begins with the formation of the world from *chaos,* how it took on order, shape, form, and purpose.

How many myths are related?

ANSWER: Ovid has collected, from multifarious ancient and contemporary sources, over 250 myths; and has retold them with superb charm and warmth, as well as with keenness of insight into human nature.

Are the 250 different myths unified in any way? Is there a continuity to such a vast canvas?

ANSWER: The myths are unified by

1. following the myths in their chronological order;

2. by the varied and intricate relationships among the characters in the myths;

3. and especially by Ovid's mastery of the technique of inventing human motivations for the passions of his characters. In this way, the myths contain unity of character and a kind of inevitable psychological logic of emotional progress.

Does Ovid, the sophisticated Roman, believe these fairy tales?

ANSWER: Ovid at no time intimates any kind of belief in the myths of the gods.

Then what makes them (and has made them) so fascinating down the ages?

ANSWER:

1. His playful tone.

2. The use of fantasy and humor.

3. The charm of Ovid's scintillating wit.

4. The graceful style.

5. The easy and light tone of the style; its half-seriousness.

6. The revelation, above all, of human character in action—in conflict with itself and with others.

7. The masterly structure gives unity to 250 myths telling—in a language suffused with charm and passion, insight and wit, tales that undoubtedly prove appealing to all literate people.

What are some of the myths he tells? Name several of the more prominent ones.

ANSWER: Creation of man, the four ages, the great flood, Apollo and the python, Apollo and Daphne, Phaethon, Narcissus, Actaeon, Pentheus, Medea and Jason, Scylla and Minos, Orpheus and Eurydice, and 240 others! See *Glossary* for a good share of the myths given in brief summary.

ROMAN HISTORY: TACITUS

LIFE (c. A.D. 55-c. A.D. 117)

Publius (?) Cornelius Tacitus (TASS ih tuss) came of good family, saw military service as a tribune, and held one of the offices of the vigintivirate (minor magistrate) under Vespasian, quaestor (tax collector) under Titus, and praetor (magistrate) under Domitian (A.D. 88). He married the daughter of the famous consul and later governor of Britain, C. Julius Agricola. Around 90-93 Tacitus was probably governor of some minor province.

When he returned to Rome, he found the city subjected to a vicious reign of terror under Domitian; this experience had a profound effect upon Tacitus, especially apparent in his later work in history.

HIS WORKS:

AGRICOLA: This is a work praising his father-in-law, C. Julius Agricola, published about A.D. 98, five years after Agricola's death. Tacitus gives his ancestry, following that with a step-by-step account of his political progress. Agricola finally became governor of Britain in A.D. 77 or 78.

Then Tacitus gives an historical account of Britain—its tribes, climate (the continual rain and fog), a rather vague and inaccurate account of its geography (Tacitus even thinks of the earth as flat!).

Finally, there is an account of the conquest of Britain by the Romans. Agricola himself secured the borders as far north as the Clyde and the Forth. The book closes with Agricola's return home, where he was prudently able to disarm the jealous Domitian. Agricola dies and Tacitus pens for his close a moving and eloquent eulogy to a great Roman.

GERMANIA: Probably published in A.D. 98, about the same time as the *Agricola*.

1. It describes the geographical features of Germany.

2. He describes the social customs of the inhabitants; their appearance, their manners, and their dress.

3. He describes their politics, the organization of their military, their religion, and system of land tenure.

4. He describes their warlike behavior which alternates with periods of sloth; their love of gambling; their general intemperance; their ideal morality pervading family life (this is contrasted ironically with the opposite of the ideal prevailing in Rome).

5. He describes the various German tribes (this included such groups as Swedes and Finns).

HISTORIES: The publication date is between A.D. 104-109. The younger Pliny revised some portions of the manuscript. The time encompassed is from A.D. 69-96; that is from the principate of Galba to that of Domitian. Only four books and a portion of a fifth survive.

Book I: He is going to tell of times "rich in tragedies, terrible with battles, torn by civil strife"—of times when Rome itself was set to the torch.

Tacitus tells of the short reign of Galba, his adoption of Piso (A.D. 69), and the death of Galba and Piso by murder, with Otho succeeding as the new ruler.

Tacitus then talks of the legions in Germany; the negotiations between Vitellius and Otho; and finally civil war.

Book II: The play of politics in the East—between Vespasian and Titus.

Then back to Rome to relate the fighting about Bedriascum and the suicide of Otho. Vitellius succeeds as ruler; his reign described; his sloth and gluttony vividly detailed; the chaos in the legions, the graft and waste in the administration; and finally the threat of Vespasian's army.

Book III: Tacitus describes the actions of the Flavian generals under Vitellius; the destruction of Cremona (in vivid detail); the battle in Rome between the two forces; the burning of the Capitol; the capture of Rome, and the death of Vitellius. This is the most sombrely cast of all the books, a genuine masterpiece.

Book IV: The reign of Vespasian; the rise of the Batavians under
(and what   Civilis; the expedition of Titus against Jerusalem (ac-
remains of   count of the siege and destruction of Jerusalem by
Book V)   Titus in 70 A.D. is lost).

ANNALS: This book was written after the *Histories,* and relates
a history of the reigns of Tiberius, Caligula, Claudius, and Nero.
It was written about A.D. 116. Books I-IV survive, parts of V and
VI, and Books XI-XVI (the beginning and end are incomplete).

1. Tacitus' style is packed and concise—almost obscure.

2. The writing is dignified and vivid.

3. There are many epigrammatic sayings, full of irony and melancholy.

4. One gets an impression of unrelieved crime, an unending line
   of sycophants, unceasing tyranny and oppression, and wide-
   spread pervasive corruption. This was not entirely true.

5. Tacitus claimed he was impartial, aiming to hold up worthy
   actions to posterity. But he was biased, indeed, Tacitus being
   a true devotee of republicanism.

6. Tiberius is overdrawn, painted uglier than life; Tiberius, the
   debaucher at Capri, the bloodthirsty tyrant suffers in the
   Annals.

TACITUS

ANNALS: OUTLINE

Tacitus' *Annals* (his most famous work) in outline, book by book:

BOOK I (A.D. 14-15):

1. Rapid review of Augustus' reign.

2. Reign of Tiberius (the suppression by Germanicus of the mutinous legions in Pannonia and Germany).

3. A famous description of the visit of the Roman army to the place where the disaster of Varus occurred.

BOOK II (A.D. 16-19):

1. The third campaign of Germanicus in which he defeats Arminius.

2. Germanicus' expedition to the East with Piso, who probably killed Germanicus in A.D. 19.

BOOK III (A.D. 20-22):

1. The return of Agrippina, the widow of Germanicus, to Italy.

2. The trial and suicide of Piso.

3. Rome grows in wealth, luxury, and sycophancy.

BOOK IV (A.D. 23-28):

1. The character and career of Sejanus.

2. He causes the poisoning of Drusus.

3. He plots against the children of Germanicus.

4. Tiberius lays aside Sejanus' proposal that he be allowed to wed Livia (the wife of the poisoned Drusus, who had assisted Sejanus in the poison plot).

5. Tiberius goes to Capri.

    a. As a result, informers are everywhere.

    b. Judicial murder is common; as in the case of Cordus.

BOOK V (A.D. 29):

1. The death of Julia Augusta or Livia, mother of Tiberius.

2. The conspiracy and downfall of Sejanus; part of this book has been lost.

BOOK VI (A.D. 31-37):

1. Tiberius at Capri; his vices and ferocity; his tortured soul.

2. The death of Drusus, the son of Germanicus, who was starved in prison.

3. The death of Agrippina, the mother of Drusus.

4. The unending bloodshed in Rome by execution and suicide.

5. The death of Tiberius, and an account-summary of his life.

BOOK XI (A.D. 47-49):

1. Begins with the seventh year of Claudius (A.D. 47: remember that Books VII-X have not survived).

2. The excesses of the vicious profligate Messalina.

    a. Her marriage with Silius.

    b. The emperor disturbed at her actions.

    c. The execution of Silius and Messalina.

BOOK XII (A.D. 49-54):

1. Claudius marries his niece, Agrippina (daughter of Germanicus).

    a. At Agrippina's insistence and influence he adopts Nero (her son), thus rejecting his own son, Britannicus.

    b. Claudius' daughter Octavia is wedded to Nero, Agrippina's son, and now Claudius' adopted son.

    c. Agrippina causes ruin and death to Silanus, beloved of Octavia.

2. Seneca recalled from exile to be Nero's tutor.

3. The British insurrection and its quelling.

4. Agrippina poisons Claudius. Nero succeeds Claudius as ruler.

BOOK XIII (A.D. 55-58):

1. The good promise of Nero in the beginning under the influence of Seneca and Burrus.

2. C. Domitius Corbulo sent to the East to fight the aggression of the Parthians.

3. Agrippina, whose influence upon her son Nero is weakening, takes up the cause of Britannicus.

    a. Nero poisons Britannicus (i.e., has him poisoned).

    b. Nero has Agrippina, his mother, removed from the palace.

4. Nero loves Poppaea Sabina.

BOOK XIV (A.D. 59-62):

1. Nero tries to kill his mother, Agrippina, finally succeeding in the direct and brutal murder of his own mother.

2. Boudicca (Boadicea) revolts in Britain, and the suppression of that revolt by the Romans.

3. Armenia is taken from the Parthians by the Roman general Corbulo.

4. Burrus dies; Seneca retires.

5. Nero marries Poppaea.

   a. He banishes his virtuous former wife (Octavia), and then has her murdered!

   b. Octavia was murdered in exile at Pandataria.

BOOK XV (A.D. 62-65):

1. Paetus takes a drubbing in Armenia, and the country is made a dependency of the Empire by the Romans under Corbulo.

2. The great fire of Rome (A.D. 64).

   a. Ten of fourteen districts are destroyed.

   b. The city is improved in the rebuilding.

3. The persecution of the Christians, whom Nero blamed as the cause of the fire.

4. The conspiracy of Piso. As a result Seneca and Lucan are put to death in A.D. 65.

BOOK XVI (A.D. 65-66):

1. Nero's wild behavior.

   a. He appears in public as a singer.

   b. The death of his wife Poppaea.

2. The suicide of the Stoic Thrasea, and his son-in-law banished.

3. In a last surviving chapter Tacitus sorrows over the long tale of melancholy and bloodshed.

4. The parts dealing with the last two years of Nero's reign are lost.

INTERPRETATION: *ANNALS*, QUESTIONS AND ANSWERS

Whose biography did Tacitus write?

ANSWER: That of his father-in-law, C. Julius Agricola.

Discuss the matter of Tacitus' bias as a historian.

ANSWER: There is no doubt that Tacitus reveals bias in his writing of history, especially in his *Annals;* and especially in his account of Tiberius. Yet, such a bias cannot be looked on as a flaw. Tacitus is primarily a moralist who writes history for didactic purposes:

1. Respect for dignity and honesty.

2. Hatred for tyranny and cruelty.

Tacitus' admiration for the Roman Republic is never hidden. He loved the freedom available under the Republic, and its hatred of tyranny.

How does Tacitus expose the corruption and cruelty of the tyrants?

ANSWER: He is brilliant at analyzing motives; it is his analyses of motives that succeed in exposing the wickedness of the tyrants. In this way too his sorrow and anger at all the corruption and cruelty is revealed, and *not* through resoundng declamations. Like the novelist, Tacitus can bring to life the complex forces that motivate human beings, even those to be found only on the pages of dusty manuscripts and records.

What is Tacitus' style like?

ANSWER: It is packed, intense, crowded, often obscure, laced with brilliant epigrams; it is highly sophisticated, conscious of form and polish, revealing a personality of dignity and high worth.

GLOSSARY

NAMES, PLACES, and TERMS IN GREEK AND ROMAN CLASSICS

ACESTES
: King of Sicily. He was friendly to the Trojans because his mother came from Troy.

ACHAEANS
: A tribe of Greeks, dominant in the southern part of Greece. The word is often used to mean all the Greeks. The terms Achaean, Argive, and Danaan seem synonymous in the *Iliad,* and are all names for the Greeks (the words Greeks, Greece, etc., are from the Latin, the Greeks' own name for their country being Hellas).

ACHERON
: A river of the underworld whose overflow was thought to form Lake Avernus and the marshy region around it. Even today there are sulphuric fumes and other signs of volcanic action in this area.

ACHILLES
: The hero of the *Iliad*. Odysseus meets him on his trip to the underworld. His sad state contrasts sharply with that of Odysseus, who was one of the few Greek heroes to return home. Achilles' death is frequently predicted in the *Iliad;* shortly after the end of the poem he will be slain by Paris with an arrow.

ACIDALIAN MOTHER
: Venus; the name came from the fountain, Acidalius, in Boeotia (central Greece), sacred to Venus and her followers, the three Graces.

ACRISIUS
: A king of Argos whose daughter Danaë, went to Italy, and married Pilumnus, an ancestor of Turnus.

ACTIUM
: One of the most famous battles in Roman history, between Augustus and Antony and Cleopatra; actually more of a naval battle than a land operation; fought off the Ambracian Gulf on the northwest coast of Greece, in 31 B.C.

541

AEACUS Ancestor of Achilles. Apollo guided the arrow which Paris shot and from which Achilles died.

AEAEA Circe's island, and also another name for Circe.

AEGISTHUS After plotting with Agamemnon's wife, Clytemnestra, to kill Agamemnon, he was later slain by Agamemnon's son Orestes.

AENEAS The hero of Virgil's *Aeneid*.

AGAMEMNON He is slain by his wife, Clytemnestra, and his cousin, Aegisthus, when he returns from Troy.

AGATHYRSI Tribe from Sarmatia on the Danube.

AGENOR Founder of Sidon, the sister city of Tyre.

AGYLLA A small Etruscan town.

AIAS (Ajax) Son of Oileus, king of the Locrians. He is fleet of foot, bold and insolent, endowed with an unpleasant character. He is subsequently drowned by Poseidon for blasphemy while returning home from Troy.

AIAS (Ajax) Son of Telamon, king of Salamis, often known as the greater Ajax (and not to be confused with Oilean Ajax). His character is stubborn, unshakeable courage, often relying on his brute strength rather than his wits. After the death of Achilles, he kills himself when he loses a contest with Odysseus for the armor of the slain hero.

AJAX See Aias.

ALBUNEA A sulphurous spring in Italy.

ALCAEUS Grandfather of Hercules, whose last labor was to bring up from the underworld the three-headed dog, Cerberus.

ALCIBIADES   An Athenian commander who showed great brilliance and audacity. He later deserted to Sparta, and aided that state in its defeat of Athens. He plotted to gain control of Athens, and hoped to become tyrant of that city-state.

ALCIDAS   A Spartan commander involved in several of the early battles of the Peloponnesian War. He fought at Mitylene, and had several victories before fleeing.

ALEXANDER   (Paris) Son of Priam, brother of Hector of Troy. Having seduced and married Helen, wife of Menelaus, he is responsible for the Trojan War. He defends himself always in the name of Aphrodite, whose deity must not be slighted. He slays Achilles with an arrow.

ALOEUS   His wife, Iphimedia, and her lover, Neptune (god of the sea), had two sons, Otus and Ephialtes, who are generally called the sons of Aloeus. Their crime was an attempt to reach heaven by piling Mount Ossa on Olympus, and Mount Pelion on Ossa—hence the expression "piling Pelion on Ossa."

ALPHEUS   The god of the river of the same name in Greece, which flows into the Ionian Sea near Olympia. He was pursuing the nymph Arethusa, and Diana, to save her, changed her into a fountain on the island of Ortygia.

AMAZONS   A warrior nation of women whose queen, Penthesilea, came to the aid of the Trojans.

AMBROSIA   The food of the immortal gods; their drink was nectar.

AMMON   God of the Egyptian city of Thebes. The Romans later identified him with Jupiter. He was the father of Iarbus by a Libyan nymph.

AMPHIMEDON   One of Penelope's suitors.

AMPHINOMUS   A suitor whom Odysseus tried to frighten away before the slaughter.

AMPHITRYON   Supposed father of Hercules. He was the husband of Alcmene, who bore Hercules by Jupiter in the guise of Amphitryon.

AMPHRYSUS   A river in Thessaly, where Apollo tended the flocks of the king, Admetus.

AMPSANCTUS   A lake east of Naples, which gave forth poisonous odors. It was therefore thought of as one of the entrances to the underworld.

AMYCUS   Son of Neptune, king of the Bebryces (a mythical people in Bithinia); had world-wide renown as a boxer.

ANAGNIA   The largest town of the Hernici, about thirty-six miles east of Rome.

ANCHISES   There was a legend that Diomedes stole the ashes of Anchises but later restored them to Aeneas, the son of Anchises.

ANDROGEOS   Son of Minos, went to Athens to take part in the games in honor of Athena. When he had won every contest, the king of Athens, Aegeus, set him to fight the wild bull of Marathon, which killed him. In consequence Minos imposed a tribute from the Athenians of seven boys and seven girls.

ANDROMACHE   Wife of Hector. Their first-born son was named Astyanax, which in Greek means "lord of the city." One of the most touching scenes in the *Iliad* is the description of Hector's farewell to his wife and son at the gates of the city. She is the representative of wifeliness. Although fighting for his wife, Hector is fighting on the side of Paris, who has defiled a wife and broken the laws of the hearth. After the fall of Troy, she is carried off by Achilles' son who takes her as his wife.

ANGITIA A goddess worshipped by the Marsi.

ANTENOR A gentle and wise Trojan, who advises the return of Helen to the Achaeans to end the war.

ANTICLEIA Odysseus' mother, who died grieving over her lost son.

ANTILOCHUS Young son of Nestor, noble but somewhat rash. By reckless driving he defrauds Menelaus of second place in the chariot race in the funeral games; but his modesty and good sense prevent exacerbation of the dispute.

ANTINOUS The boldest and most ruthless of Penelope's suitors.

ANXUR Early name for Tarracina, a town southeast of Rome.

APHRODITE Daughter of Zeus and Dione, goddess of love. She is an awesome goddess in the field of love but weak and effeminate in battle; she is wounded by Diomedes with the aid of Athena. It is her power that is responsible for the war with Troy.

APOLLO Son of Zeus and Leto, god of prophecy and poetry; he represents the defender of the walls of Troy. There is some suggestion that he is an Asian deity, perhaps connected with Lycia, a nation allied with Troy.

ARAXES A river rising in Armenia and flowing into the Caspian; the force of its current was proverbial.

ARCHIDAMUS A Spartan commander early in the war. He led the first attacks on Athens, despite his friendship with Pericles. Later on he captured Plataea. He was responsible for the winning of Lesbos for the Spartan cause.

ARCTURUS HY-ADES, & THE BEARS — Three constellations. The Hyades were associated with rainy weather.

ARES — Son of Zeus and Hera, god of war. Homer makes him blustering, unpleasant, and relatively feeble; thus he is scorned by Zeus and defeated easily by Athena. He is partial to the Trojans.

ARETE — Queen of the Phaeacians.

ARGIVES — The terms Achaean, Argive, Danaan are synonymous in Homer and are his names for the Greeks (the words "Greece," "Greeks," etc. are from the Latin, the Greeks' own name for their country being *Hellas*).

ARGOS — One of the most important cities in Greece to supply fighters to Troy in the Trojan war. It is emphasized because Juno had a great temple there.

ARISBA — A town in Asia Minor which sent allies to Troy.

ARISTAGORAS — The tyrant of Milesia who led the revolt of Ionia against Persia.

ARNAEUS — The beggar who bullied Odysseus.

ARPI OR ARGYRIPA — Town in Apulia in Italy, founded by Diomede who settled there after the Trojan War. He was the son of Tydeus who wounded Venus when she rescued Aeneas from him.

ARTEMIS — Daughter of Zeus and Leto, sister of Apollo, goddess of the hunt and wild animals. She is associated with death by disease (for women); she fights on the Trojan side.

ARTEMISIUM (BATTLE OF)

A navel battle between Greeks and Persians off the northern coast of Euboea (August, 480 B.C.)

ASIAN POND

Refers to the valley of the mouth of the Cayster river in Asia Minor, a favorite haunt of swans.

ASSARACUS

A Trojan ancestor; his Lar (Roman deity) would thus be considered the guardian deity of the whole Trojan race.

ASYLUM

Built by Romulus to house refugees and thus increase the population of Rome. It was supposed to be located between the two summits of the Capitoline hill.

ATE

Daughter of Zeus, the goddess of representation of Folly or Delusion. Ate is said to take possession of a man (or god) when he performs a sudden mad action which contradicts the ordinary pattern of his behavior; thus Agamemnon explains his rashness toward Achilles.

ATHENA

(Pallas Athena) Daughter of Zeus (alone); goddess of wisdom, crafts, cities and techniques of warfare. She fights loyally for the Achaeans, moved by her bitter hatred for the Trojans, which presumably stems from the judgment of Paris.

ATHENE

The goddess of war, wisdom and craft—in other words, the goddess of the skills Odysseus most excels in. It is no wonder that Athene likes Odysseus so much.

ATHENAGORAS

A Syracusan, enemy of Hermocrates, who doubted that Athens would attack Sicily in force (Peloponnesian War).

ATLAS

One of the Titans who rebelled against Jupiter and was forced to bear the world on his shoulders.

ATREIDES This term means "son of Atreus," and therefore refers either to Agamemnon or Menelaus.

ATTICA The region of Greece in which Athens was located.

AURORA'S SON Memnon; Aurora, goddess of the Dawn, married Priam's brother, Tithonus.

AURUNCI An early primitive tribe in Latium.

AUSONIA Another name for Italy.

AUTOLYCUS Odysseus' maternal grandfather, who named Odysseus.

BACCHUS The well-known god of wine, whose favorite home was Thrace.

BARCAEANS Wild tribes of the desert of North Africa.

BELUS Son of Neptune, father of Aegyptus and Danaus, who, according to some traditions was king over Libya and Egypt.

BERECYNTIA Mountain in Phrygia sacred to Cybele, the Great Mother. She was represented as wearing a crown of towers.

BITIAS A Carthaginian noble.

BOEOTIA A region north of Attica whose chief city was Thebes.

BRASIDAS One of the most brilliant and forceful leaders. A Spartan general, he took Megara, Thrace, and other areas in the north. Brasidas subdued Amphipolis and nearly choked the Athenian economy. He was killed near Amphipolis by Cleon's army (Peloponnesian War).

BRIAREUS A giant with a hundred hands.

BRISEIS Agamemnon demands the woman Briseis, Achilles' prize, to compensate for his loss when he returned Chryses' daughter to her father in order to end the plague sent by Apollo (Trojan War).

BUTHROTUM Located in the region of Chaonia in northern Epirus.

BYRSA The Greek word for "bull's hide." Venus is describing the founding of Carthage. The colonists had been granted as much land as a bull's hide could cover, so they cut the hide into strips and thus traced out a large piece of land (*Aeneid*).

CAENEUS Started out as a maiden, Caeneus was later changed into a boy by her lover Neptune. In the underworld she regained her feminine form.

CAERE Also called by the other name Agylla, an Etruscan town.

CAESAR Often means Augustus. His whole name was **Gaius Julius Caesar Octavius Augustus;** he was made a god even before he died. In later times emperors were usually not deified until after death (*Aeneid*).

CAIETA Town in Latium, which got its name from being the burial place of Aeneas' old nurse, Caieta.

CALCHAS Son of Thestor, chief prophet of the Achaeans. His advice is detested by Agamemnon, for it was Calchas who bade the king to sacrifice his daughter Iphigenia at Aulis before the heroes departed for Troy. He also ordered the king to give Chryseis to her father to end the plague of Apollo.

CALES A Campanian town.

CALLIOPE Muse of epic poetry.

CALYDON | A town in Aetolia in Greece famed for the wild boar which inhabited the nearby mountains. The goddess Diana sent the boar to ravage the town because its king, Oeneus, had failed to sacrifice to her.

CALYPSO | A minor goddess who kept Odysseus on her island of Ogygia. Her name has the apt meaning of "Concealer."

CAMBYSES | The Persian king who added Egypt to the Empire.

CAMERINA | A Sicilian city, which had been warned by an oracle never to drain the marsh nearby. When the inhabitants disobeyed, the enemy entering by the drained marsh was able to capture the town.

CAMILLUS | After he had been exiled from Rome on false charges, he was recalled to defeat the conquering Gauls (around 390 B.C.)

CAPE SEPIAS | A headland north of Euboea where a storm destroyed a large number of Persian warships in 480 B.C.

CAPHEREUS | A promontory in Euboea, in Greece, where the Greek ships were wrecked on returning from Troy. Athena (Minerva) sent a storm, so the king of Euboea, Nauplius, hung out false lights to guide the fleet onto the rocks.

CARINAE | Name of a wealthy section of Rome.

CARMENTIS | Mother of Evander and a prophetess (*Aeneid*).

CARPATHIAN SEA | Between Crete and the island of Rhodes.

CASTOR AND POLLUX | Half-brothers who loved each other dearly. Their mother was Leda. Castor's father was Tyndareus, king of Sparta and father of Helen.

Jupiter was the father of Pollux, which made Pollux immortal. Both were conceived the same night and were twins. When Castor was killed, Pollux was desperate with grief. Finally Jupiter allowed the twins to spend one day each in the underworld and the next with the gods.

CATALINE CON- Conspired to overthrow the Roman senate in
SPIRACY   63 B.C.

CATO   Known as the censor for his stern conservatism. He was most famous for the words he always repeated before the senate: "Carthage must be destroyed," and was thus, in some ways, responsible for the start of the third Punic War.

CAULON AND   They were cities farther along the coast of
SCYLACEUM   Italy.

CECROPS   The mythical founder of Athens.

CENTAURS   A wild race living on Mt. Pelion in Thessaly. They delighted in bull-killing; according to most legends, they were thought to be half-man, half-horse.

CERES   The goddess of harvest, crops, grain.

CHALCIDEUS   A Peloponnesian commander who was sent to Ionia with Alcibiades; he helped lead the revolt at Chios, Miletus, and other cities.

CHALYBES   A people of Pontus who lived near the shore of the Black Sea; they were famous for their iron work.

CHARYBDIS   A powerful whirlpool that could suck down ships.

CHERSONESE   The peninsula which forms the northern shore of the Hellespont.

CHIMAERA   A fire-breathing monster with the head of a lion, the tail of a dragon, and a goat's body.

CHRYSEIS   Daughter of Chryses, priest of Apollo, whom Agamemnon returns to her father to end the plague sent by Apollo.

CICONES   Allies of the Trojans, whom Odysseus plundered on his way home.

CIRCE   A goddess who tried unsuccessfully to turn Odysseus and his men into swine. Her name means "Hawk"; she resides at the island of Aeaea.

CISSEUS   King of Thrace, father of Hecuba, Priam's wife. He dreamed that before her son Paris was born that she would give birth to a flaming torch. Juno says that Venus also gave birth to a torch because her son Aeneas will bring ruin on the new Troy by marrying Lavinia, just as Paris did on old Troy by marrying Helen (Aeneid).

CLARIAN   Adjective from Claros, referring to Apollo; because at Claros in Asia Minor there was a temple and an oracle dedicated to Apollo. The laurel was a bush sacred to the god; his priestess sat on the tripod when the oracle was consulted.

CLEISTHENES   The leader who introduced democratic reforms into Athens after the expulsion of Pisistratids (see Herodotus).

CLEOMENES   The Spartan king who helped bring Sparta and Athens together in order to oppose Persia.

CLOELIA   A Roman virgin sent as a hostage to Porsena. She escaped and swam back across the Tiber, but the Romans sent her to Porsena again. He was so impressed that he set her free, along with several other hostages.

CLYTEMNESTRA The wife of Agamemnon, who plotted with his cousin, Aegisthus, to kill Agamemnon on his return to his kingdom of Mycenae.

COCLES Refers to Horatius Cocles, whose superhuman valor kept the whole Etruscan army under Lars Porsena at bay on the other side of the bridge to Rome. Behind him the Romans destroyed the bridge. He jumped into the river and swam back to the Roman side and to safety.

COCYTUS One of the rivers that bounded the Lower World. It was the river of wailing and a tributary of the Acheron, river of woe.

COEUS AND ENCELADUS Giants, known as Titans, who scaled Mt. Olympus. They were sons of Mother Earth. When one brood of Titans, represented by Coeus, was hurled down from the mountain, Earth, in anger, produced another crop, of whom Enceladus was one.

CORINTH Destroyed by Mummius in 146 B.C. (in Greece).

CORYBANTES Followers of Cybele who performed her rites with clashing cymbals and wild dancing. Lions were harnessed to her chariot.

CORYTHUS An Italian hero, son of Jupiter, father of Iasius and Dardanus. It is also a city in Italy, as well as an ancient town in Etruria, north of the Tiber River.

COSSUS An early republican hero of Rome.

CRETAN MONSTER The bull which legend says Hercules brought back alive to Eurystheus. All these are references to some of the twelve labors: he strangled the Nemean lion, carried back Cerberus, the three-headed dog guarding the entrance to the underworld, and burned off the nine heads of the Lernian Hydra.

CREUSA
Ascanius' mother, Aeneas' first wife who died at Troy.

CROESUS
The last monarch of independent Lydia. He was supposed to have been fabulously wealthy (see Herodotus).

CTESIPPUS
A suitor of Penelope's, who threw a cow's hoof at Odysseus.

CURES
A town of the Sabines, birthplace of Numa Pompilius.

CURETES
The name for the priests of Jupiter in Crete, where he was worshipped with noisy rites. He had been hidden on the island when a baby, to escape being killed by his father, Cronos. His cries were covered up by the Curetes' clashing their armor.

CYBELE
A mountain, sacred to the goddess of the same name, located in Phrygia.

CYCLOPES
A race of one-eyed giants. They forged the iron for the walls of Pluto's palace.

CYCNUS
Father of Cinyras and Cupavo, beloved of Phaethon. When the latter was destroyed by Jupiter, Cycnus' grief was so great that he was changed into a swan.

CYDONIA
Important city in Crete, rival of Knossos. Crete was famous for its archers.

CYLLENIUS
A name for Mercury, because he was born on Mt. Cyllene in Arcadia. His mother, Maia, was the daughter of Atlas.

CYRUS
The Persian King who overthrew the Medean Empire, established the Persians in power, and conquered Lydia, Ionia and Babylon.

CYTHERA
An island off the southeastern part of Greece, where a famous temple to Venus was located.

Although some legends said she rose from the sea near Paphos, others said it was near Cythera.

DAEDALUS The designer of the labyrinth, the den of the Minotaur, half-bull, half-man, for King Minos in Crete. When he incurred Minos' anger, he fled from the island on wings which he had made, and landed at Cumae.

DANAANS The terms Achaean, Argive, Danaan are synonymous in Homer and are his names for the Greeks (the words "Greece," "Greeks," etc., are from the Latin; the Greeks' own name for their country being Hellas). Another poetic name for the Greeks, coming from the name of one of the early kings of Argos, Danaus.

DARDANIAN Equals Trojan, from Dardanus, a mythical ancestor of the Trojans.

DARDANUS AND IASIUS Brothers who married daughters of Teucer, a king in Asia Minor.

DARIUS The Persian king who reorganized the Empire after the death of Cambyses, and who invaded Greece after having crushed the Ionian revolt.

DAUNUS King of Apulia and father of Turnus (*Aeneid*).

DECII Three generations of this family fought for Rome in the battles with the Latins, Samnites, and Pyrrhus respectively. (The Latin war ended in 340 B.C.; the Samnite in 290 B.C.; and the war with Pyrrhus, from Epirus on the north-west coast of Greece, 280 B.C.)

DEIPHOBUS The third of Priam's sons (Hector and Paris were the oldest). He married Helen after Paris was slain in battle, and his house was therefore the first to burn. He was also impersonated by Athena to deceive Hector in his encounter with Achilles (*Iliad*).

DELPHI   A Greek city in which was located the most famous oracle of Apollo.

DEMARATUS   The Spartan who shared ruling with Cleomenes. He was ousted and became an adviser to the Persians (Herodotus).

DEMODUCUS   A blind bard in the palace of Alcinous. His blindness may have given rise to the tale that Homer was also blind.

DINDYMUS   A mountain in Phrygia, sacred to Cybele.

DIODOTUS   An enemy of Cleon, who argued for leniency in the case of Mitylene. He won the debate and saved the day for the city.

DIOMEDES   Went with eighty ships to the Trojan War, and was the bravest of the Greeks next to Achilles. After the war he left Argos and was driven by a storm to the east coast of Italy. There legend says that he founded many cities, among them Argyripa or Arpi. He is the son of Tydeus, prince of Argos. He is brave, powerful, and a counterpart of Achilles. Diomedes, however, is a perfectly integrated member of the traditional society. He is pious toward the gods, respectful toward his elders and superiors—particularly his father—and loyal to Agamemnon. His sense of honor and duty perfectly accords with his role in the war. He is disgusted with Achilles' nonconformity and breach of discipline.

DIONE   Daughter of earth and sky, beloved by Jupiter, and thus mother of Venus.

DIS   Another name for Pluto.

DODONA   The location of the most ancient of all the oracles of Greece, in Epirus.

DOLIUS   A servant to Laertes.

DOLON

Son of Eumedes, audacious but without stead-fast courage and much attached to wealth. His soft character is emphasized by the fact that he is an only son among several sisters. He is the Trojan volunteer for the night expedition and is killed by Diomedes (*Iliad*).

DONYSA, OLEAROS, PAROS

All islands of the group known as Cyclades.

DORYCLUS

Brother of Pheneus, king of Thrace.

DRUSI

A good Roman family, but not famous for any great deeds. They are mentioned as a compliment to Augustus because his wife, Livia, was of that family.

DRYOPES

A people living in Asia Minor.

EDONI

A people living in Thrace on the Strymon River.

ELISSA

Another name for Dido.

ELPENOR

The youngest and most inexperienced of Odysseus' crew. He lost his life when he fell from Circe's roof.

ELYSIUM

According to Virgil, the portion of the lower world where the heroes went after death. Tartarus is sometimes used to mean the whole of the lower world; but often the reference is more probably to the section where bad heroes lived in constant torture.

ENCELADUS

One of the giants who fought against the gods.

ERATO

The muse of love poetry.

EREBUS

A lesser divinity, whose name signifies darkness; therefore applied to the gloomy area through which the shades must pass on their way to the underworld.

EREBUS AND CHAOS	Gods of the underworld, especially associated with magic.
ERETRIA	A city located in Euboea which helped Athens burn Sardis. It was destroyed by the Persians in 490 B.C.
ERIDANUS	Often in Virgil, a reference to the river Po, which flows underground for about two miles near its source. The ancients thought it rose in the underworld.
ERIPHYLE	After being bribed to convince her husband, Amphiaraus, to war against Thebes, she was slain by her son. The husband was killed in the war.
ERYMANTHUS	Mountain in Arcadia, Greece, where the famous boar (which Hercules killed) roamed.
ERYX	Son of Neptune and Venus; half-brother of Aeneas. He was king in Sicily. While king he built a temple to his mother Venus on a mountain in the western part of the island.
EUBOEA	A large island off the eastern coast of Greece.
EUMAEUS	Odysseus' swineherd, who remained faithful throughout his master's absence. He helped Odysseus slaughter the suitors.
EUMENIDES	A nice-sounding name for the Furies, the goddesses of vengeance. It meant "well-wishers." The most famous were Tisiphone, Allecto, and Megaera. Their mother was night. Earth was night's sister.
EUPEITHES	The father of Antinous and leader of the Ithacans who objected to Odysseus' killing of the suitors.
EUROTAS	A river near Sparta in southern Greece.
EURYCLEIA	Telemachus' nurse; she remained loyal to Odysseus.

EURYLOCHUS   The only member of Odysseus' crew to have a personality of his own. He frequently opposed Odysseus' plans.

EURYMACHUS   A leader of the suitors, he was a suave, hypo-critical liar (*Odyssey*).

EURYMEDON   An Athenian commander in the campaign against Syracuse (Thucydides).

EURYSTHEUS   King of Argos, for whom Hercules performed the twelve labors. Juno hated Hercules, as she did most of Jupiter's children, who were born of other women.

EVADNE   She jumped onto her husband's funeral pyre after he was killed in the war against Thebes.

FABRICIUS   He rejected the bribes of Pyrrhus, 278 B.C., and later defeated him (*Aeneid*).

FASCES   Rods (for whipping) and an axe were carried in front of the highest officer as a symbol of power (*imperium*). At first they were the ex-clusive right of the kings, but, after Brutus, they were taken over by the consuls. When Brutus' sons conspired to restore the king to power, he put them to death.

FATES   Three goddesses who controlled the thread of human life: Clotho held the spindle, Lachesis drew the thread, Atropos cut it.

FAUNUS   Father of Latinus, son of Picus, and grandson of Saturn. He was worshipped as the god of the fields and of oracles.

FERONIA   An old Italian deity worshipped in Etruria and the Sabine region; goddess of fields and fer-tility, and freedom from slavery.

FESCENNIUM, CAPENA, MT. SORACTE   All located in Etruria, north of Rome. Mt. Ciminus is west of Soracte. The Falisci in-habited a town near Fescennium.

FIELDS OF SATURN A third name for Italy because Saturn was supposed to have ruled Italy in the Golden Age.

FUCINUS A lake in central Italy about fifty miles east of Rome.

FURIES The avenging deities of crimes against parents, relatives, and the like. They were said to take away all peace of mind and to lead their victims to wretched misfortune. (The Greek word for them is *Erinyes*).

GABII An early Latin town not far from Rome. The legend of Caeculus' birth was that his mother was sitting by the fire and a spark jumped out; thus she conceived by Vulcan, but abandoned the child near the temple of Jupiter after it had been born.

GABINE CINCTURE A ceremonial manner of binding the toga so that it became shorter and clung closer to the body.

GARAMANTES A tribe from the interior of Africa, to which was sent an expedition in the time of Augustus.

GARGANUS A promontory on the east coast of Italy; the modern Gargano.

GATES OF WAR Gates of the temple of Janus, which were closed during times of peace, but open in war. Augustus closed them in 29 B.C. for the first time in nearly two hundred years. Janus was the early Italian god of entrances whose name is derived from the Latin word meaning door. He had two faces, one looking forward and the other back.

GELONI A Scythian people living near the Black Sea in south Russia.

GERYON A three-headed monster living on the island of Erythia, near Gades, Spain. Hercules managed to steal his oxen. Tiryinthian is an epithet of Hercules because he was brought up in Tiryns, who was slain by Hercules.

GETAE

A tribe living near the mouth of the Danube, conquered about 25 B.C.

GLAUCUS

A lesser sea-divinity, overgrown with shellfish and seaweed; he is the son of Hippolochus, prince of the Lycians under Sarpedon. His code of duty and honor, his deep respect for the noble lineage, make him a counterpart of Diomedes, whom he encounters without battle but with an exchange of pedigrees and armor, in aristocratic style (*Iliad*).

GODS, ROMAN

Refers to the household gods of the Romans, the Lares and Penates. The Lares were the spirits of the dead who protected the home where they had lived. The Penates protected the food and material prosperity of the family. Images of the Lares and Penates were placed near the hearth, and at each meal offerings were made to them.

GORTYNIA

Town in Macedonia.

GRACCHI, THE

Two brothers; Tiberius became tribune and was murdered in 133 B.C.; Gaius in 121 B.C. Both tried to bring about reforms so that the common people would have a greater voice in government.

GRAECIAN CITY

The city of Pallantium, ruled by Evander, who came from Greece. Aeneas goes to Evander for aid. Pallantium was on the Palatine hill, one of the seven hills in Rome.

GYAROS AND MYCONOS

Two islands in the group known as Cyclades. Legend runs that Apollo was supposed to have moored Delos, because it was so tiny, to the two larger islands of Gyaros and Myconos.

GYLIPPUS   The brilliant Spartan commander who led the victors in the Sicilian campaign (see Thucydides).

HADES   Son of Cronos and Rhea, lord of the underworld; the third portion of the universe, which he received by lot. Brother of Zeus and Poseidon.

HALITHERSES   A prophet of the Ithacans.

HARPALYCE   A female warrior from Thrace.

HECATE   She was associated with the moon, in the heavens; with Diana on earth; and with Persephone (the queen of the underworld) under the earth. Thus she was thought to have three heads, that of a horse, a dog, and a lion. She was worshipped at places where roads met, and came to be regarded as the goddess of witchcraft.

HECUBA   Chief consort of Priam, mother of Hector and queen of Troy. Her values are traditional and possessed of little substance, marked by fear and hatred of enemies, particularly Achilles.

HELEN   The famous wife of Menelaus (king of Sparta) who ran off with Paris, prince of Troy. Sparta was located in the Argive plain as was Mycenae (ruled by Agamemnon). This abduction led to the Trojan War.

HELICON   A range of mountains near the Corinthian Gulf in Boeotia, sacred to Apollo and the Muses. Virgil invokes the muse before listing his catalogue of warriors, as Homer does before his catalogue of ships.

HELIOS   The god of the sun, whose cattle Odysseus' men slaughtered, bringing about their own doom.

HEPHAESTUS The god of craft and son of Zeus and Hera. Demodocus told the tale of how, upon learning his wife Aphrodite was committing adultery with Ares, he trapped the two of them in bed together. In his battle with the river Xanthus, he represented the elemental force of battle (*Iliad*).

HERA Daughter of Cronus and Rhea, sister and wife of Zeus, goddess of marriage. She is cantankerous and tricky, supporting the Achaeans unreservedly, and implacably hating the Trojans.

HERCULES The most famous of mythological heroes, known especially for performing twelve impossible labors. He also boxed with Eryx and killed him. His grandfather was Alcaeus, from whom came the name Alcides.

HERMES Son of Zeus and Maia; god of roads and wayfarers, and guide of the souls of the dead (*psychopomp*); also, with Iris, a messenger of the gods.

HERMIONE The only child of Menelaus, king of Sparta (*Lacedaemon*) and Helen (daughter of Leda and Jupiter). She had been promised to Orestes, son of Agamemnon and Clytemnestra. But when Clytemnestra had murdered her husband when he returned from Troy, Orestes took revenge by killing the murderess. For this crime of matricide the Furies drove Orestes mad.

HERMOCRATES An important leader of Syracuse, who was instrumental in the defeat of Athens in the Sicilian campaign.

HERMUS A river in Asia Minor, flowing through Phrygia and Lydia.

HESPERIA A name for Italy. The word is Greek for "Western Land."

HIPPOLYTUS — Son of Theseus. His step-mother Phaedra fell in love with him, but he rejected her. In anger she accused him falsely to Theseus, who had his son dragged to death by horses. Later, when he discovered Hippolytus' innocence, Diana persuaded the god of healing, Aesclepius, to restore his body. His name was changed to Virbius, and he was placed under the protection of the nymph Egeria, in the grove of Aricia.

HOMOLE AND OTHRYS — Mountains in Thessaly.

HOPLITE — A Greek heavy-armed soldier.

HYLAEUS AND PHOLUS — Centaurs.

HYRCANEA — A province in Persia along the south-eastern shore of the world known to the ancients. It was inhabited by Parthians. The standards which the Parthians had conquered from Crassus in 53 B.C. were restored to the Romans in 20 B.C.

HYRTACUS — He married Priam's first wife, Arisba, when Priam married Hecuba.

IAPYGIA — Part of Apulia in southeast Italy.

IAPYX — The west-northwest wind blowing off the south of Italy, and thus favorable to those crossing to Greece.

IARBAS — The king of Gaetulia, which bordered on Dido's Carthage. He had sought her hand in marriage but was refused.

ICARUS — Son of Daedalus who fled Crete with his father. He flew too close to the sun so that the wax on his wings melted and he fell into the sea.

IDA

The figurehead of Aeneas' ship is a replica of Mt. Ida with Cybele's lions at its base.

IDAEUS

Old Herald of Priam.

IDALIUM

Town in Cyprus sacred to Venus.

IDOMENEUS

Cretan leader who took part in the Trojan war. On his way home a storm came up, and he foolishly vowed to Neptune the first living creature that he should meet if he arrived safely. Naturally the first thing he met was his son. Obediently he sacrificed him, but a plague followed. So Idomeneus fled from Crete to settle in Italy. He was also the king of Crete and one of Helen's suitors. The son of Deucalion, king of the Cretans. He is an aged hero of an ancient race, but still active, whose code of duty is to remain steadfast in every battle, and thus to conquer or to die. His role is prominent at the nadir of Achaeans' fortunes.

ILIUM

Another name for Troy.

ILIUS

Another name for Troy.

ILLYRIA LIBURNIA, THE RIVER TAMAVUS

All located far up the Adriatic Sea. Antenor, escaping from Troy, sailed up the Adriatic and settled near Padua.

INACHUS

River near Argos, named for the first king and most ancient hero of Argos.

INDUS

A reference to the East in general, by naming a prominent river there.

INO

A goddess born a mortal; she helped Odysseus escape the storm Poseidon had called up against him.

IRIS

Female messenger of the Gods.

IRUS

The beggar who bullied Odysseus.

ITALUS   An ancient god from whom the name "Italy" was thought to come.

ITHACA   The home of Odysseus' father, who withdrew from the city to his farm in grief over his son's absence. Naturally, also, Odysseus' island kingdom.

IULUS   Another name for Aeneas' son, Ascanius. The play with the various forms of Iulus' name is to remind the reader of the Julian house and its ancestry. Thus Augustus, adopted by Julius Caesar, is related to Aeneas, the founder of the Roman race (*Aeneid*).

JUNO AND MOTHER EARTH   They represent gods of sky and earth. Here they preceded a wedding. Juno also acts as the *pronuba,* the matron who conducted the bride to the bridal room (*Aeneid*).

LABICUM   An ancient town in Latium.

LABYRINTH   According to legend, a winding maze of paths in Crete at the end of which was the half-bull, half-man beast kept by Minos the king of Crete. Modern excavation has uncovered a huge palace at Knossos with innumerable rooms and halls from which the ancient legend may have had its start.

LACINIUM   A headland on the east coast of Bruttium on which was a temple of Juno.

LADE (BATTLE OF)   A naval battle off the Milesian coast in which the Ionians were decisively defeated at sea by Persia, 494 B.C.

LAERTES   Odysseus' father; he withdrew from the city to his farm in grief over his son's absence.

LAESTRY-GONIANS   A barbaric race of cannibals who attack Odysseus and his crew.

**LAKES
(AVERNIAN)**   The marshy area round Avernus in southern Italy, which was thought to be an entrance into the lower world.

LAODAMIA   She killed herself when her husband was killed at Troy.

LAOMEDON   He organized the building of Troy, but refused to pay Apollo and Neptune for their work. The Harpy, Xalaeno, taunted the Trojans by reminding them that they are descendants of a man famous for breaking his word.

LAPITHS   A tribe in Thessaly ruled by Pirithous, son of Ixion, whose bride was affronted by one of the centaurs. Thus arose the famous struggle between the Lapiths and the centaurs. (The most well-known portrayal of this battle was a frieze on the temple of Zeus at Olympia.)

LAURENTUM   An ancient town in Latium near the Tiber river.

**LELEGES AND
CARIANS**   Peoples in Asia Minor.

LEMNOS   One of the larger islands in the Aegean, sacred to Vulcan because it was there that he landed when Jupiter hurled him from Olympus.

LERNA   A Greek town not far from modern Naples.

LETHE   The river of forgetfulness in the underworld. The souls of the dead drank of its water before they returned to the world to inhabit new bodies; they forget their former life as mortals completely.

LETO   Mother of Apollo and Artemis; accordingly on the side of the Trojans. She plays no role in the fighting, Hermes declining to engage her in battle.

LIBER The early Italian god of fertility, connected by the Romans with Bacchus. In the legend Bacchus' chariot drawn by tigers, went as far as India.

LIBYA Used, by Virgil, to mean all of Africa under Carthaginian rule.

LICHAS Children, saved alive from dead mothers, who were dedicated to Apollo as the god of healing (also the sun-god).

LIPARA Largest of a group of islands northeast of Sicily.

LOCRIANS Colonizers of southern Italy from Narycium on the mainland of Greece, opposite Euboea. According to legend they were driven by storms to south Italy after the Trojan war. The historical fact is that all of southern Italy along the coast was settled in the ninth, eighth, and seventh centuries by Greeks. The area was known as *Magna Graecia*.

LORD OF MYCENAE Refers to Agamemnon, killed by his wife Clytemnestra, who was urged to the deed by her lover Aegisthus (*Aeneid*).

LOTUS-EATERS A people who, by eating of the lotus, drugged themselves into a complete withdrawal from reality and a permanent state of euphoria.

LUPERCAL A cave under the western side of the Palatine hill, connected with the worship of Lupercus, an Italian god of the country.

LYAEUS Another name for Bacchus.

LYCAEUS A mountain in Arcadia where Pan, the Greek god of shepherds and flocks, was born.

LYCIA District on the southwest of Asia Minor.

LYCIA   A southern district in Asia Minor.

LYCTOS   A city in Crete.

LYCURGUS   He persecuted Bacchus; his kingdom, there-
                 fore, became sterile; its fertility returned after
                 his exposure on a mountain.

LYDIAN TIBER   Tradition holds that the area around the Tiber
                 and just north of it, where the Etruscans lived,
                 was colonized by the Lydians from Asia Minor.

LYNISUS   A town in Asia Minor.

MACHAON   Son of Aesclepius, chief physician for the
                 Achaeans along with his brother, Podaleirius.
                 He is wounded in battle, where he fought
                 bravely (*Iliad*).

MAEONIA   Another name for Lydia, where legend says
                 the Etruscans originated.

MAEOTIA   In southern Russia, area around the Sea of
                 Azov.

MARATHON   A town in Attica near which the Athenians
                 and Plataeans defeated a Persian invading
                 force in 490 B.C. (Herodotus).

MARCELLUS   Consul in 222 B.C. He killed the chief of the
                 Insubrian Gauls. He is mentioned for the pur-
                 pose of adding glory to his namesake, Mar-
                 cellus. The second Marcellus, was the son of
                 Augustus' sister Octavia. He married (in 25
                 B.C.) the emperor's daughter, Julia, and was
                 adopted by Augustus as his heir (*Aeneid*).

MARDONIUS   Son-in-law of Darius who conducted the mili-
                 tary campaign against Greece. He was killed
                 at Plataea in 479 B.C.

MARPESSA   A mountain in Paros, the island famous for
                 marble.

MARS

Not the starter of the battle between Lapiths and Centaurs, but thought of as the destroyer because he was the god of war.

MASSICUS

A mountain in Campania near the frontiers of Latium, famous for its wine.

MASSYLIANS

A North African tribe from the area west of Carthage.

MAXIMUS

His whole name was Quintus Fabius Maximus Cunctator (the last means Delayer). Since the Carthaginian general Hannibal seemed impossible to beat, Fabius refused to meet him in a pitched battle. Instead he harried him from the rear and finally wore him out.

MEDON

A steward in Odysseus' palace.

MELANTHEUS

A goatherd disloyal to Odysseus, who curried favors with the suitors.

MELANTHO

A maidservant to Odysseus, as disloyal to her master as was her brother Melantheus.

MELIBOEA

A town in Thessaly famous for its purple dye.

MEMNON

He led the Ethiopean allies of Troy.

MENELAUS

Son of Atreus, King of Sparta and brother of Agamemnon. The seduction of his wife, Helen, is the cause of the Trojan war. Menelaus is the weakest and least courageous of the Achaean lords, but the fact detracts nothing from his nobility and authority. Agamemnon frequently worries for the safety of his younger brother, restraining him from taking risks. Menelaus is sensitive about his fortitude and his role in precipitating the long conflict. He receives the fate Odysseus could have had with Calypso—immortality.

MENTES

A visitor to Ithaca, actually Athena, takes on his form (*Odyssey*).

MENTOR

An Ithacan idler, loyal to Odysseus. Athena frequently takes on his shape.

MERIONES

Squire and nephew of Idomeneus, prominent in battle and competitor in Patroclus' funeral games.

METTUS

Leader of the Roman allies from Alba Longa. In a battle when he was supposed to help the Romans, he refused to join; and later as punishment for treachery he was torn apart by chariots driven in opposite directions (*Aeneid*).

MILTIADES

The Athenian general who was responsible for the victory at Marathon.

MINERVA'S HEIGHT

A hill at the top of the "heel" of Italy. The modern name is Castro.

MINOS

King of Crete who became a judge in the underworld after his death. The other two judges were Rhadamanthus and Aeacus.

MISENUS

Virgil incorporates part of an early legend which dealt with the death of a comrade named Misenus. To this day a cape at one end of the bay near Naples bears his name.

MNESTHEUS, SERGESTUS, CLOANTHUS

Prominent Roman families of Virgil's time who liked to think of themselves as having Trojan ancestors; the Memmians from Menstheus; the Sergians from Sergestus; the Cluentians from Cloanthus.

MONOECUS

Modern Monaco, one of Julius Caesar's strongholds. His daughter, Julia, was Pompey's third wife. After her death in 54 B.C., reconciliation between the two rivals was no longer possible. Most of Caesar's army came from Gaul, while Pompey recruited his from the eastern portion of the Mediterranean. Caesar claimed descent from Venus, through Aeneas, and thus was proclaimed a god after his death.

MOTHER OF THE GODS Cybele, the Great Mother goddess of Asia Minor. She is also known as Rhea.

MOUNT ATHOS A treacherous promontory at the eastern tip of a peninsula to the northeast of Greece. A Persian fleet was destroyed while attempting to round it in 492 B.C. (Herodotus).

MT. CYNTHUS Located on the Greek island of Delos and one of Diana's favorite spots; from the name of the mountain comes the other most common name of Diana, *Cynthia*. Her followers were the mountain nymphs, the Oreads.

MT. LEUCATA A mountain sacred to Apollo on the southern tip of the island of Leucadia.

MT. OLYMPUS The home of the immortal gods, located in Thessaly.

MULCIBER Another name for Vulcan.

MYCALE (BATTLE OF) The battle in which the Greeks broke the Persian power in Ionia, mid-August 479 B.C.

MYCENE AND ARGOS The homes of Agamemnon, the leader of the Greek expedition to Troy, and Diomedes, both located in southern Greece. The whole region became a Roman province in 146 B.C.

MYRMIDONS AND DOLOPIANS Soldiers of Achilles from Thessaly.

NAR A river famed for its sulphurous waters, which flowed into the Tiber.

NAUPACTUS An Athenian commander during the Sicilian campaign.

NAUSICAA The princess of Sherie, a quite charming and believable character; reminiscent of the fairy-tale princess of the middle ages. It is her misfortune that Odysseus had no wish to be her Prince Charming (although he lets her believe so, for as long as he needs favors of her).

NAUTES — Beloved of Minerva because he brought the tiny wooden statue of the goddess, the Palladium, with him from Troy. The Nautii, a prominent family during the days of the early republic, claimed descent from him.

NAXOS — The island where Theseus deserted Ariadne after slaying the minotaur in Crete. She was rescued by Bacchus; therefore the island was sacred to him.

NEOPTOLEMUS — Also called Pyrrhus, son of Achilles, killed at Delphi, his kingdom in Epirus divided, part of it going to Helenus.

NEPTUNE — Not only the sea god, but the builder of Troy for Laomedon.

NEREIDS — There were fifty of them, nymphs of the Mediterranean, daughters of Doris and Nereus.

NEREUS — Father of the sea-nymph, Thetis, mother of Achilles.

NERITUS — Mountain of Ithaca.

NESTOR — Son of Neleus, king of Pylos. He is the oldest lord of the Argives, given to lengthy advice and speeches about his gallant youth. He is a spur to the valor of the younger heroes and leads his men in the thick of battle; but age prevents his vigorous participation in hand-to-hand combat. As a representative of an older generation, his words are heeded and respected.

NICIAS — A head of the war party in Athens after the death of Cleon. Nicias was Cleon's major enemy, as both tried to take power in the city. He was a rather poor general, who was known for his vacillations. Nicias was in charge of the Sicilian campaign; he died after Athens' defeat. Before this he led an attack on Corinth, and later he took Cythera.

NOMENTUM   An old Latin town near Rome.

NUMICIUS   A small river in Latium flowing into the Tyrrhenian Sea.

NYMPHS   The Hamadryades, or nymphs of the groves, who lived in trees. They symbolized the spirit of the tree, for they were born with it, and died when it died. As lesser goddesses, Aeneas first worships them, and then Gradivus (Mars) the more important divinity of Thrace (*Aeneid*).

ODYSSEUS   (Ulysses) Son of Laertes, king of Ithaca. He is rugged in character like his native island, of short but massive build. Odysseus became legendary as a master of guile and exemplar of patient suffering. He participates with Diomedes in the raid on the Trojan camp, chosen by Diomedes for his cleverness.

OENOTRIA   Another name for Italy, "Land of Vines."

OGYGIA   Calypso's island, located in the middle of the sea. Odysseus and Calypso lived together for seven years.

OLIVE CROWNS   The traditional prizes given at the Olympic games in Greece.

OLYMPUS   The mountain home of the gods.

OMENS   It is the Roman custom of consulting the *auspices* by a Greek priest. It consisted of examining the entrails of animals, or of observing the way chickens pecked at corn which was thrown to them. The Romans very rarely did anything without consulting the *auspices* or omens. A tremendous amount of ritual was involved, and one little wrong step meant that the whole thing had to be done again.

ORCUS   The god of death and the underworld, sometimes referred to as Pluto.

ORESTES — Son of Agamemnon who killed his father's slayer, Aegisthus.

ORICUM — Town in Illyria on the Greek coast. The district was famous for its turpentine, or terebinth, trees.

ORION — The constellation which rose near sunrise in the middle of summer and was thought to cause storms. The constellation was also said to be a giant huntsman changed by Diana.

ORPHEUS — A musician-poet of mythology who descended into the lower world to get back his wife Eurydice. He played so beautifully on his lyre that his wish was granted on the condition that he not look back at her until they reached earth. At the last minute he turned around to make sure she was following, and so lost her forever.

ORTYGIA — An earlier name for Delos, the Aegean island.

PACHYNUM — Southeast promontory of Sicily. The gods were supposed to visit their favorite spots once a year.

PALAEMON — Son of Ino who was driven mad by Juno. She threw herself and her son into the sea, and they were changed to sea-gods.

PALAMEDES — Ulysses, not wishing to join the expedition for Troy, pretended madness; but Palamedes proved he was sane, which earned him the hatred of Ulysses. For his revenge Ulysses later forged a letter from Priam to Palamedes arranging for the latter to betray the Greeks. As further proof, Ulysses hid some gold in Palamedes' tent. He was therefore found guilty and put to death.

PALICI — Twin gods of Sicily, sons of Jupiter and the nymph Thalia, who was Vulcan's daughter. They were worshipped in the vicinity of Mt. Aetna.

PALINURUS   The pilot (in the *Aeneid*) who died by drowning.

PALLAS   A king in Arcadia in Greece. His city was Pallantium, and his grandson Evander used the same name for the city he founded on the Tiber in Italy. Pallantium was later incorporated into Rome.

PANOPEA   A sea nymph.

PAPHOS   A town on the west coast of Cyprus where a famous temple to Venus was located.

PARIS   Iarbas, in contempt, compares Aeneas to Paris because he is the successful suitor of another man's wife. Paris is more famous as a prize-fighter than as a warrior. Son of Priam, brother of Hector. Having seduced and married Helen, he is responsible for the war. He can be brave, but he is generally slack in warfare and prefers more gentle activity. He is scolded by Helen and Hector, but defends himself in the name of Aphrodite, whose deity must not be slighted. He slays Achilles after the close of the *Iliad*.

PAROS   A Greek island in the Aegean Sea which provided the most beautiful white marble in antiquity.

PARTHASIA   District in Arcadia in Greece where Evander came from.

PASIPHAE   Wife of Minos, and also the mother of the Minotaur.

PATROCLUS   Son of Menoetius of Opus, squire of Achilles. Patroclus is to be contrasted with Achilles. He is slow to anger, always kind and full of pity for his suffering comrades. He is thus torn between loyalty to Achilles and duty to the Achaean army; he dies in the armor of Achilles at the head of the Argives. Achilles slays Hector to avenge his death.

PAUSANIAS — The Spartan supreme commander at the battle of Plataea.

PEISISTRATUS — Nestor's son who accompanied Telemachus to Sparta.

PELASGIAN — Means "Greek" often, although the term actually refers to the race who inhabited Greece in pre-historic times before the Greeks arrived.

PELEUS — King of the Myrmidons in Phthia in Thessaly, father of Achilles.

PELOPONNESE — The peninsula on which Sparta, the most important military power in Greece, was located.

PELORUS — Northeastern promontory of Sicily on the strait of Messina.

PENATES — Aeneas took with him his own household gods, but these represented those of Troy. Hector also entrusted him with an image of Vesta, the goddess of the never-dying hearth fire.

PENELOPE — The wife of Odysseus; she has become the proverbial example of wifely faithfulness. She waited nineteen years for her husband's return, although there was very little reason for her to believe that he was still alive. In a sense, she was preventing Ithaca from going about its business, for the kingdom could not conduct its affairs without a king. She wanted Odysseus and took no substitute.

PENTHESILEA — Another queen of the Amazons who fought on the side of the Trojans. She was killed by Achilles.

PENTHEUS — A king of Thebes who hid himself so that he could watch the mysteries of Bacchus. He was discovered, and torn to pieces. His madness caused him to see everything in duplicate.

PERGAMUM — The citadel, or inner stronghold, of Troy.

PERICLES — An Athenian leader during the early part of the war, and the closest to a hero. Pericles was a moderate. He believed that Athens should defend herself through sea power and guard against those who destroy democracy by arguing that war calls for stricter forms of government. He died in the plague during the first part of the war.

PETELIA — Another city in southern Italy, said to have been founded by Philoctetes.

PHAEACIANS — Under King Alcinous and Queen Arete, they are shown to be a highly civilized and sophisticated people, as evidenced by their love of assemblies, games, and feasting. Such a high degree of civilization, coupled with their lack of enemies, had softened them so that Odysseus was more than a match for any of them in their games, and was able to win them over with his eloquence.

PHAEDRA — She hanged herself because of her love for her stepson, Hippolytus.

PHAETHON — Son of the sun-god. He begged his father to let him drive the chariot of the sun, and going too close to the earth in North Africa, began to burn everything. A thunderbolt hurled him to the earth and restored the sun.

PHEMIUS — The bard of Ithaca. He was forced to sing for the suitors and would not have done so voluntarily. Odysseus spares his life.

PHILOCTETES — A Greek hero from Meliboea in Thessaly who took part in the Trojan War. His claim to fame was the killing of Paris.

PHILOETIUS — A person who, with Eumaeus, helped Odysseus and Telemachus slay the suitors.

PHINEUS — A king of Thrace whom the gods punished by sending the Harpies to destroy his house. But two of the famous argonauts (sailors of the ship Argo who went in search of the golden fleece), Zetes and Calais, drove the Harpies off.

PHLEGETHON   River of fire in the underworld.

PHOEBUS   Another name for Apollo.

PHOENICIANS   A seafaring people, originally from the area of what is now Lebanon. They comprised the bulk of the Persian navy.

PHOENIX   Achilles' aged tutor. Son of Amyntor, King of the Dolopes. He replaced the centaur Chiron who traditionally held that position.

PHORCUS   Another sea-god, sometimes called the "Old Man of the Sea." He was the son of Neptune and father of frightful beasts who had hissing serpents for hair, claws of brass, wings, and enormous teeth. They were called Gorgons.

PHORMIO   An Athenian commander who defeated a Spartan fleet near Acarnania.

PHRYGIA   The ancient name for the country in Asia Minor where Troy was located.

PHRYGIAN SHEPHERD   Paris.

PHTHIA   The home of the Greek hero, Achilles, in Thessaly.

PILUMNUS   Ancient Italian god.

PIRITHOUS   Friend of Theseus, and originator of the idea for carrying off Proserpina.

PISISTRATUS, PISISTRATIDS   The tyrant of Athens and/or his sons and followers.

PLATAEA (BATTLE OF)	The battle (in Boeotia) in which a combined Greek force ended the Persian threat in Greece, mid-August 479 B.C.
POLYDAMAS	Son of Panthous, wise and of good counsel. His advice is ignored by Hector, who suffers for using force in overruling the counsel of a wiser man. The role of Polydamas is in part similar to that of Odysseus or Phoenix.
POLYPHEMUS	The Cyclops blinded by Odysseus. In his anger at being blinded, Polyphemus prayed to his father, Poseidon, who thereafter was hostile to Odysseus.
PORTUNUS	An Italian god of the harbors.
POSEIDON	God of the sea and an enemy to Odysseus. He was the son of Cronos and Rhea. He rules the watery portion of the universe, and is partial to the Argives, presumably because of Laomedon's treachery. He generally submits to Zeus' authority because Zeus is the elder and wiser brother.
PRIAM	The son of Laomedon and the king of Troy. His name and harem suggest an oriental figure. He is of imperious temper, yet kindly and possessed of great courage, revealed by his stealthy trip to the tent of Achilles to ransom Hector's body. He is to be contrasted with Peleus, Achilles' father. After the fall of Troy, he is killed by the son of Achilles, Neoptolemus.
PRIVERNUM	A city in Latium on the Amasenus.
PROCAS, CAPYS, MUMITOR, SILVIUS, AENEAS	Traditional kings of Alba Longa.
PROCRIS	While checking up on her husband one day to see if he was faithful to her, she was shot accidentally by one of his own arrows.

PROSERPINA (Greek name, Persephone) Pluto's queen in the underworld was supposed to cut the thread of life of women. The lock of hair refers to the custom of taking a few hairs from a victim before it was sacrificed.

PROTEUS One tradition makes him king of Egypt. He is also called the Old Man of the Sea, because he could change his shape at will, (the word "protean" comes from Proteus).

PYRRHUS His other name is Neoptolemus. He was the son of Achilles, sent for after his father was killed by Paris, with Apollo's help.

QUIRINUS Another name for Romulus, the first King of Rome and the first religious diviner.

QUIRITES Inhabitants of Cures, a Sabine town; also the "Men of Quirinus."

RACE OF HECTOR(THE) The Trojans, so named because Hector was their most famous hero.

RHESUS A Thracian king who was supposed to help the Trojans. An oracle had prophesied that the Greeks could not take Troy if the horses of Rhesus were to eat the grass around Troy and drink from its chief stream, the Xanthus. Unfortunately, Rhesus was killed by the Greeks and his horses seized by Odysseus and Diomedes.

RHOETEAN Means Trojan after the name of a small promontory north of Troy called Rhoeteum.

ROMULUS Son of Ilia (Rhea Silivia, daughter of Numitor) and Mars. According to legend, he was the founder of Rome in 753 B.C.

ROMULUS AND REMUS After floating down the Tiber River in a makeshift cradle (they were abandoned by their mother who was a vestal virgin), they were found by a she-wolf who took them to her cave and nursed them until a shepherd boy rescued them.

RUTULIANS — The people living in Latium (in Italy) when Aeneas finally landed there. Aeneas had to defeat their king, Turnus, before he could settle there.

SABAEANS — A tribe living in Arabia.

SABELLI — A lesser tribe of the Sabines.

SACRANI — A mythical people.

SAIAMIS (BATTLE OF) — The naval battle in the straits around the island of Salamis in which a combined Greek fleet destroyed a Persian fleet of superior numbers, thus forcing Xerxes out of Greece, September 480 B.C.

SALII — Dancing priests, usually associated with religious festivals dedicated to Mars.

SALLENTINI — A people inhabiting the southernmost tip of Italy.

SALMONEUS — King of Elis (southwestern Greece) who scornfully imitated the thunder and lightning of Zeus.

SAME — A town on the island of Cephallenia.

SAMOS — A Greek island in the Aegean Sea where an ancient temple to Juno was located.

SARPEDON — A son of Jupiter and a Trojan ally. He was the prince of Lycia, and was killed by Patroclus. His death at the hands of Patroclus presages Achilles' slaying of Hector.

SATICULA — A town north of Capua.

SATURA — A marshy lake in Latium, formed by the Ufens and the Amasenus rivers.

SATURN — Expelled from heaven by Jupiter, ruled Italy in the first Golden Age, when all was peace and happiness.

SCAEAN GATE The most important gate in Troy.

SCHERIA The home of the Phaeacians; also Phoeacia.

SCIPIOS A family famous for two hundred years of republican history. The ones mentioned are probably the two "Africani." Africanus, the elder, won a battle at Zama in 202 B.C. which ended the second Punic War. Africanus, the younger, destroyed Carthage in 146 B.C. at the end of the third Punic War.

SCYLLA A six-headed monster who preyed on passing ships. He lived on the Italian side of the Strait of Messina (the narrow bit of water that separates Italy from Sicily).

SCYROS An island in the Aegean which was the kingdom of Pyrrhus' grandfather, Lycomedes.

SCYTHIANS Nomadic tribesmen who inhabited what is now part of Rumania and Southwestern Russia.

SEBETHIS A nymph who lived in a small stream near Naples. Oebalus was not satisfied with his small kingdom of Caprea (Capri), and so extended it to the north. The Teleboae were a pirate tribe who settled in Caprea.

SERRANUS Nickname of Regulus, a general in the first Punic War. It comes from the Latin word to plant seed. The messengers who brought him the news that he had been elected counsel found him planting in the fields.

SHIELD The trophy given to Salius had belonged to a Greek who had dedicated it to Neptune, and then took it from the temple when he went to war (*Aeneid*).

SIBYL A prophetess whose utterances were written on palm leaves. Aeneas is warned by Helenus not to let any breeze scatter the leaves, for then the prophecy would be unreadable.

SICANI

A tribe Virgil identifies with the Siculi who first inhabited Latium and then spread south into Sicily.

SICANIAN BAY

The bay of Syracuse.

SIDICINI

A Campanian tribe in Italy.

SIGEUM

The northwestern promontory in Asia Minor at the entrance of the Hellespont.

SIMILE

This word does not appear in the story but the comparison of Neptune with the orator is a simile. It is very important in the understanding of Virgil's art to notice how he uses them. Usually his similes are drawn from the natural or spiritual worlds.

SIMOIS

A small river near Troy.

SIRENS

Minor goddesses who lured sailors to their deaths with songs that promised knowledge of the future. After Ulysses tricked them, they drowned themselves.

SIRIUS

The dog star whose ascendancy in the late summer was associated with diseases of that dry and unhealthy time.

SISTER OF PHOE-BUS APOLLO

Diana, goddess of the moon. Her favorite sports were hunting and dancing.

SNAKE

Thought of as the guardian spirit of tombs. His seven coils stress the magic number seven (*Aeneid*).

SOLON

An Athenian lawgiver and social reformer 594-3 or 592-1 B.C.

SON OF TYDEUS

Diomedes, who appears in the *Odyssey*.

SONS OF ATREUS

Agamemnon and Menelaus, the chiefs of the Greeks together with Achilles, in the Trojan War. But Achilles refused to fight at first because he was angry with Agamemnon for taking his captive princess from him.

SORACTE

A mountain in Etruria where there was a temple to Apollo. The rites consisted of walking barefoot through hot embers.

SPOILS OF ACHILLES

Hector killed Patroclus who was wearing Achilles' armor. The armor of a dead man belonged to his slayer.

STHENELUS

Son of Capaneus, squire of Diomedes. He is disrespectful toward his father, asserting that he and Diomedes excel their parents; he takes umbrage at a rebuke from Agamemnon. He is thus a foil to play up the dutifulness of Diomedes.

STRYMON

The river forming the boundary between Thrace and Macedonia.

STYGIAN KING

Pluto.

STYGIAN WAVES

Referring to the river Styx of the underworld, wherein monsters lived.

STYX

The chief river of the underworld.

SWORD-BELT

It is worn over the shoulder. Pallas' was engraved with the story of the murder of the sons of Aegyptus by the daughters of Danaus.

SYMAETHUS

Located on the east coast of Sicily.

SYRTES

Two gulfs on the eastern half of the North African coast; they were unfriendly due to their quicksands and exposure to the north winds, the rocky shore, and variable tides.

TALTHYBIUS

Famous herald of Agamemnon, whose name has come to represent a loyal herald.

TEGEA

An important city of Arcadia, in Greece.

TEIRESIAS

A blind prophet who warned Odysseus of future troubles.

TELEMACHUS — Son of Odysseus, he shows a distinct character development in the course of the poem, from an adolescent first exercising his power to a young man capable of fighting at the side of his father. When he first decides that the situation in his house calls for action, all he does is to undertake a journey in search of his father. It is not until he meets his father in Ithaca that he proves himself.

TEUCER — The mythical founder of Troy. Teucrian race is another way of saying Trojan, but it is also indicating the Roman's reverence for their ancestors. He is also considered as one of the sons of Telamon and a nephew of Priam. When he returned from Troy without his half-brother, Ajax, Telamon banished him to Cyprus.

THEMISTOCLES — The Athenian hero of the Battle of Salamis.

THEOCLYMENUS — A prophet whom Telemachus invites to Ithaca. He prophesied doom for the suitors, but went unheeded.

THERMODON — A river in Pontus, Asia Minor, in the homeland of the Amazons.

THERMOPYLAE (BATTLE OF) — The battle for a pass in central Greece in which all the defending Greek troops were killed by the Persians, August 480 B.C.

THERSITES — A rank-and-file Achaean warrior, of common birth, a birth which is emphasized by his ugliness. He protests against the war, and is struck by Odysseus for challenging his superiors. There is an implicit comparison between Thersites and Achilles.

THESEUS — He went to the underworld to rescue Proserpina who had been carried off from her mother, Ceres, by the king of the lower regions, Pluto, whose other name was Dis.

THETIS — Daughter of Nereus, immortal wife of the mortal Peleus and mother of Achilles. Zeus and Hephaestus are obligated to her for saving their lives when (in childhood) they were threatened. She supports Zeus against Cronos, and Achilles against Agamemnon.

THUCYDIDES
THRACIANS — They were noted for their skill in archery.

AND AMAZONS — The author of the book on *The Peloponnesian War* was a general in the war. He was a general during the attack on Amphipolis, and arrived too late to save the main force. He was later exiled.

THYIADS — Attic women (from near Athens) who worshipped Bacchus on Mt. Parnassus in Thebes in wild rites. The orgies were accompanied by waving a wand (the *thyrsus*) twined with ivy and topped by a pine cone. Music was furnished by a flute-like instrument.

THYMBRA — A place near Troy where Apollo had a famous temple.

TIBER — The river in Italy on which Rome is situated.

TIBUR — A town not far from Rome, said to have gotten its name from Tiburtus, one of the three grandsons of Amphiaraus. Its modern name is Tivoli.

TISSAPHERNES — The Persian leader who subsidized Sparta in the last years of the fighting, and who became a leader of the Athenian alliance.

TITANIAN STAR — The sun. Many ancient philosophies (the most famous being the Stoic) held that the primary cause of life and motion was a sort of world-soul which had a nature like that of fire.

TITHONUS — Brother of Priam who received the gift of immortality from the gods, due to prayers of Aurora, goddess of the dawn. But he was not given eternal youth, and eventually shriveled up with old age. In pity, Aurora changed him into a grasshopper.

TOPAS — Another noble who was supposed to have been taught by Atlas, the legendary first astronomer. The mountain in northwestern Africa was named after him. Topas' ballad concerns the eclipses of the sun. The ancients referred to them as "the toils of the sun" because they thought the sun was enduring great struggles at such a time (*Aeneid*).

TORQUATUS — He killed his son for disobeying orders in war.

TRIDENT — A three-pronged spear, symbol of Neptune's power. Neptune was also the patron of horses and horseracing.

TRINACRIAN SHORE — Sicily; the name came from the fact that Sicily has three promontories and is triangular in shape.

TRIREME — An ancient warship having three banks of oars.

TRITONIA — Minerva.

TRIUMPH — In August 29 B.C. Augustus celebrated a triple triumph for victories in Dalmatia, Actium, and Alexandria.

TRIVIA — A name for Diana because she was worshipped at the place where three roads crossed (*Tres Viae*).

TRIVIA'S LAKE — Modern *Lago di Nemi* where there was a grove of Diana.

TROILUS — The youngest son of Priam, King of Troy. He was killed by Achilles. The scene concerning Hector refers to Priam's ransoming Hector's body after Achilles had it dragged three times around the walls.

TROPHY

A victor's trophy was usually the trunk of some tree decked with the armor of the man he killed.

TROY AND OECHALIA

Captured by Hercules; the first because Laomedon refused to give him his reward for killing a sea-monster; the second, a town in Thessaly, because its king, Eurytus, refused to give him his daughter Iole.

TULLUS

The third King of Rome who ordered Mettus' execution.

TYDEUS, PARTHENOPAEUS, ADRASTUS

Legendary heroes of the war of the Seven Against Thebes, the most important war before the expedition against Troy.

TYNDAREUS

Husband of Leda but not actually Helen's father. Leda was her mother, Jupiter her father.

TYPHOEUS

A frightful beast with a hundred heads, hands, and eyes. He was placed beneath a volcano by Jupiter's thunderbolts.

TYRIAN TOWN

Carthage, since it was founded by settlers from Tyre.

TYRRHENIAN BAND

Another name for the Tuscans, a people living in Italy, who revolted against their tyrant Mezentius and joined Aeneas.

TYRRHENIAN SEA

It lies southwest of Italy.

ULYSSES

He went through many years of wandering to various parts of the Mediterranean after the Trojan War. Aeneas is therefore a subtle comparison with his own adventures. Ulysses is also credited by legend with being the author of the plan for the wooden horse. His home was the island of Ithaca.

UNBURIED   Aeneas reigned only three years and his body was swept away by the river Numicus. The rest of her curse involves the adventures of Aeneas in the Punic Wars. The avenger is meant to be Hannibal.

VELIA   A Greek town not far from modern Naples.

VELINUS   A lake seventy miles northeast from the Trojan camp.

VENILA   A sea-nymph, mother of Turnus; sister of Amata, the wife of Latinus (*Aeneid*).

VESTA   Goddess of the sacred hearth fire which must always be kept burning. Her priestess, Rhea Silvia, was the mother (by the god Mars) of Romulus and Remus. (Her father was the king of *Alba Longa,* Numitor, descended from Ascanius.)

VESULUS   One of the Italian Alps, Monte Viso, whence rose the Po River.

VIRGIN
DAUGHTER   Iphigenia, daughter of Agamemnon, was sacrificed to Diana at Aulis (on the strait of Euboea) in order that the Greeks might have fair winds to Troy.

VOLSCI   One of the tribes in Latium living to the southeast of Rome.

VULCAN   The god of fire.

XANTHUS   The river known to mortals as Scamander, and also the god of the river. Staunch defender of Troy, he is defeated in the battle by Hephaestus (the Greeks thought of flames destroying pools and rivers rather than water quenching fires).

XENOPHON   An Athenian commander who captured Potidaea in the early part of the war, and was later defeated at Chalcidice. Xenophon was an historian and wrote of Socrates. It is from his works that we can construct the later history of the war.

XERXES The Persian king who led a massive expedition against Greece in 480 B.C.

ZACYNTHUS, DULICHIUM Islands off the western coast of Greece.

ZEPHYRUS The west wind.

ZEUS Son of Cronos and Rhea, god of the upper air and highest Olympian deity, the "father of gods and men." He is all-powerful and all-wise, the dispenser of destiny, yet is often deceived by Hera. His role is thus a fusion of religious traditions. As chief figure of an essentially tribal family, he may be compared with Agamemnon. His rebelliousness and aloofness link him also with Achilles. His brothers, Poseidon and Hades, presided over the sea and Underworld, respectively.

BIBLIOGRAPHY

THE ILIAD, THE ODYSSEY

TRANSLATIONS

Chase, Alston Hurd, and William G. Perry, Jr. New York: Bantam Books, 1960, (pb).

Lang, Andrew, Leaf, Walter, and Myers, Ernest. New York: Modern Library, (also in pb).

Lattimore, Richmond. Chicago: University of Chicago Press, 1961, (pb).

Pope, Alexander. Oxford, England: The Oxford University Press, 1951.

Rieu, E. V. Harmondsworth, England: Penguin Books, 1961, (pb).

Rouse, W. H. D. New York: The New American Library, 1954, (pb).

Evelyn-White, Hugh G. *Hesiod, The Homeric Hymns,* and *Homerica.* ("Loeb Classical Library Series.") Cambridge, Mass.: Harvard University Press, 1959.

GENERAL

Allen, T. W. *Homer: The Origins and Transmissions.* Oxford: The Oxford University Press, 1924.

Arnold, Matthew. *On Translating Homer.* London: Routledge, 1905.

Auerbach, Erich. *Mimesis.* Princeton, N. J.: The Princeton University Press, 1953, (also in pb). (See especially Chapter 1, "Odysseus' Scar," reprinted in *Homer,* ed. by Steiner; see below.)

Basset, S. E. *The Poetry of Homer.* Berkeley: The University of California Press, 1938.

(pb) means available in paperback.

Bespaloff, Rachel. *On the Iliad*. New York: Pantheon Books, 1947, (also in pb).

Blegen, Carl W. *Troy*. Cambridge, England: The Cambridge University Press, 1961, (pb).

Bowra, C. M. *Tradition and Design in the Iliad*. Oxford: The Oxford University Press, 1950.

Carpenter, Rhys. *Folk-tale, Saga, and Fiction in the Homeric Epics*. Berkeley: The University of California Press, 1946, (also in pb).

Chadwick, John. *The Decipherment of Linear B*. Harmondsworth, England: Penguin Books, 1961, (pb).

Dodds, E. B. *The Greeks and the Irrational*. Berkeley: The University of California Press, 1963, (pb).

Finley, M. I. *The World of Odysseus*. New York: Meridian Books, 1959, (pb).

Jaeger, Werner. *Paideia: The Ideals of Greek Culture*. (Vol. I). Oxford: Basil Blackwell, 1954. (See especially pp. 3-57).

Jebb, R. C. *Homer: An Introduction*. Glasgow: J. Macelhose and Son, 1905.

Kirk, G. S. *The Songs of Homer*. Cambridge: The Cambridge University Press, 1962.

Levy, B. R. *The Sword from the Rock*. London: 1953.

Lord, Albert B. *The Singer of Tales*. Cambridge, Mass.: The Harvard University Press, 1960.

Lorimer, H. L. *Homer and the Monuments*. London: Macmillan & Co., 1950.

Murray, Gilbert. *The Rise of the Greek Epic*. Oxford: The Oxford University Press, 1960, (pb).

Myres, J. L. *Homer and His Critics*. London: Routledge and Kegan Paul, 1958.

Nilsson, Martin. *Homer and Mycenae*. London: Methuen and Co., 1933.

O'Neill, Eugene, Jr. "The Localization of Metrical Word-types in the Greek Hexameter," *Yale Classical Studies,* VIII (1942).

Page, Denys L. *History and the Homeric Iliad*. Berkeley: University of California Press, 1963, (pb).

——————. *The Homeric Odyssey*. Oxford: The Oxford University Press, 1955.

Parry, Milman. "L'epithète traditionelle chez Homère," Paris: Les Belles Lettres, 1928.

——————. "Studies in Epic Technique and Verse-making," *Harvard Studies in Classical Philology,* XLI (1929); XLIII (1932).

Platnauer, Maurice (ed.). *Fifty Years of Classical Scholarship*. Oxford: Basil Blackwell, 1954. (See especially pp. 1-38).

Porter, Howard N. "The Early Greek Hexameter," *Yale Classical Studies,* XII (1951).

Scott, John A. *The Unity of Homer*. Berkeley: The University of California Press, 1921.

Sheppard, J. T. *The Pattern of the Iliad*. London: Methuen & Co., 1922.

Snell, Bruno. *The Discovery of the Mind*. Cambridge, Mass.: The Harvard University Press, 1953. (See especially Chapter 1).

——————. *Poetry and Society: The Role of Poetry in Ancient Greece*. Indiana University Press, 1961.

Steiner, George, and Fagles, Robert (eds.). *Homer: A Collection of Critical Essays*. Englewood Cliffs, N. J.: Prentice-Hall, 1962, (pb).

(pb) means available in paperback.

Wace, Alan J. B., and Stubbings, Frank H. *A Companion to Homer.* London: Macmillan & Co., 1962.

Wade-Gery, H. T. *The Poet of the Iliad.* Cambridge, England: The Cambridge University Press, 1952.

Weil, Simone. *The Iliad or the Poem of Force.* Wallingford, Pa.: Pendle Hill, 1957, (pb).

Whitman, C. *Homer and the Heroic Tradition.* Cambridge, Mass.: The Harvard University Press, 1959.

GREEK DRAMA

GENERAL WORKS

Allen, J. T. *Stage Antiquities of the Greeks and Romans and Their Influence.* (New York, 1927).

Bieber, M. *The History of the Greek and Roman Theater.* (Princeton, 1939).

Campbell, L. *A Guide to Greek Tragedy for English Readers.* (London, 1891).

Flickinger, R. C. *The Greek Theater and Its Drama,* 4th Ed. (Chicago, 1936).

Goodell, T. D. *Athenian Tragedy.* (New Haven, 1920).

Greene, William Chase. *Moira: Fate, Good, and Evil in Greek Thought.* (Harvard, 1944).

Haigh, A. E. *The Tragic Drama of the Greeks.* (Oxford, 1896).

Harsh, Philip Whaley. *A Handbook of Classical Drama.* (Stanford University, 1960).

Kitto, H. D. F. *Greek Tragedy, A Literary Study.* (Doubleday Anchor Books, New York, 1954).

——————. *Form and Meaning in Drama.* (New York, 1957).

Lucas, D. W. *The Greek Tragic Poets: Their Contribution to Western Life and Thought*. (London, 1950).

Legrand, P. E. *The New Greek Comedy*. (London, 1917).

Norwood, Gilbert. *Greek Comedy*. (London, 1917).

Pickard-Cambridge, A. W. *Dithyramb, Tragedy and Comedy*. (Oxford, 1946).

Prentice, William Kelley. *Those Ancient Dramas Called Tragedies*. (Princeton University Press, 1942).

Sheppard, J. T. *Greek Tragedy*. (Cambridge, 1911).

Webster, T. B. L. *Greek Theatre Production*. (London, 1956).

Young, S. P. *The Women of Greek Drama*. (New York, 1953).

AESCHYLUS

Murray, Gilbert. *Aeschylus: The Creator of Tragedy*. (Oxford, 1940).

Sheppard, J. T. *Aeschylus and Sophocles: Their Work and Influence*. New York: Longmans, 1927.

Smyth, Herbert Weir. *Aeschylean Tragedy*. (University of California Press, 1924).

EURIPIDES

Appleton, R. B. *Euripides, the Idealist*. London: Dutton, 1927.

Decharme, Paul. *Euripides and the Spirit of His Dramas*. New York: Macmillan, 1906.

Grube, G. M. A. *The Drama of Euripides*. (London, 1941).

Murray, Gilbert. *Euripides and His Age*. New York: Holt, 1913.

ARISTOPHANES

Crotset, Maurice. *Aristophanes and the Political Parties at Athens*. (London, 1909).

Ehrenberg, Victor. *The People of Aristophanes*: *A Sociology of Old Attic Comedy*. (Oxford, 1943).

Murray Gilbert. *Aristophanes*: *A Study*. (Oxford, 1933).

Richards, Herbert. *Aristophanes and Others*. (London, 1909).

GREEK LYRIC POETRY

Bowra, C. M. *Greek Lyric Poetry from Alcman to Simonides*. (Oxford, 1936).

——————, and Higham, T. F. *The Oxford Book of Greek Verse in Translation*. (Oxford, 1938).

Cox, E. M. *The Poems of Sappho*. (London, 1925).

Edmonds, J. M. *Lyra Graeca*. 3 vols. (London, 1922-7).

Goldsmith, M. L. *Sappho of Lesbos*. (London, 1938).

Petersen, W. *The Lyric Songs of the Greeks*. (Boston, 1924).

Robinson, D. M. *Pindar, a Poet of Eternal Ideas*. (Baltimore, 1936).

Symonds, J. A. *Studies of the Greek Poets*. 3rd ed. (London, 1920).

Way, A. S. *The Odes of Pindar*. (London, 1922).

Wharton, H. T. *Sappho*. (New York, 1895).

GREEK HISTORY

HERODOTUS

Carter, Harry. *The Histories of Herodotus*. New York: Limited Editions, 1958.

Glover, T. R. *Herodotus*. Berkeley: University of California, 1924.

Grundy, G. B. *The Great Persian War and its Preliminaries*. *A Study of the Evidence, Literary and Topographical*. (London, 1901).

Hignett, C. *Xerxes' Invasion of Greece*. (Oxford, 1963).

How, W. W., and Wells, J. *A Commentary on Herodotus*. (Oxford, 1912).

Macan, R. W. *Herodotus. The Fourth, Fifth and Sixth Books*. (London, 1895).
—————. *Herodotus. The Seventh, Eighth and Ninth Books*. (London, 1908).
Munro, J. A. R. (in) *The Cambridge Ancient History*, vol. IV. (Cambridge, 1926).
Myres, J. L. *Herodotus, Father of History*. (Oxford, 1953).
Powell, J. E. *The History of Herodotus*. (Cambridge University Press, 1939).
Rawlinson, G. *Herodotus*. London: Nonesuch Press, 1935.
Snider, Denton J. *The Father of History*. (St. Louis, 1937).
Wells, J. *Studies in Herodotus*. (Oxford, 1923).
Wright, H. B. *The Campaign of Plataea*. (New Haven, 1904).

THUCYDIDES

Burn, A. R. *Pericles and Athens*. (New York, 1949).
Bury, J. B. *The Ancient Greek Historians*. (London, 1909).
Cochrane, C. N. *Thucydides and the Science of History*. (Oxford, 1929).
Dickinson, G. L. *The Greek View of Life*. (New York, 1930).
Finley, J. H. Jr. *Thucydides*, (Cambridge, Mass., 1942).
Hamilton, E. *The Great Age of Greek Literature*. (New York, 1942).
Henderson, B. W. *The Great War Between Athens and Sparta*, Ln., 1927.
Rostovtzeff, M. *A History of the Ancient World*. 2 vols. (Oxford, 1933).
Zimmern, A. *The Greek Commonwealth*. (Oxford, 1931).

PRE-SOCRATIC PHILOSOPHY

Appleton, R. B. *The Elements of Greek Philosophy from Thales to Aristotle*. (London, 1922).
Benn, A. W. *Early Greek Philosophy*. 4th ed. (London, 1930).
Burnet, J. *Greek Philosophy*. Part I. (London, 1928).
Fuller, B. A. G. *History of Greek Philosophy: Thales to Democritus*. (New York, 1923).
McClure, M. T. *The Early Philosophers of Greece*. (New York, 1935).
Nahm, M. C. *Selections from Early Greek Philosophy*. (New York, 1934).
Scoon, R. M. *Greek Philosophy before Plato*. (Princeton, 1928).
Zeller, E. *Pre-Socratic Philosophy*. 2 vols. (London, 1881).

SOCRATES

Cornford, F. M. *Before and After Socrates.* (Cambridge, 1932).
Forbes, J. T. *Socrates.* (Edinburgh, 1913).
Kenyon, A. R. *The Socratic Problem.* (New Haven, 1933).
Osborn, E. B. *Socrates and his Friends.* (London, 1930).
Philipson, C. *The Trial of Socrates.* (London, 1928).
Taylor, A. E. *Socrates.* (New York, 1933).
Winspear, A. D., and Silverberg, T. *Who Was Socrates?* (New York, 1939).

PLATO

Texts
Cornford, F. M. *The Republic of Plato.* (Oxford, 1941).
Jowett, Benjamin. *The Dialogues of Plato.* 2 vols. New York: Random House, 1892.
Adam, A. M. *Plato: Moral and Political Ideals.* (Cambridge, 1913).

Barker, Ernest. *The Political Thought of Plato and Aristotle.* (New York: Dover, 1959.
Bosanquet, B. *A Companion to Plato's Republic.* 2nd. ed., London, 1906.
Boyd, W. *An Introduction to the Republic of Plato.* 2nd. ed., London, 1906.
Burnet, J. *Platonism.* Berkeley: University of California Press, 1928.
Demos, R. *The Philosophy of Plato.* (New York, 1939).
Dickinson, G. L. *Plato and His Dialogues.* (New York, 1932).
Friedlander, Paul. *Plato* (Eng. Tr.). Pantheon Books, New York, 1958.
Frye, P. H. *Plato,* Lincoln, 1938.
Grene, David. *Man in his Pride.* (Chicago, 1950).
Grube, G. M. A. *Plato's Thought.* (London, 1935).
Hardie, W. F. R. *A Study in Plato.* (Oxford, 1936).
Koyré, A. *Discovering Plato.* (New York, 1945).
Leon, P. *Plato.* (London and New York, 1939).
Levinson, R. B. *In Defense of Plato.* (Cambridge, 1953).
Lodge, R. C. *Plato's Theory of Ethics.* (London, 1928).
More, P. E. *Platonism.* (Princeton, 1917).
——————. *The Religion of Plato.* 2nd ed. (Princeton, 1928).
Mueller, G. E. *What Plato Thinks.* (LaSalle, 1937).
Nettleship, R. L. *Lectures on the Republic of Plato.* (London, 1929).
Popper, Karl R. *The Open Society and its Enemies.* 2 vols. (London, 1952).

Ritchie, D. G. *Plato.* (Edinburgh, 1925).
Ritter, C. *The Essence of Plato's Philosophy.* (London, 1933).
Ross, W. D. *Plato's Theory of Ideas.* (Oxford, 1951).
Shorey, P. *The Unity of Plato's Thought.* (Chicago, 1903).
—————————. *Platonism, Ancient and Modern.* (Berkeley, 1938).
—————————. *What Plato Said.* (Chicago, 1933).
Steward, J. A. *Myths of Plato.* (Chicago, 1928).
Taylor, A. E. *Plato.* (London, 1922).
—————————. *Plato, the Man and his Work.* (New York, 1936).
—————————. *Platonism and its Influence.* (Boston, 1924).
Thomson, J. A. K. *Plato and Aristotle.* (London, 1928).
Winspear, A. D. *The Genesis of Plato's Thought.* (New York, 1940).
Woodbridge, F. J. *The Son of Apollo.* (Cambridge, 1929).

ARISTOTLE: THE WORKS

Aristotle: The Loeb Classical Library Editions. (Greek text and English translation).
"   Oxford Translation of all the works. Ed. J. A. Smith and W. D. Ross, 1908-1931.
"   *Metaphysics.* Tr. Richard Hope. Ann Arbor: University of Michigan Press, 1960.
"   *Nicomachean Ethics.* Tr. M. Ostwald, New York, 1962.
"   *Politics.* Tr. and ed. Ernest Barker, New York, 1958.
"   Butcher, S. H. *Aristotle's Theory of Poetry and Fine Art.* (New York, 1951).
In addition, there are many other excellent editions of his major works and selections from them available in paperback.

ARISTOTLE: GENERAL

Allan, D. J. *The Philosophy of Aristotle.* (New York, 1952).
Barker, E. *The Political Thought of Plato and Aristotle.* (London, 1906).
Butcher, S. H. *The Poetics of Aristotle.* 4th ed. (London, 1911).
Bywater, I. *Aristotle on the Art of Poetry.* (Oxford, 1913).
Cooper, L. *Aristotle on the Art of Poetry.* (Boston and New York, 1913).
—————————. *The Poetics of Aristotle*: Its Meanings and Influence. (Boston, 1923).
Fyfe, W. H. *Aristotle's Art of Poetry.* (Oxford, 1940).
Grote, G. *Aristotle.* 3rd. ed. (London, 1883).
Jaeger, Werner. *Aristotle: Fundamentals of the History of His Development.* 2nd. ed., tr. R. Robinson. (Oxford, 1962).

Lucas, F. L. *Tragedy in Relation to Aristotle's Poetics*. (London, 1912).

Mure, G. R. G. *Aristotle*. (New York, 1932).

Owen, W. D. *Aristotle on the Art of Poetry*. (Oxford, 1931).

Randall, John H., Jr. *Aristotle*. (New York, 1962).

Ross, W. D. *Aristotle*. (New York, 1962).

Taylor, Alfred E. *Aristotle*. (New York, 1956).

Thompson, D. W. *Plato and Aristotle*. (London, 1928).

Wallace, E. *Outlines of the Philosophy of Aristotle*. 3rd. ed. (Cambridge, 1883).

ROMAN LITERATURE

GENERAL: HISTORY AND LITERATURE

Bailey, C. (ed.) *The Legacy of Rome*. (Oxford, 1923).

Baker, G. P. *Twelve Centuries of Rome*. (New York, 1934).

Fowler, W. W. *Rome*. (New York, 1912).

Frank, T. *Roman Imperialism*. (New York, 1914).

—————. *A History of Rome*. (New York, 1923).

Greene, W. C. *The Achievement of Rome*. (Cambridge, Mass., 1933).

Harvey, P. (ed.). *The Oxford Companion to Classical Literature*. (Oxford, 1937).

Guinagh, Kevin and Dorjahn, Alfred P. *Latin Literature in Translation*. 2nd. ed. (New York, 1960).

Hamilton, Edith. *The Roman Way*. (New York, 1932).

Howe, G. and Harrer, G. A. *Roman Literature in Translation*. New York, 1924.

Laing, G. J. *Masterpiece of Latin Literature*. (London, 1936).

Rose, H. J. *A Handbook of Latin Literature*. (London, 1936).

Robinson, C. E. *A History of Rome from 753 B.C. to 410 A.D.* (New York, 1935).

Summers, W. C. *The Silver Age of Latin Literature, from Tiberius to Trajan*. (New York, 1920).

LUCRETIUS

(*See below for explanation of ODGR, ACER, WBL*).

Hadzsits, George D. *Lucretius and His Influence, Our Debt to Greece and Rome*. G. P. Hadzsits and D. M. Robinson (eds.), Longmans Green and Company. All these volumes contain a complete bibliography of each author discussed in the series. (ODGR).

Mallock, W. H. *Lucretius, Ancient Classics for English Readers*. W. Lucas Collins (ed.), 1870 and on. Twelve of the 28 volumes are devoted to latin authors. (ACER).

Sellar, W. Y. *The Roman Poets of the Republic*. (Oxford, 1889), pp. 280-407.

Shorey, Paul. "Titus Lucretius Carus," in *A Library of the World's Best Literature, Ancient and Modern*. Charles Dudley Warner (ed.), (pp. 9304-9312). 45 vols. Authors arranged alphabetically with a noted scholar devoted to each writer. (WBL).

Slaughter, Moses. *Roman Portraits*. (New Haven, 1925).

Tennyson, Alfred. *Lucretius*. (London, 1870).

Tyrrell, R. Y. *Latin Poetry*, "Lucretius and Epicureanism," pp. 59-89. (New York, 1895).

Herford, C. H. *The Poetry of Lucretius*. (Manchester, 1918).

Masson, J. *Lucretius, Epicurean and Poet*. 2 vols. (New York, 1907-9).

Sides, E. E. *Lucretius, Poet and Philosopher*. (Cambridge, 1936).

CATULLUS

Cranstoun, James. *The Poems of Valerius Catullus*. (Edinburgh, 1867).

Davies, James. *Catullus Tibullus, and Propertius*, "Catullus," pp. 1-92. (ACER).

Duckett, E. S. "Catullus in English Poetry," *Smith College Classical Studies*, No. 6, 1925.

Frank, Tenney. *Catullus and Horace*. (New York, 1928).

Gregory, H. *The Poems of Catullus*. (New York, 1931).

Harrington, K. P. *Catullus and His Influence*. (ODGR).

Tyrrell, R. Y. *Latin Poetry*. (New York, 1895).

Wright, F. A. *Catullus: the Complete Poems*. (New York, 1926). See especially the excellent introduction, pp. 3-89.

——————. *The Roman Poets*. (New York, 1938).

THE AUGUSTAN AGE: HISTORY

Allen, B. M. *Augustus Caesar*. (London, 1937).

Baker, G. P. *Augustus; the Golden Age of Rome*. (New York, 1937).

Holmes, T. R. *The Architect of the Roman Empire*. (Oxford, 1928).

Sellar, W. Y. *The Roman Poets of the Augustan Age*. (Oxford, 1892).

Winspear, A. D. and Geweke, L. K. *Augustus and the Reconstruction of Roman Government and Society*. (Madison, 1935).

VIRGIL

Bailey, Cyril. *Religion in Virgil.* (Oxford, 1935).
Collins, W. Lucas. *Virgil.* (ACER).
Comparetti, D. (tr.) E. F. M. Benecke. *Virgil in the Middle Ages.* (New York, 1908).
Connington, J. and Nettleship, H. *The Works of Virgil.* 2 vols. (London, 1884).
Duckworth, G. E. *Structural Patterns and Proportions in Virgil's Aeneid.* (Ann Arbor, 1962).
Frank, Tenny. *Virgil, a Biography.* (Oxford, 1922).
Glover, T. R. *Virgil.* (New York, 1912).
*Highet, Gilbert. *Poets in a Landscape.* (New York, 1957).
Knight, W. F. J. *Roman Virgil.* (London, 1953).
Letters, F. J. H. *Virgil.* (New York, 1946).
Mackail, J. W. *Virgil.* (ODGR).
——————. *Virgil and His Meaning to the World of Today.* (Boston, 1922).
Nettleship, H. *Suggestions Introductory to a Study of the Aeneid.* (Oxford, 1875).
Nitchie, E. *Vergil and the English Poets.* (New York, 1919).
Oxford Classical Dictionary. (Oxford, 1957).
*Pöschl, V. (tr. G. Seligson). *The Art of Vergil.* (Ann Arbor, 1962).
Prescott, H. W. *The Development of Virgil's Art.* (Chicago, 1927).
*Rand, E. K. *The Magical Art of Virgil.* (Cambridge, Mass., 1931).
Sellar, W. Y. *The Roman Poets of the Augustan Age—Virgil.* (Oxford, 1908).
Smith, W. and Anthon, C. *A New Classical Dictionary.* (New York, 1851).
Syme, Ronald. *The Roman Revolution.* (Oxford, 1939).

HORACE

Duff, J. Wright. *Roman Satire: Its Outlook on Social Life.* (Berkeley, 1936).
Frank T. *Catullus and Horace.* (New York, 1928).
Lang, A. *Letters to Dead Authors.* (New York, 1899).
Martin, Theodore. *Horace.* (ACER).
Reppelier, Agnes. "Horace," *The Atlantic Monthly,* Vol. 157, 279-287, 1936.
Sellar, W. Y. *Horace and the Elegiac Poets.* (Oxford, 1899).
Showerman, G. *Horance and His Influence.* (Boston, 1922).

---

* Especially useful.

—————————. *Horace.* (ODGR).
—————————. *Monuments and Men of Ancient Rome.*
Wilkinson, L. P. *Horace and His Lyric Poetry.* (Cambridge, 1945).

LIVY

Collins, W. Lucas. *Livy.* (ACER).
Hart, B. H. L. "Hannibal and Rome," *Atlantic,* CXLII, 532-542, 1952.
Mackail, J. W. *Latin Literature,* "Livy," pp. 145-155, 1904.
Shotwell, J. T. *An Introduction to the History of History.* (New York, 1922). See pp. 247-256.
Wilkinson, S. "Hannibal in the Alps," *Nineteenth Century and After,* CXI, 96-105, 1911.

OVID

Church, Alfred. *Ovid.* (ACER).
Mackail, J. W. *Latin Literature.* "Ovid," pp. 132-144, 1904.
Rand, E. K. *Ovid and His Influence.* (ODGR).
Rose, H. J. *A Handbook of Latin Literature,* 1936.
Sellar, W. Y. *The Roman Poets of the Augustan Age.* 3rd. ed., Oxford, 1897.
Thornton, J. C. and M. J. *Ovid: Selected Works.* New York: Everyman's Library.

TACITUS

Boissier, G. *Tacitus and Other Roman Studies.* (New York, 1906).
Donne, W. B. *Tacitus.* (ACER).
Hadas, M. *The Complete Works of Tacitus.* (New York, 1942).
Henderson, B. W. *Civil War and Rebellion in the Roman Empire* A.D. 69-70. (London, 1908).
Harvey, Paul. *The Oxford Companion to Classical Literature.* (Oxford, 1949).
Mackail, J. W. *Latin Literature.* (New York, 1904).
Sandys, J. E. *A Companion to Latin Studies.* (Cambridge, 1929).
WBL   See "Tacitus."

GREEK AND ROMAN MYTHOLOGY

Bullfinch, T. *Mythology.* (New York, 1934).
Fairbanks, A. *The Mythology of Greece and Rome.* (New York, 1907).
Hamilton, E. *Mythology.* (Boston, 1924).
Harrison, J. E. *Myths of Greece and Rome.* (New York, 1928).

Harvey, Paul. *The Oxford Companion to Classical Literature.* (New York, 1931).
The Loeb Classical Library, Cambridge, Mass.
Rose, H. J. *A Handbook of Greek Mythology.* (New York, 1928).
Tatlock, J. M. *Greek and Roman Mythology.* (New York, 1923).

PAPERBACKS, *Translations*

As an example of what is now available in paperback, I list the volumes available in the Penguin Series on some translations from the Greek classics, each volume done by a noted authority: *Aesop* (S. A. Handford), *Euripides* (P. Vellacott), *Herodotus* (A. de Selincourt), *Homer* (E. V. Rieu), *Plato* (H. Tredennick, W. Hamilton, H. D. Lee), *Sophocles* (E. F. Watling), *Thucydides* (R. Warner), *Xenophon* (R. Warner), etc. See especially Robert Graves *Greek Myths* (2 vols.) in the Penguin Series.

The listing of other paperback series (as well as individual authors) dealing with Greek and Roman literature would fill a good sized book!

NOTES

MONARCH® NOTES AND STUDY GUIDES

ARE AVAILABLE AT RETAIL STORES EVERYWHERE

In the event your local bookseller cannot provide you with other Monarch titles you want —

ORDER ON THE FORM BELOW:

Simply send retail price, local sales tax, if any, plus 35¢ per book to cover mailing and handling.

TITLE #	AUTHOR & TITLE	PRICE
	PLUS ADDITIONAL $1.00 PER BOOK FOR POSTAGE	
	GRAND TOTAL	$

Mail to: **PRENTICE HALL PRESS,** c/o Simon & Schuster Mail Order Billing, Route 59 at Brook Hill Drive, West Nyack, NY 10994

I enclose $ .... to cover retail price, local sales tax, plus mailing and handling. (Make checks payable to Simon & Schuster, Inc.)

Name _____

(Please print)

Address _____

City _____ State _____ Zip _____

Please send check or money order. We cannot be responsible for cash.